Old Testament Theology:
Flowering and Future

Sources for Biblical and Theological Study

General Editor:
David W. Baker
Ashland Theological Seminary

Old Testament Theology: Flowering and Future

edited by

Ben C. Ollenburger

Eisenbrauns
Winona Lake, Indiana
2004

www.eisenbrauns.com

Paperback reprint, 2016
Paperback ISBN: 978-1-57506-460-4

Library of Congress Cataloging-in-Publication Data

Flowering of Old Testament Theology
   Old Testament theology : flowering and future / edited by Ben C.
  Ollenburger. — 2nd rev. ed.
       p. cm — (Sources for biblical and theological study ; 1)
  Includes bibliographical references and indexes.
  ISBN 1-57506-096-5 (hardback : alk. paper)
    1. Bible. O.T.–Theology   2. Bible. O.T.–Criticism, interpretation,
etc.–History–20th Century.   I. Ollenburger, Ben C.   II. Title.
III. Series.
  BS1192.5.F564   2004
  230′.0411–dc22

                                             2004002309

CONTENTS

Part 1
The Background

Part 2
Old Testament Theology's Renaissance:
Walther Eichrodt through Gerhard von Rad

Part 3
Expansion and Variety:
Between Gerhard von Rad and Brevard Childs

Part 4
*From Brevard Childs to
a New Pluralism*

Part 5
Contexts, Perspectives, and Proposals

Appendix

SERIES PREFACE

Old Testament scholarship is well served by several recent works which detail, to a greater or lesser extent, the progress made in the study of the Old Testament. Some survey the range of interpretation over long stretches of time, while others concern themselves with a smaller chronological or geographical segment of the field. There are also brief *entrées* into the various subdisciplines of Old Testament study included in the standard introductions as well as in several useful series. All of these provide secondary syntheses of various aspects of Old Testament research. All refer to, and base their discussions upon, various seminal works by Old Testament scholars which have proven pivotal in the development and flourishing of the various aspects of the discipline.

The main avenue into the various areas of Old Testament inquiry, especially for the beginner, has been until now mainly through the filter of these interpreters. Even on a pedagogical level, however, it is beneficial for a student to be able to interact with foundational works firsthand. This contact will not only provide insight into the content of an area, but hopefully will also lead to the sharpening of critical abilities through interaction with various viewpoints. This series seeks to address this need by including not only key, ground-breaking works, but also significant responses to these. This allows the student to appreciate the process of scholarly development through interaction.

The series is also directed toward scholars. In a period of burgeoning knowledge and significant publication in many places and languages around the world, this series will endeavor to make easily accessible significant, but at times hard to find, contributions. Each volume will contain essays, articles, extracts, and the like, presenting in a manageable scope the growth and development of one of a number of different aspects of Old Testament studies. Most volumes will contain previously published material, with synthetic essays by the editor(s) of the individual volume. Some volumes, however, are expected to contain significant, previously unpublished works. To facilitate access to students and scholars, all entries will appear in English and will be newly typeset. If students are excited by the study of Scripture

and scholars are encouraged in amicable dialogue, this series would have fulfilled its purpose.

DAVID W. BAKER, *series editor*
Ashland Theological Seminary

Publisher's Note

Articles republished here are reprinted without alteration, except for minor
matters of style not affecting meaning. Page numbers of the original publication are marked with double brackets ([[267]], for example). Other editorial
notes or supplementations are also marked with double brackets, including
editorially-supplied translations of foreign words. Footnotes are numbered
consecutively throughout each article, even when the original publication
used another system. No attempt has been made to bring transliteration systems into conformity with a single style.

In the introductions to each part below, reference to works included in
the respective "additional reading" sections is made by in-text citation; bibliographic information for all other works is provided in footnotes.

EDITOR'S FOREWORD

The editors of this volume's predecessor, *The Flowering of Old Testament Theology*, intended it especially for students, as an orientation to work in Old Testament theology from 1930 until the time of its publication in 1990. It served that purpose for more than a decade, through several printings. However, the production of Old Testament theologies has not abated; indeed, and contrary to some expectations, it has accelerated. The years since 1990 have seen the publication of numerous substantial monographs and many more essays and articles on the subject. These have brought both new contributors and new perspectives to the discussion of Old Testament theology. It seemed, then, that substantial revision would be required if a second edition were to fulfill the purpose of the first.

This volume follows the format of the SBTS series. That is, it includes introductory essays and excerpts from books and journal articles in the field. I have sought to include material whose authors represent a diversity of social locations, methods, and theological perspectives. But I have not attempted to invent diversity where it does not yet exist. The only fixed criterion for selection was that a publication address the subject of Old Testament theology expressly. A number of biblical scholars, theologians, and philosophers, writing since (and well before) 1930, have published work of value to biblical interpretation and theology, including Old Testament theology. Some of them make their appearance here, by way of influence and of footnotes. The focus remains on Old Testament theology.

The contents of the book proceed, by and large, in historical order. Part 1 provides background, especially in the essays by Otto Eissfeldt (1926) and Walther Eichrodt (1929); their debate still reverberates in contemporary discourse. Except for those chapters, all of the material excerpted in this volume was previously published in English. Parts 2 through 4 draw primarily from comprehensive Old Testament theologies (the works of G. E. Wright and Rolf Knierim are exceptions). These parts of the book include two types of excerpts. The first focuses on the author's approach or method, while the second samples the content of Old Testament theology from that author's point of view. Part 5 comprises programmatic statements and critical reviews aimed at furthering, or disciplining, Old Testament or biblical theology. Not all of the diverse proposals in part 5 are new; the earliest dates from 1977. But each of them stands in some critical relation to previous approaches and continues to challenge contemporary ones.

Nine of the twenty-eight authors represented here are new to this edition. However, simply adding new material would have expanded the book beyond manageable size. Thus, some of the earlier chapters have been eliminated and others abbreviated. The aim of these changes has been to include as many excerpts as possible while still providing students, and their professors, adequate orientation and context. In recent years, John H. Sailhamer (1995), Walter Brueggemann (1997: 1–114), Paul R. House (1998: 1–57, 548–59), and James Barr (1999) have assessed, from particular and quite different points of view, Old Testament theology's history and the current state of its questions (cf. more briefly Martens 1997a; Ollenburger 1999). Students may be directed to one or more of these works, as well as to earlier assessments of the field such as those by Gerhard F. Hasel (1991), John H. Hayes and Frederick C. Prussner (1985), Robert C. Dentan (1963), and Emil G. Kraeling (1955). Elmer A. Martens has provided a very useful annotated bibliography, with coverage until 1996 (Martens 1997b). But it is especially to be hoped that students will read further in Old Testament theology, and in the Old Testament itself.

That term—Old Testament—has been controversial for some time, given its Christian provenance and possibly supersessionist (or even worse) associations. It is retained here, both because none of the proposed substitutes has proved adequate and because it figures prominently, and sometimes intentionally, among the authors here represented. When that designation is inappropriate, as in reference to Jewish authors, other terms are used. Similar considerations attach to the divine name YHWH. When authors vocalize it, it is printed that way; otherwise, it remains without vowels. The same principle obtains elsewhere: the language of the authors remains their own.

Finally, I should like to thank David Baker, series editor, for promoting a revised edition, and Jim Eisenbraun, publisher, for patiently shepherding it through publication. Beverly McCoy, editor at Eisenbrauns, is a genial model of competence and efficiency. I also owe a particular debt to my colleagues in the first edition, Elmer A. Martens and the late Gerhard F. Hasel. Professor Martens first introduced me to Old Testament theology. He also took the lead in conceiving SBTS 1 and bringing it to life. The Associated Mennonite Biblical Seminary granted time and support for my work on this volume. To the seminary and to the Bible department's assistant Amy L. Barker, who graciously performed mundane tasks and provided wise counsel, I am most grateful.

BEN C. OLLENBURGER
Associated Mennonite Biblical Seminary

ABBREVIATIONS

General

A.T.	Altes Testament
E	Elohist writings
ET	English translation
J	Jahwist writings
LXX	Septuagint
MT	Masoretic Text
NF	Neue Folge (New Series)
NIV	New International Version
NJB	New Jerusalem Bible
NJPSV	New Jewish Publication Society Version
NJV	New Jewish Version
NLB	New Living Bible
NRSV	New Revised Standard Version
NT	New Testament
OT	Old Testament
P	Priestly writings
REB	Revised English Bible
RSV	Revised Standard Version
R.V.	Revised Version

Books and Periodicals

AJBI	*Annual of the Japanese Biblical Institute*
AJSL	*American Journal of Semitic Languages*
AnBib	Analecta Biblica
ANEP	J.B. Pritchard (ed.), *Ancient Near East in Pictures*
ANET	J.B. Pritchard (ed.), *Ancient Near Eastern Texts Relating to the Old Testament*
AThD	Acta Theologica Danica
BA	*Biblical Archaeologist*
BASOR	*Bulletin of the American Schools of Oriental Research*
BBB	Bonner biblische Beiträge

BiBe	Biblische Beiträge
Bib.Int.	_Biblical Interpretation_
Bibl	_Biblica_
BiE	_Biblische Enzyklopädie_
BiKi	_Bibel und Kirche_
BK	Biblischer Kommentar
BSt	Biblische Studien
BTB	_Biblical Theology Bulletin_
BWANT	Beiträge zur Wissenschaft vom Alten und Neuen Testaments
BZ	_Biblische Zeitschrift_
BZAW	Beihefte zur Zeitschrift für die alttestamentliche Wissenschaft
CBQ	_Catholic Biblical Ouarterly_
CBQMS	Catholic Biblical Quarterly Monograph Series
CJ	_Conservative Judaism_
CJT	_Canadian Journal of Theology_
DBS	_Dictionnaire de la Bible, Supplèment_
ET	_Expository Times_
Ev. Quarterly	_Evangelical Quarterly_
EvTh	_Evangelische Theologie_
FRLANT	Forschungen zur Religion und Literatur des Alten und Neuen Testaments
HBT	_Horizons in Biblical Theology_
HSM	Harvard Semitic Monographs
HSS	Harvard Semitic Studies
HTR	_Harvard Theological Review_
IDB	_Interpreter's Dictionary of the Bible_
IDB, Suppl. Vol.	_Interpreter's Dictionary of the Bible: Supplementary Volume_
IKZ	_Internationale kirchliche Zeitschrift_
Int/Interp	_Interpretation_
JAOS	_Journal of the American Oriental Society_
JBL	_Journal of Biblical Literature_
JBTh	_Jahrbuch für biblische Theologie_
JES	_Journal of Ecumenical Studies_
JJS	_Journal of Jewish Studies_
JQR	_Jewish Quarterly Review_
JR	_Journal of Religion_
JSOT	_Journal for the Study of the Old Testament_
JSOTS/JSOTSup	Journal for the Study of the Old Testament Supplement Series
JT(h)S	_Journal of Theological Studies_
KAT	Kommentar zum Alten Testament

MSL	Materials for the Sumerian Lexicon
NBL	*Neues Bibel-Lexikon*
NGTT	*Nederduitse gereformeerde teologiese tydskrif*
OBO	Orbis Biblicus et Orientalis
OTS	*Oudtestamentische Studiën*
RTP	*Revue de thèologie et de philosophie*
SBLDS	Society of Biblical Literature Dissertation Series
SBS	Stuttgarter Bibelstudien
SBT	Studies in Biblical Theology
SJOT	*Scandinavian Journal of the Old Testament*
SJT	*Scottish Journal of Theology*
StBib	Studia Biblica et Theologica (Pasadena)
THAT	*Theologisches Handwörterbuch zum Alten Testament*
ThB	Theologische Bücherei
Theol. Lit. Zt./ThLZ	*Theologische Literaturzeitung*
ThR	*Theologische Rundschau*
ThSt	Theologische Studien
TRE	*Theologische Realenzyklopädie*
TS	Theological Studies
TWAT/ThWAT	*Theologisches Wörterbuch zum Alten Testament*
TWNT	Gerhard Kittel and Gerhard Friedrich (eds.), *Theologisches Wörterbuch zum Neuen Testament*
TZ	*Theologische Zeitschrift*
VT	*Vetus Testamentum*
VT Supp/VTS	Supplements to Vetus Testamentum
VuF	*Verkündigung und Forschung*
WMANT	Wissenschaftliche Monographien zum Alten und Neuen Testament
ZATWiss/ZAW	*Zeitschrift für die Alttestamentliche Wissenschaft*
ZT(h)K	*Zeitschrift für Theologie und Kirche*

Part 1

The Background

BEN C. OLLENBURGER

Old Testament Theology before 1933

Introduction

As the contents of this volume will document, biblical and Old Testament theology are marked by disagreement and debate. This should not surprise us. In the course of more than two centuries, disagreements are bound to emerge regarding the nature and task of any area of academic inquiry, as they have in our case. The reasons for disagreement are not only academic. According to one biblical theologian, "the current crisis in church and theology" could explain why biblical theology commands special interest. In such a situation, he wrote, "many different attempts at biblical theology will have their place." Indeed, he reported that scholars use the term biblical theology to mean six quite different things, and he tried to chart his own course through that diversity.

Even though the quotations in the previous paragraph seem quite contemporary, they come from the preface of a book by Ludwig Friedrich Otto Baumgarten-Crusius, former Professor of Dogmatic Theology at the University of Jena. His book *The Basic Characteristics of Biblical Theology* was published in 1828. At the time, near the beginning of the discipline, the number of meanings assigned to the term *biblical theology* roughly equalled the number of published works on the subject. In other words, diversity and disagreement about Old Testament and biblical theology did not simply emerge over time; they were present at the beginning. However, Baumgarten-Crusius was able to cite one unifying factor: biblical theology emerged together with a

BEN C. OLLENBURGER, born in 1948, graduated from California State University, Long Beach (1973), and the Mennonite Brethren Biblical Seminary (1975). After teaching biblical studies and philosophy at Tabor College, he took his Ph.D. in Old Testament at Princeton Theological Seminary (1982), where he continued as Assistant Professor of Old Testament. Since 1987 he has taught at the Associated Mennonite Biblical Seminary (Elkhart), where he is Professor of Biblical Theology. In addition to works included in this volume's bibliography, he is the author of *Zion, the City of the Great King: A Theological Symbol of the Jerusalem Cult* (JSOTSup 41; Sheffield: Sheffield Academic Press, 1987), and *Zechariah* in the *New Interpreter's Bible*, vol. 6 (Nashville: Abingdon, 1996).

historical interpretation of the Bible. "The idea and the execution of biblical theology," he wrote, "are joined essentially with historical interpretation, and each of them has developed in recent times in relation to the other" (1828: 4). This relation has suffered serious strain in recent years, as scholarship in both history and theology has moved in various, not always compatible, directions. But for Baumgarten-Crusius and his peers, the historical study of the Bible made biblical theology possible.

This brief review traces developments in the way scholars conceived Old Testament or biblical theology in the years prior to the publication of Walther Eichrodt's first volume, in 1933. Some remarks on Old Testament theology's eighteenth-century beginnings precede paragraphs on history and philosophy, salvation history and history of religion, and the revival of Old Testament theology.

In the Beginning

Its emphasis on historical understanding counts among the eighteenth century's more important intellectual contributions. This emphasis had a significant impact on arts and letters generally, and it was crucial for theology (Shaffer 1975). By the end of the eighteenth century it had become clear that historical interpretation—more precisely, historical-critical interpretation—offered a fresh and also different understanding of the Bible. More specifically, some Protestant theologians were convinced that the historical interpretation of the Bible provided new and much more adequate foundations for dogmatic (or systematic) theology. However, it remained a matter of controversy exactly how these two, historical interpretation and dogmatic theology, should be related. Biblical theology emerged as a consequence of this controversy. In fact, it would not be too strong to say that, at its beginning, biblical theology was this controversy: it was an inquiry into the question how a historical study of the Bible should relate itself to dogmatics. Historical interpretation made biblical theology possible, and it also raised the most pressing issues in the discipline it helped to create. Primary among these was how to determine what in the Bible remained of universal and abiding validity in view of its irreducibly historical character.

It has long been customary to date the beginning of biblical theology to Johann Philipp Gabler's inaugural address at the University of Altdorf, in 1787 (included below, pp. 497ff.). Gabler there distinguished biblical from dogmatic theology and assigned them different tasks. In subsequent publications, he proposed joining the "grammatical-historical" interpretation of scripture to a theory of human reason's "development by stages" (Hartlich and Sachs 1952: 46)—a notion he borrowed from studies of classical and biblical mythology by Heyne and Eichhorn. Gabler made it the task of biblical theology to extract from historically determined modes of expression the unchanging truth contained in them, as a kernel from its husk, so that it could be delivered to dogmatics for elaboration in contemporary, ever-changing contexts (Ollenburger 1985; 1995; Knierim 1995: 495–556).

Gabler's proposal assumed that the Old Testament occupies a lower rung than the New on reason's developmental ladder. Historically considered, then, the Old and New Testaments required separate treatments. Gerhard Lorenz Bauer, Gabler's Altdorf colleague, adopted this view already in 1796, when he published the first Old Testament theology. In his "hermeneutics," Bauer insisted that all biblical interpretation be grounded in historical investigation in order to avoid "distorting the meaning of the Bible," as "the church fathers, allegorists, and mystics" had done (Bauer 1799: 10). Only a consistently historical interpretation could prevent "every theologian finding the doctrine of his church, and every philosopher his system . . . confirmed in the Bible" (1799: 99). Historical interpretation's distinction from dogmatics could not be clearer. Even so, Bauer's Old Testament theology proceeded to set out "the religious concepts of the ancient Hebrews" in static doctrinal categories: for example, "the eternity and immutability of God" (1796: 46–47). Thus, in 1801 Bauer added a supplement (*Beylagen*), which treated the Old Testament books in historical (roughly canonical) order. This allowed him to show the development from particular to universal ideas, a development crowned by Proverbs (similarly Noack 1853: 89–90). Even though Solomon's Proverbs retain "the name of the national deity [YHWH], and he appears as the one who has revealed himself more specifically to the Israelites," Bauer read Proverbs as transcending this particularity in its depiction of God's perfections: "the most rational [*vernünfstige*], highest, wise, self-subsistent cause of the world" (Bauer 1801: 135).

In arguing that Old Testament and New Testament theology must be distinguished from each other and carried out in independence from dogmatics, and in emphasizing religious ideas or concepts and their development from particular to universal, Bauer—together with Gabler—foreshadowed the nineteenth-century discussion (Smend 1962).

History and Philosophy

The first Old Testament theologies of the nineteenth century, contained in the biblical theologies of Christoph Friedrich von Ammon, Wilhelm Martin Leberecht de Wette, and Gottlieb Philipp Christian Kaiser, adopted a philosophical framework. For Ammon, the task of biblical theology was to provide a more adequate foundation for dogmatic theology through a critical study of the texts, in order to free them from the "nimbus of illusory ideas" (1801: 8). To this end he cited the traditional proof texts of doctrinal *loci* and tested them against the criterion of rationality. This criterion, understood in a Kantian moral sense, Ammon regarded as crucial, because only what is judged rational can be carried over into dogmatics.

Ammon, while influenced by Immanuel Kant, remained cautious. He regarded interpretation on the basis of "pure practical reason" in a negative light, as a "philosophical midrash" and thus as a species of allegory (so also did Gabler, a severe critic of Kant). In Ammon's view, Kantian interpretation tended to confer equal theological value on the texts of various religions; for

Ammon, this was too universal: "my hermeneutical principles do not permit me to share in this multiplication of theological profit" (Ammon 1801:
xii–xiii).

De Wette, unlike Ammon, exercised a profound influence on subsequent
biblical scholarship and theology (Rogerson 1991; Smend 1958). And his approach was much more historical in character than was Ammon's. But like
Ammon, de Wette, in his *Biblical Dogmatics* (first edition 1813; third edition
1831), wrote under the influence of Kant, especially as mediated through the
anthropology of Jakob F. Fries. Philosophical anthropology provided de
Wette the foundation he thought necessary to understand the Bible's religious ideas in their purity. The subject matter of dogmatics (biblical or otherwise) is religion, said de Wette, and religion is a part of human spiritual life.
This anthropological starting point is grounded in the immediate "fact" of
self-consciousness, which includes a religious component. Self-consciousness
itself thus yields "the pure idea of religion." A theology, or a dogmatics, of the
Old Testament must begin, then, with the "internal organization of the human spirit as such" (de Wette 1831: 1). However, it must also include an investigation of the laws and conditions under which the inner manifestation
of religion is expressed externally. These religious expressions stem from the
convictions, feeling (de Wette was congenial toward Schleiermacher), and
faith of the Old Testament authors themselves. This anthropological foundation then provided de Wette with a critical tool for recognizing the Old Testament's pure religious ideas and for distinguishing them from the mixed
historical forms in which they are clothed (1831: 30). This two-pronged strategy, which de Wette called biblical theology's anthropological and critical
operations, employs "inner revelation"—the pure idea of religion given in
self-consciousness—as a critical principle in the study of "external revelation."
Historical interpretation is then an active effort to correct, by the criteria of
internal revelation, the historical revelation of the Old Testament's authors.
De Wette's goal was exactly the same as Gabler's, pursued according to a different strategy.

In pursuing Old Testament theology itself, de Wette began by identifying
the "fundamental idea on which everything depends" and around which everything must be ordered (1831: 38). It is, he says, "the moral idea, free of
myth, of one God as a holy will" (1831: 63). This decision determined de
Wette's presentation of Old Testament theology, or "the doctrine of Hebraism." He first differentiated Hebraism from Judaism, which represents a religious decline, and then distinguished within Hebraism between its "ideal
universalism" and its "symbolic particularism." Universal are the doctrines of
God and humankind, while particularism he identified with the theocracy:
God's particular relation to Israel. De Wette claimed that Israel showed its tendency to misunderstand this particularism by reducing the universal character
of God's rule to nationalism, thus preparing the way for Judaism. In his discussion of the philosophical or hermeneutical framework that guided his biblical
theology, and in the execution of his interpretive strategy on the Old Testament, de Wette reflected idealism's characteristic interest in the abstract and

universal rather than the concrete and particular. Idealism provided him a way to merge historical and theological interpretation on behalf of dogmatics . . . and to denigrate Judaism.

G. P. C. Kaiser provided a different kind of framework, subsuming the Old Testament under "the universal history of religion" and then ultimately under "the universal religion." The particularity of Old Testament religion (Judaism) could be understood only in relation to religion in general, and then, together with Christianity and all other particular religions, taken up into a genuine "catholicism" (1813: 12). By describing the "principal moments" of religion in a dialectical fashion and drawing random insights from philosophy, Kaiser pared from the Old Testament the temporal ideas that must be left behind in the universal religion of humanity. He also invented new categories for this task, such as geofetishology, anthropotheology, cosmocraty, demonophany. He used this monstrous vocabulary much as Ammon and de Wette used the vocabulary of philosophy and dogmatics to transcend the Old Testament's particularity, producing in his case, however, a vacant universalism. Kaiser himself found it vacant, repented of it, and announced his commitment to "the word revealed in the Bible" (1821: iv).

Alongside and occasionally in response to those philosophically grounded accounts were others that sought, by intentional contrast, to proceed in a purely historical manner. Baumgarten-Crusius made the first attempt in 1828, followed immediately by Carl Peter Wilhelm Gramberg (1829–30). Overshadowing them in both methodological clarity and influence was Daniel Georg Conrad von Cölln (1836). He modeled his Old Testament theology on de Wette but claimed that neither de Wette nor anyone else had fulfilled the strictly historical requirements of Old Testament theology laid down (as he believed) by Gabler. However, von Cölln's own work showed that he actually opposed the use of philosophical categories. His understanding of Old Testament theology's task—to differentiate the universal from the particular, or the "inexact forms of representation" from the "pure concepts" hidden in them (1836: 11)—otherwise hardly differed from de Wette's. Following G. L. Bauer, von Cölln argued that these judgments can and must be made by historical criticism itself, which follows the Old Testament's religious notions in their process of formation through the New Testament. There they are deepened and broadened to form the basis of a "universal religion" (1836: 4). Old Testament theology was for von Cölln, as it was for de Wette and Baumgarten-Crusius, the first chapter of historical theology (Dentan 1963: 33) and one foundation of dogmatic theology.

The methodological tension between the philosophical and historical approaches was resolved in a higher unity—*aufgehoben*, as he put it—by Johann Karl Wilhelm Vatke, whose *Religion des Alten Testaments* was the only part of an announced six-part biblical theology that Vatke was permitted to publish (Brömse 1984: 129–45; Benecke 1883: 188–228). Old Testament theology must be historical, Vatke insisted, because it pursues the idea of Old Testament religion, expressed in its various religious representations, through the "principal moments" of its historical development. But historical criticism by

itself is subjective; it is not concerned with truth, because it is not properly
scientific (Vatke 1835: 156). It can only achieve scientific status, and thus always only a relative objectivity, by being taken up into a philosophically
grounded conceptual analysis. Hegel provides the tools for such analysis,
which is scientific because it comprehends the most universal horizon possible: history as a whole. Conceptual analysis will necessarily be historical because the concept of a religion is unfolded in a historical dialectic: the
subjectivity of the concept and the objectivity of its manifestations are resolved in the Idea of Israel's religion. Since the same dialectic occurs in the
"knowing subject" (the biblical theologian, in this case), the subjectivism of
historical criticism is overcome. Hegel's philosophy was thus Vatke's hermeneutical foundation for understanding the history of Old Testament religion
theologically (Vatke 1835: 594–95, where he also cites de Wette 1831: 63,
quoted above).

     While Vatke's Old Testament theology was grounded in a philosophical
method, it was also the first to have a thoroughly historical character, thus exhibiting a remarkable harmony of method and form. The most notable of his
historical observations was that the system of legislation in the Pentateuch
came after and not before the prophets (1835: 204). This observation led
others, after Vatke, to elevate the prophets to the pinnacle of Old Testament
religion. However, Vatke (disagreeing with Hegel) argued that Israel's religion
reached its zenith in the postexilic period. This followed logically, since Vatke
stressed the need to understand Israel's religion from the perspective of its
completed history. His philosophical language was as dense as Kaiser's was
monstrous, but Vatke's methodological rigor and consistency were exemplary.

Salvation History and the History of Religion

Vatke's synthesis did not survive him (Bruno Bauer's equally Hegelian work
[1838] took no account of historical criticism), but his historical organicism
was taken up, apart from a Hegelian framework, by a series of conservative
scholars oriented to "salvation history": Steudel, Hävernick, Oehler, Hofmann, and Schultz (1869). Influencing them to varying degrees was a tradition of mystical Pietism and speculative history rooted in Württemberg and
Tübingen (Diestel 1869: 698–708) and absorbed by Hegel and Schelling as
well (Toews 1980: 13–26; Benz 1983). The salvation historians put particular
emphasis on the "facts" (*Tatsachen*) of God's activity in Israel, which constituted its history as an organic whole. They believed that the history narrated
in the Old Testament corresponded substantially to an actual course of
events within world history and that these should be the central subject matter of Old Testament theology. They further claimed that participation in the
spirit of revelation was a condition for understanding its history (Oehler
1845: 32–34; Schultz 1869: 72). Heinrich A. C. Hävernick emphasized the
"acts of God" and not just doctrines and specifically the subjective effects of
these acts, which reflect different stages of "religious consciousness" (1848:
17). For Johann C. F. Steudel, the "facts" of revelation in the Old Testament

were more important than either its religious concepts or the religious consciousness that lay behind them, because the facts of revelation are the source of both concepts and consciousness (1840: 18–19; cf. Riehm 1889: 8–10). Like Vatke, then, the salvation historians brought the interpreting subject into relation with its object. Steudel, Hävernick, and Oehler were unable, however, to display their historical and even narrative emphases (Steudel 1840: 11–19) in the body of their Old Testament theologies, which thus reflect a certain inconsistency between theory and execution.

Johann Christian Konrad von Hofmann overcame this inconsistency, particularly in his *Schriftbeweis* (1852–56). He wrote no separate Old Testament theology but conceived biblical and historical theology to be engaged in testing systematic theology's exposition of that of which every (Protestant!) Christian is absolutely certain: reconciliation with God through Jesus Christ. According to Hofmann, the Trinitarian life of God unfolded itself into the world's history and then Israel's, giving each biblical fact and each text its necessary place within the organic sequence of salvation history. (The term *salvation history* first occurs in Hofmann 1841–44: 1.8.) The historical form of the Bible is not accidental; it is necessarily analogous to God's trinitarian history, which expands and unfolds itself into the world's history and then Israel's. For Hofmann, biblical theology is thinking *in* our relation to God, not about it; hence, its relation to systematic theology is organic, not something to be considered separately. In the power and consistency of his thought and in the density of his language, Hofmann resembled Vatke.

Soon overshadowing the salvation historians were the historians of religion, particularly Wellhausen, as Hermann Schultz's career itself illustrates. In 1848 Schultz edited Hävernick's work, and the first edition of his own *Alttestamentliche Theologie* (Schultz 1869) reflected the influence of the salvation historians. But in his second edition (1878), Schultz adopted Wellhausen's views, and in subsequent editions (through 1896) he moved still further toward history of religion. The first to conceive Old Testament theology purely as the history of Israel's religion was August Kayser in 1886; the third and subsequent editions of his work were written by Karl Marti and entitled *History of Israelite Religion*.

Hermann Gunkel and the "history-of-religion school" (*religionsgeschichtliche Schule*) brought the production of Old Testament theology to a temporary halt, not because they were not theologians—"Biblical exegesis is theological exegesis" (Gunkel 1913: 24)—but because they conceived theology to be concerned with religion as opposed to dogmatics. Religion, Gunkel declared, is fundamentally piety, to be discovered in the Old Testament by penetrating to the "inner life" of its authors (1913: 25). Gunkel wanted to go behind the religious representations and concepts of the Old Testament in order "to be present at the birth of its deepest thoughts" (1926–27: 533). Bernhard Stade, a friend and follower of Wellhausen, wrote an Old Testament theology as late as 1905, but Gunkel and his circle had already made it an anachronism. Stade gave Old Testament theology the task of tracing the origin and progressive development of the religious notions that formed the content of Jewish faith and are "for that reason the historical presupposition of Christianity" (Stade 1905: 2). He also wanted to distinguish the Old Testament religious concepts whose development can be traced into Judaism but were not taken up by Jesus and his apostles. Consequently, "The New Testament is the best source for the theology of the Old Testament" (1899: 93).

The Revival of Old Testament Theology

The stalemate to which Wellhausen and Gunkel helped bring Old Testament theology eventually spawned a series of reflections on method by Old Testament scholars from different points of view, united only in their agreement that Old Testament theology had to be conceived anew. Justus Köberle repudiated the history-of-religion movement and suggested a return to salvation history, beginning from the NT and a concept of revelation adequate to Christian faith. Rudolf Kittel complained that in the then-current academic climate, fascinated by Mesopotamian parallels, it was as if *extra babylonem nulla salus* ("outside of Babylon there is no salvation"; Kittel 1921: 96). History-of-religion research must be expanded into Old Testament theology, he argued, by employing a philosophy or dogmatics of religion in order to penetrate to the Old Testament's essence and truth. Willy Staerk granted history of religion its due but called for systematic and philosophical reflection on the historical data from a phenomenological point of view, so that Old Testament theology might "come to its fulfillment as a component of systematic theology, which it was from the beginning and which it must remain" (Staerk 1923: 290). Staerk proposed a philosophical starting point, defining religion as "the transcendental unity of apperception in the experience of the unconditioned-personal as a synethic a priori" (1923: 292). The experience in question, for Staerk, was that of Moses, who was Israel's founder because he had a uniquely immediate experience of God. Old Testament theology would grasp the essential religious experience of Moses and follow its unfolding, as God's self-mediation, in Israel's history. Departing from Staerk, Carl Steuernagel (1925) proposed the systematic presentation of Old Testament religion in categories drawn from its historical analysis, without borrowing either these categories or Old Testament theology's methods from philosophy or dogmatics (cf. König 1922).

Steuernagel, like many of his predecessors, invoked Gabler as having defined for Old Testament theology a task from which it had lamentably departed. Steuernagel blamed history of religion. Steuernagel wrote, with reference to Gabler, "If it was then necessary to free biblical theology from the shackles of dogmatics, so it is time now . . . to free Old Testament theology from the shackles of Old Testament history-of-religion" (Steuernagel 1925: 266). Neither Steuernagel nor his peers fully appreciated the degree to which assumptions about Old Testament theology had changed since Gabler. For Gabler the task of biblical theology consisted in determining which of the Bible's ideas were universal and had abiding validity and in distinguishing them from the ideas that were merely particular or historical. By the time of

Steuernagel, the goal of Old Testament theology was thought to consist much more in penetrating to, or in grasping, the essence of Israel's religion. Somewhat ironically, the history-of-religion school was in agreement. Articulating the "dogmatics" of this school, Ernst Troeltsch wrote that it regards "the entire territory of Christian life and thought as a gradual unfolding of an immanent impelling power or fundamental ideal, realizing itself in historical Christianity. This ideal, or this 'essence' persisting in all specific manifestations, might then be taken as the subject-matter and the normative principle of dogmatics" (Troeltsch 1913: 11–12). Willy Staerk, as described above, echoed this understanding, as would Walther Eichrodt in this Old Testament theology of 1933 (see below, pp. 39–56).

This limited and very general agreement on the goals of theology, specifically Old Testament theology, concealed significant disagreement about how to achieve them. In some part, the disagreement was regarding the unity that Baumgarten-Crusius had observed and prescribed in 1828 between "historical interpretation" and biblical theology. Could a historical(-critical) discipline grasp the essence of Old Testament religion, or must Old Testament theology pursue its proper goal in some other way? Conversely, could a properly historical inquiry, as part of a critically responsible biblical scholarship, have as its object anything other than the history of (Israel's) religion? Must Old Testament theology be a historical discipline? Can it be one? Must Old Testament theology be specific to a particular confession? May specific Christian convictions play a legitimate role in historical inquiry (cf. also Sellin 1933)?

Otto Eissfeldt and Walther Eichrodt debated these and other questions in a context shaped by (among other things) the background sketched above, intellectual (including theological) currents in the aftermath of World War I, and their respective Lutheran and Reformed confessions. Their (translated) essays, of 1926 and 1929, follow immediately below. While clearly and expressly reflecting the particular time in which they were written, these essays have proved remarkably—even increasingly—pertinent to contemporary issues and debates about Old Testament theology. Hence, they provide instructive background, and also occasional foreground, to the theologies and proposals that follow in this book.

OTTO EISSFELDT

The History of Israelite-Jewish Religion and Old Testament Theology

[[1]] The tension between absolute and relative, between transcendence and immanence, is the current problem of theology. For biblical scholarship, this general problem is reduced to a particular one: history and revelation. It is with this problem that the study of both Testaments, of the New just as of the Old, has to grapple, and a new solution must be found that applies fundamentally to both. However, particular matters in the Old Testament differ from those in the New, so that a treatment restricted to the Old Testament is legitimate. The question, then, is whether the religion of the Old Testament is to be understood and presented as a historical entity like other religions of antiquity, and thus in terms of the history of Israelite Jewish religion, or as a religion which is, even if in some limited way, the true religion, the revelation of God, and thus—so the term will be understood here—as "Old Testament theology."

In the last three decades, the question has been debated repeatedly. Even if that has taken place most often in a way that has gone beyond the Old Testament and put the Bible as a whole or Christianity at the center, from the general answers given here those that apply particularly to the Old Testament can

Translated and reprinted with permission from Otto Eissfeldt, "Israelitisch-jüdische Religionsgeschichte und Alttestamentliche Theologie," *Zeitschrift für die Alttestamentliche Wissenschaft* 44 (1926) 1–12. Translated by Ben C. Ollenburger. Otto Eissfeldt (1887–1973) studied with two of the luminaries in German biblical scholarship, Julius Wellhausen and Hermann Gunkel. Eissfeldt's own work, first in Berlin, where he also served briefly as a preacher, and then in Halle (1922–54), continued the literary-critical and historical tradition that he learned from his mentors. His textbook, *The Old Testament: An Introduction* (New York: Harper & Row, 1965), became a standard work in the field; its first German edition was published in 1934. Eissfeldt also distinguished himself as a scholar of, among other things, Israel's history and religion, the Bible's Hebrew text, and the Ugaritic texts. The six-volume collection of his essays reflects the range and the depth of his scholarship (*Kleine Schriften* [ed. Rudolf Sellheim and Fritz Maas; Tübingen: Mohr, 1962–79]). Among the volumes published in his honor is *Festschrift Otto Eissfeldt zum 60. Geburtstage 1. September 1947* (ed. Johann Fück; Halle: Max Niemeyer, 1947).

be immediately derived. Two conceptions stand over against each other. The one, the *historical* or the *scientific study of religion*, requires that the religion of the Old Testament be investigated by the same means with which historical scholarship otherwise works: linguistic and historical-critical mastery of the sources, and analysis of their content on the basis of an empathic personal reliving. However, this conception understands the valuation of Old Testament religion, and the question of its truth altogether, as matters [[2]] of personal conviction; science does not proceed that far. The other conception, the *theological* (in the narrow sense of the term) or *churchly*, claims on the other hand that perception of the true essence of Old Testament religion merely by application of the otherwise typical methods of historical investigation is impossible. Rather, it discloses itself only to faith, and that is something different from empathetic reliving; it consists, namely, in being overwhelmed and humbled in inner obedience to that which has taken hold of oneself. Accordingly, in Christian theology the decisive contents of the Old Testament will be determined on the basis of Christianity, while the Old Testament will be joined to the New, and the Bible will be interpreted from a foundational experience, naturally of a Christian sort, whether this be called religious-moral renewal or justification by faith or the revelation of God in Jesus or something else. Whatever has gone into belief in the Old Testament as the revelation of God is precisely what has to be treated by Old Testament theology.

Prior to the [First] World War these two conceptions, the historical and the theological, somewhat counterbalanced each other, but in such a way that the historical appeared to be "modern." But after the war, the situation has changed completely. Among those who have since expressed themselves on these matters, the overwhelming majority have declared the historical study of the Bible, and thus also of the Old Testament, to be antiquated and outmoded, and they enlist on the side of the theological conception, to which the present and the future belong. Weary of the historicism, the psychologism, and the relativism of the scientific-study-of-religion method, one yearns for revelation and demands a scientific treatment of the Bible that does justice to its claim to be revelation of absolute worth—namely, the theological. Especially the representatives of dialectical theology have expressed this demand. But they have not yet gone much beyond criticism of the old and the basic demand for something new. More precise expositions of how the scientific presentation of the religion of the Bible or of the Old Testament should now be done have not yet appeared.[1] Alongside the representatives of dialectical

1. Worth noting are the statements in Eduard Thurneysen's article on "Schrift und Offenbarung" (*Zwischen den Zeiten* 2 [1924] 1–30), and in Karl Barth's article on "Das Schriftprinzip der reformierten Kirche" (*Zwischen den Zeiten* 3 [1925] 215–45). I can agree with a whole series of Thurneysen's propositions, since they are congruent in their intention with those I will set out. Propositions such as these:

> It is characteristic of the so-called historical-critical school of the past decade that it has at least made a point of putting into practice the method of historical psychological interpretation, which during the course of the past century has universally prevailed in the treatment of historical problems. . . . None of us can any

theology it has been [[3]] theologians of a conservative bent like Girgensohn and Procksch who have recently taken up the struggle against the scientific-study-of-religion treatment of the Bible. In its place they propose treating it pneumatically, wherein the concept pneumatic is nearly identical with what has been identified previously as theological in the narrower sense. One of the two, Procksch, has also shown how this proposal is to be worked out when applied to [[4]] the study of the Old Testament, so that his exposition must be

---

longer retreat behind this historical-psychological view. . . . What has to be asserted against liberal theology is this: that it has never taken up. . . . the question posed to it in the biblical claim of revelation. And yet, precisely this theology would have been in a unique position to approach the problem of revelation, based on the only correct assumption; namely, that revelation as such can never be established in the domain of historical events. . . . A revelation that must be defended on rational grounds—that, indeed, can really only ever be so defended—is no revelation. This attempted defense has always been made, however, and always will be made. It is the essential characteristic of that which is called orthodoxy. Orthodoxy is precisely the attempt . . . to confirm revelation. The understanding of revelation marks a transcendence of liberalism and orthodoxy; it is the crisis of them both.

And very similar expressions are found in Barth's article. But since revelation is then equated with the canon, and thus with a historical entity, and the correlative relation of the twin concepts, revelation and faith, is thereby sundered, the promising beginning is nipped in the bud. This can already be seen in Thurneysen, when he says:

The same claim of revelation is also the secret of the New Testament, the meaning of the prophets and that of the Psalms, of Job, and of the historical books. And even if often so dimmed as to be unrecognizable, it extends to the farthest margins of the Bible. . . . This claim has found its unequivocal and powerful expression in the fact of the canon.

But this is much clearer in Barth:

Even if the individual reader is able, in light of his own understanding, to distinguish between the center and the periphery of the Bible, between what he "experiences" and something else that he has not "experienced," between what in his judgment "promotes Christ," as Luther put it, and something else where he judges such to be missing, the distinctions that result from such considerations may in no way have the character of distinctions in principle. With God it is not a matter of more or less, but of either-or. The Reformed Church has long since laid special emphasis on this determination. It has fundamentally disapproved Luther's imperious way of arranging, on the basis of a most individually conditioned dogmatics, a kind of selected Bible. And we believe that in so doing, it has done well.

Here the bond between faith and revelation is completely sundered, because what Barth calls Luther's most individually conditioned dogmatics is, in truth, faith. Thus, also among the representatives of dialectical theology the two different modes of consideration, that from the outside (the historical) and that from within (from faith), are not held strictly apart. Moreover, it is significant that in Barth the Reformed confession is played off against Luther. But here, if anywhere, evangelical theology must follow the path indicated by Luther, and not that of the Reformed confession.

investigated somewhat more thoroughly as the more important contribution to our question.[2]

Procksch proposes as the ultimate task of biblical exegesis that it must expound divine revelation, whose validity is eternal, in human forms. To this end it must apply with complete thoroughness those means at the disposal of the historian in the interpretation of other literary works: philology, historical criticism, empathy. However, investigation that works only with these tools is unable to fathom precisely the decisive elements of the Old Testament's—words, historical events, the notion of God. Words like the first sentence of the Bible, events like the crossing of the Red Sea and the Sinai covenant, and most especially the notion of the transcendent, personal God, are irrational, paradoxical, and contradict any merely historical understanding. Here it is a matter of pneumatic entities that can only be understood from within, from faith.

> Faith is the organ of perception for the pneumatic world. Exegesis, historical understanding, and esthetic empathy continually come up against the world of the Bible, which discloses itself to faith as God's miracle, and which contains at the same time God's revelation.

Nonetheless, it is not the case that the pneumatic subjects pointed to in the Old Testament are by themselves able to awaken the faith which can now penetrate to their mystery. Rather, they become clear only from the perspective of faith in Christ.

> Christ is the central figure of the Bible from whom all effects of the New Testament proceed, in whom all effects of the Old Testament are comprehended. . . . In Christ [[5]] the Bible becomes a seamless whole. One can sever no member from this organism without wounding the entire organism. . . . As the Father of Jesus Christ, the God of the Old Testament is our God. Whoever denies this proposition puts himself outside the fundamental certainty of biblical religion.

It is clear from all this that Procksch is talking about a presentation of Old Testament religion drawn on the basis of faith, and even from a distinctly Christian faith. The otherwise typical methods of historical investigation are not thereby scorned, but they are nonetheless—despite every insistence on their importance—finally valued only as *ancillae theologiae*. All decisive statements about the essence of Old Testament religion are made from faith, and it is emphatically determined that faith remains the organ of historical reflection for the Christian.

If the historical approach to the Old Testament and its religion is here robbed of its independence and made subservient to the theological, as alone

---

2. "Über pneumatische Exegese," *Christentum und Wissenschaft* I (1925) 145–58; "Die Geschichte als Glaubensinhalt," *Neue Kirchliche Zeitschrift* 36 (1925) 485–99; "Ziele und Grenzen der Exegese," *Neue Kirchliche Zeitschrift* 36 (1925) 715–30. This last essay concludes with a brief debate with Barth.

able to grasp the essence of the subject completely, there is on the other hand no lack of attempts to treat the theological as an appendix to the historical, and to see the former as a direct continuation of the latter. The efforts of Schleiermacher and Hegel, by means of a historical-philosophical comparison of religions to show Christianity and thereby, at least indirectly, Old Testament religion to be the highest and absolute religion, have continued to find followers in the present.[3] And there is no lack of those who—like Hermann Schultz—are of the opinion that Old Testament religion "discloses itself in all its truth," as does any other spiritual development, "only to one who has an intrinsic appreciation of its essence, who has a love for it, and who takes delight in its specific character,"[4] but reject a particular theological method for comprehending it. Thus, they suppose that they can treat the claims of faith satisfactorily by means of a historical presentation. Over against this very [[6]] widespread inclination to tie these two approaches in one way or another, it must be emphasized that such a blending can only be harmful. Historical understanding of the Old Testament may never go beyond the relative and the immanent, while on the other hand, faith grasped by the absolute and transcendent is not the instrument that could comprehend the Old Testament as a historical entity. The theological approach reduces the diversity of historical phenomena, since it seeks to interpret them on the basis of the decisive experience of faith, and the historical approach flattens the depth of revelation that faith experiences in the Old Testament, since it arranges it alongside these other phenomena.

The historical approach on the one hand and the theological on the other belong on two different planes. They correspond to two differently constituted functions of our spirit, to knowing and to believing. Knowing consists in intensely engaged activity; as historical knowing, it is a tireless effort to inquire after what has taken place. The manner of religious believing is passivity, which allows itself to be grasped by something higher and purer, in order to surrender itself freely to it. Knowledge is aware that despite all its efforts it cannot get beyond the world limited to space and time, while faith knows that it has been laid hold of by the eternal. Knowledge strives for certain, clear evidence that will convince others even against their will, while faith always remains a completely personal venture to be undertaken anew by each individual, which is at its greatest when it signifies a not-seeing but yet believing. With this twofold intellectual function we approach Old Testament religion. Knowledge subordinates this entity to itself, since it masters it; yet, at the same time, it is stronger than we are, since it submits itself to us as believers. Thus, the necessity of both approaches is given in our intellectual be-

3. Willy Staerk, "Religionsgeschichte und Religionsphilosophie in ihrer Bedeutung für die biblische Theologie des Alten Testaments," *Zeitschrift für Theologie und Kirche* 21 (1923) 289–300; C. Stange, "Die Absolutheit des Christentums," *Zeitschrift für systematische Theologie* I (1923/24) 44–68; "Die Aufgabe der Religionsgeschichte," *Zeitschrift für systematische Theologie* I (1923/24) 301–13; "Stimmungsreligion, Stifterreligion und Christentum," *Zeitschrift für systematische Theologie* I (1923/24) 427–37; and etc.

4. *Alttestamentliche Theologie* (5th ed.; Göttingen: Vandenhoeck & Ruprecht, 1896), 1:8.

ing, and we have only to choose either to effect a compromise between them, or to recognize and attend to each in its own character and integrity.

As we have seen, compromises prove in the long run to be unsatisfactory, so it is worth leaving both approaches in their unrestricted independence and tolerating the tension that arises between them, [[7]] even should this occasionally become—and perhaps it must become—torment and temptation to the pious. But in the long run this is not fate but fortune, because the more purely the two approaches are distinguished from each other, the more they will be able to enrich each other. Powers of faith, and not of knowledge, have formed the Old Testament, and if in the successive generations of theologians knowledge turns first to one and then to another portion of Old Testament religion, this is grounded not only in the internal movement of knowledge itself but also and above all in this, that new dimensions of the religious treasure transmitted from the past always assume importance in the life of faith of individual epochs, and that knowledge then takes hold of these dimensions. If investigation now emphasizes particularly the demonic, irrational, and unfathomable with respect to Yahweh, this can be explained on the basis of the religious experience of our generation, in which this side of God has become newly apparent. And it is no accident that, at the same time, work in church history and systematics has learned anew to understand Luther's *deus absconditus*. So it is faith that has provided knowledge with its object and continually sheds new light on it.

On the other hand, knowledge can be useful for faith by enriching and relieving it. The life of faith of individuals and even of an entire generation can never appropriate more than a part of Old Testament religion; the remainder remains foreign to it. The Old Testament is too rich and too diverse for it to be otherwise. Thus, the prophets as religious personalities, that is, as heroes, remained unknown to Christianity for eighteen centuries. They supposedly lived and worked—one need only recall the paintings on the ceiling of the Sistine Chapel—as those who had predicted the Christ. Accordingly, only their isolated words were important; as personalities, they remained unknown and without effect. It was nineteenth-century historical research that taught us to understand the grand prophetic characters, since it had empathetically relived their proclamation. And who would deny that these valuable discoveries of knowledge have not also enriched the life of faith? The other side of it is that the historical consideration of the Old Testament is able to prove of [[8]] service to faith in relieving it of the burden of such elements in the Old Testament that appear to us, and must appear, as sub-Christian and immoral. Thus, it shows that the narratives of Jacob's cunning and deceitful behavior toward Esau and Laban, and the passages that attribute the ruthless and horrible extermination of the Canaanites to Yahweh's command, are emanations from a nationally restricted religiosity, which is also to be found elsewhere in history and in the present. With naive and subjective sincerity, God and nation are equated—a kind of piety that can be shared, however, only by those who feel themselves to be part of the nation concerned. Already for that reason those elements of the Old Testament are meaningless for the faith of Christians. But historical consideration shows, further, that this nationally restricted piety represents a form of religion that is overcome in the course of the history of Israelite religion itself. Prophecy severs the bond that unites God and the nation, and thereby creates space for a piety that leaves everything earthly behind and can say to God: "If I have only you, then I care nothing of heaven and earth"—a word that corresponds completely to the loftiness of Christianity. In this way, historical knowledge frees faith from sub-Christian religious forms of the Old Testament and does justice to them at the same time, since it teaches us to consider them as historically conditioned.

How dangerous it is to combine the two approaches can be shown with particular clarity from the Old Testament. It is here especially clear that Procksch's statement—that faith remains the organ even of historical reflection for the Christian—is to be questioned. We have examples in the Old Testament of historical reflection and of historical description in which faith was the decisive factor. It is what has been called religious or theological pragmatism in Judges and in the books of Kings and the Chronicler: the depiction of the period of the judges according to which Yahweh's punishment (oppression by enemies) follows on the apostasy of the nation, and then Yahweh's help (the sending of a savior or a judge) follows on the nation's conversion; and in the books of Kings and the Chronicler, the schema of the kings' success and failure, fortune and misfortune, which depends on their religious-cultic actions. [[9]] That this religious-pragmatic understanding of history has distorted and falsified reality will be universally admitted; however, it not only hinders historical knowledge but also endangers the purity of faith. The view underlying this understanding of history, that the way of the world can be evenly calculated in such a way that piety and fortune, conduct pleasing to God and success—or the reverse, sin and suffering—always go together, corresponds in no way at all to what can be recognized at the high points of Old Testament religion as the nature of faith. There, faith always entails struggle and daring, and precisely where an incongruity between piety and fortune is discovered and must be overcome, faith displays itself in its full power: "Nevertheless, I abide with you." What is clear from this example applies generally: on behalf of knowledge, just as on behalf of faith, one must guard against confusing the historical treatment of the Old Testament with the theological.

On this basis it becomes clear that the development traversed by our discipline—now usually, and significantly, designated by the double name of "history of Israelite-Jewish religion (Old Testament theology)"—from the *dicta probantia* [[proof texts]] of orthodoxy and the Bible doctrines of pietism on the one hand, to the history of religion of the nineteenth century on the other, was not accidental but necessary. In each of the two phases two modes of consideration came into view: that of faith and that of historical knowledge. To the first, the Old Testament means God's revelation, while to the second it offers itself as a historical entity. Orthodoxy and pietism allowed history to be submerged into revelation, while the historical understanding of the nineteenth century threatened to dissolve revelation into history. It is important to avoid the errors of both phases, and to carry further the appropriate starting points of each; that is, to acknowledge and to practice both approaches: history of Israelite-Jewish religion and Old Testament theology.

The first is, as the name implies, a historical discipline. It presents Old Testament religion as an entity having undergone historical development, and treats it with the [[10]] usual philological-historical tools, as has already been mentioned. To it belongs the instrument of empathy with the subject, which is especially important in this particular field. But this is then sufficient for accomplishing the historical task; it requires no other means. The historian does not answer the question of absolute value, of the "truth" of the subject. He must remain satisfied with establishing that he has to do with an entity that makes the claim to be revelation and the word of God; he does not decide whether this claim is justified. It is his responsibility to show that here men appear who assert that they have been called and commissioned in miraculous fashion by a personal power outside of and over the world, by Yahweh, and he must acknowledge that it is here doubtless a matter of a subjectively truthful assertion. Whether this assertion is also true objectively remains undecided. With respect to Old Testament religion, the historian is aware that he can never go beyond the world of space and time. Insofar as value judgments are made in the presentation of the history of Israelite-Jewish religion, in speaking of its rise and fall or its flowering and withering, they are of a relative kind, and the criterion of judgment must be derived from the history of Jewish-Israelite religion itself. It is therewith assumed that the historian must omit any forward reference to the New Testament. He may and must look beyond the historical development he has to treat only insofar as it makes its own reference beyond itself, but he leaves undecided whether the New Testament and Christianity represent its fulfillment. It goes together with this kind of history of Jewish-Israelite religion that its treatment is fundamentally independent of the scholar's form of religion, and that in this field those who belong to diverse Christian confessions, and even those of non-Christian religions, can work hand in hand, as indeed actually happens.

Quite different the theological consideration of the Old Testament! Here it is a matter of presenting that which, with respect to the Old Testament, has become revelation, God's word, for the interpreter and his religious community—because he will always be in some way the organ of his religious community. It will thus bear the character of witness, even though of a thoroughly scientific [[11]] kind, and its validity will be restricted to the circle of those whose piety is the same as, or similar to, that of the interpreter; in other words, it is relative to church and confession. There is, therefore, no possibility here of cooperation among members of different religious communities who could further their knowledge through cooperative investigation and argument; rather, here one community can convince the other only by the more powerful demonstration "of spirit and of power."

In Old Testament theology it is a question of describing the revelation of God as it has occurred and occurs ever anew for faith in relation to the Old Testament. For that reason, it can never take the form of a historical presentation, because faith has not to do with things past but with the timeless present; revelation is exalted above the category of time. Thus, a systematic form of presentation is appropriate for Old Testament theology—if systematic is understood to mean not the methodological development of everything from a first principle but, rather, the sequential arrangement of propositions in the manner of *loci*. The "attributes" of Yahweh, which have come to be, for the interpreter, revelations concerning the essence and will of his God (God the Lord, God the Holy, etc.); the estimation of the world and of humankind, which is truth for the interpreter (the world of God's creation, and the God who abides with humankind despite its insignificance in comparison with this vast creation [Psalm 8], etc.); these and others must be so treated.

Of course, this kind of Old Testament theology, structured on the basis of faith, is influenced throughout by the central faith experience of its author and his religious community, but it is not required that every assertion must be expressly related to this. In other words, Old Testament theology does not always require "fulfillment" in New Testament theology. There are elements in the Old Testament—for example, the psalms that praise God's majesty as it is unfolded in creation—that can also be direct revelation to the Christian, all the more since such are almost wanting in the New Testament. In this case, the otherwise self-evident schema of placing the religion [[12]] of the New Testament above that of the Old[5] must be replaced by a schema that sets them alongside each other. Here the Old Testament serves to complement the New.

Despite every distinction between the two approaches, the historical and the theological, it is nonetheless finally the case that, seen from a higher vantage point, they form a unity—and they do so not just to the extent that its importance to us as the source of revelation, rather than only or even primarily as the object of historical knowledge, accounts for the extraordinarily urgent historical investigation of Old Testament religion. Rather, beyond all this, we are confident that it is the one identical truth for which knowledge strives and by which faith is grasped. Knowing and believing belong, as we have seen, to two parallel planes, and they must meet each other in infinity—but only in infinity. Within the finite realm the two approaches form a unity only to the extent that one person can master them.

---

5. This applies above all, as Karl Holl has justifiably stressed ("Urchristentum und Religionsgeschichte," *Zeitschrift für systematische Theologie* 2 [1924/25] 387–430), to conceptions regarding the relation of God to sin and the sinner. The New Testament idea of a God who offers himself to the sinner is actually foreign to the Old Testament. But it is equally correct and worth noting when Holl adds this conclusion: "Indeed, in the question of evil, Judaism came to a similar recognition never attained elsewhere among humankind. Recalling only Isaiah 53 and the *anawim* in the Psalms—Judaism broke through the conventional wisdom which held that the best person must also be the most fortunate. Just the reverse: precisely the most pious can suffer the harshest troubles. The unfortunate one does not necessarily despise God; he may stand closer to God than the one who gains everything." With respect to overcoming evil, the Old Testament must here be placed *alongside* the New. In addition, compare Noll's statements with what was said above concerning the religious pragmatism of the Old Testament's historical books.

WALTHER EICHRODT

Does Old Testament Theology Still Have Independent Significance within Old Testament Scholarship?

[[83]] In the *Festschrift* for Karl Marti in 1925, Steuernagel still interceded, with noteworthy arguments, on behalf of retaining Old Testament theology as an independent discipline within Old Testament scholarship.[1] He showed that from the standpoint of the general history of religion as well as of theological scholarship, but also in the interests of research into Old Testament religion itself, an Old Testament theology in the sense of a systematic overview of Old Testament religion is indispensable. In observing the prevailing uncertainty regarding the task and method of Old Testament theology, which is leading toward the complete displacement of systematic presentations by historical-genetic ones, one can only wish that the arguments Steuernagel brought forward would gain a wider hearing.

But the justification of Old Testament theology as a historical discipline related to the history of Israelite religion, and distinguished from it only by the means of analysis and selection of material, has been most vehemently disputed in the most recent phase of theological discussion. By the dialectical theologians on the one side, and the proponents of pneumatic exegesis on the other, Old Testament theology has been assigned a completely different purpose. Precisely the historical character of the discipline elicits opposition, because one is purportedly unable by means of the usual methods of

Translated and reprinted with permission from Walther Eichrodt, "Hat die Alttestamentliche Theologie noch selbständige Bedeutung innerhalb der Alttestamentlichen Wissenschaft?" *Zeitschrift für die Alttestamentliche Wissenschaft* 47 (1929) 83–91. Translated by Ben C. Ollenburger. The footnotes have been supplied, in large part, by the translator. For information about Walther Eichrodt, see p. 39.

1. Carl Steuernagel, "Alttestamentliche Theologie und Alttestamentliche Religionsgeschichte," in *Vom Alten Testament: Karl Marti zum siebzigsten Geburtstage* (ed. Karl Budde; Beiheft zur Zeitschrift für die Alttestamentliche Wissenschaft 41; Giessen: Töpelmann, 1925) 266–73.

historical research to perceive the true essence of Old Testament religion. This latter is said to reside in the reality of revelation to which the Old Testament bears witness. However, if one wants to penetrate to this center of the Old Testament, rather than to remain on its periphery, then an approach wholly different from the historical is said to be in order, either the pneumatic or one moving within the category of existential judgment, or whatever name one may choose. By their very nature, the means of historical research extend only to the understanding of the conditional, the finite; in order to attain to the unconditional, to what is of absolute value, we are said to require a new disposition toward reality—in short, that of faith, which, as the organ for knowing the pneumatic world, is alone able to disclose the world of the Bible. A new function of our spirit thus becomes active, a new method of understanding reality is to come into play, and thereby we purportedly achieve a new discipline that is differentiated from the rest of Old Testament scholarship by its own wholly distinct character.

If one wants to do justice to the new state of affairs thus brought about, then it is appropriate first of all to admit candidly that in these new demands a completely justified requirement of our current theological situation has asserted itself. One [[84]] can take whatever position one wants regarding dialectical theology, but everyone will have to admit that it has urgently drawn theology's own attention once again to its foundation and, at the same time, to its central problem, that of the reality of revelation. It has become impossible henceforth to remain content with a historicizing approach. After Rudolf Kittel referred emphatically to this point, at the Leipziger Alttestamentlertag in 1921,[2] and to the important task of Old Testament theology that follows from it, Old Testament research of the last few years has also moved increasingly in this direction. I mention only the fine study by Hempel, *Gott und Mensch im Alten Testament*,[3] or call attention to the debates at the first Deutschen Theologentag.

However, even if the goal of achieving a deeper understanding of the religious life attested in the Old Testament is clearly before us, the question is not yet answered how this goal can be attained. In fact, it is precisely this question that seems inevitably to threaten the place of Old Testament theology within the framework of Old Testament scholarship, since Old Testament theology as a historical discipline, in Steuernagel's sense, is repudiated. It must now pose the question of truth, and must thus go beyond the phenomenology of religious life to a religio-dogmatic presentation of the essence of Old Testament religion. But thereby it doubtless leaves the ranks of empirical-historical scholarship and enters the circle of normative science. So also Staerk, in an interesting exposition of the significance of history of religion and philosophy of religion for Old Testament theology, vigorously claims the latter as

2. Kittel's lecture was published as "Die Zukunft der Alttestamentlichen Wissenschaft," *ZAW* 39 (1921) 84–99.

3. Published as volume 38 in the series Beiträge zur Wissenschaft vom Alten und Neuen Testament (Stuttgart: Kohlhammer, 1926).

part of systematic theology.[4] In a penetrating study, Eissfeldt has attempted to formulate theoretically the opposition this conception entails to the previously typical definition of the task of Old Testament research. In his presentation, "The History of Israelite-Jewish Religion and Old Testament Theology,"[5] he ultimately fixes the contrast between these two disciplines as that between history and revelation, knowing and believing. Only if these are cleanly separated and developed according to the laws internal to each does he see the possibility of preserving the legitimate interests of the historian and the theologian. Any compromise would only lead to intolerable tensions. But then we confront a momentous decision, because this new definition of Old Testament theology's task means a burden for Old Testament scholarship that not a few will think unbearable. If there were already serious reservations about the task of presenting Old Testament religion in a cross section—that is, in a systematic outline but still entirely within the boundaries of the historical discipline—then the introduction of a religio-dogmatic discipline will, it seems to me, encounter far more decisive repudiation. The feeling will not be entirely unjustified that here a task has been imposed on the Old Testament scholar which [[85]] really belongs to the dogmatician, and which only he with his particular education can satisfactorily undertake. Do we not still have the obligation to preserve Gabler's legacy and to insist on the clear distinction of Old Testament theology from dogmatics? We are thus confronted with a methodological question whose significance, not only for Old Testament scholarship but also for theological inquiry in general, demands the most serious consideration and fundamental reflection. Here are offered only a few indications of where I see the decisive point of the problem to lie, and the direction in which its solution must be sought.

I would like to begin, then, with history and its investigation, because the proposition, "We are unable by historical means to penetrate to the essence of Old Testament religion," is actually the general assumption lying at the basis of all the challenges to refashion our discipline, however opinions regarding the ways and means of this refashioning may otherwise diverge. Now certainly, this proposition contains an incontestable truth, insofar as history can say nothing about the final truth of a matter; that is, it is unable to make any claims concerning its validity for our current existence or its significance for our world view. To the extent that historical research is able to view and to describe more precisely any event—also anything of an intellectual scope— only within a system of relations, its assertions about a historical entity always remain relative; that is, they have meaning only in relation to other entities and only in this sense command assent. To judge regarding what is true and what is false, what has an absolute claim to validity and what is worthless,

---

4. Willy Staerk, "Religionsgeschichte und Religionsphilosophie in ihrer Bedeutung für die biblische Theologie des Alten Testamentes," *Zeitschrift für Theologie und Kirche* 21 (1923) 389–400.

5. Otto Eissfeldt, "Israelitisch-jüdische Religionsgeschichte und Alttestamentliche Theologie," *ZAW* 44 (1926) 1–12; English translation on pp. 12–20 above.

continues to be reserved fundamentally to the science of values, to philosophy or to dogmatics. If one takes a proper understanding of the essence of Old Testament religion to mean a judgment concerning its truth and validity claims, then this falls outside the boundaries of Old Testament scholarship as empirical-historical research, and requires a discipline related to dogmatics.

It is quite otherwise if we understand "the essence of Old Testament religion" to be, very simply, what the Old Testament means, what the essentials of its history really consist in, what constitutes the deepest meaning of its religious thought world. Historical investigation of the Old Testament will never be able to renounce the explication of "essence" in this sense if it wishes to carry out its task completely. Historical research must insist on the fullest possible understanding of the meaningful content, and the comprehending reconstruction of the actions in which this meaningful content is given—what is also called the "interpretation" of phenomena—if it does not want to forfeit its noblest task. But precisely this task entails that research may not remain content with a genetic analysis but has a vast systematic assignment to carry out: It must lay a cross section through the developed whole in order to demonstrate the inner structure of a religion [[86]] in the mutual relation of its various contents. It would be wrong to see in this systematic task an opposition to historical method. It is an impermissible restriction of the concept "historical" to relate it, as if self-evidently, only to observation of the growth process, to the genetic method; rather, "historical" may be understood as the opposite only of anything normative. Thus, the systematic consideration is to be comprehended completely within the historical.

This explicit inclusion of the systematic task within the sphere of historical research has as it consequence, of course, that there appears more sharply an epistemological problem of historical scholarship normally overlooked in such a restriction to genetic analysis: the subjective moment included within historical research. With respect to its extent and its significance there are, for the most part, only very imprecise notions. On few points is one more painfully aware of the lack of rigorous reflection, because the most precise grasp of the subjective moment bound up with it is indispensable for the correct determination of historical method and its general scientific character. Historicism's mistake is the suggestion that one can, by historical-empirical means, advance to norms or to universally valid propositions. The error of positivism is certainly no better—that a particular discipline must renounce any philosophical grounding if it is to be "objective." Today, the renewed permeation of the particular disciplinary specializations with a philosophical spirit is perceived as essential, and we recognize that the historian cannot even investigate and present discrete historical developments without the support of general concepts and notions provided by the philosophy of history.

The discussion among secular historians on this point has made it sufficiently clear that, to a certain degree, a subjective moment already plays into the determination of the *object of historical research*, insofar as the work of historical scholarship has as its presupposition that one knows what historical life is.

The subjective moment appears even more clearly if one inquires concerning the *principle of selection* by means of which the historian orders the vast quantity of individual phenomena and arranges their broad inner connections. Is there a universally valid principle of selection? Work in logic and methodology, in any event, has been unable to establish one. Presumably, it will not be able to do so in the future, either, to the extent that even here the influence of our basic value orientation, our individual world view, cannot be eliminated. Indeed, even a comparison of significant contemporary historical achievements shows that the governing category under which particular events are subsumed is not only a neutral, comprehensive key concept, but is obviously also [[87]] a value concept. All that can here be required is that the scholar, with methodological self-consciousness, be clear about his guiding conception and its standing in the world of values, and not set to work in the cheery optimism of absolute objectivity.

Closely related to the principle of selection is the *perspectival concept of purpose* under which a historical development is placed. This, too, is a particular guiding conception, determined in its content by the object in question; thus, it stands in the closest connection with the historical material. It is not determined only by the requirements immanent in this material, however, but receives its decisive character from the subjectivity of the scholar.

Let us then set these general presuppositions of a subjective kind, from which every scholar's work must proceed, alongside the particular intellectual preparation that a scholar must bring along in order to do the material justice! The current inclination is to pursue this factor more precisely, and to determine more carefully the often-used but somewhat vague notion of "congeniality." In this case it is evident that the scholar must have an internal affinity with his object, in order to overcome the distance to the unfamiliar phenomenon, and in order to comprehend its essence correctly. By no means can anyone understand everything, but only the circle of phenomena and human beings with whom one possesses an affinity.[6] For genuine understanding goes beyond empathetic reliving; genuine understanding requires a spontaneous productive action, a release of the plenitude of spiritual powers, in order to absorb the unfamiliar reality into oneself, so to speak, and then to place it once more outside oneself. But only in the encounter with a related life are these powers awakened: one comprehends only that in which one shares in some way—which one is like—and not more.

One can view this psychological conditionedness of historical work as a deficiency and fear the dangers given therein: prejudice, lack of discrimination, evident bias. And one should certainly not take these lightly, but should oppose them with every weapon that a scrupulous methodology makes available.

6. Eichrodt refers "above all" to Joachim Wach, *Religionswissenschaft: Prolegomena zu ihrer wissenschaftstheoretischen Grundlagen* (Veröffentlichen des Forschungsinstitut an der Universität Leipzig 10; Leipzig: Hinrichs, 1924). He also mentions works by Spranger, Litt, and Bächtold. See Eduard Spranger, *Der Sinn der Voraussetzungslosigkeit in den Geisteswissenchaften* (Darmstadt: Wissenschaftliche Buchgesellschaft, 1963); Theodor Litt, *Die Wiederweckung des geschichtlichen Bewusstseins* (Heidelberg: Quelle & Meyer, 1956).

But even so, one may not on that account evaluate it only negatively, seeing the ideal to consist in somehow extinguishing one's own identity. That would be to misunderstand that just in this psychological moment resides the possibility of entering into the historical event, of giving it blood and life, and thus of constructing that third [[88]] element that goes beyond the mere subject and the pure object: history elevated to a new present.

In light of these conclusions, it will come as no surprise if Eduard Spranger claims, "These days, it is simply common knowledge among all reflective historians that there is no discipline of history without a philosophy of history." And that is only one among many similar statements by recognized historical scholars. The wide-ranging consequences this has for the evaluation of historical scholarship, and for its task generally, have been drawn by C. H. Becker, in an essay on the "Change in Historical Consciousness,"[7] although we are unable here to take up his exposition in detail or to identify ourselves with it.

What, then, can this more precise conception of the subjective moment in all historical scholarship teach us regarding our particular problem? Above all, it may deter us from a fruitless opposition between history and faith's intuitive knowledge, which would be the basis for requiring, on the one hand, a dogmatic discipline of Old Testament theology and, on the other hand, an objective history of Israelite-Jewish religion chemically pure of any valuation. In reality, history and intuitive knowledge do not stand in any relation of opposition to each other, but one of mutual fulfillment. The discussion about historical scholarship in general teaches us that there just is no history of Israelite religion independent of all subjective presuppositions. In its case, as with every historical presentation, the concept of purpose and understanding's governing category, the principle of selection, are derived from considerations that stem not from empirical scholarship but from our basic value orientation. In other words, the pursuit of its lines of development must find its goal, at least for the theologian, in the thought world of the New Testament. And the selection of particular material can only occur from the perspective of the extent to which this serves to make clear and comprehensible the preparation of the historical basis of revelation in Christ, acknowledged as the supreme value. Thereby, however, we are only comprehending with fundamental clarity what was already commonly recognized among earlier historians. None other than Bernhard Stade expressed this in 1892, in his university address on "The Task of Biblical Theology of the Old Testament,"[8] saying that if the presentation of Israelite religion wants to find a center of gravity, it will have to offer as a conclusion a brief outline of the whole course of development of Jesus' preaching.

---

7. "Wandel im geschichtlichen Bewusstsein." As a reference, Eichrodt gives only *Die neue Rundschau* 38 (1927) 113ff.

8. Published as "Über die Aufgabe der biblischen Theologie des Alten Testaments," *Zeitschrift für Theologie und Kirche* 3 (1893) 31–51; also in *Ausgewählte Akademische Reden und Abhandlungen* (Giessen: Töpelmann, 1907) 77–96.

Naturally, this is not at all to deny that the history of Israelite-Jewish religion can also be portrayed from another standpoint, just as long as there, too, methodological reflection and clarification regarding this standpoint has preceded. But, of course, [[89]] a theological presentation can be given on no other presupposition than marked out above.

On this basis the task and character of Old Testament theology can be determined more precisely. If the history of Israelite-Jewish religion is a matter of the genetic understanding of Old Testament religion in the interplay of historical forces, then Old Testament theology has to do, as was already stated, with the systematic task of a cross section through the developed whole, which should illumine the entire dynamic content of the religion according to its internal structure, and which should perceive its uniqueness over against the religious environment—that is, over against the typology of the history of religion generally. For the fulfillment of this task, Old Testament theology has no tools other than history of religion; that is, it proceeds from the same subjective presuppositions, in order to arrange matters of empirical fact, and to bring them to a conclusive understanding. Thus, according to both its object and its method, Old Testament theology has its place entirely within empirical-historical Old Testament scholarship.

I would like to believe that this also meets the legitimate concern of those who would require a dogmatic discipline for perceiving the essence of Old Testament religion. Those who represent this demand are entirely right in referring to the internal relation of the scholar to his material as the presupposition of a genuine understanding, and in defining this internal relation more precisely as a basic value orientation—theologically expressed, as a relation of faith. Except that this presupposition also applies to *historical* work, if the interpretation of phenomena according to their deepest meaning is kept in mind as its goal, rather than the "drayman's work" of chronistically determining facts whose inner connection remains in the dark. Just as historical research in every regional specialization recognizes with increasing clarity that among the most important presuppositions of any significant work is fruitful cooperation between philosophy and individual empirical disciplines, so the theological treatment of history must become clear that it can proceed to the meaningfulness of Old Testament history in no other way than from a supraempirical fundamental presupposition, namely, the viewpoint gained from the reality of New Testament revelation.

To comprehend the essence of Old Testament religion in this way would certainly not involve the explicit faith statements of a *kerygma*, of a direct testimony; if that should be what is meant by the demand for a religio-dogmatic discipline of Old Testament theology, we would have to reject it. Comprehending the essence of Old Testament religion under the viewpoint of the reality of revelation can indeed occur only in such a way that one makes explicit its thoroughgoing relation to the supreme value. But once again, that can only occur on historical bases, and by historical means.

It is really superfluous to say that this demonstration of [[90]] relatedness is still no proof for the reality of revelation. Relatedness to the supreme value will say nothing to anyone who does not share the same fundamental presupposition. But for someone who is internally convinced of the reality of revelation, it is certainly essential whether historical matters of fact attested in the records of revelation stand in a demonstrable outer and inner connection to the center of revelation, for only if they do can one appropriate their intellectual content.

Admittedly, one could here raise the objection that, with everything that has been said, the specific character of theological knowledge has not yet been taken into account, to the extent that in its case it is, supposedly, not a matter of the usual kind of intuitive knowledge that is also indispensable to other disciplines. Rather, here there is said to loom the sphere of decision, in which there are only existential judgments. For that reason as well, the relation of the Old Testament scholar to his material is said to differ from that of the literary historian, in spite of all they hold in common regarding their subjective presuppositions.

However, such an objection would not have considered that proof of similarity in methodological definition cannot be a question of identity in the content of the postulated fundamental presupposition. It is self-evident that any material will once again require distinctive criteria for its own evaluation, and will disclose itself fully only to an interpreter who brings with him this requisite affinity to the object. This, then, in no way implies an alteration of theology's scientific character, but only indicates its special distinction; namely, that in its case the subjective presupposition falls in the sphere of existential decision.

However, even the recognition of this distinctiveness in no way grants that the Old Testament scholar in his biblical-theological work generally would be constrained toward existential judgments. To be sure, such a scholar makes his statements under the presupposition of an existential judgment; however, he is otherwise involved in the presentation of historical states of affairs and their inner connections. Whatever connections he shows there to be in the Old Testament between God and humankind he leaves to the dogmatician, as the representative of regulative science, to utilize in the system of Christian faith as normative knowledge.

Naturally, these claims are only intended as an attempt to establish theoretical boundaries between the individual theological disciplines. In practice, it may happen more than once that an Old Testament scholar will feel constrained at this or that point to transcend the boundaries of historical-empirical scholarship, and to state explicitly that New Testament revelation as the point of departure does not mean for him only a heuristic principle, which he applies to serve some external purpose or with reference to the common basis of the Christian church's faith; but rather, that it corresponds to a living reality which recognizes the Old Testament as normative foundation that he himself applies. The inner, living connection within which all the theological disciplines [[91]] stand may dispose them more to such a transgression of boundaries than is the case with other disciplines. But one thing would need to be stressed by way of methodological clarity: that rendering a verdict and offering proof, as is appropriate to normative science, is not thereby to be carried into Old Testament scholarship as an essential component.

It may seem desirable to consider many points further in explanation of what has been said. Nonetheless, it can only be a question here of offering a few indications of the problem, not of pursuing it in its entire scope. If I have been successful in gaining the active interest of my colleagues in the significance of our question just now, and in view of the situation of the human sciences in general, then this lecture has achieved its goal.[9]

9. Presented at the fifth Orientalistentag, Bonn, 1928.

Part 2

Old Testament Theology's Renaissance:
Walther Eichrodt through
Gerhard von Rad

Introduction

The four authors from whose work the excerpts in this section are drawn—
Walther Eichrodt, T. C. Vriezen, G. Ernest Wright, and Gerhard von Rad—
represent different, often competing efforts to revitalize Old Testament theology. Animating each of them was a concern, not only for the field of biblical
theology, but especially for the theological substance of the Old Testament
and thus, as they believed, for Christian faith and theology. As we shall see in
these introductory paragraphs, two interrelated issues were of particular interest: (a) history, including both the historical character of the Old Testament (or of Israel's religion) and the properly historical approach to its
theological interpretation; (b) what, if anything, best captured the essence,
the unifying force, or the theological center of the Old Testament (or of Israel's religion). None of the four authors viewed these issues as of strictly
methodological or "academic" importance but as related intrinsically to the
theological character and witness of the Old Testament. The stance each of
them took to these issues bore directly on his actual achievement, of course,
and also (or thus) on his characterization of God. A third issue also bore
heavily, though variously, on both of the prior two: (c) the Old Testament's relation to the New. Because especially Eichrodt and von Rad have had such enduring influence, and since, together with Vriezen and Wright, their work
reflects so many of the contested choices facing Old Testament theology into
the present, this introduction offers more-extensive exposition than do the introductions to parts 3–5.

To English readers, Eichrodt, Vriezen, and von Rad burst on the scene
almost simultaneously, between 1958 and 1962; and they came in the wake
of Wright's brief but influential volume, *God Who Acts* (1952). By 1962, English readers had much to choose from. J. Barton Payne issued his evangelical Old Testament theology in 1962, the same year that von Rad's first
volume was published in English. Edmond Jacob's *Theology of the Old Testament* had appeared in 1958 (French original, 1955). A year earlier came Ludwig Köhler's *Old Testament Theology* (1957), more than twenty years after its
first German edition (1935). A helpful prospectus of Old Testament theology
by H. Wheeler Robinson and a compact version of one, equally valuable, by
H. H. Rowley, had appeared in 1946 and 1956, respectively. Coming between
them was Otto Baab's more systematic work (1949), the first Old Testament
theology in English since the posthumous publication of A. B. Davidson's incomplete work, in 1904. Baab's volume appeared just after Geerhardus Vos's

distinctively Reformed essays on biblical theology (1948) and just before the
translated Old Testament theology of Paul Heinisch (1950; 1940), a Roman
Catholic. The first volume of Paul van Imschoot's similarly systematic, and
also Catholic, theology appeared later (1965; 1954–56). Antedating all of
these earlier works, from Köhler's in 1935 (and 1957) to Jacob's in 1955 (and
1958) and yet in its boldness, scope, and methodological consistency already
advancing beyond them was the first German volume of Eichrodt's *Theology of
the Old Testament* (1933).

The first volume of Walther Eichrodt's *Theology of the Old Testament* followed the lineaments of his programmatic essay of 1929 (translated above,
pp. 21–29). He intended it to be a comprehensive presentation "of the OT's
faith-world precisely in its quality as revelation" (1962: vi; cf. 1961: 13). For
Eichrodt, this required avoiding the "bloodless abstractions" of static doctrinal categories, while at the same time breaking the "tyranny of historicism"
that reduced Old Testament theology to the history of Israel's religion (1961:
12, 31). It also meant, then, departing from a form of presentation that separated historical or chronological rehearsals from a systematic or conceptual
treatment—G. L. Bauer, author of the first Old Testament theology, had also
been the first to adopt this twofold form (1796; 1801), which had frequently
been repeated. Eichrodt insisted, to the contrary, that the primarily systematic or conceptual—thus, as he believed, theological—exposition of the Old
Testament's religious ideas must be itself historical in character and integrated with historical-critical inquiry, which plays "a supplementary role"
(1962: 6; cf. 1961: 32). In this way, he intended the form of his *Theology* to
correspond to the nature of its object, which displays a dynamic yet "constant
basic tendency and character" through the whole course of "Israel's religious
history" (1961: 11, 32).

Epitomizing this basic tendency and character, Eichrodt argued, was the
concept of *covenant*. Covenant served especially well to articulate "the OT's
faith-world precisely in its quality as revelation," since covenant expresses
"one basic element in the whole Israelite experience of God, namely *"the act-
character of God's revelation"* (Eichrodt 1962: 10; cf. 1961: 37; Jacob 1958: 32).
That is, revelation and thus knowledge of God in the Old Testament comes
by way of God's "active intervention" in the life of Israel, and God's primal
act of intervention was the covenant. Eichrodt neither intended covenant to
serve as a static, univocal, and all-encompassing dogmatic concept nor pre-
tended that it pervades the biblical texts. Rather, he viewed covenant as the
"center [*Mitte*] of the Old Testament's message," which concerns "the real,
historically-concrete encounter of God with humankind, through which a
people of God is called into being" (Eichrodt 1964: xii). The "stock of spiritual values" established, through Moses, at the inauguration of this covenant
relationship between God and Israel persisted through Israel's history and
the Old Testament's diversity (1961: 32, 290–93; see below, pp. 49–56), including in literature that nowhere mentions covenant. As Eichrodt's English
translator, J. A. Baker, put it, "the focus of these volumes is not any one concept, but only God" (Eichrodt 1967: 10). "[T]*he irruption of the Kingship of God*

into this world and its establishment here," which covenant epitomizes, also continued into the New Testament (1961: 26, italics his). According to Eichrodt, this very continuity gave Judaism, severed from Christianity, the appearance of a torso (1962: 1; cf. 1961: 26). This judgment illustrates the degree to which the New Testament informed Eichrodt's perception of the Old.

The New Testament and Christian theology definitively and expressly informed T. C. Vriezen's *Outline of Old Testament Theology*, published first in Dutch (1949). "Old Testament theology," Vriezen wrote in his lengthy introduction, "gives an insight into the Old Testament message and a judgement of this message from the point of view of the Christian faith"; in this case, and thus "as a part of Christian theology," Old Testament theology has the New Testament as its starting point (1970: 149, 99). In other words, and contrary to Eichrodt, Vriezen did not view the task of Old Testament theology as presenting a comprehensive account of "the OT's faith world." Eichrodt had undertaken to present a cross-section of Old Testament religion in its structural unity, thereby comparing (rather, contrasting) it with its ancient "religious environment" and showing "its essential coherence with the NT" (Eichrodt 1961: 31). Vriezen assigned this to "the phenomenological branch of theological study," while insisting that Old Testament theology had to raise the question of truth—not just incidentally, but as ingredient in its method (Vriezen 1970: 146, 149). It had to offer a judgment of the Old Testament's message with regard to its truth, by which Vriezen meant "weighing against each other . . . the living Word of God and the temporal, human element in the Old Testament" (1970: 113; cf. Gabler, below pp. 497–506).

Consistent with this starting point, Vriezen sided with Eissfeldt against Eichrodt: "*both as to its object and its method Old Testament theology is and must be a Christian theological science*" (Vriezen 1970: 147, italics his; cf. 1958: 121). How else to put "the living Word of God" in mutually critical or dialectical relation with the Old Testament's "temporal, human element"? At the same time, and like Eichrodt, Vriezen assigned to historical-critical inquiry a complementary role in Old Testament theology. However, in Vriezen's case historical criticism aided precisely the critical assessment of the Old Testament's message, making clear "the truly human nature of the form in which the Revelation of God has come to us" (Vriezen 1970: 134). In this apparently negative but actually dialectical role, historical criticism served as Christian theology's ally, not in relation to the Old Testament alone, but to the whole Christian canon: all "must be submitted to the preaching of Jesus Christ"; revelation must not be identified with canon (1970: 149).

Vriezen's frequent references to revelation, in his introduction of more than 150 pages, suggest a preoccupation with the knowledge of God, which is precisely the concern of his remarks regarding "the content of Old Testament theology" (1970: 153). The content of Vriezen's theology, or his presentation of the Old Testament's, remains consistent with his introduction to it, despite critical comments to the contrary (e.g., Barr 1999: 30). To be sure, his theology also displays much more in common with Eichrodt than his introduction would have led us to believe. Vriezen dissented from Eichrodt's use of covenant as the Old Testament's theological center, instead absorbing covenant under the larger umbrella of communion—God's "intercourse" with humankind (Vriezen 1970: 170). Even so, he agreed with Eichrodt that the inauguration of God's communion with Israel was by way of concluding a covenant with them, through Moses, and that the inauguration of this relation on God's initiative, as God's intervention, was God's grant of self-knowledge and was enduringly constitutive (Vriezen 1970: 44, 168; Eichrodt 1961: 32, 37, 290-93). For Vriezen, however, such knowledge was also historically progressive, reaching its Old Testament zenith in Deutero-Isaiah, who finally articulated Israel's universal missionary vocation, present from the beginning, and revealed the life-giving power of suffering for sinners (1970: 44) Vriezen's Deutero-Isaiah displaced Eichrodt's Moses. More than any other, Deutero-Isaiah disclosed the "secret centre of all Old Testament revelation," which is prophecy—because of prophecy's closest possible, personal relation to the "Word of God" and thus to "the living God," who is the Old Testament's "foundation" (1970: 102). Prophecy itself, because of this very relation, is the critique of the Old Testament's late "legalistic element" (1970: 276). From this prophetic perspective, Jesus Christ confirms for the present the revelation of God in the Old Testament, even though the New Testament may require going even further than the Old Testament could go, for example in matters of ethics (1970: 378).

G. Ernest Wright, like Eichrodt and Vriezen, stood within the Reformed tradition, and he too stressed the coherence of the Old and New Testaments: "the understanding of God is the same in both Testaments" (Wright 1969a: 117). Further, vexing Wright as it had Eichrodt, was the dominance of dogmatic theology's bloodless abstractions—Wright refers to "systematic and propositional dogmatics"—in biblical and Old Testament theology (e.g., Wright 1952: 11, 81). The Bible, in both Testaments, lays particular stress on "history as the arena of God's activity," Wright claimed, and even on the same decisive acts of God in history; hence, "history is the revelation of God" (1952: 38, 50). Biblical theology, then, should be conceived not systematically but as confessional recital (1952: 13), as Wright conveyed in the title of his 1952 volume: *God Who Acts: Biblical Theology as Recital.* But in addition to acting in history, God also spoke—spoke through interpreters, who drew inferences, even abstract ones, from God's acts, giving those acts their meaning. Thus is God revealed and known (1952: 84-85). In remarks such as these, Wright suggested a strong analogy between the nature of the Bible itself—"the Bible exists as a confessional recital" (1952: 85)—and what biblical theology, indeed all theology, should undertake to be (1952: 107). Even biblical theology must undertake provisional "attempts to systematize the unsystematizable" if it would meet the "needs of the church" (1952: 116; 1969a: 45). Old Testament theology, then, could not simply have the recital of God's acts as its form or its content, regardless of the indispensable, foundational character of the biblical recital (cf. Kelsey 1975: 32–38).

Formally, the distance between Eichrodt, perhaps also Vriezen, and Wright was not great (compare Eichrodt 1961: 286; Wright 1969a: 45). Despite his earlier criticism of Eichrodt's arrangement of Old Testament theology in the "systematic" categories of God and the people (Israel), God and the world, and God and the individual, with covenant as the center (Wright 1952: 36), Wright himself followed a similar pattern in *The Old Testament and Theology* (1969). There, in brief scope, he treated God the Creator, God the Lord, and God the Warrior. In each case and for the Old Testament generally, covenant—the Mosaic covenant—is "central and formative" (1969a: 116; cf. 1952: 43-44). Yet Wright conducted his discussion and his argument in a discursive mode quite different from Eichrodt's. On one hand, Wright located biblical theology within what Eichrodt regarded as the normative space of theology. In both of the books excerpted below, Wright expressly engaged theological controversies that he saw as threatening the church; his positive arguments, directed also to the church, contended with and drew substantively from theologians (and philosophers). In this regard, Wright came closer to Vriezen (and Eissfeldt). On the other hand, Wright's positive theological arguments strictly depended on, and partially consisted in, historical-critical arguments of a particular kind. And in the way he framed it, Wright's theology depended on significant correspondence between the specific content of "Israel's event-confessional mode of revelation" and the reconstruction of Israel's history by archaeological, historical, and (derivatively) literary scholarship. Consequently, or in the nature of the case, a biblical theologian must also be a historian; honesty and faith require it (1969a: 116). Old Testament theology could not be strictly reduced to the history of Israel's religion, on Wright's view, but neither could the two be in any conflict. In all of these respects, Wright characterized the "biblical theology movement" of which he was a leader.

Gerhard von Rad, whose first volume (1957; 1962a) appeared between Wright's two, seemed at first glance to follow Wright's programmatic suggestion that Old Testament theology should consist in recital: the recital of God's acts (Dentan 1963: 80). Indeed, von Rad argued that "re-telling [*Nacherzählen*—recital could serve as a translation (ed.)] remains the most legitimate form of theological discourse on the Old Testament" (1962a: 121). Also like Wright, von Rad claimed that the proper object of this recital should be "the divine acts in history"; that is, "Jahweh's action in revelation" (1962a: 112, 115). Further, strongly influencing Wright was von Rad's earlier work on the history of Old Testament traditions; von Rad had argued that brief confessions of faith, "recitals of the saving acts of God," expanded and supplemented, lay behind the formation of the Hexateuch (Wright 1952: 70; von Rad 1966). However, von Rad's conception of Old Testament theology was actually quite at odds with Wright's (Wright 1969a: 50-67). By "the divine acts in history," von Rad meant God's acts as Israel narrated and thus confessed them. But Israel's confessional traditions, especially in the Hexateuch, constructed a history that, not only might be, but was in fact quite different from a history of Israel that historical-critical scholarship could reconstruct (von Rad 1960: 8). Thus von Rad divided in two what Wright insisted was one. On the other hand, von Rad's theological project strictly converged with, and was itself an exercise in, the critical reconstruction of the Old Testament's tradition history (1962a: v, 116). Consequently, recital or retelling meant, for von Rad, attending to Israel's own testimony—thus to the form and content and to the complex history of Israel's traditions, in their unmitigated particularity and diversity.

This led von Rad to two further conclusions that excited much controversy. First, von Rad argued that it was mistaken to search for a theological center of the Old Testament. Any proposed "systematizing" center, including covenant, can be but an imposition from outside and an abstraction—a "bloodless ghost" (1962a: 112, 116). Old Testament theology must remain content with describing "the Old Testament's revelation of Jahweh as a number of distinct and heterogeneous revelatory acts" (1962a: 113). Second, von Rad observed that, in the Old Testament, "Israel constantly fell back on the old traditions," reinterpreting them and "actualizing" them in different ways (1965a: 413). This amounted to a kind of continuing typological interpretation, von Rad argued, which found testimonies to God's past actions both promissory and revelatory of the present. On one hand, this placed Israel constantly between promise and fulfillment, and on the other hand it formed the very traditioning process, open to the future, of which it was a part. This "ceaseless process" continued into and concluded in the New Testament. Old Testament theology must make clear, in this way, "that the two Testaments belong together." Otherwise, it amounts only to a "history of the religion of the Old Testament" (1965a: 428-29). On Roland de Vaux's account, what von Rad produced was just that: "no more than a history of the religion of the Old Testament" (de Vaux 1972: 56).

In 1933, Eichrodt found Old Testament theology at an impasse. Three decades later, von Rad found it in the same condition (1965a: ix). In the judgment of some, that is where von Rad left it (Barr 1961; cf. Anderson 1971). Regardless, together with Eichrodt, Vriezen, and Wright, von Rad left Old Testament with substantial challenges and resources.

WALTHER EICHRODT

b. 1890   d. 1978

Covenant

After studying in several German schools, Walther Eichrodt completed his Habilitation under Otto Procksch, at Erlangen. From 1921 until his retirement in 1966, he taught Old Testament and the history of religion at the University of Basel. In 1970, Norman Gottwald called Eichrodt's Old Testament theology "the most important work of its genre in the twentieth century."

Selected Writings by Eichrodt

1929   Hat die Alttestamentliche Theologie noch selbständige Bedeutung innerhalb der Alttestamentlichen Wissenschaft? *Zeitschrift für die Alttestamentliche Wissenschaft* 47: 83–91. [English translation on pp. 21–29 above]

1933   *Theologie des Alten Testaments*. Volume 1: *Gott und Volk*. Leipzig: Hinrichs.

1935   *Theologie des Alten Testaments*. Volume 2: *Gott und Welt*. Leipzig: Hinrichs.

1939   *Theologie des Alten Testaments*. Volume 3: *Gott und Mensch*. Leipzig: Hinrichs.

1961   *Theology of the Old Testament*. Volume 1. Translated by John A. Baker. Philadelphia: Westminster / London: SCM.

1962   *Theologie des Alten Testaments*. Volume 1: *Gott und Volk*. 7th edition. Stuttgart: Klotz / Göttingen: Vandenhoeck & Ruprecht.

1964   *Theologie des Alten Testaments*. Volumes 2–3. 5th edition. Stuttgart: Klotz / Göttingen: Vandenhoeck & Ruprecht.

1967   *Theology of the Old Testament*. Volume 2. Translated by John A. Baker. Philadelphia: Westminster / London: SCM.

1969   *Religionsgeschichte Israels*. Bern: Francke.

Writings about Eichrodt

Barr, James
1999   Pp. 266–73 in *The Concept of Biblical Theology: An Old Testament Perspective*. Minneapolis: Fortress.

Gottwald, Norman K.
1970   W. Eichrodt: *Theology of the Old Testament*. Pp. 23–62 in *Contemporary Old
       Testament Theologians*. Edited by Robert B. Laurin. Valley Forge, Pennsyl-
       vania: Judson.
Sæbø, Magne
1982   Eichrodt, Walther. Volume 9: pp. 371–73 in *Theologische Realenzyklopädie*.
       Berlin: de Gruyter.
Stoebe, Hans J., Johann J. Stamm, and Ernst Jenni (editors)
1970   *Wort-Gebot-Glaube: Beiträge zur Theologie des Alten Testaments: Walther Eich-
       rodt zum 80. Geburtstag*. Abhandlungen zur Theologie des Alten und
       Neuen Testaments 59. Zurich: Zwingli.

Walther Eichrodt's
Approach to Old Testament Theology

Excerpted with permission from Walther Eichrodt, *Theology of the Old Testament* (Philadelphia: Westminister, 1961), vol. 1: 25–33.

Old Testament Theology:
The Problem and the Method

[[25]] Among all the problems known to OT studies, one of the most far-reaching in its importance is that of the theology of the OT: for its concern is to construct a *complete picture of the OT realm of belief*, in other words to comprehend in all its uniqueness and immensity what is, strictly speaking, the proper object of OT study. The tasks of this science are very various in character, but this is the crown of them all; and to this, therefore, the other disciplines involved are ancillary.

But though the domain of OT theology proper is comparatively restricted, yet it is closely linked both to the prolific variety of pagan religions and to the exclusive realm of NT belief. Thus it exhibits a *double aspect*.

On the one side it faces on to the *comparative study of religions*. To adapt a well-known dictum of Harnack[1] (which he coined in opposition to the thesis of Max Müller that 'The man who knows only one religion knows none') one might say, 'The man who knows the religion of the OT knows many.' For in the course of its long history it has not only firmly consolidated its own unique contribution, but also, by a process of absorption and rejection, has forged links with the most varied forms of paganism. Hence the study of it can become at the same time a course in the comparative study of religions. *No presentation of OT theology can properly be made without constant reference to its connections with the whole world of Near Eastern religion.* Indeed it is in its commanding such a wide panorama of the rich domain of man's [[26]] religious activity that many will prefer to see the special significance of the faith of the OT.

And yet there is this *second aspect*, looking on towards the New Testament. Anyone who studies the historical development of the OT finds that throughout there is a powerful and purposive movement which forces itself on his attention. It is true that there are also times when the religion seems to become static, to harden into a rigid system; but every time this occurs the forward drive breaks through once more, reaching out to a higher form of life and making everything that has gone before seem inadequate and incomplete. This movement does not come to rest until the manifestation of Christ, in whom the noblest powers of the OT find their fulfillment. Negative evidence in support of this statement is afforded by the torso-like appearance of Judaism in separation from Christianity.

---

1. *Die Aufgabe der theologischen Fakultäten und die allgemeine Religionsgeschichte*, 1901, p. 10.

The affinity with the NT is not, however, exhausted by a bare historical connection, such as might afford material for the historian's examination but no more. It rather confronts us with an essential characteristic, which must be taken into account if the OT is to be understood. Moreover this is an impression which is confirmed over and over again when we enter the unique spiritual realm of the NT. For in the encounter with the Christ of the Gospels there is the assertion of a mighty living reality as inseparably bound up with the OT past as pointing forward into the future. *That which binds together indivisibly the two realms of the Old and New Testaments—different in externals though they may be—is the irruption of the Kingship of God into this world and its establishment here.* This is the unitive fact because it rests on the action of one and the same God in each case; that God who in promise and performance, in Gospel and Law, pursues one and the selfsame great purpose, the building of his Kingdom. This is why the central message of the NT leads us back to the testimony of God in the old covenant.

But in addition to this historical movement from the Old Testament to the New there is a current of life flowing in the reverse direction from the New Testament to the Old. This reverse relationship also elucidates the full significance of the realm of OT thought. Only where this two-way relationship between the Old and New Testaments is understood do we find a correct definition of the problem of OT theology and of the method by which it is possible to solve it.

[[27]] Hence to our general aim of obtaining a comprehensive picture of the realm of OT belief we must add a second and closely related purpose—*to see that this comprehensive picture does justice to the essential relationship with the NT and does not merely ignore it.* Naturally this does not mean that the language of the OT must be artificially screwed up to the pitch of the New in order that both Testaments may be on the same spiritual plane. To seek to do this would merely betray a very poor idea of the difference between a process in real life and a process in logical thought. It was just at this point that the old orthodoxy, in spite of having a sound idea of the correct course, had the misfortune to lose its grasp of the living reality and to slip back into the procedures of logical demonstration, thereby concealing rather than clarifying the actual relation between the Old and New Testaments. The reaction to this was rationalism with its root-and-branch rejection of the OT.

This then is the problem that confronts us. In expounding the realm of OT thought and belief we must never lose sight of the fact that the OT religion, ineffaceably individual though it may be, can yet be grasped in this essential uniqueness only when it is seen as completed in Christ. None other than B. Stade, well known for the radical nature of his criticism, emphasized this 'homogeneity and similarity of the Old and New Testament revelations' in his own theology of the OT; and he saw in this fact the premise from which this branch of OT studies could be proved to be a necessary part of Christian theology.[2]

2. *Biblische Theologie des Alten Testaments*, 1905, p. 15.

The more clearly the shape of this problem is seen, the more apparent it becomes that it is not to be solved along the lines which OT studies have so far taken, namely the consideration of the process of historical development only. It is not just a matter of describing the all-round expansion of OT religion, or the phases through which it passed, but of determining to what extent—as B. Stade remarked—it ties up with the NT revelation and is analogous to it. But this can only be done by taking a cross-section of the realm of OT thought, thus making possible both a comprehensive survey and a sifting of what is essential from what is not. In this way both the total structure of the system and the basic principles on which it rests can be exposed to view. In other words we have to undertake a *systematic examination* with objective classification and rational arrangement of the varied material. This does not in any way imply that the historical method [[28]] of investigation is worthless, nor that it should be set aside. We ought rather to build deliberately on its conclusions and make use of its procedures. Nevertheless developmental analysis must be replaced by systemic synthesis, if we are to make more progress toward an interpretation of the outstanding religious phenomena of the OT in their deepest significance.[3]

A glance at the history of our particular discipline will abundantly confirm that this method, deriving as it does from the nature of the material, is the proper one. As we have already stated, rationalism tore to shreds the inadequate attempts of orthodoxy to demonstrate the inner coherence of the Old and New Testaments by the collation of proof-texts and an extensive system of typology.[4] It proved that it was impossible to reduce the whole realm of OT thought, conditioned as it is by such an immense variety of ages and individuals, to a handbook of dogmatic instruction without doing violence to it. Rationalism itself, however, was quite unable to offer any substitute; for in its delight in critical analysis it lost its feeling for the vital synthesis in the OT and could only see the differing teachings of individual biblical writers.[5]

Into the meaningless confusion of *disjecta membra*, into which the OT on such a view degenerated, the new approach to history which began to flower with the age of romanticism brought a unifying principle. It dismissed once for all the 'intellectualist' approach, which looked only for doctrine, and sought by an all-inclusive survey to grasp the totality of religious life in all its richness of expression. Furthermore it brought this unexpected expansion of the field of study under control with the magic formula of 'historical development', allowing all the individual elements to be arranged in one historical

---

3. I have given the main outlines of the relationship between this task and the dogmatic religious presentation, properly so called, of OT religion in my lecture, 'Hat die alttestamentliche Theologie noch selbständige Bedeutung innerhalb der alttestamentlichen Wissenschaft?', *ZAW* 47, 1929, pp. 83ff. [[See pp. 21–29 above for an English translation.]]

4. It is not possible to take into consideration in this work such exceptional cases as G. Calixt and J. Cocceius.

5. Cf. C. F. Ammon, *Biblische Theologie*, 1792; G. L. Bauer, *Theologie des Alten Testaments*, 1796, and others.

process and thus enabling the meaning of the whole to be demonstrated in its final achievement.

This method of treatment, which began with Herder[6] and de [[29]] Wette,[7] reached its high-water mark with Wellhausen[8] and his school, and for decades diverted work on OT theology into historical channels. Of what avail was it that a Beck[9] or a Hofmann[10] should attempt, about the middle of the last century, to develop a system of biblical doctrine? By making use of the OT for this purpose they were indeed standing up for its vital importance for the Christian faith, but they made no headway against the rising stream of historical investigation—to say nothing of the fact that the dogmatic system to which they harnessed the thought of the OT was seriously defective.

All the more deserving of notice, therefore, are three men who in the second half of the nineteenth century, right in the thick of the triumphal progress of historical criticism, attempted to expound the essential content of the OT in systematic form, while at the same time giving full consideration to the newly emergent problems connected with it. These were G. F. Oehler,[11] A. Dillmann,[12] and H. Schultz.[13] All three took account of the new movement by prefacing their exposition with a historical summary of OT religion. They then went on, however, to contend earnestly for a systematic correlation of the elements which had so far been examined only as they occurred in the course of the historical process. It was unfortunate that the two first-named works did not appear until after the deaths of their authors and so were already at the time of their publication no longer defensible in many details.[14] Nevertheless, repeated new editions witness to their having met a pressing need. Even today they still provide the most thorough treatment of the realm of OT belief from the systematic standpoint; and even though since that time research has brought to light much new relevant material and has introduced different ways of framing the problems, so materially altering the total picture, one can turn to them again and again. It is significant that for twenty-five years after the last edition of Schultz's *Theology* no one ventured on a further attempt to provide an exposition of this kind in the realm of OT belief. The historical approach had triumphed on every side.

[[30]] To say this is of course not to attempt to deny that this method accomplished an immense amount for the historical understanding of OT religion. It is impossible even to conceive of a historical picture that does not

6. *The Spirit of Hebrew Poetry, Letters on Theology, The Oldest Documents of the Human Race*, etc.

7. *Beiträge zur Geschichte des Alten Testaments*, 1806–7; *Biblische Dogmatik*, 1813, 3rd edn, 1831.

8. *Prolegomena to the History of Israel*, ET, 1885; originally 1878; *History of Israel*, ET, 1894; *Die israelitische-jüdische Religion*, 1906 (Kultur der Gegenwart I, 4).

9. *Die christliche Lehrwissenschaft nach den biblischen Urkunden*, 1841.

10. *Der Schriftbeweis*, 1852–55.

11. *Theologie des Alten Testaments*, 1873; 3rd edn, 1891.

12. *Handbuch der alttestamentlichen Theologie*, ed. R. Kittel, 1895.

13. *Old Testament Theology*: ET in 2 vols., 2nd edn, 1898; 5th German edn, 1896.

14. This applies also to the less important OT Theology of E. Riehm, 1889.

make use of its findings, and to that extent not one of us can help being in its debt. For this very reason, however, the method had a particularly fatal influence both on OT theology and on the understanding of the OT in every other aspect, because it fostered the idea that once the historical problems were clarified everything had been done. The essential inner coherence of the Old and New Testaments was reduced, so to speak, to a thin thread of historical connection and causal sequence between the two, with the result that an external causality—not even susceptible in every case of secure demonstration— was substituted for a homogeneity that was real because it rested on the similar content of their experience of life. How appallingly this impoverished the conception of the relationship of the two Testaments strikes one at once; but it is also clear that the OT itself, if valued only as the historical foundation or forerunner of the New, was bound to lose its own specific value as revelation, even though from the historical angle it might be assessed as highly as ever. One consequence of this is the fact that the OT has completely lost any effective place in the structure of Christian doctrine. Indeed, in the circumstances, it sometimes seems more from academic politeness than from any real conviction of its indispensability that it is so seldom denied all value as canonical Scripture[15]—a step which would enable the whole subject to be transferred from the sphere of theology to that of the comparative study of religions.

That OT theologians for their part were content to put up with this development, and thought that the value of the OT could be safeguarded even along these lines, can only be understood if we remember that the full flood of historicism, which overflowed every academic discipline, had blinded them to the fact that historical investigation, for all its glittering achievements, could yet offer no serious substitute for the concept of the essential coherence of the Old and New Testaments. The little still left to OT theology to do, viz., the historical presentation of the Israelite and Judaistic religion, was quite insufficient to conceal, even with the help of the magic word 'development', how serious the loss had been. There was no longer any unity to be found in the OT, only a collection of detached periods which were simply the reflections of as many different [[31]] religions. In such circumstances it was only a logical development that the designation 'OT Theology', which had formerly had quite a different connotation, should frequently be abandoned and the title 'the History of Israelite Religion' substituted for it.[16] Even where scholars still clung to the old name,[17] they were neither desirous nor capable of offering anything more than an exposition of the historical process.

15. Harnack (*Marcion*, 1921, pp. 247ff.) was one notable exception.

16. So R. Smend in his widely-used *Lehrbuch der alttestamentlichen Religionsgeschichte*[2], 1899; F. Giesebrecht, *Grundzüge der israelitischen Religionsgeschichte, 1904*; K. Marti, *Geschichte der israelitischen Religion*[5], 1907; K. Budde, *Die Religion des Volkes Israel bis zur Verbannung*[3], 1912; E. König, *Geschichte der alttestamentlichen Religion*[2], 1915; R. Kittel, *The Religion of the People of Israel*, ET, 1925; G. Hölscher, *Geschichte der israelitischen und jüdischen Religion*, 1922.

17. B. Stade, *Biblische Theologie des Alten Testaments*, E. Kautzsch, *Biblische Theologie des Alten Testaments*, 1911. So also A. Kuenen, *De godsdienst van Israel*, 1869ff., and the work of the same name by B. D. Eerdmans, 1930.

When, therefore, in 1922 E. König ventured to publish a Theology of the OT which attempted to take its title seriously, it was a real act of courage which deserves to be recorded. It is true that to some extent a hybrid form is still noticeable in the book. The historical-developmental method of examination, carrying over from the opening historical section into the systematic part, never allows the synthesis its rightful scope. Furthermore, the recalcitrant material is forced into a Procrustes' bed, because it has been made to fit a dogmatic arrangement foreign to the subject. Nevertheless, that the author had rightly sensed the need of the contemporary situation was proved by the grateful reception accorded to his work.

It is high time that the tyranny of historicism in OT studies was broken and the proper approach to our task re-discovered. This is no new problem, certainly, but it is one that needs to be solved anew in every epoch of knowledge—*the problem of how to understand the realm of OT belief in its structural unity and how, by examining on the one hand its religious environment and on the other its essential coherence with the NT, to illuminate its profoundest meaning.*[18] Only so shall we succeed in winning back for OT studies in general and for OT theology in particular that place in Christian theology which at present has been surrendered to the comparative study of religions.

We are not for one moment trying to make light of the difficulties that stand in the way of this undertaking. It is a fact that the unique [[32]] quality of Israelite religion obstinately resists all efforts to subject it completely to systematic treatment. For if there is one feature that it exhibits more than any other religion, it is an abundance of creative religious personalities, who are closely involved in the historical experiences of the people. In any religion where this is not so the main content of the thought is usually present at its foundation and changes but little in the course of time, being rather worn away and levelled down than made more profound or fashioned afresh. In the OT, however, we find both a stock of spiritual values firmly established at the outset and also an incessant process of growth which is continually enriching the religion by drawing into its sphere new content from without. At the same time the internal shape of the religion becomes increasingly well-defined. It is *this prominence of the personal and historical factors* in Israelite religion which constitutes a constant temptation to the writer to resort to an exposition along the historical line of development.

But though such a motive may be justifiable, it should not be overriding. A picture of the historical development of Israelite religion can equally well be conveyed by means of a History of Israel, so long as the religious life is allowed that place in the work which its close contact and interaction with the political history merits. It is true that to this extent OT theology presupposes the history of Israel. Nevertheless, in so far as the spiritual history of Israel has brought about a drastic remodelling of many religious ideas, the right way to make allowance for this is *to have the historical principle operating side by*

---

18. In this connection cf. the examination by R. Kittel of the importance of OT theology in his essay, 'Die Zukunft der alttestamentlichen Wissenschaft', *ZAW* 39, 1921, pp. 94ff.

side with the systematic in a complementary role. In treating individual religious concepts the major elements of their historical background must be taken into account. Only so can we hope to do justice to the great unitive tendency that runs through the whole religious history of Israel and makes it with all its variety a self-consistent entity.

One thing, however, must be guarded against and that is any *arrangement of the whole body of material* which derives not from the laws of its own nature but from some dogmatic scheme. It is impossible to use a system which has been developed on a basis quite different from that of the realm of OT thought to arrive at the OT belief about God. All that results is a grave danger of intruding alien ideas and of barring the way to understanding.

It has often been observed that the OT contains very little actual 'doctrine'. Nowhere are formal 'instructions' about the Being of God [[33]] or his attributes delivered to the Israelite. His knowledge of God comes to him from the realities of his own life. He learns about the nature of God by reasoning *a posteriori* from the standards and usages of Law and Cult, which rule his personal life with divine authority, from the events of history and their interpretation by his spiritual leaders, in short, from his daily experience of the rule of God. By this means he comprehends the divine essence much more accurately than he would from any number of abstract concepts. The result is that the formation of such concepts in the OT lags far behind, while the same spiritual values which they are normally the means of conveying to us are yet uncompromisingly real and effective.

In deciding, therefore, on our procedure for the treatment of the realm of OT thought, we must avoid all schemes which derive from Christian dogmatics—such, for example, as 'Theology—Anthropology—Soteriology', '*ordo salutis*' and so on. Instead we must plot our course as best we can along the lines of the OT's own dialectic. This speaks of a revelation of the God of the People, who in his rule proves himself to be also the God of the World and the God of the Individual. We are therefore presented with three principal categories, within which to study the special nature of the Israelite faith in God: *God and the People, God and the World* and *God and Man*.[19]

---

19. I owe this pregnant formulation of the three major categories to the outline by O. Procksch, which formed the basis of his university lectures on OT theology and which has provided me with many stimulating ideas. The division of the material here suggested had already been anticipated by H. Schultz in the arrangement of the second part of his *OT Theology*, except that in a way characteristic of him he treated Hope separately in a special section. . . .

Synopsis of Eichrodt's *Theology of the Old Testament* (1961, 1967)

Walther Eichrodt on Covenant

Excerpted with permission from Walther Eichrodt, *Theology of Old Testament* (Philadelphia: Westminister, 1961), vol. 1: pp. 286–96.

Affirmations about the Divine Activity:
Synthesis

[[286]] The unique character of the picture of God in ancient Israel is derived in essence from the attempt to hold together the ideas of a [[287]] divine *power without limitation* and of a divine *act of self-limitation* in the establishment of a *berît* [['covenant']]—an act where God makes himself known as *sovereign and personal will*. The conception of God's power is given its special character by its association with first the idea of the divine *holiness*, that which is annihilating and inaccessible and utterly distinct from every created thing, and secondly the divine *wrath*, God being, in his sovereign freedom, inscrutable to men. Contrasted with this is God's voluntary engagement of his sovereignty to the covenant fellowship with Israel, by virtue of which he grants men to know his *lovingkindness* as Father and Shepherd and demonstrates his *righteousness* by victoriously defending them against their enemies. Since these dealings of God with his people have as their object the establishment of his dominion in the holy land, the divine will is revealed as *power directing history*; and this implies a *fullness of personal life* which not only is different in principle from mere natural forces, but rejects as utterly alien the primitive conceptions of God attaching to the beliefs in spirits, 'power' and magic.

This unique attempt to combine the ideas of the manifest and the hidden God by way of the claim which he made upon men established itself in the succeeding period in opposition to an understanding of the world and of life which had been enriched by foreign elements, and in the process gained in force both in comprehensiveness and profundity. No longer was it simply exceptional incidents and occasions which were seen in the light of the divine presence, but every detail of life was now interpreted with increasing logical consistency in this way. As a result the *wrath of God* was ever more closely connected with his *punitive righteousness* and with *individual retribution*, while his *holiness* was understood as the *perfection of the divine being*, reflected in the Law as the pattern of life or the holy people and annihilating everything which resisted the purposes of that law. That all this was the work not of some impersonal world-order, but of the *will of a personal Lord*, was newly comprehended and expressed in the recognition of *love* as the deepest meaning of election and of *righteousness* as the power educating the pious in the attainment of their own righteous conduct. Holiness was now understood as God's supremacy over the heathen; the idea of him as Father was extended to cover the whole Creation; the concept of love now applied to God's relations with each individual member of the nation; and consequently men came to a new vision of how far-reaching might be the scope of their covenant God in his operations.

[[288]] This line of thought presented the divine activity as matched to human understanding and attuned to human needs, with the result that the 'absolute' quality of the divine, God's being by nature 'unintelligible', receded in importance. But in the prophetic preaching the superhuman and enigmatic, nay irrational liberty and superiority of God returned in force. This came about not by a revival of the ancient Israelite way of looking at the matter, but by the ascription of a superhuman character even to God's self-involvement. Indeed, *God's sovereignty* appears to be raised to the highest possible power in the proclamation of the *eschatological doom of wrath*, which reveals the ultimate depth of the abyss between God and man and characterizes the whole of this world as a temporary and provisional order incapable of standing in the presence of the Holy One. But this very act of concluding every element of earthly existence in one vast community of guilt, breaking man's link with God and hurling humanity far from his presence, becomes the means whereby *God's voluntary self-involvement* is revealed as something transcending all human standards and shattering all men's categories of retribution. It means that God's *covenant lovingkindness* now becomes the free gift of mercy; his *righteousness* becomes that redeeming activity, which pleads even for the godless and restores not only Israel but the world; his *holiness* acquires its deepest meaning as the moral governance of the universe or the inconceivable power of love which suffers for the sake of the condemned, until it has achieved his salvation. Thus the ultimate secret of the *divine personhood* is manifested as *love concealed in wrath*, redeeming righteousness, the lovingkindness that remains constant despite the instability of the covenant. The antinomies that must for human thought remain for ever insoluble are fused in the amazing truth that God is a living person; but this truth is manifested as a living reality only to the man who can apprehend by faith the breaking into this present aeon of God's new world.

The Instruments of the Covenant:
The Charismatic Leaders

The Founder of the Religion

[[289]] In the opinion of J. Burckhardt the forces at work in the emergence of a religion also determine its whole succeeding history.[1] If this is true, then the figure dominant at the outset of Israelite religion must be of decisive importance for the interpretation of the spiritual mediators of the concept of Yahweh in later times.

Now it is characteristic of Moses that it should be impossible to classify him in any of the ordinary categories applicable to a leader of a nation; he is neither a king, nor a commander of an army, nor a tribal chieftain, nor a priest,[2] nor an inspired seer and medicine man. To some extent he belongs

---

1. Cf. *Weltgeschichtliche Betrachtungen*, ed. J. Oeri, 1905, p. 42.
2. The points which P. Volz (*Mose*[1], p. 100) enumerates as marks of his priestly character are not sufficient to justify this as an exclusive classification. (In the 2nd ed. of his work,

to all these categories; but none of them adequately explains his position. In many respects he gives the impression of exercising kingly authority; he determines the direction of the line of march and appoints its destination; he gives laws and administers justice and orders the external details of the common life of the tribes. But that which is specifically characteristic of a king, prowess in war and leadership in battle, is just what is lacking in Moses. Similarly nothing is heard of his having made any arrangements for a son and successor to inherit his position. His giving of *tōrā*, that is to say his instructions at the sanctuary and the organization of the cultus attributed to him, suggest the priest; but on the other hand his office of supreme judge is not to be regarded simply [[290]] as a priestly function, and we are told nothing of his offering sacrifice, a task which seems to have been reserved to Aaron and the Levites, or to specially chosen laymen such as the young men of Exod 24:5. The seer seems to be suggested by many individual traits, such as the theophanies, his remaining forty days on the mount of God, his delivery of the divine decisions; but there is no tradition in the case of Moses of the one feature especially celebrated in other seers, miraculous foreknowledge of the future or clairvoyant explication of puzzling situations. Attempts have been made to explain him as a medicine man or magician;[3] but even if isolated features can be made to support this view, in particular the various miracle stories, it is manifestly quite inadequate to cover the whole of this man's life work and the traditions that have been connected with him.

For these reasons, and from a perfectly correct feeling that his most important work lay in the field of religion, the title of Prophet has often been conferred on him, in support of which a number of Old Testament passages from the later monarchy may certainly be quoted (Deut 34:10; 18:15, 18; Hos 12:14). Nevertheless, it should be noted that the tradition of Israel taken as a whole does not regard Moses as the prophet κατ' ἐξοχήν [['par excellence']], but portrays him, in accordance with his various achievements, as intercessor, miracle worker or lawgiver; it is only where there has been time to reflect on the analogy between Moses and prophetism, that he is explicitly displayed as the supreme preacher of the divine will, towering above all the prophets of later days (cf. Exod 4:16; 7:1; 33:11 and Num 11:24-30; 12:1-8). It is in keeping with this that Deuteronomy characterizes him as *the mediator between God and his people* (5:24-28).

Justice, then, can never be done to the full historical reality, if the attempt is made to imprison this outstanding figure in any one of the ordinary categories of 'holy men,' *homines religiosi*. It is precisely the secret of this man's greatness that he unites in himself gifts not normally found in combination, and is therefore able to work with lasting effect in the most diverse fields. If we ask, however, what is *the master key to the career* of this rarely endowed personality, the common factor which saves it from being a jumble of

---

pp. 57, 91ff., 125f., Volz advances a quite different opinion.) A similar view of Moses as priest may be found in E. Meyer, *Die Israeliten*, p. 72.

3. The view of Beer in his study *Mose*, 1912.

dissociated elements, the answer lies in *the concrete historical task* which was entrusted to him in the very hour in which he was seized of a new understanding of the whole nature of God. To bring a nation to Yahweh, the mighty Lord, a nation in which his sovereignty could [[291]] be established and his nature expressed, which furthermore he could forge into an instrument for the execution of his judgment upon the nations and the founding of a new world order[4]—that was the goal which dominated the life of this man whom Yahweh had conquered. To the service of this calling he dedicated all his wealth of gifts and became *the messenger who should proclaim God's will for social, political and cultic life*, whether in the summons to escape from Egypt and in the holy war or in the marvellous redeeming acts of the perilous wandering in the wilderness. Only such personalities as Zoroaster or Mohammed, who were themselves founders of religions, and who likewise closely combined political and national activity with their religious work, can be compared with him; and it is just the fact that it is only such leader-figures who are at all comparable that should warn us not to try to bring Moses down to the level of those more ordinary servants of God or consecrated men whose operations were confined to a restricted sphere.[5]

One thing, however, is clear at the start. This organizer who enjoyed no proper political power, this national leader who boasted no prowess in war, this man who directed the worship of God without ever having received the status of priest, who established and mediated a new understanding of God without any of the credentials of prophetic powers of prediction, this wonder-worker who was yet far above the domain of mere magic, confronts us from the very outset with one ineluctable fact: Israelite religion is not the product of a scrupulously guarded tradition, swollen with the accretions of history, nor does it rest on any sort of organization, [[292]] however cleverly or successfully devised, but is a *creation of that spirit* which bloweth where it listeth, and which in mockery of our neat arrangements unites in the richness of marvelously equipped personalities things patently incompatible, in order that it may forward its own mighty and life-giving work. *At the very beginning*

---

4. Cf. the view, long predominant in Israel, that Yahweh's battles were the execution of his judgment upon his enemies: Num 23:22ff.; 24:8ff.; 10:35; Judg 5:20, 23, 31; Gen 15:16; 1 Sam 15:2, 33; Ps 2; 45:4ff; 110 etc. It is possible to argue about how far the dominion of the new world order was thought to extend; but at least there can be no doubt that from the very beginning it was seen as extending beyond Israel, since it clearly applies to the nations overthrown by her.

5. An enterprising and most effective attempt to present this comprehensive interpretation of the figure of Moses has been made by M. Buber (*Moses*) with complete disregard for prevailing source-criticism. His penetrating religious exposition will always be of value even for those who cannot follow him in his method or in many details. E. Auerbach in his book of the same title has adhered more closely to contemporary scholarship in his attempt to portray Israel's 'mightiest genius'; on occasion his simplifications and strongly rationalist interpretation do violence to the material, but he has a sound feeling for the untenable nature of most criticism of Moses hitherto. Each of these authors has in his own way made abundantly clear the need for a new understanding of the accounts relating to the first preacher of the faith of Yahweh.

of Israelite religion we find the charisma, the special individual endowment of a person; and to such an extent is the whole structure based on it, that without it it would be inconceivable.

1. *That men's relationship with God should be founded on the activity of one specially called and equipped mediator* is of abiding significance for the whole character of their understanding and worship of God. The single historical event in which God encountered the nation becomes what the mediator declared it to be, *the point of alignment for their belief in God;* the redemption from Egypt received its definitive interpretation at the covenant-making on Sinai—and thus became *the foundation and the orientation of all the mutual relations of Yahweh and his people.* It has already been explained[6] how this meant that man's relationship with God was based on revelation in the strict sense of the word—that is to say, on God's imparting of himself through the contingency of historical circumstance—and required submission to the will of God simply as that was made known here and now; and further how this excluded any attempt to base a doctrine of God on general concepts or principles derived from human experience. It was also pointed out that this makes explicit the principle of God's being undetermined by any involvement with Nature. It remains to add here, that the very fact of the emergence of a mediator supplied further confirmation of these basic features of the new relationship with God; for the activity of the mediator was an emphatic reminder of *the distance between God and man,* a distance not in any way lessened for the chosen people. That this was indeed felt to be the significance of the mediator is indicated by the many interpretations of his work along these lines,[7] but also by the sense, which loomed so large in Israel's religion, that Yahweh was terrible and unapproachable, and that to draw near to him without such mediation was to court destruction. The frequent references to the fact that Moses' own intercourse with God was unique precisely [[293]] because it was unmediated, and that this constituted the special character of his position,[8] prove that men never ceased to meditate on the gulf between God and man which he had bridged.

2. Moreover, the way in which Moses brought God near to his people became an important model for the future. For it made clear that *the demands of God in the Law,* which strove to order every detail of the national life and to conform it to the mind of God himself, *were those of a personal will.* From thenceforward the legal regulation of the people's conduct was not only raised to the status of a religious obligation, and distinguished definitely from all merely human opinions,[9] but it was also bound up with the type of lawgiving mediated by Moses. In the Torah of Moses, regardless of whether this is held to be simply oral tradition or to have been fixed in writing, is to be found the source of all law, public and private. Deuteronomy may have

6. Cf. ch. II, The Covenant Relationship, [[Eichrodt 1961:]] pp. 37ff.

7. Exod 20:18ff.; 33:5; 33:7ff.; 34:9; 34:29ff.; Num 11:2; 11:25ff.; 12:2ff.; 17:27f.; 21:7; Deut 5:5, 22ff. Cf. also the way in which Moses is in general portrayed as an intercessor.

8. Exod 4:16; 7:1; Num 11:24–30; 12:1–8; Deut 5:24, 28.

9. Cf. chs. III and IV, The Covenant Statutes.

derived its distinctive form, the presentation of the law as an address from the founder of the religion, from the traditional practice of having a reader of the law at local assemblies,[10] but it was a real dependence which made this established form the most fitting mode of expression. Again, the constantly recurring formula of the Priestly Law—'And the Lord spake unto Moses'—in both early and late passages, bears witness to the feeling that the regulation of cultic life could only be carried out by associating it with the original giver of the Law. This means, however, that from the time of Moses onwards the will of God, as this applied to the nation, was conceived as being *normative for all human relations and remaining ideally the same for ever*; it was his proclamation of this will, and his application of it to the new problems that were arising, which brought about the submission of the people and caused the rule of God to be accepted. The whole intensity of Israel's devotion to the Law, which arises from her knowledge that she is carrying out God's unchanging will, rests ultimately on this foundation.

Combined with this, however, is a renewed sense of *the Word of God* addressed to the will as the true basis of man's association with him; it is from this, and not from any naturalistic or mystical significance it may possess, that every sacred act derives its sanction; and the obedience of the pious comes to the forefront as the only justification of the sacramental. The person of the mediator [[294]] determined for ever the personal character of man's relations with God.

3. This divine will, which was normative for the whole of life, also indicated the role of the nation in men's relationship with God, giving it on the one hand an undeniable importance, but on the other taking care that this importance should be clearly limited. Because the divine covenant did not embrace simply the Israelites as individuals or the tribes as separate entities, but the people as a whole, it was possible to recognize *the existence of the nation as rooted in the will of God*. National feeling was given an out-and-out religious colouring; under Moses' leadership the tribes learnt that they had a duty of mutual support not, primarily, because they were all Israelites, but because they were all followers of Yahweh. Loyalty to the nation was made an explicitly religious obligation.[11]

There can be no question but that this subordination of the nation to the aims of the theocracy was achieved more easily in an age which knew none but a charismatic leader, and which was learning to make national unity an effective reality under his direction, than in the period in which the Israelite nation-state was emerging. Conflict only broke out in all its fierceness when nationalist ideals were confirmed and given independent validity under a strong monarchy, and Israel awoke with pride to the fact of her national coherence and power. It must, however, have been of the most essential importance for the clashes which at this stage had to come, that the work of the

10. Cf. A. Klostermann, *Der Pentateuch* N. F., 1907.
11. That this does not imply that Yahweh was included among the purely national deities, has already been explained in ch. II: The Covenant Relationship.

founder of the religion should already have included among its principal features a definite evaluation both of the importance and of the limitations of the nation, and that this should have become the common inheritance of a wide circle.

4. These considerations may have helped to clarify the underlying importance of the activity of the founder and mediator for the whole structure of Israelite faith and worship. But they should not be allowed to obscure the fact that *the continued influence of Moses* was essentially different from that of other great founder-personalities. The revelation of God which Moses mediated did not acquire its final form in his own lifetime; his work only laid the initial foundation. From those beginnings was to develop a permanent intercourse between God and the nation, with all the possibilities which that implied of further self-imparting by God. However highly the [[295]] Mosaic interpretation of God's will was valued as determining the line of development for all succeeding ages, *it was never accorded the character of a final and definitive communication concerning God's nature and operation*; it pointed categorically to the future. It is significant in this connection that not one saying of the founder of the religion, not one λόγιον [['saying']] of Moses, has been preserved—as part of the content of the revelation; there is nothing to compare with the Gathas of Zoroaster or the Suras of Mohammed. Even the transmission of Moses' law was carried out in a spirit of freedom, as the frequent additions, transpositions and expansions of the Book of the Covenant and the various forms of the Decalogue and other basic laws make clear. *An incessant process of expanding and adapting the law* to meet the demands of changing situations was perfectly compatible with loyalty to the religious and social spirit of the Mosaic legislation. Just as little was it supposed that after Moses there would be no need of any further prophetic souls to interpret or reveal the divine will; on the contrary, an abundant provision of new men of God was regarded as the guarantee that Yahweh's favour was still guiding the destinies of his people. The figure of the mediator was never 'improved' into a hagiological portrait, even though devout and thankful minds may have taken a delight in adding a good many decorative—but non-essential—details to the traditional account of his doings. In complete contrast to the case of the Patriarchs, there is no trace of any cultus of his tomb or relics; the tradition lays particular stress on the fact that no man knew his grave. It is this, among other things, which distinguishes him sharply from the ordinary chieftain and medicine-man endowed with power, a well-known figure in the realm of primitive religion, even though certain stories, such as those of the miraculous demonstrations in the presence of Pharaoh, of his prayer prevailing in the battle with the Amalekites, or of the healing of the serpent-bites by means of a wonder-working idol,[12] might seem to suggest such an identification. It is precisely the fact that the powerful fascination of this mysterious personality did not lead popular tradition, always particularly susceptible to phenomena of this kind, to exalt Moses into a wonder-working magician or

12. Cf. on this point [[Eichrodt 1961:]] pp 112f.

tabu-man which is the most striking testimony to his belonging to a completely different sphere. Moreover, in his case magical power was quite distinct in character from that of the primitive sorcerer, for it was entirely subordinated to the activity of the Deity; hence, [[296]] even when similar in external appearance, there was no similarity whatever in significance. Furthermore, the death of the founder of the religion before the conquest of the Promised Land for which he had paved the way seemed to the Israelite historians on reflection to mean that Yahweh's first servant had been sternly recalled by his heavenly Lord, precisely because that Lord wished to crown his work of liberation without him. At no stage is there any mention of a return of Moses in the future such as was envisaged for Zoroaster or Mohammed. The God who sends his servant safeguards his own supreme sovereignty by refusing to associate his work throughout with the person of the mediator. With unconditional authority he recalls him and discharges him from his service at the very moment when, in human eyes, he would seem to have been most indispensable. The work of the founder of the religion seemed after his death to have been scattered to the winds; in fact, it was firmly established on the *charisma*, the free activity of God-inspired personalities—which is to say, on God himself.

THEODORUS C. VRIEZEN

b. 1899   d. 1981

The Nature of the
Knowledge of God

T. C. Vriezen studied in the universities of Utrecht, Leiden, and Groningen. He was a minister in the Dutch Reformed Church before becoming a professor at The Hague and then in the universities of Groningen and Utrecht. Vriezen's Old Testament theology especially addressed the Christian theological and pastoral appropriation of the Old Testament, crucial in the aftermath of World War II.

Selected Writings by Vriezen

1949   *Hoofdlijnen der Theologie van het Oude Testament.* Wageningen: Veenman & Zonen.
1958   *An Outline of Old Testament Theology.* Translated by S. Neuijen. Boston: Branford / Oxford: Blackwell.
1966   *Hoofdlijnen der Theologie van het Oude Testament.* 3d edition. Wageningen: Veenman & Zonen.
1970   *An Outline of Old Testament Theology.* 2d edition. Translated by S. Neuijen. Newton, Massachusetts: Branford / Oxford: Blackwell.

Writings about Vriezen

Clements, Ronald E.
1970   Theodorus C. Vriezen: *An Outline of Old Testament Theology.* Pp. 121–40 in *Contemporary Old Testament Theologians.* Edited by Robert B. Laurin. Valley Forge, Pennsylvania: Judson.
Dijkstra, Meindert, and Karel Vriezen (editors)
1999   *T. C. Vriezen: Hervormd Theoloog en Oudtestamenticus: Studies over Theologie van het Oude Testament, bijbelse theologie en godsdienst van Oud-Israël bij de 100e geboortedag van T. C. Vriezen.* Kampen: Kok.
Unnik, W. C. van, and A. S. van der Woude (editors)
1966   *Studia Biblica et Semitica: Theodoro Christiano Vriezen . . . Dedicata.* Wageningen: Veenman & Zonen.

Theodorus C. Vriezen's
Approach to Old Testament Theology

Excerpted with permission from Theodorus C. Vriezen, *Outline of Old Testament Theology* (2d ed.; Newton, Massachusetts: Branford, 1970), pp. 147–52. Some footnotes have been omitted.

Basis, Task, and Method of Old Testament Theology

[[147]] In this book we start from the view that *both as to its object and its method Old Testament theology is and must be a Christian theological science.*[1] That does not mean that it denies the empirico-historical, phenomenological or any other results of the other branches of Old Testament study, but that it performs its task independently while taking account of and assimilating the results attained by Old Testament scholarship in all its various aspects—the results, therefore, not only in research in the fields of phenomenology and the history of religion, but also those of archaeology, philology, literature, history, exegesis, etc. It is [[148]] not correct, therefore, to incorporate the science of religion as such into theology itself, as was done by Procksch in his *Theologie des A.T.*, for in that case the same procedure should be applied in the other branches of scholarship.[2]

It would be preferable to treat the history of religion as an independent parallel science, as was done by E. Sellin in his *Alttestamentliche Theologie auf religionsgeschichtlicher Grundlage*, the first part of which deals with the *Israelitisch-Jüdische Religionsgeschichte* and the second with the *Theologie des A.T.* It is hardly possible, though, to look upon the history of the religion of Israel as the twin brother of Old Testament theology, for the two are indeed too far apart, even if this view is understandable from a historical point of view. Old Testament theology is a form of scholarship differing from the history of Israel's religion in its object as well as in its method. In its object, *because its object is not the religion of Israel but the Old Testament;*[3] in its method *because it is a study of the message of the Old Testament both in itself and in its relation to the New Testament.*[4]

About both these aspects we shall go into more detail. Only when Eissfeldt's line of thought is followed out consistently can we arrive at a defini-

---

1. Also O. Procksch, *Theologie des A.T.*, 1950. . . .
2. Nowadays several scholars propose to incorporate the Introduction to the Old Testament into theology, as was already done to a large extent by Von Rad.
3. On what grounds this distinction can be made is evident from what has been said above on [[Vriezen 1970:]] pp. 24ff. and 51ff.
4. The English works on the theology of the O.T. (A. B. Davidson, *The Theology of the O.T.*, 1911, and H. Wheeler Robinson, [[p. 62 n. 13 below]]) give us particularly the impression that they start from a synthesis of the theological and the religio-historical methods (e.g. Davidson, p. 6) and that it is this which makes their work so fascinating; cf. also the books by Rowley [[*The Unity of the Bible*, 1953; *The Faith of Israel*, 1956]] and North [[*The Thought of the Old Testament*, 1948]].

tion of Old Testament theology which guarantees a science independent in name and content. Old Testament theology is concerned with the Old Testament; that is to say it is not the religion of Israel in its historical growth and origin, in its development and formation, that is of central importance (so that e.g. Israelite Baalism has as much right to our attention as Yahwism), but it is concerned with the Old Testament as the Holy Scriptures of the Jews, and more especially of the Christians; its task is to define the characteristic features of *the message of the Old Testament,* and for that reason many things can be left out of account which are of more importance in the study of the religions of Israel; as a theological branch of scholarship the theology of the Old Testament seeks *particularly the element of revelation in the message of the Old Testament,* it must work, therefore, with *theological standards* and must give *its own evaluation of the Old Testament message on the ground of its Christian theological starting-point.* In doing so it must guard against the error of tearing apart the *correlation between faith* [[149]] *and revelation* by identifying revelation and canon.[5] From the Christian theological point of view the canon, too, must be submitted to the judgement of the preaching of Jesus Christ. This implies that the method of Old Testament theology is not only purely phenomenological (a reproduction of the Old Testament message in context), but it also gives the connection with the New Testament message and a judgement from the point of view of that message.[6] So, as a part of Christian theology, Old Testament theology in the full sense of the word gives an insight into the Old Testament message and a judgement of this message from the point of view of the Christian faith. It includes the theological motives found in the Old Testament,[7] but it is also concerned with the whole reality of the revelation of God, as described to us in the historical conceptions and the literary testimony of the Old Testament. In doing this it is not enough to give a general survey of "sacred history," with a simple rendering of the biblical narrative in the order in which it is given to us in the Canon,[8] but it must express

5. Cf. Eissfeldt, *op. cit.* p. 3n. (continuation of p. 2, n. 1), who reproaches Barthian theology with this.

6. The programme unfolded above is an ideal objective, which could only be realized by the close co-operation of theologians in the fields of both the Old and the New Testament. Therefore any Old Testament scholar who devotes himself to this task can achieve no more than patch-work. Von Rad thinks the application of standards so problematical that he prefers to refrain from using them completely, for the present at any rate, and to go no further than allowing the Old Testament authors to proclaim their message as objectively as possible (see Th.L.Z. 1963, pp. 407f). Meanwhile in the latter part of the second volume of his Theology he meets the problem of the relationship between the two Testaments in such a way as to relate the Old Testament typologically to the New Testament. It remains to be seen if in doing so he pays sufficient attention to the critical relationship between the two Testaments and if this kind of methodical search for a solution does not imply a theological conception which does identify canon and revelation after all.

7. See [[Vriezen 1970:]] p. 153.

8. As given e.g. by A. C. Welch in his book for religious instruction, *The preparation for Christ,* 1933, or by O. Weber, *Bibelkunde des A.T.,* I, II, 1935, or by P. Heinisch, *Geschichte des A.T.,* 1950, however important this sacred history may be; (cf. that already A. J. C. Vilmar,

the message of God of the Old Testament (using the results of critical research) as it took shape in the various books and sources of the Old Testament during the history which God made Israel pass through until Jesus Christ. All this means complete absorption in the voices which bear witness in the Old Testament to the work of God and so to Him in the course of history and this is not [[150]] merely a philological and historical exercise but also a personal exercise in listening and spiritual understanding.

When the question of method is raised we must say first of all that Old Testament theology must first and foremost inquire into the kerugmatic nature[9] of the Old Testament as a whole and of its parts.[10] This should really be looked upon as a necessary preliminary. For this reason the outline of the message of the separate writings has been given in the prolegomena (Ch. III). This study must always be continued.

On the ground of the understanding of the message of the books and their authors we can expound the whole body of their testimony concerning God, His work and His relations with man and the world. Fundamentally the witness of the God of Israel, Yahweh, is the central element of the words of the Old Testament authors. There are many voices to be heard in the various writings, but the speakers and singers all want to proclaim one and the same God. He is the one focal point of all the Old Testament writings, whatever their literary character, whatever their period of origin.[11] This leads me to the

---

Theologie der Tatsachen, 3rd printing, 1938, p. 33 emphasizes the necessity of a "special acquaintance with the contents of the whole Bible, which has long since been lost"); the sacred history is an indispensable and *basic* element of all theological study, though one which is all too often lacking. If, however, theology were to stop short here, it would mainly bear witness to only one type of preaching in O.T. viz. that of the last editors of the books, and give us too little insight into the various forms of the message and its spiritual development in Israel.

9. See G. von Rad, "Grundprobleme einer biblischen Theologie des A.T.," *Theol. Lit. Zt.*, Sept./Oct. 1943, pp. 225ff.

10. Essentially von Rad would restrict the task of Old Testament theology to this latter inquiry, for the present anyway. Actually he does not, because he also raises the subject of the relationship between the two Testaments in his *O.T. Theology* (II, pp. 319ff.), where he gives theological directives which make us wonder if they sprang from the study of the tradition-theology, or rather dominate the latter (cf. also the closing remarks of von Rad's article in ThLZ, 1963, p. 416). This does not mean that all the historical sources of the Old Testament conform to a certain kerygmatic ground-plan (creed), as von Rad thinks.

11. Von Rad, too, accepts Yahweh as the element in the Old Testament common to all efforts in the field of historical theology (ThLZ, 1963, p. 409); he could hardly do anything else. It is a mystery to me, however, why he should deny that Yahweh is to be looked upon as the central element of the Old Testament. Does this imply a theological conception that makes Christ the "centre" of the Old Testament? (cf. *O.T. Theology* II, pp. 362ff.). However that may be, I am of the opinion that he lays too much stress upon the divergence between the various testimonies concerning Yahweh to be found in the books of the Old Testament. His point of view is theologically unrealistic when considered in the light of the unity that is a characteristic of the Old Testament witness to God in all its divergent traditions. In *The Meaning of Biblical Theology* (JThS 1955, pp. 210ff.) G. Ebeling expresses the view that its task consists in the inquiry into the relations between the variety of testimony and the inner unity of the New Testament.

conclusion that Old Testament theology must centre upon Israel's God as the God of the Old Testament in His relations to the people, man, and the world, and that it must be dependent upon this central element for its structure.

The attempt to understand the Old Testament in this respect demands a continuous intensive contact with the whole of Old Testament scholarship, with its philological and literary aspects as well as [[151]] with its aspects in the field of general history and the history of religion. To demonstrate this connection, this last question was expressly put in Ch. II.

It is, however, neither possible nor necessary in a theology of the Old Testament to deal with all questions concerning the *"religionsgeschichtliche"* and phenomenological background of the message of the Old Testament. It can only lightly touch on a few very important points, so that the true nature of certain elements can be understood more clearly by a comparison with this background. A synthesis of the material obtained in this way cannot be given without more ado, for the content of the message of several books, even concerning one special aspect, is not always the same; these books will have to be confronted with each other and then with the message of the New Testament, in order that we may form an idea of the deepening or decay of spiritual knowledge by seeing the mutual relations between these different elements, and in order that an impression may be obtained of the guidance of the Spirit in the history of revelation.

It is not really possible to press Old Testament theology into a complete systematical survey, though many have attempted this, including Ludwig Köhler in his well-known *Theologie des A.T.*[12] Porteous is probably right when he remarks that owing to this procedure Köhler has failed to find a satisfactory place in his scheme for the cult so that he came to relegate it to anthropology. At any rate the subjects of the Old Testament always interlock in such a way that a systematic classification of the material implies some measure of arbitrariness. A classification which expresses an existential relationship, such as that between God and people, God and the world, or God and man, attempted by Eichrodt and Procksch, has many advantages but is not wholly satisfactory either.

In view of what we said on [[pp. 60-61]] we shall have to divide up our subject as follows: communion as a relationship and the communion between God and man, communion with Yahweh in history, and the prospects for man and the world. We have always considered these subjects in their connection with each other; this feature is emphasized especially by the first chapter on the content of Old Testament theology—the nature of the Old Testament knowledge of God as a relationship between the holy God and man—in which we have tried to keep the essential characteristic of the Old Testament message to its existential plane; the chapter anticipates the next three: communion between God and man, the communion of faith and the prospects for man and the world and was intended as a summarizing introduction to these chapters.

12. Third ed. 1953.

[[152]] In this procedure repetition could not always be avoided. If the various subjects are to be considered in their true connection, certain matters must come up for discussion more than once, though from different points of view.

One thing is certain, though, that the attempt to give a living and true picture of the Old Testament message, on the one hand in its connection with the history of Israel,[13] on the other hand in its perspective in revelation in Jesus Christ, can never succeed fully, not only because our understanding of the Old Testament and the New Testament and of their mutual coherence will always remain imperfect, but above all because God's activity in the history of Israel, the history of salvation (and there is no better name to be found for it), can never be made completely perspicacious to the depths of God Himself, for if we compare this history with a line, there are only certain points of this line that are visible, the line itself cannot be copied by any man, because it is God's secret[14] and He Himself, too, remains a miraculous and essentially hidden God, also in the Old Testament, however much He reveals Himself again and again in history, personal relationship or otherwise.

---

13. This is emphasized by H. Wheeler Robinson in his contributions to the theology of the O.T. in *Record and Revelation*, and in his *Inspiration and Revelation in the O.T.*, 1946. This is done even more strongly by Von Rad, who ranks history, in the form of the traditions concerning God's activity so highly that it becomes the *source* of the knowledge of God and a separate, independent element in Israel's religious life, an element, even, of central importance. Here various objections make themselves felt, i.e. that this view is too one-sided, that it systematizes and abstracts too much ("history" is detached almost completely from the historical facts and, as the central element of the Old Testament message, it is, in fact, as much of a concept as the terms formerly derived from Christian theology). Has "history" in the Old Testament any other aim than leading man to God and to belief in Him (Exod 14:31)? On this question see also [[Vriezen 1970:]] pp. 188ff.

14. For that reason one must be careful in using the name *historia Revelationis*, which Kuyper (*Encyclopaedie* III, p. 166) wished to give to this subject and especially in using the definition of its task: "to describe the process of the Revelation of God to mankind and to throw light upon this process both in its parts and in the whole of its progress." Kraemer rightly remarks (op. cit., p. 23) that the word "process" is entirely out of place beside the word "revelation." On the other hand a Christian need not shrink back from the idea of a line of development which is implicit in the idea of history—for a Christian believes that God has a plan, and he may try to trace this plan, if only he realizes that this plan is fully known only to God.

Synopsis of Vriezen's *Outline of Old Testament Theology* (1970)

Theodorus C. Vriezen
On the Nature of the Knowledge of God

Excerpted with permission from Theodorus C. Vriezen, *Outline of Old Testament Theology* (2d ed.; Newton, Massachusetts: Bradford, 1970), pp. 157–58, 160–66, 168–72, 174–75. Some footnotes have been omitted.

The Nature of the Knowledge of God in the Old Testament as an Intimate Relationship between the Holy God and Man

[[157]] We saw that the Old Testament esteems the knowledge of God as the real, decisive element of religion, and that this knowledge can be defined as communion with God, whose Being as such remains a secret and who is holy. *The basis of Israel's conception of God is the reality of an immediate spiritual communion between God, the Holy One, and man and the world.* God is *directly* and personally concerned with the things of this world, first and foremost with Israel as a people, but by *implication* also with the individual Israelite, with the world of nations, and even with man in general and with the world at large. The experience of communion with the Holy One always implies a sense of distance between God and man, which finds expression either in the form of a confession of guilt (Isaiah 6) or of fear (Gen 28:17, Exod 20:18ff.) or of wonder (Psalm 8, Isaiah 28f.).

This certainty of the immediate communion between the Holy God and weak, sinful man may be called the underlying idea of the whole of the Biblical testimony, for in its essence this basic idea is also found in the New Testament.

It is most surprising that this has been denied again and again and that the conception of God in the Old Testament has been set against that of the New Testament, as if the Old Testament spoke of God as a hard despot and the New Testament of a merciful Father in heaven. In this way neither the Old Testament nor the New Testament was done justice: the God and Father revealed in Jesus Christ, who is love (1 John 4:8b) did not have justice done to His holiness—and Yahweh, who is the God of communion, was denied in His *chesed*, His love. The attempt of M. Buber in his book *Two Types of Faith*, to represent the *relationship to God* in the Old Testament as quite unlike that in the New Testament (in the Old Testament the relation to God rests on an immediate faith, in the New Testament on an intellectual act of faith, namely the affirmation of faith in Jesus Christ) is a misconception, too, for the Old Testament as well as the New Testament demands faith in God's work of salvation to which the prophets revert again and again, and conversely the New Testament also knows the intimate immediate relationship with God based on His work of salvation.

This communion between God and man is given a central position in the historical narratives, prophecies, the psalms and the wisdom-literature as a basic hypothesis or as an explicit testimony and may [[158]] be called the A-B-C of the Biblical religion and message. It is the spiritual presupposition and the purpose of the cult and of the other institutions of salvation (the monarchy, prophetism), the foundation-stone of creed and hymn, the starting-point of faith, ethics and expectations; it dominates the whole field of Israel's religious life and thought. For a theological interpretation of the Old Testament, not only in its historical and prophetical traditions, but also regarding its inward vital principle that integrates all the expressions of Israel's faith, we shall have to deal with this fundamental category of the communion between *this* God Yahweh and *this* people of Israel. Here we find the factual content of the Old Testament expressed most profoundly. Times without number the words: "I am Yahweh, thy God" are repeated in the historical and prophetical writings; in the latter it becomes a guiding principle for a hope of salvation in the future.[1]

. . . .

[[160]] It must remain an established fact that communion between the Holy One and man is the essential root-idea of the Old Testament message, but equally, that the knowledge concerning this relation is only the effect of God's work of revelation and the relation itself was only ordained by God in His grace (Deuteronomy 7; 9)! In this communion man may, on the one hand, realize that he does indeed stand in a personal relationship to God and may speak to God as God speaks to him;[2] on the other hand this should never make him think that his relation to God is a true "dialogue-situation."[3] Man cannot keep quarreling with God to the end: even if God does allow man to dispute with Him (cf. Job, Jeremiah 15),[4] ultimately disputing man is always silenced and condemned (Job 42, Jer 15:19). The discussion between God and man is never a dialogue pure and simple; the man who speaks must always realize and experience that he is addressing himself to the *Holy One*, and his word or answer spoken to God can fundamentally be a prayer only.

The last word, therefore, never rests with man; even in Gen 18:33 God terminates the discussion with Abraham more or less abruptly; and even Israel's prayers of penitence are not always answered by Yahweh (Jeremiah 15; Hosea 6).[5] It is for Him to take *the decision* whether or not to accept man's words. Therefore Buber just oversteps the mark when he says that in the dialogue between God and His creature man is a real partner in his own right

---

1. Cf. Jer 31:33 and elsewhere, Ezek 11:20, 26:28, 27:27; Zech 8:9. No wonder that F. Baumgärtel considered these words to be the content of the whole of the Old Testament message (cf. *Verheissung*, 1952).

2. J. Muilenburg, *The Way of Israel*, 1961, pp. 18ff. rightly points to the frequent use of the vocative where God speaks to man and conversely.

3. Buber, *Kampf um Israel*, p. 32. This view is connected with the one quoted above, [[Vriezen 1970:]] p. 158.

4. Cf also M. A. Beek, *Het twistgesprek van de mens met zijn God*, 1946.

5. Neither does He accept sacrifice—Amos 5, Isaiah 1, Psalm 1, Genesis 4, etc.

who can speak his own word independently and of his own free will.[6] This view smacks too much of modern individualism and humanism.

When the communion between the Holy God and man is taken to be the underlying idea of the Old Testament witness concerning God we must always keep in view that there is in this message a strong tension, which for the sake of truth must never be relaxed, between these two elements: the Holiness of God and His communion with man. The fact, already pointed out, that the most fundamental expression for faith or religion in the Old Testament is *yir'ath Yahweh*, the fear of the Lord, speaks for itself;[7] this need not be taken to mean, [[161]] as some commentators think, that Israel never managed to rise above the terror of God, for the word fear also occurs as a synonym for faith and expectation; but the presupposition of the glory and holiness of God is always implicit in the word. When God appears to Israel or to a prophet, the first reaction felt is always that of fear (Exodus 19f.; Isaiah 6; Ezekiel 1ff.).

All through the Old Testament we find that man cannot behold God, that man must die after having seen God or one of His messengers. God cannot, therefore, really be seen or described. There are a few exceptions to the former, where God is actually seen, so, e.g., Exod 24:10f., where the elders of Israel see God but the appearance itself is not described; it is, however, stated emphatically that God did not lay His hand upon the "nobles of the children of Israel," those who had been specially elected for this purpose. In connection with the concluding of the Covenant we are here informed of a most peculiar event (to a certain extent comparable with St. Paul's "mystical" experience in 2 Corinthians 12). Also in connection with the concluding of the Covenant God is said to have spoken to Moses face to face (Exod 33:11; Num 12:8; Deut 34:10) and the appearance of God to Moses is assumed (Exod 34:5ff., 29ff.), but on the other hand Exod 33:18ff. expressly states that even Moses could not bear to see Yahweh in all His glory; God's face could not be seen, only His back.[8] In later times the appearance of God is beheld, by prophets such as Isaiah (ch. 6) and Ezekiel, but they cannot see, let alone describe, God properly speaking; for in Isaiah's case even the seraphim shroud their faces and figures and encircle the throne of God, while in Ezekiel 1 the prophet can only describe the appearance approximately ("I saw as it were . . .").

On the other hand the anthropomorphical appearances of God, taking place especially in the stories of the patriarchs, show the other aspect: the communion between God and man. This representation of the appearance of God may be partially due to a more primitive aesthetic way of expression, going back to oral folk-tales, on which the authors draw, it is at any rate also

6. Buber, op. cit., p. 33. . . .

7. Cf., for instance, Isa 29:13c: "their fear toward me is taught by the precept of men"; another possible translation would be: "their religion is a lesson learnt by heart."

8. The end of Exodus 33, from vs. 12 onwards, looks like a discussion on the question of the reality of knowing God face to face (vs. 11) and reminds us of a later collection like the midrash; see [[Vriezen 1970:]] pp. 186ff.

partly due to the tendency of the authors to make the people of Israel participate in the experience of [[162]] the original intimacy of the relationship between God and man; this tendency is not primitive, but originates purely in religious Yahwism.

Finally we shall point out a few main ideas that dominate Old Testament religion and give expression to various aspects of the leading motif of Israel's religion, namely the direct relationship between the Holy God and man.

a. One of the most fundamental elements of the Old Testament teaching is the great stress laid on *God's activity in history.*[9] The belief in God seems to be wholly based on the experience of this activity. The background against which the image of God stands out in the Old Testament is history.[10] Yahweh is in the Old Testament rather the God of history than the Creator or the God of Nature, though these latter elements are not lacking (cf. [[Vriezen 1970:]] pp. 331ff.). This thought was expressed by Pascal in his well-known words: "Dieu! Dieu d'Abraham, d'Isaac et de Jacob! Dieu de Jésus Christ, non des philosophes et des savants." Israel derives its knowledge of God from His activity in history on behalf of His people, particularly in Egypt and in the desert. He has intervened in behalf of the oppressed and the forsaken and has thus called Israel into being. This is pointed out continually with great emphasis by the prophets. In history, by His activity for the good of His people, God has revealed Himself as the living God who is near, but who is holy, too.[11] And throughout the course of history God intervenes at critical moments; He follows His people, saving as well as judging them, and He controls their destiny. The whole life of the people passes under His eyes in times of disaster and of prosperity; both are signs of His activity. There are always these two aspects to His activity: it is majestic and inspires confidence, for it is the Supreme God who intervenes, who does as He pleases and who is terrible [[163]] even when He intervenes in behalf of His people; cf. e.g. Exodus 15; Psalm 68, 111, 114; Isaiah 45. The works of Yahweh are performed to make His people glorify Him, but also give Israel reason to extol Him because they have thus experienced His faithfulness and love (many Psalms, Deuteronomy, Deutero-Isaiah and Ezekiel).

b. Whereas God's saving activity in history is the general basis for the certainty of the direct relationship between God and man, *prophecy* is the deepest and strongest revelation of the communion between the Holy One and man. It is found throughout the history of Israel and is the most characteristic element of the structure of the Israelite religion. God is not only the God of history, who acts with and on behalf of man, but He is also the God who

9. See [[Vriezen 1970:]] pp. 26ff. and pp. 190ff.

10. A. Weiser, *Glaube und Geschichte im A.T.*, 1931; C. R. North, *The O.T. interpretation of history*, 1946, pp. 141ff.; H. Wheeler Robinson, "The Theology of the O.T.," *Record and Revelation*, 1938, pp. 303ff.; id., *Inspiration and Revelation*, 1946, pp. 106ff.; Köhler, *Theologie des A.T.*[3], pp. 77ff.; J. deGroot and A. R. Hulst, [[*Macht en Wil*, 1952,]] pp. 213ff.; R. C. Dentan, *The idea of history in the Ancient Near East*, 1955, see the contribution on Ancient Israel by Millar Burrows, pp. 99ff.

11. Cf. for example W. J. Phythian-Adams, *The Call of Israel*, 1934.

allows the man whom He has called to share in His activity by His Spirit or Word. God performs nothing without revealing His decree to His servants, the prophets (Amos 3:7), the prophet is allowed to be a witness to God's work in history and, as it were, "sees reality through God's eyes" (Heschel); that is why he is called a "seer."

It is even possible to speak of a "pathetic" theology.[12] God's work in history is accompanied by the prophetic revelation, God reveals His mind to man. *There must be an original connection between Israel's belief in God who acts in history and the prophetic experience* expressed so strongly by Amos; for this word is not merely *his* conviction, but it is the testimony of the Old Testament generally.[13] The prophets did not only explain God's work in history, but revealed it, too (often also by foretelling it).

That this certainty is found again and again through the course of the centuries can only be attributed to the fact that this connection between prophetic revelation and God's work in the history of His people formed part of Israel's religious conceptions from the very beginning: the figure of Moses must therefore have been prophetic; it is to him that the religious relationship dates back.[14] For this reason [[164]] prophecy and history are not to be separated, as some theologians are inclined to do, for that would make the prophets mere interpreters of what has already happened, and history itself would become the medium of revelation.[15]

Hempel rightly says:[16] "In the origin of the religion of Israel two elements cooperate: the miracle, the exceptional event in nature or history, experienced as a miracle, and the extraordinary man who explains this miracle; revelation and inspiration, to use dogmatic terminology."

And it is exactly in this prophetic experience focused on the history of today and tomorrow that the two elements of the knowledge of God, the Holy One, *and* of communion with Him are most closely linked; we mention here the figure of Isaiah who comes to know God as the Holy One in the vision of his vocation and announces His judgment with great force, but who on the other hand is the very proclaimer of confidence, or faith, almost more so than any other prophet (cf. Isa 7:9: "believe," 30:15: "quietness and confidence"); another such prophetical figure is Deutero-Isaiah, in whose message both elements are found very strongly supplementing each other, compare Isaiah 40 and 45 with Isaiah 55. But with Hosea, too, the preacher of God's

12. A. J. Heschel, *Die Prophetie*, Krakow, 1936; *The Prophets*, 1962. It is this reality of the knowledge of God that is denied to man by Ecclesiastes.

13. Cf. e.g. J. Bright, *Jeremiah*, 1965, pp. xxviiff.

14. The use of the word "prophetic" in this book to denote the personal and moral character of Israel's religion, is based upon this conviction that the religion of Israel dates back in the first instance to the prophetic work of Moses; besides this general broad use of the word prophetic there is the more limited sense of the word denoting the religious conviction of the classical prophets.

15. Cf. W. Pannenberg c.s., *Offenbarung als Geschichte*, 1961, particularly the contribution of R. Rendtorff, *Die Offenbarungsvorstellungen im A.T.* and the discussion between W. Zimmerli and R[[endtorff]] in *Ev. Th.* 1962, pp. 15ff and 62ff. . . .

16. J. Hempel, *Gott und Mensch im A.T.*², 1936, p. 2 n. 2 now also *Geschichten*, p. 232. . . .

love, the element of dreadfulness in the Nature of God stands out clearly. He depicts Yahweh as a lion (5:14), or even as a consuming disease (5:12), a lion or a leopard by the way (13:7ff.). The same applies to the earliest prophet Amos, who sees God as a destroyer (7:7ff., 8:1ff., 9:1ff.), and as a roaring lion (1:2, 3:8), but also as saving righteousness. To this experience of communion by the prophets clearly corresponds the message they teach, always ending in the proclamation that Yahweh shall be Israel's God and Israel Yahweh's people (e.g. Hosea 2, 14; Isaiah 2; Jeremiah 31; Ezekiel 36f; Isaiah 45, 51f.; Zechariah 8, etc., see [[p. 65 above]]). The keystone of the message of salvation is always the proclamation of the actualization of communion with God.

   c. A third typical characteristic of Israel's religion, connected with the preceding, is *the personal character of religious life.* Like the belief [[165]] in Yahweh as the God who acts in history, this element of Israel's religion may also be looked upon as closely connected with its prophetic character. Like the two preceding elements this characteristic, too, is of a very early date and it is, as it were, the product of the first two; it stands out clearly in the Yahwistic narratives of the patriarchs in the calling of Abraham and his faithful obedience in the Word of God. We may agree here with A. Alt who discovers evidence of the personal character of the relationship between the patriarchs and their God in names such as "the God of the fathers," "the God of Abraham," "the fear (relation?) of Isaac," "the Mighty One (?) of Jacob."[17] As to the stories concerning Moses, which are highly coloured by later religious conceptions, as are the patriarchal narratives, we may be brief. In Exodus 33f., Numbers 12 and Deuteronomy 34 the personal relationship is emphasized so strongly, that any sense of distance seems to have disappeared altogether. The same is true of the earliest historical work that has come down to us, the history of David and his succession; for in 2 Sam 12:16 we already find how David very personally "besought God for the child" to which Bathsheba had given birth; this chapter is a profound account of David's spiritual struggle with God to save the child's life. In 1 Sam 30:6 we read that David, in one of the most difficult moments of his life, when he stood all alone during a catastrophic event, "encouraged himself in the Lord his God." In the Psalms God is invoked again and again with the simple, direct exclamation: *"Elohai,* my God,"[18] and on comparing this appellation with the many titles and names of deities that we meet with in the initial verses of Accadian psalms it becomes quite apparent that there is a vast difference in distance between gods and men in Babylon and God and man in Israel;[19] the word "my God" bear witness to the intimacy of the communion between man and God. Many other Psalms (Psalm 33, 16, the final vss of 73, etc.) testify to the reality of the communion and to the spiritual strength radiating from it. In the prophetic type

   17. See A. Alt, *Der Gott der Väter,* 1929, pp. 42ff. and 62ff.
   18. See also Hempel, op. cit., pp. 185–86; O. Eissfeldt, " 'My God' in the O.T.," *Ev. Quarterly,* XIX, 1947, pp. 7ff. (cf. p. 83, n. 2).
   19. An exception to this in Mesopotamia is the relationship to the personal tutelary deity, a lower deity who must intercede with the mighty gods as an intermediary; see H. Frankfort, *Intellectual adventure,* 1946, pp. 203ff. . . .

of piety, especially in Jeremiah's confessions, we are struck by the directness of the relationship between man and God, which is perhaps brought out even more clearly by the way in which Micah (6:8) defines religion: "He hath shewed thee, [[166]] O man, what is good; and what doth the Lord require of thee but to do justly, and to love mercy, and to walk humbly with thy God?" The simple-farmer of Moresheth near Gath must have known a very direct contact with God. The personal relationship to God as the God of history brings with it *faith*, complete reliance on God; this is stressed by the prophet Isaiah, and it is by this faith that Abraham's life is judged in Gen 15:6.

The other side to this personal relationship between God and man is the consciousness that all lies exposed before the Holy God, who knows man in all his ways (Psalm 139; Isa 29:15ff.), and calls him to account for all his acts (Amos 3:2). Moreover, communion with God also leads to the experience of the terribly severe demand which serving God involves. It is precisely the man who has been called personally by God who is led into the fight by Yahweh (Mic 3:8; Jeremiah 1; 8:18ff.; 9:1ff.; 11:18ff.; 15:15ff.; 16; 17:14ff.; 20:14ff.; 36ff.). The prophet of the exile who experienced this personally (Isaiah 1) realized most profoundly how the true Servant of the Lord, the *ᶜebed Yahweh*, would have to suffer and die for God's people, according to God's will.

d. In the preceding more *general structure forms* of Israel's religion, as depicted in the Old Testament, it becomes quite clear that the relationship between God and man is a communion. The same holds good for the two following important *theological conceptions: the idea of the Covenant* and the doctrine of *man as the image of God.* On closer examination, however, we also see that these, too, are based on the recognition of the fundamental distinction between God and man.

We shall first deal with the *conception of the Covenant*, as this idea was the most influential in the Old Testament writings, especially in and influenced by Deuteronomistic theology.

[[168]] The doctrine of the Covenant presupposes a relationship between Yahweh and Israel which arose in history, not a natural relationship. The Covenant relation was established by Yahweh alone—in the Old Testament Yahweh is always the subject of the verb used to indicate the concluding of the Covenant. This clearly shows that Yahweh and Israel are not co-equal partners: everything originates with Yahweh, it is He who states the terms of the Covenant. The Judaic theological notion of a bilateral covenant is hardly supported by the Old Testament data, but rather by a later theological interpretation of these data. It is true, though, that especially in the Deuteronomic works such a tendency is, indeed, to be observed: we see how Israel as a partner to the Covenant confirms it and agrees with it; in this way Israel acknowledges its responsibility for adhering to the rules of the Covenant decreed by Yahweh (e.g. Deut 26:16–19; Exod 19:7, 24:2ff.).[20]

---

20. Especially in Joshua 24 the bilateral aspect seems to be emphasized, but the situation is different; this appears to be a description of the historical formation of the Yahweh-amphictyony, in which the ancient pre-Mosaic tribes enter into the Yahweh-religion and join

By concluding the Covenant with Israel Yahweh enters into communion with this people. The Hebrew word *berith* (covenant) means something like "bond of communion"; by concluding a covenant a connective link is effected[21] (by means of a sacrifice or a meal or both) between the two partners, who thereby enter into an intimate relationship.

Yahweh entered into such a relationship with Israel. To that end he has drawn up the rules that are to obtain, rules which Israel could not but accept if it wanted to be accepted or remain within this circle. Thus Israel was admitted to God's Covenant and thus it was sanctified. By allowing Israel to enter into this Covenant God by no means gives up His holiness, but Israel is admitted to His holy sphere of life (cf. Leviticus 19).

The Covenant may be 'transgressed' (*'abar*), 'left' (*'azab*), 'broken' (*hefer*), but Israel cannot meddle with its laws. We must, therefore, [[169]] certainly not represent the Covenant as a "voluntary agreement" between the two parties.[22] As we said above, and Köhler himself admits (p. 45) God is always the subject when the Covenant is concluded, and in later times He is always said to "cause the Covenant to exist," 'to establish' (*heqim*), 'found' (*sim*) or 'give' (*nathan*) it!

The Covenant is, therefore, "unilateral," not bilateral in origin: Israel is expected to obey the rules of the Covenant drawn up by God and by Him alone. After the Deuteronomic reformation Israel was called God's heritage, His own, to the glory of God in the world. Israel is elected by God, and therefore the object of His electing will, committed to this will. As the elected people Israel is the *'ebed*, the *servant*, as Deutero-Isaiah has it.

Though the Covenant is broken by Israel and God punishes His headstrong and wilful people, the Covenant itself is not set aside by God. Even if God rejects the empirical Israel in its entirety for some time, that does not mean that Israel as such is rejected. None of the prophets taught that the judgment of the people in their days implied the lasting rejection of the people as such! Each prophet was, somehow, a prophet of salvation as well as a prophet of evil and hoped that God's Covenant, which owed its existence to His love would also be restored by Him. Israel was never rejected absolutely, a conception which is found with the ancient Orientals, e.g., the Babylonians, who in their Creation-narratives supposed that the wrath of the gods had in view the complete destruction of mankind.[23]

---

the Yahweh-league. Even here, though, those who enter into the Covenant do not decide on the condition of entering.

21. According to Buber, *Königtum Gottes*, 1932, pp. 113, 231, *Berith* means "Umschränkung' ("circumscription," "confinement"). The word cannot be divorced from the Assyrian *biritu*, intervening space, in the sense of what is common, and unites (*ina birit* = between); cf. B. Landsberger, *Ana ittišu*, MSL [[1]] 1937, p. 89; W. von Soden, *Akkadisches Handwörterbuch, s.v.* and M. Noth, *Das alttest. Bundschliessen im Licht eines Mari-textes* [[in *Gesammelte Studien zum Alten Testament*, 1960]], pp. 142ff.

22. Köhler, *Theologie*, p. 52.

23. The view that the counterpart of the election of Israel in the O.T. is the rejection of Israel (Köhler, *Theologie*, p. 66) cannot be maintained in this general form. It is true that in

All this points the same way: the *Covenant* between God and the people *did not bring these two "partners" into a contract-relation, but into a communion, originating with God, in which Israel was bound to Him completely and made dependent on Him.*

The Covenant absolutely obliges Israel to do God's will. Israel cannot remain itself but must let itself be sanctified. Particularly the book of Deuteronomy emphasizes strongly the spiritual obligations while the Priestly Code stresses the fact that God has *made* the Covenant and that Israel is sanctified to the Lord.

[[170]] The priestly author considers all communion between God and man from the angle of the Covenant. In his conception of history (see [[Vriezen 1970:]] pp. 62ff.) there are three kinds of covenant: besides the Mosaic Covenant there is the Covenant with Abraham (Genesis 17) sealed by circumcision, and before that the Covenant with the whole of mankind and, indeed, with all creation—the Noachian Covenant (Gen 9:9ff.).

The doctrine of the Covenant implies, therefore (1) the absolute recognition of the reality of a true *communion* between God and people (man); (2) the absolute recognition of God, the Holy One, the Supreme, who has established and guides this relationship; (3) the absolute acknowledgment of the rules of the Covenant, given by God. Thus the doctrine of the Covenant is the clearest illustration of communion with God, the fundamental idea of the Old Testament message.

The Covenant-relationship is one of the most important forms in which the communion between God and man reveals itself in Israel's religion, but this communion is also expressed by quite different relations, such as those between father and child, husband and wife, lord and servant, king and people. For that reason the present author thinks it preferable, for various reasons, to use the much wider term "communion" in a theological exposition to denote the relationship between God and man rather than the more definite notion of the "Covenant."

e. Finally: *the doctrine of man as the Image of God.*

. . . .

[[171]] The outstanding feature of the conception of man in the Old Testament is the pronouncement of the Priestly Code that man is created *in God's image, after His likeness* (Gen 1:26f., cf. 5:1, 9:6; Psalm 8). Like other elements in Genesis 1 this wording must be considered in the light of the ancient oriental range of ideas: there man is often placed in a directly physical relationship with the deity: man is frequently represented as both from the

---

Ps 78:67 the rejection of the northern tribes—because of their idolatry—is mentioned, and in Isa 14:1 and Zech 1:17, 2:6 (R.V.12) we read of the "*further*" (Hebr. '*od* is "anew," or "further") election of Jerusalem. This implies the continuous faithfulness of the electing God rather than the possibility of definite rejection by God of what He has once elected. In any case rejection is a judgment based on the inconvertibility of man and never founded on the unwillingness of God, as may be found elsewhere, as far as Israel is concerned rejection only exists partially and temporarily as punishment. Cf. my *Die Erwählung Israels*, pp. 98ff.

mother-goddess or as created by the deity from divine blood (partially at least). This view is the expression of an "idealistic" anthropology namely the conception that man is essentially of divine origin, an idea well-known from Greece (cf. Acts 17) and inherent in naturalistic paganism which puts cosmogony on a level with theogony. According to Babylonian theory, e.g., man distinguishes himself from the gods by weakness and mortality, but otherwise man and the gods spring from the same stock (men can also be looked upon as deities, as is proved by the Mesopotamian and especially the Egyptian ideology concerning the monarch).

[[172]] This notion is utterly unknown to the Old Testament and this constitutes the essential difference between the Biblical and non-Biblical conceptions of God. In the Bible God and man are absolutely distinct, because God essentially precedes nature and is superior to it,[24] however much He may reveal His power in nature.

In spite of the fact that this absolute difference is clearly recognized in the Old Testament, the Old Testament is by no means behind any of the non-Biblical philosophies in its spiritual appreciation of man, as appears from the recognition of the communion between God and man. Whereas there is a great ideological tension in the ancient oriental world concerning the relationship between God and man (on the one hand man is the child of God, or at any rate he shares in the same life with the deity, and on the other hand he is merely a slave used by the deity) which gives rise to the typically naturalistic (ancient oriental and Greek) and tragic view of life, the Old Testament religion is founded upon the certainty of the relationship between the holy God and man.

The representation of man as the *imago Dei* is the symbol of this certainty of the communion of the Holy God who is "wholly different," with man, the creature of God. This term may be called a "critico-theological" idea which on the one hand indicates a direct, positive communion, but on the other hand excludes any equality. By this wording, the actual terms of the Father-child relationship are avoided, but the relation itself is meant, as also in the whole of the Old Testament, to denote the relationship between God and man.

. . . .

[[174]] It would be possible to add many important points to the five already mentioned; we indicate the following, without pursuing the subject further, because they are discussed more or less fully in the factual part of the book; the *cult*, whose main object is the strengthening or restoration of the communion between God and the people (see especially [[Vriezen 1970:]] pp. 255ff.); *wisdom* which in its Israelite form fully aims at keeping peace with God and leads to the proclamation of communion with Him, as we see particularly clearly at the end of the book Job;[25] *eschatology*, which proclaims the message of the kingdom of peace between God and man with God as the

---

24. In fact, the *ruach 'Elohim* is said to circle over the waters of the chaos before the creation of the world (Gen 1:2, see [[Vriezen 1970:]] p. 215.

25. See [[Vriezen 1970:]] p. 84 n. 3.

focal point of this communion (cf. [[Vriezen 1970:]] p. 204f.); the *Spirit of God* which operates in history and dominates the kingdom of God (cf. [[Vriezen 1970:]] p. 211f.), and last but not least the very *name of God* in Israel, *Yahweh*, in which both the idea of nearness, of being present and the idea of mystery are found (cf. [[Vriezen 1970:]] pp. 180f.).

Thus the Old Testament is pervaded throughout by the security contained in the name which Isaiah held up to his people: Immanuel, God with us. Right from the start, Gen 1–3 tells us, God had in view life in communion with man. The historians bear testimony to the fact that throughout history, in spite of sin and guilt, transgression and unbelief, God went with His people, to which He revealed His communion. To this the prophets add the message that at the end of time there shall be full *shalom* between God and man. And in the face of death one of the Psalmists sings; "My flesh and my heart faileth: but God is the strength of my heart and my portion for ever."

This communion is always experienced in the Old Testament as something miraculous, for God is God and no man; man is on earth, God is in heaven. Yet they belong together, because He willed [[175]] it so in His incomprehensible goodness (Psalm 8).[26] In this fundamental point of faith the New Testament is in complete agreement with the Old. And for that reason the communion between God and man is the best starting point for a Biblical theology of the Old Testament, and the following chapters will, therefore, be arranged with this aspect in view.

---

26. This relationship should never be denoted by the word "kinship," a supposition which we find all through Pedersen's *Israel*, and in H. Wheeler Robinson's well-considered work, *Inspiration and Revelation in the O.T.*, 1946, p. 190 ("there is a real kinship between God and man. Man is presented in the O.T. as a spiritual being and as such he is, notwithstanding all limitations, akin to God who is Spirit"). The former places God and man too much in a relationship of natural mysticism, the latter spiritualizes man too much.

GEORGE ERNEST WRIGHT

b. 1909   d. 1974

God the Warrior

Having done his doctoral work with William Foxwell Albright at Johns Hopkins University, G. Ernest Wright became a leader in "biblical archaeology." He founded and long edited *The Biblical Archaeologist* (since 1997, *Near Eastern Archaeology*). Wright was also a leading figure in the biblical theology movement of the 1950s and 1960s. Historical and theological concerns merge in his approach to biblical theology. Wright taught at McCormick Theological Seminary and, for many years, at Harvard University.

Selected Writings by Wright

1952   *God Who Acts: Biblical Theology as Recital.* Studies in Biblical Theology 8. London: SCM / Chicago: Regnery.

1969a   *The Old Testament and Theology.* New York: Harper & Row.

1969b   History and Reality: The Importance of Israel's "Historic Symbols" for the Christian Faith. Pp. 176–99 in *The Old Testament and Christian Faith.* Edited by Bernhard W. Anderson. New York: Herder and Herder.

1970   Historical Knowledge and Revelation. Pp. 279–303 in *Translating and Understanding the Old Testament.* Edited by H. T. Frank and W. L. Reed. Nashville: Abingdon.

1957   *The Book of the Acts of God: Contemporary Scholarship Interprets the Bible.* Garden City, New York: Doubleday. [[With Reginald H. Fuller.]]

Writings about Wright

Cross, Frank M., Werner E. Lemke, and Patrick D. Miller Jr. (editors)

1976   *Magnalia Dei—The Mighty Acts of God: Essays on the Bible and Archaeology in Memory of G. Ernest Wright.* Garden City, New York: Doubleday.

Long, Burke O.

1997   *Planting and Reaping Albright: Politics, Ideology, and Interpreting the Bible.* University Park: Pennsylvania State University Press.

G. Ernest Wright's
Approach to Old Testament Theology

Excerpted with permission from G. Ernest Wright, *God Who Acts:
Biblical Theology as Recital* (London: SCM, 1952), pp. 33–35, 55–
58; and G. Ernest Wright, *The Old Testament and Theology* (New
York: Harper & Row, 1969), pp. 61–63.

Theology as Recital
[[from *God Who Acts*]]

[[33]] Biblical theology has long been dominated by the interests of dogmatic
or systematic theology. Indeed, throughout the first three centuries of Protestantism the two disciplines were scarcely distinguished, at least among conservative churchmen. All theology was Biblical theology in the sense that it
was a system of doctrine drawn from the Bible and supported by collections
of proof-texts. While the fact of the Reformation is illustrative of the perennial tension which has always existed between the Bible and theology, nevertheless the separation of Biblical theology as an independent subject of study
occurred in a new form within pietism and eighteenth century rationalism,
when the Bible was used to criticize orthodox dogma. Johann Philipp Gabler
in 1787 seems to have been the first in modern times formally to advocate a
distinction between the two disciplines. To him Biblical theology is an objective, historical discipline which attempts to describe what the Biblical writers
thought about divine matters. Dogmatic theology on the other hand, is didactic in character and sets forth what a theologian philosophically and rationally decides about divine matters in accordance with his time and situation.[1]
Nevertheless, in organizing the data of Biblical faith the rubrics of systematic
theology continued in use, the chief of these being the doctrine of God, the
doctrine of man, and the doctrine of salvation.

During the nineteenth century, however, the historical nature of the
Bible was more clearly seen than ever before. As a result, men came to believe that Biblical theology must concern itself primarily with the development of religious ideas. This point of view made the task of the Biblical
theologian so difficult that few scholars attempted anything other than a history of religion in the Old and New Testaments. Perhaps the greatest work in
Old Testament theology produced during the last century was [[34]] that by
the German scholar Hermann Schultz.[2] He tried to solve the problem by presenting first a historical account of the development of Israel's religion and
then by giving a topical treatment in which theological concepts were traced
through the various historical periods. In other words, no attempt was made

---

1. So Robert C. Dentan, *Preface to Old Testament Theology* (New Haven, 1950), p. 8.
2. See his *Old Testament Theology* (translated from the 4th German ed. by J. A. Paterson,
in 2 vols., Edinburgh, 1892).

to present a systematic theology of the Old Testament as a whole. The growth of religious concepts through the history was thought to be too great to permit a systematic survey. A different type of treatment is illustrated by the work of the French pastor, Ch. Piepenbring, first published in 1886.[3] He presented three cross sections through Israel's history, the first being the preprophetic period beginning with Moses, the second the age of prophecy, and the third the Exilic and post-Exilic age. In each period he systematically treated the doctrines of God, man, worship and salvation under a variety of chapter headings.

It will be noted that these works are based upon two presuppositions. The first is that the evolution of religious concepts in the Bible is so great that there are virtually different theologies in different periods. The second is that the procedure of dogmatic theology is normative for all theology, including that of the Bible. If both these presuppositions are correct, then the task of Biblical theology is quite clear. It is either to trace the evolving history of religious concepts through the various Biblical periods, as did Schultz, or else it is to take a cross section through the Bible at one period and treat that as systematically as possible.

With regard to the first presupposition there is an increasingly widespread belief today that while historical development is indeed a very important factor in the Bible yet it is one which has been overemphasized. A living organism is not a blank tablet on which all writing is done by environmental, geographical and historical conditioning. If it were, then a description of a historical process might be sufficient to enable us to comprehend its inner significance. But in every organism there is something given which determines what it is and what it will become. Environment and geography can explain many things in ancient [[35]] Israel, but they cannot explain why Israel did not undergo the same type of evolution as did her pagan neighbours, nor why the early Church did not become another Jewish purist sect or Hellenistic mystery religion. One explanation for this difference in evolution which positivist scholars have been wont to give is the presence in Biblical history of remarkable series of religious geniuses: Moses, the prophets, Jesus, Paul. Yet every genius is in part a product of his historical situation in a given social context. He cannot be explained apart from certain inner, spiritual factors which are a vital part of the cultural situation in which he arose. In other words, there is in the Bible something far more basic than the conceptions of environment, growth and genius are able to depict. It is this 'given' which provided the Bible's basic unity in the midst of its variety and which sets Biblical faith apart as something radically different from all other faiths of mankind.[4]

· ·

3. *Theology of the Old Testament* (translated from the French by H. G. Mitchell, Boston, 1893).

4. See further the monograph by the writer, *The Old Testament Against its Environment*, and that by Floyd V. Filson, *The New Testament against Its Environment* (London and Chicago, 1950).

[[55]] From the above survey we are now in possession of the chief clues to the theological understanding of the whole Bible. There is, first, the peculiar attention to history and to historical traditions as the primary sphere in which God reveals himself. To be sure, God also reveals himself and his will in various ways to the inner consciousness of man, as in other religions. Yet the nature and content of this inner revelation is determined by the outward, objective happenings of history in which individuals are called to participate. It is, therefore, the objectivity of God's historical acts which are the focus of attention, not the subjectivity of inner, emotional, diffuse and mystical experience. Inner revelation is thus concrete and definite, since it is always correlated with a historical act of God which is the primary locus of concentration. Mysticism in its typical forms, on the other hand, subtly turns this concentration around, so that the focus of attention is on the inner revelation, while the objectivity of God's historical acts is either denied altogether or left on the periphery of one's vision. Important as Christian pietism has been in the Church, it has not escaped this subtle inversion with the result that the central Biblical perspective has been lost.

Secondly, the chief inference from this view of history as revelation was the mediate nature of God's action in history: that is, his election of a special people through whom he would accomplish his purposes. This was a proper inference from the Exodus deliverance; and the migration of Abraham to Canaan was believed to have been occasioned by a Divine call which involved election. In Genesis the election is portrayed as the goal of history and the Divine answer to the human problem. After the Exodus, it formed the background for the interpretation of Israel's life in Palestine and a central element in prophetic [[56]] eschatology and in the apocalyptic presentation of the Book of Daniel.

Thirdly, the election and its implications were confirmed and clarified in the event of the covenant ceremony at Sinai. Israel's sin was the breach of this covenant, which, therefore, enabled the faithful to see that election was not unalterable. It could be annulled by Israel herself. Consequently, covenant was something that had to be periodically renewed by ceremonies of re-dedication.[5] It involved the interpretation of the whole life of the people, in the social, economic, political and cultic spheres. The law of the society was the law of the covenant, given by God with the promise of justice and security within the promised land. Consequently, the central problem of Israel was envisaged as the problem of true security in the midst of covenant violation and international upheaval. This security was seen by the prophets as only to be found beyond the suffering and judgment of the Day of Yahweh. There would be a revival of the community, but only after the elect people had become scattered and dry bones (Ezekiel 37).

---

5. For a brief review of these ceremonies, see the writer in *The Old Testament against Its Environment*, Chap. II. Form criticism has led some scholars to the highly probable view that in early Israel, at least, the ceremony of covenant renewal was a yearly affair: see Gerhard von Rad, *Das formgeschichtliche Problem des Hexateuchs* (Giessen, 1938), and Martin Noth, *Überlieferungsgeschichte des Pentateuch* (Stuttgart, 1948), pp. 63f.

These three elements are together the core of Israelite faith and the unifying factor within it.[6] They have little abstract or propositional theology
within them. They are based on historical events and the inferences drawn
from them. They cannot be grasped by the abstract rubrics of dogmatic theology. And these very same elements are the centre and core of the faith of
the early church. For this reason the advent of Jesus Christ could not be understood solely or chiefly as the coming of a teacher of moral and spiritual
truths. His coming was a historical event which was the climax of God's working since the creation. All former history had its goal in him because God
had so directed it. All subsequent history will be directed by him because
God has exalted him as Lord. In so doing he will fulfill the promises [[57]] of
God in the government of Israel, assuming the royal office of David at the
right hand of God and providing the security which the sin of Israel made impossible of achievement. The election of Israel as the agent of God in universal redemption is reaffirmed in the New Israel (e.g., 1 Pet 2:9–10), the Body
of Christ, which is the partaker of the New Covenant of Christ's blood. In
Christ God has inaugurated the new age, foreseen of old; entrance into it is
by faith and by the sharing of Christ's cross, for in him our sins are forgiven
and our alienation from God done away. Thus God in Christ has completed
the history of Israel; he has reversed the work of Adam, fulfilled the promises
to Abraham, repeated the deliverance from bondage, not indeed from Pharaoh but from sin and Satan, and inaugurated the new age and the new covenant. To be sure, the world is unredeemed and the final consummation is yet
to appear. Yet Christ is the sign and seal of its coming. Hence he is the climactic event in a unique series of events, to be comprehended only by what
has happened before him, but at the same time the new event which marks a
fresh beginning in human history.

This, then, is the basic substance of Biblical theology. It is true that we
simply cannot communicate it without dealing with the *ideas* of which it is
composed. Yet to conceive of it primarily as a series of ideas which we must
arrange either systematically or according to their historical development is
to miss the point of it all. It is fundamentally an interpretation of history, a
confessional recital of historical events as the acts of God, events which lead
backward to the beginning of history and forward to its end. Inferences are
constantly made from the acts and are interpreted as integral parts of the acts
themselves which furnish the clue to understanding not only of contemporary happenings but of those which subsequently occurred. The being and attributes of God are nowhere systematically presented but are inferences from
events. Biblical man did not possess a philosophical notion of deity whence
he could argue in safety and 'objectivity' as to whether this or that was of
God. This ubiquitous modern habit of mind which reasons from axioms and
principles of universals to the concrete would have been considered as faithless rebellion against the Lord of history who used [[58]] history to reveal his

---

6. For the problem of the wisdom literature in this connection, particularly Job, Proverbs and Ecclesiastes, see the treatment in Chap. IV.

will and purpose. Hence the nearest approach to atheism which the Old Testament possesses is the fool who says in his heart there is no God (Ps 14:1; 53:1). Yet the Psalmist means by this, not a theoretical atheism, but rather the practical atheism of a sinner who calls God's works, not his being, into question.[7] Jeremiah clarifies the point when he speaks of people in his day who refuse to believe that the great events which then are happening are the work of God. They thus 'have denied Yahweh and said: "It is not he; neither shall evil come upon us; neither shall we see sword nor famine"' (5:12). To refuse to take history seriously as the revelation of the will, purpose and nature of God is the simplest escape from the Biblical God and one which leaves us with an idol of our own imagining.

Consequently, not even the nature of God can be portrayed abstractly. He can only be described *in relation to* the historical process, to his chosen agents and to his enemies. Biblical theology must begin, therefore, with the primary question as to why the Bible possesses the historical nature that it does. It thus must point in the first instance to this confessional recital of traditional and historical events, and proceed to the inferences which accompanied those events, became an integral part of them, and served as the guides to the comprehension of both past and future. Biblical theology, then, is primarily a confessional recital in which history is seen as a problem of faith, and faith a problem of history.[8]

---

7. Cf. Ludwig Köhler, *Theologie des Alten Testaments* (Zweite Auflage; Tübingen, 1947), p. 1.

8. An affirmation of Artur Weiser, *Glaube und Geschichte im Alten Testament*, p. 19, here used in a somewhat different context.

Revelation and Theology
[[from *Old Testament and Theology*]]

[[61]] Here all too briefly is the direction in which I have been moving.

By 1950 I had independently come to a position similar to that of von Rad with regard to revelation by event, the interrelation of word, event, and history (see section I of this chapter [[not reprinted here]]). In my monograph of lectures, *God Who Acts: Biblical Theology as Recital* (1952), I found von Rad's theological views, so far as they were then published, most stimulating and helpful. However, with the publication of von Rad's *Theology*, I discovered certain differences of viewpoint:

1. While I agree completely with the confessional center of revelation to Israel, it appears that von Rad, like Bultmann,[1] has carried the Lutheran separation of law and gospel back into his Old Testament scholarship so that Israel's recitals of the *magnalia Dei* are interpreted as having nothing to do originally with the Sinai covenant tradition. The welding of the two is a sec-

---

1. Cf. my analysis in "History and Reality . . . ," Chap. 10 in B. W. Anderson, ed., *The Old Testament and Christian Faith.*

ondary phenomenon, which marked the beginning of the law–gospel tension in the Bible. This viewpoint from a scholarly standpoint has been rendered highly unlikely by George E. Mendenhall's basic work, *Law and Covenant in Israel and the Ancient Near East* (1954–1955), and by the dissertation of one of von Rad's own students, Klaus Baltzer, [[62]] *Das Bundesformular* (1960),[2] the implications of which von Rad evidently cannot face. The pioneering work of Mendenhall and Baltzer means that the two forms, *magnalia Dei* and Sinai covenant tradition, are inseparable and that the covenant is the setting for the recitation of the acts.

2. This means that Eichrodt is right in insisting that Israel's testimonies find their setting and particularity only in the framework of the Sinai covenant. Von Rad's existentialist interpretation of Israel's theology has no *Sitz im Leben* apart from a people dominated by the conception of a world empire whose Suzerain has created a people, Israel, whose identity is one of vassalage by treaty in the cosmic empire. Hence Old Testament theology without a sense of this cosmic structure, which informs Israel's every testimony, is simply impossible.[3]

3. What, then, is theology? I must side with Eichrodt that it is impossible to separate testimonies to God's saving activity, reactualized in succeeding periods, from conceptual and structural elements provided by the Sinai covenant tradition. On the other hand, Eichrodt is much too wedded to older terms like "system," "systematic," which are unnecessary. "Coherence" and *sui generis* seem to me more appropriate.

In other words, theology is the effort of a man to explicate his own or someone else's tradition meaningfully in his conceptual world, so that he can understand it. To restrict theology to the proclamation of Israel's or the Christian's kerygma is too confining. What is kerygma without exposition and application? What is [[63]] the proclamation of the Word apart from the structure of "the people of God" whom it has created and whom it recreates?

2. Mendenhall's work originally appeared as Vol. XVII.2 and 3 (May and Sept., 1954) of *The Biblical Archaeologist*, and reprinted as a monograph in 1955 from the same plates. . . . The Baltzer volume was published by Neukirchener Verlag in Neukirchen-Vluyn, Germany.

3. For a proper discussion of the political form of the Bible, which so many today want to "demythologize," see, e.g., Paul Lehmann, *Ethics in a Christian Context* (New York: Harper & Row, 1963), Chap. III, entitled "What God Is Doing in the World."

Synopsis of Wright's *God Who Acts* (1952)

Synopsis of Wright's *Old Testament and Theology* (1969)

G. Ernest Wright on God the Warrior

Excerpted with permission from G. Ernest Wright, *The Old Testament and Theology* (New York: Harper & Row, 1969), pp. 121–26, 129–31, 145–50.

[[121]] A most pervasive Biblical motif is the interpretation of conflict in history as owing to the sin of man, against which the cosmic government and its Suzerain take vigorous action. Since so much of history is concerned with warfare, it therefore must be expected that one major activity of the Suzerain will be the direction of war for both redemptive and judgmental ends. That is, a major function of the Suzerain will be understood to be his work as Warrior.

Yet in our time no attribute of the Biblical God is more consciously and almost universally rejected than this one. The reason is that theologically we are unable to keep up with our emotional attitudes toward war. The latter are so shocked by the savage horror of war that it is most difficult to see any positive good in this type of conflict. As the weapons of war become more efficiently destructive, the harm caused is surely greater than the good brought by success. As a result, the Bible on this subject is simply dismissed, or at best treated in the most simplistic and superficial manner. Jesus and the New Testament portray love and the God of love, while the God of the Old Testament, especially the God of Joshua, is another deity altogether, or at least a lower, more primitive understanding of deity.

Such an attitude is more a derivative from idealism than it is from a faith that struggles with history, with the way men actually act in time and space, and seeks there the evidence of Providence. Idealism predetermines its conception of The Good, and thus ends with a "philosophy" unable to deal with human life as it is actually lived.[1] Hence, the sermons and contemporary prayers in the typical [[122]] synagogue or church have generally dealt with the inner resources of faith, though the recent civil rights and poverty problems are now receiving attention, primarily because the safety of law and order is threatened. One can see the truth in the statement attributed to Harry Golden to the effect that in his town he as a Jew can go to church for six months without hearing anything to offend him.

It is the intent of this chapter to suggest that if the conception of the Divine Warrior cannot be used theologically, then the central core of the Biblical understanding of reality is dissolved with drastic consequences for any theology which would maintain a connection with what most distinguishes and characterizes the Bible in the world of religious literature.

We begin by recalling a simple and obvious fact about the Book of Joshua. It cannot be considered to contain a "primitive" theology of God and war which later books replace with a God of love. The book in its completed

1. See Chap. 1, and esp. the quotations from Kierkegaard and William James about the classical philosophers being unable to live in the marble palaces which they had created.

form is an indispensable and climactic part of Israel's epic of her formation as a nation by the great providential acts of God in western Asia during the second millennium B.C. Formally, it stands at the beginning of the Deuteronomistic history of the ways of God with Israel in the Promised Land (Deuteronomy–2 Kings). It is a creation of the Deuteronomic historian from old sources, perhaps during the reign of Josiah at the end of the seventh century B.C., or else after the fall of Jerusalem, *ca.* 550 B.C.[2] Theologically, [[123]] it furnishes traditional details about how the initial wars of conquest were won by Joshua. Israel was victorious, not because they were marvelous fighters under a brilliant general, but because God went before Israel, threw fear into the hearts of the opposition, and wrought the victory for his own purposes.

In Israel's confessions of faith and praise to God for his marvelous works, the Conquest is closely associated with the Exodus. The slaves who were freed from Egyptian bondage are given a land. The outcasts, the powerless, the slaves of the greatest world power of the day, are now a nation with "a land of milk and honey" as a gift of God (Deut 26:9). It is the Promised Land, promised by God to Abraham, Isaac, and Jacob (Gen 12:7; Deut 6:23). The victories in the Conquest were "not by your sword or by your bow. I gave you a land on which you had not labored" (Josh 24:12–13).

Biblical references to the conquest generally omit all mention of specific battles and human activity. It is God's deed; he is the sole actor; there are no human heroes.[3] A few citations will suffice:

The prophet Amos, speaking for God, exclaimed:

It was I who destroyed the Amorite before them
    Whose height was like the height of cedars
    and whose strength was that of oaks.
I destroyed his fruit above
    and his roots below. (2:9)

[[124]] An early psalm has the following reference to God's work as Warrior:

He led them in safety and they were not terrified;
    their enemies, the sea covered over!

2. Most scholars have concluded that the history was completed at the end of the seventh century and that 2 Kings 24–25 are a subsequent addition to bring the story up to date *ca.* 550 B.C. A decision between the two views is difficult. Granted that nearly all the material used is preexilic, the period when the chief historian drew it together depends so much on one's understanding of the theological purpose of the historian.

3. In spite of the number of Biblical theologies which have been written, the task of preparing such a work, in the view of this writer, is very difficult because the basic research work has either not been done or must be redone because of the advance in research. A definitive study of the theology of the conquest theme in Biblical literature is an example; it simply has not been made—or at least not published. It is interesting that whereas Sihon and Og whom Moses conquered in Transjordan are occasionally mentioned (a tradition surviving from the liturgy of celebration once used at Gilgal?), no specifics are ever given in prophecy or psalms of battles west of the Jordan, except on a very rare occasion, Jericho. All activity is Yahweh's.

He brought them into his holy boundary,
this mountain which his right hand had acquired.[4]
He expelled nations before them;
he assigned them a measured allotment.[5]
he made the tribes of Israel to dwell[6] in their tents.
(78:53–55)

Another psalm refers to the Conquest as God's planting of a vine:

A vine out of Egypt you removed;
You expelled nations and planted it.
You cleared [the ground] for it;
its root took root;
it filled the land. . . .
Its shade covered the hills,
its branches mighty cedars.
It sent its branches to the Sea [the Mediterranean],
to the River [the Euphrates] its shoots.
(80:8–11 [Heb. 9–12])

Nowhere in the Bible is this interpretation of the Conquest challenged or corrected. Paul is cited as using the old confession in his preaching:

Men of Israel and you who reverence God, listen: The God of this people Israel chose our Fathers and made the people great in the sojourn in the land of Egypt, and with uplifted arm [great strength] he led them out of it. . . . And having [[125]] destroyed seven nations in the land of Canaan, he gave them their land as an inheritance. . . .[7] (Acts 13:16–19)

Stephen in his defense carefully and in detail reviews the same epic story, doing so, however, from the standpoint of Israel's faithless response to God's beneficence.[8] Speaking of the tabernacle in the wilderness, he is recorded as saying: "This our fathers in turn brought in with Joshua [at the time of] the dispossession of the nations whom God thrust out before the presence of our fathers" (Acts 7:45).

More generalized and oblique but nevertheless referring to the interpretation of the Exodus-Conquest events as God's mercy and salvation is such a passage as the following:

4. Or "this mountain which his power had created."

5. This colon is not clear. It could mean that he gave Israel property which had been measured out by lot for the tribes, or that he had destroyed the nations by means of a determined penalty. It can thus be interpreted as going either with the colon before it or the one after it. ("Colon" here is a technical term for one part of a Hebrew poetic line.)

6. Literally, "to tent."

7. Or "he allotted their land" (i.e., separated their land to their tribes by casting lots).

8. That is, the confessional history was recited in two ways: one to glorify God for his mighty acts (cf. Psalm 105) and the other to confess Israel's faithless response to God at each juncture (cf. Psalm 106, and Wright, "The Lawsuit of God . . . ," *Israel's Prophetic Heritage* [ed. by Anderson and Harrelson], pp. 26–67). Stephen's defense is a particularly vigorous recital in the second vein. Both are woven together, of course, in the epic.

Indeed you are an elect race, a royal priesthood, a holy nation, God's own possession,[9] in order that you may proclaim the wondrous deeds of him who called you out of darkness into his marvelous light, [you who] once were no people but now are God's people, [you who] had not received mercy but now have received mercy. (1 Pet 2:9–10)

In other words, the Conquest as God's gracious gift to those who had been outcast—this is the unanimous account of Biblical authors. In only one place is there a more rationalizing and broad perspective presented from the standpoint of the whole divine purpose in the world. That is Deut 9:4–7:

Do not say in your heart when the Lord your God drives them [the nations] out before you: "Because of my righteousness the Lord has brought me in to possess this land." It is because [[126]] of the evil of these nations that the Lord is dispossessing them before you. Not because of your righteousness nor because of the uprightness of your heart are you entering to possess their land. Instead it is because of the evil of these nations that the Lord your God is dispossessing them before you, and [also] to the end that he confirm the thing which the Lord swore to your fathers, to Abraham, to Isaac and to Jacob. And you [must] acknowledge that the Lord your God is not giving you this good land to possess because of your righteousness. Indeed, you are a stiff-necked people. Remember and do not forget how you provoked the Lord your God in the wilderness. From the day when you came out of the land of Egypt until your coming into this place you have been rebellious against the Lord.

Israel thus is an agent in God's overall purposes as the Suzerain of history. And if one is an agent in conflict, that does not necessarily involve a moral superiority. Indeed, in Israel's conquest it definitely does not involve any connotation of a superior goodness. The evidence is quite to the contrary. Yet as a result of corruption the divine government has decreed the end of Canaanite civilization.[10] At the same time, a new and redemptive purpose for mankind is expressed in the promises to the Fathers (that is, in the Abrahamic covenant; cf. Gen 12:1–3; 15:12–21; 17:1–8).

In any case, the events in Joshua cannot be attributed to primitivism in Biblical theology. The Bible's most advanced interpretations in later ages saw there nothing but a most dramatic illustration of the power, grace, and justice of God.

. . . .

9. Literally, "a people for his possession"—clearly an attempt to translate into Greek the special word *səgullāh* in Exod 19:5.

10. There is indeed evidence of the decline of Canaanite civilization during the thirteenth century B.C. On the other hand, the Israelite conquest in the thirteenth century and the Aramean and Philistine conquests of the twelfth century confined most remaining Canaanites to the coastal regions of Lebanon where in due course the remarkable Phoenician trading empire was developed.

[[129]] There is only one theological context in which the institution of holy war in early Israel can be dealt with meaningfully. Certain components are as follows:

1. Ultimate power or "the field of power" is actively experienced in history in both positive—i.e., creative and redemptive—and negative—i.e., destructive and judgmental—ways. Yet in the long run I put my faith in the creative and redemptive as the context of the whole, because of the manner in which I feel I must interpret the structure of existence.

2. The use of the Divine Monarch theme involves also that of the Divine Warrior because the Monarch's chief concern is universal order. We cannot assume, therefore, that blood and God are [[130]] contradictory terms, so that where the one is, the other simply cannot be.

3. Our human world stands in defiance of its pretensions. It is in dreadful disorder, a faithful copy of all the Apostle Paul says in Romans 1 that it becomes when men worship the creature rather than the Creator. All war is fought by sinners who are employing evil structures of power to their own ends.

4. God works in this world as it is by mediate means. He has his men, whether they know it or not, who serve as his agents, doing what is appropriate for the immediate issue. Our problem is to know and do what we are called to do. But by failure of mind and will, we seldom get our duty straight or do what we know we should.

5. From this standpoint, Israel's holy war—something that looks to us today as a kind of fanaticism—can be conceived as an agency which God made use of at one time for his own purposes and without in any way sanctifying the participants. Similarly, the world powers of Assyria and Babylon were subsequently used to destroy Israel and Judah—and for just cause, so the literature maintains. Yet each moment is unique. A past pattern of response by an agent can be used as a guide only with great caution in the present. Israel's wars of conquest become no mandate for wars by God's people today.

6. God the Warrior is the theme that furnishes hope in time. What is, cannot be sanctified for the future because a vast tension exists between the will of the Suzerain and that of his vassals. Our world is under judgment. Wars and rumors of wars are a Biblical reality, a present reality, and we see no immediate surcease of them in the future. Yet the strong, active power given language in the Warrior-Lord means that there is a force in the universe set against the forces of evil and perversity. Life, then, is a battleground, but the Divine Warrior will not be defeated.

Now if one thinks this type of language is too strong, let him only remember that God the Warrior is simply the reverse side of God the Lover or God the Redeemer. The seeking love of God is only one side of the Suzerain's activity, because, to change the figure, [[131]] divine love is a two-edged sword. It is power in action in a sinful world, and redemption is disturbing, painful, resisted.

. . . .

[[145]] The purpose of this sampling of Biblical material is not to make a bibliolatrous point. That is, just because these things are Biblical, one should not automatically assume they must be central to our own theology. Indeed, with regard to the themes surveyed in this and in the preceding two chapters it would be simple to suggest that we forget that they exist. Yet when one reviews the attempts at theology in recent years which proceed on this very suggestion, I for one find much that is not satisfying. The conscious rejection of political language as appropriate to an interpretation of my existence leaves me without a firm anchor to what appears to be my central problem as a human being. That is, how I can see my life as possessing freedom for positive ends that encompass more than myself? Since as a social and historical being I was not a person as a fetus in the womb, but only became a person in interaction within my environment of other people and institutions within a context of relatedness to fellow men with our vocational choices, and within a social organism which has its history and traditions, what is the "ground" of my life? To disregard the political is to disregard this central and social aspect of myself as a self-in-relation. To reduce the language patterns to the family and love with the family, to say that my only need is to be "brother" to my neighbor, is simply to neglect the larger contexts of my relatedness, of institutions, of other people and nations whom I do not know. Does "love" here become a passion for justice[11] which soon goes far beyond what any model drawn from the family can provide?

Shall I disregard the real structure and history of the self and assume with current existentialisms that my only duty is to myself, to courage, and to "authentic" existence, whatever I may decide that to be? But self-preoccupation is the first and basic disease of the neurotic. It is only as I give my loyalty to concerns larger than [[146]] myself that I can find freedom from the tyranny of self-preoccupation.[12]

Perhaps we should say that the first and most important thing to admit about ourselves is that we are simply an integral part of nature and of nature's process. If so, then perhaps ancient polytheism has its point and the process and power of life in all its forms should provide the chief categories for self-understanding. There is great merit in some sort of process philosophy as a background for current theology. Yet the difficulty always encoun-

---

11. See Reinhold Niebuhr, *Nature and Destiny of Man*, Vol. II (New York: Charles Scribner's Sons, 1943), pp. 244ff.

12. See the final section of Chap. I for additional discussion, esp. for the query as to whether the popular form of existentialism being used currently in theology is not just as artificial a construction, as an attempt to describe my existence, as any of the past systems, Hegelianism, e.g., that it supersedes. The attempts of several modern "sons" of Bultmann to suggest that if existential categories are drawn from "the later Heidegger," the problems of the school with regard to history would be removed, have been wordy but not very impressive: see, e.g., James M. Robinson and John B. Cobb, eds., *The Later Heidegger and Theology* (*New Frontiers in Theology*, Vol. I; New York: Harper & Row, 1963); and the critique of Hans Jonas, "Tenth Essay. Heidegger and Theology," *The Phenomenon of Life* (New York: Harper & Row, 1966), pp. 235–61.

tered is that set forth as basic presupposition by Reinhold Niebuhr in the first chapter of his *Nature and Destiny of Man*. The first thing to be said about man is that he is a child of nature. Yet one cannot stop there without making the equally important observation that man is a child of God. By the latter one refers first of all to man's power of self-transcendence and to all that distinguishes him in and from nature. Man is the creator of cultural tradition. As phenomenon he creates and lives in a present which contains its past, but he also transcends the present by foresight, planning, even controlling to some degree his own evolution. That is, historical man is equally significant with natural man, and both aspects of our being must provide the terms of basic reference. Nature's process is insufficient to expound human life and history.

Perhaps the easiest course to follow is the popular one today among Christians. That is simply to drop all talk of God and live as a Christian humanist, Christ forming a model of what the good for us can be. Yet here again the structures of historical existence are so complex that the very simple, idealized model thus created from the life of Jesus, one abstracted almost completely from its own environment, furnishes a very limited and limiting context in which I must attempt to face the human struggle with and for civilization.

[[147]] It will be suggested in the next chapter that human beings live with their fellows in a cultural environment in which communication is by a language that has a variety of symbolic expressions to convey meaning. The images or symbols are abstractions of experienced realities by which and within which thinking and action take place. To demythologize is to destroy an organism of meaning because it generally turns out to be de-symbolization instead of resymbolization. Without the latter, no thought or action is really possible. And one thing seems certain about my existence: I cannot express a sufficiently comprehensive or coherent set of meanings and values for myself, my fellow men, or my world without the use of social and political language models. Such language is simply basic to my life as a fellow man and as a member of a social organization, which includes but is ultimately much larger and more complex than the family alone or nature alone can possible provide.

Summary

The heuristic value of the Bible's version of the cosmic government has been suggested in this and in the preceding chapters. The particular conception and language pertaining to it are by no means simple, and they are so frequently misunderstood and misrepresented simplistically. However, they successfully hold together the relativity of so much of our human activities and valuations. At the same time they present a structural model which preserves the positive importance of values themselves and their relation to what can be conceived as stable and permanent in the cosmos. In this context all human activity exists in tension with ultimate goals, and thus [[148]] forbids all claims of absolution for our earthly existence. It sets forth a very realistic picture of the world and its history, holding the positive and the negative together in tension but setting forth grace, love, and justice—positive goals—as the primary context of all action. It presents a much more "secular" and realistic Christ than the simplistic improvisations to which we are prone.

One thing clear, however, is that one cannot adopt the cosmic government model for self-understanding and for communication without a creative attempt to deal with the fundamental and necessary engagement of all life in conflict for continuous adaptation to a changing environment. This conflict too often spills over into overt and often evil uses of force because of our sin and finitude. Hence, if God is Lord, he must also be Warrior. Unless he is, there is no ground for hope, for there is knowledge that human evil is not the last word, that the cards are stacked in behalf of the Kingdom of God, rather than the Kingdom of Satan.

In conclusion, I would like to summarize a conversation with a theologian about the substance of this chapter. This man is one to whom I have looked for guidance as a theological mentor since our thinking runs in parallel paths on most issues. Let me refer to him as "Mr. X." He was reared within a community of one of the historical "peace churches," a relationship which he still retains. I, on the other hand, was reared in a Presbyterian environment which has generally been more a part of the establishment in this country than its critic. Consequently, my basic question about the use of force immediately concerns its proper use, the restraints that must be employed, and some kind of casuistic analysis as to the relative weight of the positive and negative goals of the use of force in a given situation. Mr. X will indulge in much of the same kinds of consideration but in a context in which nonviolence is accepted as an absolute guide to action in conflict situations.

He also agrees with my basic thesis that God the Suzerain of cosmic government is the primary area in which the unifying threads are to be discovered in the vast variety of literature in both Testaments. He agrees that early Israel's institution of holy war was an agency which the Suzerain could be said to have used as a device for implanting Israel in Palestine, without conferring moral [[149]] value on the agent or the institution. He agrees that God as King, Judge, Warrior, Father, and Shepherd is accorded these roles, not as contradictory expressions, but as deriving from royal language which thus expresses the various activities of the Divine Monarch. He also agrees that the common attitude about that Monarch, as given expression in the quotation from Whitehead in Chapter 2, is a misunderstanding and inadequate presentation of what the Bible means.

Yet when we come to the New Testament, Mr. X says that Christ is the supreme and final revelation of the will of God for Christians. This means that nonviolence and love are always the ethical imperatives, and in situations of conflict they must always be employed in every situation. The reason we must retain the image of God the Lord and Suzerain is that only the ruling power of God actively at work in history can assure the ultimate success of the nonviolent imperative.

Yet since conflict itself must be viewed as both opportunity for change, growth, and broadening, on the one hand, and judgment for failure, on the other, why is it not true that the response of "love" is also two-edged? Love in situations of conflict obviously does not involve surrendering individual integrity, while concern for the needy and for justice to the oppressed may involve the active use of power in ways that cannot be described in every instance as nonviolent. Can it not be said that when the absolutes of the Kingdom-ethic are translated into absolutes for the present age, trouble always ensues? In the life we lead we are always involved in mental casuistry because two or more absolutes are in conflict in so many situations we have to face. Nonviolence can always be defended in a given instance as the best means to obtain a necessary and quite specific objective. Yet to absolutize it as the only form of action love can take in conflict would from my perspective and tradition be far too limiting for the flexibilities needed to reach necessary goals when we are faced with the principalities and powers of darkness.[13] In any event, such a position enables me to see far more [[150]] symbolic value in the New Testament's apocalyptic material than Mr. X has been able to appropriate. For him God the Warrior was necessary and proper in its time and setting, but it no longer can have positive use as an appropriate symbol in Christian ethics.

13. Needless to say, I am stating this in the most general of terms, and, if this means a position in general support of a given war, it would not lead me to a self-righteous support of a given "just war" theory as background for that war. Since all wars exemplify human evil in its most virulent expression, one can only set up guidelines as limits of coercive action, such as the Geneva conventions, etc.

GERHARD VON RAD

b. 1901   d. 1971

Eighth-Century Prophecy

Like Walther Eichrodt a decade before him, Gerhard von Rad came under the influence of Otto Procksch at Erlangen. Perhaps more significant was Albrecht Alt, his mentor at the University of Leipzig, where von Rad was first a professor of Old Testament. He later served in the universities of Jena, Göttingen, and then Heidelberg. Through Procksch, von Rad was related to the salvation-historical tradition of von Hofmann. From Alt, von Rad acquired the critical sensibilities of a historian. He combined these in his approach to Old Testament theology.

Selected Writings by von Rad

1957   *Theologie des Alten Testaments.* Volume 1: *Die Theologie der geschichtlichen Überlieferungen Israels.* Munich: Kaiser.

1960   *Theologie des Alten Testaments.* Volume 2: *Die Theologie der prophetischen Überlieferungen Israels.* Munich: Kaiser.

1962a *Old Testament Theology.* Volume 1: *The Theology of Israel's Historical Traditions.* Translated by David M. G. Stalker. New York: Harper & Row / Edinburgh: Oliver & Boyd. [Reprinted in 2001 with an introduction by Walter Brueggemann]

1962b *Theologie des Alten Testaments.* Volume 1: *Die Theologie der geschichtlichen Überlieferungen Israels.* 4th edition. Munich: Chr. Kaiser.

1965a *Old Testament Theology.* Volume 2: *The Theology of Israel's Prophetic Traditions.* Translated by David M. G. Stalker. New York: Harper & Row / Edinburgh: Oliver & Boyd.

1965b *Theologie des Alten Testaments.* Volume 2. *Die Theologie der prophetischen Überlieferungen Israels.* 4th edition. Munich: Chr. Kaiser.

1966   *The Problem of the Hexateuch and Other Essays.* Translated by E. W. T. Dickens. Edinburgh: Oliver & Boyd.

1972   *Wisdom in Israel.* London: SCM / Nashville: Abingdon.

Writings about von Rad

Crenshaw, James L.
1978   *Gerhard von Rad*. Makers of the Modern Theological Mind. Waco, Tex: Word.

Davies, G. Henton
1970   Gerhard von Rad: *Old Testament Theology*. Pp. 63–89 in *Contemporary Old Testament Theologians*. Edited by Robert B. Laurin. Valley Forge, Pennsylvania: Judson.
1989   Smend, Rudolf. Gerhard von Rad. Pp. 226–54 in *Deutsche Alttestamentler in Drei Jahrhunderten*. Göttingen: Vandenhoeck & Ruprecht.

Wolff, Hans W. (editor)
1971   *Probleme biblischer Theologie: Gerhard von Rad zum 70. Geburtstag*. Munich: Chr. Kaiser.

Gerhard von Rad's
Approach to Old Testament Theology

Excerpted with permission from Gerhard von Rad, *Old Testament Theology* (New York: Harper & Row, 1962), vol. 1: 105–12, 121–28.

Methodological Presuppositions

The Subject-Matter of a Theology of the Old Testament

[[105]] This belief in Jahweh, whose vitality we have described in brief outline, had very many ways of speaking about him. It never ceased speaking of his relationship to Israel, to the world, and to the nations, sometimes through the impersonal media of the great institutions (cult, law, court, etc.), sometimes however through the mouths of priests, prophets, kings, writers of narratives, historians, wise men, and Temple singers. Now, from this extremely abundant witness to Jahweh it would be perfectly possible, as has already been said, to draw a tolerably complete and, as far as comparative religion goes, a tolerably objective picture of the religion of the people of Israel, that is, of the special features in her conception of God, of the way in which Israel thought of God's relationship to the world, to the other nations and, not least, to herself; of the distinctiveness of what she said about sin and had to say about atonement and the salvation which comes from God. This has often been attempted, and needs no doubt to be attempted repeatedly. While Christian theologians may have played a decisive role in fostering this enterprise, the task in itself, however, falls within the province of the general study of religion; and it is therefore fitting that in recent times Orientalists, sociologists, ethnologists, ethnopsychologists, investigators of mythology, and others too have to a considerable extent co-operated in its accomplishment. The theological task proper to the Old Testament is not simply identical with this general religious one, and it is also much more restricted. The subject-matter which concerns the theologian is, of course, not the spiritual and religious world of Israel and the conditions of her soul in general, nor is it her world of faith, all of which can only be reconstructed by means of conclusions drawn from the documents: instead, it is simply Israel's own explicit assertions about Jahweh. The theologian must above all deal directly with the evidence, that is, with what Israel herself testified concerning Jahweh, and there is no doubt that in many cases he must go back to school again and learn to interrogate each [[106]] document, much more closely than has been done hitherto, as to its specific kerygmatic intention.[1] The tremendous dif-

---

1. It would be well to scrutinise from this point of view the chapter-headings in our translations or interpretations of the Bible, which often completely miss the intention that the specific narrators had in mind.

ferences evinced in the specific literary units will be dealt with later on in this volume. None the less we must anticipate, and mention briefly, what unites them all. They are far from comprehending equally all the wide range of statements about God, man, and the world which are conceivable and possible in the religious sphere. In this respect the theological radius of what Israel said about God is conspicuously restricted compared with the theologies of other nations—instead, the Old Testament writings confine themselves to representing Jahweh's relationship to Israel and the world in one aspect only, namely as a continuing divine activity in history. This implies that in principle Israel's faith is grounded in a theology of history. It regards itself as based upon historical acts, and as shaped and re-shaped by factors in which it saw the hand of Jahweh at work. The oracles of the prophets also speak of events, though there is the definite difference, than in general they stand in point of time not after, but prior to, the events to which they bear witness. Even where this reference to divine facts in history is not immediately apparent, as for example in some of the Psalms, it is, however, present by implication: and where it is actually absent, as for example in the Book of Job and Ecclesiastes, this very lack is closely connected with the grave affliction which is the theme of both these works.

Both at this point and in the sequel, we are of course thinking, when we speak of divine acts in history, of those which the faith of Israel regarded as such—that is, the call of the forefathers, the deliverance from Egypt, the bestowal of the land of Canaan, etc.—and not of the results of modern critical historical scholarship, to which Israel's faith was unrelated. This raises a difficult historical problem. In the last 150 years critical historical scholarship has constructed an impressively complete picture of the history of the people of Israel. As this process took shape, the old picture of Israel's history which the Church had derived and accepted from the Old Testament was bit by bit destroyed. Upon this process there is no going back, nor has it yet indeed come to an end. Critical historical scholarship regards it as impossible that the whole of Israel was present at Sinai, or that Israel crossed the Red Sea and achieved the Conquest *en bloc*—it holds the picture of Moses and his [[107]] leadership drawn in the traditions of the Book of Exodus to be as unhistorical as the function which the Deuteronomistic book of Judges ascribes to the "judges." On the other hand, it is just the most recent research into the Hexateuch that has proceeded to deal with the extremely complicated origin of the Old Testament's picture of Jahweh's saving history with Israel. Scholars are even beginning to allow a scientific standing of its own to the picture of her history which Israel herself drew, and to take it as something existing *per se* which, in the way it has been sketched, has to be taken into account as a central subject in our theological evaluation. Research into the Hexateuch has established that this picture is based upon a few very old *motifs* around which subsequently have clustered in organic growth the immense number of freely circulating separate traditions.[2] The basic *motifs* were already pronouncedly

2. M. Noth, *Pentateuch*.

confessional in character, and so were the separate traditions, in part very old, which made the canvas so very large. Thus the Hexateuch shows us a picture of the saving history that is drawn up by faith, and is accordingly confessional in character. The same holds true for the Deuteronomistic history's picture of the later history of Israel down to the exile. These two pictures of Israel's history lie before us—that of modern critical scholarship and that which the faith of Israel constructed—and for the present, we must reconcile ourselves to both of them. It would be stupid to dispute the right of the one or the other to exist. It would be superfluous to emphasise that each is the product of very different intellectual activities. The one is rational and "objective"; that is, with the aid of historical method and presupposing the similarity of all historical occurrence, it constructs a critical picture of the history as it really was in Israel.[3] It is clear that in the process this picture could not be restricted to a critical analysis of the external historical events: it was bound to proceed to a critical investigation of the picture of Israel's spiritual world, her religion, as well.

The other activity is confessional and personally involved in the events to the point of fervour. Did Israel ever speak of her history [[108]] other than with the emotion of glorification or regret? Historical investigation searches for a critically assured minimum—the kerygmatic picture tends towards a theological maximum.[4] The fact that these two views of Israel's history are so divergent is one of the most serious burdens imposed today upon Biblical scholarship. No doubt historical investigation has a great deal that is true to say about the growth of this picture of the history which the faith of Israel painted: but the phenomenon of the faith itself, which speaks now of salvation, now of judgment, is beyond its power to explain.

It would not do, however, simply to explain the one picture as historical and the other as unhistorical. The kerygmatic picture too (and this even at the points where it diverges so widely from our historical picture) is founded in the actual history and has not been invented. The means by which this historical experience is made relevant for the time, the way in which it is mirrored forth in a variety of pictures, and in sagas in type form, are those adapted to the possibilities of expression of an ancient people. But it would be a very hasty conclusion if critical historical scholarship were minded to be itself taken as the only way into the history of Israel, and if it denied to what Israel reports in, say, her sagas a foundation in the "real" history. In some respects, this foundation is an even deeper one. Only, in these traditional materials the historic and factual can no longer be detached from the spiritualising interpretation which pervades them all.

3. "The historical method, once it is applied to biblical science . . . is a leaven which transforms everything and finally explodes the whole form of theological methods." "The means by which criticism is at all possible is the application of analogy. . . . But the omnicompetence of analogy implies that all historical events are identical in principle." E. Tröltsch, *Über historische und dogmatische Methode*, Tübingen 1889 (*Gesammelte Schriften*, vol. II, pp. 729ff.) .

4. N. A. Dahl, *Der historische Jesus als geschichtswissenschaftliches und theologisches Problem, Kerygma and Dogma*, Göttingen 1955, p. 119.

We are not here concerned with the philosophical presuppositions of objective, rational, and critical scholarship, or the methods with which it works. On the other hand, the particular way in which Israel's faith presented history is still far from being adequately elucidated. Admittedly, we are acquainted with the various basic historical and theological ideas of the Jahwist, or of the Deuteronomist's history, or the Chronicler's. But we are much less clear about the mode of presentation of the smaller narrative units, although it is in fact the mass of these which now gives characteristic stamp to those great compilations. The way in which faith perceives things has its own peculiarities, and it is perhaps therefore possible to point to some constantly recurring features, certain "patterns," which are characteristic of a confessional presentation, particularly of early historical experiences. In this connexion a very common datum would have to [[109]] be taken into consideration by the theologian as well as by others—the fact that a great part of even the historical traditions of Israel has to be regarded as poetry, that is, as the product of explicit artistic intentions. But poetry—especially with peoples of antiquity—is much more than an aesthetic pastime: rather is there in it a penetrating desire for knowledge directed towards the data presented by the historical and natural environment.[5] Historical poetry was the form in which Israel, like other peoples, made sure of historical facts, that is, of their location and their significance. In those times poetry was, as a rule, the one possible form for expressing special basic insights. It was not just there along with prose as something one might elect to use—a more elevated form of discourse as it were then—but poetry alone enabled a people to express experiences met with in the course of their history in such a way as to make the past become absolutely present. In the case of legend, we now know that we must reckon with this coefficient of interpretation. But in thinking of the literary stories, which extend from the Hexateuch to 2 Kings, and which we must also regard to begin with as poetry, we have to learn to grasp this coefficient more clearly in its special features in any given story.[6] As far as I can see, Israel only finally went over to the prosaic and scientific presentation of her history with the Deuteronomistic history. Thus, right down to the sixth century, she was unable to dispense with poetry in drafting history, for the Succession Document or the history of Jehu's revolution are poetic presentations, and are indeed the acme of poetic perfection. No wonder that in Israel, and in her alone, these historical narratives could develop so profusely and in such perfection—the faith needed them. On the other hand, there is no mistaking that the effort to interpret historical events in this poetic-theological guise imposes a limit upon the possibilities of our understanding such narratives. The understanding of lists and annals is independent of the presuppositions of faith. But these poetic stories appeal for assent; they address those who are

---

5. The idea of poetry as an "organ for the understanding of life" goes back to Dilthey. Cf. P. Böckmann, *Formgeschichte der deutschen Dichtung*, Hamburg 1949, pp. 17ff.

6. A few more specific references are to be found in G. von Rad, *Der Heilige Krieg im alten Israel*, pp. 43ff.

prepared to ask questions and receive answers along like lines, that is, those who credit Jahweh with great acts in history.

If some stories, chiefly older ones bordering upon legend, represent [[110]] events which happened to a group as connected with an individual, this is doubtless mainly a poetic proceeding. They are removed from the realm of political history and projected into the wholly personal world of an individual. This usage which personalises and at the same time symbolises can be plainly seen in the stories about Ham and Canaan (Gen 9:25), and in those about Ishmael or Judah (Gen 16:12, 38:1). But exegesis probably must take still greater account of it in the patriarchal stories dealing with Abraham and Jacob. To symbolise things in a single person in this way is in itself not at all peculiar to Israel. But since it also crops up in stories which are markedly minted by faith, we must make ourselves familiar with it. In every case, through this transference into a personal picture these stories have been given an enormous degree of intensity, for events or experiences of very different times have been pulled together as a single episode in an individual's life. Thus, for our historical and critical understanding, stories such as these have from the very start only an indirect relationship with historical reality, while their relation to what was believed by Israel is much more direct. We have further to consider that in their presentation of religious material the peoples of antiquity were not aware of the law of historical exclusiveness, according to which a certain event or a certain experience can be attached only to a single definite point in history. In particular, events bearing a saving character retained for all posterity, and in that posterity's eyes, a contemporaneousness which it is hard for us to appreciate.[7] The upshot is that, in what they present, the later story-tellers blatantly make capital of experiences which, although they are invariably brought in on the basis of the ancient event in question, still reach forward into the story-teller's own day. It is only from this standpoint that the story of Jacob's struggle (Gen 32:22f.), or the story of Balaam (Numbers 22–24), or the thrice-repeated story of the endangering of the ancestress of the race (Gen 12:10ff., 20:1ff., 26:5ff.) can be interpreted as they should. What is historical here? Certainly some definite but very elusive particular event which stands at the primal obscure origin of the tradition in question—but what is also historical is the [[111]] experience that Jahweh turns the enemy's curse into blessing, and that he safeguards the promise in spite of all failure on the part of its recipient, etc. Israel did not dream up this confidence, but came to it on the basis of rich and wide experience, of her history in fact; and, symbolising it in a person, she illustrated it in a story. This of course occasions another and rather severe clash with our critical way of thinking about history. Did the historical Balaam actually curse, or did his mouth really utter blessings? We may assume that it was only

---

7. L. Köhler, *Hebrew Man*, trans. P. R. Ackroyd, London 1956, p. 39. This cannot of course be taken as meaning that "the conception of history itself hardly plays any noticeable part" for Israel. These words are incomprehensible in face of the fact that Israel's faith gave itself sanction in a series of ever vaster theological sketches of her history.

in the story that which was given to Israel's faith became presented as a visible miracle. This process of glorification is quite clear in many of the stories about the Conquest—the events are depicted with a splendour and a strong element of the miraculous which are impossible to square with older strands in the report.[8] The later story-tellers are so zealous for Jahweh and his saving work that they overstep the limits of exact historiography and depict the event in a magnificence far transcending what it was in reality.[9] These are texts which contain an implicit eschatological element, since they anticipate a *Gloria* of God's saving action not yet granted to men.

In the Old Testament it is thus this world made up of testimonies that is above all the subject of a theology of the Old Testament. The subject cannot be a systematically ordered "world of the faith" of Israel or of the really overwhelming vitality and creative productivity of Jahwism, for the world of faith is not the subject of these testimonies which Israel raised to Jahweh's action in history. Never, in these testimonies about history, did Israel point to her own faith, but to Jahweh. Faith undoubtedly finds very clear expression in them; but as a subject it lies concealed, and can often only be grasped by means of a variety of inferences which are often psychological and on that account problematical. In a word, the faith is not the subject of Israel's confessional utterances, but only its vehicle, its mouthpiece. And even less can the "history" of this world of faith by the subject of the theology of the Old Testament. Admittedly, the presentation [[112]] of the "ideas, thought, and concepts of the Old Testament which are important for theology" will always form part of the task of Old Testament theology.[10] But is this all that there is to it? Would a history confined to this leave room for discussion for example of the saving acts of grace, on which the faith of Israel regarded itself as based, and with reference to which it lived its life? A world of religious concepts later systematically arranged is of course an abstraction, for such a thing never existed in Israel in so complete and universal a way. So too the idea of a "religion of Israel," that is, the idea of the faith as an entity, appears more problematical still as a result of the investigation of the history of tradition in our own time. There were up and down the land many traditions which little by little combined into ever larger complexes of tradition. Theologically, these accumulations were in a state of constant flux. Religious thought cannot be separated out from these traditions and represented thus in abstract. If we divorced Israel's confessional utterances from the divine acts in history which they so passionately embrace, what a bloodless ghost we would be left with! If, however, we put Israel's picture of her history in the

---

8. It is well known that an older and less miraculous picture of the events is given in Judg 1:1ff. than in the larger complex in Joshua 1–9.

9. "Poetry is not the imitation of a reality which already exists in the same quality prior to it . . . ; the aesthetic faculty is a creative power for the production of a concept which transcends reality and is not present in any abstract thinking, or indeed in any way of contemplating the world." W. Dilthey, *Gesammelte Schriften*, Leipzig 1914–18, vol. VI, p. 116. In this "production," the chief force in Israel in forming tradition was Jahwism.

10. Köhler, *Theology*, p. 1.

forefront of our theological consideration, we encounter what appropriately is the most essential subject of a theology of the Old Testament, the living word of Jahweh coming on and on to Israel for ever, and this in the message uttered by his mighty acts. It was a message so living and actual for each moment that it accompanied her on her journey through time, interpreting itself afresh to every generation, and informing every generation what it had to do.

. . . .

The Oldest Pictures of the Saving History

[[121]] Even the earliest avowals to Jahweh were historically determined, that is, they connect the name of this God with some statement about an action in history. Jahweh, "who brought Israel out of Egypt," is probably the earliest and at the same time the most widely used of these confessional formulae.[11] Others are such as designate Jahweh as the one who called the patriarchs and promised them the land, etc. Alongside these brief formulae, which are content with a minimum of historical subject-matter—as a species they are generally cultic invocations—there were very certainly soon ranged confessional summaries of the saving history, covering by now a fairly extensive span of the divine action in history.[12] Among these the most important is [[122]] the Credo in Deut 26:5–9, which bears all the marks of great antiquity:

> A wandering Aramean was my father; he went down with a few people into Egypt and there he became a nation, great, mighty, and populous. But the Egyptians treated us harshly, they afflicted us, and laid hard toil upon us. Then we cried to Jahweh, the God of our fathers, and Jahweh heard us, and saw our affliction, our toil, and oppression. And Jahweh brought us out of Egypt with a mighty hand and an outstretched arm, with great terror, with signs and wonders, and brought us to this place and gave us this land, a land flowing with milk and honey.

These words are not, of course, a prayer—there is no invocation or petition—they are out and out a confession of faith. They recapitulate the main events in the saving history from the time of the patriarchs (by the Aramean, Jacob is meant) down to the conquest, and they do this with close concentration on the objective historical facts. As in the Apostles' Creed, there is no reference at all to promulgated revelations, promises, or teaching, and still less any consideration of the attitude which Israel on her side took towards this history with God. The exalted mood which lies behind this recitation is

---

11. The content of the old confessional formulae and the problem of their connexion is dealt with by Noth, *Pentateuch*, pp. 48ff.

12. In no circumstances are these historical summaries to be judged as later than those short historical epicleses, as for example in the sense of an organic development as their subsequent combination, for both are very different in respect of species and each could have its life in its own place contemporaneously.

merely that of a disciplined celebration of the divine acts, and in the process a note was struck which henceforward was to remain the predominant one in Israel's religious life. Israel was always better at glorifying and extolling God than at theological reflexion.[13] In spite of being cast in the form of words spoken by God, the retrospect of the history given in Josh 24:2ff. [[123]] is closely allied to Deut 26:5ff. Admittedly, it goes into considerably greater detail in the presentation of the saving history; but the two are alike in confining themselves to the objective facts. And, in particular, in Joshua too the starting-point is the period of the patriarchs while the end-point is Israel's entry into the promised land. Some of the psalms make it perfectly clear that, originally, this span of time, and this alone, was regarded as the time of the saving history proper. Psalm 136 is certainly a much later litany, but apart from the fact that it starts with the creation, it keeps to the same canonical pattern of the saving history. The same is true of Psalm 105, which also is certainly not old. Psalm 68 does indeed go beyond the conquest—down into the period of the monarchy. But just in so doing it serves as a proof of our thesis. While it is able to depict Israel's early period down to the conquest with a real wealth of concrete historical data (vss. 12–55), its presentation after vs. 50—that is, exactly at the point where the canonical pattern of the saving history leaves it in the lurch—is jejune and slight. (Still, it does mention the loss of Shiloh and the election of David and Zion.) Even stranger is the disproportion in the picture of the saving history in Judith 5:6ff. Its picture of the conquest takes up ten verses, but for the whole period from then down to 586 the narrator can only report trite generalities concerning constant apostasy. He jumps a span of more than 600 years in two verses! These historical summaries in hymn form are still thoroughly confessional in kind. They are not products of a national or even a secular view of history, but clearly take their stand on that old canonical picture of the saving history, the pattern of which was fixed long ago for all time.[14] They are of course no longer confessions in the strict sense of

---

13. The question of the age of this Credo in ancient Israel's life is fairly unimportant for us here. Noth emphasises the original cultic independence of the various themes out of which it is composed (deliverance from Egypt, the promise to the patriarchs, guidance in the wilderness, etc.), *Pentateuch*, pp. 48ff. The literary material seems to justify him, for in the majority of cases the "themes" seem to be independent. Nevertheless these single themes themselves always presuppose an idea of the whole. Guidance in the wilderness cannot be thought of apart from the deliverance from Egypt and vice versa. Again, the promise to the patriarchs, after it passed over from the cultic communities of the people belonging to Abraham and Jacob to Israel, was immediately referred to the deliverance from Egypt, etc. At the same time, regarding the patriarchal tradition, there is much to be said for the assumption that the Credo itself presupposes the combination of an originally independent set of traditions with the central Exodus tradition. Even afterwards the two traditions, of the Exodus and of the patriarchs, are found side by side in marked independence, and clearly discriminated in references to them. K. Galling, *Die Erwählungstraditionen Israels*, Bei[[hefte zur]] Z.A.W. No. 48, Giessen 1928.

14. On the reappearance of the saving history in the Psalms cf. A. Lauha, "Die Geschichtsmotive in den alttestamentlichen Psalmen," in *Annales Academiae Scientiarum Fennicae*, Helsinki 1945.

Deuteronomy 26. Concentration on the facts alone has been abandoned. A tendency towards epic elaboration, and also towards reflexion, is apparent: more than anything else, contrasting with the chain of the divine saving acts, the infidelity and disobedience of Israel now increasingly become objects of importance in the presentation. If we imagine a considerably greater advance still in this process of connecting a narrative to the old pattern and widening its theological range by means of all kinds of traditional material, then we find ourselves face to face with the work of the Jahwist or the Elohist. Starting as the latter does [[124]] only with the history of the patriarchs (Genesis 15), he comes closer to the old canonical pattern of salvation. But both with the Jahwist and the Priestly Document too, their allegiance to, and indeed their rootedness in, the old confessional tradition is beyond doubt. Once this process of giving a narrative connexion to the old plan and widening its scope was given free play, it is no wonder that the plan was also supplemented by theological traditions originally alien to it. The most important of these additions, of which not even a hint is to be found in the old transmitted pattern, is the prefixing to it of an account of the creation and the primeval history, and the insertion of the Sinai pericope, which as a block of tradition has a completely different derivation.[15] As far as form goes, this expansion of the ancient Credo by the Jahwist and the Elohist led to the creation of an extremely involved and highly detailed presentation of the history. Finally, the subsequent combination of the three great works J, E, and P produced a literary structure of the history, whose disproportions can only cause astonishment to anyone who looks for an artistic harmony and an inner balancing of these tremendous masses of material. There is in fact much to be learned from a comparison of how the story of Jacob or Moses is presented with that of the Homeric Odysseus, for in both cases the pictures are due to the coalescence of originally independent traditions. The main difference lies in the fact that in the rendering of her story Israel handled the old material much less freely than the Greeks. A later age could not venture to recast the old legends in respect of theme and thought and to combine them so as to give rise to what was in fact a new history complete in itself. They were bound in a much more conservative way to what had come down to them, and especially to the forms in which they had received it—that is, they handled it much more as if it were a document. The result of this for the theological elaboration of the old traditions upon which J, E, and P were indeed intensively engaged, was a completely different form of theological handling of the tradition. If the possibility of bringing the several traditions into inner unity with one another and of balancing them as they were amalgamated, was ruled out, it was nevertheless still possible to insert expressly directive passages at important nodal points in the events. And this possibility was in fact used again and [[125]]

---

15. The free variations on the old Credo do not mention the events at Sinai either. The first mention is in Neh 9:6ff. This was then the first place where the picture which J and E expanded made an impression.

again.[16] but the chief method employed in the theological unfolding of the tradition was a different one still: it was much more indirect, for it consisted in the way in which separate pieces of material were connected. The lay-out of the primeval history, the story of Abraham, the relationship of the period of the patriarchs to that of Joshua, etc., is arranged in such a way that quite definite theological tensions, which the great collector intended, arise out of the sequence of the material itself. This indirect theological way of speaking through the medium of the traditional material and its arrangement makes clear once more that remarkable preponderance of the matter-of-fact historical over the theological which is so characteristic of the witness of Israel. Even in its final form, the Hexateuch retained a confessional stamp, though not in that restrained form of celebrating the divine deeds and them alone which is found in the old Credo; for as well as dealing with them, this historical work also deals with the institution of offices and rites, and with men standing up to the test, and still more with failure and rebellion. If we say a confessional stamp, this means that the later Israel saw in the historical witness of the Hexateuch something that was typical for the people of God, and that what was there related remained of immediate concern for every subsequent generation, because of a latent contemporaneousness in it.

Meanwhile, however, something of decisive importance for the faith of Israel had come about. As early as the time when the theological elaboration of the old Credo was still at its beginnings, Jahweh had further dealings with Israel. The history with God did not come to a standstill. Jahweh had raised up charismatic military leaders to protect Israel, he had chosen Zion and established the throne of David for all time, Israel had become disobedient, and so he had sent prophets, and finally he repudiated Israel in the twofold judgments of 722 and 587. The realisation that with David something new began had certainly come to life fairly soon in Israel. This is without any doubt itself the background of the great narrative complex describing "David's rise to power" and in particular of the Succession Document, which are so [[126]] important theologically.[17] But Israel did not arrive at a clear consciousness of this new epoch in her history with Jahweh as a whole until it had, in such a fearful way, already come to its end in the exile. Then, with the help of a great mass of already available historical material, the great theological history which we call the Deuteronomist's came into being. It carried the thread of the history with God down from the conquest to the catastrophe of the exile, and presented and interpreted this period up to Israel's final shipwreck from quite definite and very individual theological points of view. The second stage

16. Gen 12:1–9, for instance, is such a unit in the story of Abraham lying outwith the saga material handed on. The prologue to the Flood in the primeval history of J (Gen 6:5–8) is to be judged in the same way. In the realm of the story of Jacob the prayer in Gen 32:10ff. [9ff.] would call for mention, and in that of the Deuteronomistic histories the freely composed discourses in Joshua 23; 1 Samuel 12; 1 Kings 8.

17. For the history of David's rise to power see Noth, *Überl. Studien*, p. 61. For the history of the succession to David see L. Rost, *Thronnachfolge*, pp. 82ff.

in Israel's history with Jahweh was clearly not simply conceived of as the uni-linear prolongation of the first; from the theological point of view, it ran its course under essentially different presuppositions. As concerns the good gifts of salvation promised by Jahweh, it does not go beyond the old one—the good gift of the land was always the ultimate for Israel, which nothing could sur-pass and which could only be won or forfeited. But this era stands rather un-der the sign of the law of judgment, and accordingly the question as to how Israel stood up to the test thrusts itself more and more into the foreground: indeed it becomes decisive for Israel for life and death before Jahweh. And the sum-total of this Deuteronomistic historical work is that Israel, possessed as she already was of all the good gifts of salvation, chose death. It is to be no-ticed that the decision about this termination of her monarchical period was thus in the Deuteronomist put in the hands of Israel. In the "canonical" sav-ing history, from the patriarchs down to the entry into Canaan, it was Jahweh who made the truth of the promise good in face of all the failure of Israel; and he did not let any part of his great plan in history, least of all the final part, be taken out of his own hands. But in the Deuteronomist's history Jah-weh allowed Israel to make the decision.

The exile was a period devoid of saving history. The Deuteronomistic his-torical work gave an authoritative interpretation of the riddle of the standstill in the divine history with Israel: the catastrophes were the wellmerited judg-ment upon the continued apostasy to the Canaanite cult of Baal. At the time, who could know whether this judgment was final or only temporary? In keep-ing with Israel's whole religious attitude, this question could in fact be an-swered only by Jahweh's beginning to act anew in history. As it happened, about 550, through [[127]] Cyrus, history began to move very mightily in the immediate surroundings of the exiles. But at this point Israel's witness parts company with itself. After Babylon had fallen, and the worship in the Temple had been reconstituted in Jerusalem, and later, when even a large section of the exiles had returned home, Israel could only see in these events a fresh act of grace; and, as the historical summaries in Neh 9:6ff. and Judith 5:5ff. show, she carried the thread of history with God which had been so abruptly snapped, down with praise and thanksgiving into the present time. This theo-logical link with the pre-exilic history with God is established by means of elaborate argumentation, especially in the Chronicler's history, the main con-cern of which is to legitimate the cultic restoration in the post-exilic period on the basis of a legacy of David's which had not been brought into effect un-til his time. But the prophets Jeremiah, Ezekiel, Zechariah, and, more than anyone else, Deutero-Isaiah, placed a very different interpretation upon the breaking-off of the history with God up to then. The tenor of their message is this: the old is done away with; now Jahweh will bring about something com-pletely new, a new Exodus, a new covenant, a new Moses. Israel's old confes-sion of faith is present now only as something which is done away with, since Jahweh is about to act along the lines of his earlier saving acts in an even more splendid way.[18]

18. Especially Isa 43:16–20; Jer 21:31ff., and also Hos 2:16ff.

Now this sequence given by the great pictures of the history, with their very different conceptions of the progress of the saving history, prescribes the way in which we too have to unfold the witness of the Old Testament. What other starting-point can we take than the colossal theological structure which Israel raised on the foundation of her oldest confession of Jahweh? We have therefore first to attempt to sketch the basic traits of a theology of the Hexateuch. This must be followed by a description of the new experience which Israel gained on her journey from the conquest to the disasters at the end of the period of the monarchy; for a description of the outcome of this second phase of the history with God was, of course, the task which the Deuteronomistic writer imposed on himself. Following on that, we shall finally have to deal with the great interpretation which Israel later drew up in the Chronicler's history of the final phase of her history with God, the period from David to Nehemiah. Then, in a second part, we will have to speak about the situation in which Israel felt herself to be placed as a result of this revelation and of God's activity in [[128]] history, and about her praises, her justice, her trials, and her wisdom. What was distinctive in the response which Israel made to the revelation of Jahweh will therefore be dealt with there.

The most accurate test of the starting-point and arrangement of a theology of the Old Testament is, however, the phenomenon of prophecy. At what point has it to be dealt with, and in what connexion? If we are resolved on giving a systematic and connected presentation of the religious ideas, then we shall have occasion to speak about prophecy throughout—in dealing with the holiness of Jahweh, the beliefs about creation, the idea of the covenant, etc. But in so doing would we do justice to its message? We should also, however, do it an injustice if we reserved treatment of it for a special section dealing with Israel's thought about her own and the nations' future.[19] This is not the way to bring the message of the prophets into organic connexion with the religious ideas of Israel. However overpoweringly diverse it may be, it nevertheless has its starting-point in the conviction that Israel's previous history with Jahweh has come to an end, and that he will start something new with her. The prophets seek to convince their contemporaries that for them the hitherto existing saving ordinances have lost their worth, and that, if Israel is to be saved, she must move in faith into a new saving activity of Jahweh, one which is only to come in the future. But this conviction of theirs, that what has existed till now is broken off, places them basically outside the saving history as it had been understood up to then by Israel. The prophets' message had its centre and its bewildering dynamic effect in the fact that it smashed in pieces Israel's existence with God up to the present, and rang up the curtain of history for a new action on his part with her. So prophecy needs separate treatment in a theology of the Old Testament.

19. So for example E. Jacob in his *Theology of the Old Testament*, London 1958.

Synopsis of von Rad's *Old Testament Theology* (1962, 1965)

Gerhard von Rad
On the New Element
in Eighth-Century Prophecy[1]

Excerpted with permission from Gerhard von Rad, *Old Testament Theology* (New York: Harper & Row, 1965), vol. 2: 176–80, 183–87.

[[176]] Careful consideration of the distinctive features in the prophecies of Amos, Hosea, Isaiah, and Micah might well lead us to the conclusion that all comparisons are dangerous, because once we have discovered the radical differences between them it is difficult to avoid the temptation of going on and smoothing these out. What, in actual fact, do Hosea and Isaiah have in common? Hosea came from the farming world of the Northern Kingdom, he was opposed to everything that in his day was implied by the word "king"; of all the prophets he was the most deeply involved in patriarchal concepts deriving from the cult, and he paid particular attention to problems in the sacral sphere and to cultic irregularities. Isaiah was a townsman, brought up in a *polis* tradition, and a sharp-sighted observer of world politics; he explained all the changes in the political kaleidoscope as part of Jahweh's rational scheme, he placed his confidence in the divinely guaranteed protection of the city, and he looked for a king who would bring peace and righteousness. Much the same can be said of Amos and Micah. Amos was apparently quite unmoved by Hosea's main topic, the threat of Jahwism from the Canaanite worship of Baal; and he is also different from Isaiah, for he does not inveigh against mistaken policies, against armaments and alliances. Finally, there is absolutely no bridge between Micah and the hopes cherished concerning Zion by Isaiah, his fellow-countryman and contemporary; Micah in fact expected Zion to be blotted out of the pages of history. Even the kind of prophetic office surprisingly discovered in the state documents of Mari, which makes it clear that the prophet could threaten even the king in God's name, does not give us any standpoint from which to summarise and categorise the prophetic role. If their close connexion with the king and their interest in political and military affairs is a particular characteristic of the "prophets" of Mari, then Israel has comparable figures not only in Isaiah, but in a whole series of prophets beginning with Ahijah of Shiloh, including Micaiah ben Imlah and [[177]] Elijah, and going down to Jeremiah.[2] On the other hand, it is impossible to bring Amos into this category. Nevertheless, in spite of all these great differences, there is a great deal of common matter which links the eighth-century prophets to one another; for their religious ideas led them to an absolutely common conviction, one so novel and revolutionary when compared with all their

1. Eichrodt, *Theology*, pp. 345–53; Vriezen, *Outline*, pp. 62–66.
2. S. Herrmann, *Die Ursprünge der prophetischen Heilserwartung im Alten Testament*, Leipzig Dissertation 1957, pp. 65ff., 73ff.

inherited beliefs, that it makes the differences, considerable as these are, seem almost trivial and peripheral. We shall now make another attempt to find out which element in the prophets' teaching struck their contemporaries as being a departure from the religious standards of the time.

To begin with a very simple statement: these men were set apart from their contemporaries and they were very lonely. Their call gave them a unique knowledge of Jahweh and of his designs for Israel. We have already seen how, apparently to a much greater degree than any of their contemporaries, they are deeply rooted in the religious traditions of their nation; indeed, their whole preaching might almost be described as a unique dialogue with the tradition by means of which the latter was made to speak to their own day. Yet the very way in which they understood it and brought it to life again is the measure of their difference from all the contemporary religious heritage of their nation. When Amos said that Jahweh presided over the migration of the Philistines and the Syrians (Amos 9:7), he was departing pretty radically from the belief of his time. This novel and to some extent revolutionary way of taking the old traditions was not, however, the result of careful study or of slowly maturing conviction; rather, these prophets were all agreed that it was Jahweh who enlightened them and led them on from one insight to another. The reason for their isolation was therefore this—as they listened to and obeyed a word and commission of Jahweh which came to them alone and which could not be transferred to anyone else, these men became individuals, persons.[3] They could say "I" in a way never before heard in Israel. At the same time, it has become apparent that the "I" of which these men were allowed to become conscious was very different from our present-day concept of personality. For first of all, this process of becoming a person was marked by many strange experiences of compulsion, and one at least of its characteristics—we have only to think of the "be still" [[178]] in Isaiah's demand for faith—was passively to contemplate and make room for the divine action.[4] Yet, at the same time, this opened up freedom upon freedom for the prophet. He could even break out into an "exultation of the spirit" about this, as Micah once did when, as his *charisma* welled up gloriously within him, he became conscious of his difference from other people:

> But as for me, I am filled with power,
>   [with the spirit of Jahweh],
>   with justice and might,
> to declare to Jacob his transgression,
>   and to Israel his sin. (Mic 3:8)

There is a very direct reflexion of the prophets' attainment of personal identity and of their religious uniqueness in their style, the way in which they speak of God and of the things of God. During centuries of reverent speech Israel had created a language of the cult, and had devised a conventional

---

3. See [[von Rad 1965:]] pp. 76f. Eichrodt, *Theology*, p. 343.
4. Eichrodt, *Theology*, p. 357.

phraseology for speaking about God; yet there were times when he might also be spoken of in the way these prophets loved to do—in monstrous similes, with an apparent complete absence of any feeling for dignity or propriety.[5] These were *ad hoc* inspirations, the provocative inventions of a single person, whose radical quality and extreme boldness was only justified by the uniqueness of a particular situation and the frame of mind of the people who listened to them.

Even if we knew still less than we in fact do of the way in which the concepts of Jahwism were still a living force at the shrines and among the broad mass of the people at the time when these prophets were active, one thing could yet be said for certain—the new feature in their preaching, and the one which shocked their hearers, was the message that Jahweh was summoning Israel before his judgment seat, and that he had in fact already pronounced sentence upon her: "The end has come upon my people Israel" (Amos 8:2). The question has recently been asked whether the prophets did not base even these pronouncements of judgment on older tradition. Were there ceremonies [[179]] in the cult at which Jahweh appeared as his people's accuser?[6] So far nothing definite has materialised; and an answer to this question would not in any way be a complete answer to the other question: why did the prophets proclaim this message? Moreover, the devastating force and finality of the prophetic pronouncement of judgment can never have had a cultic antecedent, for it envisaged the end of all cult itself.

For the proper understanding of what we have called this completely new note in the prophetic preaching, we have not least to remember the changing political situation, Assyria's increasingly obvious and steady advance towards Palestine. When in an almost stereotyped fashion Amos suggests that Jahweh's judgment will take the form of exile, this quite clearly reflects how much the Assyrians occupied his thoughts. The prophets are, however, obviously motivated not merely by one factor but by several. Let us simply say that these men spoke of the divine wrath as a fact, and designated as its proper object their contemporaries' whole way of life, their social and economic attitudes, their political behaviour and, in particular, their cultic practice. At all events, the favourite way of putting it, that this is simply the emergence of new religious ideas, and as such only a new understanding of the relationship between God and Man, does not square with the fact that in this matter the prophets most decidedly took as their starting-point the old traditions of Jahwism. It was these that formed the foundation of their attack, and time and again the prophets took them as the basis of arguments with their audiences. Thus, as far as the old Jahwistic tradition was concerned, the prophets and their hearers were on common ground: but they differed in

---

5. Jahweh, the barber (Isa 7:20), the ulcer in Israel's body (Hos 5:12), the unsuccessful lover (Isa 5:1ff.); see also [[von Rad 1965:]] p. 375.

6. So E. Würthwein, "Der Ursprung der prophetischen Gerichtsrede," in *Z. Th. K*, 49 (1952), pp. 1ff.; in a different way F. Hesse, "Wurzelt die prophetische Gerichtsrede im israelitischen Kult?" in *Z. A. W.*, 64 (1953), pp. 45ff.

their interpretation of these traditions, which the prophets believed were far
from ensuring Israel's salvation. The classic expression of this aspect of
prophecy are Amos's words—her very election made the threat to Israel all
the greater (Amos 3:1f.)! This is therefore the first occasion in Israel when
"law" in the proper sense of the term was preached.[7] This is most apparent in
the prophets' castigations of their fellow-countrymen for their anti-social behaviour, their commercial sharp-practice. Here they do not in any sense regard themselves as the revolutionary mouthpiece of one social group. Time
and again we can see them [[180]] applying provisions of the old divine law to
the situation.[8] Isaiah uses much the same procedure when he measures the
behaviour of the people of Jerusalem against the Zion tradition, and looks on
armaments or security sought for in alliances as a rejection of the divine help.
It is also used by Hosea when he takes the saving gift of the land, which Israel
still completely failed to understand, as his starting-point, and uses it to show
up the enormity of her faithlessness and ingratitude. Jahweh was known to
be the judge of sinners in early Israel also; and early Israel was equally aware
that a man's sin is more than the sum total of his several acts (Genesis 3). Yet,
the prophets' zeal in laying bare man's innate tendency to oppose God, their
endeavour to comprehend Israel's conduct in its entirety, and to bring out
what, all historical contingency apart, might be taken as typical of that conduct—this was something new, especially since its purpose was to give reasons
for Jahweh's judgment. Thus, for example, Hosea included and discussed the
whole story of the relationship between God and his people in his poem on
Israel's failure to understand that the blessings of the soil of Canaan were
gifts from Jahweh. This was a great intellectual achievement. The prophets'
chief concern was not, of course, to summarise human conduct under the
most general concepts possible by the method of abstraction, though this
does sometimes happen;[9] they reached their goal in a different way. For
while they seem to be describing only a particular failure of a particular
group of men in a particular situation, they have really depicted, by their use
of a few characteristic traits, something that was typical of Israel's general attitude to God.[10]

. . . .

7. See [[von Rad 1962:]] pp. 195ff.; see [[von Rad 1965:]] pp. 395ff.
8. See [[von Rad 1965:]] pp. 135f. H.-J. Kraus, "Die prophetische Botschaft gegen das
soziale Unrechts Israels," in Ev. Th., 15 (1955), pp. 295ff.
9. Here one might think, for example, of Isaiah's characteristic reproach of pride
(גבהות אדם Isa 2:11, 17) or of Hosea's equally characteristic term "spirit of harlotry" (זנונים רוח
Hos 4:12, 5:4), or also of Amos's word about the "pride of Jacob" (גאון Amos 6:8). The comprehensive term "return" and the statement that Israel does not return, also belong here.
H. W. Wolff, "Des Thema 'Umkehr' in der alttestamentlichen Prophetie," in Z. Th. K., (1951),
pp. 129ff.
10. The courtly monologues which the prophets put into the mouth of foreign kings
also belong to this tendency to make types, Isa 10:8ff., 14:13ff., 37:24, Ezek 28:2, 29:3, 9,
27:3.

[[183]] We may therefore describe the characteristic feature of the prophetic view of history as follows: not only does it recognise most clearly Jahweh's designs and intentions in history, it also sees the various historical forces involved in quite a different light from other people. The great powers which occupied the centre of the political stage did [[184]] not blind the prophets to God; these empires shrivel up almost into nothingness before Jahweh's all-pervasive power. It is the "I" spoken by Jahweh that pervades the historical field to its utmost limits. It is moving to see how Isaiah and his subjective certainty about his own view of history came into collision—a proof of its complete undogmatic flexibility and openness. As Assyria advanced, the interpretation he had put upon her as an instrument of punishment in the hands of Jahweh proved to be inadequate, or at least partial. The way in which she exterminated nations and the danger that she would treat Jerusalem and Judah in the same way gave rise to a question: did she not intend also to overrun Zion? Nevertheless, Isaiah was still able to interpret Jahweh's design; he explained the difficulty by saying that the Assyrians were exceeding the task assigned to them. The scope of their commission was merely to chastise, not to annihilate (Isa 10:5-7). This change in Isaiah's views is a further remarkable confirmation of the prophets' claim to be able to see history in its relation to God clearly and with perfect understanding. In Isaiah's view history can be analysed into the divine design and the co-efficient of arbitrary human power.[11] To come to this explanation—and we should make no mistake about this—Isaiah wrestled with the whole force of his intellect as well as of his faith. Written evidence of this expressly rational grappling with history is furnished by the generally accepted interpretation of the didactic poem in Isa 28:23-29, in which Isaiah makes the multifarious and carefully considered actions of the farmer's sowing and reaping into a transparent parable of the divine action in history. "Wonderful is his counsel and great his wisdom."[12]

So far, however, we have dealt almost too much with history in a general sense, with the result that misunderstanding could arise: it might be supposed that the prophets shared our concept of objective history. This is contradicted by the very fact that, as the prophets use the term, wherever history is spoken of, it is related in some sense to Israel. Even Isaiah's famous universalism still keeps to the idea that Jahweh directs history with reference to Israel. Yet, closer consideration of the prophecies of salvation shows that Jahweh's coming action in history upon Israel has still another peculiar characteristic. What comes in question here are not designs which Jahweh formed so to speak in perfect freedom, but only the fulfillment of promises he had already made to Israel in the old traditions. Whether we think of Hosea's [[185]] prophecy that Israel will once more be led into the wilderness and once more be brought through the valley of Achor into her own land (Hos 2:16ff. [14ff.]), or of the prophecy that Jahweh will once more gather nations together against Zion, though he is again to protect it, or of the prophecies about the anointed one

---

11. See [[von Rad 1965:]] p. 163.
12. See [[von Rad 1965:]] p. 163, n. 21.

who is yet to come in Amos, Isaiah, and Micah, we everywhere see to what an extent even the prophets' predictions of the future are bound to tradition; and this in the sense that on the prophets' lips the coming and, as we may safely call them, eschatological events of salvation are to correspond to the earlier events as antitype and type. Thus, even in what they say about the future, the prophets function largely as interpreters of older traditions of Jahwism.

At the same time they introduce a fundamentally new element, which is that only the acts which lie in the future are to be important for Israel's salvation. The old traditions said that Jahweh led Israel into her land, founded Zion, and established the throne of David, and this was sufficient. No prophet could any longer believe this; for between him and those founding acts hung a fiery curtain of dire judgments upon Israel, judgments which, in the prophets' opinion, had already begun; and this message of judgment had no basis in the old Jahwistic tradition. They believed, therefore, that salvation could only come if Jahweh arose to perform new acts upon Israel, an event which they looked on as certain—and they entreated those who were still able to hear not to put their trust in illusory safeguards (Mic 3:11), but to "look to" what was to come, and to take refuge in Jahweh's saving act, which was near at hand.[13] The prophets were therefore the first men in Israel to proclaim over and over again and on an ever widening basis that salvation comes in the shadow of judgment. It is only this prediction of a near divine action, with its close relation to old election traditions and its bold new interpretation of them, which can properly be defined as eschatological.[14] Everywhere there were pious hopes and confident statements about the continuance of the divine faithfulness. What the prophets foretold was something completely different theologically. They take as their basis the "No" pronounced [[186]] by Jahweh on the Israel of their day, her relationship to Jahweh which had for long been hopelessly shattered. They were sure, however, that beyond the judgment, by means of fresh acts, Jahweh would establish salvation; and their paramount business was to declare these acts beforehand, and not simply to speak about hope and confidence.

Summing up, it may be said that in regard to both their "preaching of law" and their proclamation of salvation, the eighth-century prophets put Israel's life on completely new bases. The former can only be seen in its true light when it is considered in relation to the latter. We have already emphasised the fact that the prophets did not derive their conviction that Jahweh purposed judgment from any special revelation, independent of his saving acts, but from the old saving traditions themselves; thus, they interpreted the message in a way different not only from their contemporaries but also from

13. See [[von Rad 1965:]] pp. 160ff.
14. See [[von Rad 1965:]] pp. 118f. and 239. The term "prophetic," too, urgently requires a suitable restriction. There is no profit in expanding it, as for example Vriezen does, so as to see what is prophetic as something implanted into Jahwism by Moses (*Outline*, pp. 137, 257f.). In my opinion, what is specific to the prophet only appears with the determination of his characteristic attitude towards tradition (see [[von Rad 1965:]] p. 299).

all earlier generations. For them the traditions became law. Yet, they were
not precursors of legalism; they did not reproach their fellows with not living
their lives in obedience to law; their reproach was rather this, that as Jahweh's
own people they had continually transgressed the commandments and not
put their confidence in the offer of divine protection. How little the prophets' work was aimed at a life lived under the yoke of the law is made particularly clear in those places, which are, of course, few in number, where they go
beyond negative accusations to positive demands. "Seek good, and not evil;
hate evil, love good!" "Seek Jahweh, that you may live!" (Amos 5:14f., 6). This
is not the language of a man who wants to regulate life by law. In Amos's
view, what Jahweh desires from Israel is something very clear and simple; if
not, how could he have described it by the perfectly general term "good" (cp.
also Hos 8:3; Isa 5:20; Mic 3:2)? And listen to Micah. The prophet answers
the excesses in the performance of legal and cultic rites to which Israel's anxiety was driving her: "he has showed you, O man, what is good and what Jahweh seeks from you: to do justly, to love kindness, and to walk humbly before
Jahweh" (Mic 6:8).[15] This is [[187]] the quintessence of the commandments as
the prophets understood them. There is no demand here for "ethics" instead
of a cult, as if the prophet's desire was to lead men from one set of laws into
another. No, something quite simple is contrasted with the arduous performance of works which can end only in destruction—a way along which men
can walk before God. Exactly the same is true of the verse in Hosea which
"reads like the programme of an opposition party," to the effect that what
counts with Jahweh is not the offering of the proper sacrifices, but "loyalty to
the covenant and knowledge of God" (Hos 6:6). The vow which this same
prophet puts into the mouth of those who turn to Jahweh is given in negative
terms, doubtless because it follows a literary category used in worship, but in
principle it takes the same line. It does not expect the fulfillment of a legal
demand:

> Assyria shall not save us, we will not ride upon horses;
> and we will say no more "Our God" to the work of our hands.
>
> (Hos 14:4 [3])[16]

Isaiah says practically nothing about the inner disposition of the purified
remnant, with the result that it is not easy to imagine what this is. The remnant is composed of those from whom Jahweh has not hidden his face (Isa
8:17), those who have had faith. On one occasion he calls those who take refuge in Zion "the poor of his people" (Isa 14:32).

---

15. The meaning of הִצְנֵעַ is not perfectly certain. The term seems to belong to the language of Wisdom (Ecclesiasticus 16:25, 35:3), and tends in the direction of the idea of "measured." In his study, "Und demütig sein vor deinem Gott," in *Wort und Dienst, Jahrbuch der
theologischen Schule Bethel*, 1959, pp. 180ff., H. J. Stoebe also finds the term principally in the
language of Wisdom and translates it as "to be discerning, circumspect."

16. The negative formulation of the confession corresponds to model confessional formulations; von Rad, *Ges[[ammelte]] St[[udien zum Alten Testament]]*, Munich 1958]], p. 292.

The eighth-century prophets were, of course, only the first to tread this new theological path. Their successors were to go further along it, and in particular were to have still more to say about the question of the new obedience. In general they were to take up the topics they inherited and to develop them in their own way; but they were also to enrich the prophetic preaching with new topics which for eighth-century prophecy had not as yet appeared on the horizon.

Part 3

Expansion and Variety: Between Gerhard von Rad and Brevard Childs

Introduction

Writing in 1963, in the wake of Eichrodt and von Rad, Robert Dentan predicted that "the next decade or so" would be "a period of assimilation, self-criticism, and consolidation rather than of continued expansion" (1963: 83). Three decades later, Phyllis Trible seemed to confirm Dentan's prediction: "Since 1963 few biblical theologies have appeared, and none has dominated the field" (Trible 1993: 35). In some respects, both were right. The decade following von Rad produced no dominant works, and it involved much self-criticism. In 1970, Brevard Childs's announced *Biblical Theology in Crisis* appeared. His book helped bring to an end the "biblical theology movement" that Paul Minear had called for in the inaugural issue of *Theology Today* (1944) and of which G. Ernest Wright's work was most representative (Kraftchick 1995). However, contrary to Dentan's expectation and part of Trible's observation, Old Testament theology did continue its expansion. At least ten such theologies, remarkably diverse, appeared between 1971 and 1981 (see Martens 1992; 1997a). The seven volumes excerpted in this part 3 did not aim to be exhaustive or definitive in the manner of Eichrodt and von Rad (both of whose theologies, in English, remain in print). Their authors sought rather to move Old Testament theology beyond—or to avoid—the methodological impasse that followed von Rad. They did so from different perspectives.

Walther Zimmerli (1972; 1978) and Claus Westermann (1978, 1982) continued the German line of Old Testament theology, especially in response to von Rad and, in Zimmerli's case, von Rad's students. Zimmerli made his "point of departure that focal point where the faith of the Old Testament specifically confesses the God of Israel under the name of Yahweh" (1978: 14). Zimmerli understood the name of YHWH to function as a dynamic center in relation to God's freedom and God's revelatory acts. However, Zimmerli resisted the equation of revelation and history (Pannenberg [ed.] 1968), stressing also the importance of "Yahweh's word," as illustrated especially by the prophets (Zimmerli 1978: 25, 31). Also distinctive was the emphasis that Zimmerli accorded God's "specific gifts" and blessings, including "war and victory" (sometimes granted to Israel's enemies), the gift of land, and the gift of divine presence (1978: 58, 63–70). Blessing became a defining feature in Westermann's work. Following von Rad's emphasis on narrative, Westermann acknowledged the historical, verbal character of Old Testament theology and the central place of God's acts of deliverance (1982: 9–11). However, he saw specific acts of (Israel's) deliverance in dialectical relation with blessing:

117

"something that goes on all the time and may apply to the whole world" (1982: 103). Westermann understood creation to be the basis and framework of blessing. Deliverance and blessing constituted the principal poles, or dialectic, in the Old Testament, which incorporates subsidiary ones, such as divine action and Israel's response. Zimmerli pointed directly to the New Testament only in his closing remarks on the Old Testament's openness to the future (1978: 240), while Westermann made connections to the New Testament frequently and at length (1982: 217–32).

Different contexts and concerns lay behind the volumes written outside Germany, yet they struck some of the same notes. Ronald Clements agreed with Zimmerli that God must be the Old Testament's center, or the basis of its unity (Clements 1978: 23–24), as did John L. McKenzie (Clements 1978: 26). But while McKenzie wrote "as if the New Testament did not exist" (Clements 1978: 319), Clements stressed the Old Testament's reception by two different communities, Jewish and Christian. This twofold, different reception and hope for conversation between the communities led Clements to orient his "fresh approach" around the two poles of law and promise (cf. Chapman 2000: 283–84). In this formal respect, Clements resembled Westermann. Even more was this true of Samuel L. Terrien (1978), whose biblical theology traded on the poles of divine presence and absence—hence, God's dynamic, "elusive presence," which incorporates a series of subsidiary dualities, such as the ethical and the aesthetic. It also incorporates other proposed "centers," such as covenant. Distinctive of McKenzie and Terrien was their positive attention to Israel's cult, to which McKenzie assigned definitive importance. In the emphasis he gave to divine presence, Terrien resembled Zimmerli. Also like Zimmerli, Elmer A. Martens (1981; 1998) devoted particular attention to the topics of *war* and *the land*. He encompassed these and other themes within a uniquely exegetical approach: an exegesis of Exod 5:22–6:8 yielded a four-part, biblically comprehensive "divine design." Aligning with Clements's claim that "promise" defined Christian reception of the Old Testament, Walter C. Kaiser made promise the unifying center of Old Testament theology, able to incorporate both covenant and blessing and preparing the way for the New Testament (1978). Notably problematic in earlier Old Testament theologies, and in some excerpted here, was the wisdom literature. However, Terrien found in wisdom, especially in its personification, a theological bridge joining the two Testaments.

The expansion of Old Testament theology represented below did not converge toward consensus; to the contrary, it comprised a variety of approaches, assumptions, and conclusions—as well as denominations: Baptist, Catholic, Evangelical Free, Lutheran, Mennonite, and Reformed. (Lehman, also a Mennonite, produced an Old Testament theology [1971] that followed closely the Reformed theology of Vos [1948].) None of the authors was deeply troubled by the crisis that befell the biblical theology movement. Only Terrien adverted to it; he viewed "the failure of the biblical theology movement" with favor, since it opened new opportunities (1978: 475). And none of the authors proposed a symbolic or conceptual center of the sort that

Eichrodt and Vriezen had employed. Neither did any of them adopt either von Rad's tradition-historical approach or his conclusions regarding unmitigated theological diversity in the Old Testament. Instead, there was a tendency toward more relational categories and toward a bounded diversity embracing theological tension. Westermann and Terrien especially exemplify the point, as does Clements. Like Rudolf Smend (1970) before him, and A. B. Davidson much earlier (1904: 13), Clements "correlated" "the God of Israel" with "the people of God" (Clements 1978: 79; cf. Fohrer 1972: 97–102; Otto Kaiser 1998: 24–28). But Clements also gave unprecedented attention to the bounded character of the Old Testament's diversity, which also made it theologically productive; that is, to the canon (Clements 1978: 8–19). In his argument for Old Testament theology as a theological discipline, Clements echoed Vriezen. In his emphasis on canon, he both followed and presaged Brevard Childs, who would make "canon" a clarion call.

WALTHER ZIMMERLI

b. 1907   d. 1983

Life before God

Walther Zimmerli was born in Switzerland, where he served as a Reformed pastor and then as a professor at the University of Zurich. In 1950, he was called to the University of Göttingen, where he had been a student. While his first publication was a critical edition of Calvin's *Psychopannychia* (1542), Zimmerli's outstanding achievement was his commentary on Ezekiel. His long occupation with this prophetic book was reflected in his Old Testament theology.

Selected Writings by Zimmerli

1932   (editor) *Psychopannychia, von Joh. Calvin.* Leipzig: Scholl.

1971   *Man and His Hope in the Old Testament.* Translated by G. W. Bowden. Studies in Biblical Theology 2/20. London: SCM / Naperville, Ill.: Allenson.

1972   *Grundriss der Alttestamentlichen Theologie.* Theologische Wissenschaft 3. Stuttgart: Kohlhammer.

1976   *The Old Testament and the World.* Translated by John J. Scullion. Atlanta: John Knox.

1978   *Old Testament Theology in Outline.* Translated by David E. Green. Atlanta: John Knox / Edinburgh: T. & T. Clark.

1979–83 *Ezekiel: A Commentary on the Book of the Prophet Ezekiel.* 2 volumes. Translated by Ronald E. Clements and James D. Martin. Edited by Frank M. Cross, Klaus Baltzer, Leonard J. Greenspoon, and Paul D. Hanson. Hermeneia. Philadelphia: Fortress.

1982   *I Am Yahweh.* Translated by Douglas W. Stott. Edited by Walter Brueggemann. Atlanta: John Knox.

1985   *Grundriss der Alttestamentlichen Theologie.* 5th edition. Theologische Wissenschaft 3. Stuttgart: Kohlhammer.

Writings about Zimmerli

Brueggemann, Walter
  1982 Introduction. Pp. ix–xvii in *I Am Yahweh*. Translated by Douglas W. Stott. Edited by Walter Brueggemann. Atlanta: John Knox.
Donner, Herbert, Robert Hanhart, and Rudolf Smend (editors)
  1977 *Beiträge zur Alttestamentlichen Theologie: Festschrift für Walther Zimmerli zum 70. Geburtstag*. Göttingen: Vandenhoeck & Ruprecht.
Smend, Rudolf
  1989 Walther Zimmerli. Pp. 276–89 in *Deutsche Alttestamentler in Drei Jahrhunderten*. Göttingen: Vandenhoeck & Ruprecht.

Walther Zimmerli's
Approach to Old Testament Theology

Excerpted with permission from Walther Zimmerli, *Old Testament Theology in Outline* (Atlanta: John Knox, 1978), pp. 13–14, 17–26. The footnotes have been reconstructed from the bibliographies on pp. 21 and 26–27.

[[13]] The Old Testament comprises a set of documents that came into being over a period of almost a thousand years. During this period Israel, from whose world the documents contained in the Old Testament derive, underwent many changes. Nomadic beginnings give way to settled life in Canaan. Herdsmen become farmers and also infiltrate earlier urban cultures. A loose association of the groups constituting Israel in the period before there was any state develops into a state, first as a single kingdom, then as two. The latter are destroyed by the blows of the great powers, first the Assyrians and then the Neo-Babylonians. The people lose their identity as a separate state; a major portion of the intellectual leadership lives in distant exile in Mesopotamia. Then a new entity, something like an ecclesiastical state, consolidates itself around Jerusalem, first under Persian, then under Macedonian-Greek hegemony.

The change in sociological structures produced changes in liturgical life, resulting finally in the elimination of a multiplicity of sanctuaries and focusing on Jerusalem. And of course, alongside of this, the exile forced the establishment of places of worship in distant lands. Modern scholarship has revealed how this historical movement has its inward aspect in the faith of Israel. Religious traditions in new situations find new interpretations. According to the law of challenge and response, a new historical challenge brings about a novel formulation of the response.

A presentation of Old Testament theology cannot close its eyes to all this movement and change, the more so in that it is characteristic of the faith of the Old Testament not to live with its back turned to the world and to history, turning inward to guard its arcanum, but rather to relate closely to the world and the course of events and engage in dialogue with whatever it encounters in history.

On the other hand, this raises the question of whether the "coherent whole" of what the Old Testament says about God, which it is the task of an Old Testament theology to present, consists merely in the continuity of history, that is, the ongoing stream of historical sequence.

The Old Testament itself makes a different claim: it firmly maintains its [[14]] faith in the sameness of the God it knows by the name of Yahweh. Throughout all changes, it maintains that this God Yahweh takes an active interest in his people Israel. In the face of all vexation and anguish, when "the right hand of the Most High" seems to have lost its power (Ps 77:11), the devout person takes refuge in this confession and "remembers" the former

122

works of Yahweh (Ps 77:12). Here, in Yahweh himself, who has made himself known in his deeds of bygone days, this faith believes it can find the true and authentic continuity on which it can rely.

Thus it is advisable to turn our attention first to this central focus, where alone we find the inner continuity acknowledged by the faith of Israel itself. But a second point must be added at once. This faith knows that Yahweh was not the God of Israel from the beginning of the world. In the account of how the world began, Israel does not yet appear in the great table of nations displayed in Genesis 10. Not until Genesis 12, with the beginning of the story of Abraham, and in the "fathers" descended from him, do we begin to hear distant echoes of the promise of the history of Israel. According to Gen 32:29 (35:10), the name "Israel" is given first to the patriarch Jacob. With the beginning of the book of Exodus we encounter Israel as a people.

This striking phenomenon goes hand in hand with another. As early as Gen 2:4b, that is, in the context of the story of how the world began, the earliest source stratum, J, speaks quite artlessly of Yahweh as creator of the world. But the two other narrative strands, E and P, on the other hand, know that the name "Yahweh" was first revealed to Moses, when he was commissioned to lead Israel out of Egypt. This obviously preserves the correct recollection that there can be no talk of the Yahweh of the Old Testament until he reveals himself as the God of Israel and accomplishes the deliverance of Israel from Egypt.

From this perspective, too, it is advisable to take as our point of departure that focal point where the faith of the Old Testament specifically confesses the God of Israel under the name of Yahweh. It will be clearly evident that this "focal point" does not present an "image" of God to be understood statically. The God who is invoked by the name "Yahweh" repeatedly demonstrates his freedom by dashing to pieces all the "images" in which humanity would confine him. This takes place not only in Exod 3:14, in the account of how the divine name is revealed to Moses, but to an equal degree in the great prophets, or, in the realm of wisdom, in Ecclesiastes and Job.

Zimmerli, Walther. "Alttestamentliche Traditionsgeschichte und Theologie." In *Probleme biblischer Theologie* (Festschrift Gerhard von Rad), pp. 632–647. Edited by Hans Walter Wolff. Munich: Kaiser, 1971. Reprinted in his *Studien zur alttestamentlichen Theologie und Prophetie*, pp. 9–26. Theologische Bücherei, vol. 51. Munich: Kaiser, 1974.

Smend, Rudolf. *Die Mitte des Alten Testaments.* Theologische Studien, vol. 101. Zurich: EVZ, 1970.

Hasel, G. F. "The Problem of the Center in the Old Testament Theology Debate." *Zeitschrift für die Alttestamentliche Wissenschaft* 86 (1974): 65–82.

Zimmerli, Walther. "Zum Problem der 'Mitte des Alten Testaments.'" *Evangelische Theologie* 35 (1975): 97–118.

Fundamentals

[[17]] *"I am Yahweh, your God, who brought you out of the land of Egypt, the house of servitude. You shall have no other gods beside me." (Exod 20:2–3; Deut 5:6–7)*

At the beginning of the great revelation to Israel at Sinai, the mountain of God, stands the proclamation of the Decalogue, introduced with full solemnity by the words quoted above. The God who here appears in the storm makes himself known through his name, recalling at the same time his act of delivering Israel from servitude. On the basis of this act his people may and shall know him.

The recollection of this deliverance and the subsequent journey to Canaan under the guidance of God, which re-echoes in later summaries and creed-like statements, constituted the nucleus of what is today the monstrously expanded first portion of the canon, the Pentateuch. It is therefore advisable in the fundamental exposition of this introductory section to take as our point of departure Yahweh (§1), the God of Israel since Egypt (§2). We shall then turn our attention to the discussion of the God of the fathers (§3), which precedes this nucleus, and of the creator of the world (§4), proclaimed in the primal history. We shall conclude by treating the theologoumena of election (§5) and covenant (§6), which describe in more detail the relationship between Yahweh and Israel. [[Only sections 1 and 2 are reprinted here.]]

The Revealed Name

The faith of the Old Testament knows its God by the name of Yahweh. This pronunciation of the tetragrammaton (יהוה), which is no longer recorded in the masoretic vocalization, can be shown to be highly probable on the basis of evidence from the church fathers.

The passages that deliberately avoid speaking of Yahweh by name can as a rule be understood on the basis of specific considerations. E and P do not speak of Yahweh before the time of Moses because of a specific view of the history of revelation, which will be discussed below. The elimination of the name of Yahweh from the so-called Elohistic psalter (Psalms 42–83) is the result of editorial revision probably based on a dread of pronouncing the holy name of [[18]] God. In Judaism, this tendency later resulted in a total avoidance of pronouncing the tetragrammaton. This tendency appears also to have been at work in the book of Esther. In the book of Job, the name of Yahweh is avoided in the discourses of chapters 3–37 because the discussion is between non-Israelites; it is replaced by the more general terms אלוה *ĕlôah* or שׁדּי *šaddai* The introductions to the speeches of God and the framework narrative in chapters 1–2 and 42 use the name of Yahweh without hesitation. Elsewhere, too, as in the Joseph story, the name of Yahweh is not placed in the mouth of non-Israelites. In Ecclesiastes, the name is probably avoided because the wise man in question prefers to distance himself from God (see [[Zimmerli 1978:]] pp. 161–163). In the book of Daniel, too, the final chapters show clearly that the Lord referred to as "God of Heaven" or "the Most High God" or simply as "God" is none other than he who is called by the name of Yahweh. The prayer in Daniel 9 uses the name "Yahweh" quite naturally.

For the audience of the Old Testament, a "name" is more than a randomly selected label. Those who are named are vulnerable; they can be invoked by means of their name. Two questions arise in this context:

1. How does the faith of the Old Testament come by its knowledge of the name of its God? The Old Testament can be heard to give various answers:

a) J uses the name "Yahweh" without hesitation even in the primal history and the patriarchal narratives.

In the context of J, the statement in Gen 4:26 stands out: in the days of Enosh, who represents the third human generation, people began to call on the name of Yahweh. Since the name "Enosh," like "Adam," can simply mean "man," it is possible there was an earlier version according to which Yahweh was called upon in the generation of the very first man. According to Horst, the present text can be understood on the basis of the distinction common in comparative religion between the high god present from the beginning (i.e., the creator) and the god that people call upon in the cult of the historical present.[1] The special contribution of the Old Testament would then be the statement that the creator and the god called upon in worship are the same Yahweh.

b) E and P take a different approach. Each in its own way represents a specific view of how the name of Yahweh was revealed. According to both, this takes place in the time of Moses, the initial period of Israel's history as already mentioned. According to E, it is at the mountain of God that Moses learns to invoke God by name; in the earlier narratives the general term אלהים *ĕlōhîm*, "God," was used, which could also be applied to non-Israelite deities. When Moses is commanded to lead his enslaved people out of Egypt, he asks the name of the God under whom this is to happen; the name of Yahweh is communicated to him in a veiled way that will be considered in more detail below (Exod 3:1, 4b, 6, 9–15).

c) P, whose peculiar organization of God's history with Israel will be discussed in more detail later (see [[Zimmerli 1978:]], pp. 55–57), exhibits a process by which the name of God is revealed in three stages. Like E, P uses the general term אלהים *ĕlōhîm* at the outset when referring to the acts of God in the primordial era. According to Gen 17:1, however, God reveals himself to Abraham, the earliest of the patriarchs of Israel, under the name אל שדי *ēl* [[19]] *šaddai* (see [[Zimmerli 1978:]], p. 41). Then, according to Exod 6:2ff., he encounters Moses with equal spontaneity, introducing himself of his own accord under his name Yahweh, while referring explicitly to Genesis 17: "I am Yahweh. To Abraham, Isaac, and Jacob I appeared under the name אל שדי *ēl šaddai*, but in my name Yahweh I was not made known to them." This passage expresses most emphatically the spontaneity and novelty of the revelation of the name Yahweh. The name by which Israel may call upon its God does not simply lie ready to hand for people to use. Neither, as in E, is it

---

1. Friedrich Horst, "Die Notiz vom Anfang des Jahwekultes in Gen. 4:26," in *Libertas Christiana* (Friedrich Delekat Festschrift; ed. Walter Matthias; Munich: Kaiser, 1957) 68–74.

given in response to a human question; it is the free gift of the God who sends his people their deliverer, thereby forging a bond between himself and them (Exod 6:7).

2. Does the name of Yahweh, which Israel calls upon, reveal something of the nature of this God?

To answer this question, we must distinguish two directions of inquiry. (a) Quite apart from the statements made by the Old Testament texts themselves, we can inquire whether philological investigation can give us any information about the original meaning of the name "Yahweh." But of course an answer in these terms need by no means have any relevance for the faith of the Old Testament. The name might have taken shape in a totally different context. This does not hold true in the same way, however, if (b) we ask whether the Old Testament context itself says anything about the meaning of the name. With such a statement, whatever its original philological accuracy may be, we are in any case dealing with an actual statement of the Old Testament that is significant for an Old Testament theology.

a) There is no lack of suggestions about what the name "Yahweh" originally meant.

Philological investigation must first deal with the question of whether we should take as our point of departure the long form "Yahweh," an abbreviated form "Yahu" as found in many names (ישעיהו *yᵉšaʿyāhû*; ירמיהו *yirmᵉyāhû*; יהויקים *yᵉhôyāqîm*, etc.), or the monosyllabic form "Yah," as found, for instance, in the acclamation "Hallelujah" (הללו יה *halᵉlû yâ*). Driver claimed that he could interpret the form "Yah" as a shout of ecstatic excitement, which then turned into a divine name and, in association with the deliverance from Egypt, became the long form with the meaning "he who is" or "he who calls into being." Eerdmans derives the name from a disyllabic form, in which he hears what was originally an onomatopoetic imitation of thunder. There are good reasons to consider the long form original; it probably represents an imperfect form of a verb הוה *hwh*. But is this root related to the Arabic verb meaning "blow," which would suggest the name of a storm god, or to the verb meaning "fall," which would suggest a god of lightning and hail? Or should we take הוה *hwh* as equivalent to היה *hyh* and interpret it as "he is" or "he shows himself efficacious" or "he calls into being"? And are we then to follow Cross in thinking of an abbreviated form of the more complete יהוה צבאות *yahweh sᵉbāʾôt*, "he who calls the (heavenly) hosts into being" (see [[Zimmerli 1978:]], p. 75)?[2] It is unlikely that we are dealing with a noun form having the meaning "being."

b) We come next to the actual statements of the Old Testament itself. When Moses asks the name of the God who sends him to Israel, he is given, [[20]] according to Exod 3:14, the answer: אהיה אשר אהיה *ehyeh ăšer ehyeh* ("I am who I am . . . and so you shall say to the Israelites, 'I am [אהיה *ehyeh*] has sent me to you'"). Here the name "Yahweh" is unequivocally interpreted on the basis of the verb היה *hyh* (= הוה *hwh*).

---

2. Frank M. Cross, "Yahweh and the God of the Patriarchs," *Harvard Theological Review* 55 (1962) 225–59. [[Zimmerli does not give the bibliographic data for the references to Driver and Eerdmans in this paragraph.]]

This passage, therefore, has provided the basis for most attempts to interpret the name in a way consonant with the faith of the Old Testament. The Septuagint led the way with its translation *egṓ eimi ho ṓn,* "I am the one who is," transforming the verbal expression into a nominal participle and, following Greek example, finding an ontological concept of being in Exod 3:14. It was probably sensed, however, how inappropriate this concept was within the framework of Old Testament thought. Scholars have therefore gone on to ask whether היה *hyh* might not be better taken to mean "be efficacious" (Ratschow), "be there, be present" (Vriezen), "be with someone" (Preuss).[3]

But the name "Yahweh" is here not meant to be understood on the basis of the isolated verb היה *hyh*, but rather on the basis of the figure of speech "I am who I am." This form may be compared to the lordly statement of Exod 33:19: "To whom I am gracious I am gracious, and to whom I show mercy I show mercy." In this figure of speech resounds the sovereign freedom of Yahweh, who, even at the moment he reveals himself in his name, refuses simply to put himself at the disposal of humanity or to allow humanity to comprehend him. We must also take into account God's refusal to impart his name to Jacob in Gen 32:30: "Why do you ask about my name?" According to the statement of Exod 3:14, at the very point where Yahweh reveals his true name so that people can call him by it, he remains free, and can be properly understood only in the freedom with which he introduces himself.

This knowledge, which also lies behind God's free revelation of his name in Exod 6:2 (P), coming not in response to any human question, was given further expression in certain characteristic Priestly turns of phrase. In the laws of the Holiness Code in Leviticus 18ff., the legislation is underlined by copious use of the appended phrase "I am Yahweh" or "I am Yahweh, your God." Here, in the context of proclamation of the law, this formulaic phrase of self-introduction maintains the majesty of him who issues the law, who encounters people as their Lord. It is possible to ask, even if a definitive answer cannot be given, whether there were occasions in the liturgical life of Israel when this free self-introduction of Yahweh in his name was publicly spoken (by the priests?). The preamble to the Decalogue with its אנכי יהוה אלהיך *ānōkî yahweh ĕlōhêkā* [['I am Yahweh your God']] may also support this suggestion.

In a different way this element centered into the prophetic formulation of the so-called "proof-saying" (*Erweiswort*), found repeatedly in the book of Ezekiel but apparently originating in earlier pre-literary prophecy and its messages from God in the context of the Yahweh war (1 Kgs 20:13, 28). Here a statement of what Yahweh will do with or for his people (expanded [[21]] by the addition of a motivation or stated without any motivation at all) can be concluded with the formula: "And you [he, they] will know that I am Yahweh." This formula declares the announced action of Yahweh to be the place where people will know—and acknowledge—Yahweh as he introduces himself.

3. Carl H. Ratschow, *Werden und Wirken* (Beiheft zur Zeitschrift für Alttestamentliche Wissenschaft 70; Berlin: Töpelmann, 1941); Theodorus C. Vriezen, [[*An Outline of Old Testament Theology* (trans. S. Neuijcn; Oxford: Blackwell/Boston: Branford, 1958) 235–36]]; Horst D. Preuss, " . . . ich will mit dir sein!" *ZAW* 80 (1968) 139–73.

Yahweh declares himself in what he does. This rhetorical form is also found in Joel and the late exilic Deutero-Isaiah (see Isa 49:22-26). See also [[Zimmerli 1978:]] pp. 207, 229.

This freedom of Yahweh means he is never simply an "object," even in his name which he graciously reveals—the third commandment of the Decalogue seeks to protect the freedom implicit in Yahweh's name in a very specific way against "religious" abuse. And this freedom of Yahweh must be taken account of in all other statements about the faith of the Old Testament. In the only passage where the Old Testament itself attempts to provide an explanation of the name "Yahweh," it refuses to "explain" the name in a way that would confine it within the cage of a definition. It seeks to express the fact that we can speak of Yahweh only in attentive acknowledgment of the way he demonstrates his nature (in his acts and his commandments).

. . . .

Yahweh, God of Israel since Egypt

In Hos 13:4, we hear the words: "I, Yahweh, am your God since the land of Egypt. You do not know any god except for me, or any savior except [[22]] for me." This statement corresponds in content with the beginning of the Decalogue (Exod 20:2-3); like the latter passage, it says two things. First, where Yahweh presents himself to the faith of the Old Testament, he does so as the God of Israel, who will not tolerate any other god. And even more clearly than the beginning of the Decalogue it underlines the fact that this "God of Israel" is a relationship that has existed from the beginning of time, in the sense, for instance, that the Babylonian god Shamash was the sun god by definition. Yahweh is the God of Israel by reason of certain historical events associated with the name of Egypt (to which the preamble to the Decalogue adds: "the house of servitude").

This phrase points to the events recorded in the book of Exodus, in which the people of Israel first makes its appearance. Their forebears, as Exod 1:11 maintains with historical accuracy, were compelled to perform forced labor for the building of the provision cities Pithom and Ramses during the reign of Ramses II (1290-1224 B.C.). Moses, who bears an Egyptian name, led them forth at the command of Yahweh. At the Sea of Reeds they escaped miraculously from the pursuing Egyptians, whose king had refused to let them go. This event is recorded in the earliest hymn preserved in the Old Testament, the Song of Miriam. "Sing to Yahweh, for highly exalted is he; horse and rider he cast into the sea" (Exod 15:21). What Israel experienced was no piece of chance good fortune such as might be recounted dispassionately. In this experience Israel recognized and confessed Yahweh, who refuses to be worshiped alongside others. The glorification of this initial experience of the exodus also appears in the observation that there is no other event in the entire history of Israel so surrounded by a plethora of miraculous interventions on the part of Yahweh as the event of the deliverance from Egypt. Again and again the description of the exodus makes mention of the "signs and wonders" performed by Yahweh for his people, "with mighty hand and outstretched arm." Then the road leads out into the desert, toward the land that is to be given to Israel. The Old Testament returns again and again to creed-like mentions (von Rad)[4] of this event, in detailed summaries of Yahweh's history with Israel as well as in succinct formulas like the preamble to the Decalogue. When the farmer brings his offering to the sanctuary, he speaks in his prescribed prayer of what Yahweh did for his fathers (Deut 26:5-10). When a father tries to make the commandments meaningful to his son, he tells of this event (Deut 6:20ff.). According to Joshua 24, it was spoken of when Israel assembled at Shechem. The poetry of the cult recounts the exodus immediately after speaking of Yahweh's acts at creation (Psalm 136). Commandments in the Holiness Code can be underlined by reference to it (Lev 22:32-33; 25:55). Even the prophet Ezekiel, narrating the story of Israel's sins, with the two kingdoms personified in two girls with bedouin [[23]] names, says in Ezekiel 23 that they come from Egypt, where they became Yahweh's own. Cf. also Ezekiel 20; Isa 51:9-10).

Alongside such passages, there are a few that state that Yahweh "found Israel in the desert" (Deut 32:10; Hos 9:10; cf. Bach).[5] This can hardly refer to a different story of Israel's origins; these passages must be interpreted in the same light. In Ezekiel 16, the motif of the foundling has been incorporated into the story of Jerusalem's beginnings, a story organized very differently.

. . . .

We must now consider the significance of this fundamental confessional statement for the faith attested by the Old Testament.

1. In the first place, it is quite clear that the Old Testament, however much it thinks of Yahweh as majestic and free, knows this God from the very outset as the God who wants to involve himself with Israel. In the Old Testament we never come across any attempt to inquire into the nature of Yahweh *per se*. This could be observed even in the only passage that reflected on the significance of the name "Yahweh." How the God of Israel acts with respect to his people, with respect to the individual Israelite, and later, as the horizon of religious thought expands in head-on encounter with other forms of religious belief, with respect to all of creation and the nations dominates the Old Testament statements. [[24]]

2. At the beginning of the exodus story, on which the faith of the Old Testament never ceases to reflect, stands the great deliverance from the house of servitude. It is not really accurate to turn this event into an "exodus principle,"

---

4. Gerhard von Rad, *Das formgeschichtliche Problem des Hexateuch* (Beiträge zur Wissenschaft vom Alten und Neuen Testament 4/26; Stuttgart: Kohlhammer, 1938); repr. in his *Gesammelte Studien zum Alten Testament* (Theologische Bücherei 8; Munich: Kaiser, 1958) 9–86; English translation: "The Form-Critical Problem of the Hexateuch," in *The Problem of the Hexateuch and Other Essays* (trans. E. W. T. Dicken; New York: McGraw-Hill, 1966) 1–78.

5. Robert Bach, *Die Erwählung Israels in der Wüste* (Ph.D. diss., Bonn, 1951).

which in turn produces a "principle of hope" (Bloch).[6] What is really central is not the fact of the "exodus," which would lead to new forms of "going out" into the future, but the encounter with the God who has pity on those who are enslaved. We often hear the Old Testament speak of the God who hears the crying of the oppressed and sends them their deliverer; this image becomes a category by which subsequent experiences in the history of Israel can be understood (the judges, Saul, David). Therefore even Ezekiel and above all Deutero-Isaiah can paint deliverance from the terrible distress of the exile in the glowing colors of a new exodus, in which the events of the first exodus out of Egypt return antitypically. In Trito-Isaiah we can observe how the images of exodus and roads in the desert begin to form part of the stock language of religious discourse (see [[Zimmerli 1978:]] p. 226).

3. Having seen that in the "exodus" we are dealing with an act of mercy on the part of the God who has pity on his people and delivers them, we must go on at once to say that the help Israel experiences sets it on a course on which God continues to be with it. The theme of "guidance in the desert" (Noth)[7] is intimately associated with the theme of "exodus." From the very beginning, Yahweh was known to Israel as the "shepherd of Israel," who accompanies it. Victor Maag has justifiably placed great emphasis on this heritage of Israel from its nomadic past.[8] But a sociological reference to "the nomadic heritage" will not in itself suffice for a theological understanding. We must go on to state that when Israel proclaims "Yahweh, your God since Egypt," as an element of its faith, it is also keeping alive the knowledge of the God who remains with Israel on its journey. Neither is this knowledge abrogated by all the later theologoumena about the presence of Yahweh in specific places (see [[Zimmerli 1978:]] §9). This knowledge makes it possible for Israel not to lose its God in all its subsequent "departures," when it is snatched out of the "rest" to which God brings it in the land (Deut 12:9–10), and to survive with the guidance of the "shepherd of Israel." Israel remains preeminently a people of hope.

4. In the confession of "Yahweh, the God of Israel since Egypt," Israel's faith receives an intimate association with a historical event. An initial historical deliverance, experienced by those escaping from Egypt, resounds in the earliest extant hymn of Israel. It has recently been accurately pointed out

6. Ernst Bloch, *Das Prinzip Hoffnung* (Gesamatausgabe 5; Frankfurt: Suhrkamp, 1959). For a discussion of Bloch's views, see Walther Zimmerli, *Der Mensch und seine Hoffnung im Alten Testament* (Kleine Vandenhoeck-Reihe 272S; Göttingen: Vandenhoeck & Ruprecht, 1968) 163–78; English translation: *Man and His Hope in the Old Testament* (Studies in Biblical Theology 2/20; Naperville, Illinois: Allenson, 1971) 151–65. See also Hans-Joachim Kraus, "Das Thema 'Exodus,'" *Evangelische Theologie* 31 (1971) 608–23.

7. Martin Noth, *Überlieferungsgeschichte des Pentateuch* (Stuttgart: Kohlhammer, 1948); English translation: *History of Pentateuchal Traditions* (trans. B. W. Anderson; Englewood Cliffs, New Jersey: Prentice-Hall, 1971).

8. Victor Maag, "Der Hirt Israels," *Schweizer Theologische Umschau* 28 (1958) 2–28; idem, "Das Gottesverständnis des Alten Testaments," *Nederlands Theologisch Tijdschrift* 21 (1966/67) 161–207.

(Albrektson)[9] that it is quite inappropriate to set up a contrast between Israel, with its sense of history, and the nature religions of the surrounding world, without any historical ties. The world of Assyria and Babylonia is also familiar with the intervention of the gods in the course of history and dependence on divine aid in historical crises. But it remains undeniable that Israel's basing [[25]] of its faith on that early act of deliverance, in which it knew that a single Lord was at work, not a multiplicity of powers, established a particularly intimate relationship between its faith and its historical experiences.

Having said this, we must still avoid the mistaken assumption that for Israel history as such became the revelatory word of Yahweh. Such an understanding of history as a phenomenon in its own right, to be taken as an independent quantity in God's revelation, is alien to the Old Testament. By the same token, an isolated fact of history is not as such simply a proclamation of Yahweh. Vast stretches of Israel's historical experience that come to light in the Old Testament remain silent, having nothing new to say. But then it can happen that messengers speaking for Yahweh appear unexpectedly in the context of exciting events, proclaiming the historical events to be Yahweh's call to decision. Here we recognize very clearly that "history" by no means simply proclaims Yahweh in its course of events; in the very midst of the historical disaster that is accompanied by the message of the prophets, it is especially urgent that Yahweh's word be heard. See [[Zimmerli 1978:]] §20 and §21.

Thus we must also remember in retrospect that the "deliverance from Egypt" was also accompanied by Yahweh's word. The preponderance of evidence still supports the assumption that Moses, the man with the Egyptian name, did in fact lead Israel out of Egypt "in the name of Yahweh" and thus, however we may go on to define the "office" of Moses more precisely, determined the subsequent "representation" (Noth)[10] of the acts of Yahweh in Israel.

5. In this event Yahweh declared himself for the faith of Israel. In what took place he made himself known as the deliverer of that company, which then handed on its confession to all "Israel" living at a later date in Canaan as the twelve tribes. Starting with this confession, he is the "God of Israel." Not because Israel chose him voluntarily or because he has a "primary relationship" with Israel, but simply because by a free act he delivered those who dwelt in the house of servitude in Egypt—therefore he is their God. What the self-introduction formula sought to express in its own way is defined in terms of this historical self-statement of Yahweh and given concrete meaning. Whatever those who dwelt in Egypt may previously have known of Yahweh, under this new event his name was either forgotten or subsequently incorporated

9. Bertil Albrektson, *History and the Gods* (Coniectanea Biblica, Old Testament series 1; Lund: Gleerup, 1967).

10. Martin Noth, "Die Vergegenwärtigung des Alten Testaments in der Verkündigung," *Evangelische Theologie* 12 (1952/53) 6–17; repr. in his *Gesammelte Studien zum Alten Testament* (Theologische Bücherei 39; Munich: Kaiser, 1969), 2:86–98.

into this "initial knowledge": he who is invoked in the name "Yahweh" made himself known as the God of those brought up out of the house of servitude in Egypt and became the "God of Israel" through an expansion of the circle of those confessing him in the land of Canaan. Only when this self-statement of Yahweh is recognized is the phrase "Yahweh, God of Israel since Egypt" properly understood.

6. This makes a final point clear. The event that bears significance for the beginning of "Israel's" faith in Yahweh has from the outset a political ‖26‖ dimension. The beginning does not consist in the illumination of a single individual who then assembles other individuals around him, like Buddha, but in the deliverance experienced by a cohesive group. This political dimension, relating to a people defined in secular terms, will subsequently remain a hallmark of Yahwism. The individual is not forgotten and individual responsibility is increasingly stressed as time goes on, but it remains clear even in the late statements of the book of Daniel that individuals are not isolated from the people of Yahweh as a whole, nor can they take refuge in a special relationship with their God such as might remove them from the concrete events of the "secular" world. On the special problems posed by "wisdom," see [[Zimmerli 1978:]] §18.

Synopsis of Zimmerli's *Old Testament Theology in Outline* (1978)

Walther Zimmerli
on Life before God

Excerpted with permission from Walther Zimmerli, *Old Testament Theology in Outline* (Atlanta: John Knox, 1978), pp. 141–47. The footnotes have been reconstructed from the bibliography on pp. 147–48.

[[141]] It is reasonable to ask whether a section on "life before God" belongs in an Old Testament theology. Especially in a theology that takes as its point of departure the principle that the Old Testament faith derives from Yahweh's "statement" about himself in history. But our discussion has shown how the faith of the Old Testament knows its God not in an absolute transcendence but rather in his approach to Israel and the world, and how the Old Testament, in what it has to say about God, thinks of itself as a book of God's words addressed to people. And it is also true that in the "response" God expects from those he addresses God himself can be recognized as in a mirror.

This "response" is found in people's obedience to the commandments of God as formulated in his law. But it is also found when Israel submits to the gracious governance of its God, even when no specific commandments are formulated (§16). Yahweh's nature is also recognizable in those situations when people turn to him in thanksgiving or petition (§17). Even in situations in which individuals, sensible of their relationship to the creator, order their daily course according to reasonable decisions, making thankful and obedient use of the gifts given them by Yahweh, their creator, it is possible to recognize the God who guides their lives (§18). [[Only section 16 is reprinted here.]]

The Response of Obedience

As Parts II and III have made clear, Yahweh's love for his people has two aspects, which are inseparable from each other. It expresses itself in Yahweh's gracious guidance, beginning with his deliverance of Israel out of the house of bondage in Egypt, and subsequently in all his gifts bestowed on Israel and the world. But the gift always implies a requirement. This imperative aspect takes concrete form in the words of Yahweh's commandments, which expect very specific actions in obedience to them.

The response of obedience itself has two aspects. In the first place, it consists of obedience to the concrete requirements of the law as elaborated in Part III.

[[142]] In this context, an important role is played by "hearing" (שמע *šmʿ*, which can also mean "obey"), "observing" (שמר *šmr* in the sense of "keep, follow"), and "doing" (עשה *ʿśh*; cf. the stereotyped formulas of the Sinai episode [Exod 19:8; 24:3; and 24:7 in conjunction with שמע *šmʿ*]). They refer to a clearly delineated act of obedience.

133

Likewise, the response of faith consists of the acceptance and proper stewardship of the gifts given by Yahweh, which Israel receives within the framework of having its history guided and governed by its God. It is not always clear in any particular case at what point precisely the gift to be received with pure hands turns into the commandment that requires active obedience. The discussion to follow will illustrate this point clearly with reference to certain specific passages.

1. Yahweh, who comes to his people, wishes to have his nature reflected in theirs. This point is made especially clear in the statement that introduces the core of the legal material in the Holiness Code: "You shall be holy, because I, Yahweh your God, am holy (קדוש *qādôš*)" (Lev 19:2). Here the closeness between Yahweh's gift and his commandment is unmistakable.

. . . .

2. The projection of Yahweh's divine nature upon the community living before God, and at the same time the unmistakable tension between gift and commandment, indicative and imperative, can be seen even more clearly in the term צדקה (צדק) *ṣᵉdāqâ (ṣedeq)*, translated very imperfectly as "righteousness." This circumstance conceals the fundamental theological problem of "divine and human righteousness."

Recent studies have shown clearly the "righteousness" predicated of Yahweh must not be confused with the blindfolded "justice" that strictly apportions to every person the reward or punishment he or she deserves according to an objective norm that stands above all parties. When the Old Testament speaks of "Yahweh's righteousness," it means rather the social bond existing between him and his people and Yahweh's actions based on this bond. The plural form צדקות יהוה *ṣidqôt yahweh*, found as early as the Song of Deborah (Judg 5:11; also 1 Sam 12:7 and Mic 6:5), is best rendered "saving acts." The singular forms צדקה *ṣᵉdāqâ* and צדק *ṣedeq* are often used in the Psalms and in Deutero-and Trito-Isaiah, which come from the milieu of the Psalms, to refer to Yahweh's beneficent order, which can be recognized even in the realm of [[143]] nature. According to Jepsen, the masculine form צדק *ṣedeq* means "rightness," "order," while the feminine form צדקה *ṣᵉdāqâ* means the "conduct that aims at right order."[1] Schmid prefers to understand the term in its various ramifications on the basis of its Canaanite background, where it expresses the harmony of the world in all its different realms.[2]

Now it turns out that the term "righteousness," which characterizes the sphere of divine justice, understood in Israel with specific reference to Yahweh, becomes likewise the central term for human justice. The extent to which Israel sees this human justice as a reflection of Yahweh's justice is illustrated especially well in the twin acrostic Psalms 111/112. The former extols the glorious acts of Yahweh; the latter, the actions of the person who fears God. In verse 3b, each of them uses precisely the same words to refer to both God and the person before God: "His 'righteousness' is forever."

1. Alfred Jepsen, "צדק und צדקה im Alten Testament," in *Gottes Wort und Gottes Land* (Hans-Wilhelm Hertzberg Festschrift; ed. Henning Graf Reventlow; Göttingen: Vandenhoeck & Ruprecht, 1965) 78–89.
2. Hans H. Schmid, *Gerechtigkeit als Weltordnung* (Beiträge zur historischen Theologie 40; Tübingen: Mohr, 1968).

If we go on to ask for a more detailed description of human righteousness, the fact cannot be overlooked that it is associated with keeping the commandments. Ezek 18:5ff., for example, describes righteous persons in terms of their conduct with respect to a series of commandments: "Consider the man who is righteous and does what is just and right. He never feasts at mountain-shrines, never lifts his eyes to the idols of Israel, never dishonors another man's wife. . . ." According to this passage, it is individuals' right actions, according to the norm of the law, that constitute their "righteousness."

But the list culminates surprisingly in the repeated formula: "Such a man is righteous; he shall live." The first half of this statement is composed formally in the style of a priestly "declaration," like those found above all in the legislation governing leprosy in Leviticus 13 (Rendtorff).[3] Here it pronounces a general verdict upon the man. Von Rad has pointed out that more is involved here than an analytic statement.[4] The declaration must be seen in the context of the priestly entrance liturgies, which pronounce the general divine verdict of "righteousness" upon the pilgrim, who has been examined on some of the marks of the righteous person. Thus we see in Ps 24:4–5 how the one "who has clean hands and a pure heart, who has not set his mind on falsehood, and has not committed perjury" is granted entrance to the Temple; it is further said of him: "He shall receive a blessing from Yahweh, and righteousness from God his savior." Here "righteousness" is clearly something received at the sanctuary, not simply achieved by the individual. Gen 15:6 states that Abraham believed in God and "it was counted as righteousness"; von Rad has shown elsewhere that this statement is connected with "righteousness" accorded by declaration.[5] We see especially clearly in Job 33:26 how God restores "righteousness" to the sinner who has been warned by his illnesses and then prays to God.

In sum, all talk of human "righteousness," like that heard at the sanctuary, is like the talk of Israel's "holiness": there is obvious tension between what the law given by Yahweh seriously requires on the one hand, and on the other the concomitant superabundance that is an unearned gift. Neither aspect can simply be eliminated in favor of the other. The law that in the great legal corpora of Deuteronomy and the Holiness Code culminates in the alternatives of salvation and perdition, that confronts people with a promise and a threat, is not to be abrogated. But Israel is also familiar with the will of Yahweh to exercise a beneficent "righteousness" over Israel, only rarely (as in Ps 7:12) associated with his wrath: "God is a 'righteous' judge, and a God who is daily angered." Israel, living before God, knows that it is called to the "righteousness" that is indispensable for real "life." Therefore the theme of "righteousness" also dominates the prayers of the Psalms. At the beginning of the psalter there is placed, like a call to decision, the twofold image of the "righteous" person and

---

3. Rolf Rendtorff, *Die Gesetze in der Priesterschrift* (Forschungen zur Religion und Literatur des Alten und Neuen Testaments 62; Göttingen: Vandenhoeck & Ruprecht, 1954).

4. Gerhard von Rad, " 'Gerechtigkeit' und 'Leben' in der Kultsprache der Psalmen," in *Festschrift Alfred Bertholet zum 80. Geburtstag* (ed. Walter Baumgartner; Tübingen: Mohr, 1950) 418–37; repr. in his *Gesammelte Studien zum Alten Testament* (Theologische Bücherei 8; Munich: Kaiser, 1958) 225–47.

5. Gerhard von Rad, "Die Anrechnung des Glaubens zur Gerechtigkeit," *Theologische Literaturzeitung* 76 (1951) 129–32; repr. in his *Gesammelte Studien zum Alten Testament* (Theologische Bücherei 8; Munich: Kaiser, 1958) 130–35.

the "wicked," who is blown away like chaff at the judgment (Psalm 1), so that the worshiper will always keep in mind [[144]] that the prayer of the devout can never evade the question of being in the right before Yahweh.

3. Deuteronomy grounds Yahweh's election of the patriarchs on a simple reference to Yahweh's love; see [[Zimmerli 1978:]] p. 45. The images of marriage and childhood, which involve the notion of divine love, are also used to describe the relationship of Yahweh to Israel. "When Israel was a boy, I loved him; I called my son out of Egypt" (Hos 11:1). Besides the verb אהב *'hb*, "love," used in this passage, the relevant terminology includes the noun חסד *ḥesed*, which refers to the "grace" appropriate in the context of a specific social bond, and רחמים *raḥămîm*, which means natural love like that of a mother for her child. One of Yahweh's solemn adjectival predicates is רחום וחנון *raḥûm weḥannûn* (Exod 34:6 and elsewhere).

Once again it is appropriate to cite the conclusion of the twin Psalms 111/112, where verse 4b applies the same adjectival predicate to Yahweh and to the righteous person. Here the notion is probably of compassion toward one's neighbor; elsewhere, most clearly once again in the parenetic sections of Deuteronomy, the emphasis is on human love for God. The full exposition of this theme in Deut 6:5 admonishes listeners to love Yahweh with all their "heart and soul and strength." But when this loving is immediately associated with keeping the commandments, with serving Yahweh and going by his ways (Deut 10:12; 11:22; cf. also the Decalogues: Exod 20:6; Deut 5:10), we can see how human love for God cannot simply be equated with God's love for Israel. Israel's reply is a response to Yahweh's initiative. The love for Yahweh referred to here is never simply free intrusion into the presence of God, but an approach to God along the road he has cleared. We will speak later about the "fear of God" that is associated with love for him.

Besides Deuteronomy, it is primarily several of the Psalms that speak of people's love for God (18:2 רחם *rḥm*; 116:1 אהב *'hb*[?]; 31:24 אהב *'hb*). That it is also possible to speak of loving the commandments of Yahweh (119:47) shows once more how love follows the summons of Yahweh along the paths which he maps out. Deut 30:6 transcends everything else that is said, speaking of this love in terms reminiscent of the New Testament talk of the charisma of love in 1 Corinthians 13 and calling it a consequence of a circumcision of the heart performed by God himself. Thus the Old Testament already suggests, if not especially often, at least in crucial passages, that people must respond to Yahweh's love with their own love.

4. Amos 3:2 used the verb "know" to describe Yahweh's election of Israel. Jeremiah, too, according to 1:5 realizes that Yahweh "knew" him and thus made him his prophetic instrument. Now if knowledge of Yahweh also plays a significant role in the life of people before God, it must be stressed even more than in the case of "love" for God that the human response of [[145]] knowledge does not share in the creative power of the Lord who chooses his people, but can only return to Yahweh along the road that he himself has pioneered.

. . . .

5. In Deuteronomy the requirement to love Yahweh was linked with the requirement to fear him. Far beyond the limits of Deuteronomy, this fear of Yahweh plays an important role in E (Wolff),[6] in circles antedating the writing prophets, in a series of Psalms, and above all in wisdom literature, where it practically becomes the supreme requirement. It is strikingly absent in P and Ezekiel. The juxtaposition of these two concepts may at first seem surprising. If love appears to bring people into the presence of Yahweh, "fear" appears to remove them from this presence.

Now it is doubtless true that the "fear of Yahweh" repeatedly recalls the distance that separates creatures from their creator and Lord. In all periods of its history, Israel has had a sense of awe before the Lord, who transcends all Israel's power to love and understand, and whose encounter [[146]] from time to time produces uncontrollable terror (Volz).[7] Israel encountered the mysterious side of God in its worship, which never eliminated the element of "holiness." Even when licensed into the very presence of Yahweh, people have felt something of terror (Gen 28:17; Isa 6:5; Amos 3:8). In its wisdom musings (Ecclesiastes) and its attempts to understand the mysteries of human destiny (Job), Israel never evaded the terror evoked by Yahweh's impenetrability.

But it is a striking fact that, in all its talk of the fear of Yahweh, the faith of the Old Testament never was diverted into mere trepidation before God. This is probably in part because in Yahweh Israel knew that it confronted a Lord in whom it encountered not only mystery and arbitrary caprice, but a Lord who had promised to be Israel's God and who, in his law, had shown Israel the way that made life before him possible. Therefore in the Old Testament "fear of God" often becomes synonymous with obedience to the commandments of Yahweh.

. . . .

Yahweh's law summons people into his presence. Obedience to his will promises life. This explains how the talk of fear of God as the proper attitude for people before Yahweh can, quite surprisingly, take on a decided note of confidence. "Fear of God" becomes quite generally a term for the piety that brings people within the orbit of Yahweh's protection: "In the fear of Yahweh there is confidence and trust, even for children he [Yahweh] is a refuge. The fear of Yahweh is a fountain of life, so that one may escape the snares of death" (Prov 14:26–27). Thus one might almost say: whoever fears Yahweh need have no fear, but whoever does not fear Yahweh must have fear. "The wicked are wracked with anxiety all their days, the ruthless man for all the years in store for him," says Eliphaz the Temanite (Job 15:20). How wisdom

6. Hans Walter Wolff, "Erkenntnis Gottes im Alten Testament," *Evangelische Theologie* 15 (1955) 426–31; idem, "Zur Thematik der elohistischen Fragmente im Pentateuch," *Evangelische Theologie* 29 (1969) 59–72; English translation: "The Elohistic Fragments in the Pentateuch," *Interpretation* 26 (1972) 158–73; repr. in *The Vitality, of Old Testament Traditions* (ed. Walter Brueggemann; Atlanta: John Knox, 1975) 67–82.

7. Paul Volz, *Das Dämonische in Jahwe* (Sammlung gemeinverständlicher Vorträge und Schriften 110; Tübingen: Mohr, 1924).

speaks of the fear of Yahweh will have to await detailed discussion in §18 [[not reprinted here]].

6. The term "belief" or "faith" is sometimes used to describe the proper response of people to what Yahweh does. It does not occur frequently, but it is found in a few momentous passages. As in the case of the "fear" of [[147]] Yahweh, we are no longer dealing with an attitude that reflects Yahweh's own attitude. The term refers instead to the way a person who is weak derives stability from someone else, who is strong.

The notion of mere "holding an opinion," which is one of the senses of the English word "believe," is totally absent from the Hebrew האמין *he'ĕmîn*. This word derives from the root אמן *'mn*, "be firm, stable, secure," familiar to everyone from another derivate, "amen," which can be used as a response to emphasize a curse (Deut 27:15–26; Num 5:22), a royal command (1 Kgs 1:36), a wish (Jer 28:6), or even a prayer (Ps 41:14 and elsewhere, concluding a subsidiary collection of Psalms). One theory holds that האמין *he'ĕmîn* should be understood as a declarative hiphil, so that belief represents a responsive "amen" to a promise made by Yahweh. Against this theory, it must be pointed out that the word is usually constructed not with the expected accusative but with the preposition ב *bᵉ*, "in," and sometimes with ל *lᵉ*, "to." According to Wildberger, it is to be understood intransitively; when used with ב *bᵉ* in theological contexts, it means "find security in," "place trust in."[8] Thus the statement in Gen 15:6 (quoted in Romans 4 and Galatians 3) about Abraham, to whom, though childless, God promised descendants like the stars of heaven in number, is to be understood as meaning: "Abraham found security in Yahweh, and Yahweh accounted this as righteousness." This "finding security" in Yahweh makes people "righteous" in the eyes of God. The absolute use of the term, in which Smend claims to find the origin of talk about "faith" in the Old Testament, occurs in Isaiah.[9] In an hour of great danger, Isaiah promises King Ahaz that the plans of the enemy will miscarry, using an elegant pun that employs the root אמן *'mn* twice: "If you do not believe, you will not endure"; or, literally, "If you do not find security [i.e., in Yahweh's promise], you will not be secured [= preserved]" (7:9). And Isa 28:16 refers to Yahweh's establishment of Zion (see [Zimmerli 1978:] pp. 76–77): "He who believes will not waver." Belief or faith means security, repose within God's promise. But because this promise is spoken through men sent by Yahweh, Exod 14:31 can say that the people believed Yahweh and his servant Moses. Exod 4:1, 5; 19:9 speak of Moses alone as the messenger to be believed. 2 Chr 20:20 calls upon the people to believe Yahweh and his prophets. Ps 119:66 speaks of God's commandments as the object of "belief."

In none of these passages is "belief" or "faith" to be understood as passive quietism. Jonah 3:5 says that the people of Nineveh, when they heard Jonah's message, "believed God and ordered a public fast and put on sackcloth, high and low alike." Belief effects repentance and conversion. In Exod 4:1, 5 it is signs that evoke belief among the people. Isaiah, too, offers the hesitant Ahaz such a sign (7:10ff.). In Exod 14:31 the great event of deliverance from the Egyptians is patent to the eyes of all. According to

8. Hans Wildberger, "'Glauben': Erwägungen zu האמין," in *Hebräische Wortforschung: Festschrift zum 80. Geburtstag von Walter Baumgartner* (Vetus Testamentum Supplement 16; Leiden: Brill, 1967) 372–86.

9. Rudolf Smend, "Zur Geschichte von האמין," in *Hebräische Wortforschung: Festschrift zum 80. Geburtstag von Walter Baumgartner* (Vetus Testamentum Supplement 16; Leiden: Brill, 1967) 284–90.

the Old Testament, then, Yahweh now and then gives belief the aid of a sign or even direct vision. But Gen 15:6 shows very clearly how people must venture to believe even contrary to what they can see with their own eyes—what kind of evidence is the view of the starry heavens that is given to Abraham? And yet it is possible to say that faith bears knowledge within it. Isa 43:10 states that Israel must be Yahweh's witness, "that they may gain insight and believe and know that I am He." But Ps 106:12 clearly states the purpose of belief: "Then they believed his [Yahweh's] promises and sang his praises." Belief sings God's praises.

JOHN L. MCKENZIE

b. 1910   d. 1991

Cult

Educated in Jesuit schools and ordained a priest in 1939, John L. McKenzie taught at the University of Notre Dame and at Loyola University and De Paul University, both in Chicago. He served, at different times, as the president of both the Catholic Biblical Association and the Society of Biblical Literature. Within and beyond academe, McKenzie was a lively critic of hierarchies, both sacred and secular.

Selected Writings by McKenzie

1956   *The Two-Edged Sword: An Interpretation of the Old Testament.* Milwaukee: Bruce.
1965   *Dictionary of the Bible.* New York: Bruce / London: Collier-Macmillan.
1974   *A Theology of the Old Testament.* Garden City, New York: Doubleday.

Writings about McKenzie

Flanagan, James W., and Anita W. Robinson (editors)
1975   *No Famine in the Land: Studies in Honor of John L. McKenzie.* Missoula, Montana: Scholars Press / Claremont: Institute for Antiquity and Christianity.

John L. McKenzie's
Approach to Old Testament Theology

Excerpted with permission from John L. McKenzie, *A Theology of the Old Testament* (Garden City: Doubleday, 1974), pp. 21, 23–25, 27, 29, 32–35.

Principles, Methods, and Structure

[[21]] The task of Old Testament theology may become easier and be more successfully accomplished if we remember that it is precisely the theology of the Old Testament, not the exegesis of the Old Testament, not the history of the religion of Israel, not the theology of the entire Bible, which is the object of the study. The religion of Israel included many factors which are not found in the Old Testament; some are unknown, others are poorly known. For the historian of Israelite religion, the temple and cult of Bethel are extremely important, and he is hampered in his task because so little is known of them. To the theologian of the Old Testament the temple and cult of Bethel are important only because of what Amos and Hosea said about them. To their contemporaries Amos and Hosea were not very important.

. . . .

[[23]] I have asked, but not yet answered, whether we can use the word "systematic" of biblical theology in the same meaning in which it is used of systematic theology. The most ambitious venture in this area, the work of Eichrodt, has been successful in spite of the partial failing of the system as such. Von Rad's theology is not systematic in the sense I have already described, the sense in which certain basic principles are applied to each particular question so that the entire system is brought to bear on any particular problem. This type of system seems impossible in Old Testament theology, and we must anticipate a theological statement to explain why. Basic principles emerge in a rational system, which is a thing. What emerges in the Old Testament is not a rational system but a basic personal reality, Yahweh, who is consistent as a person is, not as a rational system. No particular problem is solved without reference to Yahweh, who is not a rational principle.

One seems, then, to be forced into the approach of particular topics; and in these treatments there is order and arrangement, but no system or structure. The topics are usually selected according to the personal studies and interest of the writers; this is not in itself deplorable, but it manifests that biblical theology is an unstructured discipline. Yet there are other factors at work which deserve mention. Up to this time it has been difficult for a Catholic to write a theology of the Old Testament without an explicit section on messianism. A small essay of my own was criticized even in the editorial stage because this topic was not presented with sufficient emphasis. I have been convinced for years that messianism is a Christian interest and a Christian theme; that it is a Christian response to the Old Testament and should be

141

treated as such; that in a theology of the Old Testament, as I have described it thus far, messianism would appear neither in the chapter headings nor in the index. It is not only not a dominant theme, but in the proper sense of the word it is doubtfully a theme of the Old Testament [[24]] at all. This theme is imposed upon the theologian by theological factors foreign to his area of study. He should be free to make his own selection and to make his own errors of judgment. Yet such a work deserves a title like "Essays in the Theology of the Old Testament," or "Towards a Theology of the Old Testament," or "Prolegomena to a Theology of the Old Testament."

We have already noticed the obvious fact that the principles, methods, and style of theology change, and usually change later than they ought. The change comes because the world and the Church are asking questions which theology is not answering or not even hearing. To illustrate: I have been a fairly convinced pacifist for twenty years. This conviction began with the teaching of the prophets. I do not remember any theology of the Old Testament which dealt with the problems of war and peace. They shall certainly be treated in this work; the purpose is not to promote pacifism, but simply to discern whether in that totality which we have mentioned there emerges some insight into this problem. Those who do not accept my insight are forced either to say that their insight is contradictory or that the Old Testament does not touch the problem at all. Such problems are not simply a question of relevance, but of meeting the development of theology. If this development is not to be met, there is no need for producing an additional theology, now or ever. Those we have are fully adequate. But since it is a biblical belief that whenever man encounters man, God is present as a witness and a party to the encounter, Old Testament theology must deal with such problems as war and peace, poverty, the urban problems, industrial and technological society, and such—not directly, of course, but by stating clearly what principles may emerge from the totality of the utterances. Theology keeps reforming its principles and its contents from the course of the human adventure. This is what gives the theologian the new questions. It is also one of the things, and perhaps the most important, which distinguishes theology from the history of religion.

If any structure emerges from the totality of the God-talk of the Old Testament, it ought to arise from the emphases of the Old Testament. These emphases, which have long been recognized, are simply those themes which occur most frequently and which [[25]] appear to be decisive in giving Old Testament belief its distinctive identity. The theologian can hardly divert much from his predecessors in his titles of chapters and subdivision. Nor can he avoid personal value judgments in the weight which he assigns to various topics and themes; if he were to present the themes with perfect objectivity, as if they were coins of the same denomination, he would not be faithful to his material. The order in which they are presented is not determined by the Old Testament, but by his own judgment of the most logical and coherent arrangement of material which was never arranged by those who wrote his sources. There is no reason in the Old Testament why biblical theology should begin with creation; in our own theology creation is the belief which is presupposed by all other beliefs. Biblical theology of the Old Testament, we have said, is written for modern readers who are probably religious believers, not for the scribes of Israel and Judaism who produced the source material of biblical theology. Their categories of thought must be of some importance for the arrangement of the material. But in whatever categories the material is arranged, the theologian is not going to escape a topical treatment; his problem is to rise above the merely topical treatment, the disconnected *quaestiones*.

. . . .

[[27]] The biblical theologian can scarcely avoid value judgments in his arrangement. Like the military historian, he should be able to distinguish the accessory and the inconclusive from the central and decisive. Not all parts of the Old Testament contribute equally to the total experience. Reviewers of Eichrodt noticed that he had difficulty including wisdom in his synthesis. Yet wisdom is more central in the Old Testament than one could judge from a covenant-centered theology. Wisdom simply has no reference to the covenant; it is older than the covenant, it is so basic to human experience that it has as many nonbiblical contacts as biblical. But it is an important part of Old Testament God-talk and includes themes which are scarcely touched in other books. Some of these themes are permanent in theological discussion and literature. The theologian ought to know that such value judgments are dangerous. But neither he nor his readers can escape their own history. It is difficult to imagine any theological question asked in this generation on which the book of Chronicles is likely to shed any light. But the theologian can write only in his generation.

. . . .

[[29]] The task of Old Testament theology can now be summarized as the analysis of an experience through the study of the written records of that experience. The experience is a collective experience which covers roughly a thousand years of history and literature. The experience is one because of the historical continuity of the group which had the experience and because of the identity of the divine being which the group retained as the object of its faith throughout the experience. The analysis must be done in certain categories and not merely by a chronological recital. We seek always the totality of the utterances and the insight which can be gained by assembling them. The theology of the Old Testament has to be a study of the reality of Yahweh. The Old Testament is the sole literary witness to that reality as the record of the experience of Israel, the sole historical witness.

The Israelite Experience of Yahweh

[[32]] If we inquire in what ways Israel, according to its literary records, experienced Yahweh, certain categories suggest themselves; and these categories will furnish the structure of the theological analysis which we undertake here. With some brief remarks, we set them forth as a preliminary outline.

I place cult first as the normal and most frequent manner in which the Israelite experienced Yahweh. The importance of cult need not be measured exactly according to the space which is given it in the Old Testament, but the space given it is abundant. That the cult is a ritual encounter with the deity is a universal human belief; we do not have to validate it for Israel, but simply to see what the peculiarly Israelite understanding and practice of cult may have been. In the Old Testament we are almost always dealing with the religion and faith of a people described as such, very rarely with the phenomenon called "personal religion." Cult is by [[33]] definition the religious expression of a group and not a feature of personal religion. Cult is explicitly or implicitly a profession of faith.

Next I list revelation as the situation in which Israel experienced Yahweh. By this I mean revelation made through authentic spokesmen of Yahweh, and not revelation in an improper sense. One need know little about other religions to recognize that revelation as it was understood in Israel does not appear in other religions except those which claim some continuity with Israelite religion. Israelite revelation is distinguished both in form and content from the revelation known to us in other religions with which Israel had contact. No other religion of the ancient Near Eastern world claimed to be founded on a revelation of the deity which the community worshiped, and on a revelation of a code of conduct imposed by the deity. No other religion exhibits a type of religious spokesman which is more than remotely similar to the Israelite prophets.

In the third place I list history as the area in which Israel experienced Yahweh. The treatment of this area may overlap the treatment of revelation, for the "experience" of Yahweh in history often consisted of hearing the prophetic interpretation of history. Yet the Israelites exhibit a conviction, again without parallel, that their history was the work of the deity whom they worshiped. One sees in the Old Testament a firm belief that Yahweh acts with plan and purpose, that he is not subject to fate, that he is not hindered by other divine beings nor moved by irrational whim.

In the fourth place I list nature as an area where Israel experienced Yahweh. The religions of the ancient Near East can generally, if unsatisfactorily, be classified as "nature religions"; the perception of superhuman power in nature is another universal human phenomenon. Israel again had its own distinctive way of expressing this perception. The question of mythology arises under this heading, as well as the question of creation.

To speak of wisdom as an experience of Yahweh may seem to be stretching our principle more than we ought; yet it is a peculiarly Israelite belief that Yahweh alone is wise and that Yahweh alone gives wisdom. Most of the content of conventional Israelite wisdom can be paralleled in other ancient wisdom literature, but [[34]] not its religious quality. Similarly, the Israelite critical or "anti-wisdom" literature is not without parallel; but Job and Koheleth are recognized as two of the most original works of the Old Testament. In any scheme of Old Testament theology, wisdom is something of a deviant; it stands in its own category, and it has to be recognized as isolated from other parts of the theological structure.

With some hesitation we then take up a topic labeled the institutions of Israel. During its history the community of Israel appeared in several political forms and with variations in its social structure. The Old Testament writings present each of the developments in these fields as exhibiting theological aspects. The Old Testament is not acquainted with a purely secular politics or a purely secular sociology. One may say that it is acquainted neither with politics nor with sociology as theoretical disciplines; but the materials which we include in these disciplines present theological problems as these materials are presented in the Old Testament. Yet one hesitates to include these elements in a treatment of religious institutions.

Our final heading is a vague title: the future of Israel. This touches the topic of messianism. I have already indicated that I do not think that this topic, precisely defined, is a topic of Old Testament theology. But it is an unparalleled feature of Old Testament belief that it has a simple and impregnable faith in the survival of Israel. As long as Yahweh is, there will be an Israel. This faith is not found everywhere; Amos possibly did not have it. But the majority of the writings exhibit the conviction that there will be an Israel, and the writers are compelled to visualize this future in some way. The variations in this vision of the future are numerous and remarkable, and this is not surprising. Each writer who thinks of the future which Yahweh will grant his people must think of those things in Israel which he believes are vital to its identity. Evidently not all Israelites thought of the same things. Still less did the Christians of the apostolic age think of all these things when they professed their belief that they were the fulfillment of the future which the Old Testament writers had seen.

At this point the theology of the Old Testament must end. The arrangement, it is hoped, will include all the God-talk which students of the Old Testament have found important. It is an [[35]] artificially unified analysis of a historical experience which has a different inner unity from the unity of logical discourse. A theology is also a theodicy. The experience of the totality, which we have insisted is the objective of Old Testament theology, shows the reality of Yahweh with a clarity which particular books and passages do not have. The Yahweh who was ready to kill Moses—on an impulse apparently—is not attractive, and obscure rather than mysterious (Exod 4:24–26); and it is certainly a pseudotheology which tries to identify this manifestation with the God whose loving kindness is above all his works. Not every biblical experience of Yahweh, not every fragment of God-talk, is of equal profundity; and it is only the totality of the experience that enables us to make these distinctions. Even though the theologian seeks the detached objectivity that modern scholarship demands, he is dealing with a collection of documents that present to those who believe in the documents a God who commands faith. Even if the theologian should not share this faith, he would be less than candid if he ignored the purpose of the literature that he analyzes. There was a time when an Israelite could give his faith to a God who could kill on impulse; many Old Testament writers wrote at length on the impossibility of faith in such a deity. Neither element should be omitted.

Synopsis of McKenzie's *Theology of the Old Testament* (1974)

John L. McKenzie on Cult

Excerpted with permission from John L. McKenzie, *A Theology of the Old Testament* (Garden City: Doubleday, 1974), pp. 48–54, 58–63.

Temple and Sanctuary

[[48]] The idea of the holy place is pervasive in religion, and it is remarkable that early Israelite religion deviates from the common pattern.[1] A holy object symbolizing the divine presence appears in the traditions earlier than the holy place and the holy building. The temples of Mesopotamia and Egypt had no counterpart in Israel before the monarchy.

The holy object was the ark, called the ark of the covenant, the ark of the testimony, the ark of Yahweh or of *elohim*, and some similar titles. This was a wooden box, described in the postexilic source P (Exod 25:10–22) as three feet nine inches by two feet three inches by two feet three inches. One tradition affirms that the ark contained the two tablets of the law inscribed by Yahweh for Moses. This was a portable shrine symbolizing the presence of Yahweh; and such a portable shrine would be at home in a nomadic tribe which lives in tents, not houses. The ark was housed in a tent until the reign of David and then was permanently installed in the temple of Solomon. Some scholars have suggested that the ark and the tent were two holy objects originally independent of each other. The tent was called "the tent of meeting," signifying the meeting of Yahweh with Israel; it was the place of revelation through oracular utterance. Like the ark, it was [[49]] a portable symbol; and it is curious that there was no permanent holy place during the period of the amphictyony, when Israel was settled on the land. No explanation of this somewhat foreign usage is available except the Israelite tradition that the worship of Yahweh came into the land with an immigrant tribe. The unreal tent of the priestly source (Exodus 26), constructed according to the dimensions of Solomon's temple, is a product of scribal imagination; but the tradition of the premonarchic tent is solid. It must be conceded that the symbolism of the ark and tent overlap somewhat. Both symbols exclude the idea of a sacred area (*temenos*); the deity is present where the portable symbol is set down, and he leaves the area when it is moved. He really dwells "in the midst of his people" and not on holy ground. The ark was carried at the head of the column when the tribe moved from place to place and at the head of the battle column (Num 10:33–35; 14:44; 2 Sam 11:11).

The precise quality of the symbolic presence is ambiguous and very probably shows considerable development. Yahweh is said to be enthroned upon the cherubim when the reference is to the ark (1 Sam 4:4; 2 Sam 6:2; Ps 80:2); and in the temple of Solomon the ark stood between the images of the cherubim, winged figures of guardian genii. But the configuration of the ark does

1. Van der Leeuw [[*Phänomenologie der Religion* (Tübingen, 1956)]].

not suggest a throne, and it is possible that the ark was not a chair but a footstool. Yahweh, who cannot be represented by image, stands invisible upon the footstool. A similar explanation of the calf of the temple of Samaria as an invisible footstool has been proposed.[2]

There is no parallel in ancient Near Eastern religions to the prohibition of images.[3] The prohibition touches images for worship, but in Israel and Judaism it has been understood as a general prohibition with a few exceptions like the cherubim in the temple of Solomon and the wall paintings in the synagogue of Dura-Europos. Palestinian archaeology has disclosed nothing which could be called an image of Yahweh; it has disclosed hundreds of images which are evidently presentations of non-Israelite gods [[50]] and goddesses, in particular female figurines of the fertility goddess.[4] These images illustrate biblical references to superstitious cults in Israel. The god Ashur was represented by an archer within a winged disk, and the Egyptian Aton as the solar disk with rays terminating in hands;[5] these are schematic, not representational, but they would fall under the Israelite prohibition.

The prohibition is comprehensive, covering anything that is susceptible of representation—that is, anything which is visible. Yet to say that the Israelites conceived of Yahweh as spiritual in the sense of immaterial says more than the texts will support. The anthropomorphisms of the Old Testament speak of Yahweh's eyes, ears, hands, arms, nostrils, mouth, and feet; yet while they may be spoken of, they may not be represented in art, and were not. Yahweh was not properly conceived as invisible; the sight of him was fatal to mortal eyes, which is not exactly the same thing as invisibility.

 The implication of the prohibition is the statement that Yahweh is like nothing in the heavens above, the earth below, or the waters under the earth. These are the boundaries of the universe as the Israelites thought of them; Yahweh can be assimilated to nothing in the universe. He is "wholly other," to use the phrase of Rudolf Otto. One may find a theoretical inconsistency between the prohibition of images and the anthropomorphisms of biblical language. One may even find a theoretical inconsistency between the imageless Yahweh and the location of Yahweh symbolically where the ark reposed; the Old Testament neither sought nor achieved theoretical consistency. The prohibition of images went far towards preventing the assimilation of Yahweh to the deities of other ancient Near Eastern religions. The books of the prophets attest that the danger of assimilation was real. The god who cannot even be symbolically represented by anything in nature is above and outside nature.

Neither the throne nor the footstool suggests the covenant; and the tradition of the tables of stone very probably reflected the historical reality that the ark contained a document stating the [[51]] terms of the covenant. We

2. William Foxwell Albright, *From the Stone Age to Christianity* (2nd paperback ed., New York, 1957), 299–301; H. Th. Obbink, "Jahwebilder," *ZATWiss* 58 (1929), 264–74.

3. Exod 20:4–6; Deut 5:8–10; see also Lev 26:1; Deut 4:15–23.

4. William Foxwell Albright, *The Archeology of Palestine* (Harmondsworth, 1951), 107.

5. Pritchard, *ANEP* 536, 408, 409.

shall see in dealing with the covenant that the treaty documents on which the covenant is most probably modeled were stored in the temples. This association, however, must be a later reinterpretation of the ark, which has in itself a satisfactory symbolism of presence with no reference to covenant. As the ark of the covenant, the ark symbolizes not only the presence of Yahweh among his people but also the union of the tribes with Yahweh and with each other. It was as the symbol of Israelite unity that it was brought to Jerusalem by David and finally installed in the temple of Solomon.

The ark and the tent, which certainly came together in premonarchic Israel, whether they originally belonged together or not, were authentically Israelite symbols of the presence of Yahweh. The temple of Solomon was an imitation of non-Israelite symbols; and there is no reason to differentiate between the temple of Solomon and the temples erected at Bethel and Dan in the kingdom of Israel. The temple was the symbolic palace of the deity; like the tent, it was his residence. The ancient temple was not built for the assembly of the worshipers, who assembled in the outer courts; it was the palace of the god, and his privacy was protected by the holiness of the place. The god lived in his temple as the king lived in his palace. Both in Mesopotamia and in Egypt the temple was a symbol of celestial reality; in Egypt the temple symbolized the world in which the god reigned, and in Mesopotamia the temple was the earthly counterpart of the heavenly temple. It was a point of contact between heaven and earth; the idea is echoed in the Old Testament story of the tower of Babel (Gen 11:4) and probably in the ladder of Jacob (Gen 28:12); Jacob recognized that Bethel (the site of an Israelite temple) was the house of God and the gate of heaven (Gen 28:17).[6]

The temple of Solomon was such a deviation from traditional Israelite cult that it had to be authenticated by an oracle of Yahweh. This is found in 2 Samuel 7, pronounced by Nathan to David; the oracle had to be given to the founder of the dynasty and of Jerusalem, not to his son. The oracle clearly states that the temple was not built because Yahweh "needed" a house, and implies [[52]] that the temple is not only the house of Yahweh but also a symbol of the "house" (dynasty) which Yahweh will build for David. The selection of the site of the temple is also attributed to revelation (2 Samuel 24). There is no doubt that the site is the modern Haram esh Sharif, occupied since the ninth century A.D. by the Dome of the Rock. There is very little doubt that this was the site of a sanctuary in pre-Israelite Jerusalem, but the narrative of 2 Samuel 24 ignores this.

Few parallels have been found to the structure of the temple of Solomon; the narrative itself states that the temple was designed and built by Phoenicians, and almost no Phoenician temples from this period have survived. Compared to the great temples of Egypt and Mesopotamia, the temple of Solomon was quite small. The inner chamber, which elsewhere enclosed the image of the deity, housed the ark. In the earliest temple there is no

6. Cf. "The Significance of the Temple in the Ancient Near East," *The Biblical Archeologist* 7 (1944), 41–63.

doubt that the ark was visible through the main door as the image was visible in most other temples. Entrance, however, was prohibited to others than priests; this was normal. The altar stood in the outer court, and there the sacrificial ritual was performed.

The courts of the temple contained some symbols which are still not understood. These included the two free standing columns named Yakin and Boaz, and the enormous bronze vessel of water called the "sea." The character of these objects suggests that they were cosmic symbols—more precisely, symbols of Yahweh's cosmic dominion. It has been suggested that the names of the two columns were the first words of inscriptions. It has also been suggested that they were fire pillars, but the description seems to make them somewhat impractical for this purpose. As symbols of the pillars of the world they are perhaps more easily understood. The "sea" could hardly symbolize the monster of chaos, but rather the sea as subdued by Yahweh. This ornamentation can easily be related to the New Year festival in which Yahweh was celebrated as king and creator. Indeed, the act of creation may have been identified with the building of the temple-palace, as it was in both Mesopotamia and Canaan; the building of the temple was the climactic act of sovereignty asserted in creation.[7]

[[53]] Less explicit in the texts but implied in the architecture is a Davidic-messianic symbolism of the temple. The temple must have been notably smaller than the rest of the palace complex of which it was a part. Many find the term "royal chapel" improper for the temple of Solomon, but in spite of the uncertainties of the total design it is clear that the temple was incorporated into the buildings and courts of the palace. The description does not suggest that the temple courts had an entrance distinct from the gates of the palace courts. The covenant union of Yahweh with the house of David was effectively symbolized by the union of the temple with the palace. Furthermore, the covenant of Yahweh with Israel stood with the covenant with David. Zion, the temple mountain, was the residence of Yahweh. It will become the tallest of all mountains to which all peoples will stream (Isa 2:1–4; Mic 4:1–4). It becomes the mythological mountain of the north, the residence of the gods in Canaanite mythology (Ps 48:1–2). These are echoes of the ancient Near Eastern belief that the earthly temple is the counterpart of the heavenly temple; it is also the residence of the king of Judah.

The law of Deuteronomy 12 prescribes that the cult of Yahweh shall be carried on only at the sanctuary which he has chosen. Historians associate this law with the cultic reform of Josiah (2 Kings 22–23), instituted in 622–21 B.C. Before this reform, according to numerous allusions in the books of Kings, the people of Judah worshiped at the "high places." These high places were local shrines in towns and villages. If the name "high place" is correctly translated, they were located on hilltops and can be compared to the "high place" preserved at Petra, which is not only on an elevation but is difficult of

---

7. *Enuma Elish,* Pritchard *ANET* 68–69; Baal of Ugarit, Pritchard *ANET* 134.

access.[8] If cultic worship had been limited to the temple of Jerusalem, most Israelite males could not have been present, and this must have been the effect of the reform of Josiah. These allusions recommend the opinion that the temple of Solomon was a royal chapel and that it was a center of worship for the palace community, identical with the population of Jerusalem. The cultic experience of Israel and Judah was not [[54]] situated in the Jerusalem temple but in the local shrines of the towns and villages. Very little trace of this cult has been left in the Old Testament, in which the cult of the second Jerusalem temple has become the model of Israelite cult. There are numerous allusions to cultic abuses in the local shrines; not all of them were unfounded, it seems, but under the monarchy the standards of the Jerusalem cult were not established as normative. Indeed, it is quite clear that during the Assyrian period (735–640) the cultic abuses of the Jerusalem temple were as deplorable as any abuses elsewhere.[9]

. . . .

Prophetic Criticism of the Cult

[[58]] Cult is generally accepted in the Old Testament as the normal means by which the community encounters Yahweh. One needs little acquaintance with the history of religion or little experience with cultic worship to know that cult is open to many abuses which have often made people wonder whether cult is a legitimate approach to the deity. To many of our contemporaries cultic worship is superstition by essence. There are also some discordant voices in the Old Testament which show that the attitude of the Israelites towards cult was more complex than simple and naïve acceptance.

Criticism of the cult in varying severity is expressed in Ps 50:7–15, Amos 5:21–25, Isa 1:10–17, Jer 7:1–15 and 21–22, and Isa 66:1–4. Psalm 50 cannot be dated with any precision. Amos 5:21–25 is accepted as original by all critics. Isa 1:10–17 is not certainly from Isaiah, but it is very probably pre-exilic. Jeremiah 7 appears to be original with Jeremiah. Isa 66:1–4 belongs to the postexilic period. The criticisms come from different periods and they are not all of the same character.

Psalm 50 is the easiest to handle. The poet rather gently and ironically speaks in the person of Yahweh and tells the Israelites that he does not accept sacrifices to satisfy his hunger. It is very doubtful that any Israelite really believed that sacrifices satisfied Yahweh's hunger; they may very well have believed that Yahweh wanted sacrifices more than anything else or that they did something for Yahweh by offering sacrifice. The poet makes Yahweh prefer vows, prayers of thanksgiving, and sincere confessions of need. The Israelite liturgy did contain these elements; and the rebuke touched no more than a kind of naïve and pardonable superstition about sacrifice. The other passages are less kindly.

8. G. Lankester Harding, *The Antiquities of Jordan* (New York, 1959), 117–20.
9. Roland de Vaux, *Ancient Israel* (New York, 1961), 322.

Both Amos and Jeremiah are thought by some scholars to express an acquaintance with a tradition of early Israel which had no institution of the sacrificial ritual as we now have it in the Pentateuch. In fact most of the liturgical passages of the Pentateuch come from the priestly source, which attributed the entire cultic system of the second temple to Moses. The older sources J and E [[59]] are much less explicit concerning the institution of the cultic system by Moses; and it is possible that both the prophets knew traditions which had no ritual institutions. The Israelite sacrificial system actually does not show any sharp differences from other sacrificial systems. There is, as is well known, considerable ambiguity concerning the knowledge of Moses and his work exhibited in the prophetic writings. The point is that nothing either in the criticisms of the Pentateuch or the prophetic writings imposes upon us the existence of a tradition in the eighth and seventh centuries concerning the institution of the sacrificial system by Moses.

To be more specific than this with the rhetoric of the two prophets is dangerous, but one can hardly evade the danger. Amos seems to deny not only the institution of the sacrificial system but even the offering of sacrifice during the desert sojourn. Jeremiah, on the other hand, rather speaks of the absence of any commandment of sacrifice. Amos adds a difficulty which Jeremiah does not have. Yet it seems scarcely possible that Amos could have had a tradition in which sacrifice was not mentioned, and one must suppose that he pushed it for all it was worth.

The common element in Amos, Jeremiah and Isaiah is that Yahweh speaks as rejecting sacrifices and not merely as criticizing abuses. The reasons for the rejection are the same in all the prophets: the offering of sacrifice is not joined with righteousness within the community. Both Amos and Jeremiah elsewhere announce the total destruction of all institutions, both religious and secular.[10] For Amos and Jeremiah there is no reason to take the rejection in any other sense than absolutely. Jeremiah predicts the destruction of the temple of Jerusalem in the same context. Isaiah is less precise in his predictions of a future destruction; but there is no reason to take his rejection as conditioned by something which he does not utter. None of the prophets speak of a reform of abuses as a way of solving the problem which they present. One need not suppose that they look to a noncultic religion of the future; they simply look to the abolition of the cultic system which they knew.

[[60]] Whatever be the ambiguities of the pre-exilic prophets, there is no ambiguity in Third Isaiah. The prophet spoke in the cultic community of post-exilic Jerusalem, the community which produced the priestly code and the elaborate ritual of P. He does not speak of a distinction between legitimate and superstitious cults, not even expressly of the moral corruption of the worshiping community as the pre-exilic prophets spoke of it. He simply enumerates several ritual actions and identifies them all as superstition. Heaven and earth are Yahweh's throne and temple, not the temple of Jerusalem. The prophet clearly repudiates the temple, the cult, and the priesthood.

---

10. Amos 2:13–16, 3:12, 5:2–3, 6:1–3, 8:1–3, 9:8a; Jer 7:1–15 (the temple), 8:8–9 (the law), 22:29–30 (the monarchy), 23:33–40 (prophecy).

These passages do not surprise us by their awareness that hypocritical worship is possible; they do create something of a problem by indicating that their authors seem ready to abandon cult without replacing it. In the same book of Jeremiah, a new covenant is presented with no intermediaries between Yahweh and the individual worshiper (Jer 31:31-34). Critics have often doubted that this passage came from Jeremiah, but it is in the same line of thought with the rejection of the cult; from both there seems to follow a religion without social structure. Jeremiah and Amos both faced the possibility—indeed, the expectation—that the people of Yahweh as such would cease to exist; there would be no worshipping community of which the believer could be a member. Such a worshiping community did arise after the exile, but this was not within the vision of the prophets. In actual fact these prophets have very little to say to the Israelite who found himself uprooted from the community of his faith. These would have to find their hope and their encouragement elsewhere. For Amos and Jeremiah the judgment of Yahweh fell with the same totality upon the cult as upon the monarchy and the nation. No institution they knew would return in the form in which it disappeared. Third Isaiah expressed a rare disapproval of the restoration which was ultimately instituted. The future of Israel was not conceived as a mere revival of institutions which had failed to do their work. Yet to say that the cult had simply failed is again to say more than the texts permit. This will concern us in the sections to follow. The conclusion from the prophetic criticism is that cult did not have a [[61]] sacramental *ex opere operato* validity as a means of approaching Yahweh.

The Cultic Community

The postexilic community of Jerusalem was effectively and almost formally a cultic community. It was not founded as such, although one of the motives alleged for the restoration of Jerusalem was the restoration of temple and cult (Ezra 1:2-4, 6:2-12). But this restoration was not immediately accomplished, and, indeed until the reforms of Ezra was not firmly established. Until these reforms the community struggled to survive as a small ethnic group in a sea of foreigners. After Ezra the community felt it had achieved the ancient ideal of Yahweh dwelling in the midst of his people. For this it needed no political institutions. As we shall see elsewhere, the postexilic community saw itself as a kind of messianic fulfillment, the saved remnant.

One cannot without reservations transfer this idea of the cultic community to Israel before the exile. At the same time, it is difficult to assess the importance of the cultic ritual in the formation and preservation of the Israelite faith and community. We have observed certain prophetic criticisms which reveal massive failures in the cult. These should be balanced against certain values, which have been well set forth by Sigmund Mowinckel.[11] In the ancient world we cannot assume that religious community was instituted and

11. *The Psalms in Israel's Worship*, 2 v. (New York, 1962), 1, 97-105.

supported by doctrinal instruction. What the people believed and accepted as obligations was professed only in cultic ceremonial; as we have pointed out several times, this was the community's collective experience of the deity. The individual person could not think of a purely personal experience; ritual performances for private persons were still ritual and fulfilled through the cultic and sacerdotal system. The Israelite prophets deviate sharply from the universal patterns, but even the prophets should not be taken outside of the cultic system in which they lived and in which they formed their basic ideas and beliefs about Yahweh and in [[62]] terms of which they addressed the Israelites. The hymns, as Mowinckel points out, are the best summary of what the Israelites thought Yahweh was; the hymns have their limitations, but they show the cultic system at its best.

In modern times a comparison between the cultic systems of Israel and its contemporaries is possible.[12] The comparison is most revealing when one observes a number of highly developed rituals which had no place in Israelite cult. Such are the rituals of divination which have left such extensive remains in Mesopotamia. The Israelites had certain oracular practices; the references to these are few and disclose no extensive apparatus for discerning the future by occult means. The Mesopotamian lived in a world where demons constantly threatened his fortunes and his health. The priestly offices and functions by which demonic attacks were averted matched the divining priesthood in their numbers and complications. Mesopotamian religion cannot always be distinguished from magic, which is really anti-religion; Israelite religion was liberated from this type of superstition. What the Mesopotamians expected from the rituals of divination and incantation the Israelites expected from Yahweh or did not expect at all. The Old Testament cultic experience of Yahweh left no room for divination or demonology. Here, however, it is necessary to recall the distinction between the history of Israelite religion and the theology of the Old Testament. There is ample evidence that superstitious rites flourished in the Israelite community; the belief in Yahweh which is expressed in the Old Testament repudiates these superstitions.

Mowinckel has pointed out that the limitations of the religion of the hymns lies precisely in their exclusively Israelite character. In the cult Yahweh is experienced as the God of Israel rather than as the God of the world and mankind. His saving power was celebrated mostly in the recital of his saving acts in behalf of Israel, whether in the past of the exodus and the possession of the land or in more recent victories. One does not find expressed in the hymns the prophetic awareness of judgment. Having said [[63]] this, one perhaps has not gone beyond the prophetic criticisms of cult.

One returns, then, to the essential nature of cult as the rites by which the believing community recognizes and professes its identity and proclaims what it believes about the deity it worships and the relations between the deity and the worshipers. The Israelite cultic system did not succeed in professing the totality of Israelite belief. It failed to maintain Israelite faith in crisis.

12. Cf. Saggs, [[*The Greatness That Was Babylon* (New York, 1962)]] 299–358.

The prophetic criticisms are not the whole truth concerning Israelite cult. Cult was also the factor which sustained the framework of Israelite belief. Many modern critics believe that the cult was the most important source of the literature of the Old Testament. One must avoid premature and sweeping judgments, but the results of recent work suggest that earlier interpreters seriously underestimated the importance of cultic worship in the formation of Israelite belief and Israelite literature.

RONALD E. CLEMENTS

b. 1929

Law and Promise

Now Professor of Old Testament Emeritus at King's College in the University of London, Ronald E. Clements studied at Spurgeon's College, Cambridge University, and the University of Sheffield, where he earned his Ph.D. He was ordained a Baptist minister in 1956. His published research has ranged widely over the Old Testament canon, including its wisdom literature.

Writings by Clements

1969 *God's Chosen People: A Theological Interpretation of the Book of Deuteronomy.* Valley Forge, Pennsylvania: Judson / London: SCM.

1976 *One Hundred Years of Old Testament Interpretation.* Philadelphia: Westminster. [British edition: *A Century of Old Testament Study* (Guildford:)]

1978 *Old Testament Theology: A Fresh Approach.* New Foundations Theological Library. Atlanta: John Knox / London: Marshall, Morgan & Scott.

1990 *Wisdom for a Changing World: Wisdom in Old Testament Theology.* Berkeley, California: BIBAL.

1992 *Wisdom in Theology.* Grand Rapids: Eerdmans.

1996 *Old Testament Prophecy: From Oracles to Canon.* Westminster John Knox.

Writings about Clements

Edward Bell (editor)

1999 *In Search of True Wisdom: Essays in Old Testament Interpretation in Honour of Ronald E. Clements.* Journal for the Study of the Old Testament Supplements 300. Sheffield: Sheffield Academic Press.

Ronald E. Clements's
Approach to Old Testament Theology

Excerpted with permission from Ronald E. Clements, *Old Testament Theology: A Fresh Approach* (Atlanta: John Knox, 1978), pp. 15–19.

The Problem of Old Testament Theology

[[15]] All of these factors bring us back to a fundamental consideration about the aim and purpose of an Old Testament theology. It should be concerned to provide some degree of theological insight and significance in relation to the Old Testament literature which we have. This canonical form of the literature represents the 'norm', if only in the sense that it represents the way in which the Old Testament is read and interpreted in the Jewish and Christian communities. To probe behind this canonical form is important, and should provide a basis for obtaining a better understanding of it, as also is the way in which this canonical form has subsequently been understood and interpreted in Jewish and Christian tradition. The questions of tradition and canon are interrelated, since the canon of the Old Testament represents a kind of 'freezing' of the tradition that was central to Israelite-Jewish religion at a critical moment in its history.

The Old Testament as Canon

All of these considerations lead us to recognise the great importance that attaches to the form, function and concept of the Old Testament as canon. It has therefore been a welcome feature of recent approaches to the problem of biblical theology to have rediscovered the notion of canon as a central feature of the Old Testament, which must be allowed to play its part in the presentation of an Old Testament theology.[1] At a very basic level we can see that it is because the Old Testament forms a canon, and is not simply a collection of ancient Near Eastern documents, that we can expect to find in it a 'theology', and not just a report of ancient religious ideas. There is a real connection between the ideas of 'canon' and 'theology', for it is the status of these writings as a canon of sacred scripture that marks them out as containing a word of God that is still believed to be authoritative. There are good reasons, therefore, [[16]] why it matters a great deal that the historical and literary problems relating to the formation and acceptance of the canon should occupy a place in our discussion.

One point becomes immediately clear, and this is that the date of composition of a document, or writing, in the Old Testament does not, of itself, determine its place in the canon. Similarly where, as is supremely the case in

---

1. Cf. B. S. Childs, *Biblical Theology in Crisis* (1970); J. A. Sanders, *Torah and Canon* (1973); and D. A. Knight (ed.), *Tradition and Theology in the Old Testament* (1977), pp. 259–326.

the Pentateuch, there is evidence that a great multitude of sources have been used to create the extant whole, then we are in a real way committed to trying to understand this whole, rather than to elucidating the separate parts.

Perhaps most of all, however, the concern with canon forces us to realise that the Old Testament has a distinctive, and in many ways unexpected, shape. This becomes clearest as soon as we follow out the guideline provided by the Hebrew (Jewish) shape of the canon, which must be accorded full authority as the oldest, and most basic, form of it. The earliest Christian Church took over the Old Testament in its Greek (Alexandrine) form, whereas the separation between Judaism and Christianity led Judaism to revert exclusively to the Hebrew (Palestinian) form. In spite of many problems and historical obscurities concerning the way in which the formation of the canon developed in the first century B.C. and in the ensuing century, we may confidently recognise that this Palestinian form of the canon represents the oldest, and most basic, form of the Old Testament. In this it is made up of three separate parts: the Pentateuch, or *tôrâh*, the Prophets (later subdivided into the Former and Latter Prophets), and the Writings. These three parts correspond to three levels of authority, with the Pentateuch standing at the highest level, the Prophets below this and the Writings further down still. When therefore the New Testament characterises the entire Old Testament as a book of 'Law' (Greek *nomos* translating Hebrew *tôrâh*) this reflects the canonical priority accorded to the Pentateuch. In a similar fashion the characterising of the historical narratives from Joshua to 2 Kings as 'Prophets' is not without significance when it comes to understanding them as a whole.

From a literary perspective, enlightened by historical criticism, one feature becomes very marked in regard to the structure [[17]] of the canon. This is that each part contains material from very different ages, spread rather broadly over the period from 1000 B.C. to approximately 200 B.C., or a little later. Age is not of itself therefore a determinative factor in explaining why particular books are in the part of the canon where they are now found.

In addition to this we also discover as a result of source criticism that there are interesting areas of overlap between some of the circles to which we must ascribe authorship of parts of the Pentateuch and Prophets. This is most evident in regard to the book of Deuteronomy in the Pentateuch and the 'Deuteronomic' character of prominent editorial tendencies in the Former and Latter Prophets. Other literary affinities are also to be seen, as for example between some psalms and certain parts of the prophetic corpus.

Yet further literary puzzles reveal themselves, for historical-literary criticism shows us that the Pentateuch has in some respects acquired its canonical status in a curious reverse order. There is widespread agreement that the book of Deuteronomy, the last book of the Pentateuch, was the first to acquire canonical status, albeit in a somewhat different form from that which it now has. Furthermore it is now widely accepted that it once was joined on to form the first 'chapter' of a work which stretched from Deuteronomy to 2 Kings, and thus combined 'the Law and the Prophets'. The point need not be explored further here, although its consequences will be referred to again later. For our immediate concern it is sufficient to note that the canonical shape of the Old Testament cannot be assigned to the result of accident, nor to a simple process of aggregation of documentary material until it formed a massive whole. There is evidently some design and system about the shape that has been accorded to the material.

Our concern at this juncture is to draw attention to the way in which the structure of the canon affects its interpretation. As the canon is primarily made up of the Law and the Prophets, so its contents are broadly to be interpreted as either 'Law' or 'Prophecy'. In fact we quickly discover that 'Law' is a somewhat inadequate term by which to reproduce the Hebrew *tôrâh*, but a legal connotation is not altogether to be discounted. [[18]] So far as interpretation is concerned, we find that the categories of 'Law' and 'Prophecy' are not rigidly restricted to their separate parts of the canon, but each tends to spill over to affect other parts. Hence we find, for example, in Matt 11:13 that 'the Law and the Prophets' are both said to 'prophesy', so that parts of the Pentateuch can be treated as prophecy. Similarly we find in Mark 2:23–28, for example, that a narrative from the Former Prophets is made into an affirmation of a 'law', or *tôrâh*. Even more importantly from the point of view of understanding the New Testament use of the Old we find that numerous passages from the Psalms can be treated as prophecy (cf. Acts 2:25–28, etc.). The details of these categories of interpretation need not detain us at this point, since it is sufficient for our purpose to note the way in which the shape which is given to the canon has served to establish an elementary, but significant, basis for interpretation. The literary context inevitably serves to create a basis of ideological context, for the Old Testament was not meant to be read as a collection of independent 'proof texts', but as a series of three great literary wholes. This is in line with the contention we have already mentioned that scripture should be interpreted by scripture.

Another point also falls to be considered in relation to the canon. If Old Testament theology is intended to be an examination of the theological significance of the Old Testament as it now exists as a canon, then this supports our view that it should not be a purely historical discipline concerned only with the world of ancient Israel and Judaism in which this canon was in process of formation. Rather it must address itself to those religious communities who accept and use this canon as a central feature of their religious life. This points us to both Judaism and Christianity as the religious communities who can be expected to concern themselves with the Old Testament as theology.

In this light we cannot remain altogether indifferent to the liturgical use made of the Old Testament within these communities. This, too, provides part of the context in which the Old Testament is understood. It is inevitable that the situation in worship in which the Old Testament is read, as well as the [[19]] particular choice and ordering of it, play a part in its being heard as the word of God. The 'I and Thou' of scripture become readily identifiable with the 'I and Thou' of worship in which God addresses man and vice versa, and it is of the utmost importance that the theological justification for this identification should be considered. We cannot tolerate a divorce between theology and liturgy, and we cannot therefore be indifferent to the way in which the Old Testament is used liturgically. A very clear example of this need for a theological reflection upon liturgical use is provided by the Psalter and its extensive employment in Christian worship.

However, the issue does not end there, but affects the whole use of the Old Testament, as is most strikingly exemplified by the use of 'messianic' prophecies in Christian Advent services. A wide range of theological questions are raised, which relate to the canonical form and use of the Old Testament. We cannot in consequence leave the question of the canon out of reckoning in an Old Testament theology. On the contrary, it is precisely the concept of canon that raises questions about the authority of the Old Testament, and its ability to present us with a theology which can still be meaningful in the twentieth century. If we restrict ourselves solely to reading the Old Testament as an ancient text, and endeavour to hear in it nothing that the ancient author could not have intended, then we should be denying something of the tradition which asserts that God has continued to speak to his people through it. In reality we do not need to insist on such a rigidly historicising approach, if we believe that the Old Testament does present us with a revelation of the eternal God.

Synopsis of Clements's *Old Testament Theology: A Fresh Approach* (1978)

Ronald E. Clements on Law and Promise

Excerpted with permission from Ronald E. Clements, *Old Testament Theology: A Fresh Approach* (Atlanta: John Knox, 1978), pp. 104–10, 140–50, 153–54, 203, 205.

The Old Testament as Law

[[104]] We remarked in considering the problems of method associated with the writing of an Old Testament theology that it is of great importance to the subject that it should take fully into account the nature of the Old Testament as literature. This must necessarily include some attention to the literary form and structure of its constituent books, but also it should look at those broad categories by which the Old Testament as a whole has been understood. The importance of doing this is all the greater on account of the far-reaching consequences that develop from the way in which the unity of the canon is understood.

Two factors can assist us in finding this basis of unity. One is the structure of the canon itself with its division into three literary collections of Law, Prophets, and Writings, in a three-tier level of authority. The second factor is provided by the way in which the early Jewish and Christian interpreters of the Old Testament have set about their task, with the indications which they give of the particular assumptions and presuppositions which they bring to the literature. Here immediately we encounter the most widespread and basic category which has been employed to describe the nature of the material which the Old Testament contains. This is that of 'law', or more precisely *tôrâh* since the question of how far 'law' is a very satisfactory translation of the Hebrew *tôrâh* remains to be considered. Certainly it raises the question of what kind of law, and what legal authority and sanctions it may be thought to possess.[1]

In the New Testament a quotation from Ps 82:6 is said to be written 'in your law' (John 10:34). Thus even the third part of the Old Testament canon, the Writings, could, by a kind of extension, be regarded as falling within 'the Law'. Evidently the priority and importance of the first part of the canon was felt to be such that it carried over to affect other parts also. [[105]] Certainly we readily discover other indications that this was so for the Prophets. In Mark 2:25–26 we find the citation of an incident regarding David and the eating of the Bread of the Presence which is recorded in 1 Sam 21:1–6. This incident from the Former Prophets is interpreted as an example of the fundamental principle, applied to Old Testament laws and regulations, that the humanitarian demand for preserving life is of greater importance than the more specifically cultic demand of respect for holiness. The background and

---

1. For the understanding of the Old Testament as law, see P. Grelot, *Le sens chrétien de l'Ancien Testament* (*Bibliotheque de Théologie* Vol. 3) (Tournai, 1962), pp. 167–208.

161

assumptions of this interpretation need not detain us. It is simply a clear illustration of the way in which the record of narrative incidents, which were originally preserved for specific purposes of quite another kind, could later be interpreted out of the basic presupposition that they are *tôrâh*–law. Nor is this approach a uniquely Christian one, or we find very strikingly that it pervades almost completely the mainstream of Jewish interpretation of the Old Testament. The Mishnah, and later the Talmud, are full of citation and interpretative comment upon the Old Testament which regard it as *tôrâh*.

Certainly we cannot put aside this fundamental category by which post–Old Testament Jewish and Christian interpreters of this literature have set about understanding it as though it were imposed upon it entirely from outside. We have already noted that the literary structure of the Old Testament supports such a pattern of interpretation by its three-tier ordering of the canon. From a literary point of view the Old Testament is *tôrâh*, and the fact that it contains a great deal else in addition to this, has to be understood in some kind of relationship to this *tôrâh* structure.[2] What has evidently happened is that the concept of a *tôrâh* literature has been used to provide some element of co-ordination and unity to a very varied collection of writings. It offers a unifying guideline, or motif, which has served to impose some degree of order upon what would otherwise be a rather strange miscellany of writings.

As we move further away in time from the editorial and redactional activity which has shaped the Old Testament into its present form, so we tend to find that the assumption that it is all *tôrâh* has tended to become more and more dominating in its effect upon the way in which the material is understood. [[106]] More diverse elements tend to become submerged under the weight of conviction that all the literature is *tôrâh*. At least this is so in respect of Jewish interpretation, since we find that in the mainstream of Christian exegesis a rather different category came to predominate. This is that of 'promise', which we must discuss later. In considering the structure of the Old Testament, therefore, we find ourselves facing a number of questions about its role as *tôrâh*. How far is this category endemic to the literature itself, and how far is it simply a structural framework, lightly built around writings of a more diverse character? Secondly, if we find that the category of *tôrâh* does have a real and fundamental place in the formation of the Old Testament, what exactly is this *tôrâh*; What kind of 'law', or 'instruction' is it?

The Meaning of *Tôrâh*

The word *tôrâh* occurs very frequently in the Old Testament to denote 'instruction' of various kinds. Its etymology is contested, and two possibilities present themselves. Either it has been formed from the verb *hôrâh* (√*yārāh*) with the meaning 'to direct, aim, point out', or it is a Hebrew counterpart of the Babylonian word *tertu*, 'oracular decision, divine instruction'. Most prob-

---

2. Cf. J. A. Sanders, *Torah and Canon* (1973).

ably the former is correct, in which case the word means 'guidance, instruction'.[3] As such it could be the kind of instruction which any person might give in a whole variety of situations. However, we find that the word is predominantly used for religious instruction, and especially for the kind of instruction which could be given by a priest. The clearest confirmation of this is to be found in Jer 18:18:

> Then they said, 'Come let us make plots against Jeremiah, for *tôrâh* shall not perish from the priest, nor counsel from the wise, nor the word from the prophet. Come, let us smite him with the tongue, and let us not heed any of his words.'

The assumption here is evidently that *tôrâh* would especially be given by a priest. Yet we find in the Old Testament that others besides priests give *tôrâh*. Hence the prophet does so (cf. Isa 8:16); so also does the wise man (cf. Prov 3:1; 4:2), and also apparently the king (cf. Isa 2:3). To what extent any clear [[107]] development or extension of meaning can be traced over a period is hard to determine with confidence. Evidently a word of *tôrâh* was particularly the kind of instruction that the ancient Israelite expected to learn from a priest, so that it was a religious direction, the ultimate source of which was to be found with God.

What kinds of rulings might be the subject of such priestly *tôrôth* can only be inferred from the particular duties and concerns which fell to the priest to take care of in ancient Israel. Obviously matters concerning the protection of the holiness of a sanctuary, the obligations of worshippers at the major festivals, and what perquisites belonged to the priests and their families would form a part of this. The fact, however, that a much wider range of concerns dealing with the health of the community, the avoidance of unclean foods, and even sexual and social manners, counsels us against drawing any very narrow conclusions about the nature and scope of *tôrâh*. Cultic, ethical and hygienic interests could all be made the subject of priestly *tôrôth*. That the word could readily be extended to cover matters where the traditions of the past, most naturally thought to be in the custody of the priest as the guardian of the community's lore, could all be included is not difficult to see. What is noticeable is that it does not specifically apply to juridical traditions in the narrower sense of 'law', nor is it a broad word for general ethical admonition, although it could include this.

So far as the formation of the Old Testament is concerned a quite fundamental development is to be found in the book of Deuteronomy, where *tôrâh* becomes applied to the law-book itself:

> This is the *tôrâh* which Moses set before the children of Israel; these are the testimonies, statutes, and the ordinances, which Moses spoke to the Israelites when they came out of Egypt. . . . (Deut 4:44–45)

3. The question of the meaning and use of *tôrâh* is discussed extensively by G. A. Ostborn, *Torah in the Old Testament. A Semantic Study* (Lund, 1945).

This summarising introduction to the central part of the book of Deuteronomy is particularly helpful to us in showing the way in which the idea of *tôrâh* was developed and extended. It must once have formed an opening introduction to an edition [[108]] of the book, and so clearly was intended to apply to a written text. Hence it has carried over the idea of an orally given *tôrâh*, delivered as occasion demanded, to a more permanently recorded account of what constituted the *tôrâh* of Israel.

There is clearly also a very marked effort present to achieve comprehensiveness, as is shown by the definition which follows and the wide range of rulings and injunctions which the book contains. The definition in terms of testimonies (Hebrew *ʿedôt*), statutes (*mišpāṭîm*) and ordinances (*ḥuqqîm*) is interesting for the way in which it brings together words denoting laws, decrees, and admonitions under one all-embracing category. From this time onwards *tôrâh* came to signify the most comprehensive type of instruction in which legal, cultic, and more loosely social obligations were brought together. To obey *tôrâh* was to satisfy the demands of religious, social and family life in the broadest possible compass. Even quite directly political obligations would appear to be included.

The definition that is given in Deut 4:44f., therefore, provides a valuable summarising note about the kind of duties that are brought under the hearing of *tôrâh* in the book of Deuteronomy. When we look at the contents of this book this anticipation is fully borne out. Very decidedly the book is addressed to each and every Israelite, who bears the responsibility for bringing its contents to the attention of his children (cf. Deut 6:7; 11:19), and of reflecting upon them carefully himself (cf. Deut 11:18). No exceptions are envisaged or allowed for. Included in the book are rulings of a markedly legal character concerning the processes of law and the way in which serious crimes are to be dealt with (cf. Deut 19:14-21).

Murder, theft, adultery, and the problems arising therefrom about the trial and punishment of offenders, are all included. But so also are matters of an exclusively religious kind such as the observance of cultic festivals (Deut 16:1-17), which even incorporates notes on how the festivals are to be interpreted. Perhaps more surprising in a document of this kind, which is concerned to spell out precisely the nature of the individual's responsibilities and obligations, is that moral attitudes are commanded, particularly those of love and respect (cf. Deut 15:7-11). Even more prominently is this carried over into the [[109]] religious realm, so that it becomes a prime duty to love God, and to feel and express gratitude to him (cf. Deut 6:5; 9:4-5). Beyond these broad ethical admonitions, we find that a wide area of life comes under the heading of *tôrâh*. Obligations for military service, the care of buildings, the conservation of the environment and the protection of slaves are all included (cf. Deut 20:1-20; 21:10-17; 22:6-7; 23:12-14).

So far as the threat of punishment for disobedience to particular *tôrôth* is concerned, two points call for comment. The first is that the entire machinery of the state, with all its sanctions, is involved in dealing with all offences against the injunctions laid down. Hence religious offences, especially apostasy, are to be dealt with by the most severe sanctions (Deut 13:5, 8–11). In some cases, as for instance in that of failing to show a right attitude, it would clearly have been impossible to adjudicate the fault. Yet this highlights the second feature concerning punishment, which is that, over and above the particular punishments and sanctions that society could impose, there stood a larger sanction. This is that Israel would have shown itself to be disobedient to the covenant with Yahweh, and would forfeit all its privileged status as his chosen people. We have already considered this earlier in relation to the Deuteronomic teaching concerning Israel and the covenant.

This brings us to note the wider theological context in which the book of Deuteronomy places the notion of *tôrâh*. This is not treated simply as 'good advice', which might, through social pressure and the good sense of the hearers, be accepted by men of good intention everywhere. It is directed specifically to Israel and is the *tôrâh* of the covenant by which Israel's relationship to God is governed. It is as a consequence of belonging to the elect people of Yahweh that the Israelite finds himself committed in advance to obedience to *tôrâh*. Hence he found that it was imperative for him to know *tôrâh*, to understand it correctly, and to be reminded of it regularly, if he were to remain as a member of his people. Furthermore, it was upon the sincerity and willingness of each individual Israelite that the well-being of the whole nation was made to depend.

When we come to ask the question 'What is *tôrâh*?', therefore, the clearest and fullest answer that we have is that which is [[110]] provided by the book of Deuteronomy. *Tôrâh* is the comprehensive list of instructions and stipulations by which Israel's covenant with God is controlled. What we have now to do is to enquire further how far this understanding of *tôrâh* has affected the Old Testament as a whole.

· ·

The Old Testament as Promise

Prophecy and Hope

[[140]] The problem of the origin and meaning of the prophecies of hope and restoration for Israel must find answers to two main questions. The first concerns the circumstances in which it is possible for us to see that such a message would have been entirely appropriate. The second question concerns the reason why this message of hope has been added to each of the prophets, and why it takes very much the same form in each of them.

The first question has generally been answered by noting the real birth of the message of hope during the years of Babylonian exile, and regarding this as the first truly appropriate moment for it to have arisen. However, not all scholars have been convinced that no place for a message of hope existed in the eighth century B.C. We may consider the problem in relation to one particular text, that of Amos 9:11–12:

'In that day I will raise up the booth of David that is fallen,
   and repair its breaches and raise up its ruins, [[141]]
   and rebuild it as in the days of old;
that they may possess the remnant of Edom
   and all the nations who are called by my name,'
   says the LORD who does this.

The use of the metaphor of the 'booth', or 'shelter', of David to signify his kingdom raises a number of questions. The reference could be to the collapse of the united kingdom of David, which took place with the division into two kingdoms after Solomon's death. Or it could be to the downfall of the northern kingdom in 722, which had once been an important part of the territory ruled by David. It could, however, also refer to the fall of the Davidic dynasty from the throne of Judah, which did not take place until Zedekiah's deposition in 587 B.C. A large number of scholars have taken the reference in the latter sense, so that the promise in these two verses, as well as that which follows in Amos 9:13–15, have been ascribed to the post-exilic age. On the other hand, G. von Rad, in arguing that the reference is back to the disruption in the tenth century B.C., has defended the authenticity of the saying from Amos.[4]

In itself the saying scarcely allows a very clear-cut decision to be made. However, when we compare it with comparable sayings in Hosea (e.g. Hos 2:5), and Isaiah (e.g. Isa 9:2–7; 11:1–9; 32:1–8) regarding the restoration of the united Davidic kingdom, the picture gains a clearer perspective. The recent recognition that a very significant and substantial editing of a collection of Isaiah's prophecies occurred during the reign of Josiah (640–609 B.C.),[5] enables us to see that a very attractive case can be made out for recognising that the age of Josiah witnessed a very marked resurgence of hope for the restoration of Israel. The clearest indication of this is to be found in the Deuteronomic movement and its ambition of re-establishing a united Israel modelled after the old kingdom of David. Certainly by this time in the seventh century B.C., there were indications of the weakening of the Assyrian grip on Judah, and substantial signs of new hope and expectation abroad in the land. There is no reason, therefore, why all the hopeful prophecies to be found in Amos, Hosea and Isaiah should be later than this time. The assumption that all of them must be post-exilic is [[142]] unnecessarily rigid. In fact several scholars have concluded that, even if serious doubt remains about the presence of a clear word of hope in Amos, at least with Hosea and Isaiah these prophets looked for a restoration of Israel beyond the judgments which they foresaw.[6] There are strong reasons, therefore, why it should be fully recognised that a message of hope entered into the mainstream of Israelite-Judean prophecy no later than the seventh century B.C., and probably before this time.

4. G. von Rad, *Old Testament Theology*, Vol. II, p. 138.
   5. H. Barth, *Israel und das Assyrerreich in den Nichtjesajanischen Texten des Protojesajabuches* (Diss. Hamburg, 1974).
   6. Cf. J. Bright, *Covenant and Promise*, pp. 92ff.

It remains doubtful, however, whether this message of hope can be properly called eschatological, for the simple reason that Judah had survived to become a remnant of the old kingdom of Israel. Very possibly the beginning of the 'remnant'-theology in Isaiah is to be traced back to this time, although the original prophecy had looked in a very different direction. What was anticipated was a resurgence of Israelite power and independence after the disastrous years of Assyrian oppression and suzerainty. Such a hope could take up the themes and images which belonged to a far older stage of Israel's worship and religious life. Especially here we can see an influence from the older Jerusalem traditions associated with the Davidic monarchy and the great festivals celebrated in the temple there. All of these belong to the general theme of hope, rather than with an eschatology in the full sense.

What was lacking for an eschatology was a sense that a full and complete end had overtaken the survivors of Israel, so that an entirely new beginning needed to be made. This is the new element that came with the disaster which overtook Judah in 587, with the destruction of the temple and the removal of the Davidic king. The two institutions which seemed to have achieved most in providing a sense of continuity with the greatness of Israel's past were swept away. From this time onwards the whole direction of the prophetic faith turned to look for the return of that part of the community of Judah which had been carried into Babylonian exile in 598 and 587. We find this very fully demonstrated in the way in which the book of Jeremiah has been expanded and developed. The prophet's words of hope for a renewal of normal life in Judah (cf. esp. Jer 32:15) have been very fully and extensively elaborated by Deuteronomistic editors to show that this fulfilment could only come when the [[143]] return from exile took place (Jer 24:1-10; 29:10-14; 32:36-44). We find a similar hope of a return from the Babylonian exile at the centre of the message of Ezekiel (cf. Ezek 36:8-15; 37:15-23; 40-48), and then coming into full flower in the preaching of the prophet of Isaiah 40-55 (Isa 40:1-5; 43:1-7, 14-21; 45:20-23).

The prophets who followed after the time of Babylon's downfall, when the first company of returning Jews made their way back to their homeland, elaborate still further on this hope of a return. They do so, however, in language which becomes increasingly extravagant, and which displays a growing frustration with the political and social possibilities of the times. The prophetic hope of a return to the land and a restoration of Israel acquires a marked supernatural and apocalyptic character (cf. Isa 60:1-22; 61:1-7; 66:12-16). In this way the prophetic eschatology appears to have slipped further and further away from the realities of history, and to have moved into a strange world of apocalyptic images and themes. Yet these themes and images themselves derive from the older cult and prophecy of Israel.

When we look at the canonical collection of the Latter Prophets we find that there is a certain connectedness between the different prophets, and signs that their preaching has been treated as a part of a larger whole. It is the conviction that all the prophets were speaking about the death and rebirth of Israel that has brought together prophecies which stretch across

more than two centuries. Beginning with Amos and the onset of the threat
from Assyria in the middle of the eighth century, and continuing until the
early returns of the fifth century, Israel and Judah had suffered traumatic disasters. The specific and individual circumstances of threat and danger have
been swallowed up in a wider portrayal of doom and judgment which applies
to all Israel. History has become subsumed in eschatology. Yet in a comparable fashion, the message of hope that began no later than the middle of the
seventh century has become an all-embracing message of Israel's restoration
and future greatness. No hesitation and compunction has been felt, therefore, by the editors of the separate prophetic books in applying this message
of hope to each of the books. Such a hope belonged to the prophetic 'message', even though, from a [[144]] strictly literary viewpoint, it did not derive
from each individual prophet. Individual prophetic hopes and promises have
become part of a much greater theme of 'promise' which came to be seen as
characteristic of prophecy as a whole.

The Forms of Prophetic Hope

The particular way in which the prophetic books have been put together, supplemented and expanded to form a large canonical collection, has clearly
been the result of a very extended process. Nevertheless, within this process
a number of basic concepts and themes have played a dominant role. Where
the modern critical scholar is rightly desirous of listening to the differing
sound of each of the prophetic voices, the editors of the collection have
worked with a different aim, and have tended to obscure these different
tones by the way in which they have edited the collection into a whole. The
result now is that we frequently find difficulty in determining the authenticity
or otherwise of particular sayings, as we have already noted especially in the
case of the hope expressed by Amos and Hosea. Certainly it has not been the
needs of liturgical use alone that have determined this, but rather the conviction that the prophetic message is a unity, the ultimate author of which is
God himself. The theological student of the meaning of prophecy must consequently be content at times to accept some degree of uncertainty as to
when a particular saying was added to a book, since to note this has not been
in any way a concern of the original editors.

However, this way of treating the prophetic books, in which some consistency of pattern and ideas is evident, does enable us to see the importance of
a number of recurrent themes which form the centre of their message of
hope. We may now note briefly what these are. At the head of them we can
undoubtedly place the expectation of a return from exile (cf. esp. Jer 24:1–
10; 29:10–14; Ezek 36:8–15; Isa 40:1ff.). The plight of those deported to
Babylon has become a kind of model or symbol of the plight of all the scattered and dispossessed Jews who formed the Diaspora. The very word 'exile'
comes to take on a larger significance as a description of the scattered Jews of
every land.

[[145]] Behind this we can also detect the importance of the consequences that arose from the Assyrian deportations from the northern kingdom in the late eighth and seventh centuries B.C. (cf. Jer 31:7-9; Ezek 36:8-
15; Isa 49:6). The return of these people too, however completely they appeared to have become lost among the nations, became a part of this hope of
a return. So the return to Jerusalem and to Mount Zion became the classic
image of how Israel's restoration would take place (cf. Isa 60:1-22; Joel 3:9-
17). With this is coupled a related theme that members of Gentile nations
will join with them, to pay homage to them and to act as their servants (cf. Isa
33:1-24; 35:1-10). This theme of 'return' also implies the great importance
that was attached to the promise of the land. Never is there the slightest suggestion that Israel's misfortune of being scattered among the nations should
be a permanent condition, or that it might re-establish its national existence
in some other territory than that promised to the patriarch Abraham. This
land itself becomes central to the theme of promise.

There is, however, a very deep concern in the prophetic message of hope
that Israel should recover its status as a nation. In particular, the division into
two separate kingdoms of Israel and Judah is viewed as an act of sin, which
must not be repeated. The Israel of the future is consequently foreseen as a
single united Israel under a single ruler (cf. Ezek 37:15-23).

This brings us to the third of these basic prophetic themes of hope,
which is that the new Israel is to come under a restored king of the Davidic
line (Amos 9:11-12; Hos 2:5; Isa 9:2-7; 11:1-9; 32:1; 33:17; Jer 33:19-26;
Ezek 37:24-28). This hope, which found a basic point of reference in the
older Davidic promise tradition delivered by the prophet Nathan in 2 Sam
7:13, became the foundation of the later 'messianic' hope. Since the restored
king was to be an 'anointed' ruler (Hebrew *māšîaḥ*) of the Davidic family,
there is some basis for speaking of a 'messianic' hope. Yet this was certainly
not the full expectation of a remarkable superhuman figure such as developed in later Judaism. Rather, it was a hope of the restoration of a Davidic
ruler, based on the belief that this dynasty alone had been entrusted with this
privilege by God.

Two factors in particular belonged to this hope. In the first [[146]] place it
was important, since the renewal of the monarchy would signify for Israel the
return to full political independence. In this particular form the hope was
destined never to be realised, even though the possibility that it would be at
one time seemed real and even imminent (Hag 2:23). In the second place the
expectation of a return of the kingship, restricted to the Davidic line, was important for the concept of the unity of Israel. It is no surprise, therefore, to
discover that eager eyes must have surveyed the fortunes of the Davidic family for a long time after Zerubbabel's death (cf. 1 Chr 3:16-24). Throughout
the period when this hope was at its greatest, it is evident that the main
weight of interest lay with the belief in the divine destiny of the descendants
of David, rather than with any deep commitment to the monarchy as an institution on the part of Israel. In this form the hope appears gradually to have
waned, only to re-appear later in a more radical form with the expectation of

a messiah of more transcendent proportions, but once again descended, as prophecy foretold, from the house of David.

In relation to the messianic hope we find how the written form of prophecy lent new possibilities to the interpretations which could be placed upon it. The hope of a restoration of a Davidic kingship became transformed into a wider portrayal of the coming of a heavenly saviour figure. The prophecies on which the later hope was built, as in the Messianic Testimonia from Qumran,[7] were the earlier prophecies seen in a new context of expectation. It is in no way the special divine status of the king in ancient Israel which has aroused this pattern of interpretation, but rather the unique importance of the Davidic family in Israel's history.

A further basic theme, or model, of the prophetic hope is the belief in an ultimate glorification of Mount Zion as the centre of a great kingdom of peace. Jerusalem itself becomes a place of the greatest importance, with its rebuilt temple looked to as the place where God's 'glory' or 'presence' would appear (cf. Ezek 48:35; Mal 3:1). To this the nations would come as an act of pilgrimage and homage, rather in the way that their representatives had done long before in the short-lived kingdom of David (Isa 2:2–4 = Mic 4:1–5; cf. Isa 60:14; 61:5).

[[147]] It becomes evident on examination that all of these images of what the restoration of Israel would bring have been drawn in one way or another from the tradition of Israel's past history as a nation. The central role of Israel as the people of God is everywhere assumed and used as a basis for depicting the future. Yet this is not in any way out of a conviction that history is cyclic in its nature, and that an inevitable 'return to the past' would take place as future years unrolled. In general such a deterministic view of history appears to have been almost completely alien to the Israelite tradition of thought. It is instead the belief that Israel's election must mean something, both for Israel itself and for the nations which would be blessed through it, that lies at the heart of these convictions. In calling Abraham, God had begun a task which he had not completed. Indeed the intransigence of the old Israel and its resort to idolatry were regarded as having frustrated this purpose. Yet the purpose itself had not, and could not, be abandoned. God would bring to fruition that which he had begun. By an understandable human reaction, the very frustrations and disappointments of the post-exilic age appear to have intensified the strength and firmness of the conviction that the final goal of God's purpose—the eschatological age of salvation—would certainly come.

It is difficult, to the point of impossibility, to speak of this element of 'promise' and eschatological hope in the Old Testament in terms of a 'doctrine,' or of a rounded theology. Its literary form is primarily that of prophecy, and its ideas are expressed through images and thematic models, and not through firm doctrines or fixed schemes in which the sequence of events could be determined. The very flexibility of the literary and verbal expression

---

7. Cf G. Vermes, *The Dead Sea Scrolls in English* (1962), p. 245.

of such hopes and images meant that there could be no single form of interpretation which could be heralded as self-evidently correct.

It is against this background that we must understand the rise of certain key-words and sometimes bizarre images in Jewish hope. In some circles this gradually developed into a new literary form, which we can call apocalyptic, of which the book of Daniel is the only full example in the Old Testament.[8] This new type of literature, however, which for a period flourished extravagantly in Judaism, arose out of earlier [[148]] prophecy, and carried its images and themes to strange extremes. For this to have happened one essential prerequisite was necessary, and this was that prophecy should already have become an accepted part of a canonical literature. The new 'prophecy' was essentially the ability to discover the further messages that were believed to lie hidden in the old (cf. Dan 9:2).

With the arrival of apocalyptic the concept of God's promise to Israel acquired a new medium of expression. Yet already we find an abundance of indications that it was a medium with genuine antecedents in the way in which earlier prophecy had been studied, interpreted and re-applied by the editors of the prophetic books themselves. There is no clear and broadly acceptable definition by which the passage from prophecy to apocalyptic can be readily traced. The strange images and symbols of the latter have their antecedents in the poetry and conventional descriptions of divine activity which we find in the former. With this new literary form there went a clear pattern of interpretation which could treat all prophecy as a kind of apocalyptic, with hidden meanings contained in every word, and names and numbers used as ciphers. Hence it is no surprise to discover from the way in which the prophetic books of Nahum and Habbakuk were interpreted at Qumran that they could be regarded as though they were a form of apocalyptic.[9] All prophecy had come to be seen as a veiled form of revelation, the fundamental message of which was the judgment that still awaited the sinners of the earth and the salvation that was to come for Israel.

Already, therefore, we discover that the particular assumptions about Old Testament prophecy that we find in the New Testament are firmly anticipated in the Old. If we are to seek some defence of the early Christian claim that the prophetic message of the Old Testament had been fulfilled in the events concerning Jesus of Nazareth, then we must begin to trace critically and historically the way in which prophecy itself developed from the preached utterances of inspired individuals to become a written series of texts, collected together and edited to form great books. These were then subsequently interpreted as a vast repository of hidden truths and revelations which the [[149]] skilful interpreter and the discerning student of events could use to discover the will of God.

---

8. For the origin of apocalyptic and its relation to prophecy, see P. D. Hanson, *The Dawn of Apocalyptic. The Historical and Sociological Roots of Jewish Apocalyptic Eschatology* (1975).

9. Cf. G. Vermes, *The Dead Sea Scrolls in English*, pp. 230–40.

The Promise in the Law and the Writings

So far we have looked at the theme of promise in the Old Testament in relation to the books of the prophets. Attempts that have been made from time
to time to trace the ultimate origin of this concept of promise further back
than the prophets, to discover its roots either in an ancient mythology or a
particular tradition of the cult, must be rejected. It is the way in which the
prophets gave new hope to Israel and Judah, after the ruination of the old
kingdoms had occurred in the eighth to the sixth centuries B.C., that has
given rise to this fundamental theme of promise.

Yet when we turn to the New Testament for some guidance upon the way
in which the promise was being interpreted in the first century A.D. we find
that passages from the Pentateuch and the Writings could be interpreted as
though they were prophecy. This is most notable in the way in which royal
psalms are interpreted as foretellings of the coming of the messiah in early
Christian preaching, so that the text of the psalm, which was certainly originally composed and intended for liturgical use, is treated exactly as though it
were prophecy. The divine declaration of Ps 2:1–2 is interpreted in Acts
4:25–26, as a prophetic foretelling of the sufferings of Jesus, in precisely the
same way as though it had been preserved in a book of prophecy:

> Why did the Gentiles rage,
>   and the peoples imagine vain things?
> The kings of the earth set themselves in array,
>   and the rulers were gathered together,
>   against the Lord and against his Anointed.

Even in the case of a psalm which carries in itself no special indication
that it was a royal psalm (Psalm 118), we find that it could be treated as containing a prophecy of the rejection of the messiah by God's people in Acts
4:11. Evidently what has taken place is that the category of prophecy, and the
assumptions and [[150]] methods of interpretation that were believed to belong to it, have been carried over to other parts of the Old Testament. This
recognition is of great importance in the modern critical attempt to uncover
the origins of the messianic hope in ancient Israel. It also matters greatly in
connection with attempts to claim a far greater number of the psalms as being concerned with the kingship of Israel than any explicit statement in the
text warrants. So attempts have been carried through in which the institution
of kingship itself, and the distinctive high ideology associated with this, have
been regarded as the real basis of Israel's 'messianic' hope.[10] Yet this can be
true only by reaching a very extended understanding of what such a hope
truly entails.

We have already seen that, so far as the main essential of the 'messianic'
hope was concerned, this derived from the expectation of the restoration of

---

10. Cf. A. Bentzen, *King and Messiah* (ed. G. W. Anderson,[2] 1970); and T. N. D. Mettinger, *King and Messiah. The Civil and Social Legitimation of the Israelite Kings* (*Coniectanea Biblica. Old Testament Series* 8, Lund, 1976).

the Davidic family to the kingship of a renewed Israel after the Babylonian exile. The distinctive elements of the old royal ideology as such, difficult as this is to define on account of its highly symbolic language, came to be caught up in this, but was not its main stimulus. The prophetic interpretation of specific psalms has not arisen because these psalms were originally thought to be prophetic in their nature, but rather as a consequence of the trends and developments which were taking place in the formation of a collection of canonical texts.

. . . .

[[153]] From this perspective we can see that the early Christian claim that the whole Old Testament is a book of prophetic promise cannot be regarded as something imposed on the literature from outside. Rather it reflects an understanding which exists within the Old Testament canon itself. We find, therefore, that the Old Testament is presented to us with two major themes governing its form and establishing a basis of understanding from which all its writings are to be interpreted. It is a book of *tôrâh*—of the 'law' of the covenant between God and Israel. Yet it is also a book of promise, for it recognises the tensions that have arisen within this covenant relationship and the fact that Israel stands poised between the election of God, with all the promises that this entails of land, national life, and the tasks of bringing blessing to the nations, and its fulfilment. The law itself is both a gift and a goal. While we can see that historically the theme of 'law' belongs primarily to the Pentateuch and that of 'promise' to the Prophets, in practice all parts of the literature could be interpreted from the perspective of both themes. However, their mutual interrelationships, and the questions of priority between them, do not appear with any [[154]] rigid fixity. In their own ways, both Judaism and Christianity saw the relationships differently as they built upon the Old Testament and established their own priorities in interpreting its demands upon the continuing 'Israel of God'.

WALTER C. KAISER JR.

b. 1929

Promise

Walter Kaiser is a leading figure among evangelical biblical scholars. After a dozen years as academic dean at Trinity Evangelical Divinity School, he became Professor of Old Testament and President of Gordon-Conwell Theological Seminary. An ordained minister in the Evangelical Free Church, he took his Ph.D. from Brandeis University, in Mediterranean studies.

Selected Writings by Kaiser

1978   *Toward an Old Testament Theology.* Grand Rapids: Zondervan.
1981   *Toward an Exegetical Theology: Biblical Exegesis for Preaching and Teaching.* Grand Rapids: Baker.
1983   *Toward Old Testament Ethics.* Grand Rapids: Zondervan.
1994   (with Moisés Silva) *An Introduction to Biblical Hermeneutics: The Search for Meaning.* Grand Rapids: Zondervan.
1995   *The Messiah in the Old Testament.* Grand Rapids: Zondervan.

Walter C. Kaiser Jr.'s
Approach to Old Testament Theology

Reprinted with permission from Walter C. Kaiser Jr., *Toward an Old Testament Theology* (Grand Rapids: Zondervan, 1978), pp. 11–14, 32–35.

The Method of Old Testament Theology

[[11]] Is there, then, a distinctive methodology for this discipline? Or has all the toil of the last half century been for no real purpose? Is there an inner, persistent, distinctive, and characteristic theme or plan that would mark off the central concern for the OT? And would it aid the theological curriculum or even the general reader's appreciation of the text to have this plan laid out in its successive installments? Does all this amount to a system or a logic that builds within the Old Testament? And does this pattern give evidence that it expects additional events and meanings even beyond the range of its canonical writings? Even more critical, can it be shown from the claims of the original participants in the events and thoughts of these OT texts that they were conscious of a continuing stream of events, meanings, and ideas which preceded them and that they felt themselves obligated to acknowledge some type of permanent, normative demands laid on their beliefs and actions? These are the hard, methodological problems which the past generation and ours have found difficult to answer, especially since this discipline was viewed as the synthesis of all the "assured results" of OT study over the past two centuries. Unfortunately, some of these results represented as great bondage to grids, systems, and philosophies as those the discipline had originally attempted to evade in 1933.

Our proposal is to distinguish sharply biblical theology's method from that of systematics or the history-of-religion. There is an inner center or plan to which each writer consciously contributed. A principle of selectivity is already evident and divinely determined by the rudimentary disclosure of the divine blessing-promise theme to all men everywhere as the canon opens in Genesis 1–11 and continues in Genesis 12–50. Rather than selecting that theological data which strikes our fancy or meets some current need, the text will already have set up priorities and preferences of its own. These nodal points can be identified, not on the basis of ecclesiastical or theological camps, but by such criteria as: (1) the critical placement of interpretive statements in the textual sequence; (2) the frequency of repetition of the ideas; (3) the recurrence of phrases or terms that begin to take on a technical status; (4) the resumption of themes where a forerunner had stopped often with a more extensive area of reference; (5) the use of categories of assertions previously used that easily lend themselves to a description of a new stage in the program of history; and (6) the organizing standard by which people, places, and ideas were marked for approval, [[12]] contrast, inclusion, and future and present significance.

Not only must the job of selectivity be initiated and guided by textual controls set by the authorial truth-intentions of the writers of the OT, but these same men must also be closely followed in the evaluation of all theological conclusions drawn from these "selected" theological data.

If the value judgments, interpretations, and estimates which they placed on these key events and persons in the text be deleted, dismissed, neglected, or replaced with those of our own, we will need to blame no one but ourselves if the authority of the Bible seems to also have evaporated beneath our own best scholarly efforts. The truth of the matter, for better or for worse, is that these writers claim they were the recipients of divine revelation in the selection *and* evaluation of what was recorded. Consequently, all serious theologies will need to reckon with both aspects of this claim, not to speak of the claim itself to have received revelation.

To repeat then, in our proposed methodology, biblical theology draws its very structure of approach from the historic progression of the text and its theological selection and conclusions from those found in the canonical focus. Thereby it agrees in part with the historical and sequential emphasis of the diachronic type of OT theology and the normative emphasis of the structural type.

Yet it does more than merely synthesize or eclectically accept a new combination of what has been heretofore a set of antithetical methods. It deliberately attempts to derive its theology from the exegetical insights of canonical sections, whether it be a summarizing paragraph or chapter, a key teaching passage, a strategic event as evaluated in the context where it first appeared and in subsequent references in the canon, or a whole book or group of books which are so closely connected in theme, approach, or message as to provide an explicit unity.

Amidst all the multiplexity and variety of materials, events, and issues, it is our contention that there does exist an eye to this storm of activity. Such a starting point is *textually* supplied and *textually* confirmed as the canon's central hope, ubiquitous concern, and measure of what was theologically significant or normative. While the NT eventually referred to this focal point of the OT teaching as the promise, the OT knew it under a constellation of such words as promise, oath, blessing, rest, and seed. It was also known under such formulas as the tripartite saying: "I will be your God, you shall be My people, and I will dwell in the midst of you" or the redemptive self-assertion formula scattered in part or in full form 125 times throughout the OT: "I am the Lord your God who brought you up [[13]] out of the land of Egypt." It could also be seen as a divine plan in history which promised to bring a universal blessing through the agency of an unmerited, divine choice of a human offspring: "In thee shall all families of the earth be blessed" (Gen 12:3).

So crucial is the passage rendering of Gen 12:3 (also 18:18; 28:14—all niphal form verbs) that Bertil Albrektson[1] acknowledges that if the niphal

---

1. Bertil Albrektson, *History and the Gods* (Lund, Sweden: C. W. K. Gleerup Fund, 1967), p. 79.

form is passive here and not reflexive as most modern translations claim, then a clear reference to a divine plan by which Abraham is chosen to be God's instrument to reach all the nations of the earth is explicitly taught in the text. But, alas, he feels constrained to reject it on the basis that this formula appears in the hithpael form (usually a reflexive form) in Gen 22:18 and 26:4: "Bless oneself."[2]

But a strong protest must be raised at this point for several exegetical reasons. First of all, in Gen 12:2 the divine blessing already is said to be attached to Abraham's person: "And thou [or "it," referring either to Abraham's name or nation] shalt be a blessing." Hence, neither he nor the nation are merely to be a formula of blessing; neither will he merely bless himself! Instead, even apart from the controversial niphal of verse 3, Abraham is to be the medium and source of divine blessing. Such was his destined mission in the first set of promises of verse 2 before moving on to another and higher statement of purpose on verse 3.

All five passages in Genesis (both the niphal and hithpael forms of the verb "to bless") are treated in the Samaritan, Babylonian (Onkelos), Jerusalem (Pseudo-Jonathan) Targums as passives. Indeed, the harmonistic interpretation which insists on rendering three niphals by two hithpaels is also misinformed when it insists on a uniform reflexive meaning of the hithpael, for that is not true.[3] Thus it cannot be assumed so facilely that the sense of the hithpael is clear and therefore it should be made the basis of rendering the sense of the "disputed niphal." The sense of both of these stems changed under the pressure of polemical interest in Rashi, then Clericus, and now the greater majority of linguists and exegetes. [[14]] Meanwhile, O. T. Allis's linguistic challenge has stood unrefuted and even unacknowledged by contemporary scholars—the meaning is clearly passive and the implications for OT biblical theology are massive!

The focus of the record fell on the *content* of God's covenant which remained epigenetically constant, i.e., the accumulation of materials as time went on grew around a fixed core that contributed life to the whole emerging mass. This content was a given word of blessing and promise. It was a declaration guaranteed by a divine pledge that God would freely do or be something to a certain person(s) in Israel there and then and to later Jewish descendants in the future so that God might thereby do or be something for all men, nations, and nature, generally. The immediate effects of this word were divine blessings (happenings or arrival of persons) usually accompanied by a promissory declaration of a future work or completion of the series—a divine

---

2. For the hithpael form of this verb, see Ps 72:17 and its parallelism in context, but note the LXX and Vulgate *passive* rendering.

3. The most definitive discussion of this problem ever is O. T. Allis's "The Blessing of Abraham," *Princeton Theological Review* 25 (1927): 263–98. See especially p. 281 where he lists these possible examples of a passive meaning for the hithpael: Gen 37:35; Num 31:23; Deut 4:21; 23:9; 1 Sam 3:14; 30:6; 1 Kgs 2:26; Job 15:28; 30:16, 17; Ps 107:17, 27; 119:52; Isa 30:29; Lam 4:1; Ezek 19:12; Dan 12:10; Mic 6:16.

promise. Accordingly, men received the promise and waited for the promise all in one plan.

But in its composition, it contained such variegated interests as to include: (1) material blessings of all men and beasts; (2) a special seed to mankind; (3) a land for a chosen nation; (4) spiritual blessing for all the nations; (5) a national deliverance from bondage; (6) an enduring dynasty and kingdom that would one day embrace a universal dominion; (7) a forgiveness of sin, and on and on.

No principle foisted as an "abstract divining rod" over the text could be expected to yield so great a theological payload. Only a textually supplied claim could have pointed our attention to such a constellation of interconnected terms and contents as are found in this single plan of God—His promise. The progress of this doctrine can be historically measured and described. Further, it will include its own pattern for a permanent, normative standard by which to judge that day and all other days by a yardstick which claims to be divinely laid on the writer of Scripture and on all subsequent readers simultaneously.

· ·

Canonical Precedence for a Center

[[32]] OT theologians have missed the only way for safe passage through these treacherous waters. That way must be an *inductively* derived theme, key, or organizing pattern which the successive writers of the OT overtly recognized and consciously supplemented in the progressive unfolding of events and interpretation in the OT. If amidst all the variety and multiplexity of the text there does, as we [[33]] contend, exist an eye to this storm of activity, it must be *textually* demonstrated that it is the canon's own "starting point" and *textually* reconfirmed in the canon's united witness that it is its own ubiquitous concern, central hope, and constant measure of what was theologically significant or normative!

Such a textually derived center, what the NT eventually was to call the "promise" (*epangelia*), was known in the OT under a constellation of terms. The earliest such expression was "blessing." It was God's first gift to the fish, fowl (Gen 1:22), and then to mankind (v. 28).

For men, it involved more than the divine gift of proliferation and "dominion-having." The same word also marked the immediacy whereby all the nations of the earth could prosper spiritually through the mediatorship of Abraham and his seed: this, too, was part of the "blessing." Obviously, pride of place must be given to this term as the first to signify the plan of God.

But there were other terms. McCurley[1] counted over thirty examples where the verb *dibber* (usually translated "to speak") meant "to promise." The promised items included (1) the land (Exod 12:25; Deut 9:28; 12:20; 19:8;

---

1. Foster R. McCurley, Jr., "The Christian and the Old Testament Promise," *Lutheran Quarterly* 22 (1970): 401–10, esp. p. 402, n. 2.

27:3; Josh 23:5, 10); (2) blessing (Deut 1:11; 15:6); (3) multiplication of God's possession, Israel (Deut 6:3; 26:18); (4) rest (Josh 22:4; 1 Kgs 8:56); (5) all good things (Josh 23:15); and (6) a Davidic dynasty and throne (2 Sam 7:28; 1 Kgs 2:24; 8:20, 24–25; 1 Chr 17:26; 2 Chr 6:15–16; Jer 33:14). Also note the noun *dābār* ("promise") in 1 Kgs 8:56 and Ps 105:42.

To these "promises" God added His "pledge" or "oath," thus making the immediate word of blessing and the future word of promise doubly secure. Men now had the divine word and a divine oath on top of that word (see Gen 22; 26:3; Deut 8:7; 1 Chr 16:15–18; Ps 105:9; Jer 11:5).[2]

The case for this inductively derived center is even more wide-ranging than the lexicographical or vocabulary approach traced so far. It also embraced several epitomizing formulae which summarized that central action of God in a succinct phrase or two. Such was what we have called the tripartite formula of the promise. This formula became the great hallmark of all biblical theology in both testaments. The first part of the formula was given in Gen 17:7–8 and 28:21, viz., "I will be a God to you and your descendants after [[34]] you." When Israel approached the eve of nationhood, again God repeated this word and added a second part, "I will take you for My people" (Exod 6:7). Thus Israel became God's "son," His "firstborn" (Exod 4:22), "a distinctive treasure" (Exod 19:5–6). Finally, the third part was added in Exod 29:45–46 in connection with the construction of the tabernacle: "I will dwell in the midst of you." There it was: "I will be your God; you shall be My people, and I will dwell in the midst of you." It was to be repeated in part or in full in Lev 11:45; 22:33; 25:38; 26:12, 44–45; Num 15:41; Deut 4:20; 29:12–13; et al. Later it appeared in Jer 7:23; 11:4; 24:7; 30:22; 31:1, 33; 32:38; Ezek 11:20; 14:11; 36:28; 37:27; Zech 8:8; 13:9; and in the NT in 2 Cor 6:16 and Rev 21:3–7.

Another formula, found in Gen 15:7, "I am Yahweh who brought you out of Ur of the Chaldeans," was matched by an even greater work of redemption: "I am the Lord your God who brought you out of the land of Egypt" (found almost 125 times in the OT). Still another formula of self-prediction was, "I am the God of Abraham, Isaac, and Jacob." All such formulae stress a continuity between the past, present, and future. They are parts of God's single ongoing plan.

As the record progressed, an accumulation of various metaphors and technical terms began to emerge. Many of these focused around the Davidic descendant. He was the "Seed," "Branch," "Servant," "Stone," "Root," "Lion," etc.[3] More often than not, the text had a backward glance to previous contexts which contained parts of the same metaphors and technical terms.

Nevertheless, neither the vocabulary nor the formulae and technical terms by themselves would make the case for a unified plan to the entirety of

2. Gene M. Tucker, "Covenant Forms and Contract Forms," *Vetus Testamentum* 15 (1965): esp. pp. 487–503, for the use of "oath" with promise.

3. Dennis C. Duling, "The Promise to David and Their Entrance into Christianity—Nailing Down a Likely Hypothesis," *New Testament Studies* 20 (1974): 55–77.

the OT progress of theology. The accent must ultimately fall where it fell for the writers themselves—on a network of interlocking moments in history made significant because of their content, free allusions to one another, and their organic unity. The focus of the record fell on the *content and recipients* of God's numerous covenants. The content remained epigenetically constant, i.e., there was a growth—even a sporadic growth from some points of view—as time went on around a fixed core that contributed vitality and meaning to the whole emerging mass. The content was a divine "blessing," a "given word," a "declaration," a "pledge," or "oath" [[35]] that God Himself would freely do or be something for all men, nations, and nature, generally.

Consequently, the revelatory event and/or declaration was frequently an immediate "blessing" as well as a promissory "word" or "pledge" that God would work in the future or had already worked in some given event or situation. God had done so in a way that significance had been given to man's present history and by this, simultaneously to future generations, also.

Synopsis of Kaiser's *Toward an Old Testament Theology* (1978)

Walter C. Kaiser Jr.
on the Promise Theologian: Isaiah

Reprinted with permission from Walter C. Kaiser Jr., *Toward an Old Testament Theology* (Grand Rapids: Zondervan, 1978), pp. 204–5, 207–10, 212–19.

[[204]] Beyond all question, Isaiah was the greatest of all the OT prophets, for his thought and doctrine covered as wide a range of subjects as did the length of his ministry. While his writing can be divided into two parts, chapters 1–39 keyed mainly to judgment and chapters 40–66 primarily emphasizing comfort, the book stands as a unit with its own continuity features such as the unique and distinctive phrase "the Holy One of Israel," which occurs twelve times in the first part and fourteen times in the second part.[1]

[[205]] The second part of Isaiah's work is a veritable OT biblical theology in itself. It might well be called the "Old Testament book of Romans" or the "New Testament within the Old Testament." Its twenty-seven chapters cover the same scope as the twenty-seven books of the NT. Chapter 40 begins with the predicted voice of John the Baptist crying in the wilderness as do the Gospels: chapters 65–66 climax with the same picture as the Apocalypse of John in Revelation 21–22 of the new heavens and the new earth. Sandwiched between these two end points is the midpoint, Isa 52:13–53:12, which is the greatest theological statement on the meaning of the atonement in all Scripture.

No less significant, however, is the first part of Isaiah's writing. Its successive "books," to use Franz Delitzsch's term,[2] are the books of Hardening (chaps. 1–6), Immanuel (7–12), Nations (13–23), the Little Apocalypse (24–27; 34–35), the Chief Cornerstone and Woes (28–33), and Hezekiah (36–39).

In our view, Isaiah must be called the theologian's theologian. And when the continuing promise of God was being considered, Isaiah excelled both in his use of the antecedent theology of the Abrahamic-Mosaic-Davidic promise and in his new contributions and development of that doctrine.

. . . .

The Branch of Yahweh

[[207]] Who is the "sprout" or "branch" (*ṣemaḥ*) of Isa 4:2–6? Very few doubt that the one who is afterward called "the Branch" is the Messiah. Nor do they

---

1. Conservatives have pointed to some forty additional phrases or sentences that appear in both parts of Isaiah as evidence for its unity, cf. Gleason L. Archer, Jr., *A Survey of Old Testament Introduction*, rev. ed. (Chicago: Moody Press, 1974), pp. 345ff.

2. Franz Delitzsch, *The Prophecies of Isaiah*, 2 vols. in C. F. Keil and F. Delitzsch, *Biblical Commentary on the Old Testament*, 25 vols., trans. James Martin (Grand Rapids: Eerdmans, 1969), 1:v–vii; 2:v.

doubt that later prophets directly depend on Isa 4:2 for that title. Those products who use this title for Messiah are:

"Branch of Yahweh" (Isa 4:2)
"Branch of David" (Jer 23:5–6)
"The Branch, My Servant" (Zech 3:8)
"Branch, a man" (Zech 6:12)

In Isa 4:2 the "Branch of Yahweh" is the Davidic dynasty in its human ("fruit of the land") nature as well as its divine ("of Yahweh"). In this case "Branch" would be an equivalent term for "Anointed" or "holy One."

But many object that "Branch" was not yet a fixed designation for Messiah; besides, its parallelism with "the fruit of the land" (4:2) favored a reference to the sprouting forth of the land under the beneficent influence of Yahweh. However, as the following chapters of Isaiah show, Messiah was the Mediator of these benefits and He Himself was the greatest of all the benefits.

Is it any wonder then that the later prophets applied this title to the living personal source of all these gifts in the last days? Some of those gifts found already in this passage are (1) the promise of the fruitfulness of the land; (2) the certainty of a remnant of "survivors"; (3) the holiness of the remnant; (4) the cleansing and purification of the moral filth of the people; and (5) the radiant glory of the personal presence of Yahweh dwelling in Zion with His people forever. The "holy nation" of Exod 19:6 would finally be completely realized as would the permanent "dwelling" of Yahweh in their midst. Even the "cloud by day" and "fire by night" (4:5) were to be renewed. For just as they were the visible proofs of God's presence in the wilderness (Exod 14:19ff.), so they would be a shade by day and illuminate the night to shield the city of God from all violence.

Immanuel

What the previous "Branch [or Sprout] of the Lord" passage left indefinite was now given personal shape and definition in the Immanuel [[208]] prophecies of Isaiah 7–11. This word came against the background of the Syro-Ephraimitic War in which Pekah, king of Israel, made an alliance with Rezin, king of Syria, to advance against Ahaz, king of Judah, with a view to installing the son of Tabeal as king on David's throne. This threat to Jerusalem and Judah was countered by Isaiah's invitation to Ahaz to "believe" God in order that Ahaz himself might "be believed," i.e., established (7:9). In fact, God would validate His good offer in so improbable a situation by performing any sign (i.e., miracle) Ahaz might choose from Sheol or heaven.

But Ahaz, true unbeliever that he was, piously rejected Yahweh's help with an oblique reference to Deut 6:16 about not tempting the Lord his God. The truth of the matter was that he expected little from Yahweh; moreover, he had probably already secretly sought the support of Tiglathpileser, king of Assyria (2 Kgs 16:7ff.).

Nevertheless, the Lord proceeded to give a sign. It was: "Behold, [you] the virgin are pregnant and bearing a son; you shall call his name Immanuel" (7:14). Now it is important to note several things: (1) the word *'almâh* denotes a "virgin" in every case where its meaning can be determined;[3] (2) it has the definite article, "*the* virgin"; (3) the verb "to call" is second person feminine and not third person feminine; and (4) the wording of this verse made use of older biblical phraseology: at the birth of Ishmael (Gen 16:11); at the birth of Isaac (Gen 17:19); and at the birth of Samson (Judg 13:5, 7). Thus, the sign given to Ahaz consisted in repeating to him the familiar phrases used in promising the birth of a son.

But this passage dealt with the birth of three children, all three being signs in Israel (8:17–18). Each of the three was introduced and then was later the subject of an expanded prophecy as follows:

1. · Shear-Jashub—"remnant shall return"
   7:3 → 10:20, 21, 22; 11:11, 16
2. Immanuel—"God with us"
   7:14 → 8:8, 10
3. Mahershalalhashbaz—"haste spoil, hurry prey"
   8:1, 3, 4 → 10:2, 6

In each of these passages we have the mention of a child born in fulfillment of the promise that had been made to David, to the [[209]] effect that his seed should be eternal. . . In the second half of his discourse on the three children, Isaiah thus reiterates the promise that had been made to David, and insists upon it. He makes it the foundation of his rebuke to the people for their corruptions . . .

Those who heard him understood that when Ahaz refused to ask the offered sign, the prophet repeated to him, in a new form, Jehovah's promise concerning the seed of David, and made that to be a sign that Jehovah would both keep his present pledge and punish Ahaz for his faithlessness. It may be doubted whether any of them had in mind the idea of just such a person as Jesus, to be born of a virgin, in some future century; but they had in mind some birth in the unending line of David which would render the truth, "God with us," especially significant.[4]

Furthermore, before this son, the most recent birth in the line of David, was able to understand right from wrong (7:16–17), a political revolution of major proportions would remove both Pekah and Rezin from power. But several other facts must be borne in mind at once if one is rightly to identify this "son." According to 8:8, 10, he is addressed as the prince of the land

---

3. Besides this text, it appears in the account of Rebekah (Gen 24:43); the sister of Moses (Exod 2:8); in the phrase "the way of a man with a maid" (Prov 30:19); and in the plural in Ps 68:25 [26]; Cant 1:3; 6:8; and the titles to Psalm 46 and 1 Chr 15:20.

4. Willis J. Beecher, "The Prophecy of the Virgin Mother: Isa. vii:14," *Homiletical Review* 17 (1889): 357–58.

("thy land, O Immanuel") and as the expected anointed one of David's house in 9:6–7 [5–6] ("There will be no end of the increase of his government and peace [as he rules] on the throne of David over his kingdom . . . forevermore"). Also Isaiah, like his contemporary Micah, everywhere presupposes that a period of judgment must precede the glorious messianic age. Therefore, whatever this sign and birth is, it cannot be the completion of the "last days."

Who then was this child? His messianic dignity totally excludes the notion that he may have been Isaiah's son born to some maiden newly married to the prophet after Shear-Jashub's mother supposedly died. Still less likely is it a reference to any marriageable maiden or some particular ideal maiden present at the time of the proclamation of this prophecy since the prophet has definitely said "the virgin." It is preferable to understand him to be a son of Ahaz himself, whose mother Abi, daughter of Zechariah, is mentioned in 2 Kgs 18:2—namely, his son Hezekiah. It is well known that this was the older Jewish interpretation, but it is also supposed that Hezekiah could not be the predicted "sign" of 7:14 since on present chronologies he must have already been nine years old at that time (about 734 B.C.). That last point is to be thoroughly studied before it is adopted. The chronology of Israel and Judah has been well secured with only one minor exception—a ten year difficulty in the [[210]] rule of Hezekiah. Without arguing the point at this time, I would like to boldly suggest that only Hezekiah meets all the demands of the text of Isaiah and yet demonstrates how he could be part and parcel of that climactic messianic person who would complete all that is predicted in this Immanuel prophecy. Only in this, the most recent installment in the Abrahamic-Davidic promise, could it be seen how God was still being "with" Israel in all His power and presence.

In Isa 9:6, a series of descriptive epithets are given to this newborn son who is to climax the line of David. He is "wonderful Counsellor," "mighty God," "Father of eternity,"[5] and "Prince of Peace." These four names represent, respectively, (1) the victory due to His wise plans and great skills in battle; (2) the irresistible Conqueror (cf. 10:21); (3) the fatherly rule of Messiah and His divine attribute of eternality; and (4) the everlasting peaceful reign of Messiah. His government and the peace during His regime would know no boundaries, for He would establish His kingdom in justice and righteousness forevermore (Isa 9:7). Unique among the descriptions of peace that will be observed during that era is the picture of all nature at rest and devoid of hostility (11:6–9). Again, there is a graphic prediction of the restoration of both the north and south to the land "in that day" (vv. 10–16). And from the stump of David's father, Jesse, would come that "shoot," even a "branch" (*nēzer*), upon whom the sevenfold gift of the Spirit of the Lord would rest as He ruled and reigned righteously and awesomely (vv. 1–5). The

---

5. It is not "Father of booty," which does not match the permanent attribute of "Prince of Peace"; rather, the Hebrew *'ab 'ad* is "Father of Eternity" as *'ad* means in Gen 49:26, Isa 57:15, and Hab 3:6.

whole picture of the future person and work of the Messiah was cast in terms of the Davidic promise as a glowing encouragement for Israel.

. . . .

Short Theology of the Old Testament

[[212]] One of the most remarkable sections of all the OT is Isaiah 40-66. In its general plan, it is laid out in three enneads: chapters 40-48, 49-57, and 58-66. In each of these three sets of nine messages the focus is directed to the particular aspect of the person and work of God. It is as close to being a systematic statement of OT theology as is the book of Romans in the NT. Its majestic movement begins with the announcement of the person and work of John the Baptist and spins to the dizzy heights of the suffering and triumphant servant of the Lord by the time the middle of the second ennead is reached. But this climax is again superseded by the concluding message on the new heavens and the new earth.

In each of the three sections there is a central figure. In Isaiah 40-48 the key figure is a hero who would come from the East to redeem Israel from captivity, namely, "Cyrus." The revelation of this hero, coming as it did right in the middle of the addresses (44:28-45:10), served as a bold challenge to the idols or deities embraced in that day to do likewise for the people. However, their inability to speak anything about the future could only lead to one conclusion: Yahweh was indeed the only God, and they were nothing at all.

In Isaiah 49-57 the central figure is the "servant of the Lord," who combined in his person all the people Israel, the prophet and [[213]] prophetic institution, and the Messiah in His role as Servant. Again the climactic description and his most important work was located at the middle point of this ennead: 52:13-53:12. The salvation effected by this servant had both objective and subjective aspects (54:1-56:9); indeed, its final and concluding work would involve the glorification of all nature.

The third ennead, 58-66, triumphantly announces the dawning of a new day of salvation for nature, nations, and individuals. At the center of this ennead was a new principle of life—the Spirit-filled Messiah (61:1-63:6) who bore the powers and dignities of the prophetic, priestly, and kingly officers.

Thus in each successive ennead another aspect of the Godhead and God's work was celebrated. In order, the emphases on the persons of the Godhead are Father, "Servant" [Son], and Holy Spirit. In work, they are Creator-Lord of history, Redeemer, and sovereign Ruler over all in the "eschaton." The five major forces in Isaiah's message are God, the people of Israel, the event of salvation, the prophet, and the word of God. Finally, this message even has several distinctive stylistic features. It has a plethora of divine self-asserverations such as "I am the first and the last," or "I am Yahweh"; a long series of participial phrases after the formula "Thus says the Lord" or "I am the Lord" which continue on to detail His special character; and a profuse number of appositional words appearing after the names of Yahweh or Israel as well as a great abundance of verbs to describe Yahweh's work of judgment or salvation. Such is the style of this most magnificent section of the OT. But let us treat each of these enneads in turn to examine that theology more closely.

The God of All (Isaiah 40–48)

The theme of Isaiah's call returns in this section as the holiness and righteousness of God are praised repeatedly. God is "the Holy One" (40:25; 41:14, 16, 20; 43:3, 14; 47:4; 48:17; and it continues in the later sections in 49:7 bis; 54:5; 55:5). He also is righteous (*ṣedeq*), i.e., straight, right, and faithful to a norm, His own nature and character. His righteousness could best be seen in His work of salvation, for the prophet often joined His righteousness and His performance of the covenant promise together (e.g., 41:2; 42:6–7; 46:12–13; note later 51:1, 5, 6, 8; 54:10; 55:3; 62:1–2). Only of God could it be said, "He is right" (41:26) or He is "a righteous God and Savior" (45:21), who declares "what is right" (v. 19) and who brings men near to His righteousness (46:13).

His nature is especially to be seen in His singleness and self-sufficiency. In Isaiah's famous set of six variations on the formula of self-predication, he set forth the incomparability[6] of Yahweh: Beside [[214]] Him there was no other God (44:6, 8; 45:5–6, 21). Thus the question remained: "To whom then will you liken Me?" (40:18, 25; 46:5). The forms of self-predication[7] are:

"I am Yahweh" or "I am Yahweh your God"	41:13; 42:6, 8; 43:3, 11; 45:5, 6, 18
"I am the first and I am the last"	41:4; 44:6; 48:12
"I am He"	41:4; 43:10, 25; 46:4; 48:12
"I am God"	43:13; 46:9
"I am your God"	41:10

But God's works were likewise enumerated in this first ennead. He was Creator, Kinsman-Redeemer, Lord of history, King of all, and Discloser of the future.

Repeatedly Isaiah stressed the fact that God had "created" (*bārāʾ*); "made" (*ʿāśâh* or *pāʿal*); "spread out" (*nāṭâh*); "stretched out" (*rāqaʿ*); "established" (*kûn*); and "founded" (*yāsad*) the heavens and the earth. In this vocabulary, so reminiscent of Genesis 1–2, he established God's ability to create as part of His credentials as rightful Lord of man's present history and final destiny (40:15, 17, 23–34; 42:5; 43:1–7; and later 54:15–16).

---

6. For an excellent study on this concept, see C. J. Labuschagne, *The Incomparability of Yahweh in the Old Testament* (Leiden: E. J. Brill, 1966), esp. pp. 111–12, 123f., 142–53.

7. See the discussion by Morgan L. Phillips, "Divine Self-Predication in Deutero-Isaiah," *Biblical Research* 16 (1971): 32–51.

Yahweh was also a Kinsman-Redeemer (*gô'el*) as Boaz was to Ruth. The verb to redeem (*gā'al*) and its derivatives appear twenty-two times. Here Isaiah used the motif of the Exodus as his source (cf. Exod 6:6; 15:13; Isa 45:15, 21). Involved in this redemption were (1) physical redemption from bondage (43:5–7; 45:13; 48:20; and later 49:9, 11, 14; 52:2–3; 55:12–13); (2) inward, personal and spiritual redemption with the removal of personal sin for Israel (43:25; 44:22; 54:8) and Gentiles (45:20–23; 49:6; 51:4–5); and (3) the eschatological redemption when Jerusalem and the land were rebuilt (40:9–10; 43:20; 44:26; 45:13; 49:16–17, 51:3, 52:1, 9; 53:11–12). Yahweh was a Kinsman-Redeemer without equal.[8]

[[215]] Currently, Yahweh was in charge of history itself, and the nations did not frighten Him at all (40:15, 17). In fact, foreign leaders were raised up to do His bidding in history (as is so aptly illustrated by Cyrus in 41:1–4); and they were ransomed or conquered on His authority (43:3–14; 44:24–45:8; 47:5–9). No wonder He was called "King" on four occasions. He was "King of Jacob" (41:21); "your King," O Israel (43:15); "King of Israel" (44:6); and as 52:7 summarized, "Your God is King." Isaiah also used the additional royal titles of "Shepherd" (40:9–11), "Witness," "Commandment-Giver," and "Leader" in Isa 55:3.[9]

One more word must be added before leaving the theology of this ennead: Yahweh was the discloser of the future. Before things happened, the prophet was told about them (41:22–23, 26; 42:9; 43:9–10; 44:7–8; 45:21; 46:10–11; 48:5). The challenge to the gods, who were poor rivals and actually nonentities at best, was to declare what was to come to pass in the future, be it good or bad. The most graphic of all the predictions was the naming of Cyrus and two of his greatest works for Israel almost two centuries before they took place (44:28). On such works as these Isaiah rested his case. Yahweh was God of gods, Lord of lords, King of kings and beyond all comparison. He was the God of all.

The Savior of All (Isaiah 49–57)

Two words would summarize the second plank in Isaiah's minitheology book: servant and salvation. But it was the figure of the servant of the Lord that captured the limelight in this section.

The advances in the portrayal of this corporate figure of "servant" are already observable in the use of the singular form twenty times in Isaiah 40–53 and in the plural form ten times in Isaiah 54–66.[10] To demonstrate that the servant is a collective term as well as an individual one representing the whole group can be done from two sets of data: (1) the servant is all Israel in

---

8. See F. Holmgren, *The Concept of Yahweh as Gô'el in Second Isaiah* (Diss., Union Theological Seminary, New York: University Microfilms, 1963). Also Carroll Stuhlmueller, *Creative Redemption in Deutero-Isaiah* (Rome: Biblical Institute Press, 1970).

9. Carroll Stuhlmueller, "Yahweh-King and Deutero-Isaiah," *Biblical Research* 11 (1970): 32–45.

10. Isa 54:17; 56:6; 63:17; 65:8–9, 13 (3×), 14–15; 66:14.

twelve out of the twenty singular references (41:8–10; 43:8–13; 43:14–44:5; 44:6–8, 21–23; 44:24–45:13; 48:1, 7, 10–12, 17); (2) the four great servant songs of Isa 42:1–7; 49:1–6; 50:4–9; and 52:13–53:12 all present the servant as an individual who ministers to Israel. Therein lies one of the greatest puzzles for those scholars who reject the corporate solidarity of the servant.

[[216]] Israel, the servant, is the "seed of Abraham," the patriarchal "friend" of God (41:8). "Abraham . . . was called and blessed" when "he was but one" and was subsequently "made . . . many" (51:2; cf. 63:16). Now God had already called Abraham His servant in Gen 26:24; and so had Moses referred to Abraham, Isaac, and Jacob as servants of the Lord (Exod 32:13; Deut 9:27). In fact, all Israel was regarded as His servants in Lev 25:42, 55. Thus the seed was still the center of God's blessings (43:5; 44:3; 45:19, 25; 48:19; 53:10; 54:3; 59:21; 61:9). "The seed shall be known among the nations . . . that they are a seed whom Yahweh has blessed" (65:9, 23; 66:22). That seed was God's "servant," or as it regularly appears in Isaiah 54–66, His "servants." As John Bright noted,

> The figure of the Servant oscillates between the individual and the group . . . He is the coming Redeemer of the true Israel who in his suffering makes the fulfillment of Israel's task possible; he is the central actor in the "new thing" that is about to take place.[11]

In the four servant songs, many of the individual's titles or descriptions are matched by identical ascriptions made of Israel in the Isaianic poems, for example:

An Individual		*All Israel*
42:1	"my chosen"	41:8–9
49:3	"my servant"	44:21
49:6	"a light to the nations"	42:6; 51:4
49:1	"called me from the womb"	44:2, 24; 43:1
49:1	"named my name"	43:1b

Yet, striking as this evidence might be, the servant of the songs has the task and mission "to bring Israel back" and "to gather" Israel to Himself, "to raise up the tribes of Jacob and restore the preserved of Israel" (49:5–6). Therefore, the servant of the Lord cannot be totally equated with Israel as the servant in all respects. The apparent ambivalence is the same type of oscillation found in all the collective terms previously observed in the promise doctrine. They were all-inclusive of all Israel, but they were simultaneously always focused on one representative who depicted the fortunes of the whole group for that present time and the climactic future. The connection was to be found not in some psychological theory of personality but in the "everlasting covenant," even the "sure loyal love for David" (Isa 55:3; 61:8; cf. 2 Samuel 7).

---

11. John Bright, *Kingdom of God* (Nashville: Abingdon, 1953), p. 150ff.

The servant of the Lord was the messianic person in the Davidic line then and finally that [[217]] last new David who was to come and who was known as the Seed, the Holy One (*ḥāsîd*), the Branch, etc.

The second ennead also detailed the salvation won by the Servant. In a real turn of events, the prophet Isaiah had God take the cup of God's wrath from Israel's lips and put it to her oppressor's mouth instead (51:22–23; cf. the seventh century prophet Nahum [1:11–14]). Furthermore, a new exodus and redemption were envisaged for the future (52:1–6). This "good news" (*mᵉbaśśēr*) to Zion. Then all the ends of the earth would see God's salvation (52:9–10; cf. 40:9).

This servant who would personally rule, a fact that would startle all the kings of the earth (52:15), would also be the One who would suffer on behalf of all humanity so as to make God's atonement available. The first advent of this Servant would amaze many (vv. 13–14), but His second advent would catch the breath of even the kings of the earth (52:15)—therein lay the mystery of the Servant. His rejection followed: men would reject His message (53:1), His person (v. 2), and His mission (v. 3). But His vicarious suffering would effect an atonement between God and man (vv. 4–6); and though He would submit to suffering (v. 7), death (v. 8), and burial (v. 9), He would subsequently be exalted and richly rewarded (vv. 10–12). On the Servant of the Lord, then, was laid the iniquity of all humanity.

The result of the Servant's suffering was that the "seed" would "possess the nations"; for their tent would be enlarged, the ropes lengthened, and the pegs driven in deeper (54:2–3). Yahweh would then be "the God of the whole earth" (54:5; 49:6). Thus, as "it was in the days of Noah," so it would be when Yahweh returned to "gather Israel" and extended His "steadfast love" (*ḥesed*) and "covenant of peace" (54:5, 9–10). Meanwhile, the free offer of salvation was extended to all nations through David's son (55:3–5; cf. 55:1–2, 6–9; 49:6; and the NT comment in Acts 13:45–49; 26:22–23).

The End of All History

The inauguration of the "eschaton" was sharply demarcated by the ending of the "former things"[12] (41:22; 42:9; 43:9, 18; 44:8; 46:9; 48:3) and the introduction of God's "new thing." There would be a "new" sincere repentance (58–59), a "new" Jerusalem [60], and a "new" heavens and "new" earth (65:17–25; 66:10–24; cf. 2 Pet 3:13; Rev 21:1–4).

[[218]] This would be the aeon of the Holy Spirit according to 63:7–14. A call would go forth for a new Moses to lead a new exodus (vv. 11–14) and give them that "rest" (*nûaḥ*) promised long ago to Joshua. As the servant was empowered by God's Spirit (42:1), so was this "anointed" Person. Indeed, He was equated with the servant in Isa 61:1—"The Spirit of the Lord God is on me because the Lord has anointed me." There He described the joy of His mission (vv. 1–3) and the content of His message (vv. 4–9) including:

12. C. R. North, "The Former Things and the 'New Things' in Deutero-Isaiah," *Studies in Old Testament Prophecy*, ed. H. H. Rowley (Edinburgh: T. & T. Clark, 1950), pp. 111–26.

1. "You shall be called priests of the Lord and ministers of our God" (v. 6; cf. Exod 19:6).
2. The "everlasting covenant" will be carried out (v. 8).
3. Their "seed" would be known among the nations as those whom God had truly blessed (v. 9).

Even the equipment and character of this Spirit-filled messianic Servant were noted in 61:10–11. He would be clothed with the "garments of salvation" and "cause righteousness and praise to spring forth before all nations."

The Redeemer would come in the last day "for the sake of Zion" (Isa 59:20). He would be dressed as a warrior (59:15b–19) and would wage war on all evil and sin, especially that type of hypocritical life style described in Isa 57:1–59:15a. He would be invested with God's words and His Spirit (59:21). Then Jerusalem would experience violence no longer, for the Lord of glory would be her greatest asset (60). The wealth of the nations would pour into Jerusalem as all humanity arrived to praise the Lord (60:4–16). Then the exalted city of Jerusalem would be at peace forever, and the presence of the Lord of everlasting light would make the need for the sun or moon obsolete (vv. 17–22).

While the "day of vengeance" (63:4–6) and "year of redemption" brought judgment on the nations when God trampled down the nations in His winepress, even as Obadiah and Joel had proclaimed, God's irrevocable purpose for a rebuilt city of Jerusalem which would be inhabited by the "holy people" of God would be realized (62). Even though the clothes of the Hero were sprinkled with the blood of the winepress (63:1–6; cf. Isaiah 34; Joel 3:9–16; and later Zechariah 14; Ezekiel 38–39), He would be vindicated as this aeon drew to a close and the new aeon began.

Part of that renewed—for so the word "new" should be understood—world to come, where righteousness dwelt, included new heavens and new earth. Once again, Isaiah's paradisiacal pictures of peace in nature came to the fore (cf. Isaiah 11 and 65:17–25; 66:10–23). [[219]] Death would be abolished (cf. Isa 25:8), and the everlasting world-wide rule and reign of the new and final Davidic King would begin. Only the judgment of eternal torment on the wicked and finally unrepentant interrupted this picture, for they were perpetually in agony and forever apart from God.

So Isaiah ended his magnificent shorter theology. His dependence on antecedent theology was evident at almost every turn. While relating the "servant" to the earlier teaching about the "seed" (Isa 41:8; 43:5; 44:3; 45:19, 25; 48:19; 53:10; 54:3; 59:21; 61:9; 65:9, 23; 66:22) and to the "covenant" already given (Isa 42:6, 49:8; 54:10; 55:3; 56:4, 6; 59:21; 61:8), not to mention "Abraham" (41:8; 51:2; 63:16) or "Jacob" (41:21; 44:5; 49:26; 60:16) or "David" and the "everlasting covenant" (55:3; 61:8), Isaiah carefully systematized to a large degree the total plan, person, and work of God in the short scope of twenty-seven chapters. No wonder his theology has so profoundly affected men over the centuries.

SAMUEL LUCIEN TERRIEN

b. 1911   d. 2002

Presence in Absence

Samuel Terrien's theology was formed in the French and Swiss streams of the Reformed tradition. He studied in Paris, at the École Biblique in Jerusalem, and at Union Theological Seminary in New York. The latter school was his academic home for almost his entire career. Terrien paid unprecedented attention to the aesthetic dimensions of the Bible and its artistic interpretation. His final, posthumous work, a massive commentary on the Psalms, was published 27 years after his retirement and 92 years after his birth.

Selected Writings by Terrien

1978   *The Elusive Presence: Toward a New Biblical Theology.* Religious Perspectives 26. San Francisco: Harper & Row.

1981   The Play of Wisdom: Turning Point in Biblical Theology. *Horizons in Biblical Theology* 3: 125–53.

1996   *The Iconography of Job through the Centuries: Artists as Biblical Interpreters.* University Park: Pennsylvania State University Press.

2003   *The Psalms: Strophic Structure and Theological Commentary.* Grand Rapids: Eerdmans. Writings about Terrien

Writings about Terrien

Barr, James
1999   Pp. 323–25 in *The Concept of Biblical Theology: An Old Testament Perspective.* Minneapolis: Fortress.

Gammie, John G., Walter A. Brueggemann, W. Lee Humphreys, and James M. Ward (editors)
1978   *Israelite Wisdom: Theological and Literary Essays in Honor of Samuel Terrien.* New York: Scholars Press for Union Theological Seminary.

Samuel L. Terrien's
Approach to Old Testament Theology

Excerpted with permission from Samuel L. Terrien, *The Elusive
Presence: Toward a New Biblical Theology* (San Francisco: Harper &
Row, 1978), pp. 31–33, 39–43, 57–62. Some footnotes have been
omitted.

The Quest for a Biblical Theology

[[31]] In the face of the multiplicity of rituals and beliefs represented in the
Bible, many scholars have restricted their endeavors to describing the religious phenomena which have received literary formulation. Recent interpreters have therefore tended to present only the history of the religion of Israel
and the history of primitive Christianity. Even writers of an Old Testament
theology, like Gerhard von Rad,[1] or of a theology of the New Testament, like
Rudolf Bultmann,[2] have stressed the plurality of theological responses within
Scripture rather than run the risk of distorting historical complexity through
oversimplification.

At the same time, it is not possible to ignore the place the Bible has occupied for centuries—and still occupies today—at the heart of both Judaism and
Christianity. The books of the Hebrew Bible for Judaism and of both the Old
Testament and the New for Christianity exerted an inward stimulus and a
power of restraint on faith long before these writings received [[32]] recognition of authority by synagogue or church. It was neither the synagogue nor
the church which initially decreed that Scripture was to be the rule of faith
and order or "the Word of God."[3] Rather, the books of the Hebrew Bible and
of the New Testament imposed themselves upon Jews and Christians as the
regulating standard of their religious commitment and ethical behavior.
Canon was originally not a dogmatic structure imposed from without by institutionalized collectivities but an unspoken force which grew from within the
nature of Hebrew-Christian religion.[4] The obligations of the Sinai covenant
were remembered as the "torah" of Yahweh, a growing collection of instructions which were inserted within the context of the narratives of the Sinai
theophany. Thus, the cultic *anamnesis* of the event during which the divine

---

1. G. von Rad, *Old Testament Theology,* I–II, tr. by D. M. G. Stalker (New York, 1960–65).
2. R. Bultmann, *Theology of the New Testament,* I–II, tr. by K. Grobel (New York, 1951–
55).
3. The rabbinical college at Jamnia (ca. A.D. 97) did not promulgate the canon of the
Hebrew Bible. It decided on the canonicity of marginal or doubtful books. Likewise, it is pi-
quant to observe that the Western church lived for centuries without an official canon of
scripture, which was formulated by the Protestant Confessions of the sixteenth century and
the decrees of the Council of Trent in response to the Protestant challenge.
4. See G. E. Wright, "The Canon as Theological Problem," *The Old Testament and Theology* (New York, 1969), pp. 166ff.

presence disclosed itself to the people through the mediation of Moses prepared and promoted the development of the canon.[5] The idea of the canonicity of a "scripture" was a *fait accompli* when a written document was found in the temple of Jerusalem in 622 B.C. and led to the reform of Josiah and the renewal of the Sinai covenant (2 Kgs 22:1ff.). The "book of the law" (approximately Deut 12:1–26:19) became the nucleus of "the Bible" (*ta biblia*, "the books") because Huldah the prophetess found it conformed to the living word of the Deity (2 Kgs 22:13ff.). Canonicity went back to the cultic memories of the Sinai-Horeb theophany. It is significant that the final edition of the Deuteronomic law opened with a cultic rehearsal of those memories (Deut 1:1ff.) in which the motif of covenant is subordinated to the story of theophanic presence (Deut 5:2–4).

Likewise, it appears that the letters of Paul, which constituted the original nucleus of the New Testament, were circulated throughout the churches of the Mediterranean world and they were read ceremonially at the paracultic celebrations of nascent Christendom, side by side with the portions of the Law and the Prophets traditionally appointed for the sabbath service and the [[33]] festivals. Canonicity imposed itself from within, little by little, in the context of the Christian community at worship.

The inwardness of scriptural canonicity and of its growth in the course of several centuries suggests that a certain homogeneity of theological depth binds the biblical books together beneath the heterogeneity of their respective dates, provenances, styles, rhetorical forms, purposes, and contents. The search for the principle of this homogeneity which spanned a considerable period of time points to the dynamic aspect of a continuity of religious aim rather than to a static unity of doctrinal conformity.[6]

As soon as the historian of the Hebrew-Christian religion seeks to determine the nature of this continuity, he goes beyond a merely phenomenological description of rites and beliefs. He does not disregard on that account the historical fluidity of their origin and growth, but he asks the question of the possibility, the legitimacy, and perhaps even the inevitability of biblical theology.

The disrepute in which this discipline is held in some quarters depends on several factors, one of which is the hostile attitude which many biblical theologians of the past century displayed against modern methods of literary and historical criticism. Another of these factors is related to the denominationalism which has colored not a few treatises of biblical theology in which one or another of the scriptural themes was enlisted as the ancillary justification of a dogma peculiar to individual church, sect, or tradition.

. . . .

[[39]] In the meantime, biblical theologians have been led to work more closely with the systematic theologians and the philosophers of language in

5. See [[Terrien 1978: 51]] note 100.
6. See J. Barr, *The Bible in the Modern World* (New York, 1973), p. 181; J. A. Sanders, "Reopening Old Questions About Scripture," *In.*, 28 (1974): 322f.

raising the issue of hermeneutics. [7] The distinction between biblical theology, a historical discipline which seeks to elucidate the meaning of the Bible itself, and systematic theology, which attempts to translate biblical dynamics of faith and cultus into the contemporary idiom, needs to be carefully preserved. [8] Biblical theologians are increasingly aware of the relativity of historical research and of the dangers of *historicism*. They recognize the need of becoming critically explicit regarding their epistemological presuppositions, and they constantly remind themselves of their own limitations in attempting to penetrate scriptural meaning and to remain faithful to that meaning while seeking to translate it into the language of the cultural world view of the twentieth century. In addition, they know that to assume their proper responsibility toward the work of systematic theologian, they must perform the "descriptive task" of biblical theology, as it has been called, [9] in a way which goes beyond the mere cataloguing of the mythopoetic formulations of the biblical documents, from the Yahwist epic in the tenth century B.C. to the Johannine Apocalypse at the end of the first century A.D.

[[40]] By their parallel insistence on *Heilsgeschichte*, biblical theologians like Eichrodt, Vriezen, Jacob, von Rad, Cullmann, and Wright have offered a platform for further research. [10] The warnings of Ebeling on the problematic character of theological coherence within each Testament deserve scrupulous attention, [11] but the arguments that he directed against the unity of the Bible have now lost their sharpness, for contemporary discussion no longer attempts to expound biblical "ideas." It centers on the dynamic continuity of biblical fields of force. [12] Furthermore, general agreement has been reached

7. The problem of the interrelation of exegesis and epistemology has been revived in the past twenty-five years through the development of linguistic analysis and philosophical inquiry concerning the question of objectivity and subjectivity. See F. Bovon, et al., *Analyse structurale et exégèse biblique* (Neuchâtel, 1971); J. A. Sanders, "Hermeneutics," *IDB, Suppl. Vol.* (1976), pp. 402ff.; *id.*, "Adaptable for Life: The Nature and Function of the Canon," *Magnalia Dei: The Mighty Acts of God [In Memoriam G. E. Wright]* (Garden City, N.Y., 1976), pp. 531ff.

8. In his book, *Biblical Theology in Crisis* (New York, 1969), B. S. Childs referred not to "Biblical Theology" in the historical sense of the word (p. 18, *et passim*), but to various forms of a neoorthodox theology which appeared on the North American continent in the middle of the twentieth century and was sometimes known as "the Biblical Theology Movement." This misleading expression designates a loose group of heterogeneous trends that have been influenced by Kierkegaard, Dostoievski, Barth, Brunner, Bultmann, Tillich, R. Niebuhr, Sartre, Heidegger, and even Camus. Although several of the representatives of this theological movement have taken seriously the theological significance of the Bible, their work should not in any way be confused with "biblical theology" in the proper sense.

9. See K. Stendahl, "Biblical Theology, Contemporary," *IDB*, 1 (1962): 429ff.; cf. "Method in the Study of Biblical Theology," in *The Bible in Modern Scholarship*, ed. by J. Ph. Hyatt (Nashville, 1965), p. 199.

10. See B. Albrektson, *History and the Gods: An Essay on the Idea of Historical Events as Divine Manifestations in the Ancient Near East and in Israel* (Lund, 1967); S. Amsler, "Les deux sources de la theologie de l'histoire dans l'Ancien Testament," *RTP*, 19 (1969): 235–46.

11. G. Ebeling, "The Meaning of Biblical Theology," *JTS*, 6 (1955): 210–25; revised and rep. in *Word and Faith* (Philadelphia, 1963), pp. 79–97; see esp. pp. 91f.

12. See P. R. Ackroyd, *Continuity: A Contribution to the Study of the Old Testament Religious Tradition* (Oxford, 1962). New Testament scholars generally tend to continue presenting

on Ebeling's plea to understand Scripture in the context of the ancient Near Eastern and Mediterranean cultures, with special emphasis on the extracanonical literature of Judaism in Hellenistic, Hasmonean, and Roman times.[13]

Above all, the very use of the word "theology" in connection with the Bible requires critical scrutiny. Going beyond Ebeling's challenge,[14] the biblical theologian will refuse to apply the word *theo-logia* to the content of the Bible as if it were still overloaded with connotations that are either patristic, medieval, scholastic, or Tridentine on the one hand, or Protestant, modernist, and postexistential on the other. Instead he will seek to discover the biblical meaning of the notion which the Greek term *theo-logia* fails to convey. Plato and Aristotle employed it in the sense of "science of divine things."[15] Quite differently, the Hebraic expression *da'at Elohim*, "knowledge of God," points to a reality which at once includes and transcends intellectual disquisition. It designates the involvement of man's total personality in the presence of Yahweh through the prophetic word, the cultic celebration, and the psychological mode of communion in faith. In the Hebraic sense of "knowledge of God," theology does not mean an objective science of divine things. Although it uses the critical faculties of the mind, it proceeds both from an inner commitment to a faith and from [[41]] a participation in the destiny of a people which transcends the national and racial particularities of the times.

Theology in this sense implies the dedication of the self, its orientation toward the demands of a specific vocation, and its acceptance of a corresponding mode of living. At its highest level, it aims at promoting a stability of faith independent of the normal fluctuations of the human character, and at facilitating a transmission of that faith to the next generation. It is based on the cultic commemoration of presence and the cultic expectancy of its renewal. It is nurtured by the celebration of presence in the midst of the community of faith which extends from the theophanic past to the epiphanic end of history.[16]

Not on account of an editorial accident of juxtaposition but through a conscious intent which reveals a theological grasp have the Deuteronomists made the *Shema'* ("Hear, O Israel, Yahweh thy God, Yahweh is one") inseparable from the invitation to love God. In the words of Israel's creed (Deut

---

theological themes separately, although several of them are trying to bring these themes into a single focus. See H. Thyen, *Studien zur Sündenvergebung im Neuen Testament und seinen alttestamentlichen und jüdischen Voraussetzungen* (Göttingen, 1970).

13. See J. Barr, "Le judaïsme postbiblique et la théologie de l'Ancien Testament," *RTP*, 18 (1968): 209–17.

14. "What the Bible testifies to and strives after is not theology, but something that happens to man in God's dealings with the world" (Ebeling, *Word and Faith*, p. 93).

15. Plato, *Rep.*, 379a; Aristotle, *Meteor.*, 2, 1–2, *id.*, *Metaph.*, 2, 4, 12; 10, 7, 7; 11, 6, 6; etc. See F. Kattenbusch, "Die Entstehung einer christlichen Theologie. Zur Geschichte der Ausdrücke *theologia, theologos, theologikos*." *ZTK*, 11 (1930): 161–205; W. W. Jaeger, *Theology of the Early Greek Philosophers* (Oxford, 1947), pp. 4–5.

16. It is significant that in the revised edition of *An Outline of Old Testament Theology* (Oxford, 1970), Th. C. Vriezen emphasizes the reality of communion between Yahweh and his people above all other factors (see esp. pp. 150, 175).

6:6ff.), faith in Yahweh means love of Yahweh, first with the whole of one's mind (*lebh*), second with the whole of one's living being, its instinctual drives and its persistence in selfhood (*nephesh*), and third with the whole of one's potentiality, the abundance or "muchness" (*me'ôd*) of eros, which leads to the extension of the individual into the family, the continuation of the self into the self of one's children and the future generations of man.[17]

It is therefore not on account of a second editorial accident of juxtaposition that Israel's creed was used as a preface for the first textbook on religious education in the history of western culture: "And those words, which I command thee this day, shall remain in thy intellectual consciousness, and thou shalt teach them to thy sons by sing-song rote (*we-shin-nànetâ lebhanèkâ*)" (Deut 6:6ff. [Heb. 7ff.]). The pericope concludes with the kerygmatic summary of the *Heilsgeschichte*: "Then, thou shalt say to thy son, "We were Pharaoh's slaves in Egypt . . ." (Deut 6:21 [Heb. 20]). [[42]] Theology is the knowledge of God, but this knowledge is love with the whole of one's mind in the context of a corporate obligation toward the past and the future. Biblical theology as the biblical knowledge of God is indeed the object of science, provided that the biblical theologian is also subject to a personal involvement in the "knowledge" of that God. Biblical theology is thus indissolubly married to biblical spirituality, which in turn remains inseparable from the continuity of the cultic celebration of presence. It is the knowledge of God which provides the clue to the mystery of the people of God, whether Israel or the Church. Such a knowledge points to what has been felicitously called "the sacramental prophetism" of the Bible in its entirety.[18]

Covenant ideology and covenant ceremonial may have played significant roles at critical moments in the history of Israel, and especially in its eschatological form at the birth of the Christian church. Nevertheless, this ideology and ceremonial proved to be chiefly the means of reform in times of corruption or cultural chaos. Covenant making constituted a rite which depended on the prior affirmation of a faith in the intervention of God in a peculiar segment of history. By contrast, the reality of divine presence proved to be the constant element of distinctiveness throughout the centuries of biblical times. It is this reality which produced the power of a "canonical" Scripture, and it is this reality which may renew this power in contemporary Christianity.

Israel maintained her historical existence as a people only in so far as she remembered and expected the manifestation of divine presence. It was the presence which created peoplehood. An individual member of that people partook of the life of the community only in so far as he shared in the presence, either through cultic celebration or by associating himself with the mediators of presence who had experienced its immediacy. When the structure

17. See J. W. McKay, "Man's Love for God in Deuteronomy and the Father/Teacher-Son/Pupil Relationship," *VT*, 22 (1972): 426–35; S. D. McBride, Jr., "The Yoke of the Kingdom: An Exposition of Deuteronomy 6:4–5," *In.*, 27 (1973): 273–306.

18. J.-J. von Allmen, *Prophétisme sacramental; neuf études pour le renouveau et l'unité de l'Eglise* (Neuchâtel, 1964), p. 19; cf. S. Amsler, "Le thème du procès chez les prophètes d'Israël," *RTP*, 24 (1974): 116–31, esp. p. 130.

of the covenant exploded, as it did during [[43]] the exile in Babylon, the people remained conscious of their peoplehood only when they improvised paracultic celebrations of the presence and thereby ritually anticipated the final epiphany.

Because it brings together the divine asseverations, "I am Yahweh," of the Hebraic theophany, and "I am the Lord," of the Christian faith in the resurrection of Jesus, the motif of presence induces a magnetic field of forces which maintains a dynamic tension, in the whole of Scripture, between divine self-disclosure and divine self-concealment.[19] The proximity of God creates a memory and an anticipation of certitude, but it always defies human appropriation. The presence remains elusive.

It is symptomatic of our age that the crisis of contemporary theology is related to the problem of authority in all domains, and that the search for the perennial authority of Scripture requires new tools of semantic interpretation. The problem of responding to the biblical record of the revelation of God from Abraham to Paul moves again to the forefront of the theological enterprise. The Hebraic theology of presence leads to the Christian theology of the eucharistic presence. Because it refuses to accept a separation between cultus and faith and carries at the same time the seed of corporate continuity in history, the biblical theology of presence may provide a prolegomenon to a new biblical theology that in its turn may play a central part in the birth of an authentically ecumenical theology.

19. K. H. Miskotte, *When the Gods are Silent*, tr. J. W. Doberstein (New York, 1967), pp. 257ff.

Synopsis of Terrien's *Elusive Presence* (1978)

Samuel L. Terrien
On the Psalmody of Presence

Excerpted with permission from Samuel L. Terrien, *The Elusive Presence: Toward a New Biblical Theology* (San Francisco: Harper & Row, 1978), pp. 320-26, 347-48.

Presence in Absence

[[320]] As the kingdom of David crumbled from within and eventually fell to Babylonian imperialism, the temple psalmodists continued to praise Yahweh as the lord of Zion, the sovereign of nature, and the judge of history. With candor, they also confessed their own agonies. Although they sometimes borrowed [[321]] hackneyed formulas which went back to Sumerian laments, they also gave poetic shape to their original insights into the crucible of religious discovery. As lyrical poets of sickness, harassment, doubt, and guilt, a few became channels of divine revelation. Some of the psalmodic theologians labored under the plight of their spiritual isolation. They sang the hidden God. Others were tortured by an obsession for God. They sang the hauntingness of presence. A few reached a plateau of confident serenity. They sang the sufficient grace.

The Hidden God

When the prophet Isaiah of Jerusalem observed that "Yahweh concealed his face" (Isa 8:17) or the Second Isaiah in Exile mourned the absence of Yahweh from the fate of his own people, saying,

> Verily, verily, thou art a God that hidest thyself (Isa 45:15),

their complaint amounted in effect to a confession of faith. To be aware of divine hiddenness is to remember a presence and to yearn for its return. The presence of an absence denies its negativity.

The poet who composed Psalm 22 was a theologian of dereliction.[1] His cry, "My God, my God, why hast thou forsaken me?", has been echoed by legions who have been tormented by cosmic solitude. In a sense, the psalmist showed that he had been a poet of cultic presence, but he ignored the myth of holy space. He substituted for the category of the sanctuary the living reality of the act of praise offered by the whole community—past, present, and future—of the people of God:

---

1. See R. Martin-Achard, "Notes bibliques: Remarques sur le Psaume 22," *Verbum Caro*, 17 (1963): 119ff.; N. H. Ridderbos, "The Psalms: Style, Figures, and Structures . . . ," *OTS*, 12 (Leiden, 1963): 43ff.; L. R. Fisher, "Betrayed by Friends. An Expository Study of Psalm 22," *In.*, 18 (1964): 20ff.; R. Kilian, "Ps 22 und das priesterliche Heilsorakel," *BZ*, 12 (1968): 172ff.; H. Schmid, "Mein Gott, mein Gott, warum du mich verlassen?" *Wort und Dienst*, NF, 11 (1971): 119ff.

> . . . Thou art holy,
>   enthroned upon the praises of Israel. (vs. 3 [Heb. 4])

[[322]] It is only through exegetical legerdemain that commentators discern in this phrase an allusion to the ark upon which Yahweh of Hosts was believed by some to have been ceremonially seated. The psalmist used a spatial verb with an auditive object that belonged to the realm of humanity. The ear triumphed over the eye. The mystery of divine nearness depended less on the *hagios topos* than upon the social reality of adoration.

Now, the lamenter has been cut off from the source of his life. Not only has he been deprived of the protection he expected from the Lord of history, but he has also been dispossessed of his divine filiality.

> . . . Thou art he who took me from my mother's womb,
>   Thou caused me to feel safe on my mother's breasts,
> Upon thee was I cast from my mother's womb,
>   And from my mother's belly thou hast been my God!
>   (vss. 9–10 [Heb. 10–11])

These ritual gestures of paternal adoption may indicate that the lament was intended to be intoned by the king at the ceremonial of the New Year, if indeed such a drama of royal humiliation, torture, and execution did take place at any time in the temple of Jerusalem (vss. 19–21 [Heb. 20–22]).[2] Unfortunately, the Hebrew text of the critical lines is obscure and probably corrupt. In any case, in mid-course the lament becomes a hymn of praise, as if the hero has been raised from symbolic death to a new life (vss. 22–30 [Heb. 23–31]).

From dereliction, the perspective of the psalmist broadened its scope to include "all the families of the nations." In a reminiscence of the Abrahamic promise (Gen 12:1-3), the reborn hero hailed Yahweh's kingdom "to the extremities of the earth." His horizon has now transcended the categories of time. Both the dead and the generations yet to be born are invited either to eat at the heavenly banquet or to hear the good news of the *Opus Dei*.[3]

[[323]] Inasmuch as the motif of divine hiddenness in Psalm 22 was unrelated to any sense of sin—a most unusual omission in Near Eastern and Hebraic laments—and on account of the universalism of its eschatology, the early Christians appropriated this extraordinary poem of presence lost and regained to describe the passion of Jesus, his death in forsakenness, and his triumph over mortality and time in the life of his followers.[4]

---

2. See discussion in G. Fohrer, *History of Israelite Religion*, tr. by D. E. Green (Nashville and New York, 1972), pp.142ff.

3. See C. Krahmalkov, "Psalm 22,28–32," *Biblica*, 50 (1969): 389ff.; E. Lipiński, "L'hymne à Yahwé Roi au Psaume 22,28–32," *Biblica*, 50 (1969): 153ff.; O. Keel-Leu, "Nochmals Psalm 22, 28–32," *Biblica*, 51 (1970): 405ff.

4. See A. Rose, "L'influence des Psaumes sur les annonces et les récits de la Passion et de la Resurrection dans les Evangiles," in R. de Langhe, ed., *Le Psautier* (1962), pp. 297ff.; H. Gese, "Psalm 22 und das Neue Testament," *ZTK*, 65 (1968): 1ff.; H. D. Lange, "The Relation

Psalm 22 constitutes an exception in the psalmody of presence. Other laments which complained of the veiling of the Deity were confessions of sin. In Hebraic theology, Yahweh concealed his face from human criminality. If the hero of the poem was not a king but a single member of the community, his plight must have been the more intolerable, for he had no answer to the question "why" and he found neither justification nor meaning in his spiritual, as well as physical, agony. After his ordeal, however, he was ushered into the future. Looking back, he understood that absence was presence deferred. His dereliction had been the prelude to what Kierkegaard many centuries later called "the moment before God." The cruelty of his trial proved to be as disproportionate as the magnitude of his eventual mission.[5]

The appeal from dereliction to communion is heard in the psalter especially when laments are confessions of sins. When a guilty man asks for forgiveness and rehabilitation, he begs at the same time for the renewal of presence. The penitential psalm *par excellence*, known as the *Miserere* or Psalm 51, exhibits the intricacy of the theological transition which links the request for mercy with the request for presence.[6]

In an unexpected way, the psalmist at first used the motif of hiddenness in a reversed form. He begged the Deity to hide from his sins:

Hide thy face from my sins
    and blot out my guilt. (vs. 9 [Heb. 11])

[[324]] The exact nature of the petitioner's lawlessness is unknown. Since the worshippers of the Second Temple during the Persian centuries ascribed some thirteen psalms to specific events in the life of David, it is quite understandable that this poignant confession of criminality would have been related to the king's notorious murder of Uriah, Bathsheba's husband (Ps 51:1; cf. 2 Sam 12:14ff.). The horror of the deed and the total incapacity of its perpetrator to make amends led the poet to ask in effect for the death of his inward self and for his rebirth under the mythical trope of a cosmic creation:

Create in me a pure heart, O God,
    and make new within me a steadfast spirit,

---

between Psalm 22 and the Passion Narrative," *Concordia Theological Monthly,* 43 (1972): 610ff.; J. A. Soggin, "Notes for Christian Exegesis of the First Part of Psalm 22," in *Old Testament and Oriental Studies* (Rome, 1975), pp. 152ff.; J. H. P. Reumann, "Psalm 22 at the Cross: Lament and Thanksgiving for Jesus Christ," *In.,* 28 (1974): 39ff.

5. The MT merely reads, "that Yahweh did" (vs. 30b). Modern translators err when they supply the pronoun "it" as a direct object. The verb is used intransitively in an absolute sense. The psalm ends on the evocation of the act of God in the history of the world.

6. Among the many monographs on Ps. 51, see especially those which deal with vss. 10–12 (Heb. 12–14): R. Press, "Die eschatologische Ausrichtung des 51.Psalms," *TZ,* 11 (1955): 241ff.; P. Bonnard, "Le psaume de pénitence d'un disciple de Jérémie," *Bible et vie chrétienne,* 17 (1957): 59ff.; *id.,* "Le vocabulaire du Miserere," *Festschrift A. Gelin* (Paris, 1961): 145ff.; E. R. Dalglish, *Psalm Fifty-One in the Light of Ancient Near Eastern Patternism* (Leiden, 1962); L. Neve, "Realized Eschatology in Ps 51," *ET,* 80 (1968–69): 264ff.; P. Auffret, "Note sur la structure littéraire de Ps LI 1–19," *VT,* 26 (1976): 142.

Cast me not away from thy presence.
and take not the spirit of thy holiness away from me.
Restore unto me the mirth of thy rescue
and let the spirit of nobility uphold me.

(vss. 10–11 [Heb. 12–14])

God comes only to those who are pure of heart, but how can the heart of man be pure? God alone is able to cleanse an enormous guilt (*'awônôth*, a superlative). No ritual will suffice,[7] for man is utterly depraved.[8] More than ceremonial ablutions or characterical amelioration are needed. Nothing less than a radical innovation is required. The psalmist borrowed the verb *bara'*, "to create," from the cosmogonies of the sapiential circles,[9] and he dared to apply it to his own, minuscule, situation. As God creates a world, so also can he create a man.

The idea of the new being was articulated within the theology of presence. The poet reflected on his estrangement, no longer in terms of God's hiddenness, but according to the image of his own expulsion: "Cast me not away from thy presence!" He also developed his hope of communion through the triple use of the word "spirit." First, the newly created being needs the power [[325]] of survival, or the gift of self-maintenance. He therefore must be able to resist temptation and to overcome self-doubt: "Make new within me a steady, firmly attached, coherent spring of moral behavior!" Second, estrangement must be enduringly bridged. The power which will permanently heal the poet's alienation from God will be so penetrating that holiness itself will flow from God to him. "Do not take away from me the spirit of thy holiness!"[10]

Since the ancient notion of holiness connoted the dread of "the wholly other," the psalmist's prayer was unprecedented. He viewed the holy no longer as the *mysterium fascinans atque tremendum*, forever exterior to man as the numinous force which attracts and repels him at the same time, but as the source of vitality which sharpens conscience, activates the will to shun evil, and stirs the imagination to do the good. A world is aborning also within

7. Cf. A. Caquot, "Ablution et sacrifice selon le Ps 51," *Proceedings of the XIth International Congress of History of Religion*, II (Leiden, 1968), pp. 75ff.

8. Cf. Job 14:1 with Ps 51:7 [Heb. 9]. See J. K. Zink, "Uncleanness and sin. A Study of Job XIV and Psalm LI 7," *VT*, 17 (1967): 354ff. The statement of Ps 51:7 (Heb. 9) does not refer to the sinfulness of sexuality but implies the universality of sin and the solidarity of the human race from generation to generation.

9. The story of creation in Gen 1:1–2:4a represents ancient traditions which have affinities with wisdom poetry. See G. M. Landes, "Creation Tradition in Proverbs 8:22–31 and Genesis 1," *Festschrift J. M. Myers* (Philadelphia, 1974), pp. 279ff.

10: The traditional rendering, "thy holy spirit," risks anachronistic connotations with the Jewish and Christian hypostasis. Moreover, the context shows that the word *ruah* is used three times in the sense of "virtue" as energy. Although it is unlikely, the psalmist may have referred to "the angel of the presence," an expression which appeared after the Babylonian exile in parallel with the spirit of God's holiness (Isa 63:9; cf. vss. 10–11).

man. Creation may be microcosmic as well as macrocosmic. Presence and spirit coalesce to animate the new being.

Third, the slave of egocentricity discovers freedom from the self. "Let the spirit of nobility uphold me!" A noble man is one who assumes his obligation of social responsibility. A knight is not a knave. He helps and respects others with the ease, elegance, and style of a prince. The new being is a moral aristocrat, not of birth but of service. Freedom to be oneself implies the power to serve willingly. A fresh innocence will obliterate the murderous past. The poet has joined those

> who were so dark of heart they might not speak,
> a little innocence will make them sin. [11]

The psalmists exhibited theological maturity because they were forced to a recognition of their true selves vis-à-vis their God, even when that God was hiding from their plight. By evading [[326]] their pleas, that God became more and more manifest to them, even when he seemed to

> . . . adjourn, adjourn . . .
> To that farther side of the skies. [12]

It was that very hiding which disclosed to them not only the meaning of their existence but also the intrinsic quality of divinity. The God of the psalmists made them live in this world, and they lived without using him. It is when man tries to grasp him that God veils himself. The *Deus revelatus* is the *Deus absconditus*.

11. e.e. cummings, *XAIPE*, no. 51, in *Poems 1923–1954* (New York, 1954), p. 456.

12. Peter Viereck, "Incantation at Assisi," *The First Morning: New Poems* (New York, 1952), p. 39.

CLAUS WESTERMANN

b. 1910   d. 2002

God's Judgment and God's Mercy

Claus Westermann came to prominence through his form-critical work on the prophets and Psalms and his comprehensive work on Genesis. After serving as pastor in the Lutheran Church, Westermann began his academic career at the Kirchliche Hochschule (seminary) in Berlin. He was for many years Professor of Old Testament at Heidelberg, where his colleague was Gerhard von Rad.

Selected Writings by Westermann

1967 *Basic Forms of Prophetic Speech.* Translated by Hugh C. White. Philadelphia: Westminster.

1978a *Blessing: In the Bible and in the Life of the Church.* Translated by Keith Crim. Overtures to Biblical Theology. Philadelphia: Fortress.

1978b *Theologie des Alten Testaments in Grundzügen.* Göttingen: Vandenhoeck & Ruprecht.

1979 *What Does the Old Testament Say about God?* Edited by Friedemann W. Golka. Atlanta: John Knox / London: SCM.

1980a *The Promises to the Fathers: Studies on the Patriarchal Narratives.* Translated by David E. Green. Philadelphia: Fortress.

1980b *The Psalms: Structure, Content and Message.* Translated by Ralph D. Gehrke. Minneapolis: Augsburg.

1982 *Elements of Old Testament Theology.* Translated by Douglas W. Stott. Atlanta: John Knox.

1984–86 *Genesis: A Commentary.* 3 volumes. Translated by John J. Scullion. Minneapolis: Augsburg / London: SPCK.

Writings about Westermann

Albertz, Rainer, Hans-Peter Müller, Hans W. Wolff, and Walther Zimmerli (editors)

1980 *Werden und Wirken des Alten Testaments: Festschrift für Claus Westermann zum 70. Geburtstag.* Göttingen: Vandenhoeck & Ruprecht / Neukirchen-Vluyn: Neukirchener Verlag.

Albertz, Rainer, Friedemann W. Golka, Jürgen Kegler (editors)
1989   *Schöpfung und Befreiung: für Claus Westermann zum 80. Geburtstag.* Stuttgart: Calwer.
Barr, James
1999   Pp. 481–84 in *The Concept of Biblical Theology: An Old Testament Perspective.* Minneapolis: Fortress.

Claus Westermann's
Approach to Old Testament Theology

Excerpted with permission from Claus Westermann, *Elements of Old Testament Theology* (Atlanta: John Knox, 1982), pp. 9–12, 230–32, 235.

What Does the Old Testament Say about God?

Preliminary Methodological Considerations

[[9]] The answer to this question must be given by the entire Old Testament. A theology of the Old Testament has the task of summarizing and viewing together what the Old Testament as a whole, in all its sections, says about God. This task is not correctly understood if one declares one part of the Old Testament to be the most important and gives it prominence over the others; or if one regards the whole as determined by one concept such as covenant, election, or salvation; or if one asks beforehand what the center of the Old Testament is. The New Testament clearly has its center in the suffering, death, and resurrection of Christ, to which the Gospels are directed and which the Epistles take as their starting point. The Old Testament, however, bears no similarity at all to this structure, and it is thus not possible to transfer the question of a theological center from the New to the Old Testament.[1]

If we wish to describe what the Old Testament as a whole says about God, we must start by looking at the way the Old Testament presents itself, something everyone can recognize: "The Old Testament tells a story" (G. von Rad). With that statement we have reached our first decision about the form of an Old Testament theology: If the Old Testament narrates what it has to say about God in the form of a story (understood here in the broader sense of event), then the structure of an Old Testament theology must be based on events rather than concepts.

But how can we define this structure of events more exactly? There seems to be an obvious answer to this question. The task of a theology of the Old Testament could simply consist of re-narrating the story of the Old [[10]] Testament in an abbreviated and summarized form. This was certainly how Gerhard von Rad understood it: "Re-telling the story is therefore still the most legitimate way for theology to speak about the Old Testament." This would be possible if the whole of the Old Testament consisted of a continuous story from the first to the last chapter. However, this is not the case.

The Old Testament has come down to us in a threefold structure in which it also originated: the Torah, the Prophets, and the Writings; or the historical, prophetic, and didactic books, the nucleus of which is the Psalms.

---

1. G. von Rad, *Old Testament Theology*, p. 127f.; R. Smend, ThSt 101; G. F. Hasel, ZAW 86; W. Zimmerli, EvTh 35.

According to the traditionists' conception here, the Bible of the Old Testament includes the story narrated, but also the word of God inhering in the story and humanity's response in calling to God. The narrative of the historical books from Genesis to Chronicles does contain texts in which the word of God enters the action, and texts which contain the response of praise or lament; but the structure of the Old Testament in its three parts indicates that the narrative in the Old Testament is determined by the word of God occurring in it and by the response of those for whom and with whom this story unfolds.

It is therefore the canon of the Old Testament itself which shows us the structure of what happens in the Old Testament in its decisive elements. We have thus found an objective starting point for an Old Testament theology which is independent of any preconceptions about what the most important thing in the Old Testament is and independent of any other prior theological decisions. If one asks what the Old Testament says about God, this threefold structure shows us the way. [2]

But how can what the Old Testament says about God be viewed and described together in its many and diverse forms? How can it be expressed along broad and simple lines? In previous Old Testament theologies, this has been attempted predominantly by reducing what the Old Testament says about God to comprehensive terms such as *salvation, election, covenant, faith, kerygma, revelation, redemption, soteriology, eschatology*, etc. By using these noun concepts scholars moved away from the language of the Old Testament, which is overwhelmingly dominated by verbs. In addition, this meant a loss of the diversity in which the Old Testament speaks of God. [3]

If we wish to inquire concerning these broad lines determining the whole way in which the Old Testament speaks about God and yet not overlook the many forms in which it occurs, we shall therefore have to start from *verb structures*. This demands a complete change of our way of thinking. The story [[11]] told in the Old Testament is then not a salvation history in the sense of a series of God's salvation events, but rather a history of God and man whose nucleus is the experience of saving. It does not, however, remain only a story of deliverance. In the middle of the Pentateuch stands the confession of praise of those who experienced this saving, and in the middle of the Deuteronomistic historical section (Joshua to 2 Kings) the confession of sin of those on whom judgment was passed. The Pentateuch is further subdivided into primeval history, patriarchal history, and history of the people. Within this subdivision, the beginning of the history of the people (Exodus through Deuteronomy) receives a forestructure which encompasses God's activity in the world and human life and thus God's blessing.

2. B. S. Childs points to the significance of the canon for OT theology; see also G. W. Coats–B. O. Long.

3. The history of OT theology can show how difficult it is to present the variety of Old Testament talk about God as a whole. E. Würthwein gives an overview, ThR NF 36, 3.

In the prophetic books, the framework of the presentation does not emerge from what the individual prophets said, but rather from the structure of the judgment oracle common to all judgment prophets (to which corresponds the confession of sin in the middle of the Deuteronomistic historical work) and its correspondence within the salvation oracle. The varying individual prophetic pronouncements are then to be understood from the perspective of these constants.

In the Psalms, this constant factor is given by the structure of the Psalms of lament and praise, and two major types, from which then both the varying individual expressions and any subordinate forms are to be understood.

Wisdom has no place within this basic framework of an Old Testament theology, since it originally and in reality does not have as its object an occurrence between God and man; in its earlier stages wisdom is overwhelmingly secular. A theological wisdom develops at a later stage, and is then to be understood according to its theological statement (e.g., from the perspective of the contrast between the pious and godless). The theological home of wisdom can be found within the context of human creation; the creator gives humanity the ability to understand its world and to be oriented within it.[4]

So far we have only hinted at a few main features. They should show that from such a starting point of an Old Testament theology, the whole of what the Old Testament says about God continually stays in view. The theology of the Old Testament thus remains determined in every aspect by the outline of a story entrusted to us which includes the occurrence of God speaking and the response of those who experience these events.

With that the structure of Old Testament theology acquires a systematic [[12]] as well as historical aspect. The systematic aspect emerges from the talk about God which remains constant throughout the entire Old Testament. This constant is found primarily in an interaction between God and man (more precisely; between God and his creation, his people, humanity), and includes speaking and acting on both sides. In addition to this we find a series of other constants throughout the entire Old Testament, e.g., the fact that both saving and blessing belong to God's acts from beginning to end, or that human response finds its center in lament and praise, or that from beginning to end God is *one*.

The historical aspect emerges from the fact that this God of whom the Old Testament speaks has bound himself to the history of his people. Since this is a people like any other, it, too, is subject to historical change and historical contingency. This accounts for the fact that the elements of this interaction between God and humanity change in the course of history. So, for example, the facticity of response in service remains constant, while the worship service itself is subjected to changes during the course of this history. Or it manifests itself in the fact that the saving God is simultaneously always the

---

4. See [[Westermann 1982:]] pp. 85f; cf. C. Westermann, BK I/1, pp. 436–467 concerning Gen 4:17–26, and ThB 55, pp. 149–161; similarly: W. Zimmerli, *Old Testament Theology in Outline*, p. 141f.

judging God, although both God's saving and judging occurs in a history in which each, in and for itself, as well as their relationship to each other, changes. This simultaneity of constants and variables inhering in this talk about God also accounts for the fact that the history of God with his people as a whole—in this structure of constants and variables—is characterized by absolute singularity and uniqueness. The elements, however, out of which this whole is put together are able to represent a connection between the religion of Israel and other religions (see [[Westermann 1982:]] pp. 58–61).

. . . .

The Question of Biblical Theology

[[230]] What we have found in investigating the relationship of the Old Testament to Christ are not conceptual relations and contrasts but rather correspondences or contrasts which relate to a sequence of events, a history between God and humanity. This history, with which both the Old and New Testaments deal, occurs in two circles: the wider, which stretches from the creation to the end of the world, and the more limited one, which is the history of God with a specific section of humanity, the people of God. The Old and New Testaments deal with the history of the wider circle. Both speak about the God who created heaven and earth and who ultimately leads the world and humanity to a final goal. And both deal with the narrower circle which has two sections, the first treated in the Old Testament, the second treated in the New. The history of God's people in the Old Testament leads away from power and toward salvation on the basis of forgiveness. The new people of God can no longer preserve its existence by means of victories over other peoples, but rather only through its existence *for* the rest of humanity, as was already suggested by the servant songs in Deutero-Isaiah. The same transformation occurs in the case of the saving of the individual through God. Because Christ died on the cross even for his enemies, the [[231]] charge of the pious against their enemies is dismissed. The saving of the faithful no longer implies death for nonbelievers. This also removes the curse from the suffering of believers. The book of Job already allows the new insight emerge that human suffering does not have to be God's curse or punishment. It acquires a positive meaning through the suffering of Christ.

In the history recounted by the Old Testament we can thus see a movement toward a goal which points to what the New Testament says about Christ. In the light of Christ a Yes and Amen are spoken to the Old Testament as the way which leads to this goal. At the same time, with Christ a No is spoken to that which, through the work of Christ, is overcome and now ended: the association of God's salvation with power which is also the power of destruction, and the association of the salvation of the individual with the request against the unrighteous which aims at his destruction.

This Yes to the Old Testament from the perspective of Christ, and this No to the Old Testament from the perspective of Christ, however, are not dogmatic and not theoretical, but are rather historical. One cannot say that what the New Testament says about God is correct, and what the Old Testament says false. That part of what the Old Testament says about God which has come to an end is done away with by the historical event of the coming of Christ as God's final word and final act.

Then the history of the church or the history of the Christian churches becomes a section of the whole history of God with his people between the coming of Christ and his return, which must be seen in the light of the *entire* Bible. From the perspective of the whole Bible, we then need to ask whether the period in church history in which the church once again became associated with power is not a regression behind the extraction of the people of God from political power, as already shown in Deutero-Isaiah. The question should then be directed to New Testament theologians whether it is not possible to return from an intellectual and conceptual structure of New Testament theology to a verb-dominated or historical structure to present what happens in the New Testament between God and humanity. The first step toward this would be the recognition that what happened is more important than what was thought about it. What the New Testament says about Christ also has essentially the form of a report or story: first in the Gospels, which lead up to the death and resurrection of Christ, and then in the Book of Acts, which starts from the death and resurrection of Christ and is directed toward Christ's return, with which Revelation also deals. Here, [[232]] too, there is a correspondence to the Old Testament which should not be overlooked. While the Old Testament points from creation beyond the history of God's people to the "center of time," the New points from the center of time to the end of time. Thus Old and New Testaments belong together so that, side by side, they can report the history of God with his people and can place this history into the broader horizon of the history of God with humanity and with the world.

If this basic historical structure of what the Old and New Testament say about God were recognized in Old as well as in New Testament studies, we could return to a biblical theology which included the Old as well as the New Testament and which was based upon both. A biblical theology is necessary for the incipient ecumenical era of the Christian churches.

Synopsis of Westermann's *Elements of Old Testament Theology* (1982)

Claus Westermann
On Judgment and Mercy

Excerpted with permission from Claus Westermann, *What Does the Old Testament Say about God?* (Atlanta: John Knox, 1979), pp. 53–61, 74–80, 103–5.

God's Judgment and God's Mercy

Sin and Judgment: The Prophets of Doom

[[53]] When the Bible mentions the fact that God punishes or acts as a judge, this seems to contradict what the Bible says about God otherwise: God created men—so why didn't he just create them in such a way that he would never need to punish them? God blesses people; he saves those threatened by death—so why does he destroy his saving and blessing again and again by punishments?

Sin as a Human Phenomenon. This latter question points to an insurmountable limitation of man in deed as well as in thought. It is simply a human limitation that people transgress, that they sin. Thus they can only speak of God by including judgment and punishment. This contradiction cannot be solved; it is part of human existence. Therefore sin, human transgression and God's intervention against it, is already part of the primeval history; this indicates that this human transgression which we call sin is characteristic of human beings: no religion and no structure of society can change the fact that people of all times, all races, and all [[54]] ideologies transgress by nature. When, then, in the primeval history human sin is each time followed by God's intervention, this is motivated by the hindering, disturbing, and destruction effect of sin. An Egyptian text once called human sin "the great disturbance." By sin something or somebody is always endangered, whether this becomes immediately apparent or remains hidden for a long time.

It is the intention of the Yahwist in his narratives of guilt and punishment in Genesis 1–11 to depict human transgression in its many varied possibilities in order to make clear the impending danger to man in these possibilities: the transgression of the individual against the creator in an act of disobedience which threatens the relationship of trust between God and man (Genesis 3), fratricide (Genesis 4), and the despising of a father (Gen 9:20–27).[1]

To this has to be added the possibility of collective sin in the crossing of the border into the superhuman (Gen 6:1–4; 11:1–9) and the corruption of a whole generation (Genesis 6–9). In all these stories the narrator of the primeval history describes sin as a universal phenomenon. At the same time the

---

1. Claus Westermann, *Genesis*, 1:374–380; idem, "Der Mensch im Urgeschehen," *Kerygma und Dogma* 13 (1967): 231–246.

writer points out an important distinction in the reaction of God the creator to human transgressions. On the one hand God intervenes as judge, especially in Genesis 3 and 4, where this judicial intervention corresponds precisely to the profane trial, which can be found universally in the institution of courts (discovery of the crime—hearing—defense—sentence). It is God the creator who in the worldwide institution of the independent court opposes the transgressor and restricts evil. On the other hand the flood story shows a different reaction of God to human transgression: the flood is an act of God's judgment for the hybris of a whole generation which has grown beyond all limits (Gen 6:5a, 7a, J). But at the end of the flood the creator declares solemnly that such a destruction shall never occur again: "'I will never again curse the ground because of man, for the imagination of man's heart is evil from his youth'" (Gen 8:21). In this decision at the end of the flood the creator promises the preservation of the world in spite of all human inclination to evil. God wishes to preserve and keep humanity as it is. His reaction to the human inclination to evil is patient suffering; it is not the reaction of the judge. Jesus says likewise: "'for he makes his sun rise on the evil and on the good, and sends rain on the just and on the unjust'" (Matt 5:45). [[55]]

Sin in the History of God's People. From sin as a human phenomenon, human transgression which is part of human existence, we have to distinguish the sin of the people of God and its individual members in the mutual relationship of Israel to her God. This sin only becomes possible through the encounter of Israel with Yahweh; it is a process in the history of Israel with her God. Every possible transgression, every possible sin has already been preceded by something, namely Israel's experiences with God, the experience of the acts of saving and the receipt of his gifts.[2] It is sufficient to point out one word which makes this connection clear: the word "forget." It is often used by Jeremiah in his accusation. The transgressions of the people of Israel which lead to his accusation are rooted in this act of forgetting: only because the present generation has forgotten God's deeds and gifts for Israel could such transgressions arise.

These transgressions of Israel can only be understood in close connection with her history; they are themselves a historical phenomenon and as such subject to change (in contrast to the concept of sin in the Western Christian tradition—in which sin has become an unhistorical timeless phenomenon). The unique characteristic of the history of Israel, as described in the Old Testament, consists of the very fact that the sin of Israel towards her God has been taken so very seriously that it decisively determined the history. Israel's sin begins when Israel itself begins: the exodus from Egypt contains the event of the golden calf (Exodus 32–34). Israel's history with God is like an incline: the guilt of Israel before God grows to such an extent that it leads to his intervention against his own people in judgment. This is the very nucleus

2. Very often the prophets point to this, above all in the contrast-motif; cf. my *Basic Forms of Prophetic Speech*, pp. 181–188.

of the message of the prophets of judgment: the announcement that God will punish or even destroy his own people, based on an accusation.[3]

Remember that Israel's sin is not something which exists of necessity; Israel is *not* by its very nature a sinful people. On the contrary, at the beginning a good and intact relationship between God and his people is presupposed. This is the meaning of the frequently used image of marriage. In Deuteronomy, remaining in the promised land and the continuation of the blessing are made dependent on the obedience of the people; it is presupposed that this condition can be fulfilled [[56]] and that therefore the relationship between God and his people can remain intact. Similarly in the review of the Deuteronomistic History the idolatry of the kings of Israel and Judah, which causes God's judgment, is not general: David and a few other kings are exempt.

It is not only in prophecy that the guilt of Israel in the context of its history is seen. The Deuteronomistic History also shows this incline which led to the catastrophe.[4] The clearest sign of this incline is the fact that the prophets of judgment before Amos have voiced *no* accusation against Israel as a whole nation. Therefore the accusation against the whole nation has an added stress. It is voiced from the time of Amos up till Jeremiah and Ezekiel, and it gives the reason for the announcement of catastrophe.

The Prophecy of Judgment. There has been a phenomenon like prophecy—take in a very broad sense—in many religions. There has even been a form of prophecy that shows similarity in its very wording to the prophecy of Israel: the prophecy of Mari by the Euphrates. But only in Israel has there been this succession of prophets from Amos to Jeremiah and Ezekiel, who through this long period of time have stedfastly announced the intervention of a god against his own people in judgment. The prophecy of judgment has to be seen in close connection with the beginnings of Israel: with the saving from Egypt and the guidance through the wilderness, which only then made Israel a people. Israel obtained its very existence as a nation by God's acts of saving; if Israel forgot God, if it turned against this God and away from him, then it would thereby lose the basis of its existence.[5] This is the reason for the appearance of the prophets. Their accusations and announcements of judgment were concerned with Israel's existence. Thus the saving God is now the judging God; the judgment announced by the prophets is the necessary continuation of the saving working of God. This judgment is aimed, paradoxically, at the saving of Israel—through and after the judgment. God's acts in saving and judging his people belong closely together.

We can illustrate this point even more clearly. The prophetic accusation is not concerned with individual sins nor with the fact that [[57]] Israel is a sinner in a general and abstract way; it is concerned rather in each case with

3. *Basic Forms of Prophetic Speech*, pp. 169–175.

4. Hans Walter Wolff, "Das Kerygma des deuteronomistischen Geschichtswerkes," *Zeitschrift für die alttestamentliche Wissenschaft* 73 (1961): 171–186; also in *The Vitality of Old Testament Traditions*, ed. Brueggemann, pp. 83–100.

5. Cf. chapter II: "The Saving God and History."

transgressions which put the existence of Israel as the people of God in danger. The Old Testament knows no abstract and timeless concept of sin, which would be similar to a concept of being. Sins and transgressions are only mentioned when they threaten human existence, the human community, or the community between God and man. This threat is never the same; it is derived from the historic, economic, cultural, and religious circumstances; consequently it changes.[6]

This historic character of sin is clearly manifest in the prophetic accusation. It is not always the same, it changes from one prophet to another and also within the same prophet from one period of his ministry to another. The accusations of the prophets before Amos were mostly directed towards a king; they have to be understood against the background of the historical situation, just as the prophetic tradition afterwards is still a part of the historical tradition. Nathan's accusation against David and Elijah's against Ahab have their respective meanings only in the situation in which a threat to Israel arises from the behavior of the king; and it is against this that the accusation is directed. Thus the emphasis of the accusation changes from one prophet to another and we obtain from them a surprisingly accurate reflection of the cultural, social, economic, political, and religious events of their respective times. Sometimes the emphasis is on social accusation (especially Amos and Micah), sometimes an idolatry (Hosea and Ezekiel), on political accusation combined with an attack on hybris (Isaiah), on the deserting and forgetting of Yahweh (Jeremiah), or on worship which has become insincere (Amos, Jeremiah). These are only examples; they show the surprising liveliness of the prophet accusation. The prophets are never interested in compiling catalogues of vices to demonstrate to their contemporaries what kind of bad people they are; on the contrary, they point to the respective crises, i.e., where the threat lies in the present hour.

But this is only possible when the prophets pit their whole existence on their commission: to announce God's judgment on the basis of these accusations of Israel. The prophets' total identification of themselves with their office is a characteristic of prophecy in Israel. [[58]] This has two sides: one of them is manifest in the language of the prophets. Each speaks his own language and introduces into this language the tradition in which he has grown up, so that we can recognize more or less clearly his "geistige *Heimat*" (intellectual and spiritual home, Hans Walter Wolff). It is in most cases a profane language, differing strongly from the language of a priestly-sacral school; it is the language of a living man, whose personal fate, whose thoughts and emotions, whose involvement in the message which he has to pass on, all form part of this language. The prophets as mediators of the word of God are men of their time; while in the very midst of experiencing the present, they are under commission to accuse and to announce judgment on it. They themselves are sitting in the boat whose capsizing they have to announce. The other side has thus already been hinted at: the commission brings them no reward or

---

6. See the article "*nabi*" in *Theologisches Handwörterbuch zum Alten Testament*.

honor, but it can certainly bring them suffering. From the history of Israel's apostasy springs the history of the suffering of those individuals who in their message oppose this apostasy: the suffering of the mediator. How the suffering of the mediator forms part of the new context of God's mercy beyond judgment, we shall discuss in the following.

God's Compassion and the Prophecy of Salvation

The "Inconsequence of God" and the Prophets. In its talk about God, the Old Testament contains a very peculiar feature which makes God's actions at a certain point appear very human. As opposed to other contexts, which emphasize the holiness of God in contrast to man, here a human emotion is attributed to God: the emotion of compassion. The Hebrew word of this, *rḥm* (or its plural), actually means "mother's womb"; or the compassion of the father for his child (Psalm 103) can become the image of this divine compassion.[7] It is very often connected with an "inconsequence of God"; i.e., this divine compassion frequently occurs where a totally different reaction of God would be appropriate. This is why this divine compassion appears so human. In the narratives of guilt and punishment in Genesis 1–11, God's reaction to the human guilt never ends [[59]] simply with the punishment. Somehow he always moderates the punishment; e.g., at the expulsion from the garden, God makes skirts from skins for the man and his wife, so they need not be ashamed. This divine compassion acquires the most decisive significance after the occurrence of the divine judgment by the destruction of the state, the kingship, and the temple. The "inconsequence" of God which is connected with his compassion is most apparent at this point in the entire history of Israel: the destruction has been announced by the long sequence of prophets of judgment—but in spite of this a turning occurs for the remnant.

As the prophets had been the messengers of God's judgment, so once again the prophets were the messengers of this turning. The prophets were never messengers of doom alone. At certain times the prophets of judgment have spoken oracles of salvation too, especially Isaiah, e.g., in chapter 7. These messages of compassion are special, however, and are always connected with the prophet's message of judgment. This can be particularly recognized in Hosea and Jeremiah. The language of compassion is connected immediately with the announcement of judgment in Hos 11:8–9: "How can I give you up, O Ephraim! How can I hand you over, O Israel! . . . My heart recoils within me, my compassion grows warm and tender." Here too the same inconsequence: compassion breaks through in spite of the announcement of judgment. In Jeremiah, we find something similar in the peculiar motif of God's lament which is connected with the announcement of judgment, e.g.,

---

7. Here the whole group of words pertaining to God's mercy or goodness has to be considered, e.g., *ḥesed*, in *Theologisches Handwörterbuch zum Alten Testament*, 1:600–621. The most important references are in the descriptive praise (hymns); cf. chapter V: "The Response." The praise of God's mercy, however, is a response to the merciful intervention of God.

Jer 9:10-12, 17-22. God suffers under the judgment that he has to bring upon his people.

We have to point to a further connection: in the visions of Amos (7:1-9; 8:1-3; 9:1-6) the prophet as intercessor begs for the compassion of God upon the people's need, and in the first two visions (7:1-3, 4-6) this is granted. In the three subsequent visions, however, this compassion is denied: "'I will never again pass by them.'" (7:8; 8:2; 9:4). The announcement of judgment takes the place of God's turning towards Israel in compassion. God can now no longer show compassion, he can no longer forgive his people. Still, God's compassion is not extirpated, it is only withheld, until it breaks through again after the judgment. This is the very message of Ezekiel and Deutero-Isaiah: after judgment, there can be a message of comfort (Isa 40:1-11). As [[60]] in the visions of Amos, the lament of the people in need is presupposed; it is the many-sided lament after the catastrophe (e.g., Isa 40:27), to which the message of the prophet in the form of the oracle of salvation comes as the divine answer. And it is, once again (as in the first two visions of Amos), the answer of divine compassion (Isa 40:28-31; 41:8-16; 43:1-7).

God's Mercy and Forgiveness. But in this new compassionate turning of God towards his people, which brings the time of judgment to an end, a difference has to be noted in comparison with former demonstrations of God's compassion. Compassion is only possible in connection with God's forgiveness. The forgiveness of the guilt which had accumulated during the time of the announcement of judgment has to be explicitly stated and has to be pronounced immediately to the people of God. Compassion without forgiveness would have no meaning in this situation—it could not bring about a real change. There can only be a change when the relationship between God and his people becomes intact again, and this is only possible through forgiveness. Therefore Deutero-Isaiah's message of comfort has as its very first words an announcement of forgiveness: "cry to her that her time of service is ended, that her iniquity is pardoned!" (Isa 40:2). The complete agreement of the two exilic prophets in this is important. Ezekiel also assumes that the restoration of the people (Ezekiel 37) will be combined with a cleansing of the people from their sins (Ezek 36:16-38).

With this we have to compare what has been said about God's compassion to his people at the beginning of the history of Israel, at the beginning of the book of Exodus: "'I have seen the affliction of my people who are in Egypt, and have heard their cry because of their taskmasters; I know their sufferings'" (Exod 3:7). In this case it is God's pure compassion with these sufferers: "I know their sufferings"; this turning is brought about simply by the saving out of need, need caused by suffering. In this case no history has yet taken place and no guilt has accumulated; God's compassion is simply the compassion towards the suffering creature, in the same way as his compassion turns towards the child dying of thirst in Gen 21:17.

[[61]] It is on the basis of this compassion for the sufferer that the promise on its way through the Old Testament must be understood, beginning with the promises to the patriarchs, taken up by the prophets of salvation, and ending with the promises in the context of apocalyptic. The way of the promise through the Old Testament is the strongest expression of continuity in the history of the people of God; it holds together large epochs—for example, the promises to the patriarchs bind that period with the period of the people in Canaan.[8]

Both therefore have their place, their meaning and their necessity: God's compassion which turns towards the suffering creature and God's compassion on the basis of forgiveness which heals a broken community. It is of great significance for the Old Testament's talking about God that both are mentioned. Both are part of God's mercy: the compassion towards the sufferer and the compassion towards the sinner.

· ·

8. Claus Westermann, *Die Verheissungen an die Väter* (Göttingen: Vandenhoeck & Ruprecht, 1976).

The Response in Action

[[74]] Just as God's word and deed are both relevant in every relationship of God to man, the human response is not only in words but in deeds also; in both cases the whole being of God and the whole being of man are included.

The Commandments and Laws

The commandments and laws belong together in the context of the word of God. Moreover, they are also a part of the human response, especially that of Israel, because in the context of them Israel is shown how she can answer God through her own action.

The Connection with the Sinai Theophany. The commandments together with the laws are associated with the Sinai experience.[1] They can only become an integral part of the Pentateuch, of the Torah, through this association with the theophany at Sinai. We know that the laws in Israel had a long history; we also know that the series of commandments arose gradually. The decalogue of Exodus 20 and Deuteronomy 5 carries within itself the signs of its gradual origin. The same holds true for the history of the legal corpus.[2] Thus the association of the commandments and laws with the theophany at Sinai gives them a greater significance. Why did this happen? Israel's worship, and especially its worship of the transition to settled life, is based on

1. W. Malcolm Clark, "Law," *Old Testament Form Criticism*, ed. John H. Hayes, pp. 99–139.

2. Martin Noth, *Die Gesetze im Pentateuch* (Halle [Saale]: Max Niemeyer Verlag, 1940), also in his *Gesammelte Studien zum Alten Testament* (Munich: Chr. Kaiser, 1957), pp. 9–141. English translation: *The Laws in the Pentateuch and Other Studies* (Edinburgh and London: Oliver & Boyd, 1966), pp. 1–107.

this Sinai theophany. Significant for the worship of Israel after it is settled is the new divine relationship of Lord and servant, which is distinct from that of the period of wandering and which corresponds to that of the enthroned king and his attendant servants. As described by the Priestly writing with the concept of *kabod* (Exod 24:15–18), the majesty of the Lord belongs to the God revealed at Sinai.[3] While the guiding God is the God who directs the way, or who commands departure or indicates a direction, [[75]] the lord enthroned in majesty becomes the God who reveals his will through the series of commandments, and then through the laws and the collections of laws.[4] The people declare themselves ready to serve this lord, as the representatives of the people attest at Shechem (Joshua 24).[5] The commandments and laws explain how the people of Israel can serve their God. And then, a great arch spans from the first commandment, which bases the exclusive acknowledgment of one Lord upon the liberation from Egypt, across and beyond the series of commandments (the two tablets) which is linked to this basic command, to the gradually growing corpus of law which determines the epochs of the history of the Israelites. It spans all the way to the Priestly law, in which the law became an extensive cultic law, corresponding to the way in which the worship of Israel was established by the theophany, as the Priestly law expressly states in Exodus 24ff.[6]

The Difference between Law and Commandment. When we consider this large complex of commandments and laws, we are confronted with a difficult question for the theology of the Old Testament. Throughout the entire Jewish and Christian tradition, this large complex is understood, interpreted, and judged theologically by *one* concept, that of the Law. The question is, can we continue to maintain that in the Old Testament commandment and law have the same theological meaning and can thus be brought together under the concept of Law?[7]

The texts of the Old Testament reveal a completely clear and unequivocal distinction between commandments and laws. The commandment—or prohibition—is a single statement in which God speaks directly to people: "Thou shalt not. . . ." The law consists of two statements, an assumed situation and a determination of the consequences: whoever does this and that—such and such a thing will happen to that person. The commandment is a

---

3. Claus Westermann, "Die Herrlichkeit Gottes in der Priesterschrift," *Forschung am Alten Testament, Gesammelte Studien,* II:115–137.

4. Walter Zimmerli, *Grundriss der alttestamentlichen Theologie,* pp. 39–48. English translation: *Old Testament Theology in Outline,* pp. 48–58.

5. See the articles on *'abad* and *šērēt* in *Theologisches Handwörterbuch zum Alten Testament.*

6. Claus Westermann, "Die Herrlichkeit Gottes in der Priesterschrift," *Forschung am Alten Testament, Gesammelte Studien,* II:115–137.

7. This is the main problem with the fundamental work of Albrecht Alt, *Die Ursprünge des israelitischen Rechts* (Leipzig: Hirzel, 1934). English translation: "The Origins of Israelite Law," *Essays in Old Testament History and Religion* (Garden City, N.Y.: Doubleday, 1967), pp. 101–171. By using the same term, "Recht," for the two forms—apodictic and casuistic—he merely exchanges the governing concept of "Gesetz" for the governing concept of "Recht."

direct proceeding between God and people, and in this regard corresponds to a commandment to depart or a direction to follow, in the pre-settlement period. In contrast, the law is not a direct word of God; in every case it is tied to human institutions, since punishment requires some agency to execute the punishment. Laws about slavery presuppose a specific social order. This is also the reason why the laws within the [[76]] legal corpus of the Old Testament are much more subject to change than the commandments. The laws for sacrifices, for example, were bound to become inoperative when the temple was destroyed; the laws about slavery, when slavery was done away with. The commandments of the Decalogue, however, are not subject to such changes; commands such as "thou shalt not steal," "thou shalt not commit adultery" still stand today. This is also the reason why the Ten Commandments could be taken over by the Christian church and have retained their significance far beyond it.[8]

However, all this simply corresponds to the situation in the Old Testament itself: only in the Sinai account of the Decalogue does the word of God issue directly from the mountain of God to Israel; and the Decalogue in Deuteronomy 5 is definitely placed before the laws which follow in chapters 12–26. It was only in the late postexilic period that a comprehensive concept of the law arose which made the commandment subordinate to the law. One can only conclude from this fact that commandments and laws do not have the same theological significance in the Old Testament. Only the commandment is the direct and immediate word of God; it was only subsequently that the laws were explained as God's word. In the Old Testament as well as in the New, the *commandment,* as God's instruction for human behavior, is necessary and indispensable for the relationship of God to man. This does not apply to the *laws* in the Old Testament in the same way. They are only necessary where they develop God's commandments and apply them to the various sectors of settled life; in the process they can change, and can even become inoperative.

In view of this situation, what Paul says in his letters about the Law must be reconsidered. He uses Law in the tradition of the linguistic usage of the late postexilic period, as a general concept for commandments and laws. The negative judgment of Paul concerning the Law can no more apply to the commandments of God in the Old Testament than it does to the commands and instructions of Jesus in the New. Speaking and acting are both the response of the person who has heard God's word and experienced God's action. It is on the basis of the instructions and commandments of God that a person can act. [[77]] If the commandments which God gave to the people of Israel extend their validity and their significance into our present age, far beyond the Jewish people and the Christian church, then we may regard this as a sign of the power and quality of God's instructions which have survived the changes of history.

8. The specific meaning of the commandments finds a convincing representation in Gerhard von Rad's *Old Testament Theology,* 1:190–203.

Worship

Further, serving God has in the Old Testament—as in many other religions—the specific sense of worshiping God. Individuals can serve God insofar as they acknowledge God as their Lord in daily life, and do God's will; they can also serve God by bringing him an offering in the act of worship, at the holy place, at the sacred time. The institution of worship, however, is not solely concerned with the fact that people serve God with their offerings; it is rather that in the worship the relationship to God as a whole finds an institutionalized expression. All important parts of Old Testament theology come together in worship, which, therefore, really ought to form a special part of it.

In the Old Testament, worship is a reciprocal event between God and people. In it God acts and speaks, and people also act and speak.[9] This reciprocal event between God and people takes place at a special place at a special time, at the sanctuary on festival days. Since it happens at a special time and place, it is sacred; that is, an event removed from everyday life. As such, it requires a mediator of the holy, the priest. The worship of Israel in this form was established through the theophany at Sinai. Here, the group liberated from Egypt, on its way through the wilderness, experienced for the first time the holy place, the sacred time, and the word of God addressed to them in the theophany. Moses became the mediator of the holy in this event. What was established at Sinai was the worship of the later, settled form of life, as the Priestly writing shows: the tabernacle which God commanded to be built in the revelation at Sinai is the model for the temple. [[78]]

Viewpoints for Understanding Worship in the Old Testament

Two Types of Cult. Worship in the Old Testament has a history. The most important caesura is the transition to the settled life. Only with this transition does the *Grosskult* first arise, in which a large festive congregation comes together in the sanctuary, the "House of God," on festival days. This is preceded by the early cult which we know from the patriarchal accounts, in which the congregation consisted of only a small family group, into whose life the cult was still fully integrated. In this early cult the holy place was not yet made by hands; it was the mountain, the rock, the tree, the spring. There were no priests as yet; the father received God's word and dispensed the blessing.[10] The second caesura is the establishment of kingship, which acquires major significance for the worship of Israel. The king himself becomes the mediator of blessing (Psalm 72), he dispenses the blessing (1 Kings 8); the priests in Jerusalem become officers of the king. The third caesura is the exile, introduced by the destruction of the temple. The offering of sacrifices

---

9. In the well-known definition of Martin Luther, worship is represented as a reciprocal event between men and God. But this is limited to the spoken word.

10. Claus Westermann, Genesis, pt. 2, "Die Religion der Väter–der Gottesdienst"; Roland de Vaux, *Histoire ancienne d'Israel*, 2 vols. (Paris: Gabalda, 1971), 1:255–273; idem, *Ancient Israel: Its Life and Institutions*, pp. 289–294.

ceases; at first, worship consists of nothing more than gatherings for lamentation, then a new type of worship by word arises alongside the restoration of worship by offering. In it, many features of the early cult come to life again, and the family regains a significant role in worship.

Blessing and Saving in Worship. The action of God in worship is, first and foremost, a blessing rather than a saving action.[11] The liturgical blessing, dispensed by the priest, is an essential part of worship; the blessing flows out from the sanctuary across the land. The constant character of worship, with its regular annual cycle of returning festivals, corresponds to the blessing. The blessing is vitally important to the everyday life of the congregation gathered together in worship. The saving action of God cannot take place in worship itself. But it is present in the service, on the one hand in the announcement of saving in response to the laments of the people and of the individual (the so-called oracle of salvation); and on the other hand in the word, in the remembrance of the saving acts of God in various forms, and above all in the association of the annual festivals with the working of God in the history of Israel.[12]

[[79]] In addition to this the word of God has a decisive significance for the worship of Israel in the proclamation of the commandments, and in the representation of history in various forms and words which introduce and accompany the liturgical actions, as e.g., the words spoken for the dispensing of the blessing. How far the exhortation, as encountered in Deuteronomy, had a liturgical function is not yet certain. God's word in worship ought to be distinguished from the word of God to people outside the service—from, for instance, a messenger of God. Its particular character stems from the fact that, at a holy place and at a sacred time, it occurs against the background of quietness which hints at the presence of God, as the theophany in Exod 24:15–18 shows. The willingness of the congregation gathered in worship to hear God's word is associated with this quietness. The possibility of the transmission of God's word is based on this particular character.

The human action in worship is the offering. Rather than go into the whole history of sacrifice,[13] I should like to make only two remarks about it: Although sacrifices were originally offered by the head of the family, the priest gradually takes his place. Although originally the offering had many different functions, in the later period the sin offering takes precedence; hand-in-hand with this goes a quantitative increase in sacrifices. The prophetic criticism of sacrifices is to a large extent caused by this trend.[14] What the worshipers say in worship is, on the one hand, the words which accompany the actions, which, like the sacrificial saying at the presentation of the

11. See Gerhard Wehmeier, *Der Segen im Alten Testament*; Claus Westermann, *Der Segen in der Bibel und im Handeln der Kirche.*

12. Robert Martin-Achard, *Essai biblique sur les fêtes d'Israel.*

13. Hans-Joachim Kraus, *Worship in Israel*, pp. 112–124; Roland de Vaux, *Ancient Israel: Its Life and Institutions*, pp. 415–456.

14. H. H. Rowley, *Worship in Ancient Israel* (Philadelphia: Fortress Press, 1967), chapter 5: "The Prophets and the Cult," pp. 144–175.

first fruits, can be expanded into a creed (Deuteronomy 26). On the other hand, there is the singing of Psalms by the congregation and by the individual, the meaning of which has already been discussed.

Worship as the Focal Point in the Life of the People. The relevance of worship in Israel lies in its function as the focal point of the life of the people. What is decisive is not what happens in the isolated service, but rather what happens in worship for the whole people and the whole land. Therefore, the walk from the house to the service, and from the service back to the house, is an important factor of the service itself. What is brought into the service on these walks from the outside life, and also what is taken back into everyday [[80]] life from the service, are necessarily a part of the act of worship as well. Only in this way can worship be the center of the entire life of the people. Only in this way is criticism of worship also possible, as in the prophetic criticism of a worship which has become false. The reciprocal event of worship from God to people and from people to God receives meaning solely from the fact that it becomes the center of events outside the service.

The Universal Aspect of Worship. The Psalms show that in them the collective life of the community, and of the individual outside the service, extends into the service itself. Moreover, they show that worship in Israel had a strongly universal character. The praise of God has a tendency to expand. Even the kings and the nations are called to praise, and moreover all creatures, as is particularly evident in Psalm 148. Since the God of Israel is also the creator of heaven and earth, worship must encompass the entire span of creation. Looking back on the response of man in words and in action, we can see now how this response encompasses all of human life in speaking and in acting. There is a center of all the thousands of words each person speaks during life. This center is one's speaking to God, voicing the suffering, voicing the joy of life.

There is a center of all human actions throughout life, year after year, day after day. This center is one's doing the will of God, the obedience which seeks God's will, and the knowledge that worship can be the quiet center of all human activity.

ELMER A. MARTENS

b. 1930

Land and Lifestyle

Born in Saskatchewan, Elmer A. Martens studied at the Mennonite Brethren Biblical Seminary in Fresno, California, where he was then a pastor. Following doctoral studies at Claremont Graduate School, Martens returned to the seminary as professor of Old Testament and, for nine years, its president. His commentary on Jeremiah was the first in the Believers Church Bible Commentary series, which he served as Old Testament editor.

Selected Writings by Martens

1977   Tackling Old Testament Theology. *Journal of the Evangelical Theological Society* 20: 123–32.

1981   *God's Design: A Focus on Old Testament Theology.* Grand Rapids: Baker. [British edition: *Plot and Purpose in the Old Testament* (Leicester: Inter-Varsity)]

1986   *Jeremiah.* Believers Church, Bible Commentary. Scottdale, Pennsylvania: Herald.

1991   Biblical Theology and Normativity. Pp. 37–58 in *So Wide a Sea: Essays on Biblical and Systematic Theology.* Edited by Ben C. Ollenburger. Elkhart, Indiana: Institute of Mennonite Studies.

1994   The Oscillating Fortunes of "History" within Old Testament Theology. Pp. 313–40 in *Faith, Tradition, and History: Old Testament Historiography in Its Near Eastern Context.* Edited by A. R. Millard, J. K. Hoffmeier, and David W. Baker. Winona Lake, Indiana: Eisenbrauns.

1997   Yahweh's Compassion and Ecotheology. Pp. 234–48 in *Problems in Biblical Theology: Essays in Honor of Rolf Knierim.* Edited by H. T. C. Sun, K. L. Eades, James M. Robinson, and Garth I. Moller. Grand Rapids: Eerdmans.

1998   *God's Design: A Focus on Old Testament Theology.* 3rd edition. North Richland Hills, Texas: D. & E. Scott.

Writings about Martens

1996   Post Modernism: Honoring Elmer A. Martens. *Direction* 25: 3–85.

Elmer A. Martens's
Approach to Old Testament Theology

Reprinted with permission from Elmer A. Martens, *God's Design: A Focus on Old Testament Theology* (Grand Rapids: Baker, 1981), pp. 11–23. Some footnotes have been omitted.

A Pivotal Text about Yahweh and His Purpose

[[11]] The task of adequately stating the central message of the Old Testament is a challenging one, and that for several reasons. The diversity of the Old Testament material, quite apart from its size, offers a challenge to anyone who intends to provide a summary statement of its contents. The Old Testament includes stories, poems, laments, judgment speeches, proverbs, songs, and laws. Can one from such diversity of material written over a period of several centuries arrive at a single central theme? Is there even a single theme? Scholars have not been unanimous in their answer.

The challenge of describing the heart of the Old Testament is compounded by the variety of proposals already given by scholars, even in the last fifty years.[1] For some, God's covenant with Israel seems all-important.[2] Others organize their theological statements around the concept of God's sovereignty, or the communion of God with men, or God's promise, or God's presence.[3] Asked to summarize the Old Testament message in one sentence, a group of college graduates gave these answers: 'God acts in history'; 'God is active in reconciling fallen men to himself'; 'The central message of the Old Testament is the preparation for the first coming of the Messiah.' Some answers get closer to the heart of the Old Testament than [[12]] others. The answers are not mutually exclusive, of course, though some are more capable of embracing the bulk of the Old Testament material than others. One scholar

1. A good survey, though somewhat technical, is offered in Gerhard F. Hasel, *Old Testament Theology: Basic Issues in the Current Debate* (Grand Rapids: Eerdmans, 1972, [2]1975). A readable summary of scholarly positions is given in Robert Laurin, *Contemporary Old Testament Theologians* (Valley Forge: Judson Press, 1970). A helpful discussion of the issues facing the biblical theologian is given in Walter C. Kaiser Jr, *Toward an Old Testament Theology* (Grand Rapids: Zondervan, 1978), pp. 1–40. Cf. John Goldingay, 'The Study of Old Testament Theology: Its Aims and Purpose,' *Tyndale Bulletin* 20 (1975), pp. 34–52.

2. E.g. Walther Eichrodt, *Theology of the Old Testament*, 2 vols. (Philadelphia: Westminster Press; London: SCM Press, 1961, 1967); J. Barton Payne, *The Theology of the Older Testament* (Grand Rapids: Zondervan, 1962). An author who eschews a single concept as the centre is Gerhard von Rad, *Old Testament Theology*, 2 vols. (New York: Harper & Row; London: Oliver & Boyd, 1962, 1967).

3. E.g. on sovereignty, E. Jacob, *Theology of the Old Testament* (New York: Harper & Row; London: Hodder & Stoughton, 1958); on communion, Th. C. Vriezen, *An Outline of Old Testament Theology* (Newton, Mass.: Charles T. Branford; Oxford, Blackwell, 1956, [2]1970); on promise, Walter C. Kaiser Jr, *Toward an Old Testament Theology*; on presence, S. Terrien, *The Elusive Presence: Toward a New Biblical Theology* (San Francisco: Harper & Row, 1978).

has aptly said: 'When there is one landscape, many different pictures may nevertheless be painted.'[4] The challenge remains, however, to paint the best possible picture.

The attempt to describe the core message of the Old Testament is challenging, for clarity about the Christian faith will depend on a grasp of the Old Testament. The Old Testament supplies the fibre for the Christian faith. But unless the message of the Old Testament is clearly articulated, its relevance to the New Testament and to Christians today will remain fuzzy.

The proposal of this book is that God's design is the key to the content of the Old Testament. This proposal assumes that it is legitimate to examine the Old Testament in search of a single central message. The following chapters attempt to offer compelling reasons for such an assumption. The emphasis on a design of God as a unifying and organizing principle of the Old Testament material arises from an exegesis of several comparable biblical texts, the first of which is Exod 5:22–6:8.

The approach advocated in this book is distinctive in that the answer to the question about the central message is derived from a specific set of texts. It is in the language of the Bible itself that God's fourfold purpose is described, so that what we have here is a biblical theology rather than a systematic theology. It is with exegesis that we begin in order to get an outline for our picture.[5]

Someone might respond that selections of other texts would yield other outlines of a message. Why choose a certain text in Exodus from which to develop the central Old Testament message? The answer to this question will be clearer once the Exodus text has been understood.

A Significant Answer to a Crucial Question: Exodus 5:22–6:8

Then Moses turned again to the LORD and said, 'O LORD, why hast thou done evil to this people? Why didst thou ever send me? [23] For since I came to Pharaoh to speak in thy name, he has done evil to this people, and thou has not delivered thy people at all.'

[1]But the LORD said to Moses, 'Now you shall see what I will do to Pharaoh; for with a strong hand he will send them out, yea, with a strong hand he will drive them out of his land.' [[13]]

[2]And God said to Moses, 'I am the LORD. [3]I appeared to Abraham, to Isaac, and to Jacob, as God Almighty, but by my name the LORD I did not make myself known to them. [4]I also established my covenant with them, to give them the land of Canaan, the land in which they dwelt as sojourners. [5]Moreover I have heard the groaning of the people of Israel whom

---

4. James Barr, 'Trends and Prospect in Biblical Theology,' *Journal of Theological Studies* 25:2 (1974), p. 272.

5. See E. A. Martens, 'Tackling Old Testament Theology: Ex. 5:22–6:8,' *Journal of the Evangelical Theological Society* 20 (June 1977), pp. 123–132.

the Egyptians hold in bondage and I have remembered my covenant. [6]Say therefore to the people of Israel, "I am the LORD, and I will bring you out from under the burdens of the Egyptians, and I will deliver you from their bondage, and I will redeem you with an outstretched arm and with great acts of judgment, [7]and I will take you for my people, and I will be your God; and you shall know that I am the LORD your God, who has brought you out from under the burdens of the Egyptians. [8]And I will bring you into the land which I swore to give to Abraham, to Isaac, and to Jacob; I will give it to you for a possession. I am the LORD."'

This text presents a dialogue between Moses and God, an observation which the usual chapter division obscures. The conversation occurs after an initial attempt by Moses to seek the Egyptian Pharaoh's permission for the slave people of Israel to leave the country. Moses addresses God, primarily with questions. The larger part of the text is given to God's reply. We may already note a somewhat curious fact, namely that there are two introductions to God's speech. 'But the LORD said to Moses . . .' (verse 1) is followed, though there is no reply by Moses, by 'And God said to Moses . . .' (verse 2). The structure of this text, which consists of a twofold reply to a speech by Moses, which is also in two parts, is an important clue to the message of this text unit.

Moses' Crucial Question: Exodus 5:22-23

The situation which gives rise to the questions posed by Moses before God involves a public confrontation with the Pharaoh in the land of Egypt. Moses' initial appeal to Pharaoh to let the Israelites, for years slaves in Egypt, go to freedom to the land of promise, has been met with rebuff. Pharaoh has taunted, 'Who is the LORD, that I should heed his voice and let Israel go?' In defiance Pharaoh has responded: 'I do not know the LORD, and moreover I will not let Israel go' (5:2). Aggressive action has followed assertive word. The production quota imposed by Pharaoh on the Israelites [[14]] has remained the same, but straw for bricks is no longer provided by the Egyptians: the Israelites must secure the straw themselves. The Israelite foremen, not able to meet the new demands satisfactorily, are beaten by their Egyptian task-masters and complain to Pharaoh. The Pharaoh grants no reprieve. The foremen turn on Moses, claiming that he is to blame.

Moses takes his frustration before God, from whom he hast received the assignment to lead a people out of bondage. His speech to God consists of two parts. He asks two questions and files a complaint.

The questions are already of an accusatory nature. 'Why hast thou done evil to this people?' just as the foremen blame Moses, their superior, so the leader Moses now blames God, whose call he has reluctantly followed. As often happens in accusations of this kind, Moses overstates the case, for God has not actively brought evil upon his people. True, the events which have led to harsh treatment by the Pharaoh have been set in motion by Yahweh, but only indirectly. The second question registers impatience, if not accusation:

'Why didst thou ever send me?' This is hardly a question asking for information. After all, the directives had been clear when Moses received his commission at the burning bush: he was to bring a slave population into freedom. Is there in Moses' question a request for some further clarity, however? Is he calling for a rationale, for purpose, for objective? A hesitation, an uncertainty, underlies his question. In colloquial language one might phrase that question, 'God, what are you up to?' The whole enterprise of the anticipated deliverance is called into question. Moses has just entered into his assignment. He thought he knew what was involved, but now that opposition has set in more vehemently, he steps back and in measured cadence asks the elementary but entirely basic question about his mission: 'Why didst thou ever send me?' (5:22).

The questions, posed in a reproachful tone, are followed by a forthright complaint: 'For since I came to Pharaoh to speak in thy name, he has done evil to this people, and thou hast not delivered thy people at all' (5:23). Moses confronts God with a breach of promise. The attempts to gain a favourable response from Pharaoh have met with obstinacy on Pharaoh's part. The glorious promise of God seems at this point to be a hollow promise. With the forthrightness, if not bluntness, characteristic of some of God's servants through the ages, Moses files his complaint. Clearly Moses is in a difficult position. He has been rebuffed by Pharaoh, he has been accused by leaders of the people he is to deliver. Therefore he has turned to God for help.

God's Deliberate Reply

God's reply, like the statement of Moses, is in two parts. The first word from God is reassuring: 'Now you shall see what I will do to Pharaoh; for with a [[15]] strong hand he will send them out, yea, with a strong hand he will drive them out of his land' (6:1). A divine rebuke might be expected in response to the accusations, but Moses receives a promise instead. He is being asked to rely on the naked word of God. This initial reply addresses the last part of Moses' speech, the complaint. The procedure is reminiscent of the lecturer who says, 'I will take the last question first.' Moses charges, 'Thou has not delivered thy people at all.' God's answer is that deliverance is future but sure. The immediate agent for that deliverance will be Pharaoh himself; he will in due time virtually expel the people from his land. Thus the objection of Moses is answered by a straightforward statement, without elaboration.

God's further reply in 6:2–8 is much more extensive. It addresses the weightier part of Moses' speech, for it takes up the question of rationale and objective, a question basic for Moses. The longer reply is clearly structured. The first part revolves around the self-identification of God (6:2b–5); the second part is a series of instructions to Moses. Together the two parts speak to Moses' concern: 'God, what are you up to anyway?'

God's Self-Identification as Yahweh. God's reply to Moses begins with a simple but highly significant assertion: 'I am the LORD' (6:2). In the English translation the force of this statement is not at once apparent. It is essentially the name of the deity that is at issue. In this reply the selfidentification formula 'I am the LORD' appears three times (verses 2, 6, 8).

The name for God is given in most English Bibles as 'the LORD'. The Hebrew consonants are YHWH, and with certain vowels customarily written with these consonants, the pronunciation for the name suggested by earlier scholars was Yehovah (Jehovah). Modern scholars hold that the name of God was pronounced Yahweh. This conclusion is based on an understanding of the way in which in oral reading Jewish people came to substitute a title for the written name of God because of their deep reverence for the name of God. Yahweh, then, is the proper name for God. Some modern translations of the Bible employ the name Yahweh rather than the accustomed 'the LORD,' and perhaps for good reason. In the English language 'Lord' is a title and properly translates *'ădōnāy*, master. LORD, all in capital letters, as a translation of Yahweh,[6] does not convey the force of a personal name. In this passage it is not a title but a specific name that is revealed. Since great importance was attached to names in ancient Israel, and among Semites generally, it is of considerable importance, especially for a theology of the Old Testament, to gain clarity on the meaning of the name Yahweh.

[[16]] To answer the question about the meaning of the name Yahweh, we must reach back a little in the narrative. The name had been given to Moses earlier in connection with his call (3:1–4:17). There Moses had heard God identify himself as 'I AM WHO I AM' (3:14), a phrase that plays on the Hebrew verb 'to be.' Building on the derivation of the word Yahweh from the verb 'to be,' some scholars hold that the expressions 'I AM WHO I AM' and 'Yahweh' refer to the actuality of God's existence. The name, then, marks the certainty of Yahweh's existence. Given a western mindset, such an explanation seems plausible; yet scholars have challenged that interpretation on the basis that such abstractions as 'existence' were not characteristic of the Hebrew way of thinking.

Since linguistically the phrase could be translated, 'I cause to be that which I cause to be,' others have argued that the words refer to the creative activity of God. This view has been contested, however, on the grounds that the specific verb form involved (causative) is not found in the Hebrew for the verb 'to be.' Still others have suggested that 'I will be who I will be' indicated that God was sufficient for every circumstance. Paraphrased, this would mean, 'I will be for you the kind of God you have need of.' A Jewish scholar holds that the name El Shaddai, which also occurs in the text and is rendered 'God Almighty,' was a name that was associated with fertility. The patriarchs, this scholar says, knew God as 'God Almighty,' but did not know God as the one who fulfilled promises; now, at the time of the exodus, the name Yahweh was to be associated with the keeping of promises. That is, Yahweh represents

6. For an extended discussion of the name see G. H. Parke-Taylor, *Yahweh: The Divine Name in the Bible* (Waterloo, Ont.: Wilfrid Laurier University Press, 1975). His conclusions differ, however, from those presented here.

'He who is with his creatures, and He who is constantly the same, that is, he is true to his word and fulfills his promise.'[7]

Or, to turn to an approach that sidesteps the attempt to translate the word, some have suggested that the name Yahweh was deliberately enigmatic. To know someone by name is to have a measure of control. One can summon him, for instance. Did God give to Israel so strange a name, a name that was no name, so that Israel would not manipulate God?[8] It is a distinct possibility. Man's inclination is to use God to his own advantage. But Yahweh is not a dispensing machine from whom can be secured at will his gifts of bounty, health, wisdom, etc. No, Yahweh remains free to act. His acts are carried out in freedom. He is who he is, and is not determined, except by himself.

Attractive as some of these suggestions may be, it is best, if one wishes to know the meaning of the name Yahweh, to give close attention to the context of Exodus 3. As Eichrodt has noted, the significance of the name lies in part in the promise of his presence. Moses has already been given the assurance of God's presence earlier when God declares, in response to [[17]] Moses' objection, 'But I will be with you' (3:12).[9] The context is also one in which God promises deliverance. God says: 'I promise that I will bring you up out of the affliction of Egypt' (3:17). This promise gives support to the meaning of the name Yahweh as being the saving name. Yahweh is the name by which God represents himself as present, here and now, to act, especially to deliver. It is in this way, essentially in a new way, that Israel will experience Yahweh. Yahweh is a salvation name. This name, the most frequent name for God (YHWH occurs more than 6,800 times in the Old Testament) becomes a frequent reminder that God is the saving God.

The identity of Yahweh, as our text emphasizes, is not to be divorced from the story of the patriarchs. 'I appeared to Abraham, to Isaac, and to Jacob, as God Almighty, but by my name the LORD (Yahweh) I did not make myself known to them' (6:3). The same God who now speaks to Moses, though under a new name, Yahweh, had earlier committed himself to the patriarchs through a covenant to them, which, among other things, included the gift of the land of Canaan. With this statement the relationship of God to the patriarchs, described already in Genesis 12, is reviewed, or affirmed, or better yet, made the platform from which the further promises are now launched. The promise of land to Abraham is made in Gen 12:7. The covenant with Abraham is described in greater detail in Genesis 15 and 17 and is related to the initial blessing of a multitude of descendants promised to Abraham (Gen 12:2). Along with the promise of descendants, God promised Abraham territory. 'On that day the Lord made a covenant with Abram saying, "To your descendants I give this land, from the river of Egypt to the great river, the river Euphrates . . ."' (Gen 15:18). The triple promise of de-

---

7. U. Cassuto, *A Commmentary on the Book of Exodus* (Jerusalem: Magnes Press, ET 1967), p. 77.

8. See G. von Rad, *Old Testament Theology*, 1, p. 182.

9. W. Eichrodt, *Theology of the Old Testament*, 1, p. 191.

scendants, territory, and blessing is embraced in a covenant given to Abraham in his ninety-ninth year (Gen 17:1–8). Reiterated to Isaac (Gen 26:3) and to Jacob (Gen 28:19; 35:9–12), the promise continued to have a threefold gift of descendants, territory, and blessing. God's word to Moses is that he has remembered that covenant, not in the sense of merely recalling it, but in the sense of honouring it. One phase of the promise, that of offspring, is realized, in part, for the families of Israel have been exceptionally fruitful (Exod 1:7). Fulfillment of the remaining part of the promise, that of land, will now be brought under way.

The statement of God in Exod 6:3–5 then ties in with the patriarchs historically, by reviewing the past, and theologically by providing continuity of the name Yahweh with the name God Almighty. What follows in the Yahweh speech is directed to the future.

Yahweh's Purpose. The name Yahweh, judged by the context in which it is first given (3:14) and the special attention devoted to it in the present [[18]] passage (5:22–6:8), signals a divine presence to save. The name Yahweh, one is led to expect, will introduce a new chapter in God's work in the world. In his reply to Moses, God as Yahweh describes his intention.

Yahweh's initial design for his people is deliverance: 'I will bring you out from under the burdens of the Egyptians, and I will deliver you from their bondage, and I will redeem you with an outstretched arm and with great acts of judgment' (6:6). These three statements resemble, by reason of parallelism, lines of Hebrew poetry. Three synonyms are used to elucidate Yahweh's action. 'I will bring out' is in the causative form of 'go' (*yāṣā'*) and might be rendered: 'I will cause you to go out.' The causative is also employed in the following verb: deliver (*nāṣal*). It is the common verb used to refer to God's actions of rescue. The verbal form (*nāṣal*) is repeated with considerable frequency (135 times). The word rendered 'redeem' (*gā'al*) has its linguistic home in regulations governing tribal peoples and property. A redeemer (*gô'ēl*) was one whose responsibility it was to buy out the property of a kinsman who had forfeited it, or who was on the verge of forfeiting it, perhaps because of debt. The prophet Jeremiah purchased a piece of land from his cousin Hanamel and so acted as a redeemer (Jer 32:6ff.). A more familiar example is Boaz, who as a near relative buys the property of Naomi (Ruth 2:20; 4:4–6, 9). Or the redeemer might buy out a kinsman who had become the slave of a foreigner (Lev 25:47–54), or avenge the blood of a relative who had been murdered. The sense of restoration to a former state or the healing of tribal brokenness is an underlying component of the term. In Exodus 6 the redeemer is Yahweh, and the deliverance is specified to be of large proportion: 'from the burdens of the Egyptians' and from 'their bondage.'

Secondly, Yahweh's design is to form a godly community. 'And I will take you for my people, and I will be your God' (Exod 6:7a). God's purpose is that the people now to be formed are to be distinctly his people. But, characteristically, God's demand is not apart from his promise: he himself will be their God. This second statement makes it clear that deliverance, though it is

Yahweh's initial intention, is only preparatory to larger concerns. The re-deemed lot are to stand together as a community marked as God's special possession. The vocabulary is covenant vocabulary. The formula, slightly al-tered, occurs in the major sections of the Old Testament (e.g., Lev 26:12; Deut 26:17ff.; Jer 7:23; Ezek 11:20). The implications of this statement will receive attention later.

Thirdly, Yahweh's intention is that there be an on-going relationship [[with]] his people. 'And you shall know that I am Yahweh your God who has brought you out from under the burdens of the Egyptians' (Exod 6:7b). They are to know (that is, experience) him as Yahweh their God. This means, among other things, that he offers himself to be known. He invites his [[19]] people into the adventure of knowing him. The means by which this knowl-edge occurs and the nature of the resultant experience can be deduced from the exodus event, but further descriptions of Yahweh's encounter with his people will be in evidence later.

Finally, Yahweh's intention for his people is that they enjoy the good life. The words of the text are: 'and I will bring you into the land which I swore to give to Abraham, to Isaac, and to Jacob; I will give it to you for a possession' (Exod 6:8). The land was already earlier the object of promise, where it was the concrete part of God's blessing for his people. Elsewhere the land is de-scribed as the land flowing with milk and honey (Exod 3:17), which is to say that it is a land in which life is pleasant and in which living is marked by abun-dance. The land comes before long to symbolize the life with Yahweh in ideal conditions, a quality of life which might be characterized as the abundant life.

The divine reply to Moses' question, 'Why did you ever send me?' em-braces a discussion of the name Yahweh, and a disclosure of his purpose. Three times, as we have noted, the self-identification formula surfaces: 'I am Yahweh.' In the first instance it introduces the historical review in which em-phasis is placed on the name itself since it had not been known in earlier times (Exod 6:3). In the second part of the speech, the self-identification for-mula occurs at the outset of the four statements of divine purpose (6:6). Cu-riously, and in a sense of finality, the 'I am Yahweh' phrase also terminates the speech (6:8). Unless we think of the reply as composed carelessly, we must ask, what is the force of this thrice-repeated assertion? If in the name Yahweh there is disclosed a new feature of Yahweh, and if the covenant with the patriarchs was already made earlier, apart from the name, then we must look for a new feature other than covenant as linked in a particular way with the name Yahweh. Is that new feature not to be found in the statement of the fourfold design? Salvation, a new people, a new relationship, and the gift of the land—these are the components of the purpose. Yahweh is the name that is associated at this crucial juncture with purpose, that which God intends or is about.

One may fully affirm the remark by Brevard Childs in conjunction with this passage: 'The content of the message which is bracketed by this self-identification formula is actually an explication of the name itself and contains the essence of God's purpose with Israel.'[10] Similarly, the Jewish scholar Cassuto states in commenting on this Exodus text: 'In our passage the king of the universe announces His purpose and the amazing plan of action that He proposes to carry out in the near future.'[11] We should wish to [[20]] amend this statement only by noting that the plan is not just for the near future, but embraces a large block of time, in fact the entire history of Israel.

. . . .

A Grid for the Old Testament Message

There is general agreement that the Old Testament has Yahweh for its central subject, but we may ask, what does one say after having said that? We may posit that the text in Exod 5:22–6:8 clarifies the way in which the central subject of the Old Testament, Yahweh, is to be elaborated. Yahweh has a plan. This plan is one to bring deliverance, to summon a people who will be peculiarly his own, to offer himself for them to know and to give to them land in fulfillment of his promise. This Scripture passage asks the question posed at the outset, namely, how to understand what the Old Testament is getting at. Formulated by Moses in the context of a frustrating and perplexing experience, the question, 'Why did you ever send me?' is helpful in supplying a handle, a definite clue to our investigation about the [[21]] central message of the Old Testament. As a preliminary check we might test our suggestion that the fourfold purpose of God is a satisfactory grid by casting our eye over one block of the Old Testament, namely the Pentateuch.

The concept of purpose, quite apart from detail, already underlies the book of Genesis. The family stories of Abraham, Isaac and Jacob presage a distinct destiny, especially since they are launched with the statement of design to Abraham: 'Go from your country and your kindred and your father's house to the land that I will show you' (Gen 12:1). The Joseph narrative at the conclusion of Genesis also hints at design. Joseph says to his brothers: 'As for you, you meant evil against me; but God meant it for good, to bring it about that many people should be kept alive, as they are today' (Gen 50:20).

Deliverance, the first phase of Yahweh's intention, is particularly the subject of the first half of the book of Exodus; the covenant community, now given detailed instructions, is the subject of Exodus 19–40. Through the sacrifice and other cultic institutions in Leviticus God makes himself known and the people experience him as Yahweh. Land, and the regulations pertaining to occupancy, are the frequent subject of Deuteronomy. Thus the fourfold design serves almost as a table of contents to the Pentateuch. Might this outline be pertinent, even adequate, for the remainder of the Old Testament?

It is the thesis of this book that the fourfold design described in Exod 5:22–6:8 is an appropriate and also adequate grid according to which to

10. Brevard S. Childs, *The Book of Exodus* (Philadelphia: Westminster Press, 1974), p. 115 (= *Exodus*, SCM Press, 1974).

11. U. Cassuto, *Exodus*, p. 76.

present the whole of the Old Testament material. This is a substantial claim, proof of which must be the pages which follow. Even should it be disputed that the proposed grid is adequate as a set of categories for the presentation of the Old Testament message, the insights gained from this approach promise to be considerable.

Two points could still be raised as requiring clarification. First, it might be asked why this particular passage in Exodus rather than some other in Exodus or elsewhere was chosen. Could some other passage serve equally well? Perhaps, but not too likely. The paragraph of Exod 5:22–6:8 commends itself for various reasons. It is the text in which the revelation of the name Yahweh is differentiated from other names of God. Even though a form of it is given to Moses earlier, attention is distinctly called here to Yahweh, the form of the name by which God will be primarily known in the remainder of the Old Testament canon. Secondly, this passage speaks of the beginnings of the people of Israel, with whom much of the Old Testament [[22]] deals. It could be expected that a programmatic statement would be found here. Moreover, this text is concerned with an interpretation of the exodus event, which according to some scholars is the fulcrum event in the Old Testament.[12] Most important, however, in commending this scripture as the Old Testament message in a nutshell is the consideration that the text addresses the question of God's ultimate purpose. Moses' question is our question too: 'God, what are you up to?' More than a clue is given here. The explicit statements supply specific, even if not fully detailed, indications of Yahweh's purpose. Those indications, it may be argued, are the controlling purposes of God within the Old Testament. But someone may still object by saying, 'Is not the notion of purpose and design an import from a western civilization which, especially in our time, is fascinated by ideas such as purpose?' The notion of design is basic, for instance, to such western concepts as 'management by objective.' Since it is our intention to let the Old Testament speak in its own terms, the question is most appropriate. The remainder of the book is an attempt at an answer.

. . . .

[[23]] Yahweh is a God with a purpose. In this respect Yahweh is different from other gods represented in ancient Near Eastern literature. Already the Genesis verdict, 'God saw that it was good,' presupposes a purpose. To this fact of purpose the law gives evidence (Exod 5:22–6:8), as do the prophets (Isa 46:10; 14:26; Jer 32:18–19) and so also do the writings (Ps 33:11; Prov 19:21).

With these assertions about purpose generally, and the exegetical treatment of Exod 5:22–6:8 specifically, the shape of our task emerges with greater clarity. To comprehend Yahweh's design we shall have to talk about deliverance; about covenant and community; about the knowledge of God; and about land.

12. James H. Cone: 'The Exodus was the decisive event in Israel's history, because through it Yahweh revealed himself as the Savior of the oppressed people.' 'Biblical Revelation and Social Existence,' *Interpretation* 28 (1974), p. 423; cf. David Daube, *The Exodus Pattern in the Bible* (London: Faber and Faber, 1963).

Synopsis of Martens's *God's Design: A Focus on Old Testament Theology* (1981)

Elmer A. Martens
On Land and Lifestyle

Reprinted with permission from Elmer A. Martens, *God's Design: A Focus on Old Testament Theology* (Grand Rapids: Baker, 1981), pp. 108–15.

Land as Demanding a Specific Life-Style

[[108]] Human conduct and behaviour are understood to have a bearing on land, and conversely, land occupancy demands a particular quality of life-style. This association between life-style and land is found in scattered references through the books of Leviticus, Numbers, and Deuteronomy; but these references occur in sufficient number to command notice and have shown a point of view that is unique to the Bible. For a glimpse of this association between land and life-style we look in turn at moral and cultic responsibilities, specific rules relating to land use, and the cultic festivals which had an agricultural orientation. A discussion of these moral, economic and cultic regulations will clarify the theological aspects surrounding land.

As to moral, civil and cultic instructions, their association with the land needs first to be established biblically and then assessed. Various statutes are announced for observance at the time of entry into the land, often introduced by a general statement of which Deut 12:1 is typical: 'These are the statutes and ordinances which you shall be careful to do in the land which the LORD, the God of your fathers, has given you to possess' (cf. 11:31–32; 4:5, 14; 5:31; 6:1). From these statements it is obvious that a prescribed form of conduct is appropriate for life in the land. Thus the land is not only a promise or a gift; fulfilled responsibility is integral to land tenure.

These regulations range broadly. They deal with governance, for they speak to the possibility of the people's desire for a king and give direction for the establishment of a monarch (Deut 17:14). Cities of refuge are to be established for murderers in the land as a part of the civil-law complex regulating blood revenge (Deut 19:7). Religious and moral instruction in the Torah is to be undertaken in a family setting, and Moses, visualizing a permanent residence, commands that 'these words' are to be written on the doorposts of the house and on the gates (Deut 6:9). Dietary instructions are also given (Deut 12:20ff.). To occupy the land, as in modern occupancy of rental property, a willingness to submit to regulations of the owner is required. Israel is not at liberty to set its own behavior guidelines. Residence in the land means paying attention to what is fitting in the land.

But the case for law and land association is stronger than the words 'fitting' or 'propriety' indicate. Wrong behaviour, for instance, is not only unbecoming but it defiles the land. Harlotry is forbidden, for example, lest [[109]] 'the land fall into harlotry and the land become full of wickedness' (Lev 19:29). Shedding of blood pollutes the land and no expiation for it is possible, except the death of the murderer (Num 35:29-34). A man who is hanged for an offence is not to remain on the tree into the night—he must be buried, for a 'hanged man is accursed by God; you shall not defile your land which the LORD your God gives you for an inheritance' (Deut 21:23). Divorce is permitted, but not the remarriage of the husband to his divorced wife who has already married another. Not only is such a practice an abomination before the LORD, but it will 'bring guilt upon the land' (Deut 24:4). Marriage and family ethics are not in themselves associated directly with land—yet violations of these family—related moral and civil regulations are said to defile the land. In what sense? In the sense that Yahweh dwells in the midst of the land (Num 35:34). And in another sense also. Land is the 'middle term' between Israel and Yahweh. Land is a tangible symbol of Yahweh. It would not be conceivable that Yahweh could be defiled, therefore the negative consequence could best be stated by saying that the land will be defiled. So close is the association between Yahweh and land that an infraction against Yahweh has the effect of polluting or defiling the land. The land therefore symbolizes in a forceful way Israel's relationship with Yahweh.

Yet it is not only Israel, to whom the Torah belongs, who defiles the land: the Canaanites who are strangers to the Torah have by their abominations defiled the land. Israel is cautioned not to defile herself with such things as child sacrifice, for 'by all these the nations . . . have defiled themselves; and the land became defiled' (Lev 18:24-25). Pollution of self and pollution of land result from unlawful behaviour. Even apart from revelation the non-Israelite should know to abstain from such sexual perversion as bestiality and homosexual activity and from human sacrifice. These evils defile the land. Though they did not possess the Torah, peoples outside Israel are held responsible for their conduct in the land. It is not therefore that the land is rendered impure because of its relation to Israel. Again, it is defiled almost in its own right, or, perhaps more accurately, because of the close relationship of the land to Yahweh.

The case for the interdependence between moral behaviour and land is even stronger than the preceding discussion has suggested. There is more to be said than that obedience to Yahweh is fitting in the land and that disregard of Yahweh's instruction defiles the land. Continued occupancy of the land is itself conditioned by observance of the law. This means on the one hand that by faithful adherence to the admonitions, Israel can continue in the land. Motivation for such observance of law includes the promise of continued residence: 'All the commandment which I command you this day you shall be careful to do, that you may live and multiply, and go in and possess the land' (Deut 8:1). Moses says: 'Justice and only justice you shall [[110]] follow, that you may live and inherit the land which the LORD your God gives you.' Obedience to the law brings blessings, which, as the catalogue of blessing indicates, are primarily prosperity and fruitfulness in the land (Deut 28:1-14).

But if blessing follows obedience, curse within the land and even deportation from it will result from disobedience (Deut 28:15-68). Lack of rain, defeat by enemies, internal confusion and disease are only a few of the disasters which may be expected, and the ultimate disaster, apart from ruin, is that 'you shall be plucked off the land . . . And the LORD will scatter you among all peoples' (Deut 28:63–64). Again, such drastic treatment as removal from land is not reserved only for a people like Israel with a revealed Torah. It was because of the sinfulness of the Canaanites that they were expelled from the land (Lev 18:24). Indeed, so much are these infractions directly against the land that the land personified is described as vomiting out Canaanites (Lev 18:24). The threat for Israel too is that unless she keeps the statutes and the ordinances, the land may vomit up the people in it (Lev 20:22–26). By this one is to understand that violation of norms is so reprehensible that, quite apart from Yahweh's displeasure, the land itself cannot tolerate them: the land will spew out the population.

It may seem at first glance that the stipulations accompanying the gift of the land make the land not altogether a gift. A few passages indeed give the impression that obedience to God's ordinance was a condition of entry into the land (e.g., Deut 8:1). But these are not to be understood as qualifying people in a fundamental sense for the gift; rather they are to be taken, as are the many statements cautioning Israel lest through disobedience they forfeit the right to continue on the land, as accompanying the gift. To a gift, even a gift totally the result of grace, there is not inconsistently attached stipulation for its use. A British company director who at his death left £33,000, speci-fied that £5,000 be given to each of his two grandchildren—provided they did not spend the money on motorcycles. This twentieth-century example, while not the norm for interpreting ancient Israelite practice, may still illustrate the basic principle that a gift may have conditions. The land gift was unique in that Yahweh remained the owner. He disposed of it, but not in a final sense by giving it over to Israel. As the proprietor of the land, his right to make stipulations, along with his claim to Israel, is everywhere assumed. Life in the land can continue provided a certain life-style, one marked by obedience, is maintained.

The subject of life-style is far too large to survey with any depth, but the regulations about land use can move us from generalities to specifics and can illustrate the tenor of conduct pleasing to Yahweh. [[111]]

Sabbath and Jubilee

Two regulations dealt with land use: the sabbath and the jubilee. From Mount Sinai Moses issued this instruction: 'When you come into the land which I give you, the land shall keep a sabbath to the LORD' (Lev 25:2; cf. 23:10f.). By this, as the explanation which follows shows, is meant that whereas for six years the land is to be sown and vineyards cultivated, in the seventh it is to be fallow. There is to be no seeding of the land, and vineyards are not to be pruned, nor is there to be reaping of that which grows by itself. The practice of leaving the land fallow for the purpose of rejuvenation was not uncom-mon among Israel's neighbours. The reason for such a practice in Israel, how-ever, takes a decidedly different shape. The sabbatical year is for the benefit of the poor and for the benefit of wild life, 'that the poor of your people may eat, and what they leave the beasts may eat.' This purpose could be achieved if for individual farmers the seventh year came at different times. In Leviticus there is assumed a universal and uniform observance of the fallow year. But the purpose, while humanitarian, is not exclusively so. A religious motivation is announced in the terminology, 'a sabbath to Yahweh.' The land, by being left fallow, bears witness to Yahweh's ownership. The direct link between Yahweh and land is left intact; the land's rest is not disturbed by human intervention of tilling.

It is argued by some scholars that Deut 15:1–3 couples a regulation about the release of all debts every seven years to the command to fallow the land. While complicated in details, Deut 15:1–3 is best considered not as a cancellation of debts generally but as a case where land was mortgaged to a creditor. In the seventh year the creditor was not to demand annual payment of the land's harvest. This provision, also humanitarian, allowed the debtor some hope of meeting his obligations. If a loan were taken in the sixth year and not fully paid, it would not be payable till after the harvest of the eighth year, thus giving the impoverished Israelite an extended period of credit. The sabbath for the land was for Yahweh (Lev 25:2) and the practice of charity to the debtor was also performed 'before Yahweh' (Deut 15:2). The sabbath regulation, while clearly given as an obligation unto Yahweh, pointed two ways: to the land, and to the debtor whose land had been encumbered. Failure to observe these statutes is given as reason for drastic action of God's removal of people from the land (Lev 26:32–33, 43; 2 Chr 36:21).

A second ordinance that dealt especially with land use is the jubilee. The instructions about jubilee also require that the land be left fallow, not only every seven years but during the fiftieth year, namely after seven sevens of years (Lev 25:8ff.). It was unlike the seventh fallow year in that in the jubilee year the land was to revert to the family that originally claimed ownership. An impoverished Israelite, once he had mortgaged his land and his crops, [[112]] might find it necessary to 'sell' the land to his creditor, and even if a relative redeemed it, the unfortunate Israelite would still in all likelihood be working it for the benefit of his kinsman (Lev 26:36ff.). The purpose of the kinsman provision was to retain the land within the particular family of the clan; otherwise descendants of the unfortunate Israelite would be condemned to be property-less. The jubilee year, coming every few generations, was to remedy this eventuality, for in the jubilee year, even had the land remained in the clan through redemption, it was now to be returned to the particular family within the clan. The jubilee year also had provisions for the release of slaves. It is therefore clear that the regulations of the jubilee affected the economic life of a people by demanding magnanimous action by the well-to-do for the benefit of the less capable or unfortunate man. Without such a provision as a jubilee, territories of a clan could come into the hands of a few families, and the remaining clans people would be serfs. The jubilee aimed at the preservation of household units, ensuring their economic viability. The land belonged inalienably to the householder. This right of the household landowner to regain his property was not due to some belief about the right of property *per se*, but a belief in land as a gift from Yahweh, whose regulation stabilized the people's relationship with each other and with their God. It is not hard to see that in the Old Testament, [[113]] land, Israel and Yahweh belonged together, and that in this triad the rights of the family were particularly safeguarded.[1]

Festivals

With such agricultural practices as the sabbath year and the jubilee year, a life-style characterized by non-exploitation of land and of people was inculcated. A considerate and caring attitude was encouraged.

In addition a set of festivals, primarily agricultural, established yet another orientation and life-style attitude: thanksgiving and joy. Instructions about these festivals appears in each of the four law books (Exodus 23; 34; Leviticus 23; Numbers 28; Deuteronomy 16).

All of the three major annual festivals, each a week long, were held in connection with the harvest from the field. The festival of unleavened bread was held in the spring of the year immediately following the passover observance. Scheduled for the beginning of the barley harvest in late April/early May, its important feature was the baking and eating of unleavened bread. The bread of the harvest was deliberately not prepared with yeast, so that the firstfruits would be eaten untouched by a foreign element. The second festival, called a feast of harvest in the book of Exodus but more commonly a feast of weeks (Deut 16:10), came fifty days after the sickle was first put to the spring grain. It was observed at the end of the wheat harvest, corresponding to our month of June. At this time the firstfruits of the farmer's labour were presented before Yahweh. Either the whole crop, the first of several in the agricultural year, or the first fruits of the barley grain harvest preserved from their first cutting to the end of the season, were brought to the sanctuary. The third agricultural festival was the feast of ingathering, known also as the feast of booths or tabernacles, because of a provision that during the week people should live in tents. This festival followed the day of atonement in the month of October, and centred on the harvest of fruits, especially olives and grapes.

Though agrarian-based, these festivals were not pagan orgies. They were religious occasions. In all three, males of the country were to present themselves at the sanctuary. Although social in character, with feasting and celebration, these were more than social events. The festivals were festivals 'to Yahweh.' The religious orientation emerged in the presentation of animal offerings to Yahweh and also in the gift of first fruits of the grain and fruit to Yahweh. The detailed instruction for such a presentation of agricultural pro-

1. I am indebted for material in this chapter and for the diagram to C. J. H. Wright's careful analysis of regulations governing land, 'Family, Land and Property in Ancient Israel—Some Aspects of Old Testament Social Ethics' (unpublished dissertation, University of Cambridge, 1976).

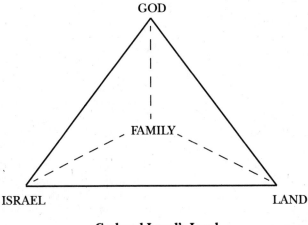

God and Israel's Land

duce is given in Deut 26:1, and, while given for the particular occasion of the very first harvest, the instruction may also have been ritually [[114]] applied, especially at the feast of weeks and the feast of ingathering.

At these festivals the Israelite was not to appear before Yahweh empty-handed (Exod 34:20; 23:15). The worshipper with his produce in his basket would appear before the priest and begin his statement by saying: 'I declare this day to the LORD your God that I have come into the land which the LORD swore to our fathers to give us' (Deut 26:3). After rehearsing the history of his people, with emphasis on Yahweh's grace to them, he concluded with the words: 'And behold, now I bring the first of the fruit of the ground, which thou, O LORD, hast given me.' The priest either set the basket before the altar (Deut 26:4) or waved the sheaf before Yahweh (Lev 23:10–11, 20). The character of the festival as a festival to Yahweh was safeguarded through this ritual at the sanctuary in which through word and act Yahweh was acknowledged. The worshipper expressed his thankfulness and gratitude to Yahweh.

Now it is highly significant that the speech the worshipper made at the presentation of his offering is a rehearsal of the deeds of Yahweh in history. The dedication of the produce was motivated by recognition of Yahweh not so much as creator, but as deliverer. It was not as a creature who enjoys the yield of creation that the worshipper came before Yahweh, but as one who had experienced deliverance from oppression. His history was a history of salvation, and here the land is remarkably in focus. His ailing forefather Jacob migrated to Egypt with but a small family and without land. The population in Egypt had no land they could call their own. But now, the worshipper concluded, Yahweh had brought them into the land. The pagan worshipper by contrast addressed a god related to nature, from whom he expected the benefits of fertility in field, flock and family. But in Israel these ideas of God so closely and so exclusively associated with nature are absent. While Yahweh is a God of nature, and is so celebrated in the Psalms, he is a God of history; and his connection with the land is not only or even primarily as a God who makes it fertile, but as one who in response to his promise has brought his people to enjoy the abundance that the land offers. To this God of history, the worshipper offered his thanksgiving.

Judged by the instruction in Deuteronomy, the festivals, while foremost festivals for Yahweh, were also festivals for the people. The males appeared at the sanctuary but the festivals involved all—sons and daughters, servants and Levites. The fatherless and widow are singled out for special mention, but, more arresting from a sociological point of view, the sojourner was also to participate in the celebrations (Deut 26:11, 14). These celebrations were not to become exclusivist—the non-Israelite was to be included. The festivals, related so closely to the land, display, as did the land use regulations, a humanitarian concern. Israel was to recall that she had been a slave in Egypt (Deut 26:12). Love to God and love to neighbour came to expression in the [[115]] festivals.

Finally, the mood of the three-week-long annual festivals deserves mention. 'You shall rejoice before the LORD your God' (Deut 16:11). 'You shall rejoice in your feast' (Deut 16:14). 'You shall rejoice before the LORD your God seven days' (Lev 23:40). The imperative to rejoice, like the imperative to love, while strange, nevertheless indicates the basic posture for the Israelite. Philo, the Jewish philosopher-exegete of the first century A.D., described even the day of atonement as the 'feast of feasts.' Israelite worship was a worship of joy and praise. In the light of the ancient Near Eastern record and practice, no doubt, one scholar has gone as far as to say, 'There is hardly a word so characteristic of the Old Testament as the word joy.'[2] Festivals, as ordered by Yahweh, were an expression of this joyful mood.

Land, then, is more than acreage or territory. It is a theological symbol, through which a series of messages are conveyed. It is the tangible fulfilment of the promise. Land is a gift from Yahweh, and Israel, through preoccupation with it, has her attention continually called to Yahweh. Land requires a specific and appropriate life-style. Responsibilities concerning social behaviour are enjoined upon the people for the time when they will occupy the land, and they are warned that disobedience defiles the land and may result in loss of their privilege of tenancy. The specific regulations about land use, such as the sabbatical year and jubilee, take ecological and humanitarian concerns into account. Finally the festivals, associated with the production from the land, once again link land and Yahweh, point to social responsibilities, and portray the joyful spirit in which this people lives its life on the land, always before Yahweh.

But if land is more than acreage or territory and symbolic of promise, gift, blessing and life-style, it is nevertheless still soil and territory. It has theological aspects, but it is not thereby an ethereal thing, nor should it be spiritu-

---

2. Ludwig Koehler, *Old Testament Theology* (Philadelphia: Westminster; London: Lutterworth, 1957), p. 151.

alized. Land is real. Earth is spatially definable. Life with Yahweh takes place here and now. The quality of that life is all-embracing—it relates to Yahweh, to neighbour, to environment. Life with Yahweh cannot be compartmentalized, as though his interest lies only within a small area. No, his interest extends to the total man and to the total society and to the total environment. He is misrepresented, and his people's life misshaped, if the wholeness of life is not emphasized. The promise of land and all that it signifies keeps the entire design rooted in history and is thoroughly reality-related. We shall find the this-worldly and earth-affirming aspect strong and marked once again in the wisdom literature, especially in Proverbs. In the New Testament, the concept of discipleship is equally all-embracing.

Part 4

From Brevard Childs to
a New Pluralism

Introduction

In the final two decades of the twentieth century, Old Testament theology became increasingly diverse—in more than one respect. The range of orientations and approaches expanded, as did the contributors. Not strictly on Old Testament theology, Paul Hanson's historical-critical study of "community" in the Bible reflected its American context (1986). Similarly, F. H. Breukelman's incomplete biblical theology (1988) drew on a Dutch tradition of biblical scholarship, including in its appeal to the Jewish scholars Martin Buber, Franz Rosenzweig, and Max Kadushin (Deurloo 2000). In Germany, Gisela Kittel (1989) wrote *against* the shadow of National Socialism, while also becoming the first woman to write an Old Testament theology. And in Italy, Marco Nobile (1998) considered the task of Old Testament theology in relation to Judaism after the holocaust and drew on the hermeneutics of Gadamer and Ricoeur—also, critically, on Brevard Childs.

No single decade in the history of Old Testament theology witnessed more voluminous production than did the years 1993–2003. The two-volume work of Horst Dietrich Preuss (1991, 1992) appeared in English translation (1995–96); following were Rolf Knierim's collection (1995) and the theologies of Walter Brueggemann (1997) and Bernhard W. Anderson (1999). James Barr reviewed and critically assessed Old Testament theology's recent history, proposing as well a future for biblical ("pan-biblical") theology (1999). Erhard S. Gerstenberger's *Theologies in the Old Testament* (2001) also appeared in English (2002). In German, the single volumes of Antonius H. J. Gunneweg (1993) and Josef Schreiner (1995) preceded Rolf Rendtorff's two volumes (1999, 2001) and the completion of Otto Kaiser's three (1993–2003; cf. Rendtorff 1996). Evangelical scholars in North America were also productive. Ralph Smith (1993) and Paul House (1998) issued comprehensive works, while John Goldingay published the first part of his three-volume *Old Testament Theology* (2003), and Elmer A. Martens issued a third and revised edition of his (1998, see above, p. 222). John H. Sailhamer, while not producing an Old Testament theology, offered a substantial review of its history and proposal for its method (1995).

Just preceding the decade was Brevard Childs's *Biblical Theology of the Old and New Testaments* (1992). Childs had earlier proposed assigning central importance to the canon (1970), a proposal on which he elaborated massively in his *Introduction to the Old Testament as Scripture* (1979). There he stressed both the "final form of the text," as alone bearing "witness to the full history of revelation," and the texts' "canonical shaping," as having crucial theological importance (1979: 75–76, 79). This involved Childs in critical engagement with, and in relativizing, the dominant historical-critical approaches—making their use relative to Christian theological interpretation and appropriation (Moberly 1999: 446–47). Subsequently, Childs extended his canonical approach into Old Testament and then biblical (and dogmatic) theology (1986, 1992), in works excerpted below. While no other Old Testament theologians fully embraced his revisionist approach and some were strongly critical of the way he carried it out, Childs contributed significantly to the vitality of the discipline. Even if measured only by the scale and temper of criticism directed toward him (Barr 1999), Childs ranks in importance with Eichrodt and von Rad.

The positive influence of Childs may be perceived in the work of Rendtorff (1993, 1999) and House (1998; cf. Nobile 1998, according to Boadt 2001). From quite different perspectives and for different theological reasons, both Rendtorff and House focused on the canon—including the Masoretic Text's canonical order and tripartite arrangement (law or Pentateuch, prophets, and writings)—and what Childs called "the final form of the text." House agreed with Childs's theologically robust, indeed theocentric, understanding of the term "canonical" (House 1998: 57) but departed from Childs in allowing no role to historical criticism (cf. Childs 1992: 379). Also contrary to Childs, Rendtorff invoked von Rad in claiming that "retelling remains the most legitimate form of theological discourse on the Old Testament" (Rendtorff 1999: 2). However, Rendtorff's canonical, largely synchronic retelling differed from von Rad's tradition-historical work, and in his second volume (2001) Rendtorff, like Childs, followed a thematic arrangement (Childs 1986).

Others, too, proceeded thematically but around a conceptual center or focus. Preuss, like Eichrodt, saw his task as presenting the Old Testament's "world of faith and witness" in its structural unity. For Preuss, who worked within the mainstream of German historical-critical scholarship, that structure centered on "YHWH's historical activity of electing Israel for communion with his world," which is an action obligating both Israel and the nations (Preuss 1991: 29; cf. 1996: 25, 249). With somewhat different accent, then, Preuss followed Zimmerli and Smend in focusing Old Testament theology around God, Israel, and their relation (see above, pp. 118–19). Similar in this respect were Kittel (1989: 19), Schreiner (1995: 17), House (1998: 56), Anderson (1999: 39–78), and Otto Kaiser. Kaiser grounded the Old Testament's (and the Bible's) unity in the first commandment, the Decalogue within the Torah forming the Old Testament's center (O. Kaiser 1993: 350; 1998: 19). Reminiscent of Eichrodt, Anderson structured his theology around covenant—but stressed three different covenants: Abrahamic, Mosaic, and Davidic.

Criticism of these and other approaches to Old Testament theology took at least two contrasting tacks. Knierim argued that they were insufficiently systematic, since they could not solve the problem of the Old Testament's plural theologies. Knierim proposed to discern semantic priorities among these various theologies, in order to correlate them systematically while preserving their individual character. He argued that, from within the Old Testament itself, "Yahweh's universal dominion in justice and righteousness" constitutes the criterion by which all themes and theologies may be evaluated (Knierim 1995: 1–20). By contrast, Gerstenberger insisted on the irreducible plurality of "conflicting" Old Testament theologies, which have to be related to their respective historical and social contexts—as do their interpreters (Gerstenberger 2000: 120–34; 2002: 5–18). Knierim and Gerstenberger—both of whom referred to and reflected their experience in Brazil—agreed that criteria are required for evaluating the truth or appropriateness of the Old Testament's theologies (Gerstenberger 2002: 280) but not on what these criteria may be or how to acquire them. Gunneweg, who more closely resembled Gerstenberger in his emphasis on Israel's religion and its history, was explicit about the source of these evaluative criteria: the New Testament (Gunneweg 1993: 35; cf. Stade 1899: 93; Vriezen 1970; Hermisson 2000: 59).

These latter works, like those of Childs, raised fresh questions about the relation between Old Testament theology and history. Gunneweg and Kaiser shared little of the concern to distinguish Old Testament theology from the history of Israel's religion that exercised many of their predecessors, including Eichrodt and von Rad. Rainer Albertz went beyond them in arguing for the historical study of Israel's religion "in place of" Old Testament theology (1995a; 1994: 16). He thereby provoked lively response (Schmitt 2001: 346–67; cf. Keel 2001; Janowski 2002). Further, both Gunneweg and Kaiser departed from the prevailing theological and conceptual vocabulary to write of Israel's "existential orientation" (Gunneweg 1993: 34; cf. Fohrer 1972: 93–94) or of the Old Testament "as existential interpretation" (O. Kaiser 2003: 393, 400–401, citing Heidegger and Kierkegaard; cf. O. Kaiser 1993: 86–87, citing Bultmann). While Brueggemann expressed his own aversion to the "cognitive-ideational" character of theology (1997: 45), he was just as critical of the "Enlightenment rationality," with its putative "autonomous reason" that underwrote historical criticism and muted the Old Testament's authoritative or theological claim—its "normativeness" (1997: 14–15, 53). For Brueggemann, Old Testament theology could not be conflated with, and neither could it depend on, the critical reconstruction of Israel's history, regardless of debates about any such reconstruction (Ollenburger 2000).

Like Childs, Brueggemann focused attention on the text itself and on its character as witness—more specifically, in Brueggemann's case, as testimony. Prescinding from any "essentialist" attempt to identify a theological center in the Old Testament, which would amount to excessive closure, Brueggemann construed the Old Testament, and Old Testament theology, as a "process" in the legal sense—thus as a trial, in which "core testimony" (e.g., God's action) and counter-testimony (Israel's questions), even unsolicited (e.g., the nations) and embodied testimony (e.g., the cult), are proffered. Testimony consists finally in rhetoric, and "God is given to us . . . only by the dangerous practice of rhetoric." In other words, "there is no Yahweh outside the text" (Brueggemann 1997: 66, 576). As this allusion to Jacques Derrida suggests, Brueggemann's was the first Old Testament theology expressly to embrace certain postmodern currents (cf. Adam 1995, 2001; Penchansky 1995). Brueggemann also incorporated feminist perspectives and saw his rhetorical approach as respecting the "Jewishness of the text" (1997: 80–83).

The works of Childs and Brueggemann have much in common, including a stress on intertextuality (Childs 1986: 13, 237; Brueggemann 1997: 78–80) and a correlative conviction about "the collapse of history," so that history can no longer serve as Old Testament theology's governing paradigm (Perdue 1994: 155–65, 285–98) or the condition of its validity (contrast Baumgarten-Crusius 1828). Even so, and to the surprise of some (Olson 1998), Childs and Brueggemann have been among each other's most strident critics (Childs 1992: 72–73; Brueggemann 1997: 89–93). They, in turn, have each come under searing criticism from other quarters. Regardless, their respective contributions and the vigorous debate that they have provoked bode well for Old Testament theology's vitality in this new century.

BREVARD S. CHILDS

b. 1923

Canon

Brevard Childs began teaching at Yale Divinity School in 1958 and was designated Sterling Professor of Divinity at Yale University in 1992. Childs studied with both Walther Eichrodt and Gerhard von Rad; like each of them, he has made signal contributions to the field of biblical theology and to theology more broadly. His canonical and resolutely theological approach continues to elicit affirmation and criticism. In either case, the influence of Childs on biblical theology has been vast.

Selected Writings by Childs

1970 *Biblical Theology in Crisis*. Philadelphia: Westminster.
1974 *The Book of Exodus: A Critical, Theological Commentary*. Old Testament Library. Philadelphia: Westminster / London: SCM.
1979 *Introduction to the Old Testament as Scripture*. Philadelphia: Fortress.
1984 *The New Testament as Canon: An Introduction*. Philadelphia: Fortress.
1986 *Old Testament Theology in a Canonical Context*. Philadelphia: Fortress.
1992 *Biblical Theology of the Old and New Testaments*. Minneapolis: Fortress.

Writings about Childs

Barr, James
1999 Pp. 32–39, 47–50, and 387–438 in *The Concept of Biblical Theology: An Old Testament Perspective*. Minneapolis: Fortress.
Brett, Mark G.
1991 *Biblical Criticism in Crisis? The Impact of the Canonical Approach on Old Testament Studies*. Cambridge: Cambridge University Press.
Noble, Paul R.
1995 *The Canonical Approach: A Critical Reconstruction of the Hermeneutics of Brevard S. Childs*. Leiden: Brill.
Seitz, Christopher, and Kathryn Greene-McCreight (editors)
1999 *Theological Exegesis: Essays in Honor of Brevard S. Childs*. Grand Rapids: Eerdmans.
Tucker, Gene M., David L. Petersen, and Robert R. Wilson (editors)
1988 *Canon, Theology, and Old Testament Interpretation: Essays in Honor of Brevard S. Childs*. Philadelphia: Fortress.

Brevard S. Childs's
Approach to Old Testament Theology

Excerpted with permission from Brevard S. Childs, *Old Testament Theology in a Canonical Context* (Philadelphia: Fortress, 1986), pp. 10–17.

A Canonical Approach to Old Testament Theology

[[10]] The profile of the discipline of Old Testament theology which I am suggesting can perhaps be made more precise by briefly sketching its relationship both to Judaism and to biblical theology. I have emphasized that Old Testament theology is a Christian discipline which reflects on the scriptures held in common with the synagogue. One of the main reasons for the Christian use of the Hebrew text of the Old Testament rather than its Greek form lies in the theological concern to preserve this common textual bond between Jews and Christians. Historically, Christianity confronted first-century Judaism through the Greek form of the Jewish scriptures, and thus the New Testament is stamped indelibly by the Septuagint. Yet the theological issue of how Christians relate to the Jewish scriptures cannot be decided biblicistically by an appeal to New Testament practice, but must be addressed theologically. The debate transcends the historical moment of the first-century encounter, and turns on the church's ongoing relation to the authoritative scriptures which Israel treasured and continues to treasure in the Hebrew. A canonical approach takes the Hebrew scriptures seriously because of its confession that Israel remains the prime tradent of this witness. It remains an essential part of the church's theological reflection on the Old Testament to continue in dialogue with the synagogue which lives from the common biblical text, but often construes it in a very different manner. The goal of the dialogue is that both religious renderings be continually forced to react to the coercion of the common text which serves both to enrich and to challenge all interpretations.

The discipline of Old Testament theology also differs from biblical theology in several important ways. Biblical theology provides a disciplined reflection on the scriptures of both Old and New Testaments. Its emphasis differs because of the overriding problem of relating the witnesses of the two different Testaments. Moreover, because of its concern to interpret the entire Christian Bible theologically, it tends to be in dialogue more with the traditions of dogmatic theology than with the discrete problems which arise from the separate Testaments. However, the theological approaches to the text of both Old Testament theology and biblical theology do not differ hermeneutically. Both are disciplines arising from within [[11]] Christian theology and both involve the application of descriptive and constructive tools in order to execute the task.

It is a basic tenet of the canonical approach that one reflects theologically on the text as it has been received and shaped. Yet the emphasis on the

250

normative status of the canonical text is not a denial of the significance of the canonical process which formed the text. The frequently expressed contrast between a static canonical text and a 'dynamic' traditio-historical process badly misconstrues the issue. Similarly, to claim that attention to canon elevates one specific historical response to a dogmatic principle utterly fails to grasp the function of canon. Rather, the basic problem turns on the relationship between text and process. The final canonical literature reflects a long history of development in which the received tradition was selected, transmitted and shaped by hundreds of decisions. This process of construing its religious tradition involved a continual critical evaluation of historical options which were available to Israel and a transformation of its received tradition toward certain theological goals. That the final form of the biblical text has preserved much from the earlier stages of Israel's theological reflection is fully evident. However, the various elements have been so fused as to resist easy diachronic reconstructions which fracture the witness of the whole.

The controversy with the traditio-historical critics is not over the theological significance of a depth dimension of the tradition. Rather, the issue turns on whether or not features within the tradition which have been subordinated, modified or placed in the distant background of the text can be interpreted apart from the role assigned to them in the final form when attempting to write a theology of the Old Testament. For example, to seek to give theological autonomy to a reconstructed Yahwist source apart from its present canonical context is to disregard the crucial theological intention of the tradents of the tradition, and to isolate a text's meaning from its reception.

Even more controversial is the usual method of reconstructing an alleged traditio-historical trajectory which does not reflect actual layers within Israel's tradition, but is a critical construct lying outside Israel's faith. To draw an analogy, it is one thing to trace the different levels within the growth of the New Testament parables. It is quite another to reconstruct putative earlier levels apart from their reception and transmission within the community [[12]] of faith. The canonical approach to Old Testament theology is insistent that the critical process of theological reflection takes place from a stance within the circle of received tradition prescribed by the affirmation of the canon.

The canonical approach to Old Testament theology rejects a method which is unaware of its own time-conditioned quality and which is confident in its ability to stand outside, above and over against the received tradition in adjudicating the truth or lack of truth of the biblical material according to its own criteria. Of course, lying at the heart of the canonical proposal is the conviction that the divine revelation of the Old Testament cannot be abstracted or removed from the form of the witness which the historical community of Israel gave it. In the same way, there is no avenue open to the Jesus Christ who is worshipped by the Christian church apart from the testimony of his fully human apostles. To suggest that the task of theological reflection takes place from within a canonical context assumes not only a received tradition, but a faithful disposition by hearers who await the illumination of God's

Spirit. This latter point has been developed so thoroughly by Calvin as to make further elaboration unnecessary (*Institutes*, I, ch. VII).

Then again, a canonical approach envisions the discipline of Old Testament theology as combining both descriptive and constructive features. It recognizes the descriptive task of correctly interpreting an ancient text which bears testimony to historic Israel's faith. Yet it also understands that the theological enterprise involves a construal by the modern interpreter, whose stance to the text affects its meaning. For this reason, Old Testament theology cannot be identified with describing an historical process in the past (*contra* Gese), but involves wrestling with the subject-matter to which scripture continues to bear testimony. In sum, Old Testament theology is a continuing enterprise in which each new generation must engage. An importapt implication of the approach is that the interpreter does not conceive of Old Testament theology as a closed, phenomenological deposit—Eichrodt spoke of a 'self-contained entity' (*Theology* I, 11)—whose understanding depends on the discovery of a single lost key. Much of the recent discussion of the so-called 'centre of the Old Testament' seems to have arisen from a concept of the discipline which views it simply as an historical enterprise (cf. Reventlow).

One of the important aspects within the shaping process of the [[13]] Old Testament is the manner by which different parts of the canon were increasingly interchanged to produce a new angle of vision on the tradition. The canonical process involved the shaping of the tradition not only into independent books, but also into larger canonical units, such as the Torah, Prophets and Writings. For example, law was seen from the perspective of wisdom; psalmody and prophecy were interrelated; and Israel's narrative traditions were sapientialized (cf. Sheppard). The canonical process thus built in a dimension of flexibility which encourages constantly fresh ways of actualizing the material.

There are some important implications to be drawn from this canonical process for the structuring of a modern Old Testament theology. This canonical structuring provides a warrant for applying a similar element of flexibility in its modern actualization which is consonant with its shape. In other words, a new dynamic issues from the collection which maintains a potential for a variety of new theological combinations. Even though historically Old Testament law was often of a different age and was transmitted by other tradents from much of the narrative tradition, a theology of the Old Testament according to the proposed canonical model seeks to exploit a theological interaction. Therefore, regardless of the original literary and historical relationship between the Decalogue and the narrative sections of the Pentateuch, a theological interchange is possible within its new canonical context which affords a mutual aid for interpretation. Of course, there are rules which control and govern the interaction which derive from the literature's structure, content, and intertextuality, but these can be best illustrated in practice. The recognition of this dimension of a canonical approach further sets it apart from the usual descriptive method which is bound to original historical sequence.

One of the hallmarks of the modern study of the Bible, which is one of the important legacies of the Enlightenment, is the recognition of the time-conditioned quality of both the form and the content of scripture. A pre-critical method which could feel free simply to translate every statement of the Bible into a principle of right doctrine is no longer possible. Of course, it is a caricature of the history of Christian theology to suggest that such a use of the Bible was universal in the pre-Enlightenment period. Augustine, Luther and Calvin—to name but a few—all worked with a far more sophisticated understanding of the Bible than the term 'pre-critical' [[14]] suggests. Nevertheless, it is still true that the issue of the Bible's timeconditioned quality became a major hermeneutical problem in the wake of the Enlightenment and the rise of the historical-critical method.

Modern Old Testament theologians have applied various hermeneutical approaches to the text in order to accommodate the problem. One sought critically to abstract the 'abiding truth' or 'elements of lasting value' from the literature. Or a history of moral progress was discerned which slowly sloughed off its primitive inheritance in order to reach its ethical goal, often found in the Sermon on the Mount. Finally, some mode of consciousness, egalitarian ideology, or elements of liberation were discovered and assigned a normative theological function. However, in spite of the tendentious nature of many of these proposals, it is significant to observe that a concern was always expressed to retain at least some understanding of biblical authority for the modern church, and to resist its complete relativity.

The hermeneutic implied in a canonical understanding of the Old Testament moves in a strikingly different direction in seeking its resolution to the problem. The emphasis on scripture as canon focuses its attention on the process by which divine truth acquired its authoritative form as it was received and transmitted by a community of faith. Accordingly, there is no biblical revelation apart from that which bears Israel's imprint. All of scripture is time-conditioned because the whole Old Testament has been conditioned by an historical people. There is no pure doctrine or uncontaminated piety. Any attempt to abstract elements from its present form by which, as it were, to distinguish the kernel from its husk, or inauthentic existence from authentic expression, runs directly in the face of the canon's function.

Moreover, to take seriously a canonical approach is also to recognize the time-conditioned quality of the modern, post-Enlightenment Christian whose context is just as historically moored as any of his predecessors. One of the disastrous legacies of the Enlightenment was the new confidence of standing outside the stream of time and with clear rationality being able to distinguish truth from error, light from darkness.

In conscious opposition to this legacy of the Enlightenment, the canonical approach seeks to approach the problem with a different understanding of how the Bible functions as a vehicle of God's [[15]] truth. By accepting the scriptures as normative for the obedient life of the church, the Old Testament theologian takes his stance within the circle of tradition, and thus identifies himself with Israel as the community of faith. Moreover, he shares in that hermeneutical process of which the canon is a testimony, as the people of God struggled to discern the will of God in all its historical particularity. Its shaping of the biblical tradition indicated how it sought to appropriate the tradition as a faithful response to God's word. In an analogous context of a received witness, the modern biblical theologian takes his stance within the testimony of Israel and struggles to discern the will of God. Fully aware of his own fraily, he awaits in anticipation a fresh illumination through God's Spirit, for whom the Bible's frailty is no barrier. Although such understanding derives ultimately from the illumination of the Spirit, this divine activity functions through the scriptures of the church; that is to say, completely within the time-conditioned form of the tradition. There is no one hermeneutical key for unlocking the biblical message, but the canon provides the arena in which the struggle for understanding takes place.

Canonical Approach and the Modern Debate

Space is too limited for a lengthy discussion with many of the classic issues which currently agitate the field. However, I would like briefly to suggest ways in which a canonical approach seeks to overcome some of the major problems at present under debate (cf. Reventlow).

(*a*) In respect to the disagreement between Eichrodt and von Rad, among others, as to whether an Old Testament theology should be organized 'systematically' or 'traditio-historically,' I suggest that both of these alternatives arise from a view of a closed body of material which is to be analysed descriptively. Both writers have worked hard to discover innerbiblical categories, which is an effort not to be disparaged. Nevertheless, when Old Testament theology is viewed in its canonical context as a continuing interpretative activity by that community of faith which treasures its scriptures as authoritative, the issue of organization is sharply relativized. At times the shaping process introduced systematic features; at times it structured the material historically. However, even more significant, there are innumerable other options within the [[16]] theological activity of interpreting scripture which are available for grappling with the material. The real issue lies in the quality of the construal and the illumination it brings to the text.

(*b*) A canonical approach once again attempts to overcome the sharp polarity in the debate whether the object of an Old Testament theology is a faith-construal of history (*Geschichte*), according to von Rad, or based on a reconstructed scientific history (*Historie*), according to Hesse and others. It reckons with the fact that Israel bore witness to its encounter with God in actual time and space, and yet registered its testimony in a text through a complex multilayered manner which far transcends the categories of ordinary historical discourse. The canonical approach views history from the perspective of Israel's faith-construal, and in this respect sides with von Rad. However, it differs in not being concerned to assign theological value to a traditio-historical trajectory which has been detached from the canonical form of the text. To put the issue in another way, the canonical approach seeks to follow the biblical text in its theological use of historical referentiality rather than to construct a contrast between *Geschichte* and *Historie* at the outset. At times, the nature of an Old Testament passage has been so construed as to register little which is accessible to objective historical scrutiny. At other times, an event which is grounded in common historical perception, such as the destruction of Jerusalem in 587 B.C., is of central importance for the theological task. In sum, although different dimensions of history are freely recognized, by focusing on Israel's historical role as the bearer of the traditions of faith, these two aspects of Israel's experience are held together in a subtle balance within the shape of the canon, and should not be threatened by some overarching theory of history.

(*c*) Finally, in respect to the position of Pannenberg which has sought to identify history with revelation, the canonical approach looks with suspicion on any view of history as a bearer of theological value which is divorced from the concrete reality of historical Israel. Far more is at stake here than simply making an academic point. Rather, scripture serves as a continuing medium through which the saving events of Israel's history are appropriated by each new generation of faith. Thus God's activity of self-disclosure is continually being extended into human time and space, which lies at the heart of the debate over the nature of revelation through scripture. [[17]]

The Importance of Old Testament Theology

Lastly, a word is in order to justify the importance of the discipline of Old Testament theology even when it is conceived of as a modest and restricted enterprise within the larger field of biblical theology.

(*a*) First, in terms of strategy, to focus solely on the Old Testament in theological reflection allows one to deal with the subject in much more detail and depth than if one sought to treat the entire Christian canon at once. It seems wise at some point to focus primary attention on the Old Testament before coming to grips with the sheer mass of material and the overwhelming complexity of issues which arise when the New Testament is also included.

(*b*) Attention to the Old Testament within a theological discipline provides a major check against the widespread modern practice of treating it solely from a philological, historical or literary perspective. The inability of most systematic theologians to make much sense of the Old Testament stems in part from the failure of the biblical specialists to render it in such a way which is not theologically mute.

(*c*) It is a major function of Old Testament theology to treat the Old Testament in such a manner as to guard it from being used simply as a foil for the New Testament. Rather, it is theologically important to understand the Old Testament's witness in its own right in regard to its coherence, variety and unresolved tensions.

(*d*) Finally, theological reflection on the Old Testament makes possible a more correct hearing of the New Testament by clarifying the effect of the Hebrew scriptures on the Jewish people from whom Jesus stemmed, to whom he preached, and from whom the early church was formed. As the history of exegesis eloquently demonstrates, a Christian church without the Old Testament is in constant danger of turning the faith into various forms of gnostic, mystic, or romantic speculation.

Bibliography

Eichrodt, W. *Theology of the Old Testament* (2 vols.; ET: London/Philadelphia 1961–1967).

Hesse, F. *Das Alte Testament als Buch der Kirche* (Gütersloh 1966).

Pannenberg, W. *Revelation as History* (ET: New York 1968/London 1969).

von Rad, G. *Old Testament Theology* (2 vols.; ET: Edinburgh/New York 1962–1965).

Reventlow, H. Graf. *Problems of Old Testament Theology in the Twentieth Century* (ET: London/Philadelphia 1985).

Sheppard, G. T. "Hearing the Voice of the Same God through Historically Dissimilar Traditions," *Interp* 36 (1982) 21–33.

Synopsis of Childs's *Old Testament Theology in a Canonical Context* (1986)

Brevard S. Childs
On Covenant, Election, People of God

Excerpted with permission from Brevard S. Childs, *Biblical Theology of the Old and New Testaments: Theological Reflection on the Christian Bible* (Minneapolis: Fortress, 1992), pp. 413–24.

The Old Testament Witness

Covenant in the Old Testament

[[413]] According to traditional Christian theology a major feature which binds the Hebrew scriptures to the New Testament is that of covenant. The Hebrew scriptures therefore received the name of the Old Testament or Old Covenant, and it was thought that its content could be structured within the category of a unified covenantal theology, which received its fulfilment in the new covenant inaugurated by Jesus Christ.

The initial problem emerged from the side of Old Testament scholarship which failed to find support for this traditional view of the Old Testament. Not only did the idea of covenant seem highly diverse within the Old Testament, but large sections did not appear to make use of the category. Moreover, within the last hundred years the result of intense critical research has greatly exacerbated the problem. Since this history has been reviewed many times and is readily available (e.g., Nicholson, *God and His People*), a brief summary will be adequate.

At the end of the nineteenth century, J. Wellhausen (*Prologomena*) and his school sought to show, largely on the basis of a new literary critical dating of the sources, that the concept of covenant was a late theological innovation which was originally associated with the Deuteronomic reform of the seventh century. Then in the early 1920s a strong reaction to this understanding set in, mediated in part from new traditiohistorical and form critical impulses of Gunkel, Mowinckel, Alt and their students (e.g., Noth, von Rad, etc.). A case was made that covenant had very strong institutional roots within Ancient Israel which greatly antedated its later literary formulations by Deuteronomy. For a time this consensus of antiquity was thought to be supported in addition by Ancient Near Eastern evidence from the so-called Hittite suzerainty treaties (Mendenhall, "Covenant Forms"). As a result, for several decades in the period from the 1930s through the early 1960s countless [[414]] theological treatises appeared which seemed to support traditional Christian theology in seeing the centre of the Old Testament to be located in covenant theology (Eichrodt, Muilenburg, Wright, Bright, Kline). However, once again the pendulum swung in another direction, initially stimulated by L. Perlitt's monograph of 1969 (*Bundestheologie*). He was then followed by many others (e.g., Nicholson) who have largely returned to Wellhausen's position in regarding the idea of covenant to be a Deuteronomic innovation of the late monarchial period without deep institutional roots in Ancient Israel.

257

It should be obvious that this critical debate within Old Testament scholarship has widespread implications for any biblical theological reflections on the
subject of covenant and also for the broader issues of God's relation to Israel
and the church. The recent study of Nicholson offers one attempt to construct
a theology of covenant on the basis of the Wellhausen/Perlitt position. Nicholson argues that Israel's relation with God was initially derived from a mythological world view, akin to the Canaanites, in which Israel's well-being was
secured by Yahweh in terms of a natural bond through an ideology of kingship. Only through the preaching of the eighth-century prophets and later was
this mythological view of God and the world "desacralized" and transformed
into a new covenant relationship based on the ethical claims of Yahweh's righteousness and Israel's pledge of loyalty. In a sense, Nicholson has returned to
the traditional, positive interpretation of Israel's "true" faith as covenantal (Jer
31:31). But what are the theological implications in seeing covenant as a late
theological "idea" which functions largely to criticize and replace the basic historical and theological foundations of Israel's faith developed over much of its
history? To what extent have all the problems of Wellhausen's reconstruction
of Israel's early religion been once again re-introduced, such as his concept of
an original "natural bonding" between God and people? Have the prophets
once again assumed the role of innovators of "ethical monotheism"? It would
appear that a fresh historical and theological analysis is called for to move beyond the present impasse. In my opinion, there are some fresh methodological
avenues into the material which might serve to open new interpretive options.

First, James Barr ("Some Semantic Notes") has raised a set of new questions from the perspective of a fresh semantic analysis of the terminology of
covenant. He has questioned whether etymology, especially of such an
opaque word as covenant (*bĕrît*), provides any real value for understanding
the semantic function of the word. He has thus greatly relativized the philological theories of scholars such as E. Kutsch (*Verheissung und Gesetz*). Even
more important, he wonders whether in [[415]] the light of the syntactical
and linguistic restrictions on the use of the term *bĕrît* it might suggest that "a
current of tradition that used *berith* in one kind of linguistic context might
use other terminology in another" (p. 38). In sum, the lack of occurrence of
the vocabulary of covenant does not exclude the possibility of a related covenant concept whose vocabulary has its own functional integrity within another linguistic context.

Barr's semantic observations offer a warrant for investigating a variety of
other relational terms and concepts, such as election, people of God, and
land, which although related in very different ways to covenant, may aid in
providing a more complete picture of Israel's relationship to God than by focusing only on the term *bĕrît*. A serious weakness in Wellhausen's reconstruction of Israel's early history was that when he failed to find the vocabulary of
covenant in the early strands, he concluded that the theology of election was
unknown. He thus posited a theory of a natural bond for early Israel. The issue will be critically to determine whether this hypothesis is congruent with a
wider field of related concepts.

Secondly, there is a basic hermeneutical issue at stake which has been previously discussed, but emerges with the greatest clarity in respect to the problem of the covenant. On the one hand, it is evident from critical research that Israel's religion underwent a history of development. Its pre-exilic form differs from the post-exilic, and Deuteronomic theology is also distinct from that of Isaiah's. At times a historical trajectory can be traced with reasonable certainty. On the other hand, it is equally evident that the compilers of the Old Testament did not collect and order their material from the perspective of modern critical scholarship. Rather, the Hebrew scriptures were formed and structured for predominantly theological concerns. I have used the cipher "canonical" to describe the forces at work which rendered the material toward serving a theological function within a community of faith (cf. Childs, *Introduction to the Old Testament as Scripture*). Often late post-exilic material was projected back into Israel's earliest patriarchal and Mosaic periods, and the writings of early prophets were edited with the language and concepts of a different age.

The hermeneutical issue at stake is how to evaluate this process when constructing a theology of the Old Testament. The critical method of a Wellhausen tends to disregard any non-historical shaping as fictional and to view the canonical form of the text with suspicion as a self-serving ideology. Accordingly, a proper critical approach to the Old Testament is one which conforms to a reconstruction of Israel's religious growth within a genuine historical context. My alternative suggestion is one [[416]] which seeks rather to interpret the canonical shape both critically and theologically, not as fictional self-serving, but as one which truly reflects the perspective from within the community of faith of how Israel understood its relationship with God. In short, a theology of the Old Testament is not to be confused with a description of Israel's religion, but is Israel's own testimony, a perspective from within the faith (emic). Israel's "history with God" reflects a different dimension of reality (*Dichtigkeitsgrad*) from a scientifically reconstructed history. Nevertheless, a critical canonical approach does not reject out-of-hand the use of the "outside" (etic) perspective of a historical critical reconstruction. Indeed recognition of the subtlety of the relationship is one factor which sets the canonical approach apart from fundamentalism on the right and liberalism on the left. Historical critical reconstructions can aid the interpreter in understanding Israel's own witness by seeing how its witness to the content of its experience with God over generations led to a reshaping of its faith in a manner often very different from the actual historical development, at times overriding, subordinating, or recasting the noetic sequence in the light of a new and more profound ontic interpretation of the ways of God with Israel. The exegetical discussion of covenant which now follows is an attempt to illustrate this suggested approach to the text.

It has long been observed that the terminology of covenant (*bĕrît*) is overwhelmingly clustered about the book of Deuteronomy and the writings of the Deuteronomic school, whereas in contrast it appears sparingly in the earlier epic sources of the Pentateuch. Again, it is a major feature in the debate over establishing the date and origin of the covenant tradition that the term is largely missing in the pre-exilic prophets, but then emerges in the sixth-century prophets, particularly in the Deuteronomic redactional layers of Jeremiah. Finally, it occurs as a major theme in the Priestly material and in the Chronicler.

As we have seen, two major scholarly hypotheses continue to compete as how best to explain this evidence and to interpret both the dating and provenance of the covenant tradition. On the one hand, the literary critical theory of Wellhausen/Perlitt finds in the predominance of covenant language in Deuteronomy and in the silence of the pre-exilic prophets a clear warrant that the tradition arose in the late monarchy. It seeks to show that this Deuteronomic understanding was then projected back into the earlier period, particularly in terms of a covenant with the Fathers and at Sinai, whereas in actual fact the covenant theology first arose as an attempt to combat the threat to the religious identity of the nation in the crisis of the seventh century. On the other hand, the form critical, traditio-historical approach of Alt and his school [[417]] sought to show ancient covenant tradition which was rooted in various cultic festivals and activated through recurring rituals. Even though the later literary sources were only indirectly influenced by this oral tradition, it was argued that vestiges of cultic patterns demonstrated that the covenant traditions were everywhere assumed, even when largely ignored by the early prophets.

The difficulty is that both theories, in spite of respective strengths, suffer also from weaknesses which continue to evoke the controversy. On the one hand, Wellhausen was able to recover a very sharp profile of the covenantal theology of Deuteronomy. Yet it is not clear to what extent earlier usages of covenant, such as found in Genesis 15, Exodus 24, and Hos 8:1, are really retrojections from a later period or are actually early historical precursors of Deuteronomy's fully developed concept. The debate, for example, between Perlitt and Lohfink on Genesis 15 offers a classic example of the inability of modern critical Old Testament scholarship to establish a consensus. On the other hand, the form critical, traditio-historical approach has in its favour its attempt to ground covenant in a concrete sociological context of religious institutions, which has a historical warrant in all ancient cultures. Conversely, its effort remains highly speculative, and the theory has failed to explain adequately why such allegedly important cultic ceremonies have been almost entirely subordinated within the present Old Testament text, thus requiring massive conjectural reconstructions (e.g., Noth's amphictyony; von Rad's "Credo").

There are two important points to make which may provide a way out of the impasse. First, many of the crucial texts relating to the covenant which in their literary context within the Old Testament are set in the early, pre-exilic period (patriarchal, Sinai, settlement) are multilayered and show signs of a lengthy development and reworking. Even if one cannot always determine with certainty the extent of each layer or the age of the traditions, one can recognize elements of theological continuity within the trajectory. For example, even if one were to accept Perlitt's theory that the covenantal language of Gen 15:18 respecting Abraham reflects a Deuteronomic redaction, it is highly significant to observe that the combination of a promise of the land, sealed by a divine oath, is widespread throughout the uncontested early levels of the Pentateuch (Gen 50:25; Exod 13:5, 11; 32:13; Num 11:12; 14:23). In sum, it is not the case that the later redactor has imposed an alien category on his material by creating a hitherto unknown relationship with the Patriarchs, but in this case, he provided a more precise theological formulation of a relationship already described in different language. For this reason I cannot agree with the statement of [[418]] C. F. Whitley, cited approvingly by Perlitt (p. 153): "The terms by which the prophets conceived of Israel's relationship to Yahweh . . . are those of the ties of natural kinship."

A similar point can be made in respect to the ritual pictured in Exod 24:3–8. Perlitt has made out a strong case for seeing Deuteronomic influence in the passage which is now clearly a covenantal ceremony. The parallels to the Deuteronomic material of 19:3–6 are striking as is also the reference to reading from the "book of the covenant" and the people's response. Yet the passage as a whole is not typical of Deuteronomy's understanding of the sealing of the covenant by a pledged word rather than a cultic rite. There is clearly an earlier version of a covenantal rite of some sort which through a blood ritual binds God and people together. Perlitt's attempt to disassociate the two levels of the text is very forced and appears to be dictated by his larger hypothesis.

A final illustration is found in the very difficult text of Exod 24:1–2, 9–11. Moses and the elders are invited into the presence of God and before this *visio dei*, they ate and drank. The contested issue is whether the description is to be understood as a covenant meal. If the passage is isolated from its present literary context—indeed there are some obvious literary seams—then the exact function of the meal is uncertain. Yet once again what is striking are the parallels with the initial revelation of God to Moses at the burning bush (Exod 3:1ff.). The setting is at the same holy mount. The God of the Fathers identifies himself as the God of Israel ("my people") before a terrified Moses. Moses is given a sign of the liberation from Egypt, namely, that Yahweh would be worshipped on this very mountain (3:12). Likewise in Exodus 24 the God of Israel (v. 10) condescends to reveal himself to the people's representatives and they are not destroyed, but continue to live and even to rejoice before God. Even with this minimalist interpretation of the meal, a relationship between God and people is described which stems from the divine initiative and gracious condescension. When this tradition was then joined to vv. 3–8, the move to see a covenantal meal in the eating and drinking occurred as if by reflex.

To summarize, even though the Deuteronomic formulation of covenant dominates whenever the topic arises, this theology consistently rests on earlier tradition which, though far from identical, has a very strong theological continuity in its earliest witness to a relationship between God and his people. There is no evidence of a sharp break between a relationship established by natural bond and one of gracious election.

My second major point is of equal, if not of more importance, for the theological treatment of Old Testament covenant, and it has been equally neglected by both competing groups of scholars within this [[419]] controversy. I am referring to the effect of the Deuteronomic redaction on the shape of the entire Old Testament understanding of covenant. It distorts the theological significance of covenant if one literary level is isolated and historicized within a developmental trajectory of Israel's religion. Rather, the various levels have been fused into an authoritative, literary composition—that is the meaning of canon—in which one particular theological formulation of God's relation to Israel in terms of a covenant has become normative, namely Deuteronomy, and then read into the entire tradition. The shapers of the scripture were uninterested in preserving the historical lines of the development of Israel's covenantal theology, much to the frustration of modern research. Rather, they interpreted the tradition in terms of its substance which they assumed to be best expressed as a covenant regardless of when or how God established his relationship with Israel. It is therefore quite impossible to speak theologically of Old Testament covenant without reckoning with the perspective of the final editors of the collection who shaped the literature as a whole.

One can discern the effect of this shaping process at every point within the Old Testament. Israel's primaeval history is construed as a series of covenants, starting with Noah (Gen 9:8ff.), and continuing with the promise of land and posterity sealed in a covenant to Abraham and his descendents (Gen 15:1ff.; 26:1ff.; 50:24). The covenant with Moses at Sinai, which is both introduced and concluded with the Deuteronomic formulation (Exod 19:3–8; 24:3–8), interprets the entire event as a covenant with Israel, repeated in chap. 32–34 of Exodus, and given a unified covenantal interpretation of both Israel's past and future in the book of Deuteronomy (5:2ff.; 7:6ff.; 26:16; 29:1ff.). The Deuteronomistic historian pursues Israel's tragic history of covenantal disobedience through the destruction of the nation (Josh 24:19ff.; 2 Kgs 17:7ff.). Israel incurred the righteous wrath of God because of the disobedience of God's covenantal law. Finally, Israel's prophets speak of a restoration of the nation in covenantal terms. For Hosea it will be a covenant with the creation and a betrothal in steadfast love (Hos 2:16ff., ET), for Jeremiah a new covenant (31:31ff.), and for Ezekiel a "covenant of peace" (34:25) for blessing and security (cf. Isa 42:6; 49:8; Mal 3:1). Daniel is confident that in spite of those who violate God's covenant, there remain those who stand firm in faith awaiting their promised deliverance (11:32; 12:1–3). In sum, regardless of the age and circumstances lying behind the Deuteronomic covenant formulation, its theology became the normative expression of God's relation to Israel and served as a major theological category for unifying the entire collection comprising the Hebrew scriptures.

[[420]] There is one final topic to be discussed which relates to the theological implications of taking seriously the canonical shape of the Old Testament in respect to covenant. I have argued that the Old Testament has received a unifying theological redaction in characterizing Israel's relationship to God under the categories of a Deuteronomic formulation. Yet this does not imply for a moment that the concept of covenant has become fully homogenized—a criticism constantly hurled at the canonical approach. Indeed there are certain consistent notes sounded throughout scripture such as the stress on the divine initiative in establishing the covenant, and on the unity of law and covenant. Yet in other respects, the theological rubric of covenant continues to tolerate a wide variety of meanings and functions which stem from its long and diverse history. At times the covenant is conceived of as conditional and its maintenance dependent upon Israel's obedient response (Exod 24:3–8). At other times the covenant appears as a unilateral act of divine grace, a complete act of divine mercy (Gen 17:1ff.). Certain texts imply that the covenant can be repudiated by God's righteous judgment (Deut 28:36–57, 63); however, others speak of an "everlasting," "eternal covenant" (Gen 17:13; 2 Sam 23:5). Sometimes the emphasis falls on the covenant of the past, but other times on a continuing relationship to be actualized in the present (Deut 5:2ff.). Finally, there is a dialectical relation often expressed between the one covenant as a medium of blessing as well as conversely one of curse (Deut 28:1ff.). The theological task is not resolved by sorting out these tensions according to reconstructed historical or sociological settings, but rather in seeking to understand how such diversity functions within a community which hears in scripture these different notes as the one will of God for Israel.

Bibliography

A. **Alt**, "The God of the Fathers," ET *Essays on Old Testament History and Religions*, Oxford 1966, 1–77; K. **Baltzer**, *The Covenant Formulary*, ET Oxford 1971; J. **Barr**, "Some Semantic Notes on the Covenant," *Beiträge zur Alttestamentlichen Theologie, FS W. Zimmerli*, ed. H. Donner et al., Göttingen 1977, 23–38; J. **Begrich**, "Berit—Ein Beitrag zur Erfassung einer alttestamentlichen Denkform," *ZAW* 60, 1944, 1–11; J. **Bright**, *Covenant and Promise*, Nashville and London 1977; S. S. **David**, "Rethinking Covenant in the Late Biblical Books," *Bibl* 70, 1989, 50–73; W. **Eichrodt**, *Theology of the Old Testament*, ET vol. 1, London and Philadelphia 1961; "Darf man heute noch von einem Gottesbund mit Israel reden?" *TZ* 30, 1974, 193–206; J. **Harvey**, "Le 'rîb-Pattern,' réquisitoire prophétique sur la rupture de l'alliance," *Bibl* 43, 1962, 172–96; D. J. **Hillers**, *Covenant: The History of a Biblical Idea*, Baltimore 1969; M. **Kline**, *The Structure of Biblical Authority*, Grand Rapids 1972; R. **Kraetzschmar**, *Die Bundesvorstellung im Alten Testament in ihrer geschichtlichen Entwicklung*, Marburg 1896; E. **Kutsch**, *Verheissung und Gesetz: Untersuchungen zum sogenannten "Bund" im Alten Testament*, BZAW 81, 1973; "Bund," *TRE* 8, 1980, 397–410.

C. **Levin**, *Die Verheissung des neuen Bundes in ihrem theologiegeschichtlichen Zusammenhang ausgelegt*, FRLANT 137, 1985; N. **Lohfink**, *Die Landesverheissung als Eid: Eine Studie zu Genesis 15*, SBS 28, 1967; *The Covenant Never Broken*, ET Mahwah, N.J. 1991; D. J. **McCarthy**, *Treaty and Covenant*, AnBib 21A, ²1978; G. E. **Mendenhall**, "Covenant Forms in Israelite Tradition," *BA* 17, 1954, 50–76; J. **Muilenburg**, "The Form and Structure of the Covenantal Formulations," *VT* 9, 1959, 345–65; E. W. **Nicholson**, *God and His People: Covenant and Theology in the Old*

Testament, Oxford 1986; M. **Noth**, *A History of Pentateuchal Traditions,* ET Englewood Cliffs 1972; *The Deuteronomistic History,* ET JSOT Suppl 15, 1981; L. **Perlitt**, *Bundestheologie im Alten Testament,* WMANT 36, 1969; J. G. **Plöger**, *Literarkritische, formgeschichtliche und stilkritische Untersuchungen zum Deuteronomium,* BBB 26, 1967; G. **von Rad**, "The Form-Critical Problem of the Hexateuch," ET *The Problem of the Hexateuch and Other Essays,* Edinburgh and London 1966, 1–78; R. **Rendtorff**, "'Covenant' as a Structuring Concept in Genesis and Exodus," *JBL* 108, 1989, 385–93; R. **Smend**, *Die Bundesformel,* ThSt 68, 1963.

M. **Weinfeld**, "berith," ET *Theological Dictionary of the Old Testament,* ed. G. J. Botterweck and H. Ringgren, vol. 2, Grand Rapids 1977, 253–79; J. **Wellhausen**, *Prolegomena to the History of Israel,* ET Edinburgh 1885; G. E. **Wright**, "The Lawsuit of God: A Form-Critical Study of Deuteronomy 32," *Israel's Prophetic Heritage, FS J. Muilenburg,* ed. B. W. Anderson, New York and London 1962, 26–67.

Israel as the People of God

The most basic Old Testament term to describe God's special relationship to Israel is the expression "people of Yahweh" (*ʿam YHWH*). Frequently it is formulated with the suffix in divine and prophetic speeches ("my people," "his people"). The classic formulation of the relationship, often named *die Bundesformel* (cf. Smend), occurs in both early and late periods: "I will be your God, and you shall be my people" (Exod 6:7; Lev 26:12; Jer 11:4; Ps 95:7). For Wellhausen, this formulation of Yahweh as the God of Israel and Israel as the people of God was the essence of Israel's religion.

Originally the term "people" did not designate a political entity, but rather a relationship within the context of a household, family, or tribe. In possibly the earliest occurrence (Judg 5:13) the term refers to [[422]] the army which marched for Yahweh against the enemy. Lohfink ("Beobachtungen," 283ff.) further argues for its early connection with the office of *nagîd* (leader) which long preceded the rise of the monarchy (1 Sam 9:16; 10:1ff.; 2 Sam 5:2). A leader such as Saul was called forth charismatically for the deliverance of Israel in times of crisis. In the same context Yahweh is pictured metaphorically as a shepherd of his people (2 Sam 5:2) who leads his people in safety (cf. Ps 28:9). Indeed when God fixed the inheritance of the peoples, "Yahweh's portion is his people, Jacob his allotted heritage" (Deut 32:9).

Within the Pentateuchal periodization of Israel's history, the story of Israel's deliverance from Egypt is the point in which the term "people" becomes central. Exodus 1 marks the transition from the sons of Jacob to the people of Israel. Yet Israel does not become a people because it was delivered, but rather it was delivered because it was the people of God. Throughout the struggle the "people of Yahweh" are set in opposition to the "people of Pharaoh" (Exod 12:31), and Yahweh's people become increasingly identified with a nation.

It has long been observed that the most extensive and profound theological reflection on the subject of the people of God is found in the book of Deuteronomy. It was the great contribution of von Rad in his dissertation of 1929 to have demonstrated the centrality of the term for interpreting the entire book (*Das Gottesvolk*). Chapter 4 sounds the note of astonishment—Did such a thing ever happen before? (v. 33)—that God brought out of Egypt a people of his own possession (cf. Exod 19:3ff.). Nor is this some distant event of the past, but a special relationship was established which continued to be constitutive of Israel's present life "as at this day" (4:20; 5:3ff.). Because Israel has this special heritage, its life must now reflect God's holiness. Israel is to be a "holy people," not in order to become the people of God, but because this is what her election entails. The absolute loyalty to Yahweh, the repudiation of all rival deities, the purity of worship, are all derivative of God's claim on his people. Moreover, the signs of being God's people are realized in the promise of the land with all the blessings of the covenant.

The people of God according to Deuteronomy consists of "all Israel," and is fully coextensive with empirical Israel. Deuteronomy is not addressing some pious portion of Israel, but the unity of all Israel is an essential feature of his portrayal. Similarly, the concern for the weak and vulnerable within the nation is not a humanitarian impulse, but an essential response to the claims of the covenant on the people of God. It is a misunderstanding of Deuteronomy to suggest that the author paints an impossible ideal toward which the nation is continuously to strive. Rather it is the reverse. The holy people of God is the actuality. Israel [[423]] lacks nothing (Deut 8:9). Yet there is always the threat of forgetting God, losing the heritage, and perishing like the other nations (8:18ff.). There are no eschatological notes sounded in Deuteronomy's understanding of the people of God, but there is a dialectic somewhat akin to Paul: "Be what you already are."

The portrayal by the Priestly writer of the people of God is remarkably different. Here the basic formulation "Be ye holy," is joined with the clause "for I, Yahweh, your God am holy" (Lev 19:2). The dialectic between the divine action and the human response is expressed differently, but in respect to the substance is similar. God is the sanctifier, but Israel must strive for holiness (Lev 20:8). In the Priestly writings the term *'am* has been replaced by *'ēdâ* (congregation). The people is that cultic congregation whose life is centred in the divine presence of God (cf. Rost, *Die Vorstufen*). Moreover, Israel can still be the people of God without possession of the land.

In the earlier discussion of covenant, it was noted that the term covenant appeared infrequently within the prophets. On the grounds of this alleged "prophetic silence" elaborate theories were constructed to describe Israel's early relationship to God as a natural bond. Now it is striking to note that the prophets represent more than half of the frequent occurrence of the terminology of people of God. It is a major category by which the prophets portray the rupture between God and Israel. Amos addresses the people of Israel: "You only have I known of all the families of the earth; therefore, I will punish you for your iniquities" (3:1-2). Isaiah compares Judah to rebellious sons: "Israel does not know, my people does not understand" (1:2-3). Hosea reverses the *Bundesformel* to highlight the breaking of the relationship: "Call his name Not-my-people (*lo' 'ammî*) for you are not my people and I am not your God" (Hos 1:9) (cf. Mic 1:2; 6:3; Joel 2:17ff.; Hos 11:1; Jer 2:2ff.).

Likewise it is of importance to note that the Psalter reflects the voice of the people, usually in the form of communal complaint, who, in spite of the signs of a broken relationship, still pleads for God's intervention and for a restoration of divine favour (Psalms 44; 77; 80, etc.). Similar communal complaints are found throughout the prophets (Isa 63:15ff.), often joined with a reiteration of divine judgment for Israel's failure to understand what is involved in being God's people (Isa 65:1–7; Hos 6:1–6; 7:1–7).

What distinguishes the prophetic message from both Deuteronomy and the Priestly writings is the eschatological hope for the people of God. Isaiah had first spoken of a remnant personified in his son (7:3) and in his disciples (8:16) which would survive the destruction (1:9; [[424]] 6:13). However, in the later levels of the Isaianic tradition the theme of a return of the remnant (10:20ff.), of the healing of the wounded people (30:26), and of the blessings of the people in the land (32:15ff.) became dominant. Israel will again be called "the holy people" (Isa 62:12). Likewise Jeremiah envisions a return to the land and a reconstitution of the *Bundesformel*: "I will give them a heart to know that I am Yahweh; and they shall be my people and I will be their God" (24:7). Also Hosea sees a reversal of the judgment of "not-my-people" to being "sons of the living God" (1:10ff., ET).

Some of the theological implications of the Old Testament's understanding of the people of God can be briefly summarized:

(i) Although the Old Testament describes the relationship of the people of God in terms of qualities of response (holiness, obedience, gratitude), the theological emphasis on a quality of existence never dissolves the formal identification of empirical Israel and the people of God. To be sure, in the Hellenistic period with the rise of various forms of sectarian Judaism, much controversy turned on this very issue.

(ii) The problem of understanding the concept of a people of God both in terms of its particularistic and universal dimension is handled in different ways. In Genesis 12 God's promise to Abraham of a great nation is specifically focussed on its goal to mediate a blessing on all the families of the earth (12:1–3). Deuteronomy seems to recognize the problem (4:15ff.) by sharply distinguishing between what is legitimate for the nations, but not for Israel, without pursuing the issue at length. In contrast, the prophets are a major witness to God's concern for all peoples and a vision of all nations worshipping God (Isa 2:1ff.; 56:7) and there being no foreigners separated from God's people (56:3ff.). However, it is consistent for the Old Testament never to use Israel's special prerogative as a negative foil over against a universal vision. Here again the rise of new forces in the Hellenistic period will introduce a new intensity to the issue.

(iii) The problem of understanding the people of God as a present reality and as an eschatological hope is handled differently by Deuteronomy from that of the prophets. Yet both witnesses firmly resist identifying God's people either with merely a political entity, or a timeless community of believers. It is thus not surprising that this issue will again erupt in the New Testament with a vengeance.

Bibliography

R. E. **Clements**, "People of God," *Old Testament Theology: A Fresh Approach*, London 1978, 79–103; N. A. **Dahl**, *Das Volk Gottes*, Darmstadt ²1963; G. A. **Danell**, "The Idea of God's People in the Bible," *The Root of the Vine*, ed. A. Fridrichsen, London 1953, 23–53; H. F. **Hamilton**, *The People of God*, 2 vols., Oxford 1912; J. **Høgenhaven**, *Gott und Volk bei Jesaja: Eine Untersuchung zur biblischen Theologie*, AThD 24, 1988; A. R. **Hulst**, "ʿam/goj Volk," *THAT* II, 290–325; E. **Lipiński**, "ʿam," *TWAT* VI, 177–94; N. **Lohfink**, "Beobachtungen zur Geschichte des Ausdrucks ʿam YHWH," *Probleme biblischer Theologie: FS G. von Rad*, ed. H. Wolff, Munich 1962, 275–305; N. W. **Porteous** "Volk und Gottesvolk im Alten Testament," *Theologische Aufsätze: FS Karl Barth*, Munich 1936, 146–63; G. **von Rad**, *Des Gottesvolk im Deuteronomium*, BWANT 47, 1929; L. **Rost**, *Die Vorstufen von Kirche und Synagogs im Alten Testament*, BWAT 76, 1938; "Die Bezeichnungen für Land und Volk im Alten Testament" (1934), reprinted *Das kleine Credo*, Heidelberg 1965, 76–101; R. **Smend**, *Die Bundesformel*, ThSt 68, 1963; J. M. P. **Smith**, "The Chosen People," *AJSL* 45, 1928/9, 73–82; S. D. **Sperling**, "Rethinking Covenant in the Late Biblical Books," *Bibl* 70, 1989, 50–73.

ROLF KNIERIM

b. 1928

Cosmos and History

Rolf Knierim is professor emeritus at Claremont School of Theology and Claremont Graduate University, where he was the Avery Professor of Religion. He has also taught in Brazil. Earlier, he was Gerhard von Rad's student in Heidelberg. However, Knierim has departed in important respects from his mentor, as the selections included here indicate. Note: several of Knierim's significant publications are incorporated in *The Task of Old Testament Theology* and in *Reading the Hebrew Bible for a New Millennium.*

Selected Writings by Knierim

1992   *Text and Concept in Leviticus 1:1–9: A Case in Exegetical Method.* Forschungen zum Alten Testament 2. Tübingen: Mohr.

1995   *The Task of Old Testament Theology: Substance, Methods and Cases.* Grand Rapids: Eerdmans.

Writings about Knierim

Kim, Wonil, Deborah Ellens, Michael Floyd, and Marvin A. Sweeney (editors)

2000   *Reading the Hebrew Bible for a New Millenium: Form, Concept and Theological Perspective.* Vol. 1: *Theological and Hermeneutical Studies.* Harrisburg, Pennsylvania: Trinity.

Sun, Henry T. C., Keith L. Eades, James M. Robinson, and Garth I. Moller (editors)

1997   *Problems in Biblical Theology: Essays in Honor of Rolf Knierim.* Grand Rapids: Eerdmans.

Rolf Knierim's
Approach to Old Testament Theology

Excerpted with permission from "On the Task of Old Testament Theology," in *Reading the Hebrew Bible for a New Millenium: Form, Concept and Theological Perspective*, vol. 1: *Theological and Hermeneutical Studies* (edited by Wonil Kim et al.; Harrisburg, Pennsylvania: Trinity, 2000), pp. 21–32.

Introduction

[[21]] This essay will focus on a method for doing Old Testament theology. In order to see this focus in its proper perspective, I will first discuss what I perceive to be the necessary distinctions between the disciplines of biblical exegesis, biblical theology, and biblical hermeneutics. In the process of interpretation, these three disciplines are closely related. Nonetheless, they must be distinguished because each confronts us with a different set of problems.

We first need to understand the individual texts to be examined, each on its own terms and in its own right; this is the process of exegesis. But since the Bible consists of many texts, small and large, we need to explain the meaning of each text in the light of all texts. This task presupposes but goes beyond exegesis. *Biblical exegesis* explains what the texts themselves say. In contrast, *biblical theology* must explain what is not, at least not sufficiently, said by the texts of the Bible, namely, the relationship among the different theologies of the texts. And *biblical hermeneutics* then needs to explain what the encounter between the worldview of the Bible and our modern worldview means for us today.

Each of these tasks is distinct. But since we cannot interpret the encounter of the biblical worldview and our own worldview without understanding each, the task of biblical theology is not only distinct from but also precedes the task of biblical hermeneutics, just as it follows the task of biblical exegesis. Hence, biblical interpretation moves from the exegesis of the texts to biblical theology and then to a biblical hermeneutic.

In light of my topic, I leave aside discussing the question of the relationship between ancient and modern worldviews. But I will elaborate [[22]] on some specific issues that are important for the distinction between biblical exegesis and biblical theology. These issues concern first of all the task of exegesis.

Author's note: This essay is dedicated to Professor George Coats, a scholar totally committed to Old Testament scholarship and a good personal friend, on the occasion of his retirement, with heartfelt good wishes. The essay represents a slightly revised version of a lecture given at the annual meeting of the Korean Society of Old Testament Studies in Seoul on May 21, 1994, and at the annual meeting of the Japanese Society of Old Testament Studies in Tokyo on May 25, 1994. It was previously published in *A Biblical Itinerary: In Search of Method, Form, and Context: Essays in Honor of George W. Coats*, ed. Eugene Carpenter. Reprinted by permission of Sheffield Academic Press Limited.

The methods of exegesis are well known and need no reiteration at this point. I need only to highlight four aspects that are intrinsic to exegetical work because they are also intrinsic to the nature of the biblical texts.

First, the texts are not quarries of words or sentences but entities *(Ganzheiten)* within which all elements are related in hierarchical semantic systems. These text systems must be explained holistically rather than solely, as is often done, verse by verse, sentence by sentence, or word by word. Without a holistic explanation of a text's overall system, the meaning of a text cannot be understood properly.

Second, and in particular need of attention, is that in each text, its story or message and its concept, idea, or doctrine are indissolubly connected and interdependent. While a text's story or message is explicit in what it says, its concept is basically inexplicit, infratextual or subtextual, but nevertheless operative in the text. It is presupposed and only coincidentally signaled by a word or phrase in the text itself as, for example, in "Let my people go!" (e.g., Exod 5:1). In this sentence, the possessive pronoun "my" is vital and reveals the conceptual presupposition for the liberation theology of the story: Yahweh liberates the oppressed because they are Yahweh's own people. Yahweh does not liberate all people who are oppressed. There is a theology of liberation in this text, but this theology is based on and controlled by the theological concept of Israel's exclusive election. Where this concept is overlooked in exegesis, the story and its concept of liberation are not correctly understood. The *concept* of a text controls its story, while the story actualizes its concept or idea. Sometimes, of course, the concepts are expressed directly in particular nominal phrases, as in the statement "God is gracious."

The recognition of the concepts or ideas of the texts has nothing to do either with a withdrawal from the texts into a world of abstract ideas or with an abstraction of the ideas from the texts. On the contrary, this recognition is exegetically indispensable because the ideas are the ideas of the texts themselves. Ideas and thoughts are just as real as stories in human history and existence, and the fact that they may be considered as abstract ideas does not mean that the idea of a text is abstract. There is no text without an idea. Its idea as well as its story belongs to the concreteness of a text. Both are to be exegeted together. In a text both language and thought, or its story and its concept, belong together, and the emphasis on the need to interpret the text's thought and concept has nothing to do with removing thought and concept from language and story or with replacing narrative by abstract concept. What is called for is the interpretation of the *conceptualized* narrative, not just narrative. It [[23]] is in this sense that the focus on concept is understood in this essay. It is important, however, that we distinguish between the ideas of texts and the ideas of the biblical worldviews. Many texts share the same worldview, such as, for example, the dynamistic ontology (Klaus Koch's *Tatspharedenken* or my own category of the concept of the holistic dynamic). While by and large sharing such a common worldview, many texts nevertheless have different conceptual foci, such as justice, judgment, liberation, forgiveness, election, corporateness, individuality, and so on. And while it is necessary for us to be aware of their common ancient worldview, this awareness interprets only what is common among them and not yet those varying concepts that are directly operative in them. The exegesis of the individual texts must interpret their specific concepts, or these texts cannot be distinguished from each other.

Third, the exegesis of texts includes each text's theology. The biblical texts are essentially theological in nature. Without this nature they would not exist. Exegesis that fails to include a text's theology is not exegesis in its proper sense. The interpretation of the theology of the texts is not something done in addition to exegesis. We exegete each text's own inherent theology. We do not theologize the texts. Were the texts not theological, exegesis should not say more about them than what they are. Inasmuch as exegesis may be called theological exegesis, it may be so called because of the theological nature of the texts themselves, and not because of our interest in theology. Yet precisely because of that nature of the texts, the attribute "theological" added to "exegesis" is pleonastic and should be avoided.

Attention to the theology of the texts is especially important because the theological task starts already with exegesis and is not reserved for biblical theology. Biblical theology is not theological because it is a discipline distinct from exegesis but because it evolves from the results of the exegesis of the theological nature of the texts. Whereas the theological task is common to both disciplines, the two differ in that exegesis interprets the theologies of the texts while biblical theology interprets the relationship of these theologies.

Fourth, exegesis not only describes the texts and their theologies, but also includes in its descriptions the fact that the texts claim to be true, valid, and authoritative. The Bible does not understand itself as a lexicon of science, history, or sociology, but as a collection of books that may in any of these aspects refer to what it claims to be divine truth that is therefore valid and authoritative for the world and certainly for its readers. We may use the Bible for all sorts of purposes, but if we ignore this claim, we certainly ignore its own raison d'être.

Thus, we exegete the theologies and truth claims of the Pentateuch, the Deuteronomistic and Chronicler's history works, of Job, each of the [[24]] Psalms, the Proverbs, and so on, and of each of the prophets, just as we exegete the theologies and truth claims of the Synoptic Gospels, of John, Paul, and the rest of the New Testament books. And the more we do careful exegesis, the more we learn that the Bible is a compendium of many theological concepts and their stories, of theologies that sometimes agree, sometimes differ even as they complement each other, and sometimes disagree. Every good student of the Bible is familiar with this fact. This situation is true not only for the relationship of the two Testaments, but also for the various theologies within each Testament.

After we have done our exegetical work, we write books in which we describe each theology or selected theological aspects, juxtapose our descriptions in anthologies of theologies, each bound in one volume, and call such a volume an Old or New Testament theology.

It is clear, however, that a theology of the Old or New Testament, let alone a biblical theology in the singular form, must be more than a collection of juxtaposed theologies derived from exegesis, a collection analogous to the collection of the juxtaposed biblical books, even where those juxtapositions rest to some extent on organizing principles such as the tripartite Tanak, or the distinction between the Gospels, Luke's Acts, and the letters in the New Testament. A theology in the singular must do what neither the biblical writers nor those who canonized the Bible have done: it must *interpret the relationship of the various theologies in the Bible.* This task presupposes the totality of exegetical work. But it involves *more* than the sum total of exegesis. Indeed, it is not solved but generated by that sum total. It is a task sui generis. The sum total of exegesis shows the diversity and even the divisiveness of the theologies in the canon. It reflects the theological pluralism of the biblical canon and the pluralism of its truth claims.

The Old Testament Defines Its Own Agenda

In the Christian tradition the reading of the Old Testament has in one way or another always been controlled by the theological criteria expressed in the New Testament. Whether these criteria contributed to keeping both Testaments together in the one Christian Bible, or whether they contributed to separating the theology of each Testament from that of the other, they were in either case the basis for the judgment of the Christian movement that the Old Testament, whatever it may mean for Christians and humanity, is fundamentally different from and less important than the New Testament. And in whatever sense one may want to speak of a *biblical* theology, the burden for such an advocacy lies always on the shoulders of Old Testament scholars.

Of course, for at least the last two hundred years all biblical scholars [[25]] have asserted that the Old Testament must be afforded the right to speak on its own terms. It especially must not be forced to speak against what its exegesis reveals. Still, the validity or truth of such exegetical results has always been adjudicated by the Christian perspective. Whether you say with Bultmann that the Old Testament, precisely when exegeted correctly, reveals how Christians or humans must not believe, or with von Rad or any similar interpreter that the kerygmatic axis of the Old Testament's salvation history leads to Jesus Christ, the Old Testament is in either case exegetically said to be theologically irrelevant without the decisive Christian perspective. It must have the right to its own position, but only as long as it defines its position in response to the predetermined Christian agenda. This situation amounts to a double standard for the Old Testament's freedom, a standard, both unconditional and conditional, which has no integrity. Instead, what is necessary is an Old Testament theology in which the Old Testament itself may define its own agenda vis-à-vis the New Testament rather than be dependent on it, a theology that would precisely for this reason also be of benefit for the Christian faith.

The Old Testament Is One

The Old Testament is one not only because it is the first part of the bipartite Christian Bible but also because it is the only Bible of the Jewish people. Its oneness is especially constituted by the fact that it is the original compendium of ancient Israel's Yahweh religion. Take Yahweh out of it, and it collapses. The Tanak represents ancient Israel's wisdom as reverence for and knowledge of God Yahweh.

The oneness of the Old Testament does not mean that its Yahweh wisdom is conceptually uniform and that everything in it has the same degree of validity. Just as it is a collection of many literary works, so it is also a collection of diverse theologies. Exegesis has long since established that Israel's Yahweh religion is theologically pluralistic. This pluralism became decisively established in the final juxtaposition of the theologies of the Yahweh religion at the same historical level during the late postexilic period. The theological traditions put together in this period had emerged diachronically, in the course of Israel's historical process, and to a large extent separately. But once they were juxtaposed, the meaning of the traditions was no longer determined by the diachronic but by the synchronic order of their relationship. What had formerly had a certain meaning because of its distinct time came to have a different meaning as it was placed side by side (i.e., synchronically) with traditions of earlier times. This synchronization of the traditions amounted to the canonization of theological diversity. For the [[26]] heirs of the Tanak or the Old Testament, be they Jewish or Christian, this pluralism is its inevitable legacy.

What is generally recognized to be the case in the New Testament is also true for the Old Testament. Its theological diversity, like the New Testament's diversity, is inherently connected to the Old Testament's claim to truth and validity and, hence, with the quest for truth and validity in Old Testament theology. This quest amounts to more than merely describing the Old Testament's texts and their theological concepts. Also, it is something different from a type of interpretation based on a confessional stance. It must explain why and in what sense any of its theologies are true and should be affirmed or confessed as true. Only this kind of explanation qualifies the discipline as theology. Otherwise it represents a phenomenology, history, or sociology of Israel's religion, or our confession of truth regardless of what is said.

In the history of the discipline, one has for too long attempted to overcome the Old Testament's theological diversity by focusing on its unifying aspects, on the unity in diversity. Thus, one has emphasized that the Old Testament is Yahwistic, monotheistic, word of God, inspired, revealed, the religion of holiness, covenantal, of the believing community, and so on.

All of these aspects exist, whereby some represent unifying factors while others, such as the aspects of holiness, covenant, or even—strictly speaking— word of God, do not, as we have learned. Decisive, however, is that none of the evidently unifying factors solves the problem of the theological diversity within each of them. The Old Testament is monotheistic, but its monotheism is theologically diverse and even divisive. It is divinely inspired and revealed, but the contents and concepts of inspiration and revelation (including theophany and epiphany) are diverse. It is altogether the witness of the believing community, but the beliefs of this community are diverse and the community itself has from its beginning been divided precisely because of its different beliefs.

The unifying aspects of these theologies belong to the Old Testament's oneness and must be interpreted in this respect. However, if we want to know in what sense the Old Testament is true and valid, even with respect to its unifying aspects, it is imperative that the discipline of Old Testament theology shift from its focus on the Old Testament's theological diversity. Rather than focus on unity in diversity, we must explain the diversity within the unity, indeed, the diversity within each unifying concept. This shift is basic, and amounts to a change in direction compared to the direction of many approaches during the last two centuries.

This approach is not completely new. Gabler proposed in 1787 that [[27]] we should describe the biblical books, interpret each of their concepts, compare them, and arrange the results of their comparison in a system of biblical theology in which the validity of each can be determined precisely in its relationship to the others. Gabler thought of a biblical theology conceived from the doctrine of salvation expressed in the New Testament alone. Yet his method remains valid, indeed the best, for an Old Testament theology on its own terms. This method accounts for the relativity of each theological concept in its relation to all others. While none is irrelevant, the degree of validity of each is discerned in its relation to all others.

The basic approach to Old Testament theology is guided by our need to identify the Old Testament's theological concepts individually, to compare them, and thus to arrive at an integrated theological value system of the Old Testament. In what follows I give some examples.

No system of positive values can exist without its opposite, a system of antivalues. In Old Testament studies, the system of antivalues is basically established through Old Testament hamartiology, the doctrine of sin and guilt. The Old Testament speaks neither only of what is good nor only of what is evil, but of both as opposites. When it speaks of what is valid, it is always aware of what is destructive and, hence, invalid. Indeed, it essentially derives its judgments about evil from its knowledge of what is good. Evil is what is not good. The distinction between good and evil, even terminologically, is widespread and fundamental. For this reason, Old Testament hamartiology is an indispensable part of Old Testament theology, even though it is subservient to the positive side of Old Testament theology.

Within Old Testament hamartiology both the diverse terminology and the many texts have one uniting feature: no matter how diverse, the aspects always point to what is destructive. And this also shows that all aspects are not equally destructive. Someone who steals is not a murderer. Someone who holds a grudge against a neighbor or covets a neighbor's property does not publicly slander or rob that neighbor. Someone who inadvertently causes damage does not commit a crime. The murder of a person by an individual is a severe crime, but it is not as severe as genocide or the destruction of the whole earth by humanity's all-pervasive violence.

When we come to the theology of the positive concepts in the texts, we encounter concepts such as liberation, justice, blessing, mercy, goodness, holiness, peace, and so on. Each of these concepts is indicated by its own word field, and all word fields signal an already conceptualized understanding of the constructive side of reality.

It is clear that these words and the concepts they signal do not all mean the same thing. Each has a distinct meaning. These meanings, [[28]] including where they overlap, are interpreted in commentaries, dictionaries, monographs, and articles. But Old Testament theology must interpret the relationship of these concepts and discern their degrees of validity within this relationship.

For example, the semantic fields and concepts of liberation, or salvation, and justice and righteousness are related but not identical. When compared, liberation appears as an element of justice, namely, as liberation either from injustice suffered by others or from self-inflicted sin. Justice is distinct in that it involves more than liberation alone. Justice also means that the liberated are freed in order to do what is just. It is not only more inclusive than liberation, but is also the criterion for the truth of liberation because it is both the reason for and the purpose of liberation.

When applied to the story of the Pentateuch, the result of this distinction becomes painfully clear. Israel's liberation from Pharaoh's oppression is an act of justice. But Israel, at Yahweh's and Moses' command, is to subjugate or ban the free Canaanites. Those liberated from oppression are commanded to use their freedom for the oppression of others. The reason for Israel's transition from being the liberated to becoming the oppressors is well known: it is the theology of Israel's exclusive election for its possession of and multiplication in the promised land. Also clear, however, is that in this kind of liberation theology, the principle of indivisible justice is destroyed. Justice, especially God's justice, cannot mean both liberation and oppression at the same time. And other Old Testament traditions, especially in the wisdom traditions, disagree with this concept in the Pentateuch.

It is known that the Old Testament does not represent a religion of judgment compared to a religion of grace in the New Testament. It is also known that the concept of judgment, present everywhere and not only in the prophetic literature, is an inevitable element of the concept of justice. No justice can do without judgment. But judgment itself must be valid. And the criterion for its truth is not emotional, irrational, or based on the mood of a tyrant. Rather, the criterion for judgment is the rationality of justice to which even the freedom of God is bound. The Old Testament texts demonstrate this rationality very clearly.

Is there also a criterion for the truth of justice itself, even for the truth of its rationales? I have in mind many texts that in various ways speak about judgment on the one hand, and about mercy or pardon on the other hand. The relationship of these two concepts pervades the entire Old Testament and the history of Israel's theology. Where there is judgment, there is no forgiveness. And where there is mercy, pardon, or forgiveness, judgment is replaced. And just as judgment must be justifiable, so can mercy not be unjustifiable. The Yahweh of Hos 11:1–9 is [[29]] caught in the tension between the justice of judgment and the justice of mercy, and is forced to replace his just judgment by just mercy because mercy is the better justice. Why is it better? Because allowing his people to live is better than destroying them. Justice itself is relative. A similar conceptual dynamic is also found, among others, in the primeval history and in the Joseph novella.

The Old Testament speaks about peace (*šālôm*) and war, especially Yahweh's wars, which are perceived to be just wars. And while it is obvious that the notion of war is in need of theological evaluation, it is also obvious that no war, not even Yahweh's just wars, has the same validity as the condition of peace. The fact that there is "a time for war, and time for peace" (Qoh 3:8) does not mean that the times of war are as good as the times of peace. The Old Testament theology of war is, at any rate, subject to the distinction between just and unjust war. Even so, no war is as just as peace; nor is war ever considered just when compared with peace. The theology of war is evaluated sufficiently only when compared to the theology of peace.

What is the relationship between justice and peace? This question is important not only today; its importance is also reflected in the Old Testament itself. The texts speak about both peace and justice. God fashions justice (Jer 9:24) and also peace (Ps 147:14). Humans are to seek both. The world is in good shape when "righteousness and peace will kiss each other" (Ps 85:10). But peace and justice are not the same, and they do not always kiss each other. The two realities differ and often conflict. What is their relationship? Is peace a precondition for justice, so that justice depends on peace, and there can be no justice unless there is peace? Or is justice a precondition for peace because there can be no peace without justice? Is the theology of peace subordinate to or the criterion for the theology of justice, or are both related on the assumption that justice and peace rotate about each other in a bipolar tension and complementation?

The evidence seems to support the view that, at best, there may be false but no true peace where there is no justice, whereas there can be a degree of justice even where there is no peace. Justice appears to be the criterion for true peace, whereas peace is not the criterion for justice, and it does not necessarily create justice. But more important than my opinion is the need for us to clarify their relationship in the horizon of Old Testament theology.

Finally, in this series of examples, which can be expanded almost ad infinitum, what is the relationship between justice, liberation, mercy, or peace on the one hand, and blessing *(běrākâ)* on the other? The importance of the reality of blessing, and the difference between blessing and liberation, have especially been emphasized in the work of Claus [[30]] Westermann. Blessing is the perpetual presence of the goodness of life, or of life as goodness, for all living beings and in everything that belongs to their earthly welfare.

Rather than merely being the *fact* of life, blessing is what we call the *quality* of life, as good rather than bad life, or life without any quality at all. And it is a gift because we have not created life but are sustained by it. The reality of blessing not only differs from the reality of liberation, but is also more fundamental than that reality. Whereas the event, or the events, of liberation presuppose conditions of oppression, fallenness, or sin, the goodness of blessing is the original condition of life. Whereas liberation may or may not be experienced by all and at all times, blessing is the basic experience of all at all times. Blessing can be absent, as in the case of hunger. Such absence amounts to the threat to, or loss of, created life itself. The absence of blessing, as in the lack of food, represents an attack against the order of creation. And liberation from hunger amounts to the restoration of the blessing of food.

Blessing belongs to the theology of creation, whereas liberation belongs to the biblical soteriology that is connected with the theology of history fallen out of the order of creation. The theology of creation is not replaced by soteriology. Rather, it is the reason for soteriology. Liberation is necessary only where the order of creation has been corrupted. The restoration of the old or the vision of the new creation is the reason for the need for and truth of salvation.

Finally, Genesis 1, important psalms, the deity's speeches in Job, and other texts say that the created world is good, or very good. These qualifying judgments are themselves acts of justice. They confirm that the creation of the world out of chaos and its sustenance above chaos are acts of God's universal justice. It has been said that creation theology is soteriology. It is more appropriate to say that the Old Testament's creation theology represents the first, and fundamental, chapter in the theology of universal justice, whereas its soteriology represents that theology of justice which deals with the restoration of creation.

The comparison of the biblical concepts involves a heuristic process through which we can establish their relationship systematically. We can discern the place of each concept in a hierarchy of values and, hence, the degree of validity or truth of each concept in its relation to all others. This heuristic process is systematizing in nature, and its results amount to a systematic Old Testament theology in which the relationship of the concepts is the basis for the evaluation of all that is said and presupposed, and also for the evaluation of all other kinds of systematization, such as, for instance, tradition history or sociology.

Thus far, all the concepts mentioned are qualitative in nature. The texts show, however, that correlated to the qualitative aspect of each [[31]] concept is also a quantitative aspect. Mercy, justice, blessing, liberation, and peace apply to individuals, to groups, to Israel, to humanity, and even to nature on earth and the cosmos. Each of these aspects is everywhere evident in the Old Testament. They range from the narrowest to the widest situations. Their varying boundaries indicate the Old Testament's differentiating awareness of reality. None of the qualities is important only for the world and not also for each individual and every quantity in between.

The problem arises, however, of whether, for example, justice and liberation are considered valid for individuals regardless of, or because of, their validity for all. If they are true for all, they are therefore also true for each
person. If they are true only for one person, justice and liberation are divided,
and what is justice for one party is injustice for another. The widest boundary,
which includes all equally, is the quantitative criterion for the validity of the
positive qualities, just as the widest boundary is the quantitative criterion for
the antivalue of the negative aspects in Old Testament hamartiology.

The most inclusive aspect is directly important theologically. If God's
peace is only for me, such a god is only my God and not the God of all. This
god is my idol. If God's peace is for all, it is therefore also for me, and God is
the God for me because God is the God of all. God is the deity of the total
world, or god is not God. The universality of God is the criterion for the
truth of God's presence in each particular situation.

This criterion is critically important for the evaluation of those texts in
the Old Testament in which Israel's election is not seen as functioning for
God's universal justice equally for all but at the expense of the other nations,
or in which even the creation is seen as serving the purpose of Israel's election. Nothing is said against anyone's election. But in a particularistic theology of election, Israel subjects the nations to the interest of its own benefit
rather than serving God's universal goodness for the benefit of all nations.
This theology of Yahwism represents the opposite of a theology according to
which God works out the same justice for all. It amounts to a nationalistic religious idolatry.

The Old Testament does not simply speak about God. From its first page
to its last, it speaks about the relationship between God and world. Its focus
on this relationship lies at the heart of its understanding of reality. In this understanding, the deity is considered as the ground of the truth of the world's
existence, and the world is therefore considered as created and sustained by,
and dependent on, this ground. If the world, including especially the humans, remains in accord with this ground, it actualizes it in its existence. The
actualization of the ground of the truth of existence is represented especially
in human ethos.

When speaking of ethos theologically, we normally use words such [[32]]
as "response" or "reaction" to God's word or action. God acts and we "react"; God speaks and we "re-spond." This language is questionable. It means
that by responding or reacting, we do on our part something that God does
not do. I know that the Old Testament itself very often says that humans responded to Yahweh's speeches. Even so, the problem is deeper. It is clear that
when responding properly, humans accept what God says or does. They then
transmit this content into, or actualize it in, their own existence and, hence,
carry on God's own work and word. Rather than doing what God does not
do, they continue God's own work by actualizing it. The actualization of
God's own work in the world is both the matrix of and the criterion for the
Old Testament's ethos.

Finally, the Old Testament focuses overwhelmingly on the affairs of this existing and ongoing world. With this focus it speaks about God's presence in the originally created world, whereas its passages about the new creation are not only minimal but also textured in the sense of the restoration of the depraved world to the shape of its original creation. All of this is clearly distinct from the New Testament. The New Testament considers the original creation from the vantage point of its replacement by the new creation and the expectation that this replacement is impending.

Thus far, the new creation—though considered as already arrived in Christ's resurrection—has not replaced the old creation. Regardless of when, or whether, this will happen, the millennia of the ongoing original creation teach us that we must pay attention to the presence of God in this original creation as long as it lasts. They teach us that the corruption in, and even the fallenness of, the original creation are no longer sufficient reasons for a theology of the *absence* of God from the structures of this creation, whether original or fallen. Indeed, if God were not present also in these structures, the deity would not be the God of the total reality, both new and old.

Thus, we realize that the total Bible teaches us this: God is not present because God comes out of the future, but God comes out of the future as well as out of the past because God is always present. When we come to these fundamental theological realizations, we will have to realize that the Old Testament, with its focus on the ongoing presence of God in this ongoing creation, original or fallen, represents in its totality an independent and critical complement to the worldview of the New Testament. This function constitutes the legitimacy of the Old Testament theology in its own right in a truly bipolar theology of the Christian Bible.[1]

1. I am indebted to Brenda Hahn and Mignon R. Jacobs for editorial assistance.

Rolf Knierim
On World Order and History

Excerpted with permission from Rolf Knierim, *The Task of Old Testament Theology: Substance, Methods and Cases* (Grand Rapids: Eerdmans, 1995), pp. 175, 205–9.

Cosmos and History in Israel's Theology

[[175]] Israel's history did not simply fail as history; it failed because of Yahweh, so that Israel would look and wait for Yahweh and quit hoping for the future reenactment of its past.

To be sure, not all the Old Testament texts reveal this understanding. However, those that do can be taken as the Old Testament's own canon for its understanding of Israel's (tradition) history. They reveal that when looking at its history, or at the history of the nations, Israel encountered Yahweh as the *crisis* of all history. Thus, Israel had to give up mythologizing its own historical institutions and looking at them as the scene of a perfect world. Moreover, Israel had to accept history for what it was, not as the stage of the revelation of God's ultimate glory, but as the realm in which the struggle for the meaning of creation is waged. The vision of the ultimate glory was to be found elsewhere.

World Order

The theological interpretation of God's relationship to the world has long been governed, at least in Old Testament studies, by our preoccupation with history. We have believed this preoccupation to be justifiable because of the intensive attention to history in the Old Testament. Under the influence of this preoccupation, however, we have by and large underestimated the role of another aspect in the Old Testament, namely, Yahweh's relationship to and presence in the order of the world. Here I refer to the Old Testament texts regarding the creation and sustenance of the world by God.

To be sure, this aspect does not command as much space in the pages of the Old Testament as does its attention to history. Even so, the texts refer to it much more than is commonly assumed. More importantly, the statistical infrequency says little about the importance of Yahweh's relationships to history and to world order in the total horizon of an Old Testament theology.

. . . .

Yahweh, World Order, and History

[[205]] The Old Testament says not only that Yahweh acts in history, but above all that Yahweh himself creates and sustains history. More specifically, it sees Yahweh as the Lord of Israel's history and of the history of the nations

280

as well. As is well known, this fact is amply documented, in the sources of the Pentateuch, in the historical and prophetic books, and in the Psalms.

Generally, it is exegetically assumed that Yahweh's intentions for history are salvific, even in those situations in which his judgment is necessary either to prevent history from collapsing or to bring failed history to a collapse in order to enable a new beginning. History was seen as guided by a salvific intentionality despite the frequent hiddenness of this intentionality behind or in the numerous catastrophic historical events. Israel always clung to the conviction that in human actions and decisions there was a meaning and a purpose at work to which those actions and decisions became subservient, even as they determined the course of history. The story of Ahithophel and Hushai (2 Sam 16:15–17:23), Isaiah's view of the Assyrians (Isa 5:26–30; 7:18–20; 10:5–11), Jeremiah's view of the enemy from the north (Jeremiah 4) and of Nebuchadnezzar (Jeremiah 23–28), Deutero-Isaiah's view of Cyrus (Isa 45:1–6; 44:28), and many other examples illustrate this point. Israel was convinced that, ultimately, human actions and decisions were more the result of history than history was the result of human actions and decisions.

At the same time, Israel knew that involvement of humans in history entails being inextricably confronted with a critically discerning factor before which human actions and decisions stand in judgment. Humans may make history, but it is the meaning and purpose of history that judges the historical creations of humans. Thus, human actions and decisions are not deemed good and justified on the ground that they are historical, but human historical involvement is judged in view of how human actions and decisions serve the meaning and purpose of history. History has [[206]] no ultimate legitimacy or validity by virtue of being history. Its legitimacy and validity are themselves subject to a criterion which is independent of history even as it is at work and can be recognized in history, whether in human history in general or in Israel's history specifically. The criterion for either the truth or the perversion of history, however, is the salvific intentionality to which history is to be subservient, which determines the purpose and meaning of history, and which at the same time is the judge of history.

What has been said amounts to a type of historical consciousness in which Israel distinguished between the historical events and the meaning of those events. Moreover, while it occasionally saw the meaning of history expressed in the events, it frequently protested against, or pointed beyond, the actual course of history precisely because of its perception of true history. The reason for this critical historical consciousness, for this sense of the potential or actual tension between true and perverse history, was undoubtedly the fact that Israel did not perceive the ongoing course of history exclusively as the revelation of Yahweh's great enterprise on earth. Israel also perceived it as the singularly genuine mode for the self-realization of humans on earth. Two questions arise at this point. First, how does the Old Testament understand the relationship between human history and the salvific meaning of history? And secondly, if the meaning and purpose of history is the factor for the critical discernment between true and perverse history, then on what ground does the Old Testament determine what salvation is most universally and most fundamentally?

Generally speaking, the search for the answers to these questions leads us to those texts that reflect the relationship between Yahweh's creation of the world and Yahweh's lordship of history. A few examples may illustrate this point. As far as the history of humanity is concerned, the most obvious case for illustration is the primeval history in the Yahwistic and the priestly versions in Genesis 1–11. The primeval history clearly raises the question of the relationship between creation and human history. The case may not be so clear in the Yahwistic history because this narration emphasizes human history after the fall—paradise on earth lost for humans—while saying nothing about the remainder of paradise itself. Even so, the Yahwist considers human history as fallen out of paradise, the earthly sphere of the order of creation. In this consideration, paradise apparently means more than only the beginning of human history. It is the mirror of true reality, the reality of creation in view of which human history is evaluated. The relationship between creation and history in the Yahwist's view is hardly only chronological in nature. It is systematic in that creation provides the criterion by which the meaning and also the purpose of history, even and especially the purpose of the history of Israel's election, can be determined. Paradise may be lost as history. However, it is not lost as the constant reminder of the true place to which history belongs—creation—nor as the reminder of the fact that history is removed from creation, and not creation from history.

[[207]] A more specific interpretation of the Yahwistic history would yield further evidence for this systematic understanding of the relationship between creation and history. Suffice it to point out that after the flood Yahweh finds it meaningless to curse the ground again and once more to destroy the living creatures because "the inclination of the human heart is evil from youth" (Gen 8:21). In addition, he guarantees the intactness of the cosmic cycle on earth forever. This guarantee by no means excuses evil human history, nor does it ascribe any legitimacy to its autonomy. On the contrary, by affirming that realm which human history cannot pervert and which, at the same time, is the indispensable basis for the existence of all creatures throughout all history, Yahweh again makes clear that history truly belongs to creation, and not creation to history. Moreover, he makes it clear that, while history cannot destroy creation and creation will not destroy history, history can destroy both life and itself.

The case is even clearer in the priestly version of the primeval history. In addition to what has been said earlier, it is sufficient to mention that the priest knows that the earth is "filled with violence" and that it remains so after the flood (Gen 6:9, 11; 9:1–7). And while he, too, speaks about God's guarantee for the cosmic order (Gen 9:1–7), he adds one more divine decree given for the protection of human life itself (Gen 9:5–6). It is doubtful that the purpose for this protection is to provide the basis for human history. Unavoidably as history springs from life, it is much more probable that the purpose for this protection is to guarantee the continued existence of that realm of the order of creation on earth without which creation itself would be meaningless, i.e., human life. Human life is not a product of human history; it is a product of creation and belongs to the continued existence of the order of creation. In being blessed in creation with the power for its self-perpetuation, human life represents once more the ongoing presence of the order of creation in the sphere of human existence itself.[1] There can be no doubt that the priestly writer sees creation and human history as systematically related, and that, in this relationship, creation appears as the salvific reality to which history genuinely belongs, from which it is actually separated, and in view of which it is evaluated.

[[208]] Isaiah, the Psalms, and the wisdom literature speak about the plans and counsels of humans and nations, the political philosophies devised especially by human governments for the purpose of world domination. These policies often conflict with Yahweh's own plan (Psalms 2; 33:10–11; 35; 37; 46; 48; Isa 7:1–9; 8:10; 28:23–29; 29:15; 30:1; 46:11; Job 12:13–25; 38:2; Prov 8:14, et al.). In most of the references, the conflict between the two parties is concerned with their historical plans. One must investigate specifically the presuppositions on which these historical blueprints rest. As for Yahweh's plan, two passages in which this plan appears in the context of creation may be mentioned. One is Job 38:2, where Yahweh's plan refers to his creation and sustenance of the world itself.[2] The other is Ps 33:10–11, where the conflict between Yahweh's counsel and the nations' counsel is mentioned directly after the passage that speaks about the creation of the world: "The LORD brings the counsel of the nations to nothing; he frustrates the plans of the peoples. The counsel of the Lord stands forever, the thoughts of his heart to all generations." Particularly in this psalm, the question arises regarding the relationship between Yahweh's creation and the nations' historical plans which are frustrated by Yahweh. More specifically, what are the objectives of the plans of the two parties, and what are the foundations on which these objectives rest? As for the nations, we may assume what is said elsewhere in the Old Testament, that their objective is to create and control world history, and that the basis for achieving this objective is their reliance on the "great army,"

---

1. This understanding is also implied in the Old Testament genealogies, e.g., Genesis 5; 10; 11, in which the constant component reflects the creational aspect, and the variable component the historical aspect, as Westermann has shown [[C. Westermann, *Genesis 1–11: A Commentary* (trans. John J. Scullion; Minneapolis: Augsburg, 1984) 347]]. Westermann is certainly correct when saying that a science of history which ignores the constant components in the genealogies and, one must add, in the structure of human procreation becomes questionable. One may ask, however, whether this constant component is to be considered an element of human history at all. Instead, it seems to belong to the structure of creation in human existence which is different from and at the same time the presupposition for those components in human existence that belong to its historical structure. Persons are not born and alive because they have individual names; rather, they have names because they are born and alive. Furthermore, humans do not have the right to live because they are historical beings. Rather, they can be historical beings because they have the right to live.

2. See also Prov 8:22–31, where wisdom was established before creation and was at work in it.

the "great strength," and on the "warhorse," the "hope for victory" (Ps 33:16–17). By contrast, Yahweh's plan "stands forever, the thoughts of his heart to all generations" (v. 11). What are Yahweh's own thoughts, and what guides them? Verse 5 seems to give the answer, "He loves righteousness and justice; the earth is full of the steadfast love of the LORD." This statement contrasts Yahweh's objectives with the objectives of the nations. Of equal importance is the fact that Yahweh's or his world's[3] love of "righteousness and justice" is mentioned within the passage about Yahweh's creation. It must be understood as the substantive qualification of creation itself. This qualification of creation is apparently the basis that guides Yahweh's thoughts and plans in his conflict with the nations. Psalm 33 as a whole seems concerned with the question of the principles and criteria according to which history on earth is to be governed. In the conflict of governing principles, Yahweh's own criterion is said to be "justice and righteousness." This principle is embedded in and in accordance with his creation of the world. When verse 5b affirms that "the earth is full of the steadfast love [חסד] of the LORD," it most probably refers to the steadfast and loyal presence of justice and righteousness in the stable cosmic condition of the earth itself, and not to the historical plans of the nations. Therefore, our psalm systematically [[209]] relates the theology of creation and the theology of history. In its attempt to validate justice and righteousness as the true guidelines for human history on earth, Psalm 33 must go back to creation and associate "justice and righteousness" (including Yahweh's חסד in the ongoing existence of the cosmic order of the earth) with the creation of the world. Hence, creation theology not only offers the most comprehensive aspect, it also offers the most foundational criterion for the conduct of universal human history and for the critical evaluation of actual human history. History either fails or is justified to the extent that it is in line with the just and righteous order of creation. Yahweh is the God who loves history as justice and righteousness instead of as power and might because he is the creator whose love for justice and righteousness is the basis for the initial and ongoing order of the world. As the creator, "the LORD looks down from heaven; he sees all humankind. From where he sits enthroned he watches all the inhabitants of the earth—he who fashions the hearts of them all, and observes all their deeds" (Ps 33:13–15).

The question of the systematic relationship between the creator of the world and the judge of the nations would also have to be raised with respect to the so-called Yahweh enthronement Psalms: 47; 93; 96–99. This question is different from the traditio-historical problem concerning the chronological sequence in which Israel came to know Yahweh as the creator. It arises at the moment in which the notion of the God of history was combined with the notion of the God of creation. From that moment on, the question is unavoidable as to whether Yahweh is understood as the God of creation because he is the God of history, or whether he is the God of history and the judge of the

---

3. [[So K. Koch, "Wort und Einheit des Schöpfergottes in Memphis und Jerusalem," *ZThK* 62 (1965) 274–75.]]

nations because he is the God of creation. At close examination, the answer given or suggested in these psalms should be quite clear. Yahweh is not the God of creation because he is the God of history.

It is true that Yahweh acts in and through history, often in quite mysterious ways. On the whole, however, it seems as if Yahweh's own plan is more effective in bringing the plans of the nations to nought than in implementing the order of his creation in or through human history, or in reintegrating human history into the order of his creation. It seems that the order of creation cannot be restored via human history. It seems that human history cannot bring about or lead to the kingdom of heaven, but on the contrary, human history will come to its end when the kingdom of heaven comes.

Synopsis of Knierim's *Task of Old Testament Theology: Substance, Method, and Cases*, 1995

HORST DIETRICH PREUSS

b. 1927   d. 1993

Exodus and Election

Horst Dietrich Preuss was Professor of Old Testament at the University of Göttingen and, after 1973, at the Augustana-Hochschule (Lutheran seminary) in Neuendettelsau, Germany. His published work ranges from technical and lexical studies to a volume on the Old Testament in Christian preaching. Preuss's was the first large-scale Old Testament theology to appear in German since von Rad's.

Selected Writings by Preuss

1968   *Jahweglaube und Zukunfsterwartung.* Stuttgart: Kohlhammer.
1984   *Das Alte Testament in christlicher Predigt.* Stuttgart: Kohlhammer.
1991   *Theologie des Alten Testaments.* Volume 1: *JHWH's Erwählendes und verpflichtendes Handeln.* Stuttgart: Kohlhammer.
1992   *Theologie des Alten Testaments.* Volume 2: *Israels Weg mit JHWH.* Stuttgart: Kohlhammer.
1995–96 *Theology of the Old Testament.* 2 volumes. Translated by Leo G. Perdue. Old Testament Library. Louisville: Westminster John Knox.

Writings about Preuss

Barr, James
1999   Pp. 461–67 in *The Concept of Biblical Theology: An Old Testament Perspective.* Minneapolis: Fortress.
Hausmann, J., and H.-J. Zobel (editors)
1992   *Alttestamentlicher Glaube und biblische Theologie: Festschrift für Horst Dietrich Preuss.* Stuttgart: Kohlhammer.

Horst Dietrich Preuss's
Approach to Old Testament Theology

Excerpted with permission from Horst Dietrich Preuss, *Old Testament Theology* (Old Testament Library; Louisville: Westminster John Knox, 1995), vol. 1: 19–25. Some footnotes have been omitted.

Setting the Boundaries for Methodology

[[19]] Seven major problems in setting forth a theology of the Old Testament have been mentioned.[1] On the basis of these problems, it is time to determine and define in a precise manner the position represented by the present description of Old Testament theology.

First, this description seeks to set forth, not a history of Israelite religion, but rather a systematically oriented and structured theology of the Old Testament. This occurs quite naturally, not because theology per se is systematic rather than chronological,[2] but because there are other reasons. One should mention at the beginning that a systematically structured description is more capable of seeing the total picture, not only of Old Testament theology but also of its relationship to that of the New Testament. Since both Old Testament and New Testament theology must provide the basis for Christian theology, a systematic description is more conducive to this larger hermeneutical enterprise. Thus one is more easily able to determine where there are similarities, [[20]] variations, approximations, and significant differences in the theological understandings between the Old Testament and the New Testament, and between the Old Testament and contemporary theology. If one wishes to discover analogous or different basic structures of the witness and faith, a systematic description that provides a comprehensive overview is more helpful. It is also more possible to move from a systematic description into necessary issues concerning the value and validity of Old Testament understandings within the larger structure of Christian theology. Even so, on the whole, a "theology of the Old Testament" still remains a historically oriented as well as a descriptive undertaking.

Second, in regard to the above, evaluations occur, not within the description of a theology of the Old Testament but within the sphere of hermeneutics and fundamental theology.[3] Furthermore, questions of value belong to

1. See [[Preuss 1995–96: vol. 1]] pp. 67 and 14–15.
2. A. H. J. Gunneweg correctly places in question and criticizes such a position. See his *Understanding the Old Testament* (OTL; London and Philadelphia, 1978), 78.
3. For a different view, see the previous work of F. Baumgärtel, "Erwägungen zur Darstellung der Theologie des Alten Testaments," *ThLZ* 76, 1951, cols. 257–72. For more contemporary scholars who represent a different view from mine on this issue, see G. F. Hasel (*Old Testament Theology* [[1991]]) and E. Otto ("Erwägungen zu den Prolegomena einer Theologie des Alten Testaments" [[*Kairos* 19 (1977) 53–72]]). According to Otto, Old Testament theology endeavors to proceed from modern questions concerning the contribution of the Old Testament to the contemporary and salutary form of existence.

the contemporary task of hermeneutical reflection on the exegesis of a particular concrete text. A theology of the Old Testament certainly must assist in answering these questions, should take into consideration the entire spectrum of theology in the formation of its own description, and ought to clarify the place of the Old Testament within a comprehensive theology. To work in the field of Old Testament studies requires one to be responsible to the present by bringing this part of the canon into the contemporary, theological debate. Such matters are also important in making the Old Testament accessible to contemporary proclamation and religious instruction.

Third, a systematic description is set forth, because the Old Testament in the final analysis probably does have a center.[4]

Fourth, on the basis of the above it is evident that this systematic presentation, if at all possible, should approach the description of an Old Testament theology, by moving, not from the outside to the inside, but rather from within the Old Testament to the outside. This means then that an Old Testament theology seeks to describe "what the Old Testament says about God as a coherent whole."[5]

Fifth, the systematic formulation must be suitable for setting forth the material in a comprehensive fashion and must bring the distinctive Word of the Old Testament as far as it is possible to clear expression. Necessary historical particularities should not be dropped; rather, they must be integrated into this systematically oriented presentation. After all, God's manner of being and acting with his people is a historical process, indeed a part of history. The drawing in of history includes necessary or accentuating comparative side-glances at the religious environment of the Old Testament. Gerhard von Rad's *Old Testament Theology* almost completely omitted this consideration. "The critical position taken here leads to the recognition that the Old Testament, in spite of its rootedness in the ancient Near East, still in its essential structure cannot be understood by reference to its environment. Rather, the Old Testament may [[21]] be compared to an erratically shaped boulder that has all the appearance of lying in a particular landscape and belonging to it, but upon closer examination can still be understood only as out of place."[6] Israel's faith has assimilated much from its environment in a form more or less recast. This faith lives, however, at the same time in a polemical debate with this environment. Thus it is not unimportant to observe that the Old Testament does not contain many kinds of religious literature that were dominant and significant in Israel's environment. The Egyptian literature dealing with the afterlife and the typical omen literature of Mesopotamia are both absent in the Old Testament. Also missing in the Old Testament are royal inscriptions and military reports that mark the self-understanding of monarchy in the ancient Near East. In addition, the Old Testament contains neither myths of gods nor astrological and astronomical texts.

---

4. See the discussion [[pp. 289–91]] below.
5. W. Zimmerli, [[*Old Testament Theology in Outline* (1978)]], 12.
6. H. Wildberger, *EvTh* 19, 1959, 77.

As a consequence it is not possible to set forth the various parts of the entire Old Testament on a continuum. Even when one is speaking of a center of the Old Testament, it is necessary to recognize the consequences that derive from the fact that there are some writings and texts that stand close to this center, while others do not. The particular nuances of faith or even the diverse judgments found in the variety of the Old Testament witnesses are therefore not to be eliminated. Nevertheless, there are still typical representations of the witness of faith that predominate in the "central structure of Old Testament faith."[7] The expression of such a center should not ignore either the historical breadth of the Old Testament or the variety of the literary texts and sociological considerations of different kinds. One should be aware of the danger that a systematic description of Old Testament theology represents. A systematic presentation could well conceal the historical diversity of the Hebrew canon. Still, a systematic formulation seeks to offer both the occasion and the context for inquiring after the "unity of the divine activity behind the multifaceted character of events and the *one* Word that resides behind many words."[8]

Concerning the Center of the Old Testament

Accordingly, we now address the problem of whether there is a possible[9] "center of the Old Testament." In earlier research, as R. Smend has shown in an instructive way, this center was referred to as the "fundamental principle," "fundamental thoughts," "fundamental character," "fundamental idea," or "kernel." The center has included the following: salvation, redemption, knowledge of YHWH (H. Ewald); the holiness of God (A. Dillmann; J. Hand); YHWH as a living, acting God (E. Jacob); YHWH as providential Lord (L. Köhler); theocracy[10] or covenant (W. Eichrodt);[11] community between the holy God and humanity (Th. C. Vriezen); community with God and the sovereignty of God (G. Fohrer); promise (W. C. Kaiser); God's presence and mystery;[12] and God's plan and his purposes (E. A. Martens).

[[22]] Evoking the name YHWH is accompanied by the inherent problem of setting forth specific language about God. Zimmerli has spoken of the oneness of Yahweh in the multiplicity of traditions, whose revealed name

---

7. Ibid. 78.

8. W. Zimmerli, *VT* 13, 1963, 105.[[. . .]]

9. See, above all, G. von Rad, *ThLZ* 88, 1963, col. 405; and idem, [[*Old Testament Theology* (1965)]] 2:362. Nevertheless, even von Rad inquires after representations of the faith "typical of Yahwism" (*Theology*, 2:428; cf. *ThLZ* 88, 1963, col. 406).

10. In this regard, see R. Smend, "Die Mitte des Alten Testaments," *Gesammelte Studien* 1 (1986), 57ff.

11. D. H. Odendall wishes to renew this attempt ("Covenant—the Centre of the Old Testament?" *NGTT* 30, 1989, 143–51).

12. Accordingly, see S. Terrien, *The Elusive Presence: Toward a New Biblical Theology* (San Francisco, 1978).

means "I am who I am." Yet, how does one speak of God, and how does Israel come into his presence? Moreover, is there within the Old Testament overall a way of speaking about God that remains constant?[13] For example, is the YHWH of Amos identical with the YHWH of Proverbs 10–29? In contrast to Zimmerli, must not the "YHWH from Egypt" be introduced before one can say anything about this YHWH, since it is there, in the event of the exodus, that Israel had experienced in a fundamental way YHWH as its God? Is it possible for one first to speak of "God in and of himself" before one speaks of "God for humanity"? Moreover, how does one evaluate the continuing efforts by Zimmerli to demonstrate that the content of the divine name is understood as the direct(!) self-revelation of God? How much is Karl Barth responsible for this contention?[14] What is one to think or believe about the "self-disclosure of YHWH" (in history)? In addition, the efforts to set forth "YHWH" or "YHWH's self-revelation" as the center of the Old Testament does not provide much further help (see Reventlow; Hasel), since they are in any case too general. In the Old Testament's speaking of YHWH, how does it come to know something of him? How does the revelation of God take place? Surely this occurs, not within the nature of God's own self, but rather in a personal "You." Revelation is not a purpose deriving from within the divine self; rather, it occurs when the community is addressed by this "You." This "You" in the Old Testament is addressed primarily to Israel and through Israel then to the world, that is, the nations. Are Yahweh's acts on behalf of Israel and the world not more precisely describable when they are brought within the "center of the Old Testament"?[15]

One should not attempt to make an "idea" the center, since abstract thinking is foreign to the Old Testament. Westermann[16] has correctly pointed out that the structure of the Old Testament's God language involves events. In addition, this center should not be "static" in nature,[17] since the Old Testament involves historical progress.

On occasion, scholars have pointed to a particular book as the center of Old Testament theology. S. Herrmann thought with good reason that the

13. Cf. also in regard to this W. S. Prinsloo, *The Theology of the Book of Joel* (BZAW 163; 1985), 1–2.

14. See, e.g., K. Barth, [[*Kirchliche Dogmatik* (1939)]] 1/1, 334ff.

15. One rejoices in the fact that one now has Jewish conversation partners who have entered the discussion about the "center of the Old Testament." Cf. the collection of essays, M. Klopfenstein et al., eds., *Mitte der Schrift? Ein jüdisch-christliches Gespräch* (1987); and E. Brocke, "Von den 'Schriften' zum 'Alten Testament'—und zurück?" in E. Blum et al., eds., *Die hebräische Bibel*, FS R. Rendtorff (1990), 581–94. It is Brocke's opinion that the search for a center of the Old Testament may not be an exegetical or a methodological problem but rather a "Christian-existential" one (p. 584). This opinion, however, has already been brought into question by the Jewish contributions in the above-mentioned collection. E.g., the Jewish interest in determining a center is clear from the emphasis given to the Torah as the most important corpus of texts within the Tanak. This view derives from the value and placement of the Torah within the Tanak as a whole.

16. C. Westermann, *Elements of Old Testament Theology* [[1982]], 9.

17. R. Smend, "Die Bundesformel," 23 (= *Gesammelte Studien* 1, 1986, 55).

Book of Deuteronomy served in this capacity.[18] And von Rad from time to time came rather close to this position. As will become apparent, the design of this present volume also seeks to take a good deal from this approach.

Smend sought to set forth the so-called covenant formula ("YHWH the God of Israel"; "Israel the people of YHWH"), including its prehistory and description of present reality in relationship to its expression of future hope, as the center of the Old Testament. This approach also offers important insights, but the question immediately arises as to how the two partners in the covenant [[23]] formula came to find each other and "what the relationship of Yahweh and Israel actually includes."[19] This question forms the basis for the work of W. H. Schmidt[20] who looks to the first commandment as both the center of the Old Testament and the introductory guide for its theology. This proposal includes the affirmation of YHWH as a God who acts in history (see the preamble of the first commandment) and a God who requires obedience from his people. Indeed, this proposal comes very close to the one suggested in this volume. However, it appears unlikely that the first commandment, with its demand for the exclusive worship of YHWH, is appropriate for the entire Old Testament. Rather, what is addressed in the preamble is more precisely the presupposition for all that follows.

Two other efforts to define the center of Old Testament theology should be mentioned. W. Dietrich's proposal[21] that "justice" is the "red thread" that is woven through the fabric of the Old Testament is not particularly convincing, since this theme is missing in many corpora of texts, especially narratives, that comprise the Hebrew Bible. J. W. Rogerson understands as central the contributions of the Old Testament to the "contemporary questions about the nature and destiny of the human race."[22] However, this statement requires more precise explication lest it remain too general.

The Present Inquiry

The present effort to set forth a "theology of the Old Testament" seeks to inquire after several related elements: the appropriate center for the Old Testament, the typical features of YHWH faith, and the decisive and formative components that comprise its fundamental structures. How does the Old Testament speak of God, that is, how is "theology" expressed? How does the Old Testament present God as speaking and being spoken to? What is the basis that makes this type of language possible? We certainly do not have before us in the

18. See, above all, S. Herrmann, "Die konstruktive Restauration: Das Deuteronomium als Mitte biblischer Theologie," in H. W. Wolff, ed., *Probleme biblischer Theologie*, FS G. von Rad (1971), 155–70. Cf. also A. Deissler, *Grundbotschaft* [[1972]], 91–92.

19. W. H. Schmidt, *VuF* 17, 1972, 12 (n. 25).

20. W. H. Schmidt, *Das erste Gebot* (ThEx 165; 1969); and idem, *Alttestamentlicher Glaube in seiner Geschichte* (6th ed.) [[1st ed., 1975]]; etc.

21. W. Dietrich, "Der rote Faden im Alten Testament," *EvTh* 49, 1989, 232–250.

22. [[J. W. Rogerson, "What Does It Mean to Be Human?" in David J. A. Clines et al., eds., *The Bible in Three Dimensions* (JSOT Suppl 87; Sheffield, 1990),]] 298.

Old Testament God's revelation as such; rather, we have testimonies to this revelation and the various responses to them. We have "data" only in the form of a *kerygma* [['proclamation']] coming to expression within the wonderment of believing witnesses, along with texts that give voice to their testimony, texts that say that here or there YHWH, according to the conviction of the faith of these witnesses, may have acted and may have revealed himself. Even so, this testimony is not uniform throughout the history of Old Testament faith. This testimony continues to be altered and to allow for new interpretations grounded in the experiences of later witnesses that evoke once more a response.

The Old Testament witnesses primarily, not to the "nature" of YHWH, but to his divine activity. This means that in seeking the center of the Old Testament one must speak of divine activity and not of fundamental concepts or of one idea as pivotal. Rather, one must speak of a fundamental activity and how [[24]] this activity is comprehended within the language of its witnesses. One should not separate external from internal history or act from interpretation,[23] for these historical happenings now exist *only* as and in language. Furthermore, the tradition history of these interpretations, which are shaped by doxological, soteriological, and polemical considerations, is a part of both the history of Israel and the history of its faith. Thus, insofar as it is exegetically supportable, one may make the effort to differentiate between an event that yields a testimony and an event that has its testimony deleted.

According to the Old Testament, YHWH's activity has to do with Israel, but his actions are not once and for all. Rather, it is through his historical activity that YHWH elects a group, a people, to enter into community with him. In and through this action, YHWH at the same time requires this people to be responsible. In this manner "community with God and divine sovereignty" (G. Fohrer) receive their expression and consequently find their basis. The "election" of Israel took place originally in the foundational events of the exodus out of Egypt and the deliverance at the sea, but election also came to be experienced and then confessed in terms of other events, for example, the installation of the monarchy or the incorporation of Zion within the world of Israel's faith. Accordingly, "election" is open to additional, new acts of YHWH on behalf of his people, provides the model for interpreting new experiences with this God, is a fundamental structure of the Old Testament witness to YHWH,[24] gives the Old Testament its inner unity (Hasel), designates what is typical for the Old Testament and its God, and thus expresses the "foundational dimension" of Old Testament faith.[25] Therefore the necessary integration of systematics and history or of the synchronic with the diachronic is already demanded by the Old Testament itself. Indeed, this foundational structure of Old Testament faith makes this integration possible.

23. M. Oeming (*Gesamtbiblische Theologien der Gegenwart*, 2d ed., 1987, 139–40) has discussed the degree to which von Rad's understanding of history was influenced by the circle of W. Pannenberg (*Revelation as History*, trans. D. Granskou; New York, 1968).

24. Cf. G. von Rad, [[*Old Testament*]] *Theology*, 2:425: "Ancient Israel found something of importance for herself expressed in [the election]."

25. Thus A. Soete, *Ethos der Rettung–Ethos der Gerechtigkeit* (1987), 41.

This "center" must be related to the additional, pivotal, foundational structures of Israelite faith that include, for example, the Old Testament witness of revelation, the cult, history, and the ancestors.[26] This present volume will seek to accomplish this task insofar as it is possible, justified, and correct to do so. While one must seek to position writings and texts in varying degrees of proximity to a designated center, one should still remember that "the center of the Old Testament . . . is not the entire Old Testament."[27] There are various corpora of texts in the Old Testament that in and of themselves attempt to set forth their own "theology."[28] This is the case for Deuteronomy, Deutero-Isaiah, and perhaps also the Priestly document. Subsequently, one should have this in view in attempting to keep one's own effort, as far as possible, in close proximity to these earlier theological formulations in the Old Testament.

Furthermore, one should ask whether this articulation of Old Testament theology, including the arrangement of the fundamental structures of Old Testament faith in relationship to a designated center, may be open to the formulation [[25]] of a comprehensive biblical theology conducive to a Christian perspective without the suspicion arising that this would lead to a denial of the Old Testament to Jews.[29] It would be rather ill-conceived for Christian readers or even Christian scholars to attempt to read the Old Testament as though they knew nothing at all of the message of the New Testament.[30] It is true that a "theology of the Old Testament" is still neither a "biblical theology" nor even a normative theology for Christians after it has been evaluated in terms of the New Testament witness. Nevertheless, even by means of historical, descriptive questions concerning the fundamental structures of Old Testament faith, an Old Testament theology still ought to prepare the way for a biblical theology. This being said, one may hope that many Jewish readers who are concerned with an overview of the "Tanakh" may still be able to view this presentation of Old Testament theology as an appropriate one.

The following presentation views the center of the Old Testament and thus the fundamental structure of Old Testament faith to be *"YHWH's historical activity of electing Israel for communion with his world"*[31] and the obedient activity

---

26. Cf. H.-J. Hermisson, "Zur Erwahlung Israels," in H. Schroer, ed., *In Memoriam Gerhard Krause* (1984), 37–66. He says on p. 37: "The theme of the election of Israel belongs to the central expressions of Old Testament theology. One could even see in this theme the (or, more precisely, a) center of the Old Testament." However, he then remarks on p. 39: "It is already a rule of good taste that one should not seek to comprehend the entire Old Testament under it" (i.e., election). As everyone would agree, one cannot debate what may be a matter of "taste."

27. R. Smend, "Die Mitte des Alten Testaments," 55 (= *Gesammelte Studien* 1, 1986, 81).

28. For an analysis of this question, although with different emphases, see R. Smend, "Theologie im Alten Testament," in E. Jungel et al., eds., *Verifikationen*, FS G. Ebeling (1982), 11–26 (= "Die Mitte des Alten Testaments" *Gesammelte Studien* 1, 1986, 104ff.).

29. In this regard, see J. Blenkinsopp, "Old Testament Theology and the Jewish-Christian Connection," *JSOT* 28, 1984, 3–15; cf. also W. Dietrich, *EvTh* 49, 1989, 249.

30. Cf. B. S. Childs, *Theology* [[1985]], 8f.

31. Cf. the similar views of H. Wildberger, "Auf dem Wege zu einer biblischen Theologie," *EvTh* 19, 1959, 70–90.

required of this people (and the nations). This presentation will seek to determine whether this center (or fundamental structure) may organize the other fundamental structures of Old Testament faith attaching to or resulting from it, as, for example, the Old Testament ways of speaking about God or the actions of humanity. Yet, even a modest degree of reflection leads to the critical question of how this center relates either to YHWH's activity in creation or to wisdom literature. This presentation will attempt to answer questions such as these.

Synopsis of Preuss's *Old Testament Theology*

Horst Dietrich Preuss
On Exodus and Election

Excerpted with permission from Horst Dietrich Preuss, *Old Testament Theology* (Old Testament Library; Louisville: Westminster John Knox, 1995), vol. 1: 40–49, 137–38. Some footnotes have been omitted.

The Election and Obligation of the People

[[40]] Israel knew its God YHWH as "YHWH from the land of Egypt" (Hos 12:10; 13:4). As the important preamble of the Decalogue indicates (Exod 20:2; Deut 5:6), this confession about YHWH refers to the exodus from Egypt and the deliverance at the sea as the decisive, divine action leading to the establishment of a community between YHWH and Israel in both its outward beginnings and its inward foundation. In this decisive act, the Old Testament witness to God finds both its origins and its center. This means that the primary definition of the divine name in the expression, "I am YHWH, your God," is captured in the statement that follows: "who has led you out of the land of Egypt, out of the house of slaves." This explanation of the divine name is not "added as a secondary definition,"[1] for the relationship between YHWH and Israel did not originate either in a mythical prehistory or from some natural bond. Rather, Yahweh's entrance into history to act on behalf of his people became for Israel an enduring pristine confession (M. Noth). This deliverance was, at the same time, an election; indeed, in this deliverance Israel saw its "primal election." Now we turn to consider how the Old Testament witness speaks about these experiences.

The Exodus Event as the Primal Election

"When Israel went forth from Egypt, the house of Jacob from a people with a strange language, Judah became his sanctuary, Israel his dominion" (Ps 114:1–2). "Has ever a god sought to come to a nation and to take it from the midst of another . . . , as YHWH, your God, has done for you in Egypt. . . . Because he loved your ancestors, he has chosen all of their descendants after them and has led you out of Egypt with his own presence, by his great power" (Deut 4:34, 37). "YHWH your God has chosen you to be a nation for his own possession out of all the nations" (Deut 7:6).

The oldest texts that witness to this *exodus event as the primal election* celebrated (Exod 15:21) and described (the J portion of Exod 13:17–14:31) it as a military action of Yahweh on behalf of his people. With direct language

---

1. In agreement with R. Smend, "Der Auszug aus Ägypten: Bekenntnis mid Geschichte," in *Zur ältesten Geschichte Israels (Gesammelte Studien* 2; 1987), 27–44.[[. . .]]

unencumbered by metaphor or simile, the Song of Miriam[2] extols with thankfulness [[41]] and praise YHWH as a God who acts: "horse and rider he has thrown into the sea." This song, patterned after a victory song, probably originated within the context of this deliverance. Here Yahweh is spoken about in words of adoration and confession.[3] In the form of thankful praise, the song is a direct response to a divine deed, in this case a historical act of deliverance. The event and the response of praise point to the establishment of trust. Finally, the future under this God is extolled at the same time that the past is remembered. [[. . .]]

[[42]] In this manner, YHWH had fought for the people and rescued them, showing himself to be powerful in war, powerful in ruling over nature, and powerful in defeating a foreign nation (Exod 14:30–31). Israel learned that "the Lord will fight for you, and you are to be still" (Exod 14:14; cf. 15:21), according to the testimony of J, who described the event that was to follow in the style of YHWH war. Yet one may also see something of the miraculous in J, for an east wind normally pushes the waves against the west coast, not away from it. "Thus YHWH fights for his own" is the motto that the Yahwist uses, not in turning backward to the deliverance at the sea, but rather for speaking emphatically about the present, telling how this YHWH in this way is important at the present time (cf. Num 24:8). This datum is integrated fully into the *kerygma* [['proclamation']]; the past is described as decisive for the present.

The basic text of the exilic Priestly document, by contrast, accentuates the supernatural character of the event, presenting it as a miracle *in* the sea and [[43]] making clear that YHWH liberates in a marvelous way. Also here the referring of what is narrated to the present is more important than presenting a report that looks to the past. What is reported in P is more of an event between YHWH and "Egypt" in which YHWH prevails (Exod 14:4, 8, 17–18). YHWH's act, in addition, has a pedagogical effect for Israel (Exod 14:15), and, as already seen in P (cf. Genesis 1), the narrative attests to the power of the divine word (Exod 14:26). And if the entire description of P comes close to the promises of a new, second exodus from Babylonia in Deutero-Isaiah, that would be no accident (cf. Exod 14:28ff. with Isa 43:16ff.). P desires to awaken a confidence in an analogous, marvelous liberation of the community in exile, and, like J, is oriented more to the present than to the past. Therefore the lack of concern with data about places and other details is not surprising. P was in agreement with what was really essential, and that was nothing other than what the oldest text, Exod 15:21, had extolled: YHWH was a deity who acts with power in history, who is able to liberate and deliver, and who has his

---

2. It must be stressed that there is not another setting in the history of Israel that is appropriate for this song. The terse language and the fact that neither the place nor the time needs to be mentioned suggest that the song belongs to this literary and historical context. For a different view, see P. Weimar and E. Zenger, *Exodus*: [[Geschichten und Geschichte der Befreiung Israels (SBS 75; 1975)]] 71ff. They argue that the song originates in Jerusalem during the early period of David's rule.

3. "All true, living confession, however, occurs in *one* sentence" (*Praise and Lament in the Psalms*, trans. Keith R. Crim and Richard N. Soulen [Atlanta, 1981], 107).

own way. The redactor who brought together these narratives by different authors also recognized and testified to this fact. In the redactional process, the description by P was given a certain predominance, even though it was often modified by the incorporation of J. YHWH reveals himself in an epiphany as one who works wonders and carries out his judgment against both his and Israel's enemies. Thus he becomes the legitimate, only God of the people of Israel who are now finally constituted as a nation, and Moses is his true, authorized representative. The constituent features of the event of the exodus, namely, oppression, the appeal to YHWH, and deliverance, become intrinsic features of further historical writing and of the confession of Israel (cf. Deut 26:5–9). That a people, nevertheless, would describe the earliest stage of its history as one of bondage ("strangers in Egypt"[4]) in order to be able to emphasize the redemptive act and salvific nature of its God, who, for example, liberates "out of the house of slavery (Egypt)"[5] or has delivered them from the burdens of the Egyptians (Exod 6:67), deserves to be closely noted.

It is no wonder that the Old Testament often and readily reaches back to the exodus event, especially in important contexts, and thereby develops the "exodus tradition(s)." Already in the two oldest festival calendars, the first festival is the Passover festival. This festival not only is oriented to an agricultural economy but also is associated with remembering the exodus (Exod 23:15; 34:18; cf. Deut 16:1 for the Passover). Ancient texts that mention the exodus include the sayings of Balaam (Num 23:21b–22; 24:8) and Amos 9:7. As for Hosea, we have already mentioned the references to "YHWH from the land of Egypt" (Hos 12:10; 13:4). In addition, there are the words of YHWH who has called his son Israel out of Egypt (Hos 11:1) and the remembrance of Israel's "youth" when it was brought out of Egypt (Hos 2:17). It is debated whether Judg 6:13 is an ancient text in Gideon's lament, although it does mention the [[44]] exodus out of Egypt as a reason for his prayer to be answered. This text also looks back at this earlier act of salvation by YHWH in order to make it possible to hope for a new deliverance. Jer 2:6 also reaches back to the exodus in order to explain Israel's foolish apostasy from God. By his action in Egypt, YHWH made himself known (Ezek 20:56); he will act against Assyria even as he has against Egypt (Isa 10:26). Because YHWH led his people out of Egypt in order to be their God and to dwell in their midst (Exod 29:45–46 = P), Israel must be holy, for YHWH also is holy (Lev 11:45). And for the Deuteronomistic redaction of the Book of Jeremiah, the reference to the exodus from Egypt sets forth the hope for a gathering and return home from the exile and the diaspora (Jer 16:14–15). With this we are close to Deutero-Isaiah, who could speak of a new exodus out of Babylonia, an idea anticipated by Hosea (Hos 2:1 6ff.; 9:1–4; 11:1ff.; and 12:10). This new exodus should and would surpass the old exodus from Egypt (Isa 40:3–5; 41:17–20; 43:16–21; 48:20–21; 49:7a,

---

4. Cf. F. A. Spina, "Israelites as *gērîm*, 'Sojourners,' in Social and Historical Context," in C. L. Meyers and M. O'Connor, eds., *FS D. N. Freedman* (Winona Lake, Ind., 1983), 321–35.

5. This occurs thirteen times in the Old Testament, often in Deuteronomistic texts (e.g., Deut 5:6; 6:12; 7:8; 8:14; 13:6, 11; Jer. 34:13).[[. . .]]

9–13; 51:9–10; and 52:7–10, 11–12; cf. 58:8).[6] In Isa 51:9–10 (cf. Pss 74:13; 77:17–21; 136:11; and Isa 63:13 תהום, = *tĕhôm*, "depths") the historical act of deliverance in the crossing through the sea (cf. Zech 10:11) is compared with the primeval act of YHWH at creation and his victory over Rahab. By contrast Ezekiel connected this new exodus to a judgment of rejection (Ezek 20:32–44). The reference back to the exodus in the unfolding of elements of salvation history in Mic 6:3ff. allows YHWH himself to speak of his saving deeds. The preamble to the Decalogue, already mentioned, goes about its arguments in a similar fashion, placing YHWH's reference to his saving act in the exodus prior to his commandments. Thus, as the Gospel precedes the Law, so election is prior to obligation in both time and substance. One not only experienced in the exodus out of Egypt and the miracle at the sea who and what YHWH *was*, one also understood who YHWH invariably *is*. The God of election is also the God who saves and liberates. If one interprets the liberating exodus out of Egypt in distinct terms, then one would speak often of "wonders" or "signs and wonders" that Israel may have experienced.[7] At the same time, however, the extensive use of this language makes clear that "wonders" during the time of the exodus were not isolated events limited to that time; rather, in the continuing providential history of Israel additional "wonders" continued to occur. Individuals and the nation both would hope and could hope for "wonders" to occur in the future.[8] The exodus event proves itself also here to be both the outer and inner foundation of Old Testament faith and hope. These divine actions during the exodus are "particularly the special manifestations of God's works, which, as such, have a fundamental significance that point beyond themselves."[9]

Among the Old Testament legal texts the Covenant Code mentions the exodus only in connection with the "stranger," who should not be oppressed, for Israel itself was a stranger in Egypt (Exod 22:20; 23:9). In Deuteronomy, [[45]] the exodus event is positioned prominently in the center of the book's theological arguments. The event is mentioned frequently not only in the paraenetic sections of the book but also in the actual legal corpus (cf. Deut 13:6, 11; 15:15; 16:1; and 24:18, 22). Election and the gifts of both the commandments and the land are related to the exodus out of Egypt. F. Crüsemann[10] has pointed to what important roles the references to the exodus play in the Holiness Code (Leviticus 17–26). Here the exodus is bound up with the categories of holiness and sanctification (Lev 11:44–45; 18:3; 19:36; 20:24–26; and 22:32–33). Through means of the exodus, Israel becomes

6. Cf. H. D. Preuss, *Deuterojesaja: Eine Einführung in seine Botschaft* (1976), 42–45. [[. . .]]

7. Exod 3:20; Judg 6:13; Neh 9:17; Pss 78:11–12; and 106:7, 21–22. Then Deut 4:34; 6:22; 7:19; 26:8; and 29:2 (מופת [*môphēt*, "wonder"] and אות [*'ôt*, "sign"]. [[. . .]]

8. Exod 34:10; Jer 21:2; Mic 7:15; Pss 9:2; 26:7; 40:6; 71:17; 72:18; 86:10; 96:3; 105:2, 5; 107; 111:4ff.; 136:4; and 145:5. The understanding is characteristically different in the Book of Job: Job 9:10; cf. 5:8–9; and 37:5, 14, 16.

9. D. Conrad, *ThWAT* 6, col. 578. [[. . .]]

10. F. Crüsemann, "Der Exodus als Heiligung," in E. Blum et al., eds., *Die hebräische Bibel*, FS R. Rendtorff (1990), 117–29. What follows is related to this essay.

YHWH's ("separated from": Lev 20:24b) people, and he becomes their God. The exodus is understood as an act of sanctification, a term that is interpreted to mean "set apart." YHWH's deed is both the presupposition and the foundation for everything. There were priestly circles in the time of the exile who reserved for all Israelites this separation or sanctification as both gift and commission and who therefore created an important basis for the Israelite law of the postexilic period.

· ·

[[46]] The narratives of the guidance in the wilderness that follow Exodus 13–14 made clear that this action of divine election placed Israel on an extended journey with YHWH. That Israel showed and continued to show itself to be an ungrateful people toward YHWH is demonstrated in the fact that these stories of the guidance in the wilderness are compelled to speak about the "murmuring" of the people several times and not simply as a single narrative digression. It was only at YHWH's initiative and only by his free gift of grace, grounded in love, that he elected Israel to be his people. Deut 7:7–11 brings this conviction later into a conceptually concentrated, thankful, theological reflection.

. . . [[47]] The event of the exodus was grounded then in Israel's relationship with God and in its knowledge of God."[11] The consequential and necessary rejection of foreign gods is based as well on this event.[12] YHWH's activity of salvation in the exodus event is also the foundation of his commandments to his people.[13] In the exodus out of Egypt, which certainly aims at the entrance into the land, YHWH's gift of the land to Israel has its grounding.[14] Standing in contrast to the exodus event as a demonstration of divine grace is the evidence of Israel's sin.[15] This sin provides the motivation for YHWH's threatened punishment,[16] and this could take the form of a "reverse exodus," namely, being taken out of the land of Israel, into the wilderness, and back to Egypt.[17] Israel's way of life, including, for example, its orientation to kingship, to luxury and urban existence, to the cult, and to other nations, is grounded in and illuminated by the exodus event.[18] It was naturally on the

11. Deut 6:12; 7:6ff.; 8:14 (and often in Deuteronomy); Hos 2:10, 22; 11:3; 12:10; 13:4; Mic 6:6–8; 7:8–20; Amos 3:1–2; Pss 105:37–41; 114:1–8; and 136:10–16.

12. Hos 11:1ff.; 13:4; Exod 20:2–3. (= parallel); Deut 6:14; 7:4; 13:6, 11; and often (also in the Deuteronomistic literature).

13. Cf. the preamble of the Decalogue; Amos 3:1–2; Hos 12:7, 9, 15; and Mic 6:4–5. Cf. also 1 Kgs 8:9; 2 Kgs 21:8; Ezek 20:10–11; Pss 81:6; and 105:43–45.

14. Hos 12:10; Amos 2:10; Deut 6:10–12, 15; and 8:6–10. Cf. already Exod 3:8; 34:10 (J); and Exod 13:17 (E?).

15. Amos 3:1–2; and Mic 6:3–4. Cf. the "murmuring stories" in Exodus and Numbers, and, in addition, 1 Sam 8:7ff.; and 10:17–18. Also cf. 1 Sam 15:1ff.; 2 Sam 7:5–6; and 1 Kgs 12:28.

16. Amos 2:6–10; 3:1–2; Hos 2:4ff.; 7:15–16; 11:1ff.; 12:10; 13:1ff.; Mic 6:5; Jer 2:4ff.; and 11:1ff.

17. Hos 2:16; 11:5; 12:10, 13–14; Amos 9:7, 9–10; and Mic 6:13ff.

18. Lev 19:33–34, 35–36; 25:35ff.; Deut 6:12, 21, 23; 7:8, 19; 8:6–16, 17b; 10:19; 13:6, 11; 15:15; 16:1, 3, 6; 23:5, 8; 24:18, 22; 25:17; 26:8; Hos 2:10, 13; 11:5; 12:10–11, 12; 13:4a,

basis of the exodus event that history as a whole was viewed and interpreted (Amos 9:7; Deuteronomy; Deutero-Isaiah). Often the reference to the exodus has a key place in the context of the passages that have been mentioned. What was to be legitimated or critically evaluated had to be measured by Israel's early period, that is, by the exodus event, the time of Moses, and the journey through the wilderness. This is true of the Sabbath according to the Decalogue in Deuteronomy (Deut 5:15), of the bull idols of Jeroboam I (1 Kgs 12:28), of the prophetic criticism of the sacrificial cult (Amos 5:25; Jer 7:22-23; cf. the rationale for the cultic [[48]] ordinances in Josh 5:1-8; 1 Kgs 8; 9:21), of the Passover, which originally had nothing to do with the exodus (Exodus and parallels),[19] and even of the "bronze serpent" (2 Kgs 18:4). The Deuteronomic literature especially judged many things by the standard set by the exodus and the period that immediately followed. This standard provided the basis for judgment or for the threat of judgment (Judg 2:1-5; and 2 Kgs 17:7-23, 34b-40),[20] for the critical evaluation of Israel's behavior, both during the time of the exodus and in the present (1 Sam 8:7-9; 10:17-19; 12:6-11; and 2 Sam 7:1-7), and for motivating additional saving activity (Judg 6:7-10, 11-13; 11:12-28; 1 Sam 15:1-6; and 1 Kgs 8:21). No apparent consideration was given to the historical accuracy or even probability of what happened. Theology was more important than history.

Particularly succinct is the characterization of "Israel as an exodus community" in Psalm 114. Here, the exodus and the institution of Israel as the sanctuary and dominion[21] of YHWH (vv. 1-2) and the "Lord" and the "God of Jacob" (v. 7) are closely connected. Verse 8 builds on Deutero-Isaiah (Isa 41:18; cf. Ps 107:35). "With a succinctness that is almost unrivalled, the history of salvation is here gathered up in a singular manner," and this indeed occurs through the dimension of temple theology's "negation of time," that is, the cult. "This was nothing other than the psalm theology of the postexilic period finally being successful in its efforts to transform entirely, according to its own theological standards, the history of salvation."[22]

The exodus event also provided significant meaning for expectations concerning the future. The importance of the exodus for the language of Ezekiel (Ezek 20:33ff.) and Deutero-Isaiah has already been indicated.[23] The Holiness Code, exilic in its core, also anchors its expectation of salvation (Lev 26:40ff.) in this event, for it commemorates YHWH's action in the exodus ("before the eyes of the nations") and in the establishment of the covenant. One believes and hopes in the God of the exodus that his grace will endure forever (Ps 136:10-16). He continued to guide his people (Ps 136:16; cf.

11; Amos 2:8; 3:1, 12, 14; 9:1, 7, 8; Mic 6:7, 13ff.; Jer 7:21ff.; and often. Cf. also Exod 22:20; and 23:9, 15. [[. . .]]

19. Cf. Vol. 2: 13.4.

20. Cf. Ezek 20:13ff., 34ff.; also Jer 2:4ff.

21. Thus with H. Spieckermann, *Heilsgegenwart* (FRLANT 148; 1989), 150-51, who on pp. 150-57 offers an engaging interpretation of Psalm 114.

22. The citations are from H. Spieckermann, *Heilsgegenwart*, 151, 155, 157.

23. Cf. above, pp. [[297-98]].

Exod 15ff.), and even after their apostasy he continued to be present by means of his angel, his tent, and his countenance (Exodus 33). It deserves to be noted that any reference to the exodus, covenant, and guidance in the wilderness is completely missing in the wisdom literature (Proverbs; Job; Qoheleth). The people of God and their history play no role in this literature. The books of Jesus the Son of Sirach and the Wisdom of Solomon are the first wisdom texts to take up these themes of salvation history and election, and this was probably due to the recognition of a deficiency in sapiential thinking.

Finally, the so-called credo (Deut 26:5-9; 6:20-24; and Josh 24:2b-13) stresses the reference to the exodus event by building it into the structure of its text. The exodus is given a theologically determinative position that marks the turn to salvation. Although they possibly may have been edited pieces, these [[49]] texts today are certainly no longer viewed as ancient or as the kernel from which the Hexateuch's narratives were developed, as von Rad above all had argued.[24] Num 20:14b-16, perhaps an older creedal text, already gives a central place to the exodus.

The attention given to the salvific acts of YHWH is decisive for these creedal texts, in their present form so clearly influenced by the Deuteronomistic School that certainly uses them as a summation of its own theology. Accordingly, there was a way, acknowledged in thanksgiving and prayer, on which YHWH had guided his people, a path from the threat of wandering to the gift of the land, from an ancestor to a people, and from imprisonment, oppression, and wilderness through the deliverance of the exodus to the gift of the land for the liberated. YHWH demonstrated that he hears their cry and turns to them when they are in need and that in the course of history, seen as purposefully directed, he brings promises to fulfillment by means of designed acts of salvation. Here the theological consideration of the exodus event reaches its high point in the Old Testament (alongside Deutero-Isaiah).

24. For the scholarly discussion (with literature), cf. H. D. Preuss, *Deuteronomium* [[EdF 164; 1982]], 144-47; S. Kreuzer, *Die Frühgeschichte Israels in Bekenntnis und Verkündigung des Alten Testaments* (BZAW 178; 1989); and D. R. Daniels, VT Suppl 41, 1990, 231-42.

. . . .

Excerpt from Chapter 3:
Yahweh as Warrior and Yahweh War

YHWH War against Israel

[[137]] According to the witness of the prophets, the YHWH who fought and fights for his people can and will turn military *against* them.[1] YHWH becomes

1. Cf. J. A. Soggin, "Der prophetische Gedanke über den heiligen Krieg als Gericht gegen israel," *VT* 10, 1960, 79-83 (= *Old Testament and Oriental Studies*, Rome, 1975, 67ff.); and D. L. Christensen, *Transformations of the War Oracle in Old Testament Prophecy* (Missoula, Mont., 1975).

the military leader also of foreign nations, including the Assyrians against Israel (Isa 5:26–30; 10:5–6; 22:7–8; 30:17; 31:1–3; 29:1ff.; Mic 3:12; and 2 Chr
33:11), the "foe from the north" (Jer 1:15; 4:6–7; 6:1ff.; cf. 5:15–16; 22:7), the
Babylonians against Jerusalem and its temple (Jeremiah 27; 51:20–23; and
Ezek 7:21), and, according to Ezekiel (26:7; 28:7; and 29:18–20), Nebuchadrezzar against Tyre. The summons to flee is issued no longer to Israel's oppo-
nent but to Israel itself (e.g., Jer 4:5–6; and 6:1); on the contrary, now it is
Israel's enemies—however, not Israel itself—who are called to battle (e.g., Jer
5:10; and 6:4–6).[2] YHWH now carries out his military judgment against his
own people.[3] The "Day of YHWH" is or already was a war against Israel (Ezek
7:12; 13:5; 34:12; cf. Deut 28:25–26; etc.). The man of war, YHWH, therefore
can fight also against his own people. In spite of what certain prophets
thought (Jer 28:8), YHWH does not simply lead only on the side of and to the
benefit of Israel (cf. Numbers 13/14; 1 Samuel 4). In Lam 2:2ff. this is brought
to stunning and shocking expression. He does not interject anymore his
"hand" and his "arm" for the benefit of his people (e.g., Ps 81:15) but rather
lifts his hand and arm against them (Lam 2:4; 3:3; and Ps 74:11; cf. Job 30:21).
Also, he does not allow the king to be victorious anymore in battle, causing
then his enemies to rejoice (Ps 89:43–44).

War and Peace

With its witness to YHWH as warrior, to YHWH war, and to the ban, the Old
Testament stands within the context of an understanding of the world at that
time while keeping its own distinctive features. There can be no discussion of
a complete overcoming of military thinking within the Old Testament or of a
development to an ever clearer emphasis upon "peace" (שלום = *šālôm*), or of
a journey of Israel away from force, or even of its withdrawing from [[138]]
[[violence—ed.]].[4] The military annihilation of the nations is found also even
in many postexilic texts (Zechariah 14; Joel 4; etc.) on down to the apocalyptic elements in the Book of Daniel. While שלום = *šālôm* is indeed the greatest
possible contrast to war,[5] it must in no way always be identified with "nonwar" (Judg 8:9; 2 Sam 11:7; 1 Kgs 2:5).[6] The word שלום = *šālôm* goes far beyond "nonwar." And if YHWH effectuates "peace," then this extends even over
cosmic disasters (Psalm 29). If he wipes out war and war materiel from the
world, then he also does this through war (Isa 9:3f.; Pss 46:10; 76:4; etc.)[7] and

---

2. See R. Bach, *Die Aufforderungen zur Flucht und zum Kampf im alttestamentlichen Pro-
phetenspruch* (WMANT 9; 1962).

3. Isa 3:25; 13:4; 21:15; 22:2; 30:32; 42:25; Jer 4:19; 6:4, 23; 18:21; 21:4–5; 28:8; 46:3;
49:2, 14; Ezek 27:27; 39:20; Hos 10:9, 14; Joel 2:5; Amos 1:14; Obad 1; and Zech 14:2.

4. Thus often N. Lohfink, e.g., *IKZ* 18, 1989, 105.

5. Cf. 1 Kgs 20:18; Mic 3:5; Zech 9:10; Ps 120:7; Qoh 3:8; then also Deut 20:10–12; Josh
11:19; 2 Sam 8:10; 11:7; 1 Kgs 2:5; Isa 27:4–5; and 1 Chr 18:10.

6. See H. H. Schmid, "Frieden. II: Altes Testament," *TRE* 11, 605–10 (literature).

7. See R. Bach, ". . . , der Bogen zerbricht, Spiesse zerschlägt und Wagen mit Feuer ver-
brennt," in H. W. Wolff, ed., *Probleme biblischer Theologie*, FS G. von Rad (1971), 13–26. Cf.
also Hos 1:5; 2:20; Jer 49:35; Mic 5:9–10; and Zech 9:10.

exterminates by means of war the enemy nations. An addition in Hosea (Hos 1:7) is the first description of the salvation of YHWH in terms that are expressly nonmilitaristic, while Zech 4:6 stresses that the removal of opposing things should happen not through power or force but through YHWH's spirit. However, faith in this nonmilitaristic activity of YHWH cannot be maintained even to the end of the Book of Zechariah (Zech 10:3ff.; 14). That YHWH delivers from the power of the sword (Job 5:20) is directly contested by Qoh 8:8 ("no one is spared in war"). The often-cited reforging of the swords into plowshares (Isa 2:4; Mic 4:3) is neither the only nor the last word of the Old Testament concerning the theme of war and power, as, for example, the formulations of contrast in Joel 4:9ff. show. It is not so certain whether and, if so, to what extent Old Testament Israel even in this area was actually a "society in opposition to" its cultural environment,[8] even if there was no hero worship in Israel. In addition to the hope in eschatological peace,[9] there remains the so-called eschatological power of God. The New Testament is also aware of this. The hermeneutical question concerning the significance and validity of the texts (Mark 13 par.; Revelation) that speak about this matter is passed on there. One can perhaps[10] say that Israel exposes power, looks at it as *the* central human sin, and helps also to dismantle it. It is not correct to see the last prophets, to which Zechariah 9–14 and the Book of Daniel belong, as viewing God's definitive society as a powerless one.[11] Whether the image of God more and more was stripped of its characteristics of power is doubtful even for N. Lohfink, in spite of the Book of Jonah, the Servant of God, and several other texts faced with holding on to judgment against the nations. He writes: "Thus the Old Testament continues to be ambivalent toward power and powerlessness even in its imaging of God."[12] Both Testaments are evaluated in Lohfink's substantial presentation on the theme of power.[13] The central, theological question is stated: How do God and human beings proceed in their quest against evil? And Christians will add what significance the word and work of Jesus Christ have for this question.

---

8. Thus N. Lohfink, "Der gewalttätige Gott des Alten Testaments und die Suche nach einer gewaltfreien Gesellschaft," *JBTh* 2 (1987), 119–20.

9. Isa 26:3, 12; 32:14ff.; chap. 60 (cf., however, also 60:12); 65:17ff.; Ezek 34:25ff.; and 37:26ff.

10. With N. Lohfink, *IKZ* 18, 1989, 106–7.

11. Thus N. Lohfink, "Der gewalttätige Gott des Alten Testaments und die Suche nach einer gewaltfreien Gesellschaft," 133.

12. 721. N. Lohfink, *IKZ* 18, 1989, 108. What Lohfink further says then about power and powerlessness reaches (both significantly and legitimately) beyond the Old Testament.

13. N. Lohfink, "Der gewalttätige Gott des Alten Testaments und die Suche nach einer gewaltfreien Gesellschaft," 106–36, esp., e.g., 107, 121, 133–34, etc. He certainly draws throughout on R. Girard's view of [[violence—ed.]] and freedom from [[violence—ed.]].

WALTER BRUEGGEMANN

b. 1933

Israel's Testimony

After studying with James Muilenburg at Union Theological Seminary, Walter Brueggemann taught for many years at Eden Theological Seminary. He is now the William Marcellus McPheeters Professor of Old Testament Emeritus at Columbia Theological Seminary. Brueggemann has published commentaries and a host of other studies that cover much of the Old Testament. His work has drawn widely from disciplines beyond biblical studies to address contemporary theological, social, and pastoral issues.

Selected Writings by Brueggemann

1992   *Old Testament Theology: Essays on Structure, Theme, and Text*. Edited by Patrick D. Miller. Minneapolis: Fortress.

1993   *Texts under Negotiation: The Bible and Postmodern Imagination*. Minneapolis: Fortress.

1997   *Theology of the Old Testament: Testimony, Dispute, Advocacy*. Philadelphia: Fortress.

2002   *The Land: Place as Gift, Promise, and Challenge in Biblical Faith*. 2d edition. Overtures to Biblical Theology. Minneapolis: Fortress.

2003   *Awed to Heaven, Rooted in Earth: Prayers of Walter Brueggemann*. Edited by Edwin Searcy. Minneapolis: Fortress.

Writings about Brueggemann

Barr, James
1999   Pp. 541–62 in *The Concept of Biblical Theology: An Old Testament Perspective*. Minneapolis: Fortress.

Linafelt, Tod, and Timothy K. Beal (editors)
1998   *God in the Fray: A Tribute to Walter Brueggemann*. Minneapolis: Fortress.

Walter Brueggemann's
Approach to Old Testament Theology

Excerpted with permission from Walter Brueggemann, *Theology of the Old Testament: Testimony, Dispute, Advocacy* (Philadelphia: Fortress, 1997), pp. 117–26. Some footnotes have been omitted.

Israel's Practice of Testimony

[[117]] The primal subject of an Old Testament theology is of course God. But because the Old Testament does not (and never intends to) provide a coherent and comprehensive offer of God, this subject matter is more difficult, complex, and problematic than we might expect. For the most part, the Old Testament text gives us only hints, traces, fragments, and vignettes, with no suggestion of how all these elements might fit together, if indeed they do. What does emerge, in any case, is an awareness that *the elusive but dominating Subject of the Old Testament cannot be comprehended in any preconceived categories.*[1] The God of the Old Testament does not easily conform to the expectations of Christian dogmatic theology; nor to the categories of any Hellenistic perennial philosophy. As a result, most of our categories are unhelpful for the elucidation of this Subject, and we shall have to proceed concretely, a text at a time, a detail at a time. The Character who will emerge from such a patient study at the end will still be elusive and more than a little surprising.

To cite God as the subject of theology; however, is to take only the *theos* of theology. There is also the speech (*logos*) element of theology. Thus our proper subject is *speech about God*, suggesting yet again that our work has to do with rhetoric. The question that will guide our work is, How does ancient Israel, in this text, speak about God? In addition to Israel's speech about God, much in the Old Testament is *spoken by God* to Israel. For our purposes, I do not make a distinction between the two modes of speech, because even where God speaks, the text is *Israel's testimony* that God has spoken so. Perhaps a greater distinction should be made, but in terms of our discussion, both sorts of speech function in the same way as testimony. It is remarkable that the Old Testament does not accent thought or concept or idea, but characteristically *speech*. God is the One about whom Israel speaks. Thus, in the formulation of Gerhard von Rad's credos, the introduction to the formula is "you shall make this response" (Deut 26:5), "then you shall say" (Deut 6:21), "And Joshua said" (Josh 24:1).[2] In Israel's more intimate practice of faith in the Psalms, moreover, the key activity is speech. It is "a joyful

---

1. See Samuel Terrien, *The Elusive Presence: Toward a New Biblical Theology* (New York: Harper and Row, 1978).

2. Gerhard von Rad, "The Form-Critical Problem of the Hexateuch," *The Problem of the Hexateuch and Other Essays* (New York: McGraw-Hill, 1966) 1–8.

noise" (Ps 100:1), "I will sing" (Ps 101:1), "I said in my prosperity" (Ps 30:6), "To you, O Lord, I cried" (Ps 30:8). [[118]] What we have available to us is the speech of this community, which has become text, and which is our proper subject of study.

Note well that in focusing on speech, we tend to bracket out all questions of historicity.[3] We are not asking, "What happened?" but "What is said?" To inquire into the historicity of the text is a legitimate enterprise, but it does not, I suggest, belong to the work of Old Testament theology. In like manner, we bracket out all questions of ontology, which ask about the "really real." It may well be, in the end, that there is no historicity to Israel's faith claim, but that is not a position taken here. And it may well be that there is no "being" behind Israel's faith assertion, but that is not a claim made here. We have, however, few tools for recovering "what happened" and even fewer for recovering "what is," and therefore those issues must be held in abeyance, pending the credibility and persuasiveness of Israel's testimony, on which everything depends.

For this community and its derivative ecclesial communities that purport to stand with and under this text, the speech is the reality to be studied. Therefore while our subject is limited, it is not modest. For in this text, there is ample utterance about God, much of it on the lips of Israel, some of it on the lips of God, and some of it on the lips of God's (and Israel's) adversaries. We shall be asking, *what* is uttered about God? And this will require us to pay attention to *how* Israel [[119]] uttered about God, for the "what" of Israel's God-talk is completely linked to the "how" of that speech.[4]

I suggest that the largest rubric under which we can consider Israel's speech about God is that of testimony. Appeal to testimony as a mode of knowledge, and inevitably as a mode of certainty that is accepted as revelatory, requires a wholesale break with all positivistic epistemology in the ancient world or in the contemporary world. In an appeal to testimony, one must begin at a different place and so end up with a different sort of certitude.[5] Here

3. Clearly Israel's speech about Yahweh is deeply embedded in lived socioeconomic-political realities—the stuff that comprises history. The exilic experience, for example, clearly impinged on what Israel said about Yahweh and, conversely, on how Yahweh addressed Israel. Israel's speech about Yahweh is characteristically situated historically. [[. . .]]

4. No doubt the "how" and the "what" of biblical testimony are intimately related. One of the problems of much Old Testament theology is that it has been too cognitive and ideational, paying insufficient attention to the ways of Israel's rhetoric. We have the curious situation of rhetorical critics who pay primary attention to the ways of Israel's speech, but who look askance at theological claims; and, conversely, theological interpreters so focused on content that they neglect mode of speech. For a way to relate the two, see Gail R. O'Day, *The Word Disclosed: John's Story and Narrative Preaching* (Philadelphia: Fortress Press, 1987); and *Revelation in the Fourth Gospel: Narrative Mode and Theological Claim* (Philadelphia: Fortress Press, 1986).

5. The most helpful discussion of these issues known to me is C. A. J. Coady, *Testimony: A Philosophical Study* (Oxford: Clarendon Press, 1992). Coady argues for an alternative mode of knowledge and certitude, which for being alternative is no less legitimate. Coady undertakes a serious critique of R. G. Collingwood's dominant positivistic objectivism.

I am much informed by an essay of [[120]] Paul Ricoeur.[6] Nevertheless, testimony as a metaphor for Israel's utterance about Yahweh is deeply situated in the text itself. Specifically, the disputation speech is a dominant form of witness in Second Isaiah, precisely in the exile when truth is in crisis and evidence is uncertain. Thus I regard testimony not simply as a happy or clever convenience for my exposition, but as an appropriate way to replicate the practice of ancient Israel.[7]

Testimony and Trial Metaphor

The proper setting of testimony is a court of law, in which various and diverse witnesses are called to "tell what happened," to give their version of what is true. In any trial situation the evidence given by witnesses is a mixed matter of memory, reconstruction, imagination, and wish. The court must then determine, with no other data except testimony, which version is reality. It is on the basis of *testimony* that the court reaches what is *real*.

As subpoints of the general rubric of testimony, I note the following:

(a) The appeal to testimony as a ground of certitude has particular and peculiar importance for the thought of Karl Barth. (I am grateful to Mark D. J. Smith for specific references.) See *Church Dogmatics* 1/1 (Edinburgh: T. & T. Clark, 1975) 98–124; *Church Dogmatics* 1/2 (Edinburgh: T. & T. Clark, 1956) 457–740, especially 457–72, 514–26. See also Martin Rumscheidt, *Revelation and Theology: An Analysis of the Barth-Harnack Correspondence of 1923* (Cambridge: Cambridge University Press, 1972) 29–53, especially 45–47. For efforts to understand Barth's peculiar assumptions, see David Kelsey, *The Uses of Scripture in Recent Theology* (Philadelphia: Fortress Press, 1975); David Ford, "Barth's Interpretation of Scripture," *Karl Barth—Studies of His Theological Method* (ed. S. W. Sykes; Oxford: Clarendon Press, 1979); and Ford, *Barth and God's Story* (Frankfurt: Peter Lang, 1981).

(b) Andrew Lincoln has helpfully pointed out that testimony is of crucial importance in the Fourth Gospel. See Andrew T. Lincoln, "Trials, Plots, and the Narrative of the Fourth Gospel," *Journal for the Study of the New Testament* 56 (1994) 3–30; A. A. Trites, *The New Testament Concept of Witness* (Cambridge: Cambridge University Press, 1977) 78–127; and Robert V. Moss, "The Witnessing Church in the New Testament," *Theology and Life* 3 (1960) 262–68. The importance of the linkage to the Fourth Gospel is the recognition that the epistemological claims made for Jesus in the early church also depend on the acceptance of testimony. The elemental case for this is the list of witnesses to the resurrection in 1 Cor 15:3–6. [[. . .]]

6. Paul Ricoeur, *Essays on Biblical Interpretation* (Philadelphia: Fortress Press, 1981) 119–54. Ricoeur's study has been carefully exposited by Jean-Daniel Plüss, *Therapeutic and Prophetic Narratives in Worship* (New York: Peter Lang, 1988), especially chap. 2. On the problems and possibilities of testimony in the pursuit of establishing "truth," see Richard K. Fenn, *Liturgies and Trials: The Secularization of Religious Language* (Oxford: Blackwell, 1982); and *The Death of Herod: An Essay in the Sociology of Religion* (Cambridge: Cambridge University Press, 1992).

7. Second Isaiah surely stands at the center of Israel's effort to utter Yahweh faithfully and effectively, in a most demanding and dangerous situation. Israel gave testimony to "the truth of Yahweh," which intended to subvert and undermine the dominant truth of Babylon's preeminence and Israel's commensurate despair. On this genre and its cruciality for Second Isaiah, see Claus Westermann, "Sprache und Struktur der Prophetie Deuterojesajas," *Forschung am Alten Testament: Gesammelte Studien* (ThB 24; Munich: Christian Kaiser, 1964) 124–44. . . .

Working with the metaphor of trial, we consider first the peculiar phenomenon of a witness. Here I make general comments, without particular
reference to Israel's peculiar witness about Yahweh. The situation of a trial
means that there is a reality in question, and there are different, competing
accounts of what that reality is (or was). In the trial situation, presumably,
some actual event or experience occurred, to which appeal is made and
which is under dispute. The witness allegedly had access to that actual event,
was there, saw it and experienced it, and so is qualified to give testimony. The
actual event, however, is enormously supple and elusive and admits of many
retellings, some of which are only shaded differently, but some of which are
drastically different.

[[121]] The court, however, has no access to the "actual event" besides
the testimony. It cannot go behind the testimony to the event, but must take
the testimony as the "real portrayal." Indeed, it is futile for the court to specu-
late behind the testimony.

From the perspective of the witness, we may observe three matters. First,
the witness is able to choose the version of construal to be uttered. This
choice may be made on advice of counsel or under the coaching of an attorney. It may be a calculated utterance, designed to produce a certain outcome,
or it may be a happenstance utterance, made with no intentionality, but one
by which the witness must subsequently stand. It is important to recognize
that the witness had other options and could have spoken differently, could
have chosen other words and images to portray reality with another nuance.

Second, when the witness utters testimony, the testimony is a public presentation that shapes, enjoins, or constitutes reality. In this sense, the testimony is *originary*: it causes to be, in the courtroom, what was not until this
utterance. In this sense, the utterance leads reality in the courtroom, so that
the reality to which testimony is made depends completely on the utterance.

Third, when the court makes a decision and agrees to accept some version of reality based on some testimony, the testimony is accepted as true—
that is, it becomes true. In the decision of the court, by the process of the verdict, the testimony is turned into reality. The defendant is pronounced to be
acquitted or guilty. In the parlance of the court, the verdict is the establishment of a legal reality.

If we describe this process theologically—or, more specifically, in the
practice of the Old Testament—we may say that testimony becomes revelation. That is, the testimony that Israel bears to the character of God is taken
by the ecclesial community of the text as a reliable disclosure about the true
character of God. Here we touch on the difficulty of the authority of Scripture, which has usually been articulated in the scholastic categories of inspiration and revelation. It is simpler and more helpful, I believe, to recognize
that when utterance in the Bible is taken as truthful, human testimony is
taken as revelation that discloses the true reality of God.[8]

---

8. The phrase "taken as" is informed for me by the analysis of David Bryant, *Faith and
the Play of Imagination: On the Role of Imagination in Religion* (Macon, Ga.: Mercer University

Thus, much of the Old Testament, the part that von Rad listed under "response," is explicitly human utterance.[9] For example, the familiar utterance of Ps 23:1, "The Lord is my shepherd," is a human utterance, and a metaphor at that. That utterance is taken by the faithful as revelation, as a true and reliable disclosure of who God is. In less direct fashion, historical criticism has seen that all utterance in the Old Testament about God, even utterance placed in the mouth of God, has [[122]] a human speaker or writer as its source. But that human utterance, as for example in Isa 40:1–11 or Job 38–41, is taken as a true and reliable disclosure. It is by no means clear how this odd transposition from testimony to revelation is accomplished, though we assume it all the time in our theological treatment of the Bible. This means that witnesses, who had other options available, who for whatever reasons chose to utter the matter in just this way, established through their utterance what is "true" about the character of God.

Our purpose in examining this strange transposition from testimony to revelation, from utterance to reality, is to indicate that for Old Testament faith, *the utterance is everything.*[10] The utterance leads to the reality, the reality of God that relies on the reliability of the utterance. Presumably other utterances could have been accepted as true, but these particular utterances are the ones that have been preserved, trusted, treasured, and given to us. The upshot of this process is, first, that Israel's claim of reality is as fragile as an utterance, and we must be exceedingly wary of flights from utterance to some presumed pre-textual reality. Second, this process makes it clear that a student of Old Testament theology must pay close attention to the shape, character, and details of the utterance, for it is in, with, and under the utterance that we have the God of Israel, and nowhere else.

Normative Shape of Israel's Utterance

We may now consider the peculiar and characteristic way in which Israel formulates its testimony about God. Here I suggest what appears to be a normative way in which such utterance is given in Israel, a way that constitutes the primary witness of Israel. We shall have to make important allowances, however, for much in Israel's testimony that does not conform to this way of speech. We must pay attention to Israel's characteristic speech about God.

Press, 1989) 115 and passim. Bryant sees that to "take" something as reality is an active process of establishing reality. A lesser verb is "to see as," as exposited by Garrett Green, *Imagining God: Theology and the Religious Imagination* (San Francisco: Harper and Row, 1989) 139–42 and passim.

9. Gerhard von Rad, *Old Testament Theology* (2 vols.; San Francisco: Harper and Row, 1962), 2:355–459, treated the Psalms and wisdom under the rubric of "response." The rubric does not fit the material very well, as has often been noted, but the notion employed by von Rad is important.

10. On the cruciality of utterance, see the general accent on "articulacy" for moral discourse in Charles Taylor, *Sources of the Self: The Making of the Modern Identity* (Cambridge: Harvard University Press, 1989), chap. 4.

The term *characteristic* is important for my argument.[11] I do not say *earliest* or *most original*, as I do not want to become enmeshed in the difficulties that von Rad had with his insistence on the "early" credos of Israel. Rather, by *characteristic*, I mean the most usual modes of speech, so that one test is the quantity of use. Beyond quantity, I mean by *characteristic* the ways Israel spoke in its most freighted, exalted, or exposed situations. Israel's most characteristic testimony is the speech to which Israel reverted when circumstance required its most habituated speech.

[[123]] It is important, first of all, to recognize that Israel's utterance about God is characteristically stated in full sentences, and the sentence is the unit of testimony that most reliably is taken as revelation. Here we do well to follow James Barr in his warning against overreliance on isolated words.[12] I insist that God is embedded in Israel's testimony of full sentences and cannot be extracted from such full sentences. Moreover, we may identify the characteristic form of such sentences, even if they can be arranged in a variety of imaginative ways. The full sentence of testimony, which characteristically becomes revelation in Israel, is organized around an active verb that bespeaks an action that is transformative, intrusive, or inverting.[13] Thus special attention may be paid to causative verbs in the *hiph'il* stem. In what follows, we shall give detailed attention to the regular stock of verbs used by Israel in its testimony. Each of these verbs regularly attests to the claim that the enactment of the verb creates a new situation or a changed circumstance that did not exist prior to its enactment.

Second, Yahweh the God of Israel, who may variously be designated by many titles and metaphors, is characteristically the subject of the active verb.[14] Thus the characteristic claim of Israel's testimony is that Yahweh is an

11. I use the term *characteristic* to recognize that one cannot say "always" about such speech, because exceptions are inevitable. On the notion of characteristic speech, see Walter Brueggemann, "Crisis-Evoked, Crisis-Resolving Speech," *BTB* 24 (1994) 95–105.

12. James Barr, *The Semantics of Biblical Language* (Oxford: Oxford University Press, 1961). It is Barr's now well-established urging that words can only be understood in the context of their usage in sentences. In what follows, my consideration of verbs, adjectives, and nouns that speak of Yahweh is an effort to treat Israel's characteristic terms in context.

13. On the privileged function of the verb, see Michel Foucault, *The Order of Things: An Archaeology of the Human Sciences* (trans. A. M. S. Smith; New York: Vintage Books, 1973) 92–96. Foucault observes on p. 93:

> The verb is the indispensable condition for all discourse; and wherever it does not exist at least by implication, it is not possible to say that there is a language. All normal presuppositions conceal the invisible presence of the verb.

Foucault also reflects on the verb *to be*, a matter that interests us in terms of nominal sentences. On the cruciality of verbs for Old Testament theology, see Terence E. Fretheim, "The Repentance of God: A Key to Evaluating Old Testament God-Talk," *HBT* 10 (1988) 47–70.

14. My way of approaching the character and identity of Yahweh provisionally precludes other approaches. Thus, for example, I will not deal with the several titles for Yahweh that reflect Israel's history of religion. On these, see Tryggve N. D. Mettinger, *In Search of God: The Meaning and Message of the Everlasting Names* (Philadelphia: Fortress Press, 1988). I am aware of the complex history of the antecedents of Yahweh; see Mark S. Smith, *The Early*

active agent who is the subject of an active verb, and so the testimony is that Yahweh, the God of Israel, has acted in decisive and transformative ways.[15] Remember that we are [[124]] here paying attention to the utterance of testimony given by Israel as witness. This strange grammatical practice serves to give a version of reality that flies in the face of other versions of reality, and most often it wants to defeat the other versions of reality, which it judges to be false. There is, to be sure, a large and vexed literature about "the acts of God," literature that tends to proceed either by recognizing that such utterances make no sense historically, or by reifying the phrase into a philosophical concept.[16] Israel's testimony, however, is not to be understood as a claim subject to historical explication or to philosophical understanding. It is rather [[125]] an utterance that proposes that this particular past be construed

---

History of God: Yahweh and Other Deities in Ancient Israel (San Francisco: Harper and Row, 1990); and Tryggve N. D. Mettinger, *The Dethronement of Sabaoth: Studies in the Shem and Kabod Theologies* (Lund, Sweden: CWK Gleerup, 1982). These antecedents to Yahweh, in my judgment, belong to questions of the history of Israel's religion and do not directly concern Old Testament theology.

15. I have arranged my discussion of Israel's God-talk around the issue of verbs. It is important to recognize that in Israel's God-talk and in God's talk to Israel, an important body of material is expressed in nominal sentences, sentences without verbs. While I will not deal with these extensively or explicitly, what I have said of verbal sentences applies, *mutatis mutandis*, to nominal sentences. That is, Yahweh is, in nominal as in verbal sentences, embedded in full sentences and cannot be extracted from them. In these sentences, however, the consequence for characterizing Yahweh tends to be presence rather than action. It may be that Foucault's general judgment that nominal sentences conceal hidden verbs does not apply directly to Hebrew usage, but I do not doubt that the usages in verbal and nominal sentences are commensurate. [[. . .]]

16. The notion of "God acting" is a long-honored one in Old Testament theology, especially with reference to the work of Gerhard von Rad and G. Ernest Wright. See especially Wright, *God Who Acts: Biblical Theology as Recital* (SBT 8; London: SCM Press, 1952). More recently, the notion has been recognized as having immense problems. The literature is as immense as the problems. The notion of "God's action in history" has been a privileged reference point in Old Testament theology, especially under the influence of von Rad and Wright. But while Old Testament theology had gone a long while with rather innocent reference to such a notion, it had at the same time been deeply problematized by theologians.

The familiar reference point for that problematizing is an early article by Langdon Gilkey, "Cosmology, Ontology, and the Travail of Biblical Language," *JR* 41(1961) 194–205. The subsequent discussion has largely been conducted by philosophically inclined theologians, with Scripture scholars contributing little. The most helpful discussion known to me is Thomas Tracy, *God, Action, and Embodiment* (Grand Rapids: Eerdmans, 1984). [[. . .]]

It is evident that a naive biblical notion of God's action is not plausible in the categories of modernism. Thus one is faced with either abandoning the notion of God's action or trimming it down to irrelevance, which an Old Testament theology can scarcely do, or refusing the categories of modernity that make one susceptible to the charge of fideism. The rich and suggestive discussion now available does not go far beyond these choices. In what follows, I have sought to explicate the rhetoric of ancient Israel in terms of its own claims, without submitting that rhetoric to the critique of modernist epistemological categories. I am aware that such a procedure begs the most difficult questions. I have taken this tack because, in terms of explicating Old Testament faith, any other strategy would end in being immobilized.

according to this utterance. For our large purposes we should note, moreover, that such testimonial utterance in Israel is characteristically quite concrete, and only on the basis of many such concrete evidences does Israel dare
to generalize.

The third element of this standard testimony of Israel is that the active
verb has a direct object, the one acted on, the one for whom transformation
has been wrought. In the first instant, the direct object may be a personal
pronoun—me, us—as the witness speaks about his or her own changed circumstance. Or this direct object may be expressed more formally as "Israel,"
who is regularly the recipient of Yahweh's direct activity. But then, as we shall
see, the direct object may vary greatly to include all of creation or even non-
human parts of it, or the nations who are acted on by God in this rhetoric.

In this complicated grammar, we are close to the core claim of Israel's
faith. In this faith, all of reality is comprehended in this simple sentence, organized around the verb. It is the verb that binds Yahweh to the object—variously, individual persons, Israel, creation, or the nations. The two parties,
however, are bound in a relation that is profoundly asymmetrical, for Yahweh, as the subject of the verb, is the party who holds the initiative and who
characteristically acts on the other party. The object is in the sentence to receive whatever Yahweh chooses to enact.

We notice immediately the manifold oddness of this claim, which constitutes the central fascination of Old Testament theology. First, the sentence
governed by the verb promptly refuses any autonomy for the object, for all of
the objects (which comprehend everything) are subject to the force of the
verb and to the intent of the Subject. Second, God as the subject of the sentence is engaged in activity that binds God to these objects. Israel rarely and
only belatedly can speak about God per se, but regularly speaks about God
engaged transformatively with and on behalf [[126]] of the object. Third, the
linkage of the subject God to the active verbs, while not unfamiliar to us, is
intellectually problematic. It appears, according to our conventional horizons, to be an ill match of categories because the verb bespeaks forceful activity, whereas God is classically understood as Being or Substance. But of course
Israel's way of utterance is not restrained by our conventional assumptions.
Clearly Israel in its utterance is up to something that it is not willing to accommodate to our more commonsense notion of reality. And clearly it is willing to make such an utterance because the Subject so compels Israel that
Israel must render a version of reality that is odd, given our more static or
controlling ways of speech.

Thus while we recognize this peculiarity and Israel's repeated insistence
on it, we must also recognize the fragility of the witness. No doubt other, more
credible witnesses to reality were always available, even in the ancient world.
The Old Testament is that literature which has in large rendered a verdict accepting this testimony as reliable. While we are paying attention to this testimony and hosting it as revelation, we must be aware that within and outside
of Israel, alternative construals of reality were always more readily credible.

Synopsis of Brueggemann's *Theology of the Old Testament*

Walter Brueggemann
On Israel's Testimony

Excerpted with permission from Walter Bruggemann, *Theology of the Old Testament: Testimony, Dispute, Advocacy* (Philadelphia: Fortress, 1997), pp. 145–51, 746–47.

Testimony in Verbal Sentences

[[145]] At the core of Israel's theological grammar are sentences governed by strong verbs of transformation. Such sentences are so familiar to us that we may fail to notice the oddity of their grammar and therefore neglect such a theological beginning point. This focus on sentences signifies that Israel is characteristically concerned with the action of God—the concrete, specific action of God—and not God's character, nature, being, or attributes, except as those are evidenced in concrete actions. This focus on verbs, moreover, commits us in profound ways to a *narrative* portrayal of Yahweh, in which Yahweh is the one who is said to have done these deeds. In what follows, I will consider, as a beginning point, the verbs that stand characteristically at the center of Israel's narrative testimony to Yahweh's action.[1] This is not to claim that such narrative testimony is the only way or even the most important way that Israel witnessed to Yahweh. It does, however, provide us with a basic orientation from which to begin, an orientation that I will critique in subsequent discussion.

Yahweh, the God Who Creates

In its most mature testimony, the witness of the Old Testament asserts of Yahweh,

> . . . who created (*bara'*) the heavens and stretched them out,
> who spread out the earth and what comes from it,
> who gives breath to the people upon it
> and spirit to those who walk in it:
> I am the Lord. . . . (Isa 42:5–6a)

---

1. It will be evident that I am here close to the ways in which Gerhard von Rad, "The Form-Critical Problem of the Hexateuch," *The Problem of the Hexateuch and Other Essays* (New York: McGraw-Hill, 1966) 1–78; and *Old Testament Theology* 1 (San Francisco: Harper and Row, 1962), presented the faith of the Old Testament. A major difference exists, however, between von Rad's presentation and the approach taken here. Von Rad (perhaps inevitably) was trapped in the conventional insistence of scholarship that the claims for God in the Old Testament were rooted in history and in God's actions in history. It should be clear at the outset that my concern is with the rhetoric of the claims as testimony. It is entirely plausible that von Rad's hypothesis of credo and recital can be understood as uttered testimony, but the categories then operative in scholarship precluded such a lean perspective.

[[146]] Israel's testimony to Yahweh as creator concerns Yahweh's ultimate power to work an utter *novum*, one that on any other terms is impossible. In this testimony, the world is characterized, according to Yahweh's intention and action, as a hospitable, viable place for life, because of Yahweh's will and capacity to evoke and sustain life.

Verbs of Creation

In this doxology, as in many assertions in Isaiah of the exile, the governing verb is *bara'*, the most majestic of terms for God's action as Creator, a verb used with no other subject except Yahweh, the God of Israel. It is Yahweh, the God of Israel, who creates the heavens and the earth and all that is, who summons, orders, sustains, and governs all of reality.[2] In this poetic assertion, as in many other uses, the awesome verb *bara'* is supported by parallel verbs that bear roughly the same witness but that lack the singular majesty of *bara'*. In this text the other verbs are "stretch out" (*nṭh*), "spread out" (*rq'*), "gives" (*ntn*), all in the participial form, indicating Yahweh's continuing action.

Among the more important verbs that are employed alongside *bara'* in the testimony of Israel are the following:

(a) By the word of the Lord the heavens were made (*'śh*),
    and all their host by the breath of his mouth . . .
    For he spoke (*'mr*), and it came to be;
    he commanded (*ṣwh*), and it stood firm. (Ps 33:6, 9)

Yahweh causes to be by utterance. The imagery is of a powerful sovereign who utters a decree from the throne, issues a fiat, and in the very utterance the thing is done. In this psalm, three words are used, *dbr*, *'mr*, *ṣwh*, all concerning powerful, sovereign, generative speech. Even in the verses we cite, however, we note also the supportive verbs "gather" (*kûn*) and "put" (*ntn*), so that God's speech is not apart from action.

(b) . . . who created (*bara'*) the heavens (he is God!),
    who formed (*yṣr*) the earth and made (*'śh*) it,
    (he established [*kûn*] it;
    he did not create [*bara'*] it a chaos,
    he formed [*yṣr*] it to be inhabited!). . . . (Isa 45:18)

---

2. It can be insisted on that the generative capacity to bring to being what was not (cf. Rom 4:17) belongs intrinsically to Yahweh's character, so that where Yahweh is, that generative power is in effect. The ground for such an elemental claim for Yahweh is the judgment that the name YHWH derives from the verb *to be* (*hyh*), which may be taken as a *hiph'il*, causative assertion, i.e., cause to be. That reading of the divine name has been most fully argued by Frank M. Cross, who follows the arguments of Paul Haupt and William Foxwell Albright. On such a reading, it is suggested that it is impossible to host the name Yahweh without being aware of Yahweh's generative capacity and inclination. For a helpful survey of the pertinent themes and issues, see Richard J. Clifford, "The Hebrew Scriptures and the Theology of Creation," *TS* 46 (1985) 507–23.

In this text, along with *bara'*, the verb *yṣr* occurs twice. This verb reflects the imagery of a potter forming clay, thus working an existing material. The term [[147]] bespeaks active, material engagement with the stuff of creation, in an artistic endeavor. The term is used most often by Israel in the creation of humankind, or more especially in the creation of Israel. In this text, however, "the earth" in parallel to "the heavens" is the object of the verb. These two verbs, *bara'* and *yṣr*, each used twice, are supported by the verbs *kûn* and *'śh*.

> (c) O Lord of hosts, God of Israel, who are enthroned above the cherubim, you are God, you alone, of all the kingdoms of the earth; you have made (*'śh*) heaven and earth. (Isa 37:16)

This verb, *'śh*, often used in parallel to *bara'* and *yṣr*, refers to the process of actual manufacture of the product, thus portraying God as a working agent who produces heaven and earth as the outcome of work.

> (d) The same field of imagination is operative with the verb *qnh*:

> Blessed be Abram by God Most High,
> maker (*qnh*) of heaven and earth. . . .
> I have sworn to the Lord, God Most High,
> maker (*qnh*) of heaven and earth. . . . (Gen 14:19, 22)

This doxology likely referred to an earlier God (El Elyon) and was taken over for Yahweh. The usage here (as in Deut 32:6) suggests a generative act of begetting, and perhaps thereby establishing ownership and property rights to creation.[3]

> (e) Was it not you who cut (*ḥṣb*) Rahab in pieces,
> who pierced (*ḥll*) the dragon? (Isa 51:9)

This text reflects an ancient tradition that God, in the act of creation, engages in combat with the dragon of chaos and defeats the threat of chaos.[4] Two reservations about this usage in the Old Testament may be registered. First, the imagery of struggle in combat, as it relates to creation, is subdued and marginal in the Old Testament.[5] In this text, what must have been creation imagery is tilted toward the specificity of Israel's Exodus memory, so that "the sea" and "the waters of the great deep" serve doubly in Israel's rhetoric as the watery, threatening chaos in the arena of creation and as the escape route of the Exodus.[6] In both usages, the God of Israel is confessed to be in

---

3. On the term *qnh*, see Gale A. Yee, "The Theology of Creation in Proverbs 8:22–31," *Creation in the Biblical Traditions* (ed. Richard J. Clifford and John J. Collins; CBQMS 24; Washington, D.C.: Catholic Biblical Association of America, 1992) 89 n. 7.

4. On chaos as monster, see John Day, *God's Conflict with the Dragon and the Sea: Echoes of a Canaanite Myth* (Cambridge: Cambridge University Press, 1985); and Mary K. Wakeman, *God's Battle with the Monster* (Leiden: E. J. Brill, 1973).

5. Jon D. Levenson, *Creation and the Persistence of Evil: The Jewish Drama of Divine Omnipotence* (San Francisco: Harper and Row, 1988), has well summarized the data.

6. Frank Moore Cross, *Canaanite Myth and Hebrew Epic* (Cambridge: Harvard University Press, 1973) 112–44, has shown how reference to the waters of chaos and the "historical

ready control, able to administer the waters. We [[148]] also note the parallel verb "pierce" (*ḥll*), which testifies to the motif of combat (cf. Job 26:13).

(f) You were unmindful of the Rock that bore (*yld*) you,
    you forgot the God who gave you birth (*ḥll*). (Deut 32:18)

Before the mountains were brought forth (*yld*),
or ever you had formed (*ḥll*) the earth and the world,
from everlasting to everlasting you are God. (Ps 90:2)

These two texts have in parallel the verbs *yld* and *ḥll*. In each case, the first verb refers to the paternal role in begetting, and the second refers to the maternal role of birthing. These terms for creating are not common in the Old Testament witness. I cite them because they are pertinent in current discussions concerning adequate metaphors for God, and they exhibit the remarkable range of verbs used in Israel's testimony concerning evidence that Yahweh creates.

(g) By the word of the Lord the heavens were made,
    and all their host by the breath of his mouth. (Ps 33:6)

Then God said, "Let there be light"; and there was light. (Gen 1:3)

Israel attests that Yahweh creates the world by speech—by royal utterance, a powerful decree that in its very utterance is eagerly and dutifully enacted. This "theology of the word" is exceedingly influential in subsequent theological reflection. It is important to recognize, however, that even this most exalted way of speaking about Yahweh's generative sovereignty is not unique to Israel. Even this mode of creation, given in the testimony of Israel, has important antecedent and parallel in the ancient Egyptian theology of Memphis concerning the god Ptah.[7] Israel uses a variety of terms in this presentation of Yahweh as Creator by speech, all of which bespeak the unquestioned authority of the sovereign to effect a genuine newness in the world, simply by making desire and intention known to the royal court so eager to obey.

This list of verbs is a fair representation of the primary terms Israel used in its testimonies concerning God's agency as one who creates. The list is by no means comprehensive but is sufficient for our purposes. In its ongoing stylized usage, this range of testimony does not require that each term should be taken at its most particular, concrete reference. Nonetheless, these concrete reference points are present in the text and should not be ignored. In this range of terms (to which others might be added), Israel appealed to all of the models of creation that were already present and available in the ancient Near East, including royal fiat, combat struggle, artistic rendering, material productivity, economic purchase, and the process [[149]] of birthing. It is also clear that

---

waters" of the Exodus converge and are identified. Thus it is not possible to make a clean distinction between what is myth and what is history.

7. See James Pritchard, *Ancient Near Eastern Texts Relating to the Old Testament* (2d ed.; Princeton, N.J.: Princeton University Press, 1955) 5.

Israel, with the exception of *bara'*, had no special, privileged category for creation, but made use of terms from many arenas of ordinary daily life.

Israel settled on no single articulation of creation as a proper one, but daringly made use of rich and diverse vocabulary in order to make its normative utterance about God. As we shall see repeatedly, *Old Testament theology, when it pays attention to Israel's venturesome rhetoric, refuses any reductionism to a single or simple articulation*; it offers a witness that is enormously open, inviting, and suggestive, rather than one that yields settlement, closure, or precision.

It was not difficult for Israel to make its testimony concerning Yahweh as "the God who creates." The religious world of the ancient Near East was already permeated with such talk of creation and such conviction about the creation work of the gods. It is plausible to assume that Israel could readily appropriate such speech and conviction.

We must recognize, however, that the great liturgical rhetoric of creation was sponsored by the great royal regimes, which easily co-opted the evocative theological assertions of created order for their specific political accomplishments and interests. Thus creation faith was recruited for royal ideology and propaganda. There is no reason to imagine that the royal establishment in Jerusalem was immune to this temptation (cf. 1 Kgs 8:12–13, Ps 89:3–37). In Psalm 89, the guarantees given by God to the house of David come easily along with the celebration of the goodness and reliability of Yahweh's created order.

Given the easy utilization of creation rhetoric and creation faith, Israel nonetheless faced a demanding task. The demanding element in this testimony is not to claim creation faith as its own; it is to claim creation for the God of Israel, as willed, gifted, and governed by Yahweh and made for glad dependence and fruitful obedience to Yahweh. It is to articulate creation faith in a peculiar way, so that it is congruent with the rest of the normative testimony that Israel would utter about its God. We shall consider in some detail a series of texts that indicate the ways in which Israel's testimony fashioned rhetoric to meet this important theological demand.

The Context of Exile

In the Old Testament, creation faith receives its fullest articulation in Isaiah of the exile.[8] In the context of exile, Israel faced a twofold crisis that invited Israel to despair and to abandonment of its confidence in Yahweh. The concrete ground for the despair is the formidable reality of Babylonian military-political power. Behind that visible authority, however, is the legitimating power of the Babylonian gods who guaranteed the regime and who appear to be stronger than the counterpower of Israel's own God.

[[150]] In the face of that challenge, Israel's despairing doubt is countered by the witness of faith that asserts that Yahweh is stronger than the

---

8. See, for example, Carroll Stuhlmueller, *Creative Redemption in Deutero-Isaiah* (AnBib 43; Rome: Biblical Institute Press, 1970).

Babylonian gods, and therefore that Israel's capacity for liberated action is stronger than the restraining coercion of the Babylonian regime. It is testimony to Yahweh's work as Creator that counters the ostensive power of Babylon.

> I made ('*sh*) the earth,
> and created (*br*') humankind upon it;
> It was my hands that stretched out (*nth*) the heavens,
> and I commanded (*swh*) all their hosts.
> I have aroused Cyrus in righteousness,
> and I will make all his paths straight;
> He shall build my city
> and set my exiles free,
> not for price or reward,
> says the Lord of hosts. (Isa 45:12–13)

> Have you not known? Have you not heard?
> The Lord is the everlasting God,
> the Creator (*br*') of the ends of the earth.
> He does not faint or grow weary;
> His understanding is unsearchable.
> He gives power to the faint,
> and strengthens the powerless.
> Even youths will faint and be weary
> and the young will fall exhausted;
> but those who wait for the Lord
> shall renew their strength,
> they shall mount up with wings like eagles,
> they shall run and not be weary,
> they shall walk and not faint. (Isa 40:28–31)

In these cases, the large claim is made for Yahweh as the subject of the verb: Yahweh created heaven and earth. In each case, however, the large claim moves from cosmic scope to the reality of Israel. Thus in Isa 45:12–13, the rhetoric moves quickly to Cyrus and the freedom of the exiles. In Isa 40:28–31, the large claim is aimed at the faint and powerless in Israel who will be given strength. The rhetorical combat with the other gods is undertaken in a series of disputation speeches, which assert Yahweh's power and in turn assert the weakness and impotence of the Babylonian gods who have neither authority nor power (Isa 40:12–13; 41:1–5, 21–29; 43:8–13). The purpose of this testimony concerning the Creator is to assert (and so to establish) that Yahweh is the only God who has demonstrated power as Creator, and therefore the other gods merit no obedience or deference.

[[151]] Creation faith is used in the testimony of Israel in order to dismiss the claim of the other gods. This function of testimony is matched by a second purpose: the affirmation of Israel. This God created not only heavens and earth, as the other gods could not; this God created Israel as a special object of Yahweh's attentive faithfulness:[9]

> But now thus says the Lord,
> he who created (*br'*) you, O Jacob,
> he who formed (*yṣr*) you, O Israel:
> do not fear. . . . (Isa 43:1)

> Do not fear, for I am with you;
> I will bring your offspring from the east,
> and from the west I will gather you;
> I will say to the north, "Give them up,"
> and to the south, "Do not withhold;
> bring my sons from far away and my daughters from the end of the
>   earth—
> everyone who is called by my name,
> whom I created (*br'*) for my glory,
> whom I formed (*yṣr*) and made (*'śh*)." (Isa 43:5-7)

> I am the Lord, your Holy One,
> the Creator (*br'*) of Israel, your King. (Isa 43:15)

> Thus says the Lord who made (*'śh*) you:
> who formed (*yṣr*) you in the womb and will help you:
> Do not fear. . . . (Isa 44:2)

This way of speaking of God's creating activity utilizes the same verbs as cosmic creation. Only now the rhetoric appeals directly to Israel, inviting Israel to confidence in Yahweh, and therefore to derivative confidence in its own capacity to act in freedom, apart from the threat of Babylonian intimidation and coercion.

. . . .

The Idiom of Israel's Faith

[[746]] I am helped by a recent phrase of Christopher Bollas, who, in his reflection on personality theory, has transposed Freud's id as the most elemental dimension of self into "idiom."[10] Bollas suggests that health, well-being,

---

9. Rolf Rendtorff, "Die theologische Stellung des Schopfungsglaubens bei Deutero-jesaja," *ZTK* 51 (1954) 3–13; and Rainer Albertz, *Persönliche Frömmigkeit und offizielle Religion: Religionsinterner Pluralismus in Israel und Babylon* (Calwer Theologische Monographieren Series A 9; Stuttgart: Calwer Verlag, 1978), have suggested that a distinction can be made between Yahweh's creation of the world and Yahweh's creation of Israel, or of individual human persons. The distinctions should not be drawn too rigorously, but it is clear that Israel spoke differently about these matters in different genres, depending on the need being served.

10. Christopher Bollas, *Being a Character: Psychoanalysis and Self Experience* (London: Routledge, 1993) 17, 64–65, 70–71. Bollas considers the psychic process as one of deconstructing and then constructing a new "form of existence."

and maturity depend on identifying, embracing, and practicing the peculiar, distinctive idiom of life with which one is born. *Mutatis mutandis,* I suggest that responsible Old Testament theology in an ecclesial community of interpretation is interpretation done in an idiom that is congruent with the life setting of the community, but that is drawn from, informed by, and authorized by the idiom of the testimony of the text. For all its variation through time and in different circumstances, there is a recognizable idiom to Israel's testimony, especially as some texts take great liberties with it.[11] That idiom is the one we have identified in the core testimony, made fuller and richer by the countertestimony that is evoked in response against the core testimony and its power. The combination of core testimony and countertestimony constitutes the idiom of Israel's faith. It is, then, this idiom that may be practiced in an ecclesial community of interpretation.

In contemporary ecclesial communities of theological interpretation, that ancient idiom is recoverable when the community accepts that its own cadences and dialect are derivative from that idiom. That is, such a community of interpretation moves past the Cartesian dilemma—now aware of the great suspicions of Freud and Marx, fully present to the great ruptures of Auschwitz and Hiroshima—to a buoyant "second naïveté," in the end convinced that no cadence of speech, no dialect of communication, no idiom of self-discernment is as powerful, as compelling, as liberating, or as transformative as this one, whereby one may speak and live unencumbered in a world of threat.

In the end, my appeal to ecclesial communities, and especially to their leaders and pastors, is that there be a serious reengagement with this idiom, which is the *Muttersprach* [["mother tongue"]] of the church (as of the synagogue). It is my impression that the church in the West has been sorely tempted to speak in everyone's idiom except its own. Liberals, embarrassed by the otherness of the biblical idiom, have kept [[747]] control of matters through rationalistic speech that in the end affirms that "God has no hands but ours," issuing in burdensome self-congratulations. Conservatives, fearful of speech that is undomesticated, have insisted on flattening biblical testimony into the settled categories of scholasticism that freezes truth.[12] In both sorts of speech, the incommensurate, mutual One disappears. Neither liberal rationalism nor scholastic conservatism will yield any energy or freedom for serious, sustained obedience or for buoyant elemental trust. Old Testament theology is, in an ecclesial setting, an activity for the recovery of an idiom of speech and of life that is congruent with the stuff of Israel's faith. Where that

---

11. The extreme cases are the Song of Solomon and Ecclesiastes. The canonizing and interpretive processes no doubt have drawn these texts into the orbit of Israel's more characteristic testimony, so that in canonical location and form one may perhaps hear echoes of standard Israelite cadences. Admittedly this requires some stretch of hearing, but that is what Israel characteristically undertakes, though the push to consensus must not be overstated.

12. It will be evident that in my own practice of a cultural-linguistic perspective, my opposition is to perspectives and approaches that George A. Lindbeck, *The Nature of Doctrine: Religion and Theology in a Postliberal Age* (London: SPCK, 1984), has termed, respectively, "expressive-experiential" and "propositional."

idiom is engaged and practiced, openings may appear in the shut-down world of contemporaneity, openings for core testimony revisited and for counter-testimony reuttered.

PAUL R. HOUSE

b. 1958

Ruth in the Canon

Paul R. House taught at Taylor University, Trinity Episcopal School for Ministry, and the Southern Baptist Theological Seminary, where he earned his Ph.D., in 1986. He is currently Professor of Old Testament at Wheaton College, in Illinois.

Selected Writings by House

1988   *Zephaniah: A Prophetic Drama.* Journal for the Study of the Old Testament Supplements 69. Sheffield: Almond.

1990   *The Unity of the Twelve.* Journal for the Study of the Old Testament Supplements 97. Sheffield: Almond.

1992   (editor) *Beyond Form Criticism: Essays in Old Testament Literary Criticism.* Sources for Biblical and Theological Study 2. Winona Lake, Indiana: Eisenbrauns.

1998   *Old Testament Theology.* Downers Grove, Illinois: InterVarsity.

Paul R. House's
Approach to Old Testament Theology

Excerpted with permission from Paul R. House, *Old Testament Theology* (Downers Grove, Illinois: InterVarsity, 1998), pp. 53–57. Some footnotes have been omitted.

A Methodology for Examining Old Testament Theology: Basic Principles

[[53]] This survey of literature makes it quite clear that several methodologies for composing Old Testament theology exist. Every serious analysis of the discipline makes this point. The question arises, then, of how to proceed in a manner true to the Old Testament itself.

Certain definitions and convictions undergird this volume's approach to Old Testament theology. No doubt the most important definition is of *theology* itself. This Greek word means "the study of God" and implies that those who undertake to study God will learn a great deal about God's nature, actions and attitudes. From learning about God they will in turn discover how God relates to the created world, including the human race. All analyses begin with God and flow to other vital subjects. Thus Old Testament theology itself can be defined as "the task of presenting what the Old Testament says about God as a coherent whole."[1] Only by keeping God at the forefront of research can one compose a viable and balanced theological work.

As has been stated, a few basic convictions have generally characterized Old Testament theology. First, it must have a historical base. Second, it must explain what the Old Testament itself claims, not what preconceived historical or theological systems impose upon the biblical material. Third, when part of Christian theology, as this book attempts to be, Old Testament theology must in some way address its relationship to the New Testament. Fourth, by joining with the New Testament to form biblical theology, Old Testament theology offers material that systematic theologians can divide into categories and topics for discussion. Fifth, by stating what the Old Testament says about God's nature and will, Old Testament theology moves beyond description of truth into prescription of action. After all, if interpreters agree that the Old Testament teaches that God commands certain behavior, it seems evident that a description has discovered a norm. One may obey the normative command or not, but the fact that a norm has been uncovered remains unchanged.

Beyond these shared convictions lie some concepts this volume holds in common with many, though not all, other similar works. First, Old Testament theology must be presented in a clear, coherent pattern so its readers can in-

1. [[Walther]] Zimmerli, *Old Testament Theology* [[*in Outline* (trans. David Eliot Green; Atlanta: John Knox, 1978),]] 12

corporate its findings into their lives and ministries. Second, Old Testament theology must try to display the Old Testament's theological unity within diversity. Difficult ideas must not be hidden, but the text's wholeness should have priority for the preceding objective to be reached. Third, authors must be honest about their established mindset. These mindsets are developed over time and after careful consideration. This volume is written by an [[54]] evangelical Christian who has come to this position only after serious study, reflection and struggle. Certainly those of a different mindset also went through a similar process.

Because of these definitions and convictions, Old Testament theology should not include certain tasks. For instance, though historical studies undergird Old Testament theology, it is not the discipline's role to write a history of all Israelite religious beliefs. Old Testament theology should focus on what the Bible's authors believed, while historians of Israelite religious beliefs must, among other things, take into serious consideration what Israelites who did not agree with the Bible's authors believed. Such data informs Old Testament theologians, but is not their main priority when they present their findings. These disciplines intersect at key points, but they are not identical.

To cite another example, though Old Testament theology has a close relationship to the New Testament the two have discrete witnesses of their own.[2] Therefore Old Testament theology must state the Old Testament's unique message before incorporating the New Testament perspective. The ultimate goal is still to produce biblical theology yet to unite the testaments at the proper moment. This procedure is sound on historical, canonical and exegetical grounds and will make scriptural unity plainer than starting from the opposite end of the canon. It will also help [[make]] the Old Testament's unique value for theology clearer.

Finally, if the text is allowed to dictate theological reflection, then it is not Old Testament theology's task to incorporate its results into a formal system. Old Testament theology must not be written in order to justify Calvinism, Arminianism or some other time-honored system of belief. If the results are congenial to a system, then proponents of that system may use the data. The goal is to avoid forcing the text into a mold before the text is studied. Scholars of all faiths and ideological convictions have committed this error, and to some extent this failing is universal, so it is necessary to attempt to be careful in this area.

A Methodology for Examining Old Testament Theology: Specific Principles of a Canonical Approach

With all these considerations in mind, it is possible to move toward stating this book's methodology. Gerhard Hasel claims that there have been ten

---

2. This conclusion lies at the heart of Childs's *Biblical Theology*. [[Brevard S. Childs, *Biblical Theology of the Old and New Testaments: Theological Reflection on the Christian Bible* (Minneapolis: Fortress, 1992).]]

different methodologies used in the history of Old Testament theology. These include

1. the dogmatic-didactic method, which organizes Old Testament theology along the lines of systematic theology (Bauer, Köhler, Jacob)
2. the genetic-progressive method, which traces the growth of Israel's faith in history (Clements)
3. the cross-section method, which utilizes a single theme to explain the [[55]] Old Testament's contents (Eichrodt, Vriezen, Kaiser)
4. the topical method, which focuses on major ideas regardless of their historical emergence or ability to unify the Old Testament (McKenzie, Fohrer, Zimmerli)
5. the diachronic method, which charts the use of basic traditions in the Old Testament (von Rad)
6. the "formation of tradition" method, which goes beyond von Rad's arguments to claim that a series of traditions unify both testaments (Gese)
7. the thematic-dialectic method, which arranges its studies around "opposing" ideas such as presence/absence (Terrien), deliverance/blessing (Westermann) and structure legitimation/embracing of pain (Brueggemann)
8. recent "critical" methods, which is Hasel's category for scholars who question whether Old Testament theology can be done at all (e.g., James Barr and John J. Collins)
9. the new biblical theology method, which attempts to relate the testaments to one another; the chief proponent of this method is Childs, who utilizes a canonical approach to biblical theology (Hasel also places Vriezen and Clements in this group and notes Terrien's, Westermann's and Gese's interest in the discussion as well)
10. the multiplex canonical Old Testament theology method, which is Hasel's own program for the discipline (it consists of four main points: a study of the canonical Scriptures rather than a history-of-religions approach, a summary of the canon's concepts and themes, a utilization of more than one methodological scheme and an analysis of blocks of material without following the specific order of Hebrew canon).[3]

Hasel's excellent list makes the methodological possibilities and difficulties in Old Testament theology evident. He is correct in stating that a combination of methodologies must be used but incorrect in which combination works best.

First of all, Old Testament theology that seeks to contribute to biblical theology should indeed analyze the Hebrew canon, for it is this canon that the New Testament mentions (see Luke 24:44) and quotes as divine revelation. Since it is the three-part (Law, Prophets, Writings) scheme that the New

---

3. Hasel, *Old Testament Theology*, 21–93 [[Gerhard F. Hasel, *Old Testament Theology: Basic Issues in the Current Debate* (4th ed.; Grand Rapids, Mich.: Eerdmans, 1991)]].

Testament mentions, the general order of the canon ought to be followed as well. Because it is an unfolding canon, intertextual connections between the books must be duly noted. Since the apocryphal books are not so quoted and described, they should not be included in Old Testament theology.[4] Analyzing the canon offers the best chance for the Old Testament to speak for itself.

Second, following the canonical order keeps the Old Testament's historical context before the reader. This principle is generally true for any reader who thinks Vatke's and Wellhausen's reconstruction of Israelite history and biblical composition faulty. Also, many scholars who agree broadly with Wellhausen [[56]] and his successors believe that the Pentateuch and Prophets at least contain many materials that are quite ancient, so they also appreciate the canonical text's stated historical sequence. Other experts hold to Mosaic authorship of the Pentateuch and that the stated authors of biblical books are indeed those books' authors. They, too, find historical progression in the canon. This volume adopts a conservative approach to Israelite history and biblical composition yet hopes its comments on the canon can at least aid those who disagree at many points.

Third, despite the current reluctance among some scholars to adopt a single centering theme,[5] Old Testament theology needs focal points. The key here is to argue for *a* main focal point, not necessarily for *the* central theme of the Old Testament. A focal point is valuable as long as it is true to Scripture and actually helps the theologian's analysis hold together. Attempting to argue a certain theme as the only major uniting idea can succeed only if all other motifs are proven secondary, and this volume makes no such exclusive claims for its centering theme. Surely such an argument would require an extended discussion before the theologian could begin. This book uses the Old Testament's insistence on the existence and worship of one God as a major, normative, theological and historical emphasis. Several theologians mention this theme's centrality [[. . .]], though none uses it to the extent employed here. This fundamental concept helps explain the Old Testament's ideas about God, Israel and the human race. It also provides an extremely important theological link between the Old and New Testament communities of faith.

Fourth, this wedding of canonical and thematic approaches also has a practical goal. One of the drawbacks of a noncanonical, or non-book-by-book, approach is that many current students do not have extensive biblical knowledge. Therefore it is quite difficult for these students to use a systematic or dialectic approach that assumes they have already mastered the theological details in individual Bible books. Such students are not intellectually weak; they lack exposure to and experience with the material for a systematic

---

4. On this point I agree with [[Ronald E. Clements, *Old Testament Theology: A Fresh Approach* (London: Marshall, Morgan & Scott, 1978)]], 16; and Childs, *Biblical Theology*, 91–92. I have set forth my own conclusions about the propriety of using the Palestinian canon in "Canon of the Old Testament," in *Foundations for Biblical Interpretation: A Complete Library of Tools and Resources*, ed. David S. Dockery, Kenneth A. Matthews and Robert B. Sloan (Nashville, Tenn.: Broadman, 1994), 134–55.

5. Cf. Hasel, *Old Testament Theology*, 112.

analysis of Scripture. I hope, then, this book's approach will be both accurate and appropriate for a majority of theological students.

Given these assertions, this volume adopts a canonical approach to Old Testament theology that can be summarized by the following principles. First, the Old Testament canon accepted by the first-century Palestinian Jewish/Christian and Jewish/non-Christian communities will be examined. The canon will be treated in the general order accepted by those groups: Law, Prophets and Writings. Analysis of specific groupings within these three parts will follow the Masoretic text found in *Biblia Hebraica Stuttgartensia*, an imperfect but reasonable procedure that keeps faith with the contours of each section as they have been handed down through the centuries. Second, [[57]] each book of the canon will be examined to show its unique theological contribution to the Old Testament. Then intertextual connections between the individual book and the rest of the canon will be noted. The thematic wholeness of Hebrew Scripture will thereby be illuminated.[6]

Third, the treatments of single books will at times include brief comments about historical details such as authorship, date and audience. The canon's contents did not emerge in a vacuum, nor is their historical context irrelevant to their message. Choosing the Law, Prophets, Writings sequence allows the basic outlines of Israelite history to be followed without a history of religion approach taking over the study. Fourth, the Old Testament's insistence on monotheism will be used as a historically attested centering theme to give focus to the text's many emphases. This emphasis will also aid the volume's attempt to focus on God's character and acts more than on other matters. Fifth, the canon will be treated as Scripture, as divinely inspired texts that claim and are accepted as having authoritative status. Neglecting this principle in effect leads to approaching the Old Testament in a manner foreign to the history of its interpretation and foreign to its own subject matter.

Thus by "canonical" this volume means analysis that is God-centered, intertextually oriented, authority-conscious, historically sensitive and devoted to the pursuit of the wholeness of the Old Testament message. It means theological reflection that intends to deal carefully with the uniqueness of the Old Testament so that its influence on the New Testament and systematic theology can be better understood. Of course such goals may not be attainable by any author, much less by this one. Still, this sort of canonical analysis may make a small contribution to the practice of Old Testament theology during an era in which the discipline seems to be seeking an identity. It may also help remove a few of the barriers that keep biblical and systematic theology unnecessarily apart from one another.

No methodology for writing Old Testament theology is flawless, and the one proposed here is no exception. Still, the suggested format is valid on historical, canonical and literary grounds. It offers a chance to read the Old Tes-

---

6. I have outlined the Old Testament's broad thematic coherence in *Old Testament Survey* (Nashville, Tenn.: Broadman, 1992). This volume addresses specific intertextual matters as well.

tament as communities of faith have done for centuries: as authoritative
Scripture born in history, intended for the ages. It also attempts to keep theological reflection focused through the use of a theme recognized by large
numbers of scholars as central to the Old Testament's message. In short,
then, it may be one way to break through the common problems with the
Old Testament's historicity, authority and unity. If so, it may also be an approach that bridges gaps between the testaments and thereby contributes to
an informed and valid biblical theology.

Synopsis of Paul House's *Old Testament Theology*

Paul R. House
On God in the Book of Ruth

Excerpted with permission from Paul R. House, *Old Testament Theology* (Downers Grove, Illinois: InterVarsity, 1998), pp. 455–62. Some footnotes have been omitted.

The God Who Extends Mercy to the Faithful: Ruth

[[455]] Ruth has long been lauded as a wonderful story that shows people overcoming life's tragedies through devotion and strong character. R. K. Harrison represents many kindred statements when he writes, "This charming tale of human devotion and kindness is one of the most beautiful in the entire Old Testament, constituting a model of the art of storytelling."[1] The book does include all the elements of excellent writing: strong characters, plot development that includes suspense and resolution, interesting use of setting and subtle narrative technique.[2] Read on a literary level, alone Ruth offers stimulating ideas about pain, loyalty, kindness and reversal of fortunes.

It is also true that Ruth yields vital canonical and theological insight. As the book that follows Proverbs,[3] it presents a woman who embodies the description of the virtuous wife set forth in Proverbs 31. Further, it describes the eventual joyous vindication of the faithful, a theme that is decidedly important in Psalms, Job and Proverbs. Those who trust God, serve the community and aid the poor eventually enjoy Yahweh's favor. As part of the Writings, Ruth examines the bitterness of pain in a manner similar to the laments in Psalms and in Job 3. Yet it also describes the joy of restoration, a subject that dominates Job 42:7–17. Because of the Davidic genealogy in Ruth 4:18–22, David's life and the prophecies connected to the Davidic covenant are also brought to mind. The application of statutes found in Leviticus and [[456]] Deuteronomy ties Ruth to the Law. All these elements are linked in a way that

1. R. K. Harrison, *Introduction to the Old Testament: With a Comprehensive Review of Old Testament Studies and a Special Supplement on the Apocrypha* (Grand Rapids, Mich.: Eerdmans, 1969), 1059.

2. Note the excellent treatments of these details in Adele Berlin, *Poetics and Interpretation of Biblical Narrative*, Bible and Literature Series 9 (Sheffield, U.K.: Almond, 1983), 83–110; and Barbara Green, "The Plot of the Biblical Story of Ruth," *Journal for the Study of the Old Testament* 23 (1982): 55–68.

3. Ruth is placed in different sections of the canon in different Hebrew traditions. For a discussion of these matters read Edward Fay Campbell Jr., *Ruth: A New Translation with Introduction, Notes and Commentary*, Anchor Bible 7 (Garden City, N.Y.: Doubleday, 1975), 32–36; Brevard S. Childs, *Introduction to the Old Testament as Scripture* (Philadelphia: Fortress, 1980), 564; and Robert L. Hubbard Jr., *The Book of Ruth*, New International Commentary on the Old Testament (Grand Rapids, Mich.: Eerdmans, 1988), 4–7. This volume holds that the canonical order of the Masoretic Text deserves priority. At the least Campbell is correct in saying, "Modern commentators agree that, whatever the internal order, the tradition which places Ruth among the Writings rather than after Judges must be original" (*Ruth*, 34).

demonstrates that Yahweh extends mercy to the faithful and offers grace to all who will embrace the faithful's convictions.

Ruth's purpose is best explained in light of the text's theological outline. The book falls into five clear parts. In 1:1-22, Ruth's two major characters and the main plot conflict are introduced. Two women, bereft of husbands and children, cling to Yahweh and one another. As they do so they encounter the God who extends mercy to the bereaved, though Naomi does not think so at first. Next, 2:1-23 introduces the third major character and by doing so begins to solve the plot's dilemma. As Naomi awakens to new possibilities she conveys faith in the God who extends mercy to the bitter. Then, in 3:1-18 Boaz learns of the possibility of marriage to Ruth. Thus, along with the women, he experiences Yahweh as the God who extends mercy to the humble. Consequently, in 4:1-17 Boaz and Ruth marry, have a child and thereby provide plot resolution. The God who extends mercy to the childless meets the needs of all three main characters. Finally, 4:18-22 offers a genealogy that includes David. This material indicates that God extends mercy to the whole nation.

Robert Hubbard is right to contend that Ruth highlights how God blesses one family and by doing so blesses multitudes.[4] Edward Campbell properly emphasizes the giving of mercy by God to the characters and by the characters to one another. The main characters embrace "a style of living which can be blessed by the God who would have it so among his people."[5] Ruth's purpose is to show the glory of God's mercy acted out in the lives of faithful people. Yahweh's faithful ones love their God (Deut 6:4-9) and their neighbor (Lev 19:18), thereby fulfilling the intent of the Law, the Prophets and the Writings (cf. Mark 12:28-34).

The God Who Extends Mercy to the Bereaved:
Ruth 1:1-22

This account is familiar to most Bible readers. Naomi, her husband and her two sons migrate from Bethlehem to Moab to avoid a famine during the era of the Judges (1:1-2). While there, the husband and the sons die (1:3-5). Naomi is left with two Moabite daughters-in-law, Ruth and Orpah. Childless, grieving, she hears of better times in Judah, decides to return home and tries to send the other women back to their homes in Moab (1:6-13). Orpah leaves, but Ruth commits herself to Naomi (1:14-18). Naomi and Ruth return, and Naomi expresses bitterness over her situation (1:19-22). The main problem the plot must solve is how these husbandless, childless women will survive in ancient Israel.

Upon closer examination, several theological principles help shape the action. First, 1:1-5 ascribes no action to the Lord, but 1:6 says that Naomi [[457]] determines to return to Bethlehem because she hears God has visited

4. Hubbard, *The Book of Ruth*, 39-42.
5. Campbell, *Ruth*, 30.

the people and given them food. This narrator's comment makes sure that readers realize that God is sovereign over all these events. God's visits in the Old Testament may occur for either blessing or punishment. In 1:6 God blesses,[6] but Naomi, Ruth and Orpah have learned that life does not always result in pleasant events.

Second, because she believes God blesses as well as takes away, Naomi asks Yahweh to bless the younger women with new husbands and homes. Thus they will be secure. Willem Prinsloo observes that Naomi bases her blessing on the kindness the women have shown her and the deceased men, an idea that reappears regularly in the story.[7] Naomi's expectation is that the Lord blesses the faithful, and a good bit of Ruth explores whether this belief is well founded.

Third, in committing herself to Naomi, the Moabite woman Ruth also commits to Israel and to Yahweh (1:16–17). She converts to covenantal faith as Rahab (Josh 2:8–14), Naaman (2 Kgs 5:1–18) and Jonah's Ninevites have done earlier in the canon. Israel is open to those who forsake other gods, desire to offer sacrifices to Yahweh (cf. Lev 22:25) and wish to pray in the temple (cf. 1 Kgs 8:41–43).[8] Though temple worship is not yet available in the era of the judges, the other principles hold true. Monotheistic faith is not the sole property of Israel or any other nation, and Israel must remain open to those who choose to embrace covenantal beliefs. Ruth's seriousness is marked by her swearing by Yahweh's name, an oath 1:17 indicates she considers binding, permanent and dangerous to break.[9]

Fourth, Naomi attributes her dilemma to the Lord in 1:20–21. She tells the Bethlehemite women to call her Mara ("bitter") instead of Naomi ("pleasant") because of how God has dealt with her. Though she does not know it, however, Yahweh has already extended mercy in her bereavement through Ruth's commitment to her. Her help has arrived. The same is true of Ruth, for God's solution to her present and future lies in her clinging to Naomi and to Yahweh. Each woman is a conduit of divine grace to the other, though stating this fact means running ahead of the story. The statement in 1:20–21 is at least as oriented toward God's sovereignty as is 1:6. Naomi certainly believes that Yahweh is Lord over both affliction and deliverance.[10] Whatever hap-

---

6. Leon Morris, "Ruth," in Arthur Ernest Cundall and Leon Morris, *Judges and Ruth: An Introduction and Commentary*, Tyndale Old Testament Commentaries (Downers Grove, Ill.: InterVarsity Press, 1968), 252.

7. Willem S. Prinsloo, "The Theology of the Book of Ruth," *Vetus Testamentum* 30 (1980): 332. This excellent article provides a foundation for much of this chapter.

8. Yehezkel Kaufmann, *The Religion of Israel: From Its Beginnings to the Babylonian Exile*, trans. and abridg. Moshe Greenberg (Chicago: University of Chicago Press, 1960), 130–31, 301.

9. Hubbard, *The Book of Ruth*, 118–20. For a discussion of how Ruth's commitment to Naomi led to a commitment to Yahweh, see Danna Nolan Fewell and David M. Gunn, *Compromising Redemption: Relating Characters in the Book of Ruth*, Literary Currents in Biblical Interpretation (Louisville, Ky.: Westminster/John Knox, 1990), 94–96.

10. Cf. Prinsloo, "The Theology of the Book of Ruth," 333.

pens in the remainder of the account must derive ultimately from the character of God.

Canonical Synthesis:
Suffering and the Righteous

Naomi stands in a long line of canonical figures who suffer through no fault of their own. This group includes, to name a few, Joseph, Joshua, Hannah, David, Jeremiah, Ezekiel, many psalmists and Job. They will be joined later by [[458]] Esther, Daniel and others. Like Job and the lamenting psalmists, Naomi is not silent in her affliction. She feels abandoned. Still she affirms God's goodness (1:6). Therefore, as Campbell writes, "looked at from this perspective, it [her discussion of God in 1:20–21] is in a very real sense a profound affirmation of faith."[11] Naomi's faith includes expressing pain, knowing that the one God who visits the land in mercy (1:6) may also visit her in mercy. Like the Job of Job 3–37, though, she does not yet know what will come of her beliefs.

The God Who Extends Mercy to the Bitter:
Ruth 2:1–23

Ruth 2 is framed by morning (2:2) and evening (2:17–22) conversations between Ruth and Naomi and by the introduction of Boaz in 2:1 and the explanation of how Ruth worked in his fields in 2:23. Between the frames Ruth meets Boaz, is blessed by him and works hard to provide food for herself and Naomi. This part of the account begins to solve the problems the women face, by both explaining how they will be fed and suggesting that a prospective husband may be available for one of them.

As was true in Ruth 1, Ruth 2 is marked by theologically oriented statements that enrich the description of events. Deftly the narrator mentions that Boaz is a relative of Elimelech and that he is wealthy (2:1). It is wonderful that without specifically knowing this information Ruth gleans in his field (2:3). The text says "she happened" (2:3) to work there, a phrase that has sparked some scholarly debate. R. M. Hals writes, "For Ruth and Boaz it was an accident, but not for God. The tenor of the whole story makes it clear that the narrator sees God's hand throughout."[12] J. M. Sasson thinks Hals reads too much into this text, noting that the book's author does not hesitate to mention direct divine activity at other points in the story. He believes this meeting simply saves time.[13] M. D. Gow disagrees with Sasson, for he considers the

11. Campbell, *Ruth*, 32.

12. Ronald M. Hals, *The Theology of the Book of Ruth*, Facet Books Biblical Series 23 (Philadelphia: Fortress, 1969), 12.

13. Jack Murad Sasson, *Ruth: A New Translation with a Philological Commentary and a Formalist-Folklorist Interpretation*, 2nd ed., Johns Hopkins Near Eastern Studies ([[reprinted;]] Sheffield, U.K.: JSOT Press, 1989), 45.

omission of God's name secondary to the fact that Boaz and Ruth's meeting is much like other providential male-female introductions (cf. Gen 24).[14] All these interpreters agree that the book affirms God's sovereignty over events, so it is not necessary to consider God absent simply because things work out well with no mention of God's directly determining events. God's sovereignty remains in effect, even when the text uses common human expressions to describe events.

The descriptions of Boaz and Ruth in 2:4–7 also carry theological weight. Ruth is depicted as laboring diligently at all times, which is noticed and praised by others. She embodies the work ethic that is so central to Proverbs' description of the righteous. Boaz's willingness to let the poor and the widow glean in his fields reveals that he keeps the Law (cf. Lev 19:9–20; 23:22; Deut 24:19–22).[15] He is the sort of person who places human need above mere [[459]] financial gain. Both characters are faithful and righteous by any canonical standard.

When they meet, Boaz blesses Ruth in unquestionably covenantal terms. He promises she will be safe as she works, whereupon she humbly asks why he favors her this way (2:8–10). Boaz says he is helping her because of her kindness to Naomi. Mercy is being rewarded with mercy (2:11), just as it was in 1:8–9.[16] Noting her new identification with Israel, he hopes she will find shelter in Yahweh (2:12). Boaz's personal theology may be summarized in this blessing. He believes that God does reward all who take shelter in the Lord. Wilhelm Rudolph and H. W. Hertzberg consider this conviction the main theme of the book and a central theme in the whole Old Testament.[17] To the extent that they imply God's mercy is expressed in 2:12, they are correct. Boaz sincerely desires for Ruth to be blessed as much as any of God's people. His wish for her to be a full covenant partner who receives God's best represents a personal mercy that transcends racial or national barriers.

Certainly the events in 2:1–16 affect Ruth and Boaz. For the moment, though, they have the greatest effect on Naomi. Upon hearing of Boaz's attentiveness she emerges from her bitterness to bless Yahweh for unceasing kindness, or mercy (2:20). Naomi reveals that Boaz is more than a relative or acquaintance (2:1). He is a "near relative," a "kinsman redeemer" (2:20). Thus he is one whom the Law says may marry the widow, redeem the deceased's land, father a child and give the land to the child. This process keeps ancestral lands within a clan and provides an heir to provide for the widow (cf. Gen 38; Deut 25:5–10). It is also possible for the redeemer to father the child

---

14. Murray D. Gow, *The Book of Ruth: Its Structure, Theme and Purpose* (Leicester, England: Apollos, 1992), 48–50.

15. Morris, "Ruth," 270.

16. Prinsloo, "The Theology of the Book of Ruth," 335.

17. Cf. Wilhelm Rudolph, *Die Bücher Ruth, Hohelied und Klagelieder: Übersetzt und Erklärt*, 2nd ed., Kommentar zum Alten Testament 17 (Gütersloh, Germany: Gerd Mohn, 1962), 32–33; and Hans Wilhelm Hertzberg, *Die Bücher Josua, Richter und Ruth*, Das Alte Testament Deutsch: Neues Göttinger Bibelwerk 9 (Göttingen, Germany: Vandenhoeck und Ruprecht, 1953), 257.

without marrying the woman, in which case the benefits to the child and woman remain.[18] Naomi's excitement is justifiable, since such a marriage could solve the women's financial problems. That she attributes this turn of events to God demonstrates her faith. That God works in this way shows that Yahweh intercedes for all hurting faithful ones, even those whose belief in divine sovereignty turns to bitterness.

The connections of Ruth 2 to earlier canonical texts has the effect of highlighting God's consistent mercy and the importance of wise living based on covenantal principles. God has seen to the needs of the suffering in this story as surely as in previous books. Naomi, Ruth and Boaz live in a way that Deuteronomy 27–28 and Proverbs promise will result in blessing, not punishment. The whole tenor of the account so far underscores that the Law and the Writings can be lived out by those who choose (1:16–17), confess (2:11–12) and praise (2:20) the God who acts mercifully.

The God Who Extends Mercy to the Humble:
Ruth 3:1-18

If Naomi is the most pleased person at the end of part two, then Boaz must [[460]] certainly have this standing at the end of part three. Here the women decide to let Boaz know that Ruth will marry him (3:1–8), he rejoices in this possibility (3:9–13), and they agree to attempt to arrange the union (3:14–18). A complication arises in that a closer relative than Boaz exists, but this problem will be met directly (3:18). Events are moving ever more swiftly now, with a resolution to the problems announced in 1:1–15 in view. Boaz acts with the determination of one who has inherent integrity and who believes he is in the process of receiving divine blessing.

Prinsloo observes that 3:1–18 demonstrates that God often answers prayers through human initiative. Ruth's desire for Boaz to spread his garment over her (3:9) fulfills Boaz's wish that she be protected beneath God's wings (2:12). Naomi's hopes for Ruth's blessings in 1:8–9 are partially met by her own plans in 3:1–4 for Ruth to meet Boaz at the threshing floor.[19] Boaz's swearing by Yahweh in 3:13 also shows that his heart for God matches that of Ruth, for her own confession in 1:16–17 includes an oath to Yahweh. Finally, the possibility of marrying Ruth vindicates Boaz's personal theology stated in 2:11–12. A humble man, he had not expected Ruth's affection (3:10). Receiving her proposal means that his personal righteousness, integrity, kindness and humility have brought him blessing under the shelter of God's wings. Ruth becomes an altogether wonderful blessing for this man who has trusted in God.

It is important to mark the fact that Boaz decides to provide for both Ruth and Naomi (3:16–18). Naomi has always spoken of "our redeemer"

---

18. For a discussion of this custom in Ruth, consult H. H. Rowley, *The Servant of the Lord and Other Essays on the Old Testament* (London: Lutterworth, 1952), 163–86.

19. Prinsloo, "The Theology of the Book of Ruth," 337.

(2:20), and Boaz's pledge and subsequent gift (3:11–18) express his willingness to do all Ruth wants done for herself and Naomi.[20] Once again all his
desire for Ruth is grounded in his convictions about her character.[21] He
chooses a "good wife" based on Wisdom standards (Prov 31:10–31) and includes in his generosity the one (Naomi) to whom and for whom Ruth
proved her worthiness.

The God Who Extends Mercy to the Childless: Ruth 4:1–17

As Naomi expected in 3:18, Boaz moves quickly in securing the right to become the nearest kinsman redeemer (4:1). To facilitate matters, though at
some risk to herself, Naomi includes Elimelech's land as a part of the redemption costs. To gain the land one must redeem it and care for the
woman. But which woman? Hubbard theorizes that the man thought he must
support Naomi, who could not have children who would share his other children's inheritance. To get good land he had "only" to care for an older wife.
Ruth, however, could have "several sons, the first eligible to claim Elimelech's
property as his heir, others perhaps to share in the kinsman's own inheritance (v. 6)."[22] Thus he rejects the opportunity, and Boaz [[461]] announces
his intentions (4:1–10).

The last seven verses in this section contain four distinct theological
points. First, the women of the town offer their own blessing. They hope Ruth
will be like Leah and Rachel, the matriarchs of the twelve tribes of Israel
(4:11). They also pray that this clan will be significant in Bethlehem and that
it will prosper like that of Tamar, the heroine of Genesis 38 who must trick a
near kinsman into fathering her child. These references to Genesis show that
Ruth has been accepted as a full member in Israel's covenantal traditions.

Second, 4:13 says that the Lord gave Ruth conception so that she could
bear a son. This child is God's gift.[23] Yahweh is said to act directly for only
the second time in the book (cf. 1:6), this time as a way of bringing resolution
to the plot.[24] Human beings can extend mercy to one another, but only God
can give life. Third, Ruth gives this child to Naomi as a restorer of family and
a financial protector for her old age (4:14–17). This gift of divinely given life
finalizes Ruth's commitment to Naomi and proves one last time her own righteousness and enormous capacity for merciful love.

Fourth, the women of Bethlehem bless God for how Naomi's fortunes
have turned. No more are she and Ruth childless. No longer is their future in
doubt. Their mercy toward one another and Boaz has resulted in a joyous
conclusion. Prinsloo concludes that

---

20. Cf. Sasson, *Ruth*, 91–92.
21. Prinsloo, "The Theology of the Book of Ruth," 338.
22. Hubbard, *The Book of Ruth*, 61.
23. Morris, "Ruth," 312
24. Cf. Hubbard, *The Book of Ruth*, 267.

the fourth pericope can be summarized as follows: although human initiative is emphasized and great stress is laid upon man as a collaborator with Yahweh, the focus naturally falls on the fact that there are limits to human initiative. Yahweh is the one who resolves the crisis and to whom praise ought to be given.[25]

Canonical Synthesis: Hope for the Childless

This section echoes earlier canonical accounts of God's opening wombs. The most famous case is that of Sarah, the mother of all Israel (Gen 21:1-7). Yahweh makes sure that the unloved Leah has children in Gen 29:31 and then opens the beloved Rachel's womb in 30:22. Samson's mother is similarly blessed (Judg 13:1-3), as is Hannah, Samuel's mother (1 Sam 1:1-2:10). In these instances God acts as the Creator of life. Yahweh offers hope to those who desire the joy and security of children yet are not able for a time to experience this blessing. God removes pain and uncertainty and replaces these with honor and praise.

The God Who Extends Mercy to All Israel:
Ruth 4:18-22

Ruth concludes with a genealogy of David's family. This ending transforms the book from an account that expresses God's mercy toward certain righteous persons to a statement about how God acts mercifully on Israel's [[462]] behalf by giving them their greatest monarch. Ruth recounts the fact that God takes pains to keep David's lineage from dying out before it can even begin. The one who brings the family and Bethlehem lasting renown is now in place.[26] By giving birth to David's ancestor, Ruth contributes as much to Israel as did Leah and Rachel. She is as blessed as Tamar.

Canonical Synthesis: The Davidic Promise

The canonical witness is that this birth will eventually extend mercy throughout the world. 2 Sam 7:1-17 promises an eternal kingdom for David's heir, and Isa 9:2-7 and 11:1-10 state that this kingdom will reach around the world. Zechariah 9-14 affirms this universal vision too, as does the New Testament in general and Paul's writings in particular. Through the work of the Davidic king God's mercy will be known in all the countries Yahweh has created. This much comes from mercy offered to a pair of righteous widows.

In every conceivable way this small book proves a worthy successor to Proverbs. Ruth confirms Job's belief that God vindicates and Proverbs' contention that the Lord blesses the righteous. The text demonstrates how laws

---

25. Prinsloo, "The Theology of the Book of Ruth," 339.

26. Oswald Loretz, "The Theme of the Ruth Story," *Catholic Biblical Quarterly* 22 (1960): 392.

found in Leviticus and Deuteronomy ought to be obeyed and illustrates once again how the women blessed with children in Genesis, Judges and Samuel are not beneficiaries of happy coincidence but are recipients of divine pleasure. Covenants made with Abraham, Moses and David are honored here. It is hard to imagine a book so short doing more to maintain the faith of the whole canon.

BERNHARD W. ANDERSON

b. 1916

Royal Covenant

Like Walter Brueggemann, a student of James Muilenburg and influenced by his rhetorical criticism, Bernhard W. Anderson earned his doctorate at Yale University; his mentor there was Millar Burrows. He became Professor of Old Testament and Dean of the School of Theology at Drew University, where he was influenced by the Jewish philosopher Will Herberg. With G. Ernest Wright, Anderson was a leader in the biblical theology movement. He is now professor emeritus of Old Testament at Princeton Theological Seminary. Anderson's book *Understanding the Old Testament*, first published in 1957, has been a standard introductory text.

Selected Writings by Anderson

1971 The Crisis in Biblical Theology. *Theology Today* 28: 321–27.

1976 Introduction. Pp. 9–28 in Will Herberg, *Faith Enacted as History: Essays in Biblical Theology.* Edited by Bernhard W. Anderson. Philadelphia: Westminster.

1984 (editor) *Creation in the Old Testament.* Issues in Religion and Theology 6. Philadelphia: Fortress.

1986 *Understanding the Old Testament.* 4th edition. Englewood Cliffs, N.J.: Prentice-Hall.

1987 *Creation versus Chaos: The Reinterpretation of Mythical Symbolism in the Bible.* 2d edition. Philadelphia: Fortress.

1994 *From Creation to New Creation: Old Testament Perspectives.* Overtures to Biblical Theology. Minneapolis: Fortress

1999 *Contours of Old Testament Theology.* Minneapolis: Fortress.

Writings about Anderson

Butler, James T., Edgar W. Conrad, and Ben C. Ollenburger (editors)

1985 *Understanding the Word: Essays in Honor of Bernhard W. Anderson.* Journal for the Study of the Old Testament Supplements 37; Sheffield: JSOT Press.

Bernhard W. Anderson's
Approach to Old Testament Theology

Reprinted with permission from Bernhard W. Anderson (with
the assistance of Steven Bishop), *Contours of Old Testament Theology* (Minneapolis: Fortress, 1999), pp. 29–33. Some footnotes
have been omitted.

Brevard Childs's Approach

[[29]] A decisive turning point was reached in 1970 with the publication of
Brevard Childs's *Biblical Theology in Crisis*.[1] Childs showed the weaknesses of
a biblical theology resting on the revelation of God in historical events. During the days of the so-called biblical theology movement (just after World
War II), this view had been set forth preeminently by George Ernest Wright
in his monograph *God Who Acts*, in which he took a stand against a doctrinal
approach and emphasized historical recital, that is, the narrative of God's acting in the world.[2] Childs was critical of any attempt to base biblical theology
on objective historical events (the Albright school), and he extended his criticism to history in the sense of "history of traditions" (Noth, von Rad, and
others). He insisted that there must be "a still more excellent way."

Canon and Biblical Theology

The even better way, in Childs's view, involves taking seriously the final form
of the tradition, not just as it is shaped by redactors but as set forth in the
canon of biblical books that the community of faith accepts as authoritative.
Against his critics, he insists that emphasis on the canon does not mean a flat
interpretation of Scripture, which lacks the dynamic of a diachronic movement. The interpreter, he declares, must take seriously the "depth dimension," that is, the stages of [[30]] development that took place in the long
period before the tradition was given its final scriptural form. However, the
purpose of studying the depth dimension through source criticism, form
criticism, tradition history, and redaction criticism is not to recover the theological interpretation that lies behind the present text but to understand the
Bible in its final canonical shape. "One can better appreciate a symphony," he
says in this connection, "if one has been trained to recognize the contribution of each of the various musical instruments involved."[3]

---

1. Brevard S. Childs, *Biblical Theology in Crisis* (Philadelphia: Westminster, 1970).
2. Wright, *God Who Acts*, SBT 1/8 (Chicago: Regnery, 1952). Wright's valid concern for
the acts of God—not just the word(s) of God—has been considered anew by Patrick D. Miller,
"Revisiting the God Who Acts," *TToday* 54, no. 1 (1997) 1–5.
3. See Brevard Childs, *Biblical Theology of the Old and New Testaments* (Minneapolis: Fortress Press, 1992), "Methodological Problems," 104–6, quotation, 105.

Childs's exposition of biblical theology is governed by the following considerations:

1. In the canon of the Christian Bible, Old and New Testaments are bound together christologically, that is, each bears witness to the God revealed in Jesus Christ.

2. This interrelationship of the Testaments respects the discrete witness of both. The Old Testament, specifically, has a quasi-independent status in the canon.

3. When turning to the discrete witness of the Old Testament, Childs follows a historical outline as far as possible, that is, from Genesis through Ezra. Thus he discusses theologically, in conversation with biblical scholars: "Creation," "From Eden to Babel," "Patriarchal Traditions," "Mosaic Traditions," "The Possession of the Land and the Settlement," "The Tradition of the Judges," "The Establishment of the Monarchy," "The Divided Kingdom," "Exile and Restoration." When this chronological outline runs out, he turns to special materials: "Prophetic," "Apocalyptic," "Wisdom," and "Psalms."

4. After treating the discrete witness of the New Testament following a similar chronological sequence ("The Church's Earliest Proclamation" to "The Post-Pauline Age"), Childs turns to "theological reflections on the Christian Bible," considering in parallel the Old Testament witness and that of the New Testament. Here he abandons historical sequence and turns to a topical discussion: "The Identity of God," "God the Creator," "Covenant, Election, People of God," "Christ the Lord," "Reconciliation with God," and so on. One can see clearly that, in Childs's view, biblical and dogmatic theology are closely related.

This is truly a monumental work that will be discussed for years to come. For two decades I have struggled with Childs's canonical approach, finding in it things to agree with and to differ over. On the positive side, it has been a major influence in moving me to concentrate on the final form of the Scriptures that we have received. Also, I welcome the insistence that the Old Testament has a relatively independent place in the Christian Bible, although I would emphasize more the dialectic of continuity/discontinuity between the Testaments.[4] My major difficulty is that this approach, being so close to dogmatic theology, does not give sufficient theological attention to the "discrete witness of the Old Testament," and especially to the pattern of symbolism that governs literary units in their final [[31]] form (e.g., Pentateuch, Deuteronomistic history). As noted above, biblical theology finally turns out to be a discussion of theological topics. Perhaps there is another way that follows more closely the Old Testament canonical structure.

4. See [[Anderson 1999]] chapter 2.

Hermeneutical Considerations

The following presentation also begins by taking a firm stand in the community of faith known as the church. At the same time, I give due consideration to the way the Jewish community reads this common Bible and, from time to time, engage in Jewish-Christian dialogue.[5] There is a great deal of affinity between this presentation of Old Testament theology and the "entry into the Jewish Bible" given by Jon Levenson in *Sinai and Zion*.[6]

In this venture, I recognize that the Old Testament contains a diversity of materials that resists being pressed into a coherent, structural unity (the weakness of Eichrodt's approach). Nevertheless, theological understanding is aided by an organization of the diverse materials, rather than just reading the Bible "from cover to cover." Other organizations may be helpful too, such as the work of Christoph Barth, *God with Us*, which is organized in a sequence of narrative statements, "God Created Heaven and Earth," "God Chose the Fathers of Israel," "God Brought Israel out of Egypt," and so on.[7] Also, I recognize that invariably we read the past through the lens of our own experience or categories. We are sociolinguistic beings who want to bring the past into our world and appropriate it on our terms. This epistemological limitation, however, does not justify a deliberate reading of the past through a particular lens (as in the case of some liberation theologies); it only warns us to be deliberate about allowing the past, in so far as possible, to speak to us with its own voice, rather than being ventriloquists who project our voice onto the Bible. We must allow the Old Testament to be a different, even an alien, voice that speaks to us from another world of discourse.

Moreover, as Karl Rahner[8] has well said, the interpreter must have a poetic sense that yields to and appreciates biblical imagery if she or he is to hear in the Bible "the Word of God." This view is echoed in Walter Brueggemann's Yale Lectures on Preaching, in his introductory essay, "Poetry in a Prose-Flattened World," where he effectively quotes Walt Whitman:

> After the seas are all cross'd, (as they seem already cross'd,)
> After the great captains and engineers have accomplish'd their work,
> After the noble inventors, after the scientists, the chemist, the
>   geologist, ethnologist, [[32]]
> Finally shall come the poet worthy of that name,
> The true son of God shall come singing his songs.[9]

---

5. See Rolf Rendtorff, "Toward a Common Jewish-Christian Reading of the Hebrew Bible," chap. 4 in *Canon and Theology* [[Minneapolis: Fortress, 1993]].

6. Jon D. Levenson, *Sinai and Zion: An Entry into the Jewish Bible* (Minneapolis: Winston, 1985).

7. Christoph Barth, *God with Us: A Theological Introduction to the Old Testament* (Grand Rapids: Eerdmans, 1985).

8. Karl Rahner, *More Recent Writings*, trans. Kevin Smyth, Theological Investigations 4 (Baltimore: Helicon, 1966), 363.

9. See Walter Brueggemann, *Finally Comes the Poet: Daring Speech for Proclamation*, especially the introduction, "Poetry in a Prose-Flattened World" (Minneapolis: Fortress Press,

Singing a new song (Ps 96:1) requires avoiding, on the one side, the Scylla of literalism and, on the other, the Charybdis of historicism. The texts of the Bible invite us into a world—a real world—that is construed by poetic imagination. Therefore, we shall give due attention to the covenantal patterns of symbolization (Priestly, Mosaic, Davidic) that govern Old Testament books or blocks of material (e.g., the book of Isaiah, the Chronicler's history).

God's Covenants with Israel

Accordingly, let's start with a clue found in the New Testament, specifically Paul's discussion of the relation between the Jewish and Christian communities in the economy of God's purpose in Romans 9–11. In a context where Paul expresses sadness that his own people, the Jews, do not accept Jesus as God's Messiah, he lists seven historic privileges that belonged to Israel as the people of God:

> They are Israelites, and to them belong the adoption, the glory, the covenants, the giving of the law, the worship, and the promises; to them belong the patriarchs, and from them, according to the flesh, comes the Messiah, who is over all, God blessed forever. Amen.[10]
>
> —Rom 9:4–5

This is a very solemn statement, as indicated by the concluding "amen." Its solemnity is heightened by Paul's use of the term "Israelites" (rather than "Jews")—the ancient sacral term for Israel as the people of God (Gen 32:28). He lists seven prerogatives of Israel—eight if one counts the last statement that the Messiah sprang out of Israel.[11]

1. Sonship, that is, Israel was adopted or elected as God's son, according to important Old Testament passages: Exod 4:22; Deut 14:1; Hos 11:1.
2. The glory, or "glorious presence." This refers to the resplendent manifestation of God's presence (*kabod*, "glory") during the wilderness wanderings (Exod 16:10; 40:34) or in the Jerusalem temple (1 Kgs 8:10–11; Ezekiel 10, etc.).
3. The covenants—the Abrahamic (Genesis 17), Mosaic (Exod 19:5; 24:1–4; renewed at Shechem, Joshua 24), and the Davidic (2 Samuel 7; Psalm 89). Some manuscripts read singular, *diatheke*, in which case the reference would probably be to the Mosaic covenant. But most translations render the plural *diathekai*. [[33]]
4. The giving of the law: the revelation of God's will, as given to Moses (e.g., Ten Commandments in Exodus 20 and Deuteronomy 5).

1989) 1–11. The lines are from Walt Whitman's "Passage to India," 5:101–5, in *Leaves of Grass* (New York: New American Library, 1954), 324.

　　10. The last words could be punctuated, "who is God over all, forever praised," as in NIV.

　　11. See the discussion by J. A. Fitzmyer in *New Jerome Biblical Commentary*, ed. Raymond E. Brown et al. (Englewood Cliffs, N.J.: Prentice-Hall, 1990), 856.

5. The worship, that is, the cult—worship in the tabernacle or the temple, where God chose to be present as "the Holy One in your midst." The book of Psalms is the book of worship for the praises of Israel.
6. The promises—primarily the promises made to Abraham (land, posterity, relationship with God that would benefit other peoples), although promises of grace were also made to Moses and to David (Deut 18:18–19; 2 Sam 7:11–16).
7. The patriarchs, that is, the ancestors of Israel who were invited into special relationship with God, so that God was known as the God of Abraham, Isaac, and Jacob (Exod 3:6). The Israelites, Paul could say (Rom 11:28), were loved by God on account of the patriarchs.

Thus election, promises, covenant, law, God's holy presence in the midst of the people, as they gathered in the temple for worship—these are some of the major subjects of the Old Testament. Instead of taking these up one by one, I propose an organization according to the major covenants with Israel: the Abrahamic, the Mosaic, the Davidic.

The term "covenant" (Hebrew *berith*) points to a fundamental reality in Israel's experience: God's special relationship with the people. After a thorough review of the controversial discussion of this subject, especially since the time of the founder of modern biblical criticism, Julius Wellhausen (from 1878 to 1918), E. W. Nicholson concludes that "covenant" expresses "the distinctiveness of Israel's faith":

> So, far from being merely one among a wide range of terms and ideas that emerged, flourished, and had their day, "covenant" is a central theme that served to focus an entirely idiosyncratic way of looking at the relationship between God and his chosen people, and indeed, between God and the world. As such it deserves to be put back squarely on the agenda for students of the Old Testament.[12]

Our interest will fasten not on covenant itself but on a *pattern of symbolism*—or perhaps one should say, a theological perspective—that is expressed in each of the covenants. Each covenant, considered in its scriptural context, nuances in symbolic terms what it means to live in the presence of the holy God, who has entered into special relationship with the people Israel.

12. E. W. Nicholson, *God and His People: Covenant and Theology in the Old Testament* (Oxford: Clarendon, 1986), v.

Synopsis of Anderson's *Contours of Old Testament Theology* (1999)

Bernhard W. Anderson
on David and Zion

Excerpted with permission from *Contours of Old Testament Theology* (Minneapolis: Fortress, 1999), pp. 195–97, 209–17. Some footnotes have been omitted.

The Promises of Grace to David

[[195]] So far we have considered two major covenant perspectives found in the Old Testament: one associated with Abraham, and one with Moses. On the one hand, the Abrahamic covenant, we have seen, is unilateral in the sense that it expresses God's absolute commitment to a people, unconditioned by their behavior. This covenant, grounded in *sola gratia* [['grace alone']], assures that the people will have a land and that they will increase on the land. It is a covenant of promise.

The Mosaic covenant, on the other hand, is more bilateral, for God and people are partners, having made a contractual agreement with each other. A heavy responsibility falls on the people, for they are called on to decide to serve their liberating God and to live in accordance with covenant obligations—God's commandments. If—and the conditional is important—if they prove unfaithful, deciding to live in a way that betrays the covenant relationship, they will suffer severe consequences—indeed, the whole thing could be called off. While the Abrahamic covenant is a covenant of promise of land and increase, the Mosaic covenant has to do with the behavior of the people on the land. It is a covenant of law, under the sanctions of blessing and curse.

The contrast between these two covenants is obvious, as it was to Paul, who draws a contrast between the Abrahamic covenant of promise and the Sinaitic covenant of obligation, which puts people under the blessing or the curse (see Gal 5:6–14).

A Royal Covenant

We turn now to another way of symbolizing God's relation to the people and to the world: the royal covenant associated with David and with Zion. "Zion" is the ancient name for the southeastern ridge of the hill on which the city of Jerusalem was founded (mountain climbers will regard "mountain" as an extravagant translation). According to 2 Sam 5:6–10 David's warriors took "the stronghold of Zion" from the pre-Israelite citizens (Jebusites) and David made it his capital, "the city of David." The temple was later built immediately to the north of this area, and because this shrine was regarded as God's chosen dwelling place (Ps 132:13), it came to be known also as "the city of God" (Pss 46:4–5; 87:3).[1] I have previously observed that Jon Levenson, in *Sinai*

1. See Karen Armstrong, *Jerusalem: One City, Three Faiths* (New York: Knopf, 1996), for an early history of Jerusalem.

and Zion, regards Zion as one of the two symbolic mountains that dominate the Scriptures of ancient Israel.[2]

A Symbolic Vista

[[196]] Like the Abrahamic and Mosaic covenants, this one too has its own symbolic vista or imaginative construal. Here the key elements in the pattern of symbolization are monarch and temple.

These two institutions, so basic to the cultures of the ancient Near East, were alien to Israel's "root experiences" of exodus and Sinai. Indeed, the Davidic covenant perspective was a "new theology," not easily absorbed into Israelite tradition. Conservatives who stood in the Mosaic tradition, like the prophet Samuel, opposed the new theology. In 1 Samuel 8, Samuel is portrayed as warning the people of the dangers of having a king "like the nations": this innovation would entail the loss of civil liberties enjoyed during the tribal confederacy. Further, the ideology of sacred kingship, known throughout the ancient Near East, would be a theological challenge, for it threatened the rejection of Yahweh as king, that is, the repudiation of Israel's theocracy.

Moreover, conservatives opposed the policy of building a temple (house) for Yahweh such as the great gods of the ancient world had. In 2 Samuel 7 the prophet Nathan is portrayed as opposing, at least initially, David's plan to build a house for Yahweh. In a dream, so the story goes, Nathan was told to say to David:

> Are you the one to build me a house to dwell in? I have not dwelt in a house from the day I brought the Israelites up out of Egypt to this day. I have been moving from place to place with a tent as my dwelling.
> —2 Sam. 7:5–6 (NIV)

The task of David's theologians was to adapt these two institutions that originally were alien to Israelite experience—dynastic kingship and sacramental temple—to Israel's faith so that they could become symbols for expressing the relationship between God and people, indeed, between God and the world. Their success is evidenced in the fact that David escorted the ark, the Mosaic symbol of Yahweh's presence in the midst of the people, into Jerusalem (see the processional ritual in Ps 24:7–10). In the book of Psalms, the temple is regarded as the place where Yahweh "tabernacles" or "tents" in the midst of the people:

> How lovely is your dwelling place (tabernacle),
> O LORD [Yahweh] of hosts!
> My soul longs, indeed it faints
> for the courts of the LORD [Yahweh];
> My heart and my flesh sing for joy
> to the living God.
> —Ps 84:1–2

---

2. John D. Levenson, *Sinai and Zion* (Minneapolis: Winston, 1985). On the mountain symbolism, see above, chapter 17 [[not reproduced here]].

Moreover, the king was regarded as God's special agent or "messiah" (1 Sam 24:6), anointed for the leadership of the people, and in this sense the proto-type of the one who is to come, the ideal ruler. The term "anointed one" (He-brew *mashiah*, Greek *christos*) refers to *function* as God's instrument, not to the divine nature of the officeholder. (Notice that the Persian king Cyrus is called Yahweh's "messiah," or anointed one, in Isa 45:1, for he is the agent of God's purpose.)

⟦197⟧ Thus here we have a perspective that embraces urban symbolism (Zion, the city) and royal symbolism (the king, "Yahweh's anointed one"). Of course this covenant perspective or "trajectory" had a profound influence on the New Testament portrayal of the Messiah, God's chosen agent to intro-duce God's dominion on earth, starting at Jerusalem (Zion).

. . . .

The Cosmic Rule of Yahweh in Zion

⟦209⟧ No covenantal perspective is more prominent in the Bible, both the Old Testament and the New, than the one associated with David. To be sure, it is not found explicitly in the Priestly Torah, though, as we have noted, there are affinities between the everlasting covenants made with Abraham and with David. Furthermore, the Davidic covenant is a subordinate theme in Deuter-onomy and the Deuteronomistic history, which on the whole is governed by the Mosaic covenantal perspective. In other literature, however, the theology of the Davidic covenant provides the major perspective: the book of Psalms, the book of Isaiah, and the Chronicler's history. Each of these units of Scrip-ture we shall consider in successive ⟦sections⟧.

Psalms: A Davidic Hymnbook

We have already found that the Davidic covenant is the subject of some of the psalms. Psalm 89, for instance, is a poetic celebration of the promises of grace to David given in Nathan's oracle (2 Sam 7:4–17, echoed in Ps 89:28–37), first in the major key of hymnic praise (vv. 1–27) and then in the minor key of lament (vv. 28–51) with its poignant question:

> Lord [Yahweh], where is your steadfast love [*hesed*] of old,
>   which by your faithfulness you swore to David?
>
> —Ps 89:49

Also we have touched on the storytelling Psalm 78, which reaches a climax in God's choice of David and of Zion, and Psalm 132, where the twin themes of Davidic king and Jerusalem temple are treated side by side. Having looked at a few trees, however, we now must stand back and look at the forest as a whole: the Psalms as a book.

The book of Psalms as a completed whole is attributed to David, "the sweet singer of Israel" (2 Sam 23:1, as some translate). David is specifically associated with some psalms whose superscriptions relate the psalm to a particular event in David's career. For instance, Psalm 51 is associated with David's "sin with Bathsheba" (2 Samuel 11). The Hebrew expression *ledawid*, found at the head of a number of psalms, may mean "dedicated to David" or "belonging to a Davidic collection" (e.g., Psalm 11). The composition, singing, and collection of some psalms can undoubtedly be traced back to the man who was reputed to be a favorite singer of songs. However, the attribution of the book of Psalms to David does not mean that he was the author of the whole collection. Rather, Davidic "authorship" must be understood theologically. David symbolizes the king who represents the people as they come before God in worship.

[[210]] Also, the structure or arrangement of the book of Psalms is significant theologically. The preface to the Psalter consists of two psalms, one a psalm in praise of God's torah or "instruction" (Psalm 1), and the other a royal psalm, dealing with the installation of Yahweh's "anointed" (messiah) on the holy hill of Zion (Psalm 2). Since both of these psalms stand outside the first Davidic collection, which comprises Psalms 3–41, and unlike other psalms in this collection they have no headings ascribing them to David, we may safely assume that they were located here by an editor for the purpose of sounding major themes of worship: rejoicing in the torah and the hope for a messianic king to rule in Zion. Mixed in with hymns, laments, and thanksgivings are a number of royal psalms that highlight the imagery of kingship (e.g., Psalms 45, 110, 118).[3]

The Theological Center of the Book of Psalms

Just as the organization of a modern hymnal may indicate its overall theological flavor, so the canonical shape of the book of Psalms may contribute to our theological understanding of the book as a whole. Gerald H. Wilson has suggested an interesting way to understand the present shape of the book of Psalms.[4] He notes that the Psalter opens with a psalm of the Davidic covenant (Psalm 2), that there is a royal psalm at the end of book II (Psalm 72), also that there is another royal psalm at the end of book III (Psalm 89), though this one, as we have seen, shifts from praise to lament about the failure of the promises of grace to David. Looking at books I–III, Wilson suggests that the placement of these psalms is intended to display the failure of the Davidic covenant and the need for a larger theological view. The problem is resolved, he maintains, in book IV, which he calls "the editorial center of the final form of the Hebrew Psalter," especially the psalms of God's dominion clustered in Psalms 93, 95–99. In these psalms, sovereignty is lifted from the human level (trust in kings and princes) to the cosmic level (trust in the God who is cosmic king and creator).

3. See my classification of the psalms in *Out of the Depths* (rev. ed.; Philadelphia: Westminster, 1983; [[3d ed., 2000),]] especially the outline in appendix A.

4. Gerald H. Wilson, *The Editing of the Hebrew Psalter,* Society of Biblical Literature Dissertation Series 76 (Atlanta: Scholars Press, 1985).

This is an attractive, even tempting, hypothesis. It enables us to see that the book of Psalms was not just thrown together but was composed in its final form to make a theological statement. The hypothesis is challenged, however, by the structure of the book of Psalms itself, for Psalm 132, which comes after the psalms of Yahweh's enthronement, presents a restatement of the tenets of the Davidic covenant: election of the Davidic king and choice of the temple of Zion. The truth is that Israelite interpreters never regarded the Davidic covenant as superseded, but held on to the promises of grace to David, though lifting them above the level of prosaic historical reality. It is noteworthy that Augustine in his great work, *The City of God* (book 17), devoted great attention to Psalm 89.

The Cosmic Dominion of God

[[211]] Despite its vulnerability, this hypothesis has the merit of drawing attention to a central teaching of the Psalms as an edited hymnbook. While the Mosaic covenant emphasizes the dimension of Israel's history, the Davidic covenant is deeply rooted in mythopoetic symbolism. Davidic covenant theology explodes beyond the limitations of Israel's sacred history and Israel's covenant community by announcing that the God whom Israel worships is not Israel's God in a narrow, possessive, or exclusive sense, but the God who is creator of heaven and earth and the sovereign of all nations. This is an ecumenical theological perspective.

Located at the center of the Psalter, the psalms of Yahweh's dominion sound forth the central message of the whole book: the sovereign rule (kingdom) of God. Today the word "kingdom" sounds foreign, especially in the United States, which has had no experience with monarchy, and for some the language is too heavily laden with masculine imagery. Is there another word in English that conveys the interrelated meanings of (a) the power of a sovereign (b) who rules over a territory and (c) is accorded allegiance by subjects? "Rule" stresses the sovereign's control, but lacks the spatial dimension. "Realm" conveys the spatial dimension but lacks the emphasis on sovereignty. "Regime" suggests a system of management but lacks a personal dimension of loyalty. The "monarchy" or "empire" of God sounds forced and is too political. For the sake of being honest with Scripture the word "kingdom" should be retained, as in most modern translations (NRSV, REB, NIV, NJB). If we shift terminology to soften the emphasis on divine sovereignty, perhaps the best word is "dominion of God."[5]

In the psalms of Yahweh's dominion, then, the horizon expands from the praise of "our God"—the God revealed in Israel's historical experience—to an ecumenical vision of God's worldwide sovereignty, which is not bounded by politics or geography.

---

5. Proposed in [[Victor Gold et al., ed.,]] *The New Testament and Psalms: An Inclusive Version* (New York: Oxford Univ. Press, 1995), as in the Lord's Prayer: "Your dominion come." On the larger question of how divine sovereignty is exercised, see my essay, "The Kingdom, the Power, and the Glory: The Sovereignty of God in the Bible," *TToday* 53 (1996) 5–14.

To be sure, these psalms do not lose contact with the plane of history, even Israel's history. There are occasional references to episodes of Israel's story, such as the years of testing in the wilderness (Ps 95:8–10), the leadership of Moses, Aaron, and Samuel (99:6–7), or the choosing of a heritage (land) for Israel (47:3–4; cf. 98:2–3). By and large, however, the primary axis of these psalms is the vertical relation of heaven and earth, not the horizontal one of the fulfillment of God's promise in history. "The real center of action, in the Covenant of David," remarks J. C. Rylaarsdam, "lies in the primordial, the cosmic, and the pre-temporal world that antedates the world of human contingency."[6] These Davidic psalms, he goes on to [[212]] say, move in a mythical dimension: they "sing about the triumph of God as Creator by recalling his establishment of order (*sedeq*), by the overcoming of chaos and anarchy in struggles that lie in that mythical past." Therefore the social order—especially the Davidic dominion—is securely founded.

> Yahweh's Kingship, and the Davidic kingship as well, rests on a series of decrees which are eternal and unchangeable: the world is established, it will not be moved. Yahweh is King forever; mightier than the breakers of the many waters [i.e., the forces of chaos]. He decrees the place of the nations in the scheme of things; and by that same immutable decree David is his first-born. He [David] has set his right hand over the sea and the rivers [cf. Ps. 89:25], a token which coordinates his rule with that of Yahweh himself.

He concludes this summary by saying that Davidic theology soars above the contingencies and changes of human history.

> The focus is on the Alpha of the beginning; and the psalms repeatedly appeal to this *me'az* [from time of old], this primordial *illo tempore* [those ancient times], as the rock of assurance amid the instabilities of time and history.[7]

Israel's Theology of Divine Kingship

Several things deserve attention in this summary of Davidic theology. First, these psalms move in the spacious horizon of creation—not just creation in the primordial past (as in Genesis 1), but the whole creation that is radically dependent on the Creator for its order and permanence. The earth belongs to Yahweh who made it, founding it securely on the waters of chaos (Ps 29:10). Creation is not just an event of the remote past but also includes the present cosmic order that the Creator sustains against continuing disruptions

6. J. C. Rylaarsdam, "Jewish-Christian Relationship: The Two Covenants and the Dilemmas of Christology," *JES* 9, no. 2 (1972) 249–70, quotation 261. Reprinted in [[James I. Cook, ed.,]] *Grace upon Grace: Essays in Honor of Lester J. Kuyper* (Grand Rapids: Eerdmans, 1975), 70–84, quotation 78. In this essay Rylaarsdam compares the Mosaic and Davidic covenants.

7. Ibid.

of the powers of chaos. In this creation theology, the whole *'erets* (earth), not narrowly *'erets yisra'el* (the land of Israel), belongs to the Lord (Yahweh) who made it, founding it on the waters of chaos (Ps 24:1). Hence worship becomes ecumenical. All peoples are invited to join Israel in worshiping the God who is Creator and king.

> For he [Yahweh] spoke and it came to be;
> he commanded, and it stood firm.
>   —Ps 33:9

Moreover, the invitation to praise God is extended to the whole realm of nature: heaven and earth, the sea and fields, the trees and the forest. Here we do not find the dichotomy between "history" and "nature" that has contributed to the present ecological crisis. God's dominion embraces the great whole.[8]

Creation versus Chaos

Second, these psalms celebrate Yahweh's dominion by recalling divine triumphs that occurred in the primordial era, "those ancient times." The language moves [[213]] beyond historical recital, found for instance in the storytelling Psalms 105 and 106, into the imaginative realm of mythical exploits of creation. Yahweh is portrayed as the Divine Warrior who came, comes, and will come to overcome the powers of chaos symbolized by the sea, the rivers, the floods. An ancient Israelite hymn displays strong influence of Canaanite poetry:

> Yahweh sits enthroned over the flood,
> Yahweh sits enthroned as king forever!
>   —Ps 29:10 (BWA)

The same language occurs in one of the hymns of Yahweh's dominion (93:3–4), where the poet portrays "the floods," "many waters," and "the sea" lifting up their stormy waves, as though seeking to challenge the sovereignty of Yahweh. But the tumult is in vain:

> More majestic than the thunders of mighty waters,
> more majestic than the waves of the sea,
> majestic on high is the LORD [Yahweh]!
>   —Ps 93:4

Establishment of Cosmic Order

Third, the result of these mythical victories in the primordial past is that Yahweh the Creator has established right order or "righteousness." The cosmic King has issued a series of eternal decrees that shape and govern the future, including the establishment of the Davidic throne and the assignment of lands to Israel and other peoples (Pss 93:5; 97:8). Therefore the dominion of Yahweh, the Creator and cosmic King, is to be proclaimed among all nations:

---

8. See Rosemary Radford Ruether, *Gaia & God: An Ecofeminist Theology of Earth Healing* (San Francisco: HarperSanFrancisco, 1993), chap. 11.

Say among the nations, "The LORD [Yahweh] is king!
  The world is firmly established,
    it shall never be moved.
  He will judge the peoples with equity."
                                        —Ps 96:10

To be sure, there are flare-ups of disorder, when it seems that God has lost control. Israelite poets, however, are confident that Yahweh is sovereign, even though that sovereignty may be hidden at present or seemingly threatened by powers of chaos, evident in attacks of foreign enemies, disruption of fertility, or social breakdown. Confident that God is fully in control, poets looked to the future in the expectation that God would come to judge (rule) the earth with righteousness and truth (Ps 96:10–13). Thus God's dominion provides "the rock of assurance amid the instabilities of time and history" (Rylaarsdam). The worship of "the King, all glorious above," resounds in Christian worship services even today, as in our hymn, "O, Worship the King."

The earth with its store of wonders untold,
  Almighty, thy power hath founded of old; [[214]]
hath established it fast by a changeless decree,
  and round it hath cast, like a mantle, the sea.

Current Battles against the Powers of Chaos

Finally, the founding of the Davidic kingdom is seen to be part of the cosmic order that God has established. As the "son of God," or in some ancient Near Eastern texts "the image of God," the earthly ruler is God's representative through whom the cosmic order is mediated to earthly society, so that there may be justice and peace (Psalm 72). The king's battles against his enemies are seen in the perspective of God's warfare against the powers of chaos:

I will set his hand on the sea
  and his right hand on the rivers.
                              —Ps 89:25

Although the Israelite king is not considered divine or an incarnation of God, in some sense his task is to make the dominion of God a reality in human society. Through the king, the social order is related harmoniously to the cosmic order.

In one respect, New Testament portrayals of the coming of God's dominion are similar to this worldview. Jesus' battles against Satan's dominion, as portrayed in the Synoptic Gospels (especially Mark), are part of God's ongoing warfare against the powers of evil in order that there may be a "new creation." In apocalyptic visions, which we will consider later, faithful people are called to take part in the struggle against evil and, as in the conclusion to the Lord's Prayer, to pray that God will deliver persons "from the evil one."[9]

9. See the discussion of "The Dominion of God versus the Dominion of Evil," [[Anderson 1999]] Chapter 33.

The Enthronement of God

It is appropriate that the songs of God's dominion belong in a hymnbook, for it is in worship that people are invited to leave the ordinary world, with its illusory values and misleading ways, and to enter imaginatively into God's world, where God is "enthroned on the praises of Israel" (Ps 22:3).[10] Perhaps it is in imagination that we discern the real world that belongs to God and, as we sing in one of our hymns, affirm "That though the wrong seems oft so strong, God is the Ruler yet."[11]

The psalms of Yahweh's kingship (Psalms 47, 93, 94–99) reflect a cultic festival, perhaps analogous to the New Year's festivals celebrated in surrounding countries such as Babylonia. On that occasion, as the great Scandinavian scholar Sigmund Mowinckel proposed, the dominion of Yahweh was not just expressed hymnically; it was celebrated in a ritual drama of Yahweh's ascension to the divine [[215]] throne.[12] The ritual included a reenactment of David's bringing the ark to Jerusalem (Ps 132:6–10; cf. 2 Samuel 6), the triumphal procession through the gates of the city (Ps 24:7–10), and the placement of the ark in the Holy of Holies of the temple, where Yahweh "sits enthroned upon the cherubim" (99:1).

Psalm 47 is an excellent witness to this view. Here the theme of Yahweh's ascension is announced: God (Yahweh) has "gone up" (ascended) amid shouts of acclamation and with the sound of the shofar (trumpet):

> God has gone up with a shout,
>   The Lord [Yahweh] with the sound of a trumpet.
> Sing praises to God, sing praises,
>   sing praises to our King, sing praises.
>
> —Ps 47:5–6

Since, however, the earthly temple was regarded as the counterpart of the heavenly, on the principle of the relationship between the macrocosm and the microcosm, the drama symbolized Yahweh's ascension to the heavenly throne. Thus "the great king" (47:2) not only reigns in Zion, where anthems of praise are sung, but over the whole earth.

> God is king over the nations;
>   God sits on his holy throne.
> The princes of the peoples gather
>   as the people of the God of Abraham.
> For the shields [rulers] of the earth belong to God;
>   he is highly exalted.
>
> —Ps 47:8–9

10. See the insightful study by Walter Brueggemann, *Abiding Astonishment: Psalms, Modernity, and the Making of History* (Louisville: Westminster/John Knox, 1991).

11. "This Is My Father's World," by Maltbie D. Babcock (1858–1901).

12. Sigmund Mowinckel's view is set forth in *The Psalms in Israel's Worship*, trans. D. R. ApThomas, 2 vols. (Nashville: Abingdon, 1962), summarized in my *Out of the Depths*, "The Festival of Zion," Chapter 6. The whole subject is discussed helpfully by Ben C. Ollenburger, *Zion, City of the Great King*, JSOTSup 41 (Sheffield: JSOT Press, 1987), 33.

The throne ascension, analogous to the coronation of an earthly monarch, was accompanied by trumpet fanfare, shouts of acclaim, and songs of joy. Emissaries from foreign nations ("the princes of the peoples," 47:9) were apparently included in this ecumenical celebration.

The Lord Is King!

The keynote in these psalms is the cultic exclamation, YHWH *malak* (93:1; 96:10; 97:1; 99:1), which may be translated 'The LORD [Yahweh] has become king" (so REB), a translation that refers to an event that has happened. Alternatively, the cultic cry may be rendered "The LORD is king" (so NJPSV, NRSV; cf. NJB) or "the LORD reigns" (NLV), a translation that indicates Yahweh's eternal kingship.

The first-mentioned translation, while grammatically justifiable, is questionable if it implies regaining a kingship that has been lost. Unlike Baal in the [[216]] Canaanite religion, Yahweh is not involved in "the myth of the eternal return"[13]—a dying-rising god who is subject to the powers of death and darkness. Some suggest that the language is existential, referring to the confession that God has been dethroned in human life and needs to be re-enthroned; but this is rather forced. In all probability the exclamation refers to God's eternal kingship: Yahweh is king forever! God was king "from of old" (Ps 93:2), God is acclaimed as king now (47:7), and God will come as king to judge the earth (98:9). All the tenses—past, present, and future—must be employed to praise the God who was, who is, and who is to come.

In this language the biblical poets express the faith that human security is grounded in the rule of God who is transcendent—beyond the historical realm where powers of chaos are at work. From our human point of view, the disorder and suffering in the world seem to challenge the sovereignty of God. But above the waters of chaos—so faith affirms poetically—God sits enthroned as the eternal King, holding the cosmos in being and maintaining the order of cosmic law. It is the eternity of God, who remains God even though the earth be destroyed, that inspires a poet to affirm in a well-known Zion psalm:

> God is our refuge and strength,
>   a very present help in trouble.
> Therefore we will not fear, though the earth should change,
>   though the mountains shake in the heart of the sea;
> though its waters roar and foam,
>   though the mountains tremble with its tumult.

> —Ps 46:1-3

13. See Mircea Eliade, *Cosmos and History: The Myth of the Eternal Return* (New York: Harper and Bros., 1959).

God's Dominion as Future Horizon

God's dominion has a future horizon; for God's kingdom has *not* come on earth as it is in heaven. People still experience the threat of chaos, the shaking of earth's foundations, the sinister powers of death and darkness. In faith's imagination, however, the King, whose throne is securely established from of old, will come.

> Let the sea roar, and all that fills it;
> the world and those who live in it.
> Let the floods clap their hands;
> let the hills sing together for joy
> at the presence of the LORD [Yahweh], for he is coming
> to judge the earth.
> He will judge the world with righteousness,
> and the peoples with equity.
> —Ps 98:7–9; cf. 96:10–13

The Christmas carol, "Joy to the World, the Lord Is Come," echoes the jubilant notes of this psalm (see Ps 98:4–9).

[[217]] These psalms, as we have noticed, may reflect a cultic festival that was celebrated in the Jerusalem temple during the period of the monarchy. If so, in the final form of the Psalter the poetic language bursts beyond the limitations of the cult and becomes an expression of praise for all times and all peoples. Imagination portrays the eschatological coronation of God!

This imaginative portrayal is found in the magnificent passage, Isa 52:5–7, where language transcends historical reality. The poet gives a concrete picture, such as people of the time probably experienced. The countryside beyond the walls of Jerusalem is desolated by war; the people are huddled in the city, anxiously wondering how the battle goes with those fighting against hopeless odds; the sentinels are on the ramparts of the city gate, scanning the surrounding territory for any sign of activity. Suddenly in the distance the watchmen spy a single runner, a herald who approaches to announce that the war is over, that peace is at hand, that a new day is breaking. In Hebrew the word of the herald of good news is described in four participles (translated "who . . ."):

> How beautiful upon the mountains
> are the feet of the messenger:
> who announces shalom,
> who proclaims tidings of good,
> who publishes victory [salvation],
> who says to Zion: Your God reigns!
> —Isa 52:7 (BWA)

Here too the herald's exclamation may be translated, "Your God has become king" (REB), although more likely the poet refers to the imminent display of God's royal rule that is everlasting: past, present, and future. It is noteworthy, however, that in this passage the poet envisions the triumphant return of God to Zion (52:8). The Divine Warrior has "bared his holy arm before the eyes of all the nations" (52:10), with the result that God's people in the ruined places of Jerusalem experience deliverance, and "all the ends of the earth shall see the salvation of our God."

The theological overtones of this language of God's dominion, specifically God's coming to the temple of Zion with saving power, are picked up in the New Testament.[14] The Gospel of Mark begins with the announcement of the imminent coming of God's kingdom:

> Now after John was arrested Jesus came to Galilee, proclaiming the good news of God, and saying, "The time is fulfilled, and the kingdom of God has come near; repent, and believe in the good news."
>
> —Mark 1:14–15

14. See [[Anderson 1999]], chapter 35.

ERHARD S. GERSTENBERGER

b. 1932

One God, Changing Theologies

Erhard S. Gerstenberger completed his doctorate with Martin Noth and Otto Plöger at Bonn University, and his Habilitation with Hans Walter Wolff at Heidelberg. He was a parish minister in Essen for six years and Professor of Old Testament at the Lutheran seminary of São Leopoldo, Brazil, for another six. He retired in 1997 as Professor of Old Testament at Marburg University. Long a leader in the form-critical study of the Old Testament, Gerstenberger has also argued for the "contextualizing" of both the biblical texts and their interpreters.

Selected Writings by Gerstenberger

1988   *Psalms, Part 1, with an Introduction to Cultic Poetry.* Forms of the Old Testament Literature. Grand Rapids: Eerdmans.

1996   *Yahweh the Patriarch: Ancient Images of God and Feminist Theology.* Translated by Frederick J. Gaiser. Minneapolis: Fortress.

2000   Conflicting Theologies in the Old Testament. *Horizons in Biblical Theology* 22: 120–34.

2001   *Psalms, Part 2, and Lamentations.* Forms of the Old Testament Literature. Grand Rapids: Eerdmans.

2002   *Theologies in the Old Testament.* Translated by John Bowden. Minneapolis: Fortress.

Gerstenberger, Erhard S., and Wolfgang Schrage

1981   *Woman and Man.* Translated by Douglas W. Stott. Nashville: Abingdon.

Writings about Gerstenberger

Kessler, Rainer, Kerstin Ulrich, Milton Schwantes, and Gary Stansell (editors)

1997   *"Ihr Völker alle, klatscht in die Hände!" Festschrift für Erhard S. Gerstenberger zum 65. Geburtstag.* Exegese in unserer Zeit 3. Münster: LIT-Verlag.

Erhard S. Gerstenberger's
Approach to Old Testament Theology

Excerpted with permission from *Theologies in the Old Testament* (Minneapolis: Fortress, 2002), pp. 12–18.

What Is the Status of the Old Testament Writings?

[[12]] Why do we study the biblical writings at all? That is something that has to be explained. In fact such study, and the pressure to engage in it, has declined [[13]] steadily over the last few decades. Even in preaching, which is the traditional core of Protestant pastoral activity, and religious education, at least at a secondary level, it is often thought that we can dispense entirely with the Bible, or at least the Old Testament.

Why do we turn to the Old Testament anyway? In short, because we have to investigate our origin, i.e., compare the influence of the Bible on us with its origin and its tradition, in order to understand ourselves. In addition there is a critical element: those who define themselves only in terms of the present will be able neither to understand nor to correct themselves, and the theological element of "God" or "the Unconditioned" or "the Whole" or our "Ultimate Concern" (to use Paul Tillich's phrase) encounters us in the biblical testimonies to faith.[1] Thus the study of biblical theology functions for us as illumination and criticism. Moreover, and above all, the Old Testament/Hebrew Bible contains such a mixture of human self-knowledge and such a critique of both society and religion, which is still not exhausted, that time and again repeated reading can only prove life-giving.[2]

What do we find in the Old Testament? First of all we come upon a very complex book which has been in this form for almost two thousand years and has been declared by our own Christian tradition to be the binding basis of faith.[3] In more recent times the number of scholarly voices which want to content themselves with this has increased: they claim that the canon of the Old Testament scriptures has been presented to us by decisions of the early church; it says what we have to believe and therefore it is the written document of our tradition. In its existing final and fixed form it is both the object of our interpretations and the subject from which we receive orientation.[4]

1. Cf. Erhard S. Gerstenberger, [["Warum und wie predigen wir das Alte Testament?" in Bernard Jendorff and Gerhard Schmalenberg (eds.), *Theologische Standorte*, Giessen 1989, 33–45.]]

2. Cf. Ernst Bloch, *Atheismus im Christentum*, Frankfurt 1969. Bloch reads the Bible against the grain of official theology and the church and opens one's eyes much as biblical exegesis by the marginalized of the Third World and clear-sighted feminist theologians does.

3. The decisions were taken early in the history of the church and in the face of strong opposition (e.g., Marcion), which wanted to exclude the Old Testament as the makeshift work of a subordinate, mere creator God, but not the God of the Spirit.

4. To mention only a selection of names and some works which represent this "canon-critical" view of things: Brevard S. Childs, *Introduction to the Old Testament as Scripture*, London

However much some representatives of this integralist approach reject the idea, in their canonical theology they are in fact following a fundamentalist path. For they are attempting through the decision of the [[14]] early church to prescribe an intrinsically coherent, unitary doctrine as binding, or as a revelation given once and for all and timelessly valid. Thus the canonical approach is dictated by the need for unity and binding force. It is a very short-sighted, unhistorical and self-seeking principle, as it suppresses all that we now know about the origin of the biblical writings and wants a priori to exclude everything that does not fit into our own previously established pattern of thought and faith.

Against "canonical" interpretation we must object, first, that there is no one uniform coherent canon, however much attempts are made to construct it. And secondly, it is impossible for us to ignore the preliminary stages prior to the completion of the book of books, i.e., individual collections and individual texts, or the thousand-year-old historical depth-dimension of the corpus of scripture that we have received as canon. Thirdly, the present with its structure and questions has to be brought into theological statements.

On the first point: scholars very much want to tie the decision on the canon to a hypothetical Jewish synod of Jamnia which is said to have taken place around 100 C.E.: however, this is probably a pious invention. What help would it be to establish a day and hour for the collection of the corpus of scripture if the corpus itself is quite disparate? For the Jewish canon itself is not completely undisputed: the canonical status of individual books (like the Song of Songs or Koheleth) was challenged time and again. But it is more important that the Christian churches attached themselves to a completely different corpus (which also was never wholly undisputed) with an essentially _different_ internal structure (Pentateuch – Writings – Prophets) and the addition of apocryphal writings. If the formation of the canon is an internal decision on doctrine (a religious group fixes the scriptures which are to be its own criterion), then it is quite impossible to see why the church should want to base itself on the Hebrew collection and not on the Graeco-Jewish Bible exclusively used by the early Christians, the Septuagint (LXX), which existed in parallel.

Furthermore, it is impossible for a canon of writings which has grown up in history over generations to represent a coherent theological doctrinal structure. Even then, the times and situations in which people spoke and sang of God were so different that there simply cannot be any question of a uniform picture of God. And more than two hundred years of research into

---

1979; Rolf Rendtorff, _Kanon und Theologie. Vorarbeiten zu einer Theologie des Alten Testaments_, Neukirchen-Vluyn 1991; idem, _Theologie des Alten Testaments_ (2 vols.), Neukirchen-Vluyn 1999ff.; Erich Zenger, "Was wird anders bei kanonischer Psalmenauslegung?", in Friedrich V. Reiterer (ed.), _Ein Gott, eine Offenbarung_, Würzburg 1991, 397–413; Norbert Lohfink, "Was wird anders bei kanonischer Schriftauslegung?", _JBTh_ 3, 1988, 29–53; idem, "Der Psalter und die christliche Meditation: Die Bedeutung der Endredaktion für das Verständnis des Psalters," _BiKi_ 47, 1992, 195–200.

the Old Testament have exposed many different forms and strata in the texts, each of which needs to be evaluated as an independent testimony of faith at a particular time. It is quite clear that finally redactors of the early Jewish community went into action and brought together the collections which had been handed down, revised them by also incorporating much [[15]] material of their own and creating whole new consecutive histories (e.g., the Deuteronomic and Chronistic histories), and this must also be taken into account. So certainly—and we owe this recognition to the canonical critics—there was a communal final redaction of considerable theological importance. It must be considered and discussed. But it has no special theological status over and above the earlier collections and revisions or even the later commentators.[5] For each time people are speaking and acting in a particular situation, in specific conditions. And what emerges here is always a contemporary testimony to the faith by which these people lived at this particular time.

If these reflections are right, then in looking for the theologies in the Old Testament we are not so much going behind the written testimonies from the ancient Israelites of those times as attempting as far as possible to recognize the faith that they were practising in their everyday life and social group, in order to be able to enter into conversation with such expressions of faith. We are dealing with faith and life, not the "paper pope," a term which in some circumstances Martin Luther could apply to the Bible.[6] The faith of individuals and groups is lived out in specific historical and social situations. That is why these situations in life are so important and must be brought out with and behind the texts if we are to have better knowledge of people's beliefs.

If our concern is with the faith of ancient Israel in its contemporary environment and in everyday life, then in our interpretation we cannot want to limit ourselves to the great historical acts, as so-called "salvation-historical" theology has often done.[7] Life as it was lived in Israel at every social level and in all realms of life is interesting and important to us. Nor is it accessible to us solely through the writings which have come down to us—in their final versions they certainly derive from particular groups and were composed by particular professional classes which of course were expressing their own interests and views. We can also openly resort to the testimony of archaeology: artefacts and inscriptions similarly tell us something about the faith and everyday life of the people of the time. Sometimes these [[16]] sources serve to supplement

---

5. Cf. Erhard S. Gerstenberger, "Canon Criticism and the Meaning of Sitz im Leben," in Gene M. Tucker et al. (eds.), *Canon, Theology, and Old Testament Interpretation*, Philadelphia 1988, 20–31.

6. Luther was much more tied to this point of reality than the later orthodox Lutherans; but cf. the even more impressive attempt by Carlos Mesters to make "life" the criterion in biblical exegesis: *Vom Leben zur Bibel, von der Bibel zur Leben*, Munich 1983.

7. Von Rad is an example: his *Old Testament Theology* begins from the history of Yahweh with his people, i.e., it always presupposes "all Israel" as a sociological entity. The faith of the small groups and the individual is discussed in an appendix, but still under the heading "Israel's Response," whereas wisdom theology in fact came later in a late work of von Rad's (Gerhard von Rad, *Wisdom in the Old Testament*, London 1972).

written sources, but increasingly frequently from archaeological material we make new and independent discoveries about the people whose texts we read or about whom we read texts. Thus the cautious and appropriate interpretation of finds makes an important contribution to knowledge of the theologies of the Old Testament.[8] Moreover the counter-voices to the "official theology" (which never existed as a uniform world-view) that can be heard in the Old Testament must also have a say.[9]

From what has been said so far it emerges that we may not read the biblical texts as a uniform norm of faith. They did not have that function when they were composed, even where there are demarcations from "pagans," "aliens" and the "godless." For these demarcations are always made in particular historical conditions and thus can be explained and understood from the situation. That means that they have no absolute claim to validity. Moreover, on closer inspection all texts without exception are deeply woven into the world of the ancient Near East, so it is no longer possible to understand them without in principle bringing in the neighbouring cultures and religions. That is even true of the core statements of the faith of ancient Israel, that "Yahweh is one and only one" and reserved for Israel (Deut 6:4). Of course it is right that in their historical situation people in Israel should and may have worshipped the God who was exclusively real to them because he was near to them and cared for them. But we cannot conclude either from this exclamation or from the theological explanations of Deutero-Isaiah that Yahweh had an objective uniqueness which was equally clear to all other groups and which they accepted as binding. In a concrete way, the exclusiveness of Yahweh remains the hope and expectation of limited communities who are fond of transferring their claim to others. It is not an objective fact that can be verified, from which we may simply proceed in our theology. There were often monolatrous and indeed monotheistic claims in the history of the ancient Near East.[10] If my view is correct, such claims cannot conceal the fact that in principle any belief in God is limited to a [[17]] particular group and that equally fundamentally in many Old Testament texts there is

---

8. Rightly, archaeology and extra-biblical evidence are increasingly being included in the historical and theological debate, cf. Gösta W. Ahlströhm, *The History of Ancient Palestine*, Minneapolis and Sheffield 1993; Niels Peter Lemche, *Die Vorgeschichte Israels*, BiE 1, Stuttgart 1996; Volkmar Fritz, *Die Entstehung Israels im 12. und 11. Jahrhundert v.Chr.*, BiE 2, Stuttgart 1996.

9. Cf. Walter Brueggemann, *Theology* (ch. 1 n. 2), 317–403.

10. Monolatry is the term used for preferential worship of one God while recognizing other deities for other groups and peoples; monotheism is the claim that there is exclusively one God for all human beings. Cf. Mark S. Smith, *The Early History of God*, San Francisco 1990; Herbert Niehr, *Der höchste Gott*, BZAW 190, Berlin 1990; Othmar Keel, *Monotheismus im Alten Israel und seiner Umwelt*, BiBe 14, Fribourg 1980; Bernhard Lang (ed.), *Der einzige Gott. Die Geburt des biblischen Monotheismus*, Munich 1981; Walter Dietrich and Martin Klopfenstein (eds.), *Ein Gott allein?*, OBO 139, Göttingen and Fribourg 1994 (bibliography).

an almost unlimited openness to the neighbouring ancient Near Eastern cultures and religions.[11]

What Are Our Aims in Interpreting the Ancient Traditions?

It is quite legitimate also to reflect on the direction that this work is to take. Unless we do so, unperceived hidden desires will become established and direct exegetical efforts and theological results. One can demonstrate at every turn how that happens, even among the great scholars of our discipline (cf. Julius Wellhausen, Bernhard Duhm, Hermann Gunkel, Gerhard von Rad, etc.). In retrospect it then seems a matter of course that even the great were "children of their time."[12] Only for the present does everyone concerned keep asserting how tremendously objective his or her own view is. Here it is significantly better for us to be clear from the start that we are not approaching the Old Testament with absolutely no intentions, but are bringing along quite specific ideas which we shall be reading into the texts.[13]

I have already indicated that we do not read the Old Testament and attempt to discover its theological statements because we are interested in them as museum pieces. The Old Testament is not to be put in a stained-glass window, so that a wondering posterity can file past it. It is not to be laid up in a mausoleum. No, the Old Testament has always been a living book and has been constantly used, read, read aloud, sung and played; it has also entered into graphic art and the literatures of the peoples in a rich and fruitful way, and also into music and drama (and into law, politics, philosophy, ethics, etc.). Be this as it may, the Old Testament is a book which is full of life and which belongs to life; as such we need to pick it up and keep it with us. It will be our dialogue partner in the most difficult questions of life and faith. From this book we hope for clarifications of what is good and evil today, of how God and human beings, world and future, nature and culture are to be defined and treated today. So after duly analysing the [[18]] conditions of faith, arrived at with all the scholarly means at our disposal, our aim is to attempt a conversation with the urgent demands of today. Only in this way, in my view, can we arrive at theological results which are viable in our apocalyptic times.

11. I have attempted to describe how demarcations can be constructed in an article entitled "Andere Sitten"–"Andere Götter," in Ingo Kottsieper et al. (eds.), *"Wer ist wie du, Herr, unter den Göttern?"* FS Otto Kaiser, Göttingen 1994, 127–41.

12. Biographical research into previous generations always produces extraordinarily interesting connections between methods and results of research on the one hand and the places of socialization and socio-cultural conditions on the other; cf., e.g., Rudolf Smend, Jr., *Deutsche Alttestamentler in drei Jahrhunderten*, Göttingen 1989; Werner Klatt, *Hermann Gunkel. Zu seiner Theologie der Religionsgeschichte und zur Entstehung der formgeschichtlichen Methode*, Göttingen 1969; Burke O. Long, *Planting and Reaping Albright. Politics, Ideology and Interpreting the Bible*, University Park, Pennsylvania 1997.

13. Few scholars see this necessary process of "eisegesis" as clearly as J. Severino Croatto, *Hermeneutics of Freedom*, Maryknoll 1978.

Synopsis of Gerstenberger's *Theologies of the Old Testament*

Erhard S. Gerstenberger
On One God, Changing Theologies

Excerpted with permission from *Theologies in the Old Testament* (Minneapolis: Fortress, 2002), pp. 215–21, 276–81. Some footnotes have been omitted.

Yahweh, the Only God

[[215]] How are we to explain the fact that after the collapse of 587 B.C.E. and the deportation of the upper class to Babylon (national!) worship of Yahweh with a claim to total exclusiveness became established in the newly formed religious community of Judah? To shed a little light on the darkness we must take into account the living conditions of the defeated, humiliated and dispersed people. Even then plenty of questions may remain. The theology of the Old Testament which can be brought out in connection [[216]] with the contemporary documents is the theology of the early Jewish community—diverse and also contradictory. At this point, too, we must not abandon the historical insight that the writings that we have arose in long processes of growth and usage. And all recognizable phases, stages and groupings of this growth have their independent significance. They are witnesses to a faith which in each case is contextual, of which no form became final. So however much the theological concern of the final revisers and collectors of the holy scriptures must be noted and taken seriously, they are not—and this has to be said against some kinds of integral or holistic exegesis—the only spokesmen, who set the standards for all times. But the greatness of the final stages of the collection and formation of the canon, which is often misunderstood, is that they reflect community theology from the sixth or fifth centuries B.C.E. And the writings from that phase which have been left to us came into being under the special conditions of Israel and the peoples and cultural world of the ancient Near East which predominated in the late Babylonian and Persian empire. (One has only to compare the legendary or historical collaboration with the Persian imperial government over the introduction of the Jewish law, Ezra 7; Nehemiah 8.) According to the principles which guide us, none of the theological statements of that time are absolutely and unchangeably valid so that they could easily be transferred to our time. But everything that people then thought, knew and experienced is extraordinarily significant. That is because, first of all through the written tradition, such great importance has come to be attached to the decisions of the early Jewish theologians and communities that today we are still living by them and to some degree suffering under them. All the basic theological concepts, e.g., the notion of God, the doctrine of salvation and redemption, the basic ethical norms (cf. the Decalogue), the understanding of history (which begins and ends at a particular point), the religious and liturgical forms (e.g., Psalms, ideas of holiness, etc.), numerous social and political concepts, etc.—like the written collections of

Torah and Prophets—come from that time and from these roots. The formation of the exilic and post-exilic Yahweh community briefly sketched out above [[not reproduced here]] is thus an integral element—the main factor, as it were the backbone, of this theology. Even now it is not a matter of presenting some abstract belief in Yahweh as the primal model of all later faith which is unchanging because it is suprahistorical. Rather, the belief of that time and that society is an important elaboration of the tradition of faith in which we and also the New Testament Jesus community, like all later forms of the Christian community, stand, and through which in fact we are first involved. By contrast, no power in the world can take from us the notions and decisions of faith that are expected of us. They have to be ventured afresh [[217]] in the light of the tradition and in dialogue with it, and also in dialogue with the other religions and our present-day reality.

Thus the social structures of the conquered Judahites at home and in the Diaspora come from the clan and village association. Those who had been subjected and integrated into the Babylonian or Persian empire no longer had to assume any responsibility at the level of wider society, even if insulted national pride sees Jehoiachin and Zerubbabel, Ezra and Nehemiah at the centre of imperial power, and in literary fiction crowns Queen Esther empress of Persia. The communities which were forming were small-scale, and found an appropriate expression of their identity and their cohesion beyond a particular region only in the tribal and national cult of Yahweh. The emigrant mentality, e.g., of German emigrants to the two Americas, is sociologically comparable. In the New World, the new settlers clung to their Germanhood because they were politically helpless and dispersed as micro-societies in an alien environment. This "virtual" identity with the homeland and its political ideologies gave such "foreign" communities a framework of identity in which everyday life with its demands could be led.[1] So we should not be surprised that the state religion of Judah became the basic foundation of the new reality after the dissolution of the state and its far-reaching transformation and adaptation to the conditions of small societies. The pluralistic traditions of family, clan and village were unable to produce a common denominator both for those who had been deported and those who had remained behind. And the figures in the new order predominantly came from the national elites of the shattered monarchical society.

The question still remains why after the loss of the war another deity known in Israel but less compromised, like, e.g., Asherah or the Queen of Heaven, did not take on integrating and protective functions for the community. In fact women in Jer 33:16–18 argue in precisely this direction (since "we have omitted to sacrifice to the queen of heaven . . . we have suffered all want and have perished through the sword and hunger"). I can only repeat

---

1. As an example, mention might be made of Martin N. Dreher, *Kirche und Deutschtum in der Entwicklung der Evangelischen Kirche Lutherischen Bekenntnisses in Brasilien*, Göttingen 1978; cf. also Hans-Jürgen Piren, *Die Geschichte des Christentums in Lateinamerika*, Göttingen 1978, 742–843.

the hypothesis that the traditional ideas of the male elites became established in the communities (in Elephantine manifestly with the retention of Yahweh) because the new community of faith was organized as a public corporation. In the public sphere men had the say. For them the old state god Yahweh was the most natural religious choice. The exclusiveness of his worship corresponded to the need to protect the new communities resolutely against all tendencies towards integration.

The Name and Exclusiveness of Yahweh

[[218]] So after the collapse of the monarchy, on the urging of the upper class, which had been stripped of political power but internally continued to set the tone, the community of the people of Judah clung to the god Yahweh whom they had worshipped since tribal times and also under the monarchy.[2] Many people were haunted by the idea that in the foreseeable future Yahweh would restore the dynasty of David and the state of Judah in more splendour than before—dreams of an impotent minority:

> In that day I will raise up the booth of David that is fallen, and repair its breaches, and raise up its ruins, and rebuild it as in the days of old; that they may possess the remnant of Edom and all the nations who are called by my name, says Yahweh who does this. (Amos 9:11-12)

> And I will set up over them one shepherd, my servant David, and he shall feed them; he shall feed them and be their shepherd. And I, Yahweh, will be their God, and my servant David shall be prince among them; I, Yahweh, have spoken. (Ezek 34:23-24)

> Behold the days are coming, says Yahweh, when I shall raise up for David a righteous branch, and he shall reign as king and deal wisely, and shall execute justice and righteousness in the land. In his days Judah will be saved, and Israel will dwell securely. And this is the name by which he will be called, "Yahweh our righteousness." (Jer 23:56)

With the delay over this restoration, hope for the new kingdom under a descendant of David then assumed increasingly more utopian and more eschatological features (cf. Isa 9:5-6; 11:1-9),[3] whereas presumably at the same time belief in Yahweh also liberated itself from the thought-patterns of the state and was transformed in the direction of the new community structures.

2. Even under the monarchy it seems to have been customary to worship Yahweh as a family god. At any rate the clear increase in personal names containing Yahweh in the late period of the monarchy would seem to point to that. These names have either been handed down in biblical texts or are attested by contemporary inscriptions. Naturally both sources predominantly mention representatives of the ruling elite. Cf. Jeffrey H. Tigay, *You Shall Have No Other Gods*, Atlanta 1986.

3. For the whole complex of expectations of king and Messiah, cf. Sigmund Mowinckel, *He That Cometh*, Oxford and New York 1954; Bernard Lang and Dieter Zeller, "Messias/Christus," *NBL* 2, 781-86.

The belief in Yahweh which arose anew after the collapse of power was ori-
entated on the parochial community and the dispersed religious community
of the Judahites, who had been relieved of all responsibility for wider society.

Thus the catastrophe of 587 B.C.E. had not totally destroyed belief in the
God who united the people and safeguarded its political existence. Or to
[[219]] put it the other way round, despite all the disappointments, in the exile the hard-hit officials, priests and other functionaries of the monarchy
maintained their orientation on Yahweh or the faith which created identity in
the upheaval of turbulent times. Compare Psalm 89; Isa 40:27: "Why do you
say, O Jacob, and speak, O Israel, 'My way is hid from Yahweh, and my right
is disregarded by my God?'" Ps 44:12–13 is even sharper: "You have made us
like sheep for the slaughter, and have scattered us among the nations. You
have sold your people for a trifle, demanding no high price for them." But
the national, monarchical level of society had collapsed and under the super-
vision of the world empires could not be regained. For the newly-arising communities, which sociologically were more like family clans, belief in Yahweh
took on a fundamental significance and provided meaning.

However, as has been said, a fixation on belief in Yahweh did not come
about without clashes with other levels of faith. The text Jer 44:15–19, which
has already been mentioned, is testimony to the opposition to Yahweh-alone
worship from the sphere of family religion. But the elite stratum, which had
really been discredited, won through. The time came when Judahites no
longer identified themselves by people, fatherland, dynasty or even abode,
but by Yahweh. When the sailors ask Jonah the quite normal question, "From
what land are you and from what people are you?", the fugitive replies: "I am
a Hebrew (ʿibrî) and fear Yahweh the God of heaven, who has made the sea
and the dry land" (Jonah 1:8–9). Here a man is (almost) exclusively defining
himself by faith and confession, which, as far as we can ascertain, is something new in the history of ancient Near Eastern religion. That such a confession of Yahweh made in Israel down to the exile was at the same time
strongly transformed, in other words that the notion of God fundamentally
changed, can already be seen from the formula used by Jonah (and later in
many different attributes of God). The expression "I fear Yahweh" echoes a
stereotyped formula, "those who fear Yahweh," which is used especially in the
Psalms of the totality of the members of the early Jewish community.[4] Ps
15:3; 22:24, 26; 31:20; 60:6; 61:6; 66:16; 85:10 may be mentioned as examples
of this:

> In whose eyes a reprobate is despised, but who honours those
>   who fear God,
> who swears to his own hurt. . . . He who does these things will never be
>   moved. (Ps 15:4–5) [[220]]

---

4. Cf. Hans Ferdinand Fuhs, *ThWAT* 3, 869–93, esp. 885–93. "Thus belonging to
YHWH will be expressed in this phrase (i.e., *yirʾē yhwh*). 'Those who fear YHWH' always denotes the community of YHWH worshippers" (ibid., 887).

> Surely his salvation is at hand for those who fear him,
> that glory may dwell in our land. (Ps 85:10)

Yahweh is the God of those who are loyal to Yahweh, who are united in the early Jewish community. Here it is presupposed that every member has made a personal decision for the God of Israel. Presumably in "fear" of Yahweh there is also an allusion to the bond to the Torah, so that only the chosen self-designation represents a clear reference to belonging to the Torah community under the God Yahweh. The Deuteronomistic writings also use the verb *yārē'* 'fear', in stereotypical fashion to express the sole orientation of believers on Yahweh (cf. Deut 4:10; 5:29; 6:2, 13, 24; 8:6; 10:12, 20, etc.).

The exclusive bond with Yahweh which applied to community and individual members then found its classic form in the "Shema Yisrael" of Deut 6:5–8, which has been influential down to present-day Judaism and in Christianity through the New Testament:

> Hear, O Israel: The Lord our God is one Lord; and you shall love the Lord your God with all your heart, and with all your soul and with all your might. And these words which I command you this day shall be upon your heart; and you shall teach them diligently to your children, and shall talk of them when you sit in your house, and when you walk by the way, and when you lie down, and when you rise. You shall bind them as a sign upon your hand, and they shall be as frontlets between your eyes. And you shall write them on the doorposts of your house and on your gates.

The sole claim of Yahweh to his people was the means of holding together the defeated and dispersed people, giving it new self-confidence and hope for the future. Every individual is addressed and at the same time referred to the community. In the course of history, both ancient and modern, many Jews have not observed the religious commandment to be united and have been integrated into other societies and faith communities. By contrast, the loyal Yahweh community preserved itself as an independent cultural and religious entity at the cost of encapsulating itself from its environment (cf. the dissolution of mixed marriages in Ezra 10 and Nehemiah 13, also in Numbers 25) and separating from divergent groupings (like the Samaritans or the Qumran community) as an independent cultural and religious entity. Minorities and emigrant groups, including the German emigrants mentioned above, have at all times produced similar phenomena in asserting their identity; one might think of the Amish or the Dutch people in Pennsylvania, indigenous peoples in industrial societies, Celtic [[221]] groups in Great Britain, Indians in South Africa, Chinese in the Western industrial states, Malays in Indonesia or in the Philippines, and so on. The special feature of the community of Judah in antiquity was that for the first time belief in God, mediated through the possession of sacred scriptures and their continuous exegesis, proved to be the dominant motif of self-assertion.

. . . .

Changes: The Accumulation and Interdependence
of Images of God

[[276]] If we look back at the history of Israelite religion from the beginnings in the twelfth to tenth centuries to the consolidation of the Yahweh community [[277]] in the Persian period and attempt to understand the changing theologies, we will inevitably get the impression that Yahweh (for once apart from the other deities known in the Old Testament) fundamentally changed, or better that the ideas of God in individual epochs and groups have to a great degree converged syncretistically and have also been driven apart syncretistically. Werner H. Schmidt has recognized that quite correctly.[5] There is no characteristic from the known religions of the environment which did not accrue to Yahweh. Or better, taking into account our principle of not wanting to argue deductively from the side of God, time and again there are only the opportunities of the particular time and the intellectual and linguistic means and models which are available from the situation and the environment. Our own tradition and experience is available, but it is already linked a thousandfold with the experiences and insights of all our neighbours, from whom we cannot completely shut ourselves off, even in the most acute case. The complete isolation of human groups from other hominids is an extreme exception—at least in the historical period—and therefore preoccupies the Robinson Crusoe fantasy of the literati. Moreover through communication with neighbours even the most recent religious currents always arrive at a given part of the population, though relatively limited. When, for example, the Indians from the tribe of the Desana (in the region of the Rio Negro) introduce into their creation story the white man with his flints alongside the priest with a book,[6] this is the indication of an actual momentous syncretism. For at some point in the twentieth century C.E. the world of the Desana came to include the whites, who wanted to rule others with force of arms. The unbelieving understanding of the Indians for the white mentality represents a syncretistic invasion of their own picture of the world.[7] Thus the existence of the invaders also has to be explained in the creation myth. Similarly, when the Zulu magician Madela retells the creation story of his tribe in a creative way he has to refer to the present changed circumstances of life, including white colonization.[8] Similar examples of rewriting and adaptation to new

5. Werner H. Schmidt, *The Faith of the Old Testament*, Oxford 1983.

6. Umúsin Panlon Kumu and Tolaman Kenhíri, *Antes o mundo não existia*, São Paulo 1980, 74, 213.

7. In the Indian myth, the creator says to the seventh creature to leave the underworld: "You are the last. I have given everything that I had to the first creatures. Now because you are the last, you must be a being without fear. You must be able to wage war in order to take their riches away from others. Then you will make money" (Umúsin Panlon Kumu and Tolaman Kenhíri, *Mundo* [[n. 19]], 74).

8. Katesa Schlosser, *Die Bantubibel des Blitzzauberers Laduma Madela. Schöpfungsgeschichte der Zulu*, Kiel 1977; cf., e.g., 231–35: "Has Matela created Sibi [the counterpart of Mvelinqangi] in parallel to Satan?," under the chapter heading "The Destruction of Mvelinqangi's Creation by his Brother Sibi." The question is answered with a cautious affirmative (ibid., 235).

[[278]] facts can be found in the Hebrew scriptures. When in Israel the question arose whether Yahweh was also responsible for growth and flourishing—in addition to warlike occasions—this theological problem was posed by a new agricultural way of life, but secondly also by an existing confrontation between Yahweh the god of the tribe and Baal the god of vegetation. We do not know precisely when both conditions were fulfilled; at any rate an important passage from Hosea seems to depict a later state of revision. (Lady) Jerusalem is presumably being addressed:

> Upon her children also I will have no pity, because they are children of harlotry. For their mother has played the harlot; she that conceived them has acted shamefully. For she said, "I will go after my lovers, who give me my bread and my water, my wool and my flax, my oil and my drink." Therefore I will hedge up her way with thorns, and I will build a wall against her, so that she cannot find her paths. She shall pursue her lovers, but not overtake them; and she shall seek them, but shall not find them. Then she shall say, "I will go and return to my first husband, for it was better with me then than now." For she did not know that it was I who gave her the grain, the wine, and the oil, and who lavished upon her silver and gold which they used for Baal. (Hos 2:6–10)

So at least theoretically the text plays through the situation assumed—Israel has now settled in cultivated land—and asserts that Yahweh has a new responsibility for agriculture and fertility.[9] On this frontier between seminomadism and a sedentary life, if it ever really existed, an extraordinary great amount of syncretistic work was necessary to shape belief in God from and for the necessities of peasant and village life.

That applies equally to the transition from tribal religion to state religion. The new social structures which have been described (centralism; a system of taxation; imperial military service, etc.) call for new definitions of the image of God which are expressed most clearly in the use of court titles and court etiquette for the religious sphere. "King," "King of all Kings," "Most High," etc., are designations of the monarch which were adopted in Israel (and above all in Jerusalem) in a necessary and completely legitimate way. But with them the earlier faith founded on a society which was not a state changed. It has to be said that in the time of the monarchy a new faith developed from the "syncretisms" of the new social structures which was composed from tradition with the old name Yahweh; that is perhaps the only authentic, deliberately syncretistic [[279]] feature. So here I would prefer to begin from the human perspective and say that in the new circumstances, in the time of the monarchy in Israel, as a result of syncretism, a new type of religion came into being, primarily on the level of the state or the official level. The new ideas about God then certainly also made themselves felt in the traditional family and local cults. Therefore the term syncretism is not quite

9. That is the current interpretation; cf. Hans Walter Wolff, *Hosea*, Hermeneia, Philadelphia, 1974; Wilhelm Rudolph, *Hosea*, KAT 13.1, Gütersloh 1966.

suitable for describing the phenomenon. It presupposes the attachment of some new features from outside to what is good, long known and homogeneous. Only with many qualifications is that the case. It is more important and more accurate to imagine creative processes at many levels on the basis of changing structures, goals and values. Every group and society works at shaping its faith and image of God with the traditions which come from the past (and therefore often also from different, outdated conditions), with influences from outside, and with the urgent questions and demands of the time and the particular interests of the group. However, it is always the case that the last point, the challenge of the present, is least perceived in the conception of the substance of faith. People think that the prefabricated elements of the images of God can break completely with the past and be brought into our present. And that is an illusion. In reality, for example in the present day, however evangelical and true to the Bible one may be, one always gains the substance of an understanding of God from one's own present, from one's own environment or in deliberate segregation from it. What is present and seems important in the traditional material is fused with modern requirements, not vice versa. However, to reassure themselves—and here there is always also an element of self-deception—people want to present their theology and ethic as "old," "well-tried" and "objective"; not as produced by themselves, but with the label "revealed." The longing for a fixed, irrevocable ground of faith drives us far into the remote past, where we want to give our own constructs of God safe anchorage. But in seeking to be responsible to the God of the present or the ground of being, it is our task to try to engage in constant, corrective dialogue with the old witnesses; we must look for the new form and formulation of faith which is valid today, appropriate to present conditions and human groupings, and "right" for them.

A third example of a revolution in Old Testament belief in God is the rise of exclusive worship of Yahweh after the deportations at the beginning of the sixth century B.C.E. The new version of religion in Judaea and among the exiles in Babylon produced the holy scriptures and left a deep mark on them. This whole chapter has been about this reshaping which accompanies the reconstruction of the community of faith and so we need not go into details here.

Tensions between the Theologies of Ancient Israel

[[280]] It should be said once again that because every situation and every human social grouping is mainly responsible for its faith, and because no human formation is completely homogeneous, but always carries around within itself its own internal contradictions, the statements of faith made in a particular era are contradictory, and each has to be taken seriously on its own terms. The question of true or false faith or images of God does not arise from assertions aimed at self-preservation along the lines of "We are right and the others wrong." Such claims to exclusiveness are usually coupled with the ideologies of power and rule and are therefore in themselves deserving of criticism. Those who claim to want to determine the true faith universally for all peoples of all times must arouse suspicion, because it is a basic human insight that our discourse is always limited and conditioned and cannot be universal. That also applies to central terms like "God." The mere history of the designations of God in the Old and New Testaments, not to mention further religious writings of humankind, shows with an unavoidable clarity how changeable and transitory the statements of faith are. The transition from the personal name "Yahweh" to the general Hellenistic term "Kyrios," to the German "Herr," the English "Lord," the French "Seigneur" and the Christian "God Christ" is a striking demonstration of how attitudes of faith are conditioned by time and culture. Each term has to be investigated and understood in its own context, with the tensions and contradictions prevailing there. Then of course we have to raise the question of truth, which we do according to mixed criteria. Some criteria have to be developed from the time of the documents, as far as that is possible. We can and may ask whether the articulated theological statements of the situation of the time were appropriate to the knowledge and state of the problem. The other criteria derive from our own surroundings and the theological (political, social, etc.) questions and values of our time. They put the theology of the witnesses of the time to the test in terms of our day. And that opens up the theological discussion beyond times and cultural spheres.

In all societies, attitudes of faith and cultic practices exist quite peacefully side by side on different social levels, often even within the same organization. Thus despite some ostracism from the side of "official" religion, family faith has never completely died out in the Jewish-Christian tradition. But in the Old Testament writings there are also signs of conflicts between [[281]] the currents of faith on a social basis. From a historical perspective, the family patriarchal religion is supplemented by local and tribal cults. The interests of the different groupings cannot always be harmonized (cf. Judges 6, Gideon). That becomes even clearer when the monarchy overlays and modifies all other formations of society (cf. Judges 9, Jotham). There will have been resistance from the tribal religions here and there. The more resolutely a social group or stratum puts forward its faith and claims to power, the more there is an internal clash over the toleration of parallel cults. That is the case in an extreme way in the exilic/post-exilic community. Under the pressure of conditions the community leaders (with the assent of the members?) decree the absolute incompatibility of any alien cult with Yahweh worship. Religious intolerance is born—as a means of self-assertion in a minority situation which seems hopeless. Down to the present day it has unleashed orgies of persecution and extermination from the side of the dominant majority and state religions, time and again, and with explicit reference to the religious sources of antiquity.

Part 5

Contexts, Perspectives, and Proposals

Introduction

In 1951, reviewing work in Old Testament theology during the first half of the twentieth century, Norman Porteous remarked that "there is no general agreement as to what a theology of the Old Testament should aim at providing" (1951: 311). That rich dissensus not only persisted but intensified, as previous chapters in this volume will have shown. Indeed, the range of approaches and proposals, including mutually incompatible ones, was never greater than at present. Several interrelated reasons could serve to explain why this is so.

First, options available for studying the Old Testament have proliferated. Many years ago, von Rad pointed to a "mutual intersection . . . between introductory studies and Biblical theology" (1962: v). By "introductory studies" von Rad meant investigation of and conclusions regarding the history and composition of the biblical material. His own tradition-historical studies were introductory in that sense, and they provided the foundation of his Old Testament theology. His remark regarding a mutual intersection remains instructive, even though introductory studies have gone in many different directions since von Rad made it. He did not anticipate the diversity of methods and approaches that the field of biblical studies now comprises.

Second, but in relation to the first point—a relation Leo G. Perdue demonstrated (1994)—Old Testament theology has drawn on a wider range of resources outside of biblical studies. Here again von Rad may serve as an example. One of his interpreters, Manfred Oeming (1987), associated von Rad's approach with Hans-Georg Gadamer—an association von Rad himself suggested (von Rad 1962a: 12). Gadamer and Paul Ricoeur, the past century's principal figures in philosophical hermeneutics, also appeared in Brueggemann's work. Above, in introducing part 4, I pointed to Otto Kaiser's use of Heidegger. To be sure, both Brueggemann and Kaiser, as examples, referred to many (in Kaiser's case, to a great many) philosophers, theologians, and scholars in various fields, whether to provide support for particular arguments, to cite influences, or to suggest instructive analogies in other areas of inquiry. Neither of them, and none of the Old Testament theologians, excerpts of whose work this volume includes, granted any particular philosopher, theologian, or "school" the foundational role that de Wette gave Kant (through Fries) and Vatke gave Hegel. Neither did Dale Patrick (1999), in his explanatory appeal to J. L. Austin and speech-act theory. On the other hand, Hans-Peter Müller posed again the question, once thought settled, "Does Old

Testament Theology Require a Philosophical Foundation?" (1992). Robert K. Gnuse was less guarded in promoting Whitehead and process thought as foundational (2001). Mark G. Brett's study of Childs (1991) perhaps best exemplified the eclectic and critical use of philosophical, theological, and literary-critical scholarship in a discussion of Old Testament theology. Regardless, Old Testament theology, in at least some regions, abandoned an earlier, transient anxiety about relating itself to currents of thought outside the putative mainstream of biblical scholarship (see Collins 1990 to the contrary). But the relations it chose or reflected, including with Christian theology, had much to do with how, in concrete instances, it conceived its own diverse aims (Ollenburger 1995).

Third, Old Testament theology came to include a wider range of participants in its discussions. The excerpts below reflect some of that greater diversity.

While Franz Rosenzweig (1921, 1970), Martin Buber (1950, 1967), and Abraham Joshua Heschel (1955) produced monumental works of Jewish biblical theology and philosophy—so also, more recently, Michael Fishbane (1989, 1998)—none of them discussed the methodological issues that had occupied Christian Old Testament theologians. Thus, in an essay first published in 1987, Jon D. Levenson could explain "Why Jews Are Not Interested in Biblical Theology" (1993a: 33–61). In the same year, Matitiahu Tsevat compared Jewish Old Testament theology with the "zoology of a unicorn" (1987: 329): a "non-existent beast," as Whybray (1987) described Old Testament theology in the same year. However, also in the same year appeared Moshe H. Goshen-Gottstein's essay arguing that "Jewish Bible scholarship cannot but [*sic*] attempt to create its alternative position" (1987: 242)—alternative, in this case, to Eichrodt and von Rad. Levenson's own work, excerpted below, has been described as illustrating "biblical theology at its best" (Murphy 1997: 271). Tikva Frymer-Kensky and Marvin Sweeney (2000), among others, carried the discussion further. Meanwhile, Isaac Kalimi provided a comprehensive review of "Jewish Interest in Biblical Theology" (2002: 107–34; cf. also Barr 1999: 286–311).

In a somewhat different direction, one that recovers Rosenzweig and Buber—but also, e.g., Emmanuel Levinas and Karl Barth—in postmodern or "postcritical" conversation, Peter Ochs has given primary leadership in "textual/scriptural reasoning" (1993, 2002). In its collaborative nature, including Jews, Christians, and Muslims in actual dialogue; in its collaborative attention to primary texts and their interpretation; in its alternative to both academic and fundamentalist reductionisms; and in its inclusion of the concrete particularities and practices of the religious communities and confessions for whom the texts are diversely primary—even its apparent conviction, expressed by Heschel, about the Bible: "It is a book that cannot die" (1955: 242)—"textual reasoning" may be a harbinger of biblical theology's future.

As Levenson gave reasons why Jews are (or were) not interested in biblical theology, Mary H. Schertz explained a similar lack of interest among feminist interpreters of scripture. In her terms, biblical interpretation, and thus biblical theology, "must take place within an ethical discourse that opposes models of domination and subjugation" and recognizes that "reading the Bible and describing its meanings are political acts . . . that involve the use of power and authority . . . not equally available to all . . ." (1991: 75). Phyllis Trible, in her essay excerpted below, shared much of Schertz's "liberationist" imperative (Schertz 1991: 66). So especially did Gunther H. Wittenberg (1996), writing in Natal and against the dominant paradigm of Old Testament theology. His essay, too, is excerpted below, as is one of Mark G. Brett's (2000). While essaying the field of Old Testament theology, Brett made reference to his Australian context and the social and political issues it presents to theological reflection and biblical interpretation.

In urging serious (re)consideration of the purposes biblical theology serves and, thus, for whom it is done, Brett joined others—including some already named—who have proposed that it may begin from the "burning problems of the present" (Brett 2000c: 477; cf. Ollenburger 1985; Albertz 1995b). Those problems themselves assume different shapes depending, in part, on "for whom it is done"—for whom biblical and Old Testament theology are done. R. W. L. Moberly suggested that "the primary and explicit purpose of a biblical theology should be to relate the Bible to the needs and concerns of the spirituality of the Christian church" (1992b: 149). As Moberly showed, in a work excerpted here, serving this purpose also involves criticism of the church (2000: 182–83). More concretely, the practices of certain communities may provide the context and purpose of Old Testament theology (Ollenburger 2003).

James Barr, while sharing Moberly's view that Old Testament (or biblical) theology includes more than just comprehensive, great books on the subject (Barr 1999: 54–55), otherwise differed. In a massive, often perceptive, and contentious review of contemporary Old Testament theology, one pointedly reproving of Childs and Brueggemann, Barr proposed an analogy with historical theology (1999: 209–21). In this he was seconded by Norbert Lohfink (2001) and anticipated by de Wette, Baumgarten-Crusius, and von Cölln. Barr's most recent arguments (as in the excerpts below) for distinguishing biblical/Old Testament theology from doctrinal or "real" theology make interesting comparison with Gabler; fittingly, then, Gabler's inaugural essay concludes this volume.

Like Gabler, Barr also considered the prospects for a biblical theology that would include both Testaments (a "pan-biblical theology"). From different perspectives—different especially from Barr's—Hartmut Gese and John Sailhamer (both excerpted below) were also concerned with the (Christian) Bible's unity. Gese, beginning from von Rad and proceeding beyond him, argued for the New Testament as "the goal and end . . . of biblical tradition" (1977: 322; cf. Hasel 1991: 80–85; Schmid 1977). Sailhamer, drawing critically on Rendtorff and Gese, and on text-critical considerations, argued that a "focus on the final shape of the Hebrew Bible . . . moves us into the world of the NT canon" (Sailhamer 2002: 37). Hermann Spieckermann has proposed to bring the two worlds close together by drawing the Septuagint (and thus the New Testament) into the discussion, and focusing on "God's Steadfast Love" as the avenue for reconceiving Old Testament theology (2000, 2001).

It remains to be seen whether any one of the perspectives and proposals represented in this (or any other) part of the current volume will have defined "the way forward" (Hasel 1992). But this seems unlikely. Old Testament theology has become too diverse in its aims, its conceptions of the material with which it works, its methods and contexts, assumptions and convictions, participants and publics (Brueggemann 1999) to permit confident predictions about the shape of its future. While this wild, undisciplined diversity may appall some moderns (Irwin 1945), it serves also to remind that Old Testament theology trades on something beyond its control, its discipline. This may be the best guarantee of its future.

Hartmut Gese

b. 1929

Tradition History

Hartmut Gese went beyond his teacher, Gerhard von Rad, by incorporating the New Testament within the process of tradition formation that began in the Old Testament. In this way, Gese moved toward a biblical theology. He was aided in this project by his New Testament colleague Peter Stuhlmacher, at the University of Tübingen. Gese was Professor of Old Testament there, beginning in 1958, until his retirement.

Selected Writings by Gese

1974   *Vom Sinai zum Zion: Alttestamentliche Beiträge zur biblischen Theologie.* Munich: Chr. Kaiser.

1977   Tradition and Biblical Theology. Pp. 301–26 in *Tradition and Theology in the Old Testament.* Edited by Douglas A. Knight. Philadelphia: Fortress.

1981a *Essays on Biblical Theology.* Translated by Keith Crim. Minneapolis: Augsburg.

1981b Wisdom, Son of Man, and the Origins of Christology: The Consistent Development of Biblical Theology. *Horizons in Biblical Theology* 3: 23–57.

1983   *Zur biblischen Theologie: Alttestamentliche Vorträge.* 2d edition. Munich: Chr. Kaiser.

1987   Die dreifaltige Gestaltwerdung des Alten Testaments. Pp. 299–328 in *Mitte der Schrift? Ein jüdisch-christliches Gespräch.* Edited by Martin Klopfenstein, Ulrich Luz, Shemaryahu Talmon, and Emmanuel Tov. Bern: Peter Lang.

Writings about Gese

Barr, James
1999   Pp. 362–77 in *The Concept of Biblical Theology: An Old Testament Perspective.* Minneapolis: Fortress.
Schmid, Johannes H.
1988   *Biblische Theologie in der Sicht heutiger Alttestamentler: Hartmut Gese, Claus Westermann, Walther Zimmerli, Antonius Gunneweg.* 2d edition. Giessen: Brunnen.

Hartmut Gese
Tradition and Biblical Theology

Excerpted with permission from Hartmut Gese, "Tradition and
Biblical Theology," in *Tradition and Theology in the Old Testament*,
edited by Douglas A. Knight (Philadelphia: Fortress, 1977), pp.
301–26. Translated by R. Philip O'Hara and Douglas A. Knight.

[[301]] The appropriate form for presenting biblical theology or even Old
Testament theology alone is a controversial subject. In fact, it is even problematic to determine exactly how its subject matter should be distinguished
from a systematic-theological (dogmatic) presentation of biblical *doctrine*.
Nevertheless, we can proceed from the justification given biblical theology in
Johann Philipp Gabler's Altdorfer inaugural address in 1787, *"De iusto discrimine theologiae biblicae et dogmaticae regundisque recte utriusque finibus"* ("On
the correct distinction between biblical and dogmatic theology and the
proper determination of the goals of each" [[English translation on pp. 497–
506 below]]). According to Gabler, biblical theology has a basically historical
orientation and should clarify the different theological positions of the writings and (as we would say today) of the traditions combined in the biblical
corpus: *"Est theologia biblica e genere historico, tradens quid scriptores sacri de re-
bus divinis senserint"* ("Biblical theology is of an historical nature, transmitting
what the holy writers thought about divine matters"). Systematic theology
can present dogmatics supported by biblical texts, but in contrast to this, biblical theology emerges from historical analysis of individual texts and should
therefore present the historical differences. With the impressive discovery
and expansion of historical knowledge in the nineteenth century, this biblical
theology progressively took on the form of a history of religion. Not only an
historical but increasingly also a dogmatic distinction [[302]] fundamentally
between the Old and New Testaments accompanied these discoveries. As a
result, the comprehensive biblical-theological perspective gave way to separate Old and New Testament theologies. The New Testament discipline maintained a conscious tie to the canon, thus setting limits to the disintegration of
New Testament theology into a history of primitive Christian religion. In part
this was due to the proximity of the discipline to dogmatics, but also because
the New Testament materials had gone through a much shorter historical expansion than had those of the Old Testament. In comparison, the Old Testament field often lost sight of its connection with the canon. As a "collection
of the national literature of Israel," the Old Testament became the main
source for reconstructing a history of Israelite religion, and this took the
place of a biblical theology.

Since the 1920s this development, which had been particularly evident
within Protestant circles, has been replaced by a general effort to reflect
upon the distinctive tasks involved if one is to make a description that is both

historical and also theological. The various contributions and suggested solutions cannot be reviewed here, but it would be well to mention the essential viewpoints and their consequences:

(1) In contrast to a history of Israelite religion, Old Testament theology must relate to Old Testament literature as *canon*. However, it is not enough for this theology to adopt—simply for practical reasons—the canon and its historical affirmation. Instead, this canon must be theologically grounded in the heart of the Old Testament itself.

(2) Only the *testimony* of the Old Testament—and not Israel's piety—can constitute material for Old Testament theology. Depending on one's proximity to Kerygmatic Theology, this basic premise was underscored and the testimonial character determined. However, such a premise derives from the very relation of Old Testament theology to the canon—regardless of one's own theological position. This is true to the extent that [[303]] the canon as such is characterized as a binding witness and consequently a religious "foundation"— and thus is more than a document of religious piety or religious "praxis."

(3) In contrast to a dogmatic presentation of theological doctrine, a theology of the Old Testament must be *historically* derived from the Old Testament itself. However, that cannot mean merely describing the historical character of a *theologoumenon* but must also involve determining its historical conditionedness, indeed its very essence which resides in its origins and in its historical crystallization and development. This historical character must be preserved regardless of whether Old Testament theology takes the form of a more or less systematically structured design, or describes the content in the form transmitted in the Old Testament, or presents its historical development, or is conceived as some combination of these approaches.

(4) It is not simply that in an Old Testament theology the relation of the materials to *history* must not become lost; indeed, this relation must determine its very structure. The historical path (*"Heilsgeschichte"*) witnessed to in the Old Testament is not merely one among several features of the Old Testament, but is of fundamental significance for every element of Old Testament theology. However, with respect to its content it does not suffice simply to understand Old Testament theology as a theology of *"Heilsgeschichte,"* especially since some important Old Testament materials cannot be subsumed under the rubric of history. Rather, theology must be understood essentially as an historical process of development. Only in this way does such a theology achieve unit, and only then can the question of its relationship to the New Testament be raised. Thus when individual *theologoumena* can be located in history, they acquire thereby a significance extending beyond historical precision and delimitation; they become classified functionally in this developmental process.

Contributions to Old Testament theology since the 1950s [[304]] illustrate progress in two directions. On the one hand, G. von Rad, drawing on the previous work of several predecessors, utilized the results of form criticism for the method of Old Testament theology. Since the Old Testament as a literary work develops from kerygmatic intentions, form criticism can to a considerable extent expose this kerygmatic structure, and a presentation of the traditions recovered by modern form criticism leads automatically to a presentation of the Old Testament kerygma. Thus, "retelling" ("*Nacherzäh-lung*") can be the "most legitimate form of speaking theologically about the Old Testament." The lively discussion following von Rad's work questioned whether form criticism was not being taxed too greatly in its significance for theology since the content behind the form should be more important than the form itself. Furthermore, the question was raised whether simply accepting the Old Testament view of history, instead of assessing the Old Testament traditions critically, would do justice to the task of Old Testament theology. Nevertheless, this whole discussion was not able to eliminate the impression that theological relevance resides not only in the "content" of Old Testament materials but also in its form-critical assessment and formation—and indeed that distinguishing between these two aspects is itself no mean problem.

On the other hand, the question of the unity or center of the Old Testament became acute as a result of the awareness, emerging from form criticism and tradition history, that the Old Testament displays a variety of elements and lines of tradition. Careful attention had been paid the Old Testament witness in its individual parts, and this raised the question about some overriding content. It was thought that a systematic presentation transcending historical description would become possible if one could somehow determine the center of the Old Testament. Yet there is still a problem of how this complies with the basic character of the Old Testament as a witness to a specific history and not simply to human historicality [[305]] ("*Geschicht-lichkeit*"). Moreover—and this question is felt to be especially urgent—how can both Testaments be related to each other if New Testament theology is presented in an analogous manner?

This aspect of biblical theology has been expressed increasingly clearly in recent years, although the means for accomplishing it are more contested now than ever before. As much as it is emphasized that the Old Testament is open to the New Testament, viewing the Old Testament as an entity *sui generis*, fundamentally different from the New Testament in many ways, nonetheless has just as great a countereffect. It is often felt that the Testaments are separated by a sizable historical gulf, occupied by the so-called apocryphal literature. This gulf is made even wider by the usual habit of devaluating the post-exilic Old Testament texts. With all of this, little is to be gained by referring to the subsequent history of Old Testament texts in the New Testament or by pointing out the complementary function of the New Testament with respect to the Old Testament. For if the New Testament is not simply to become an appendage to the Old Testament, then the Old Testament, if fundamentally different, must remain behind at the threshold of the New Testament. The demand for an historically, not dogmatically, oriented biblical theology, however, arises from the feeling that our present historical and theological knowledge and methods could disclose the internal and external coherence between the Old and New Testaments. This would transcend the fundamental distinction between Old and New Testament theology, which is affected essentially by systematic points of view, and it would transcend also the nonbinding character of a mere history of Israelite religion.

If we are to do justice to the above-mentioned demands on an Old Testament theological method, then out of necessity we must look to tradition history, which has gained special importance in modern research of the Old Testament. For, if (1) Old Testament theology needs to proceed from the canon and [[306]] yet also to understand this canon as something which is theologically grounded and not just historically given, then it must appeal to the theological development which led to the formation of the canon, and this is the history of tradition. (2) This makes it evident that not only the individual text but also the whole Old Testament has a testimonial character. Tradition does not grow as a document of piety but in its function for the life of faith—namely, as a witness to revelation and to its history. Tradition with no compelling character is unthinkable. (3) Tradition history resulted from a refinement of historical work on the tradition corpus in the Old Testament. And (4) precisely this structure of the Old Testament articulates the relation of the Old Testament to the history of Israel: what is handed down does not deal only with its experience of history; rather, stretching throughout history, tradition reflects Israel's experience of God in its history, and this historical character of revelation assumes tangible form as a process of tradition formation. The most recent development in the discipline of Old Testament theology confirms this significance of tradition history. Von Rad is particularly concerned not to bring foreign criteria to bear on an Old Testament theology but to let the Old Testament, in light of its formal structure, speak for itself in a "retelling" manner. This approach is essentially founded on traditio-historical research of the Old Testament. And with a possible traditio-historical connection between the two Testaments, the question about the relation of the Old Testament to the New could finally be liberated from the fruitless conflict over references and antitheses between their respective contents. As a result, one could instead turn to the question of how the Old Testament may provide a traditio-historical foundation for the New Testament.

Consequently, it is absolutely necessary for the method of biblical theology to become aware of the significance, indeed the essential function that tradition history can have for it. We can attempt to determine the importance of tradition history [[307]] for biblical theology in three directions: (1) with respect to the text as a whole; (2) with respect to the total subject matter of biblical theology, the canon, and the relationship between the Old and New Testaments; and (3) with respect to the theological consequences of laying a traditio-historical foundation for biblical theology-revelation history.

The Text as a Whole

The basic task of biblical theology consists in facing the multiform complex of texts, which differ sharply in their history and subject matter, and attempting to describe the theology of this complex. Simply setting out what all the texts might have in common would mean losing essentials which appear in the individuality of a text. But even for practical reasons such a process of reduction is quite impossible since a text's theological whole is more than the sum of its individual theological parts. On the other hand, we also cannot get at this plurality of theologies through merely juxtaposing them all in a biblical theology, for example, in historical order. For there is undoubtedly an internal connection among the texts (or their theologies) which gives this plurality a character extending far beyond their simple compilation.

This fundamental problem of biblical theology, that of comprehending unity in plurality, does not exist only with respect to the extensive complex of texts, but as a rule is present even in a single original text. For a biblical text is not the product of an author in the literary sense, even if we ignore all redactional arranging and reworking. For instance, a psalm is affected by a certain range of form, language, and ideas—existing antecedent to the psalm and having its own theological import—even though the author expresses his own, occasionally even his very personal "position" in this psalm. These antecedent theological elements are by no means mere externalities, as if they were only the media used for the author's real message. Rather, in his selection of precisely this form and formulation [[308]] we can perceive how the author classifies his own message. There is such a variety of formal and linguistic structures that the author is not compelled to follow a simple schema, but appropriates selectively and affirmatively. In fact, the structures of form and language are so much alive that with their inherent power they can actively convey the author's message. The author stands within a particular tradition both unconsciously and consciously.

We are advocating that biblical theology has the task of determining the theology of the whole tradition and that it can accomplish this neither by isolating a dogmatic doctrine as the unifying factor of the whole, nor by descriptively rendering historical diversity as the assemblage of the whole, but only by attempting to grasp the totality as a cohesion. Consequently, this task confronts (a) the individual text with its preliterary antecedents, (b) the development of the text as literature with its own literary classification, and (c) the growth of the text tradition into a corpus embracing the whole.

The Individual Text

The genesis of Old Testament texts usually includes an early stage of oral tradition. And even when the text appears in writing from the very outset, it is possible to speak of a prior stage, viz., its basis in the antecedent traditions. Tradition history in the narrower sense describes the preliterary, oral transmission of the text or its contents; in its broader sense, tradition history describes a text's formal and substantial presuppositions, taken from tradition. So ascertained, this formation of the text is of decisive theological importance—by no means simply a *quantité négligeable* or just a factor of very limited or circumscribed significance. The reason for this great importance is that the biblical texts grow out of *life processes* and exist in *life contexts*.

In the first place, this is true in the immediate sense in which form criticism and genre criticism speak of the "*Sitz im Leben.*" [[309]] Certain life processes in Israel lead to certain texts. The fact that the older historical traditions are totally under the influence of the legend-form ("*Sage*") can be traced back to the life situation in which historical events were narrated (and heard). The background for the collections of priestly instructions, the *tôrôt*, is the process of educating and instructing; for the laws it is that of adjudication. The prophetic reproaches and warnings derive from the process of prophetic proclamation of judgment. Cultic songs, whether lament, hymn, or song of thanksgiving, grow out of the vital process of cultic celebration. Even artistic wisdom sayings are unimaginable without the didactic discourse of the sages or without the ancient schools. This list of examples can be expanded as desired. In this regard, even late, purely literary appropriation of a genre should not be automatically excluded on principle from such basis in life processes. For even if at this point there is no longer an actual life process behind the text, this artificial connection to a suitable form shows that the writer is endeavoring to associate consciously, in a sublimated manner, with this life process. It is therefore not surprising when such texts, cut off from their direct processes in life, later find their way back to these life processes (e.g., when songs expressing individual piety become cultic songs again).

Thus we see that biblical texts relate to life processes in that these texts in their early stages grow out of such processes, or at least can be understood form-critically in terms of such processes. This is true in a deeper sense as well: what takes place in these life processes is what makes Israel into the biblical Israel. In these situations Israel's faith takes on form; revelation becomes apparent as lived life ("*gelebtes Leben*") and can be articulated and proclaimed. As the great historical events are narrated and heard, Israel's memory is formed, and it becomes conscious of divine guidance in its history. Objective reporting of history can never manage to express history as it is lived or experienced, yet this is possible for the legend, which [[310]] grows out of the living process of narrating and listening. The life process of prophetic preaching is an immediate effluence of divine inspiration. Israel's piety survives in the processes of cultic life, giving birth to the cultic song. And the regulations of Israel represent its life lived, or at least perceived, under the aspect of revelation.

The Bible does not teach us revealed truth in doctrinal form. Revelation comes in the form of truth experienced in Israel's life processes—and even at that, this lived life is almost immeasurably diverse and even seemingly contradictory. This fact, of course, is connected with the very nature of this revelation. It is not revelation of the deity as such. It is the revelation of God as Self, in a self-disclosure to his personal counterpart, Israel. It is the revelation of the divine "I" in association with the "Thou." It is revelation in an exclusive relation, in an ultimate union between God and humanity: "I am YHWH, your God." Revelation in this exclusive personal relationship therefore enters into the very life of this Israel and is rooted in Israel's life processes. And the secret of Israel and of its historical path all the way to the point of identifying with all humanity—this is the essence of biblical revelation as truly human revelation, of divine selfdisclosure projected into human life.

The biblical text thus begins in the life process of Israel. And only the traditio-historical approach can constitute the method for tracing this dimension of a text back into the lived life of Israel. Only tradition history opens up, as it were, the basis of the text in Israel's life processes. Yet this is not limited to the point of origin. Just as the individual legend develops into a literary form, into the form of a text, and just as the corpora of Torah and law are crystallized from the life context, and just as the process of prophetic preaching assumes a form amenable for transmission, and just as the various possible and actually spoken proverbs converge into the form of a text which stands the test of practical instruction, and just as apostolic parenesis [[311]] leads to the church epistle, and just as apostolic tradition yields the peculiar form of gospel—so also it is essential to describe the traditio-historical path all the way until the text is formed, and not only to penetrate back to some original situation. For the life context of the text unfolds fully on this very path to the textual whole. This is true first of all because only those life processes which the future also finds important can leave transmitted texts; only that which has proved itself can become stable tradition. Secondly, it is true because certain bodies of material develop which alone present the form appropriate for the subject.

This can be clarified with the help of an example. We can certainly assume that there were very many prophetic incidents in Israel about which no text reports because these incidents did not lead to the formation of some text. As decisive as these events may have been in the particular situation, their importance was too ephemeral for a long-lasting tradition or for transmission in the form of a text. On the other hand, inclusion of incidents in the continuing tradition must be differentiated from the determination of their form. Quite similar life processes can lead to completely different forms of tradition. The prophetic proclamation of Elijah and Elisha unfolded in historical processes, were "fulfilled" in them, in such a way that the legitimate form for tradition was the prophetic legend, presenting the living experience of these processes. However, prophetic proclamation in the eighth century was not "fulfilled" solely in the events of Assyrian domination. These historical processes constitute only the beginning, and the fullness of what was proclaimed would not be actualized until the future. Accordingly, in this case tradition usually had to retain the prophetic word in its direct form. It is especially interesting how the forms of tradition overlap in Isaiah. We can see clearly that the legendform in Isaiah can single out only one element of the Isaianic proclamation, the positive reference to the Zion tradition. Thus while tradition is being formed [[312]] into a text, significant processes of selection and interpretation are occurring, and the life of Israel is as much behind these processes as it is behind the initial formation of tradition.

The Literature

With literary fixation of a text, tradition relates to it differently in several respects. In contrast to the rather fluid preliterary form, it is possible to change the fixed form only through a conscious act of intervention. The transmitted text carries its own authority, and a traditionist who engages this text must reckon with this, especially since he will in most cases be related to the circle preserving the tradition of this text. However, this does not mean that the tradition is confined to only editorial corrections and compositions and that otherwise the formation of tradition is terminated. On the contrary: since only those items are transmitted which meet the demands of life, literature does not exist for itself but has vital functions in life; therefore by being true to these functions it assumes a new form in the context of life. Deuteronomy does not attain significance only for the Deuteronomic reform; it represents a theological movement which affects and forms life in Israel long after the time of Josiah. Complexes of historical texts cannot be characterized simply as biblical archives; they give an account of Israel's past in order to provide a point of orientation for present self-understanding. Prophetic traditions describe future expectations as events which already begin to be fulfilled now in the real present.

The continued authenticity of a text is reflected in its redaction, composition, reinterpretation, and above all its selection and incorporation into new text complexes that are being formed. Only tradition history, which includes this viewpoint and thus embraces also redactional and compositional history, is in a position to describe and assess properly the theological developments occurring here. This continuing history of tradition [[313]] can show how, for example, additions to a text—beyond simply replenishing it as may be necessary—can result in an actualization of the text which opens it up to a totally new theological perception. Through apocalyptic additions a complex of prophetic texts can acquire an altogether new character, representing old truth on a new ontological level. This is more than merely requisite modernizations or adjustments to modern ways of thinking; preservation of the truth of the old text is at stake. Thus if apocalyptic thought significantly broadens the perspective in which revelation is perceived, then prophetic tradition, which of course had led to this expansion, can be viewed in this new light. If in a new ontology the Davidic king becomes the messiah, then the ancient Davidic traditions can be understood anew—indeed have to be understood in a new way if one wants to comprehend the truth retained in them. Psalm 110 does not maintain old truths out of necessity, but directs them toward a new plateau. We find ourselves today in the wake of an historical research which is interested primarily in the origin of an historical phenomenon and which exists in order to reconstruct "historically" this origin, in contrast to the later tradition; in this approach we are governed by our own modern perception of reality. Consequently, we are accustomed to evaluating this continuing history of tradition as something which is of secondary importance in comparison with the actual origin of the text. Yet as valuable as this historical viewpoint is, it will not do justice to the character of biblical literature as tradition. The import of additions and supplements, of redaction and composition, is not that "genuine" and "nongenuine" materials are mixed together or that a "counterfeit" impression according to the interests and taste of the successors is created—as if we should be grateful that all of this can be annulled by critical analysis. Rather, the texts incorporated into the tradition were living phenomena, and the point is for us to preserve them in their life context and not allow them to be reduced to [[314]] merely historical documents. This conservative character in tradition formation becomes understandable when we consider how tradition grows toward a whole.

The Totality

Tradition does not represent a series of individual stages in the material and formal evolution of truth. In such a case each stage would have to eliminate antiquated, no longer adequate elements, or at least "modernize" them rigorously. On the other hand, tradition is also not a compilation of materials perceived as truth at some point in time. In such a case it would have to confine itself to a rigid, non-innovative preservation of ancient texts. In contrast, tradition is like a living process of growth in which the old is preserved while being understood as the new. For example, a new understanding of the creation event is recorded in the Priestly text of Gen 1:1–2:4a, but this does not require that an older notion, such as that in Gen 2:4bff., be regarded as untenable and be eliminated. The edition retains the older tradition because it is still truth; indeed the story of the so-called Fall could not be understood at all without it. Yet through a definite form of complementary coordination the older tradition is not without relation to the younger. In this way tradition becomes a polyphonic choir of voices without relativistically surpressing any part. Intelligible co-ordination and subordination yield a totality and not merely coexistence. Tradition does not attempt simply to compile but also to mold a whole.

This formation of a totality is a necessary consequence of the fact that tradition grows along a continuum of meaning. New truth exists in revelatory identity with old truth: the same Israel experiences the same God, even when this experience becomes more advanced. This later experience, also immersed and amplified in being, does not suppress and replace the earlier experience, and this is in accord with the growing structure of history in which the past affects the present and the future is [[315]] embryonically existent in the present. Just as revelation is tied to Israel's history and is fulfilled in it, so also Israel's formation of tradition is connected with its history, and the path is retraceable only through traditio-historical means. As little as history is a mere succession of incidents, so little is tradition a mere juxtaposition of materials. A totality must necessarily emerge.

This growth toward a whole comes into view most clearly in the material ties between tradition strata. At this point we can perceive a developmental continuum of notions, motifs, elements, and structures, and this can describe content-related tradition history in its wider sense, embracing the history of a concept, the history of a motif, and similar entities. A line leads from the Davidic king to the messianic ideal-king of Isaiah 9 and of Isaiah 11, to the messiah of peace in Zechariah 9, to the heroic messiah of Zechariah 13; this is not a development in which one stage replaces another, but in which the former is retained so that a whole is formed. The notion of Moses as the ʿebed

YHWH ("servant of YHWH"), which in turn corresponds to the prophetic conception of Elijah, constitutes a representation of revelation in man; this becomes understood as the personification of Israel and thus leads to the Deutero-Isaianic *'ebed*-notion and, on the other hand, paves the way for the conception of the Son of Man. Wisdom theology can conceive of wisdom as a preexistent, personal, mediating figure, as the "co-enthroner of God," which is transformed into *logos*-Christology. These developments are often described today along merely religio-historical lines, whereby one considers the diverse possibilities of foreign, external influences as a basic impetus for development. But this manner of viewing the situation does little justice to the essence of tradition formation. Only that which promotes the growth process, that which is already implicit in the present, that which accords with the entirety of tradition can be appropriated or can have influence. And referring to external, political-historical conditions as the decisive basis for [[316]] the theological "superstructure" (*"Überbau"*) of tradition fails to recognize that precisely the theological tradition determines how external history will be experienced; only this subjective experience and not an objective historical event itself could be relevant for the "superstructure." For example, the Assyrian domination can be "processed" according to the view of an Isaiah or that of an Ahaz. Only traditio-historical description related to the contents can understand tradition formation as such. It does not get lost in the quest for individual historical factors, for these cannot be properly evaluated by themselves but only in the total structure.

Against this viewpoint of the growing whole it cannot be objected that formation of tradition, like any historical occurrence, is subject to an untold number of contingencies which prohibit us from viewing the result as a developed whole. For by regarding the persistence of traditions as a result of chance one overlooks the life process which is active in the formation of tradition and which creates a totality. To be sure, the history of tradition is replete with contingencies; how much has been destroyed through external influence, how significantly have expansions and developments been hindered from without! Yet we do not disturb the contingent character of history if we pay attention instead to the lively thrust of tradition, replacing omitted elements, compensating for discontinued developments, eliminating meaningless and disruptive elements and wrong directions. If tradition formation is the living answer to the challenges of history in this external sense as well, then we have no grounds for speaking of accidental results. On the contrary, historical catastrophes appear to have benefited the formation of tradition considerably.

One could ask whether irreplaceable elements did not become lost in the course of history, as filled with misfortune as it is. What would it mean if, through an improbable occurrence, archaeology would supply us with an original testimony from a familiar Old Testament prophet? Should this document [[317]] properly belong to the prophet's canonical traditions? As important as such a discovery would be for historical research, it cannot correct the formation of tradition. For this prophetic utterance—not "heard," not esteemed, not transmitted—did not enter the life process of tradition formation. Only preaching which was heard, understood, and received constitutes the truth which sustained the life of Israel. This utterance found subsequently may be as "correct" as it can be, yet it is not truth in the sense of revelation to the Israel that lived. Revelation obtains its *organon* only in the formation of tradition.

This example makes it evident how different the historical viewpoint can be from the traditio-historical perspective, and we must recognize that only tradition history (to be sure, in its double sense) can describe biblical theology. It is only by these means that the historical as well as the kerygmatic character of revelation becomes manifest; it is only by these means that revelation can be understood as something which entered Israel's history and yet which forms a totality. Tradition history can become the method of biblical theology because it goes beyond historical facts and religious phenomena and describes the living process forming tradition.

The Canon and the Relationship between
Old and New Testament

Canonization is the final result in the formation of tradition. The path from the text's origin in life situations, via complexes of tradition in the form of literature, and on to a comprehensive corpus of tradition leads to the final collection and compilation, the canon. Of course, this progressive consolidation of tradition is not possible without a substantive process behind it which directs the development of tradition toward a goal. But at this point we need to restrict our attention to the more formal side of the phenomenon.

Just as a long process is needed in order to accomplish the precanonical consolidation of tradition, so also canonization itself is [[318]] to be understood as a process. At the outset, the canonized text is neither a plumb-line of orthodoxy nor a sacred, inviolable text. Rather, the textual corpus in the precanonical period passes almost imperceptibly over into the canonical period. There is less change in the character of the text than there is in the Jewish community which is maintaining it. What is the nature of this process?

In the context of a comprehensive theocratic reorganization of the postexilic Jewish political structure, Nehemiah's administration achieved relative independence through direct subordination to the Persian province of Transeuphrates, but under Bagoas internal difficulties resulted from conflicts between civil and religious powers (fratricide by the high priest within the temple, defilement of the temple, sacrificial tax, and more). Against this background, Ezra in 398 B.C. leads the Jewish community into a binding relationship to the codified Jewish "law," and this obligation is given external and legal form. This new obligatory character of the corpus of tradition represents the transition to the stage of canonization. At first little change occurs in the manner of relating to the more or less fixed textual tradition of the Pentateuch; even after Ezra the Pentateuchal text can be submitted to limited additions and redactions. We can observe the new relation to the text most clearly in the liturgical phenomenon of word-oriented worship ("*Wortgottesdienst*"), introduced by Ezra. The community, that is, "all who were able to hear with understanding," gathers not in the temple but in the square before the Water Gate. Following specific liturgical forms of giving reverence to God, the reading and interpreting of the text begin; indeed the present text in Nehemiah 8 speaks of Levitical instruction on the text, that is, preaching. This marks the beginning of sermons in synagogal and Christian worship, and this new liturgical relation to the text is the actual sign of canonization. The binding character of the text is expressed, and so is its authoritative and closed totality. In the face of this, any actualizing now is [[319]] understood as interpretive preaching. Alongside worship in the temple, a new form of obligatory and conscious appropriation of the revelation retained in tradition comes to the fore. The process of tradition formation had prepared the way for this long in advance, especially in the Deuteronomic demand for consciously internalizing tradition, but now it finally became possible by the virtual end of the development of the Torah.

One might think that the canonization effected at this point is tied to the preceptive character of the Torah, that is, that the form of the binding text derives from the character of the precepts themselves. However, we are dealing here with more than just commandments, which are of course a priori compulsory and which had for a long time been practiced as such in the form of the Decalogue and other legal collections. In addition to the law in its strict sense there is a plentitude of other materials in the Pentateuch which can by no means be regarded as accessories. Through the establishment of the Priestly document as the foundation and through the addition of older materials in the Tetrateuch, the *heilsgeschichtliche* structure acquired essential significance from the outset. And on the other hand, the legal material, even in Deuteronomy, often has a didactic character (for teaching "order") and thus extends beyond the normal practice of law. The understanding of Torah current in Ezra's age could have affected Pentateuchal canonization, but it is so complex (consider the influences from sapiential theology) that more was at stake in this canonization than simply elevating a certain legal tradition to the position of binding law. Instead, we must consider that the essence of revelation, the bestowal of being in community before God and with God, includes law at a decisive point, and we must comprehend the obligation being expressed in canonization in terms of this essence of revelation.

For this reason we can also understand that the canonization of the Pentateuch was only the beginning of a canonization process [[320]] and that this process did not apply to the Torah tradition alone but to the entirety of tradition: the historical tradition about the prophets succeeding Moses in the period following the Mosaic *Urzeit*, the prophetic tradition itself, the sapiential tradition, the "cult-lyrical" tradition, and the rest. With the conclusion of the prophetic age—the first signs of the end of this tradition formation can be sensed in Zechariah—the second part of the canon takes its place beside the Torah, before the close of the third century B.C.: the completed prophetic tradition, including both the historical tradition of the post-Mosaic age (which is understood as a prophetic period) as well as the tradition of the prophetic utterances. But it was never doubted that canonization did not end here. The Psalter was practically closed already, yet it could not be fitted into this prophetic section. The formation of apocalyptic tradition, which had previously occurred in direct contact to the prophetic traditions for the purpose of adding to and editing them, was continued in independent form. Sapiential tradition, as old as it might have been, now came to full bloom for the first time. These were joined by the historical tradition of the post-exilic period and many other elements. The extent and form of a third part of the canon remained open for a long time, even though the fact of such an additional section was recognized and recorded, for example, in the prologue to Sirach where mention is made of "the other books coming down from the fathers," "the remaining books" besides the law and the prophets.

When was this third part completed, and what was its extent? This question is controversial primarily for dogmatic reasons. According to the late Jewish (after A.D. 70) theory of the canon, the third part is also delimited by the traditio-historical boundary-line of Ezra, or the time of Artaxerxes; in fact, determination of all three canonical sections is attributed to Ezra (4 Ezra 14:45). Here the third part of the canon has the small scope of the Masoretic tradition, and this is attested to by Josephus (*Against Apion* I,40) who in all probability stands [[321]] chiefly in Pharisaic tradition. We are informed that in Jamnia ca. A.D. 100 an affirmative decision was made that these controversial writings belong to this third canonical section. This indicates that this delimination of the canon per se is not early, but at most the principle may be early insofar as only those writings were accepted which appeared old and enjoyed a certain respect. Synagogal worship does not usually have the third part of the canon in its scriptural readings, and this fact shows that for this stage of liturgical development the third section cannot in its entirety be presupposed as canonical.

The New Testament is familiar only with the law and the prophets (e.g., Matt 5:17; 7:12) as completed parts of the canon, and possibly also the psalms (Luke 24:44) as the beginning of a third section. However, the number of writings that are cited or that are implicitly presupposed extends far beyond the later Masoretic limit, and it can indeed even surpass the normal Septuagint circle, which is more comprehensive than the Masoretic (cf., e.g., the citation from 1 Enoch 1:9 in Jude 14–15). This corresponds entirely to the archaeologically ascertainable evidence of tradition formation prior to the upheavals of A.D. 70: a flowering formation of tradition with a plentitude of writings, especially apocalyptic and sapiential but also historical and other types, with a variety of mixed forms. Disregarding perhaps the psalms, one cannot draw a line between writings which have acquired definitive canonical status and those which have not or have not yet achieved canonical maturity. At the most, inferences can be made about common recognition on the basis of circulation.

These circumstances can permit only one judgment—that a third part of the canon was in the process of being formed in the period prior to the New Testament. Certain individual writings had already attained greater or quasi-canonical recognition; others were only beginning to win recognition and distribution or were even still in the developing stage, and still others clearly in a traditio-historical marginal position were [[322]] not able to move beyond a narrowly limited circle of tradition and therefore had to withdraw from the common formation of tradition. In this traditio-historical stage of the development of the Old Testament, the events of the New Testament take place and are then followed by the formation of the New Testament tradition. In other words, there existed no closed Old Testament prior to the New Testament, and—provided that we do not reject the formation of the New Testament tradition in principle—we can speak really of only one single tradition process at the end and goal of which the New Testament appears.

A unity of the Bible is not to be established artificially through exegetical cross-references between the Old and New Testaments. A unity exists already because of tradition history. The gulf supposedly between the Old and New Testaments does not exist traditio-historically at all, and no dubious bridges are needed to span it. There is a difference between the Old and New Testaments insofar as the New Testament represents the goal and end, the *telos* of the path of biblical tradition. With the death and resurrection of Jesus, that event takes place toward which the earthly *Heilsgeschichte* of biblical revelation is moving. The apostolic principle, tied to those who witnessed Jesus' resurrection (for Paul, the Damascus incident), defines the end of forming the New Testament and thus the biblical tradition. In the process, of course, the apostolic tradition can be shaped by the circle forming around the apostle, as is only to be expected when considered traditio-historically; as a rule it is only in this way that the total amplitude of apostolic testimony can assume the form of tradition. There is no opposition in content or in tradition history between the Old Testament and the New Testament. The Old Testament prepares for the New in every respect: the doctrine of the new covenant, the structure of Christology, etc.

Objections to this view could be raised on formal and fundamental grounds. Formally, the New Testament seems to separate itself from the Old Testament through the Greek [[323]] language and through new literary forms. In answer to this, we can point out that even during the forming of Old Testament tradition a transition could be made to "ecumenical" languages, Official Aramaic and then Greek. Certainly, deeper reasons, not just superficial ones, lead to this transition, which we find, for example, in Daniel 7 and in Wisdom of Solomon. Yet we must note that the intellectual world of Hebrew does not simply disappear with this but helps to determine thinking in these trans-cultural languages. Regarding the other point, the new literary forms of gospel and apostolic epistle result traditio-historically of necessity from the subject matter itself; they are developed for the first time in the formation of New Testament tradition. But aside from these, the individual parts of the New Testament are to be understood form-critically entirely in terms of the Old Testament.

On fundamental grounds, the post-Christian Jewish viewpoint must result in rejecting the unity of biblical tradition because the legitimacy of the

New Testament tradition is repudiated. Remarkably, though, Judaism does not continue developing Old Testament tradition parallel to the Christian forming of tradition (the latter would then appear to be a digressive, premature conclusion to the biblical tradition; cf. the Samaritan tradition). On the contrary, it leads to as extensive a reduction as possible and to a canonization of the third part of the canon, thereby terminating the whole tradition process. Through this reduction to the indispensable texts, which moreover as *kĕtûbîm* ("Writings") were not even made cultically equal to the first two parts of the canon, they rejected developments which appeared to be faulty from their perspective after A.D. 70. They appealed entirely to Ezra as the starting-point of the canon. Thus the Old Testament was closed through a reform in the spirit of Pharisaism, which rejected the Hellenistic Old Testament. Alongside the Old Testament, halakhic and aggadic explication of the Torah emerged as a new formation of tradition.

[[324]] This later Jewish view of the Old Testament has, strangely enough, also become a widespread Christian view in modern times. To a certain extent, one has carried out the same canonical reduction, has ceased regarding the later Old Testament traditions as genuinely biblical, and has thereby made it impossible to preserve the continuity from the Old to the New Testament. In turn, even the pre-Hellenistic Old Testament was thought to be more strongly affected by "Jewish legality," which one was unable to understand at all. Actually, the preaching of the literary prophets was the only point where one dared to draw close connections to the New Testament. Consequently, the New Testament's whole understanding of the Old Testament was brought under suspicion, even though the method with which the New Testament interprets the Old Testament is in principle no different from that of later strata of the Old Testament, and is fully consistent traditio-historically. A biblical theology had become impossible through this view; two entities were set in juxtaposition: the Old Testament leading to Jewish religion and the New Testament leading to Christian religion. Access to a biblical theology can be opened only by revising, through the traditio-historical perspective, this fundamental evaluation of the relationship between the Old and New Testaments. This would also affect the way we perceive the relationship between Judaism and Christianity. We would have to recognize that the relation is not a juxtaposition (*"Nebeneinander"*) but an interpenetration (*"Ineinander"*). Christianity would have to perceive itself as old-new Israel and would have to identify with the Old Testament history of experience. Judaism would have to recognize that it has not moved past Christianity, but that it has consciously taken a holding position prior to the messianic encounter.

Revelation History

Biblical theology can be described traditio-historically; it can be comprehended as a continuous, holistic process. In this totality, [[325]] no single level or element can be torn out of its context and absolutized. For example, as useful and important as it is to determine the theology of the historical

Isaiah, biblical theology cannot be content with this historical viewpoint nor with translating this historical view into a systematically developed theology. It must perceive Isaiah's traditio-historical roots not simply as an historical condition but as an essential classification and connection: without the truth of the theology of Zion we cannot understand the truth of Isaiah, who transcends the old theology of Zion. Biblical theology must also see that the biblical Isaiah is not the historical Isaiah but the dynamic force, the Isaiah tradition, which stems from Isaiah and achieves its effect traditio-historically, stretching from the first redaction all the way to the New Testament view of "fulfillment."

Just as we cannot, in view of the holistic character of biblical theology, absolutize preliterary tradition, or the formation of the text, or certain redactional stages, or the canonical composition—so also we cannot understand the *telos* of the New Testament as the "final" form which has surpassed and thus done away with all prior forms. The New Testament has absolute character with regard to the *telos* which appears in it—but not absolute over against the Old Testament traditions leading up to it. Precisely because the Old Testament is "contained" in the New, we cannot divorce it from the latter. Practically speaking, the New Testament is not understandable without the Old because the New Testament lays its foundation in the Old. We often fail to realize this because we are no longer conscious of the Hellenistic Old Testament and because we regard "Hellenistic" and "Old Testament/Jewish" actually as strict alternatives. Without Sirach 24 *logos*-Christology is cut off from older wisdom theology, and theological evaluation of such development within revelation history has become impossible. Also, setting different theologies within the New Testament in sharp and mutually exclusive contrast to each other, which then leads to a desperate search for a "canon within the canon," [[326]] stems from this disengagement of the New Testament way of thinking from that of the Old Testament. On the one hand, one does not see the multiplicity of traditio-historical starting-points or the linguistic and interpretational fields which must be appropriated from the late Old Testament. And on the other hand, one often presupposes a much too simple and exaggerated theology within late Old Testament texts; this could be shown especially for the concept of the law. A New Testament theology is not feasible until it becomes a part of biblical theology.

Tradition history renders a biblical theology possible because it can describe revelation as history—not as a history of stages which relieve each other and are annulled in succession, but as a total process in which being is made known in the self-disclosure of God. As revelation is truly humanoriented disclosure of God, it does not appeal to a specific human situation but seizes the human entirely, that is, in one's historical dimension. This full revelation can only be revelation *history*. God's self-disclosure in union with the "Thou" can unfold only as a *process*, as a proceeding toward the goal—that God himself appears in the deepest depth of the human, in his uttermost distance from God.

Biblical theology is the comprehending presentation of this revelation history, which leads through all stages of human existence in the historical process. It is the secret of Israel to have been shown this path all the way to the inclusion of the whole world, to have perceived it, and to have handed down this truth. Biblical theology has the task of teaching us to comprehend this tradition, this path.

PHYLLIS TRIBLE
b. 1932

Overture for a Feminist Biblical Theology

James Muilenburg's influence on Walter Brueggemann and Bernhard W. Anderson was noted above. Phyllis Trible, another of Muilenberg's students, earned her Ph.D. at Union Theological Seminary. After teaching at Wake Forest University and Andover Newton Theological School, she returned to Union, where she became the Baldwin Professor of Sacred Literature. Since 1998, Trible has been University Professor of Biblical Studies at Wake Forest Divinity School.

Selected Writings by Trible

1978   *God and the Rhetoric of Sexuality*. Overtures to Biblical Theology 2. Philadelphia: Fortress.

1984   *Texts of Terror: Literary-Feminist Readings of Biblical Narratives*. Overtures to Biblical Theology. Philadelphia: Fortress.

1994   *Rhetorical Criticism: Context, Method, and the Book of Jonah*. Guides to Biblical Scholarship. Minneapolis: Fortress.

1995   *Feminist Approaches to the Bible*. Symposium at the Smithsonian Institution. Washington, D.C.: Biblical Archaeology Society.

Phyllis Trible
Feminist Hermeneutics and Biblical Theology

Excerpted with permission from Phyllis Trible, "Five Loaves and Two Fishes: Feminist Hermeneutics and Biblical Theology," *Theological Studies* 50 (1989) 285–95.

Feminist Hermeneutics and Biblical Studies

Perspectives and Methods

[[285]] Joining biblical studies in the early 1970s, feminism has brought gender to the foreground of discussion.[1] It has exposed the androcentric bias of [[286]] Scripture and scholarship. Different conclusions result.[2] Some feminists denounce Scripture as hopelessly misogynous, a woman-hating document beyond redemption. Some reprehensibly use patriarchal data to support anti-Jewish sentiments. They maintain that ascendancy of the male god Yahweh demolished an era of good-goddess worship. A Christian version holds that whereas the "Old" Testament falters badly, the "New" brings improved revelation. Some individuals consider the Bible to be a historical document devoid of continuing authority and hence worthy of dismissal. In contrast, other feminists despair about the everpresent male power that the Bible and commentators promote. Still others, unwilling to let the case against women be the determining word, insist that text and interpreters provide more excellent ways. Thereby they seek to redeem the past (an ancient document) and the present (its continuing use) from the confines of patriarchy.

Whatever their conclusions, feminist biblical scholars utilize conventional methods in studying the text. Historical criticism, form criticism, tradition history, literary criticism, sociology, anthropology, archeology, history of religions, and linguistics—all these and others illuminate the document, contributing variously to theological formulations. Though traditionally tied to patriarchal interpretation, the methods produce different results when feminist hermeneutics appropriates them. A sampling indicates the terrain.

---

1. For a historical investigation, see D. C. Bass, "Women's Studies and Biblical Studies: An Historical Perspective," *Journal for the Study of the Old Testament* 22 (1982) 6–12; cf. E. W. Saunders, *Searching the Scriptures: A History of the Society of Biblical Literature 1880–1980* (Chico, Cal.: Scholars, 1982). For an overview of some recent developments, see K. Doob Sakenfeld, "Feminist Perspectives on Bible and Theology," *Interpretation* 42 (1988) 5–18.

2. Recent collections exemplifying or discussing many of these conclusions include *The Bible and Feminist Hermeneutics*, ed. M. A. Tolbert (Chico, Cal.: Scholars, 1983); *Feminist Perspectives on Biblical Scholarship*, ed. A. Yarbro Collins (Chico, Cal.: Scholars, 1985); *Feminist Interpretation of the Bible*, ed. L. M. Russell (Philadelphia: Westminster, 1985); *Reasoning with the Foxes: Female Wit in a World of Male Power*, ed. J. C. Exum and J. W. H. Bos (Atlanta: Scholars, 1988).

Working as a historical critic, Phyllis Bird has called for "a new reconstruction of the history of Israelite religion, not a new chapter on women."[3] A first step seeks to recover "the hidden history of women." She has contributed to this immense task in two articles examining women in ancient Israel and in the Israelite cult.[4] Similarly, Jo Ann Hackett locates her research in "the new women's history."[5] It attempts [[287]] to recover the stories of females in their own right rather than measuring them by the norms of male history. In an examination of Judges 3–16, e.g., Hackett explores the leadership roles of women during a period of decentralized power. Paucity of evidence, difficulty of analysis, and resistance from established scholarship lead her to a pessimistic assessment about the impact of such work on so-called mainline scholarship.

More sanguine about the possibilities, Carol Meyers has recently prepared the first book-length study of Israelite women.[6] Using the tools of social-scientific analysis combined with the new archeology, she seeks "to discover the place of women in the biblical world apart from the place of women in the biblical text."[7] She argues that "the decentralized and difficult village life of premonarchic Israel provided a context for gender mutuality and interdependence, and of concomitant female power."[8] She sharply questions the validity of the description "patriarchal" for ancient Israelite society. Yet to be tested, this revisionist thesis enlarges options within feminist biblical scholarship.

Literary analyses also show the diversity. In considering the mother figure, Esther Fuchs avers that the Bible is riddled with "patriarchal determinants."[9] It "uses literary strategies in order to foster and perpetuate its patriarchal ideology."[10] By contrast, in a close reading of the Exodus traditions, J. Cheryl Exum detects "positive portrayals of women."[11] Examining mothers of Israel, she finds "strong countercurrents of affirmations of women" within the "admittedly patriarchal context of the biblical literature."[12] Thus she calls for

3. P. Bird, "The Place of Women in the Israelite Cultus," in *Ancient Israelite Religion* [[ed. P. D. Miller, et al.; Philadelphia: Fortress, 1987]] 397–419.

4. The above note identifies one article; for the other, see "Images of Women in the Old Testament," in *Religion and Sexism*, ed. R. Radford Ruether (New York: Simon and Schuster, 1974) 41–88.

5. J. A. Hackett, "Women's Studies and the Hebrew Bible," in *The Future of Biblical Studies* [[ed. R. E. Friedman and H. G. M. Williamson; Atlanta: Scholars Press, 1987]] 141–64.

6. C. Meyers, *Discovering Eve: Ancient Israelite Women in Context* (New York: Oxford University, 1988).

7. Ibid., 23.

8. Ibid., 187.

9. E. Fuchs, "The Literary Characterization of Mothers and Sexual Politics in the Hebrew Bible," in *Feminist Perspectives on Biblical Scholarship* (n. 2 above) 117–36.

10. Idem, "Who Is Hiding the Truth? Deceptive Women and Biblical Androcentrism," in *Feminist Perspectives on Biblical Scholarship* (n. 2 above) 137–44.

11. J. C. Exum, "'You Shall Let Every Daughter Live': A Study of Exodus 1:8–2:10," in *The Bible and Feminist Hermeneutics* (n. 2 above) 63–82.

12. Idem, "'Mother in Israel': A Familiar Figure Reconsidered," in *Feminist Interpretation of the Bible* (n. 2 above) 73–85.

"reassessment of our traditional assumptions about women's roles in the biblical story."[13] A similar view governs the work of Toni Craven.[14] She compares Ruth, Esther, and Judith, recognizing the social dominance of the male in these [[288]] stories but nevertheless asserting that "within this patriarchal milieu, the three women emerge as independent, making their own decisions and initiating actions in unconventional ways." Of whatever persuasions, these and other literary readings provide an exegetical base for theological reflection.

Feminist scholars who specialize in Wisdom literature also provide data for the theologian. With a multidisciplinary approach, Claudia V. Camp has explored female wisdom in Proverbs.[15] Viewing "woman Wisdom" as metaphor, she has isolated roles and activities within Israelite culture that influenced this personification. They include the figures of wife, lover, harlot, foreigner, prophet, and wise woman. The research joins the efforts of historians, sociologists, and literary critics.

This sampling, focused on the Hebrew Scriptures, concludes with three books that differ widely in interest, approach, and purpose but share a common grounding. Particular experiences motivated their authors. Unlike traditional male scholars, feminists often spell out hermeneutical connections between life and work. Citing an episode within her Jewish heritage as pertinent to her study, Athalya Brenner probes the familiar thesis that, as a class, women in Scripture are a second sex, always subordinate and sometimes maligned.[16] Her approach covers social roles and literary paradigms. Writing as a womanist, Renita J. Weems "attempts to combine the best of the fruits of feminist biblical criticism with its passion for reclaiming and reconstructing the stories of biblical women, along with the best, of the Afro-American oral tradition, with its gift for story-telling and its love of drama."[17] Recounting unpleasant experiences within Roman Catholicism, Alice L. Laffey has prepared a "complement" to standard introductions of the OT.[18] She approaches texts, for weal or woe, with the principle "that women are equal to men." However scholarly judgments measure these works, the experiences that prompted their authors and the methods they employ show yet again the diverse terrain of feminist biblical studies.

All these samplings but hint at perspective and methods. Studying Scripture from the viewpoint of gender, feminism explores ideas and advances these shunned in traditional interpretations. Conventional methods produce unconventional results. Not all of them will endure. [[289]] Yet the ferment

13. Idem, " 'You Shall Let Every Daughter Live' " 82.

14. T. Craven, "Tradition and Convention in the Book of Judith," in *The Bible and Feminist Hermeneutics* (n. 2 above) 49–61. See also idem, "Women Who Lied for the Faith," in *Justice and the Holy*, ed. Douglas A. Knight and Peter J. Paris (Atlanta: Scholars Press, 1989).

15. C. V. Camp, *Wisdom and the Feminine in the Book of Proverbs* (Sheffield: Almond, JSOT, 1985).

16. A. Brenner, *The Israelite Women* (Sheffield: JSOT, 1985).

17. R. J. Weems, *Just a Sister Away* (San Diego: LuraMedia, 1988). The combination proposed gives more weight to storytelling than to biblical criticism.

18. A. L. Laffey, *An Introduction to the Old Testament: A Feminist Perspective* (Philadelphia: Fortress, 1988). Regrettably, factual errors mar this book.

can be salutary, for the storehouse of faith has treasures new as well as old. They necessiate the perennial rethinking of biblical theology.

Overtures for a Feminist Biblical Theology

As a student of Scripture, I read biblical theology from duty and sometimes delight. As a student of feminism, I read feminist biblical scholarship from duty and sometimes delight. And then I ask: Can feminism and biblical theology meet? The question seems to echo Tertullian, "What has Athens to do with Jerusalem?" After all, feminists do not move in the world of Gabler, Eichrodt, von Rad, and their heirs. Yet feminists who love the Bible insist that the text and its interpreters provide more excellent ways. And so I ponder ingredients of a feminist biblical theology. Though not yet the season to write one, the time has come to make overtures.

At the beginning, feminist biblical theology might locate itself in reference to the classical discipline. Assertion without argumentation suffices here. First, the undertaking is not just descriptive and historical but primarily constructive and hermeneutical. It views the Bible as pilgrim, wandering through history, engaging in new settings, and ever refusing to be locked in the past. Distance and difference engage proximity and familiarity.[19] Second, the discipline belongs to diverse communities, including academy, synagogue, church, and world. It is neither essentially nor necessarily Christian. Third, formulations vary. No single method, organization, or exposition harnesses the subject: an articulation of faith as disclosed in Scripture. From these points of reference feminism takes its first step.

1) *Exegesis.* Mindful of the androcentricity in Scripture and traditional biblical theology, feminist interpretation begins with exegesis. It concentrates on highlighting neglected texts and reinterpreting familiar ones. The approach does not guarantee the outcome. Exegesis may show how much more patriarchal or how much less is a text. I start with passages that exhibit the latter.

Prominent among neglected passages are female depictions of deity.[20] Hebrew poetry describes God as midwife and mother (Ps 22:9f.; Deut 32:18; Isa 66:13). The Hebrew root *rhm,* meaning womb in the singular and compassion in the plural, provides an exclusively female metaphor for the divine that runs throughout the canon. Supporting contexts [[290]] strengthen this meaning. Thus, Jer 31:15–22 constitutes a poem replete with female imagery. It moves from the mother Rachel weeping for her lost children to the mother Yahweh promising to show mercy (*rhm*) upon the virgin daughter Israel.

Among familiar passages, depictions of deity may require reinterpretation. Hosea 11 illustrates the point. Verses 3–4 describe God the parent teaching Ephraim the child to walk, picking him up, and feeding him. Patriarchal

---

19. See E. Schüssler Fiorenza, "The Ethics of Biblical Interpretation: Decentering Biblical Scholarship," *Journal of Biblical Literature* 107 (1988) 3–17.

20. See P. Trible, *God and the Rhetoric of Sexuality* (Philadelphia: Fortress, 1978). Throughout the discussion I draw upon this book.

hermeneutics has long designated this imagery paternal, even though in ancient Israel mothers performed these tasks.[21] Reclaiming the maternal imagery affects yet another verse (11:9). After announcing judgment upon wayward Ephraim, the Deity returns in compassion. A poignant outburst begins, "How can I give you up, O Ephraim!" It concludes, "I will not execute my fierce anger . . . for I am *'ēl* and not *'îš*, the Holy One in your midst." Traditionally, translators have understood the words *'ēl* and *'îš* to contrast the divine and the human. Though correct, the interpretation misses the nuance. Rather than using the generic *'ādām* for humanity, the poet employs the gender-specific *'îš*, male. Thus the line avows: "I am God and not a male."

This translation makes explicit a basic affirmation needed in ancient Israel and the contemporary world. By repeatedly using male language for God, Israel risked theological misunderstanding. God is not male, and the male is not God. That a patriarchal culture employed such images for God is hardly surprising. That it also countenanced female images *is* surprising. If they be deemed remnants of polytheism, the fact remains that nowhere does Scripture prohibit them.

Shifting from depictions of deity to the human scene, feminist hermeneutics highlights neglected texts about women. The Exodus narratives provide several instances. So eager have traditional interpreters been to get Moses born that they pass quickly over the stories leading to his advent (Exod 1:8–2:10). Two midwives, a Hebrew mother, a sister, the daughter of Pharaoh, and her maidens fill these passages. The midwives, given the names Shiphrah and Puah, defy the mighty Pharaoh, who has no name. The mother and sister work together to save their baby son and brother. The daughter of Pharaoh identifies with them rather than with her father. This portrait breaks filial allegiance, crosses class lines, and transcends racial and political differences. A collage of women unites for salvation; with them the Exodus originates. But existing biblical theologies fail to tell the tale.

[[291]] Likewise, these theologies neglect the distaff conclusion of the Exodus story (14:1–21). The figure Miriam provides continuity between beginning and end. First appearing discreetly at the Nile River, later she reappears boldly at the Reed Sea. With other women she leads Israel in a triumphal song. Though biblical redactors would rob Miriam of her full voice by attributing the Song of the Sea to Moses (Exod 14:1–18) and only a stanza to her (15:20–21), historical criticism has recovered the entire song for Miriam.[22] Feminist hermeneutics utilizes this work to show a conflict of gender embedded in the text. Miriam counters Moses. In time she questions his right to be the exclusive speaker for God (Numbers 11). Though the establishment censures her, fragments in Scripture yield another view. Unlike their leaders, the

21. Cf., e.g., "The Divine Father," in J. L. Mays, *Hosea* (Philadelphia: Westminster, 1969) 150–59; also H. W. Wolff, *Hosea* (Philadelphia: Fortress, 1974) 197–203. For a recent attempt to hold fast to the paternal image, even while acknowledging the maternal, see S. Terrien, *Till the Heart Sings* (Philadelphia: Fortress, 1985) 56f.

22. See esp. F. M. Cross, Jr., and D. N. Freedman, "The Song of Miriam," *Journal of Near Eastern Studies* 14 (1955) 237–50.

people support Miriam (Num 12:15). At her death nature mourns; the wells in the desert dry up (20:1-2). Centuries later Micah proclaims her a leader equal to Moses and Aaron (Mic 6:4). Jeremiah alludes to her prominence in his eschatological vision of restoration (Jer 31:4). Ramifications for biblical theology run deep when neglected Miriamic traditions emerge to challenge the dominant Mosaic bias.[23] Small things undermine patriarchal faith.

Even as it recovers neglected texts about women, feminist interpretation re-examines familiar ones. Genesis 2-3 is a prime example. Contrary to conventional understanding, this narrative does not proclaim male domination and female subordination as the will of God. Attention to vocabulary, syntax, and literary structure demonstrates no ordering of the sexes in creation. At the beginning "Yahweh God formed the human from the humus" (Gen 2:4b). Sexual identification does not obtain. At the end this creature becomes female and male in the sexually explicit vocabulary *'išša* and *'iš* (Gen 2:21-24). They are bone of bones and flesh of flesh, the language of mutuality and equality.[24] No concept of complementarity sets roles for them. The troublesome word *'ēzer*, usually translated "helper" and applied to the woman as subordinate, actually connotes superiority. The phrase "corresponding to" or "fit for" tempers this connotation to signal equality.

But with disobedience the mutuality of the sexes shatters. In answering the serpent, the woman shows theological and hermeneutical astuteness. She interprets the divine command faithfully and ponders the benefits of the fruit. By contrast, the man is mindless and mute. Opposing [[292]] portraits yield, however, the same decision. Each disobeys. The judgments that follow disobedience describe, not prescribe, the consequences. Of particular interest is the description, "Your desire is for your man, but he rules over you" (Gen 3:15). This condition violates mutuality. Thus it judges patriarchy as sin, a judgment that Scripture and interpreters have failed to heed.

Despite the passages cited thus far, feminist exegesis does not hold that all neglected and reinterpreted texts turn out to be less patriarchal than usually perceived. (Indeed, some feminists would disavow altogether the hermeneutics pursued here, to argue that patriarchy controls all biblical literature.) Exegesis also shows how much more patriarchal are many texts. The sacrifice of the daughter of Jephthah, the dismemberment of an unnamed woman, the rape of Princess Tamar, and the abuse of the slave Hagar constitute but a few narrative illustrations.[25] In prophetic literature the use of "objectified female sexuality as a symbol of evil" forms another set of passages.[26] Hosea employed female harlotry to denounce wayward Israel in contrast to the male fidelity of Yahweh (Hosea 1-3). Ezekiel exploited the female with demeaning sexual images (Ezek 23; 36:17). Zechariah continued the process by

23. See P. Trible, "Bringing Miriam Out of the Shadows," *Bible Review* 5 (1989) 14-25, 34.

24. See W. Brueggemann, "Of the same Flesh and Bone (Gen. 2, 23a)," *Catholic Biblical Quarterly* 32 (1970) 532-42.

25. See P. Trible, *Texts of Terror* (Philadelphia: Fortress, 1984).

26. See T. D. Setel, "Prophets and Pornography: Female Sexual Imagery in Hosea," in *Feminist Interpretation of the Bible* (n. 2 above) 86-95.

identifying woman with wickedness and envisioning her removal from the restored land (Zech 5:7-11). Legal stipulations also evince an overwhelming patriarchal bias.[27] Addressed only to men, the law viewed woman as property with concomitant results (Exod 20:17; Deut 5:21). While not excluded altogether from cultic functions, females were deemed inferior participants, obeying rules formulated by males. Not a few feminist exegetes find it sufficient to expose and denounce all such texts, asserting that they determine the biblical view of woman. Others recount them on behalf of their victims, thus establishing memorials in the midst of misery. However they are treated, such passages pose the question of authority—a central issue for all biblical theologies.

2) *Contours and Content.* Beyond exegesis, the next step envisions the contours and content of a feminist biblical theology. Following neither the systematic-covenant model of Eichrodt nor the tradition-historical model of von Rad, it would focus upon the phenomenon of gender and sex in the articulation of faith. Without thoroughness and with tentativeness, the following proposals come to mind.

a. A feminist theology would begin, as does the Bible, with Genesis 1-3. Recognizing the multivalency of language, interpretation exploits the [[293]] phrase "image of God male and female," relating it positively to Genesis 2 and negatively to Genesis 3.[28] Allusions to these creation texts, such as Hos 2:16-20, would also come into play. This passage envisions a future covenant between God and Israel that disavows the hierarchical ordering of husband and wife. To base understandings of gender in mythical rather than historical beginnings contrasts what female and male are and are meant to be with what they have become. Creation theology undercuts patriarchy.

b. From a grounding in creation, feminist interpretation would explore the presence and absence of the female in Scripture, also taking into account relevant literature of the ancient Near East. Organization of this material remains unsettled. Narratives, poetry, and legal formulations need to be compared; minor voices, hidden stories, and forgotten perspectives unearthed; categories of relationships investigated. They include kinship ties of daughter, sister, wife, aunt, niece, and grandmother; social and political roles of slave, mistress, princess, queen mother, prostitute, judge, prophet, musician, adulterer, foreigner, and wise woman; and religious functions in cult, theophany, and psalmody.

c. Though it awaits sustained research, Israelite folk religion would become a subject for theological reflection. Denied full participation in the cult, some women and men probably forged an alternative Yahwism. What, e.g., is the meaning of worship of the Queen of Heaven (Jer 7:16-20; 44:15-28), of

27. See Bird, "Images of Women in the Old Testament," 48-57.
28. Contra P. Bird, " 'Male and Female He Created Them': Gen 1:27b in the Context of the Priestly Account of Creation," *Harvard Theological Review* 74 (1981) 129-59, a study that assigns the text but a single meaning and that a narrow one (procreation). Such restriction the text imposes neither upon itself nor upon the reader.

inscriptions that link Yahweh and Asherah,[29] and of female figurines at Israelite and Judean sites? What effect does folk religion have upon the character of faith, particularly debate about the unique versus the typical? Probing differences between the orthodoxy of the establishment and the religion of the people might bring the female story into sharper focus.[30]

d. Feminist theology would be truly biblical in exposing idolatry. Under this rubric it investigates language for God. Juxtaposing verbal images, animate and inanimate, shows that Scripture guards against a single definition. Further, passages like the sacrifice of Isaac (Genesis 22), Elijah [[294]] on Mt. Horeb (1 Kings 19), and selected prophetic oracles (e.g., Isa 43:18f.; Jer 31:22) demonstrate that no particular statement of faith is final. Without rewriting the text to remove offensive language, feminism opposes, from within Scripture, efforts to absolutize imagery. The enterprise uses the witness of the Bible to subvert androcentric idolatry.

e. Similarly, the pursuit would recognize that although the text cannot mean everything, it can mean more and other than tradition has allowed.[31] Warrant for altering words and meanings runs throughout the history of interpretation and translation. No small example lies at the heart of Scripture and faith: the name of the Holy One. When Judaism substituted *Adonai* for the Tetragrammaton YHWH, it altered the text, "Thus is written; but you read." Christianity accepted the change. The authority of believing communities superseded the authority of the written word.[32] *Mutatis mutandis,* feminist theology heeds the precedent in wrestling with patriarchal language. The verb "wrestle" is key. In the name of biblical integrity, interpretation must reject facile formulations; in the name of biblical diversity, it must reject dogmatic positions. And like Jacob (Gen 32:22–32), feminism does not let go without a blessing.

f. Biblical theology would also wrestle with models and meanings for authority.[33] It recognizes that, despite the word, *authority* centers in readers.

---

29. See Z. Meshel and C. Meyers, "The Name of God in the Wilderness of Zin," *Biblical Archaeology* 39 (1976) 11–17; W. G. Dever, "Consort of Yahweh? New Evidence from Kuntillet 'Ajrud," *Bulletin of the American School of Oriental Research* 255 (1984) 21–37; J. M. Hadley, "Some Drawings and Inscriptions on Two Pithoi from Kuntillet 'Ajrud," *Vetus Testamentum* 37 (1987) 180–213.

30. Cf. P. D. Miller, "Israelite Religion," in *The Hebrew Bible and Its Modern Interpreters* [[ed. Douglas A. Knight and Gene M. Tucker; Philadelphia: Fortress, 1985]] 201–37.

31. Cf. A. Cooper, "On Reading the Bible Critically and Otherwise," in *The Future of Biblical Studies* [[ed. R. E. Friedman and H. G. M. Williamson; Atlanta: Scholars, 1987]] 61–79.

32. An appeal to canon as the prohibition to alteration is questionable, because canonization is a fluid as well as stabilizing concept, subject to the continuing authority of believing communities, including the power of translators; *pace* P. A. Bird, "Translating Sexist Language as a Theological and Cultural Problem," *Union Seminary Quarterly Review* 42 (1988) 89–95.

33. See L. M. Russell, *Household of Freedom: Authority in Feminist Theology* (Philadelphia: Westminster, 1987); C. V. Camp, "Female Voice, Written Word: Women and Authority in Hebrew Scripture," in *Embodied Love*, ed. P. M. Cooey et al., (San Francisco: Harper & Row, 1987) 97–113.

They accord the document power even as they promote the intentionality of authors. To explicate the authority of the Bible, a feminist stance might well appropriate a sermon from Deuteronomy (30:15–20). The Bible sets before the reader life and good, death and evil, blessing and curse. Providing a panorama of life, the text holds the power of a mirror to reflect what is and thereby make choice possible. Like the ancient Israelites, modern believers are commanded to choose life over death. Within this dialectic movement, feminism might claim the entire Bible as authoritative, though not necessarily prescriptive. Such a definition differs from the traditional. In the interaction of text and reader, the changing of the second component alters the meaning and power of the first.

[[295]] These tentative proposals only initiate a discussion that seeks to join feminist hermeneutics and biblical theology. The descriptive and historical task would explore the entire picture of gender and sex in all its diversity. Beyond that effort, the constructive and hermeneutical task would wrestle from the text a theology that subverts patriarchy. Looking at the enormity of the enterprise, critics of all persuasions might well ask, "Why bother?" After all, east is far from west; Athens has nothing to do with Jerusalem. At best, constructive interpretations offer no more than five loaves and two fishes. What are they among so many passages of patriarchy? The answer is scriptural (cf. Matt 14:13–21). When found, rightly blessed, and fed upon, these remnant traditions provide more than enough sustenance for life.

JON D. LEVENSON

b. 1949

Creation and Covenant

Jon D. Levenson graduated with a Ph.D. from Harvard University, in 1975. After serving on the faculties of Wellesley College and the University of Chicago Divinity School, he returned to Harvard as the Albert A. List Professor of Jewish Studies. Levenson has addressed differences and tensions between Jewish and Christian interpretations of scripture. His work has also shown how both critical biblical studies and the rabbinic tradition may illumine understanding of the biblical texts.

Selected Writings by Levenson

1985   *Sinai and Zion: An Entry into the Jewish Bible.* San Francisco: Harper & Row.

1988   *Creation and the Persistence of Evil.* San Francisco: Harper & Row.

1993a *The Hebrew Bible, the Old Testament, and Historical Criticism.* Louisville: Westminster / John Knox.

1993b *The Death and Resurrection of the Beloved Son: The Transformation of Child Sacrifice in Judaism and Christianity.* New Haven: Yale University Press, 1993.

1997   *Esther: A Commentary.* The Old Testament Library. Louisville: Westminster John Knox.

Writings about Levenson

Barr, James
1999   Pp. 291–302 in *The Concept of Biblical Theology: An Old Testament Perspective.* Minneapolis: Fortress.

Jon D. Levenson
Idioms of Creation and Covenant

Excerpted with permission from Jon D. Levenson, *Creation and the Persistence of Evil: The Jewish Drama of Divine Omnipotence* (San Francisco: Harper & Row, 1986), pp. 131–39, 174–75; and Jon D. Levenson, *Sinai and Zion: An Entry into the Jewish Bible* (Minneapolis: Winston, 1985), pp. 38–41, 80–86.

The Two Idioms of Biblical Monotheism
[[from *Creation and the Persistence of Evil*]]

[[131]] In the subordination of the other gods to Marduk in the *Enuma elish*, we see the emergence of a pattern that can, with appropriate qualification, be termed monotheism. Marduk, it will be recalled, demanded as the terms for his taking on Tiamat that his father Ea "convene the assembly and proclaim my lot supreme" so that he, instead of them, might "determine the destinies" and whatever he creates "shall remain unaltered."[1] Anxious to avert the lethal threat, the gods hold court and, in an atmosphere of bibulous festivity, carefree and exalted at last, they proclaim him their lord and erect him a royal dais.[2] The keynote of the homage that they then pay him is his incomparability: "You are [the most] important among the great gods" and "none among the gods shall infringe upon your prerogative. "To you," they announce, "we have given kingship over the totality of the whole universe."[3] This preliminary exaltation of Marduk at the expense of the other gods is ratified and established in perpetuity when he wins his victory and receives his temple and temple-city. In building these, the gods demonstrate their gratitude to Marduk for having beaten back the threat of chaos and for having liberated them from drudgery through the creation of humanity.[4] His acts of prowess, together with the gods' formal acknowledgment of the legal implications of them, thus become the basis of both cosmic and political order. They are the foundation of Babylon's very existence and the ground of her claim to world dominance.

As it appears in the *Enuma elish*, the creation of the world involves a movement from plurality to unity, from the fragile and cumbersome system of "primitive democracy" among the gods to the tougher and more efficient monarchy of the divine military [[132]] hero, Marduk.[5] Consensus is not, how-

---

1. *Enuma elish* 2:122–129 (Alexander Heidel, *The Babylonian Genesis*, 2nd ed. [Chicago: University of Chicago, 1963], 29–30).
2. *Enuma elish* 3:138; 4:1 (Heidel, *Babylonian Genesis*, 36).
3. *Enuma elish* 4:5, 10, 14 (Heidel, *Babylonian Genesis*, 36, except that I have modernized Heidel's archaic second person forms).
4. *Enuma elish* 6:49–54 (Heidel, *Babylonian Genesis*, 48).
5. See Thorkild Jacobsen, "Primitive Democracy in Ancient Mesopotamia," in *Toward the Image of Tammuz and Other Essays on Mesopotamian History and Culture*, ed. William L. Moran, HSS 21 (Cambridge: Harvard University, 1970), 157–70, esp. pp. 163–169.

ever, abolished. Rather, the endless and tiresome process of deliberation is reduced to the formulation of only one resolution—whether to accept Marduk's offer, whether to make him king. On this alone is consensus necessary and, it must be noted, easy to reach in light of the certain defeat that lies ahead without his leadership. In short, their choice for him is not much of a choice at all, the alternative being death. This is underscored by the imprisonment of those who confederated with Tiamat and the obvious absence of neutrality as an option. It is, nonetheless, remarkable that even the emergence of monarchy is here presented as having required a vote, as it were, and the supremacy of Marduk is not seen as primordial, self-evident, and self-sufficient, but as dependent upon the consent of the other gods.[6] In practice his elevation ends their autonomy, but in theory it does not nullify it. In full autonomy, they choose to subordinate themselves forever in order to live and be free. The paradox of world order is, to adapt Paul Ricoeur's characterization of Pharisaism, that it rests on "voluntary heteromony."[7] It is the gods' glad willingness to *choose heteronomy* that allows order, safety, and even liberty to appear.

The periodic public recitation of the *Enuma elish*, especially during the New Year's festival, indicates that this choice of heteronomy, the willing acceptance of Marduk's lordship, was never so final as a superficial reading of the great creation poem might suggest. Tzvi Abusch has recently opposed the conventional view that the *Enuma elish* is simply a reflection of the ascent of Babylon to hegemony, preferring instead to date it to "some time during the early first millennium in a period of political *weakness* of the city Babylon."[8] This fits nicely with my argument that in Israel the combat myth of creation increasingly tended to appear in moments in which YHWH and his promises to the nation seemed discredited.[9] In both cases the myth and its ritual reiteration would have had a compensatory or restorative role, serving to counter the persistence of the dark forces identified with the chaos monster. By reciting the *Enuma elish*, the cultic community overtly casts its lot with the gods acclaiming Marduk and differentiates [[133]] themselves from the army of Tiamat, destined for perdition. Covertly, they acknowledge the incompleteness of Marduk's supremacy and the persistence and resilience of the evil whose destruction *in illo tempore* they celebrate. The recitation of the *Enuma elish* is, in part, a reestablishment of social consensus, which readily dissolves when the community evades their task of self-subordination. Only the inextinguishable urge to do so accounts for the continuing pertinence of the poem.

In spite of the commonplace that Israel was monotheistic and thus radically distinct from the rest of the ancient world, clear echoes of this subordination of the pantheon to its king are to be heard in the Hebrew Bible as well:

6. On the theory and practice of acclamation in both Mesopotamia and Israel, see Baruch Halpern, *The Constitution of the Monarchy in Israel*, HSM 25 (Chico: Scholars, 1981), esp. pp. 51–148.

7. Paul Ricoeur, *The Symbolism of Evil* (Boston: Beacon, 1969), 127.

8. I. Tzvi Abusch, "Merodach," in *Harper's Bible Dictionary*, ed. Paul J. Achtemeier (San Francisco: Harper & Row, 1985), 627 (my italics).

9. See [[Levenson 1988a:]] pp. 17–25.

[1]Ascribe to the LORD, O divine beings,
  ascribe to the LORD glory and strength.
[2]Ascribe to the LORD the glory of His name,
  bow down to the LORD when He appears in holiness.
[10]The LORD sat enthroned at the Flood;
  the LORD sits enthroned, king forever. (Ps 29:1-2, 10)[10]

That Psalm 29 is a YHWHistic adaptation of Baal hymns has long been recognized.[11] This, together with the context, makes it all the more certain that the "Flood" in v. 10 is not the great deluge of Noah's time, but rather the assault of chaos upon order in the form of the sea monster's bellicose challenge to the pantheon. It is possible that this allusion hints at a time when YHWH had not yet attained to supremacy, becoming, like Marduk, king only upon his victory. Even if this be so, the emphasis in the hymn is not upon the old and presumably failed arrangement of "democracy" in the pantheon, but upon the awesomeness of YHWH's mastery and the corollary obligation of the lesser gods to render him homage. Were those gods nonexistent or that homage never in doubt, Psalm 29 would have no point.

In Exodus 15, the Song of the Sea, we again read the hymnic affirmation of YHWH's incomparability: [[134]]

Who is like You, O LORD, among the gods;
Who is like You, majestic among the holy ones,
Awesome in splendor, working wonders? (Exod 15:11)[12]

The difference is that here YHWH's band of loyal confederates is not divine, but human, the people he acquired through manumission and settled on his mountain, the site of the sanctuary in which his everlasting kingship is proclaimed. Similarly, the confederates of the vanquished enemy are also human—Philistia, Edom, Moab, and Canaan, all of them panicked and aghast at the sight of YHWH's deliverance of Israel at the sea.[13] Israel's indomitability follows from her identification with the cause of YHWH, just as the defeat of her neighbors follows from their failure to submit to him and their choice of other gods. This too becomes explicit in the Psalter:

[7]All who worship images,
  who vaunt their idols,
  are dismayed;

10. The translation departs from the NJV at the end of v. 2 for reasons laid out by Frank Moore Cross, "Notes on a Canaanite Psalm in the Old Testament," *BASOR* 117 (1950): 21.

11. See especially Theodore H. Gaster, "Psalm 29," *JQR* 37 (1946): 55–65. The earliest observation of the Canaanite roots of the psalm was that of H. L. Ginsberg, *Kitve Ugarit* (Jerusalem: Bialik, 1936), 129ff.

12. Again, the translation departs from the NJV in order to bring out the full implications of *'ēlîm* and *qōdeš*. See Frank Moore Cross, *Canaanite Myth and Hebrew Epic* (Cambridge, Mass.: Harvard University, 1973),129, n. 61.

13. Exod 15:13–18.

all gods bow down to Him.
[8]Zion, hearing it, rejoices,
    The towns of Judah exult,
    because of Your judgments, O LORD,
[9]For You, LORD, are supreme over all the earth;
    You are exalted high above all gods. (Ps 97:7–9)[14]

The other gods and their worshipers are forced into submission, even as
Judah and its Temple Mount, Zion, rejoice at the decrees (*mišpāṭîm*) of YHWH,
great king and greatest God.

If we bear in mind this partial replacement of the other gods with the
people Israel, then we shall see that in its broadest outlines, the Exodus-Sinai
narrative conforms to the same pattern as that of the *Enuma elish*. An enslaved people calls out to YHWH to rescue them, and he responds in a wondrous way, saving them at the sea and drowning the picked troops of the god
incarnate of Egypt. Israel acclaims YHWH as incomparable, their king forever,
and he, having brought them to Sinai, offers them a covenant, by which they
may become his "treasured possession among all the [[135]] peoples . . . a
kingdom of priests and a holy nation." Unanimously they accept: "All that the
Lord has spoken we will do."[15] The entire revelation at Sinai is a specification
of what that commitment entails. First and foremost is the demand that no
other god infringe upon the claim of him who redeemed Israel from the
house of bondage.

In spite of some demurrals, there is today wide agreement among scholars that the theology of the Pentateuch is deeply imbued with the idiom of the
Near Eastern suzerainty treaty: YHWH, acting in the role of an emperor, cites
the record of his benefactions to his needy vassal Israel and elicits from her a
sworn commitment to observe the stipulations he imposes, to the benefit of
both so long as she keeps faith.[16] As persuasive as the treaty analogy is, it
should be noted that much the same pattern can be detected in mythic literature, such as the *Enuma elish* and its Canaanite and Israelite parallels: the
gods willingly and gladly accept the kingship of their heroic savior, grant him
the right to determine the destinies, and redefine themselves as his servitors.
It is this act of voluntary heteronomy that, by establishing his kingship and ensuring their survival, works to the benefit of both lord and liege. There is, of
course, a vast formal difference between the covenant and the combat myth.
The first originates in the world of diplomacy, the second in cult. But when
the language of diplomacy is transposed into theology, YHWH replacing the
emperor, and the language of cult is substantially historicized, people (largely)
replacing gods, the convergence is remarkable. In the Hebrew Bible, covenant

14. "Gods" in vv. 7 and 9 is a departure from NJV's pale and misleading "divine beings."
15. Exod 19:5, 8.
16. The most exhaustive discussion is Dennis J. McCarthy, *Treaty and Covenant*, AnBib
21A (Rome: Biblical Institute Press, 1978). See also Jon D. Levenson, *Sinai and Zion* (San
Francisco: Harper & Row, 1987), esp. pp. 23–80. The most recent survey from a revisionist
perspective is Ernest W. Nicholson, *God and His People* (Oxford: Oxford University, 1986).

and combat myth are two variant idioms for one ideal—the exclusive enthronement of YHWH and the radical and uncompromising commitment of
the House of Israel to carrying out his commands. If "monotheism" refers to
anything in the conceptual universe of biblical Israel, it refers to that ideal.

The great threat to monotheism, so understood, is defection. In the
mythic idiom defection takes the form of a challenge to YHWH's supremacy
among the gods. The allusions to YHWH's composure in the face of the angry,
roiling sea reflect such a challenge, although in a rather demythologized
way.[17] More pertinent [[136]] are the instances in which YHWH pronounces a
verdict upon other gods, as in Psalm 82, in which the failure of the others to
practice justice (in the classic form of special protection for the poor and the
orphan) results in a death sentence. In a few other passages, mostly in the
prophets, we find allusions to a lost myth in which, having failed to make
good on his claim of sovereignty, a god is ejected from the pantheon.[18] Later
this story of the excommunicated deity will fuse with the biblical figure Satan, the heavenly attorney general, to produce the myth of Lucifer, the fallen
angel who rules hell in Christian demonology. But in the Hebrew Bible, the
fusion has not taken place, and the myth of the primordial theomachy or the
revolt in heaven (*which* of them is unclear and must be determined in each
case) is barely recoverable. That snippets of it are indeed to be found evidences profound insecurity about YHWH's kingship even within the world of
Israelite myth. The absence of the full-blown myth has been taken by Kaufmann and others as proof of the radical demythologized character of Israelite
religion.[19] To me it seems more consistent and more reasonable to conclude
the opposite: it is precisely what is most dangerous and most alluring that
must be repressed. That the myth of theomachy or rebellion has been repressed rather than destroyed accounts for the fact that we now have snippets,
and only snippets.

In the other idiom of monotheism, the idiom of covenant, defection takes
the form of Israel's worship of other gods, either in place of YHWH or alongside him. This aspect of biblical monotheism derives from the demand of ancient Near Eastern covenant lords (suzerains) that the vassal forswear
allegiance to rival suzerains, taking special precautions to avoid the appearance of obeisance to any but his own lord in covenant. "Do not turn your eyes
to anyone else," Mursilis, Hittite emperor of the fourteenth century B.C.E.,
warned his vassal, Duppi-Tessub of Amurru.[20] One of the great breakthroughs
in the study of covenant occurred when William L. Moran identified "love" as
one of the central items in the vocabulary of this idea of exclusive allegiance.[21]
In an Assyrian treaty of the seventh century B.C.E., King Esarhaddon, anxious

17. E.g., Ps 93:3–4.
18. E.g., Isa 14:9–14.
19. See Yehezkel Kaufmann, *The Relgion of Israel* (New York: Schocken, 1972), 60 and
142–147; and Jon D. Levenson, "Yehezkel Kaufmann and Mythology," *CJ* 36 (1982): 36–43.
20. *ANET*, 204.
21. William L. Moran, "The Ancient Near Eastern Background of the Love of God in
Deuteronomy," *CBQ* 25 (1963): 77–87.

that [[137]] his vassals may break faith with his designated successor, Assurbanipal, stipulates that "You will love Assurbanipal as yourselves." Elsewhere, the vassals swear that "the king of Assyria, our lord, we will love."[22] It is this covenantal use of "love" that makes the transition between the first two verses of the great Jewish affirmation, the *Shema'* smooth and natural:

> [4]Hear, O Israel! The LORD is our God, the LORD alone. [5]You shall love the LORD your God with all your heart and with all your soul and with all your might. (Deut 6:4–5)

The threat to covenant love is the allure of the other gods. By and large, the texts in the Hebrew Bible that show the most affinities with the suzerainty treaties also regard the other gods as extant, real, and potent:

> [2]If there appears among you a prophet or a dream-diviner and he gives you a sign or a portent, [3]saying, "Let us follow and worship another god"—whom you have not experienced—even if the sign or portent that he named to you comes true, [4]do not heed the words of that prophet or that dream-diviner. For the LORD your God is testing you to see whether you really love the LORD your God with all your heart and soul. [5]Follow none but the LORD your God, and revere none but Him; observe His commandments alone, and heed only His orders; worship none but Him; and hold fast to Him. [6]As for that prophet or dream-diviner, he shall be put to death; for he urged disloyalty to the LORD your God—who freed you from the house of bondage. (Deut 13:2–6)

In this text, a false prophet is defined by his allegiance, to a god other than YHWH, and that allegiance, in turn, is defined by disregard for YHWH's directives or obedience to the other deity. Had that god been only a lifeless, storyless fetish in the Israelite mind, as Kaufmann thinks, then the temptation to abandon YHWH for him would have been slim, and the centuries of hard-fought competition between YHWH and his rivals for the heart, soul, and mind of Israel would never have been. In fact, however, texts such as this one are struggling to neutralize the *power* in Israel of deities other than YHWH by providing a YHWHistic explanation of their appeal. The supernatural gifts of their prophets and [[138]] diviners testify not to the power of those gods (unlike the supernatural gifts of exclusively YHWHistic prophets and diviners), but to the desire of YHWH to test Israel's exclusive allegiance to him: will Israel abandon him and his *mitsvot* for the other gods and their cults, or will they cleave devotedly to him even in the face of the dramatic and persistent inducements to do otherwise?

The fact that the urge to serve the other gods continues and is, to all appearances, validated by compelling empirical evidence, is itself proof that Israel's consent to serve YHWH alone was never so final and unshakable as a

22. Ibid., 80.

reading of the passages about revelation at Sinai would suggest. Instead, YHWH's kingship in Israel, like his kingship in the pantheon and his mastery over creation, remained vulnerable and in continual need of reaffirmation, reratification, reacclamation. The re-presentation of the Sinaitic moment on the plains of Moab, which is the burden of Deuteronomy, is born of a profound awareness of the waywardness of Israel, on the one hand, her indispensability to the suzerainty of YHWH, on the other. The covenant of Sinai has not the fixity and irrevocability of a royal decree; demanding human participation, it is fully realized only with the glad consent of the cultic community of Israel, a consent that is often denied—such is the risk that the consensual basis of the covenant entails—yet never destroyed. Texts like the one in Deuteronomy 13, previously cited, are attempting to make the consent to obey YHWH alone the prime and irreducible element in Israel's collective and individual life. Obedience is not to be predicated upon YHWH's ability to work miracles and predict the future; the prophets of the other deities can do these as well, and when they do, this empirical evidence on behalf of those deities is to be disregarded in the name of an increasingly nonempirical faithfulness, a faithfulness founded upon YHWH's acquisition of Israel through the nonrepeating foundational event of the exodus. The failure of the present to match the glories of the past, in which YHWH did his work in a pyrotechnic spectacular, is no grounds for defection or faithlessness. The very existence of the non-YHWHistic Israelites is to be seen as treasonous;[23] they and their gods are classified in Deuteronomy [[139]] as intolerable and unassimilable foreigners. Only the fragility of YHWH's covenantal lordship can account for this nervousness and defensiveness with the presence of an alternative to him and his cult. The theology of the fragile lordship of YHWH is, in turn, partly a reflection of the fragility of religious consensus within Israelite society in biblical times.

A long process of development lies between this theology and the mature Rabbinic thought of the Talmud. One difference is that the later is more rigorously monotheistic, treating the other gods as unreal and nonexistent This, however, makes it all the more remarkable that the ideas of the fragility of God's reign in Israel and the continual necessity of Israel's active consent to it remain central to Rabbinic Judaism. The recitation of the *Shema'*, already the watchword of the faith, became early on in Rabbinic law an obligation incumbent upon the Jew every morning and every evening. Its covenantal acclamation of the uniqueness of YHWH and his exclusive claim upon Israel, a claim honored by observance of his *mitsvot*, became known as the "acceptance of the yoke of the kingdom of heaven." The Jew begins and ends his day with a miniature covenant renewal ceremony.[24]

More striking still this late midrash:

---

23. See Moshe Weinfeld, *Deuteronomy and the Deuteronomic School* (Oxford: Oxford University, 1972), 91–100, esp. pp. 92–93.
24. See Levenson, *Sinai and Zion*, 80–86.

"So you are My witnesses
—declares the Lord—
And I am God." That is, if you are My witnesses, I am
God, and if you are not My witnesses, I am, as it were, not God.[25]

Here the consensual basis of the divinity of the God of Israel and the fragility of his reality in the world appear with shocking clarity. God depends, "as it were," upon the witness of Israel: without it, his divinity is not realized. The actualization of the full potential of God requires the testimony of his special people. Like Marduk in the *Enuma elish* or YHWH himself at Sinai, the elevation of the God of Israel is partly a function of those who elevate him. In the covenantal idiom of monotheism, Israel is the functional equivalent of the pantheon,[26] wisely and joyfully acclaiming their lord and deliverer.

25. *Sifre Deuteronomy* 346 (Finkelstein ed.). The biblical quote is Isa 43:12.

26. This is probably to be associated with the democratization of kingship and even divinity in Israel, as attested, for example, in Psalm 8 and Gen 1:26–27. See [[Levenson 1988a:]] pp. 114–16.

Sinai, the Mountain of the Covenant
[[from *Sinai and Zion*]]

The Theology of the Historical Prologue

[[38]] It is significant for our understanding of the nature of the religion of Israel among the religions of the world that meaning for her is derived not from introspection, but from a consideration of the public testimony to God. The present generation makes history their story, but it is first history. They do not determine who they are by looking within, by plumbing the depths of the [[39]] individual soul, by seeking a mystical light in the innermost reaches of the self. Rather, the direction is the opposite. What is public is made private. History is not only rendered contemporary; it is internalized. One's people's history becomes one's personal history. One looks out from the self to find out who one is meant to be. One does not *discover* one's identity, and one certainly does not forge it oneself. He *appropriates* an identity that is a matter of public knowledge. Israel affirms the given.

The given that is affirmed in the covenant ceremony is not a principle; it is not an idea or an aphorism or an ideal. Instead, it is the consequence of what are presented as the acts of God. Israel accepts her place in the suzerain-vassal relationship. "YHWH our God we will serve; him alone we will obey" ([[Josh 24:]]24). In other words, those who come to the Hebrew Bible in hopes of finding a philosophical system flowing smoothly from a theorem will be disappointed. The religion of Israel was not a philosophical system; it had no such theorem. To be sure, every religion is the heritage of a particular community with a history of its own, and this element of history introduces a factor that frustrates the philosophical impulse in every religion. But in the religion of the Hebrew Bible, the philosophical impulse, if it exists at all, is stunted. We see no profound observation at the base of it, like the observation in Buddhism that desire is the source of suffering. Even the oneness of God, we shall soon see, is a consequence of other factors and not a proposition from which the essential religion of Israel can be derived.

Israel began to infer and to affirm her identity by telling a story. To be sure, the story has implications that can be stated as propositions. For example, the intended implications of the historical prologue is that YHWH is faithful, that Israel can rely on God as a vassal must rely upon his suzerain. But Israel does not begin with the statement that YHWH is faithful; she infers it from a *story*. And unlike the statement, the story is not universal. It is Israel's story, with all the particularities of time, place, and *dramatis personae* one associates with a story and avoids in a [[40]] statement that aims at universal applicability. In other words, if there is a universal truth of the sort philosophers and even some religions aim to state, Israel seems to have thought that such truth will come *through* the medium of history, through the structures of public knowledge, through time, and not in spite of these. History, the arena of public events (as opposed to private, mystical revelation and to philosophical speculation), and time are not illusions or distractions from essential reality. They are means to the knowledge of God. The historical prologue is a miniature theology of history.

When did the history summarized in the prologue commence? If one wishes to read the entire Torah as a covenant text, history begins at the beginning, the creation of the world and the story of primordial humanity (Genesis 1–11). But this is not where the historical prologues in the proper sense start their story. In Exod 19:3b-8, the story begins and ends with the Exodus from Egypt, when YHWH brought Israel, as on eagles' wings, to himself. In Joshua 24, the horizon is larger: history begins with the backdrop to Abraham's migration, the generation of his father, the Mesopotamian Terah. Most of the recapitulations of the sacred history begin, like Joshua 24, some time in the Patriarchal period. "An Aramean about to perish was my father," begins one little summary (Deut 26:5) in an allusion to Jacob/Israel, from whom the nation took its name, and it is the descent into Egypt by the eponymous ancestor which tends to function there as the trigger for the action of the whole history of redemption, what German scholars call *Heilsgeschichte*.[1] Theologically this means that Israel's identity is not rooted in cosmic symbols, such as those that appear in the first account of creation in the [[41]] Torah (Gen 1:1–2:4a). Her identity is not cosmic and primordial, but historical in a sense not so distant from that in which modern people use the term. Israel was not created on day one or at any other moment in the seven days of creation. In-

---

1. On these summaries of *Heilsgeschichte*, see the title essay in G. von Rad, *The Problem of the Hexateuch and Other Essays* (New York: McGraw-Hill, 1966) 1–78. I do not endorse von Rad's belief that the *Heilsgeschichte* narratives grew out of short historical credos, but I do believe that he rendered a service in drawing attention to them. They are abstracts of the *Heilsgeschichte* stories presented in order to evoke an affirmation of covenant.

stead, she was called into existence at a moment in ordinary time and at a specifiable place, Haran (11:31). Israel is to carry a metahistorical identity through her journeys in history.

. . . .

The Ever-Renewed Covenant

[[80]] The renewal of covenant was a central aspect of Israel's worship in biblical times. Psalm 81, chanted today on Thursday mornings, seems to have related the Sinaitic experience in some kind of regular liturgical celebration, also in its original setting. Although much of this psalm is obscure, v 4 would seem to locate its context in the celebration of the first day of the lunar month, on analogy with the celebration of New Year's Day (*Rosh Ha-Shanah*) so well known from later tradition, and comparable festivities for the day of the full moon, two weeks later.[2] What is most pertinent to us is that the liturgy for these holy days seems to have stressed the Decalogue. Vv 10–11 are a transparent restatement of the Second and First Commandments, according to the Jewish enumeration.[3] Vv 6b–8, in which YHWH becomes the speaker, perhaps through the mouth of a priest or prophet, and v 17 restate the the historical prologue, with its emphasis upon all that the suzerain, in his graciousness, has done for his vassal. The curses of covenant can be heard in vv 12–13, in which YHWH disowns a disobedient people, but in vv 14–16, the blessings balance this with their promise of victory if only Israel walks YHWH's path.[4] In short, Psalm 81 evidences a regular liturgical occasion in which the Sinaitic covenant and the great choice it entails were re-presented to the Israelite congregation.[5]

[[81]] In the case of the book of Deuteronomy, the book of covenant *par excellence*, this insistence upon the relevance of the covenant of Sinai ("Horeb" in Deuteronomy) to the present generation reaches a pitch of intensity:

> [1]Moses called together all Israel and said to them: Hear, Israel, the laws and ordinances which I am proclaiming to you personally today. Study them, observe them, put them into practice. [2]YHWH our God made a covenant with us on Horeb. [3]It was not with our fathers that YHWH made this covenant, but with us—us!—those who are there today, all of us, the living. [4]Face to face YHWH spoke with you on the mountain, from the midst of the fire. (Deut 5:1–4)

---

2. See [[Roland]] de Vaux, *Ancient Israel* [[New York and Toronto: McGraw-Hill, 1965]], 2:469–70, 476.

3. Exod 20:2–3 and Deut 5:6–7. See also Exod 20:5 and Deut 5:9.

4. Cf. Lev 26:7–8 and Deut 28:7.

5. On the psalms and covenant renewal, see S. Mowinckel, *The Psalms in Israel's Worship* (New York and Nashville: Abingdon 1967) 1:155–61. On covenant renewal in general, see Mowinckel, *Le Décalogue* (Paris: Félix Alcan, 1927) 114–62; H.-J. Kraus, *Worship in Israel* (Oxford: Blackwell, 1966) 141–45.

The concern in this passage is that Israel may come to think of themselves as obliged in a distant way by the covenant of Sinai/Horeb, but not as direct partners in it. Lest the freshness of the experience be lost, v. 3 hammers home the theme of contemporaneity in *staccato* fashion, with no fewer than six separate expressions: "with us"—"us!"—"those who are here"—"today"—"all of us"—"the living." The goal of this speech, as of the covenant renewal ceremony in which it probably originated,[6] is to induce Israel to step into the position of the generation of Sinai, in other words, to actualize the past so that this new generation will become the Israel of the classic covenant relationship (cf. Deut 30:19–20). Thus, life in covenant is not something merely granted, but something won anew, rekindled and reconsecrated in the heart of each Israelite in every generation. Covenant is not only imposed, but also accepted. It calls with both the stern voice of duty and the tender accents of the lover, with both stick (curse, death) and carrot (blessing, life) in hand. But it biases the choice in favor of life (Deut 30:19).

It is conventional to trace the influence of the covenant renewal ceremony and the formulary until the time of the disappearance [[82]] of the Dead Sea community (first century C.E.) and no further.[7] The tacit assumption is that these institutions did not survive into the next phase of Jewish history, the rabbinic era. In this, there is a certain truth. The idea of covenant does not seem to have had in rabbinic religion the centrality it had held since at least the promulgation of Deuteronomy in the seventh century B.C.E., although its importance for the rabbis must not be minimized.[8] There is no rabbinic ceremony in which the Jews are said explicitly to be renewing their partnership in the Sinaitic covenant, as the eight day old boy is said, for example, to be entering the covenant of Abraham (Gen 17:1–14) during his circumcision. There is, however, a text which is central to the rabbinic liturgy, in fact arguably *the* central text of the rabbinic liturgy, which is composed of three Pentateuchal passages (Deut 6:4–9; 11:13–21; Num 15:37–41)[9] expressive of the classical covenant theology. The prayer is known as the *Shma*, after its first word. The first verse of the *Shma* is correctly rendered, "Listen, Israel: YHWH is our God, YHWH alone" (Deut 6:4).[10] It is manifestly an echo

6. See von Rad, *Studies in Deuteronomy*, SBT 9 (London: SCM, 1953).

7. See [[Klaus]] Baltzer, *Covenant Formulary* [[Oxford: Blackwell, 1971]].

8. See E. E. Urbach, *The Sages* ([Hebrew] Jerusalem: Magnes, 1975), 466–77.

9. The verse, "Blessed be the name of his glorious kingship forever and ever," is whispered between Deut 6:4 and 5.

10. The verse is conventionally rendered into English as, "Hear, O Israel, the Lord our God, the Lord is one," an interpretation that reflects the philosophical monotheism of a later tradition more than the covenantal monotheism of the Torah in its original setting. My translation essentially follows that of the Jewish Publication Society new Torah translation (1962), which draws attention to the commentaries of Ibn Ezra and Rashbam in support of the rendering. The remarks of Rashbam (ca. 1080–1174, northern France) are especially apt: "HaShem alone is our God, and we have no other god with him. Thus the Book of Chronicles: 'We will serve HaShem our God, and we have not abandoned him,' That is to say, HaShem is our God and not the calves to whom you bow down. 'HaShem alone': Him alone we will serve, and we will not add any other god to serve with him. . . ."

of [[83]] the requirement of the old suzerainty treaties to recognize one lord alone. Since in the biblical case the lord is divine, the verse is a classic statement of covenantal monotheism, i.e., the prohibition upon the service of other suzerains.

In fact, we sense apprehension about the possibility of just such defection in each of the three paragraphs. In the second one, we hear of the danger of seduction, in language that recalls the career of Hosea (Deut 11:16–17), and in the last paragraph, such defection is termed "whoring" (Num 15:39). It is this passage from Numbers which establishes the ground of obedience to YHWH precisely where we expect it, in the redemption from Egypt (v 41). This verse, like the First Commandment of the Decalogue (Exod 20:2), is a condensation of the historical prologue. The central stipulation of the *Shma* is one familiar to any student of Near Eastern covenants, the obligation to love YHWH, which is inextricable from the requirements to carry out all his commandments. As we shall see, the rabbis, like the more ancient architects of covenant, saw in the acclamation of divine lordship and the love commandment of the first paragraph the basis for the acceptance of all other commandments. The second paragraph, which stresses performance of the stipulations, derives mostly from the blessings and curses of the covenant formulary. Fidelity to YHWH and the exclusive service of him will bring abundance; defection will result in drought, famine, and death. Finally, we should note that the insistence that the "words" be constantly recited, bound to one's body, written upon one's house, and the commandments symbolized in one's clothes, is also a reflex of part of the covenant formulary, the deposition of the text and the requirement for its periodic reading. In short, the idiom and the theology of covenant permeate the *Shma*.

What is interesting in light of the putative disappearance of the covenant renewal ceremony is that the rabbis selected these three texts to make up one prayer, for the three are not contiguous in the Torah, and the first of them there, Num 15:37–41, appears last here. What links the three paragraphs is that they constitute [[84]] the basic affirmation of covenant. They confront us with the underpinnings of the entire Sinaitic dimension of the religion of Israel. The link between them is theological, and it is that theology that the rabbis considered basic to their own appropriation and adaptation of the biblical heritage. For they made the *Shma* a staple in the liturgy they wove for Jewry. In the requirement to "recite them . . . when you lie down and when you get up," they saw a *mitsvah* to recite the *Shma* twice daily, in the morning and evening every day of the year.[11] The *Shma* thus became one of the pillars around which those two services developed.

What, precisely, did the rabbis think happened when one recites the *Shma*? We find an answer in the reply of the Tannaitic master Rabbi Joshua ben Korhah to the question of why Deut 6:4–9 is positioned before 11:13–21:

---

11. *m. Ber.* 1:3.

so that one might accept upon himself the yoke of the kingdom of heaven first; afterwards, he accepts upon himself the yoke of the commandments.[12]

"Heaven" in Talmudic language is usually a more delicate way of saying "God." Rabbi Joshua sees the *Shma*, therefore, as the acclamation of God's kingship. Only in light of such an acclamation do the *mitsvot* make sense. In light of the biblical ideas, we can say that one must first accept the suzerainty of the great king, the fact of covenant; only then can he embrace the particulars which the new lord enjoins upon him, the stipulations. If God is suzerain, his orders stand. But his suzerainty is not something irrational and threatening. It follows from his gracious character:

> *I am the Lord Thy God.* Why were the Ten Commandments not said at the beginning of the Torah? They give a parable. To what may this be compared? To the following: A king who entered a province said to the people: May I be your king? But the people said to him: Have you done anything good for us that you should rule over us? What did he do then? [[85]] He built the city wall for them, he brought in the water supply for them, and he fought their battles. Then when he said to them: May I be your king? They said to him: Yes, Yes. Likewise, God. . . .[13]

His past grace grounds his present demand. To respond wholeheartedly to that demand, to accept the yoke of the kingdom of heaven, is to make a radical change, a change at the roots of one's being. To undertake to live according to *Halakhah* is not a question of merely raising one's moral aspirations or of affirming "Jewish values," whatever that means. To recite the *Shma* and mean it is to enter a supramundane sovereignty, to become a citizen of the kingdom of God, not simply in the messianic future to which that term also refers (e.g., Dan 2:44), but also in the historical present. Thus, one can understand the horror a rabbinic Jew would have of failing to say the *Shma*, as exemplified in this story: There was a law that a bridegroom was exempt from the commandment to recite the *Shma*, probably because he was in no mental condition to give the prayer the concentration it required. But concerning one early rabbi, we read this exchange in the Mishnah:

> It happened that Rabban Gamaliel got married and recited the *Shma* on the first night. His students said to him, "Our master, have you not taught us that a bridegroom is exempt from the recitation of the *Shma* on the first night?" He said to them, "I am not going to listen to you and annul the kingdom of Heaven from myself for even a moment!"[14]

In other words, one who neglects the *Shma* when its recitation is due is rebelling against the sovereignty/suzerainty of God. Or, to put it positively, the

---

12. *m. Ber.* 2:2.

13. *Mek., Baḥôdeš,* 5. The translation is from *Mekilta de-Rabbi Ishmael,* ed. J. Z. Lauterbach (Philadelphia: Jewish Publication Society, 1933) 2:229–30.

14. *m. Ber.* 2:5. On the significance of the *Shma,* see Urbach, *Sages,* 348–70.

Shma is the rabbinic way of actualizing the moment at Sinai when Israel answered the divine offer of covenant with the words "All that YHWH has spoken we will do" [[86]] (Exod 19:8). In short, the recitation of the *Shma* is the rabbinic covenantal renewal ceremony. It is the portal to continuing life in covenant.

There is, therefore, no voice more central to Judaism than the voice heard on Mount Sinai. Sinai confronts anyone who would live as a Jew with an awesome choice, which, once encountered, cannot be evaded—the choice of whether to obey God or to stray from him, of whether to observe the commandments or to let them lapse. Ultimately, the issue is whether God is or is not king, for there is no king without subjects, no suzerain without vassals. In short, Sinai demands that the Torah be taken with radical seriousness. But alongside the burden of choice lies a balm that soothes the pain of decision. The balm is the history of redemption, which grounds the commandments and insures that this would-be king is a gracious and loving lord and that to choose to obey him is not a leap into the absurd. The balm is the surprising love of YHWH for Israel, of a passionate groom for his bride, a love ever fresh and never dulled by the frustrations of a storm courtship. Mount Sinai is the intersection of love and law, of gift and demand, the link between a past together and a future together.

JOHN H. SAILHAMER

b. 1946

Canon and Composition

John H. Sailhamer has taught at Bethel Theological Seminary, Trinity Evangelical Divinity School, Western Seminary (Portland), and is now Senior Professor of Old Testament at Southeastern Baptist Theological Seminary. His Ph.D. in Semitics is from the University of California, Los Angeles. Sailhamer, past president of the Evangelical Theological Society, has argued for an evangelical and confessional approach to a canonical Old Testament theology.

Selected Writings by Sailhamer

1992 *The Pentateuch as Narrative: A Biblical-Theological Commentary.* Grand Rapids: Zondervan.

1995 *An Introduction to Old Testament Theology: A Canonical Approach.* Grand Rapids: Zondervan.

1996 *Genesis Unbound: A Provocative New Look at the Creation Account.* Sisters, Oregon: Multnomah.

2002 Biblical Theology and the Composition of the Hebrew Bible. Pp. 25–37 in *Biblical Theology: Retrospect and Prospect.* Edited by Scott J. Hafemann. Downers Grove, Illinois: InterVarsity / Leicester: Apollos.

John H. Sailhamer
Canon and Composition

Excerpted with permission from John H. Sailhamer, "Biblical Theology and the Composition of the Hebrew Bible," in *Biblical Theology: Retrospect and Prospect* (edited by Scott J. Hafemann; Downers Grove, Ill.: InterVarsity / Leicester: Apollos), pp. 25–37.

[[25]] In recent years OT studies have seen many changes. Hardly an area is untouched by new approaches and new perspectives. If there is a common theme, it is the shift from a focus on the earliest stages of the biblical text to that of its final shape. Already a major work on the theology of the Tanak[1] has been published by a leading biblical scholar, Rolf Rendtorff.[2] The results, in my opinion, are impressive and exciting.

Amid the many aspects of a theology of the final shape of the Hebrew Bible, one important question stands out: What prospects remain for a biblical theology that includes the Tanak and the NT? Can a theology of the Tanak be written as part of a biblical theology? Is there an exegetically warranted unity between the Hebrew Bible and the NT?

A Definition of the Final Shape of the Old Testament

What I understand as the final shape of the OT is *the compositional and canonical* [[26]] *state of the Hebrew Bible at the time it became part of an established community.* By "compositional and canonical" I mean how an author put a book together and how it was attached to a collection of books. The idea of its being a "part of a community" is what I would call consolidation. The notion of consolidation is an attempt to respond to recent observations about the nature of texts. Communities like Judaism and Christianity, for example, derive their essential identity from texts. Yet the biblical texts often receive their final shape from those same communities. Communities endorse and impose canonical restrictions on their foundational texts. However, the consolidation of OT texts includes elements of composition as well as canonization. Communities not only produce canonical texts; they also create new texts. They do so, I would suggest, by producing the real-life authors of those texts.

Problems of Biblical Theology

There are many well-known problems and issues associated with biblical theology. Since the focus in this essay is on a biblical theology of the final shape of the Hebrew Bible, two problems that directly relate to it must be raised.

1. The Tanak is the rabbinical name given to the Hebrew OT, the Law (Ta = *Torah*), the Prophets (na = *Nebi'im*) and the Writings (k = *Ketubim*). It is the same OT as in the Christian Bible, but the order of the individual books is different. The term is used in this chapter to refer to the OT canon and the order of its books at the time of Christ.

2. Rolf Rendtorff, *Theologie des Alten Testaments: Ein kanonischer Entwurf* (Neukirchen-Vluyn: Neukirchener Verlag, 1999).

The first problem is the need for a text model. A text model is a description of the formation of the Hebrew Bible that adequately explains its present shape. This is what Wolfgang Richter has called a "Theory of Literature."[3] If we are going to talk about the final shape of the Hebrew Bible, we had better have some idea of how it arrived at that shape and how that shape changed over time. All biblical studies work with such theories, whether consciously or not. Our aim is to develop such a model consciously and to do so along lines that are consistent with an evangelical view of Scripture.

The second problem is the need to relate that shape to the NT. We will return to that problem later. At the moment let us first turn to a description of a text model of the OT.

A Text Model of the Old Testament

The text model, or general understanding of the text proposed here, is drawn directly from my understanding of the nature of the final shape of [[27]] the Hebrew Bible. In the definition of the final shape mentioned above, there are three central components:

1. the notion of the composition of a specific biblical text
2. the notion of the canonical shaping of biblical texts and its influence on communities
3. the notion of the consolidation of a text within a specific community.

Our text model thus views the biblical text at the point of intersection of these three coordinates: its composition, its canonization and its consolidation within a community.

Composition

The model proposed here takes seriously the notion that biblical texts have authors and that the meaning of authors can be discovered by reading their texts. The notion of authorship also represents a decisive moment in the history of a text. In this way of thinking about the final shape, composition is viewed neither in terms of a dynamic process nor a rigid status quo. The composition of a biblical book, like any other book, represents a creative and decisive moment in the history of the text.

The phenomenon of the two texts of Jeremiah offers a helpful example. It is fairly clear from comparing the Masoretic Text and the Septuagint that the book of Jeremiah comes to us in two final shapes. Both shapes appear destined for quite different communities.[4]

---

3. Wolfgang Richter, *Exegese als Literatur Wissenschaft, Entwurf einer Alttestamentlichen Literatur Theorie und Methodologie* (Göttingen: Vandenhoeck & Ruprecht, 1971).

4. See Emanuel Tov, *Text Criticism in the Hebrew Bible* (Minneapolis: Fortress, 1992), 320–21, and Eugene Ulrich, *The Dead Sea Scrolls and the Origins of the Bible* (Grand Rapids, Mich.: Eerdmans, 1999), 69.

In Jer 27:16, for example, the prophet Jeremiah confronts the false prophets. The message of the false prophets was that Judah's troubles would not last much longer. Relief was in sight. The temple vessels that had been taken to Babylon would soon be returned.

Jeremiah, however, offered another word. The captivity would *not* soon be over. There would be seventy years of captivity before the vessels were returned. Jeremiah thus proclaimed, "Do not listen to the words of your prophets who are prophesying to you, saying, 'Behold, the vessels of the LORD's house will *now shortly* be brought back from Babylon,' for it is a lie which they are prophesying to you" (author's translation [throughout the essay]).

A glance in the apparatus of *Biblia Hebraica* shows that the words "now shortly" were not in the Septuagint and also probably not in the Hebrew manuscript used by the translator.[5] In that text the false prophets affirm that [[28]] the vessels of the Lord's house will be brought back from Babylon. There is no mention of "shortly." Since that eventually happened, the false prophets appear to speak the truth! How could they be false prophets if their words came true? In the Masoretic Text, the false prophets say that the temple vessels would be returned *shortly*—which, of course, did not happen.

This is not a serious exegetical problem. Within the context, the false prophets clearly meant the vessels would be returned shortly. They were not thinking of Jeremiah's seventy years. If this were a mere text-critical problem, we would and should say the Masoretic Text offers a longer and therefore secondary text. It is a gloss of a scribe who wanted to supply a helpful comment. Thus the Septuagint represents the more original text.

The larger question, however, is what we make of this gloss in light of the composition of the book of Jeremiah. Is this an isolated textual gloss, or is it the work of an author? To address that question, two additional observations are necessary. First, this gloss is part of many similar glosses in Jeremiah that seem to fill in for the reader numerous historical details. This has led some scholars to suggest that the two versions of Jeremiah represent a preexilic and a postexilic edition of the book. That in fact may be the case, but if it is, it is not the whole story. To see the whole story one must take a closer look at the interpretations of Jeremiah's words reflected in these two texts. That leads to the second observation. These two versions of the book of Jeremiah both survived the exile and were thus a part of the canon of two distinct postexilic communities.

When we take the other textual variants into consideration, it becomes apparent that the community represented by the Masoretic Text had focused Jeremiah's prophecies on the events of the return from Babylonian captivity When, in some texts, Jeremiah merely speaks of a people "from the north," the Masoretic Text identifies them as Babylon and King Nebuchadnezzar.[6]

---

5. Tov, *Text Criticism*, 320.

6. William McKane, *A Critical and Exegetical Commentary on Jeremiah*, ICC (Edinburgh: T. & T. Clark, 1986), xxi: "The intention of the exegetical expansions in MT is to identify Judah's enemy with Babylon and, more particularly, with Nebuchadrezzar, whereas in Sept[uagint] there is no further elucidation of the 'enemy from the north.' "

In the text of the Septuagint, however, Jeremiah's words are not tied to specific historical events, in spite of the fact that the edition continued for several hundred years as a part of the canon in its community. The implication appears obvious. Even after the exile, this community seemed little [[29]] concerned about the relation of Jeremiah's words to the historical realities of his day. Their focus remained on Jeremiah's words about an invasion of the land by a people from the north. There was, at least in *their* Bible, still the possibility of a future referent for Jeremiah's words—a referent that looked beyond the seventy years of the Babylonian captivity. For this community, Jeremiah's words had not been exhausted in the events of Israel's past.[7]

What is remarkable about the Septuagint version of the book of Jeremiah is how well it fits with Daniel 9. In Daniel 9, we see a godly Israelite, still in exile, pondering the meaning of these chapters of Jeremiah. His question is not merely whether or how Jeremiah's words have been fulfilled, but also why his own words will not be fulfilled "for many days hence" (Dan 8:26). He is dismayed that he must now seal up the vision until a later time. In Daniel 9, Daniel tries to understand Jeremiah's prophecy of the seventy years in this new light. The answer he receives is that Jeremiah's vision of the future was to be fulfilled not in seventy years but in seventy *weeks* of years. In Daniel, Jeremiah's words point beyond the events of the return from exile. The author of Daniel 9 would have had no use for a book of Jeremiah with glosses about Nebuchadnezzar. For him there was still a future for Jeremiah's word.

These texts illustrate the nature of biblical composition. The kinds of differences that exist between these two editions of Jeremiah are compositional in nature. Daniel 9 shows the kind of situation that could possibly give rise to the two compositions. The simultaneous existence of both texts suggests multiple communities and diverse interpretations of the same OT book.

We should also note that the differences in the text of Jeremiah are accompanied by a rather large rearrangement of the contents of the book. For example, the oracles against foreign nations in the Masoretic Text, Jeremiah 46–51, are located in the Septuagint version of Jeremiah just after the prophecy of the seventy years (Jer 25:15–38).[8] Moreover, the Dead Sea [[30]] Scrolls show us that the Septuagint translators were following closely their own Hebrew texts of Jeremiah. These differences between the two texts of Jeremiah were likely already in some early Hebrew texts.[9]

Hence, these two versions of Jeremiah are not merely distinct editions. Both texts are unique books in their own right. Furthermore, both books

---

7. Ibid., 627: "In Sept[uagint] . . . there is no further elucidation of the enemy from the north. According to Sept., Judah, because of its lack of trust in Yahweh and disobedience (v. 8), is about to be vanquished by an enemy from the north who will devastate both Judah and the countries surrounding her, and leave behind a scene of desolation which will evoke astonishment and terror (v. 9)."

8. At this point in the book (Jer 25:13b–14a) somebody, presumably the narrator or the author, begins to speak directly to the readers about the book we are now reading. In text linguistics this is called a metacommunicational gloss. This comment is not in the LXX.

9. Tov, *Text Criticism*, 320.

were part of communities that in all likelihood accepted them as canonical in the late postexilic period. They show that the composition of a biblical book represented a distinct moment in time and a particular point of view.

Canonization

Canonization, the next coordinate in our text model, looks at the point where a book becomes part of a larger collection and contributes to its overall shape. In current biblical studies, composition has generally been taken to precede canonization. Books received their final shape before they became part of a canon. Composition is seen as a historical process, while canonization is a theological one. I would agree to some extent with those who separate canon from composition in this way. The final literary shape of the OT books is not always identical with the canonical shape. It does not follow, however, that the formation of the OT canon was the result of purely theological forces. The two versions of Jeremiah, for example, show that composition occurs even after canonization. The nature of harmonistic textual variants like the addition of "now shortly" in Jer 27:16 shows that the earlier version was already considered canonical, since they are attempts to harmonize an authoritative text. To the extent that such glosses are compositional, we can say there are compositional elements in the final canonical shape of the Hebrew Bible. Composition continues after canonization. It is also clear that such compositional elements were theologically motivated. This means that in classical terms of authorship, the shape of the OT canon as a whole must be taken seriously and integrated into our text model. Not only do the books of the Hebrew Bible have authors, but also the Hebrew Bible as a whole and as a canon is the product of composition and authorship.

Thus, in our understanding of the final text, the concept of canon does not follow a single trail to each and every canonical shape. Rather than speaking of a process of canonization, I would like to borrow a term from the field of biology and speak of the OT canon as a "punctuated equilibrium." It is "punctuated" in that it is the result not of a continuous process of development but of creative moments of formation that arise within [[31]] multiple canonical contexts. It is an "equilibrium" in that once established, the canonical shape continued in a more or less steady state until something triggered a major shift.

One further observation about canonization needs to be made. What we have said and will say about the compositional formation of the OT canon suggests it was the work of an individual, not a community as such. Individuals are part of communities and speak for communities, but, in the last analysis, the work of composition and canonization was the work of individuals.

Consolidation

The third notion in our model of the final shape of the Hebrew Bible is consolidation. Here the issue is the further development of a canonical text within a community. An example would be the well-known adjustment of the

Septuagint to NT quotations of the Old, or to Origen's fifth column in the Hexapla, as well as the adjustment of the Masoretic Text along the lines of the emerging rabbinical exegesis.

A good deal of the Masoretic activity in the Hebrew Bible seems to cluster around texts that form the exegetical basis for established beliefs. For example, the two *yod*s in the account of the creation of man (Gen 2:7, *wyysr*) were likely preserved in the Masoretic Text because they reflected the rabbinical notion that man was created with two natures (*ysrim*; cf. Rashi). In the same way, the single *yod* in the identical verb used for the creation of the animals (Gen 2:19, *wysr*) supports the rabbinical doctrine that the animals have only one nature (*ysr*). I am not suggesting this was the intent of the author of Genesis. That would be a question of composition. The preservation of a form of the Masoretic Text that supports a specific element of rabbinical exegesis is a function of consolidation. The notion of consolidation means that once texts become a part of a community, they take on essential characteristics of the beliefs of that community.

Thus the final shape of the Hebrew Bible is best described in terms of three intersecting coordinates: composition, canonization and consolidation. Composition preceded canonization but did not stop there. Canonical books took on varying compositional shapes that reflected theological viewpoints. Moreover, once established within a specific community, OT texts began to take on essential characteristics of those communities in a way that stopped short of actual new composition. The result was the production of the Hebrew Tanak: the Law, the Prophets and the Writings.

If our text model is valid, it suggests that lying behind the varying shapes of the Hebrew Tanak were various text communities drawing their [[32]] theological identity from those shapes. Elsewhere I have suggested that the Hebrew Tanak is shaped around two sets of seams, Deuteronomy 34 and Joshua 1, as well as Malachi 3 and Psalm 1.[10] Deuteronomy 34 and Malachi 3 look forward to the return of an age of prophecy. Moses, the prophet, is dead, and his place has been taken by Joshua. Joshua is characterized in these seams not as a prophet but as a wise man. The wise man who meditates on written Scripture has taken over the role of the prophet who speaks directly with God. Scripture is now the locus of divine revelation. Yet the hope for a return of prophecy in the future still exists. The Scriptures themselves (e.g., Deuteronomy 18) point in that direction. In the meantime, however, one prospers and becomes wise by meditating on the written Scripture.

These canonical seams suggest a conscious composition of the whole. Its ranking of a collection of written texts over the gift of prophecy strongly suggests its threefold shape was the form in which it was first received as canon. Finally, we know from the history of the Hebrew Bible within Judaism that it was in the shape of the Tanak that the Hebrew Bible was consolidated within

---

10. John H. Sailhamer, *Introduction to Old Testament Theology: A Canonical Approach* (Grand Rapids, Mich: Zondervan, 1995), 239–352.

medieval Judaism. Indeed, the whole of the Masorah that accompanied the Hebrew Bible was oriented toward this threefold division.

The Tanak and Biblical Theology

This leads now to the second problem raised by a biblical theology of the final shape of the text. How does the theology reflected in the Tanak relate to the NT?

Few would contest the notion that the Hebrew Bible existed in a threefold form at some place and time during the pre-Christian period. This was not its only form or even its most durable or authoritative form. It did exist in that form, however, for a considerable period of time and for a significantly large portion of Judaism. According to Luke 24:44, it appears the Tanak was the final shape of the Bible Jesus read. Judging by the prologue to Ben Sirach, it already had that shape a century earlier.[11]

[[33]] The so-called history of salvation[12] approach to biblical theology has largely ignored the question of the shape of the Tanak. The primary reason, of course, is that the arrangement of the books in the Tanak does not always follow the history of salvation. Ruth, for example, is not listed with Judges but with Proverbs. Chronicles falls at the end or with Psalms. In contrast, the salvation-historical approach answered the question of the unity of the two-part Christian Bible by locating that unity in the historical events leading from Judaism to Christianity. In that historical development, the OT reached its final goal in the events of the life of Christ and the early church. The unity of the two Testaments thus lies not in the shape of the Hebrew Bible but in the revelatory progression of salvation history.

The second attempt to link the Tanak with the NT is represented by Rendtorff's recent theology of the OT. Rendtorff has pressed the point that the OT (as the Tanak) was already a distinct entity in its final shape before the formation of the NT.[13] There is thus an inherent diversity between a theology of the Hebrew OT and NT theology. Such diversity stems, Rendtorff suggests, from the fact that the Tanak is a product of pre-Christian Judaism. Nevertheless, Christian theologians are obligated to treat the Tanak as the OT component in a biblical theology together with the NT.[14] As a result, the

11. An important implication of the prologue is that even the OT in Greek was read in a threefold form. This still does not tell us anything about the specific makeup of the Tanak at these various times. There continued to be considerable discussion about the details of which books were in and how they were to be arranged.

12. I have in mind here those approaches to biblical theology that focus on the salvific events of Israel's history as revelatory in addition to the biblical text. See Sailhamer, *Introduction to Old Testament Theology*, 54–85.

13. Rendtorff, "Die Hebräische Bibel war aber bereits davor die jüdische Heilige Schrift," *Theologie*, 4.

14. Rolf Rendtorff, "Toward a Common Jewish-Christian Reading of the Hebrew Bible," *Canon and Theology: Overtures to an Old Testament Theology* (Minneapolis: Fortress, 1993), 31–45.

Jewish Tanak exerts a kind of gravitational pull on the NT. Its effect is to reposition the center of gravity of biblical theology away from the purely Christian NT.

A third attempt to link the Tanak with the NT is that of Hartmut Gese.[15] Gese sees the Tanak as a past stage in the OT's revelatory tradition history. The OT that is to be linked to the NT in a biblical theology is a distinct entity only in the final shape given it by the early church. The OT that has been shaped and embraced by the NT is the final form of its tradition history. The inherent diversity of the tradition in the OT is resolved in the tradition-historical process that culminated in the reading of the OT by Jesus, the early church and ultimately the NT canon. Unity comes out of a complex [[34]] but singular line of reinterpretation.

I would like to suggest a fourth response. First, Rendtorff is right that the "final (threefold) shape" of the Tanak is already fixed in the pre-Christian period and that it is the form of the OT we must unite with the NT. However, there was not one but at least two (or multiple) versions of the Tanak within ancient Judaism (see below). We thus should ask not simply how the Tanak relates to the NT, but which form of the Tanak we should read with the NT. While it may be correct to say the NT does not wholly conform to the Tanak of later Judaism, it may also be correct to say the NT does conform to a Tanak of a slightly different shape and texture—one that perhaps developed in a different community. I am thus in agreement to some extent with Gese in that I believe the OT, in the form we now have it as the (pre-Christian) Tanak, shows real similarity to and unity with the NT. But unlike Gese, I take the (pre-Christian) Tanak, not the OT of the early church (the Alexandrian LXX), to be the canonical form in which it was received by the first Christian communities.

Daniel and the Tanak

Let me illustrate by returning to the example of Daniel's reading of Jeremiah. Canonically and compositionally, the book of Daniel raises a perplexing question. What is the appropriate location of Daniel within the Tanak?

David Noel Freedman has addressed this question in his study of the shape of the Tanak in the pre-Christian period.[16] Freedman finds a great deal of symmetry and order in the Tanak,[17] but he also shows that the symmetry is largely missing if Daniel is included. In effect, Freedman's observations suggest that within the history of the OT canon we must reckon with the possibility of both a "Tanak with Daniel" and a "Tanak without Daniel."

---

15. Hartmut Gese, *Alttestamentliche Vorträge zur biblischen Theologie* (Munich: Chr. Kaiser Verlag, 1977), 23–30.

16. David Noel Freedman, *The Unity of the Hebrew Bible* (New York: Vintage, 1993).

17. Ibid., 79–80: "The correspondences among the major segments are so close, and the symmetry so exact, that it is difficult to imagine that these are the result of happenstance, or that a single mind or group of individuals was not responsible for assembling and organizing this collection of sacred works."

The book of Daniel is not one of those books whose omission or inclusion would make little difference. This is especially true if the larger question is the relationship of the Tanak to the NT. Freedman shows that the major fluctuations in the order of the Writings largely turn on the position assigned to Daniel.

In the earliest complete medieval manuscript (Codex B19a), Daniel falls [[35]] nearly at the end of the Tanak. It is followed only by Ezra/Nehemiah, a single book in the Hebrew Bible. With that arrangement, the edict of Cyrus (Ezra 1:2–4), which was the decree to return and rebuild the temple and which plays a central role in the "messianic" schematic of Daniel 9, immediately follows the book of Daniel and provides the introduction to the last book, Ezra/Nehemiah. In that position, the edict of Cyrus identifies the historical return under Ezra and Nehemiah as the fulfillment of Jeremiah's vision of seventy years. It is as if Daniel 9, and its view of seventy weeks of years, were nowhere in sight.

In another arrangement of the last books of the Tanak (*Baba Bathra* 14b), the book of Chronicles comes last and closes with a repetition of the edict of Cyrus (2 Chr 36:23). As Freedman points out, this arrangement of Chronicles and Ezra/Nehemiah is noticeably out of chronological sequence. After the close of Nehemiah, the Chronicler begins his narrative with Adam! [18] This suggests the book of Chronicles was deliberately placed at the end of the Tanak, after the books of Ezra/Nehemiah and after the book of Daniel. It also suggests a conscious effort to close the Tanak with a restatement of the edict of Cyrus at the end of Chronicles.

There thus appears to have been at least two contending final shapes of the Tanak. The one closes with the book of Ezra/Nehemiah. In that version, the edict of Cyrus finds its fulfillment in the historical return from exile. The other shape of the Tanak closes with Chronicles and a repetition of the edict of Cyrus. In this arrangement, the edict of Cyrus has been shortened from that in Ezra/Nehemiah (Ezra 1:2–4), so that it concludes with the clause "Let him go up" (2 Chr 36:23). In the book of Chronicles, the subject of that clause is identified as he "whose God is with him." For the Chronicler this is possibly also a messianic image (cf. 1 Chr 17:12). Cyrus says, in effect, "let him (whose God is with him) go up to Jerusalem." To arrive at that dramatic conclusion the Chronicler has had to omit nearly two verses from the original edict in Ezra/Nehemiah. It is those verses that link the edict to the historical events of the return from exile. [19] Without them, the fulfillment of the Tanak's final words is left open.

---

18. The order of the OT books followed by the English translations has corrected this by placing Ezra at the end of Chronicles, with the consequence of a redundant and immediate repetition of Cyrus's edict (2 Chr 36:23 and Ezra 1:2–4).

19. In contrast to 2 Chr 36:23, the subject of the verb "let him go up" in Ezra/Nehemiah is "the heads of fathers' households of Judah and Benjamin and the priests and the Levites . . . even everyone whose spirit God had stirred to go up and rebuild the house of the LORD which is in Jerusalem" (Ezra 1:5).

[[36]] The central role of the edict of Cyrus at the conclusion of the Tanak appears to be motivated by the expectation injected into the end of the Tanak by Daniel 9. In Daniel 9, Jeremiah's expectation of a return to Jerusalem is projected beyond the immediate return from Babylonian captivity. Jeremiah's promise of a return after seventy years is extended to seven times seventy years, or 490 years.

Regardless of how one might interpret these events, it is clear that they all hinge on the timing of "the publication of the word to restore and build Jerusalem" (Dan 9:25). The fact that one version of the Tanak ends with just such a decree (the edict of Cyrus) can hardly be coincidental. Moreover, in the introduction to the edict, the Chronicler consciously links the edict to Jeremiah's prophecy of the seventy weeks, which is the passage Daniel is pondering in Daniel 9.

Two final shapes of the Tanak thus appear to emerge. One concludes with Ezra/Nehemiah and identifies the return from Babylonian exile as the fulfillment of Jeremiah's prophecy of seventy years. This is a historical fulfillment. The other Tanak features Daniel and closes with the book of Chronicles. In doing so, it extends Jeremiah's seventy years beyond the time of the return from Babylon—a future fulfillment. That shape fits well with what appears to be the Hebrew text (*Vorlage*) of the Septuagint of Jeremiah and the reading of these texts by the NT. Both are open to events that look beyond the return from Babylonian exile.

Conclusion

The points raised in this essay show that changing attitudes toward the OT have opened the door to a range of new possibilities for constructing a biblical theology of the Old and New Testaments. While there continue to be those who will seek the earliest forms of the OT texts, there is a growing number of others who have turned their attention to the final shape. This should not be construed as a turn away from an interest in history. It is rather a focus on a largely overlooked stage of Israel's history, namely, the history of Israel immediately prior to the coming of Christ and the writing of the NT. Along with an interest in the final shape of the OT has also come a renewed focus on composition. Rather than seeking to discover the literary strata behind the biblical text, attention has shifted to the literary strategy of the biblical text. The quest for strategy has replaced the quest for strata. The convergence of these two interests leads to a necessary recasting of the basic questions of a biblical theology of the Old and New Testaments. [[37]] This is true in at least three important ways.

In the first place, a focus on the final shape of the Hebrew Bible and its link to the notion of canon leaves little doubt that the OT can and should be approached theologically. In the past, biblical theologies have devoted much attention to that question, with largely negative results. It has been negative because composition has been viewed apart from the stage in which Scripture was recognized as authoritative (canonization). By contrast, Rendtorff's recent OT theology has only one sentence devoted to this question. In that sentence, which is the first sentence in the book, Rendtorff says, "The OT is a theological book."[20] Had Rendtorff been seeking any level other than the final canonical shape, he would have been obliged to say much more.

A focus on the final shape of the Hebrew Bible considerably reduces the time gap between the OT and the NT. If the formation of the Tanak took place during the second century B.C. or later, the OT is virtually laid at the doorstep of the NT. In a real sense, the OT, as the Tanak, belongs to the intertestamental period. The Tanak does not conclude in the same way as the history of Israel, that is, with the Babylonian captivity. Nor does the OT first come into being with Judaism, that is, in the priestly circles of the Second Temple. Our discussion has shown that at the end of at least one version of the Tanak we find ourselves already in the world of ideas of the NT.

A focus on the final shape, or final shapes, of the Hebrew Bible raises the possibility of an early (pre-Christian) version of the OT that intentionally links the book of Daniel with the edict of Cyrus in 2 Chr 36:22–23. To be sure, there are surface disturbances in that shape, such as the variant Hebrew versions of Jeremiah and the canonical location of the books of Daniel and Chronicles. But these very disturbances reveal the deep-seated disagreements over the meaning of Scripture that existed in the postexilic period. If we follow closely the nature of those disagreements, a picture begins to emerge. The line that runs through and divides the early versions of the Tanak is the same line that separates John the Baptist from the religious leaders of his day. The Tanak closes with the expectation of a new work of God. This work includes the return of prophecy characterized by Moses and Elijah and extends beyond the events that immediately surround Jerusalem and the Second Temple. It is along that story line that the NT writers pick up the narrative thread and take us into the world of the NT canon.

20. Rendtorff, "Das Alte Testament ist em theologisches Buch," *Theologie*, 1.

GUNTHER HERMANN WITTENBERG

b. 1935

Contextual Theology and Resistance

Gunther H. Wittenberg holds doctorates from both Tübingen (1972) and the University of KwaZulu-Natal in Pietermaritzburg (1979), where he is Professor Emeritus of Old Testament. At the conclusion of his academic career he became Chaplain of the Community and Chairman of the Board of Trustees of the Kenosis Community Trust, in rural Natal. Wittenberg's published work has attended to his context in southern Africa, while arguing for the importance of social and economic conditions to theology.

Selected Writings by Wittenberg

1988　*King Solomon and the Theologians.* Pietermaritzburg: University of Natal Press.

1991　*I Have Heard the Cry of My People: A Study Guide to Exodus 1–15.* Bible in Context 1. Pietermaritzburg: Institute for the Study of the Bible with Cluster Publications.

1993　*Prophecy and Protest: A Contextual Introduction to Israelite Prophecy.* Bible in Context 2. Pietermaritzburg: Institute for the Study of the Bible with Cluster Publications.

1996　Old Testament Theology, for Whom? *Semeia* 73: 221–40.

2000　Alienation and "Emancipation" from the Earth: The Earth Story in Genesis 4. *The Earth Story in Genesis.* The Earth Bible. Edited by Norman C. Habel and Shirley Wurst. Sheffield: Sheffield Academic Press / Cleveland, Ohio: Pilgrim.

Gunther Wittenberg
Old Testament Theology for Whom?

Excerpted with permission from "Old Testament Theology, for Whom?" *Semeia* 6 (1984) 221–22, 228–40.

Introduction

[[221]] At annual congresses of the Old Testament Society of Southern Africa it has often been observed that participation in the Society is an almost totally white affair with little black participation. Although the point has often been made that blacks have a natural affinity to the Old Testament, there are almost no black Old Testament scholars in South Africa and few have chosen the Old Testament as a discipline of study.

Nonetheless we see that the Bible still plays a significant role in black communities. There is general agreement that the Bible is of fundamental importance for their life and faith; indeed, that the Bible can and does play an important role in the empowerment of communities for liberation. But ordinary black parishioners have little biblical knowledge, and [[222]] there is little material which could make the insights of biblical scholarship available to ordinary members of congregations.

It is obvious that theological education, especially as far as biblical scholarship is concerned, has to play a crucial role in bridging the gap. Black students will one day be the leaders of their communities and will have to perform the function of bridge-building. But experience shows that this is seldom achieved. As presented in most textbooks, Old Testament Theology seems inaccessible to black students.

The question needs to be asked: Old Testament Theology for whom? Who is the dialogue partner? Is it the international academic community, or is it the ordinary people in the grassroots communities, particularly the poor and oppressed?

. . . .

[[228]] In recent years there has been an extensive debate about the question of methodology in Old Testament theology (see Hasel 1991: 28–114). The established paradigm in Old Testament theology has come under increasing attack. But really new approaches have not yet emerged. On the whole, Old Testament theology still follows the paradigm established by Gabler, although there is a recognition that it is no longer adequate. Brueggemann (1984: 1) therefore remarks in this connection: "The only two things sure about Old Testament Theology are: (1) The ways of Eichrodt and von Rad are no longer adequate. (2) There is no consensus among us what comes next." And Gerhard Hasel (1985: 34) comments: "There is today a greater variety than ever before in Old Testament Theologies. There is still no consensus on methodology for Old Testament Theology and none seems to be emerging."

Knowledge Systems

What would be the essential ingredients of a new approach to Old Testament Theology? Perhaps basic considerations in liberation theology can point the way. Per Frostin (p. 3) has drawn attention to the fact that liberation theology starts with an epistemological break from the established methodology of First World theology. Third World theologians have argued persistently for a new method of doing theology which differs from the academic theology practiced in the West.

> We reject as irrelevant an academic type of theology that is divorced from action. We are prepared for a radical break in epistemology which makes commitment the first act of theology and engages in critical reflection on the praxis of reality of the Third World. (p. 3)

Frostin notes that epistemological issues are continuously stressed at Ecumenical Association of Third World Theologians (EATWOT) conferences, because epistemology is related to the most fundamental aspect of scientific work, defining the ground rules of the quest for truth. There is [[229]] no single epistemology, but specific epistemologies which belong to distinct ways of knowing. The economist Marglin (p. 232) therefore speaks of *systems of knowledge*, each with its own epistemology, that is, its own theory of what counts as knowledge, and its mode of transmission dealing with the manner of receiving and distributing knowledge.

The comparison between Schmidt and Gabler has shown that theology is also governed by respective systems of knowledge. Drawing mainly on Marglin's work, I therefore want to look at Gabler's work from the perspective of its basic system of knowledge, and then to contrast it with a system of knowledge in which commitment to the poor and oppressed is fundamental. Following Marglin I will call the knowledge system which determines Gabler's approach and which has dominated the approaches to Old Testament Theology up to the present day, *episteme,* the Greek term for "knowledge." This term is particularly appropriate because the study of ideas in theology is a heritage of Greek philosophy. The five points which we listed as being characteristic of Gabler's approach are also characteristic of *episteme* according to Marglin.

Dominating Knowledge—episteme

Gabler was looking for certainty. His ideal for the development of biblical theology was therefore the systematic presentation of God's eternal truths or the unchanging ideas found in the Bible. This is characteristic also of *episteme.* "Episteme lays claim to *universality*, to being applicable at all times and places to all questions. Indeed adherents of *episteme* do not in general see it as one system of knowledge among many, but as knowledge pure and simple" (Marglin: 233).

Gabler emphasized sound method for developing an Old Testament theology. Method is also essential for *episteme.* It is knowledge based on *logical deduction from self-evident first principles.* The best model is perhaps Euclidean geometry (Marglin: 233). The rationalist theologians of the Enlightenment aimed at a theology which would be equally sure and axiomatic. Gabler advocated a "true biblical theology" which would ensure a sound basis for the work of dogmatic theology. "Logical deduction" implies a method according to which one proceeds by small steps with nothing left out, nothing left to chance or to the imagination (Marglin: 233). Gabler, and the historical critics after him, advocated a method proscribing each step by which they hoped to achieve assured results.

Gabler's interest was in religious ideas. Epistemic knowledge, accordingly, is purely cerebral. Since Descartes, mind is separate from body, and *episteme* pertains to the mind alone (Marglin: 233). *Episteme* is theoretical knowledge generally acquired through formal schooling based on books. Indeed, knowledge in the West has more and more come to be [[230]] equated with what is taught in the schools. This applies equally to theological education.

Gabler realised that the Old Testament contains the work of many theologians. But his concern was to extract from their works those ideas which had eternal validity. *Episteme* is therefore *impersonal* knowledge (Marglin: 234). Eternally valid theological ideas cannot be personal. They have to be abstract if they are to be applicable in all places and at all times. The impression that Old Testament theologies are often abstract is entirely in accordance with this basic characteristic of *episteme.*

"Epistemic knowledge is *analytic.* It decomposes, breaks down, a body of knowledge into its components. It is thus directly and immediately reproducible. It is fully *articulate*, and within *episteme* it may be said that what cannot be articulated does not even count as knowledge" (Marglin: 233). Historical criticism, especially the method of source criticism, which has had such a profound effect on the development of Old Testament theology, belongs to this category of analytic knowledge, often breaking down texts into a number of sub-units which are critically analysed. It determined Gabler's view of history as being something to be discarded without direct relevance for Old Testament Theology proper.

Episteme is the dominant knowledge system of the West. It is also the established, hegemonic paradigm (Frostin) of the theological disciplines taught in the academy. Since Gabler, Old Testament Theology developed as a discipline in accordance with the methods and basic criteria of the dominant paradigm.

Knowledge "From Below"—da'at

In an illuminating passage Gustavo Gutiérrez. has identified the difference between the dominant theology of the West and the new theological project of liberation theology developed in Latin America. He states that the challenge to Western theology is posed by non-believers whereas the challenge in Latin America "does not come principally from the non-believer, but from the non-person, i.e., the person who is not recognized as human by the dominant social order: the poor, the exploited, the one who is systematically and legally despoiled of his human nature, the one who hardly feels human" (Gutiérrez: 69; cf. Gibellini: 13). In order to speak meaningfully of God to the poor in an inhuman world Gutiérrez demands a theology "from the underside of history" (p. 169).

Graham Philpott, working in the informal settlement of Amawoti, near Durban, South Africa, makes a similar point when he notes that

> members of the oppressed community are often the invisible participants of society, the superfluous unknown people marginalised by the dominant sectors of society. . . . They have no access to the institutions that are responsible [[231]] for the production of knowledge, and have no way of influencing the development of appropriate and useful knowledge, let alone determining which questions and issues are researched. (p. 17)

He emphasizes that the theologian should

> hear, understand, and learn from those who are usually excluded from the enterprise of the production of theological knowledge, and to allow this "invisible" knowledge and experience to challenge and reshape traditional theological formulations which were generated from within the context of the dominant. (p. 17)

This "knowledge from below" arises from the reflection on the Christian praxis in confrontation with the Bible. The outcome of this communal reflection on the Bible in which the concerns of the poor are taken seriously is recorded in Philpott's book. Cochrane observes:

> . . . we have here a prime example of the new paradigm for doing theology at local base ecclesial community level. . . . Theology, properly understood, is not mere theory, but the reflection of Christians on their faith in the world. Theology cannot therefore be ripped out of a practice of ministry in the world without in the long run self-destructing or without losing its reason for being. (p. 8)

A project with a similar aim is the Institute for the Study of the Bible (ISB), linked to the School of Theology at the University of Natal, Pietermaritzburg. It seeks to establish an interface between biblical studies and ordinary readers of the Bible in the church and community in order to facilitate social transformation. Through the input from grassroots communities the process of Bible studies not only aims at empowering the poor and oppressed who take part in this process, but also seeks to transform the teaching of Biblical Studies at the School of Theology. In this process a new approach to the discipline of Old Testament Theology is emerging. It belongs to a different knowledge system which I term *da'at* to distinguish it from *episteme*.

Drawing again on Marglin's work, I want to concretize the discussion by contrasting "dominating knowledge" (*episteme*) with "knowledge from below" (*da'at*).[1]

---

1. Marglin contrasts the two different types of knowledge using the two different Greek terms *episteme* and *techne*.

While dominating knowledge (*episteme*) makes universalist claims and "disenfranchises those outside," knowledge "from below" makes no such claim (Marglin: 234) It is "local knowledge";[2] it is the knowledge about "the kin-dom of God in Amawoti" (Philpott). Only in its particularity [[232]] and specificity does it have any significance. The same applies to *da'at*. Knowledge of God according to Hebrew conceptions changes according to historical circumstances. God's Word is always directed at a particular historical situation, *da'at* is *contextual*.[3]

Knowledge "from below" "belies the mind/body dualism which is basic to *episteme*" (Marglin: 234). In the contextual Bible studies in Amawoti and in the ISB one knows with and through one's hands and eyes and heart as well as with one's head, because the biblical knowledge of God, *da'at*, is not "objective" and abstract, removed from the whole realm of emotions. "Taste and see that the Lord is good" (Ps 34:8).

Knowledge of God, *da'at 'elohim*, involves commitment. That is as true for the knowledge "from below" among the community in Amawoti or ISB Bible study groups, as it is for the Hebrews according to the Old Testament witness: "Know that the Lord is God!" (Ps 100:3). This is no theoretical knowledge, but it demands a decision for God and against the idols. This is one of the most fundamental themes of Old Testament theology.[4] Knowledge of God—theology—therefore does not arise out of a collection of abstract ideas which are brought into a system, but it arises in *conflict*, in struggle. Therefore *da'at* is intensely *practical*, to the point that, one could almost say, it reveals itself only through practice (Marglin: 235).

Where *episteme* is impersonal, knowledge "from below," *da'at*, is intensely personal and communal. It depends on networks of relationships and cannot be transmitted or even maintained apart from these relationships. This is certainly the experience of grassroots communities studying the Bible together, but it can easily be demonstrated from the Old Testament as well. *Da'at* is therefore community-based and cannot be understood apart from the communicative process within that community.

In contrast with the basis of *episteme* in logical deduction from self-evident axioms, the basis of *da'at* is varied (Marglin: 234). Knowledge "from below" needs its "organic intellectuals" charged with understanding the faith of the poor and oppressed people (Segundo: 23), just as knowledge of God in Hebrew thinking is based on the instruction of the priest or the revelation of Yahweh's word to the prophet.[5] Not only the content but also the bearers of the Word are important.

2. Cf. the title of the book by Clifford Geertz: *Local Knowledge: Further Essays in Interpretive Anthropology*.

3. According to Exod 7:7 Israel will know that Yahweh is God through his historical act of liberation. The prophet Ezekiel also emphasizes Yahweh's acts in history as the basis of "knowledge" of God. Cf. Zimmerli.

4. Cf. the struggle of Elijah against Baal worship and the challenge he posed for or against Yahweh.

5. Hosea attacks the priests for having rejected the *da'at 'elohim* (Hos 4:6, see also 4:1; 10:12). Cf. Wolff: 182–205.

[[233]] In contrast with the analytic nature of *episteme*, which breaks down knowledge into parts, *daʿat* is concerned with the whole. Its preferred means of transmission is the story, not the theological treatise. Bible studies in communities live from stories just as Israel again and again retold its own story to obtain a view of the whole, of what God had done and was planning to do with the people of God.

Towards a New Approach in Old Testament Theology

I do not believe that it is possible to get rid of *episteme* in theology. But we need to retrieve some of the basic characteristics of *daʿat* if we want to develop an Old Testament theology which is truly contextual and relevant not only for the academy but also, most importantly, for poor and oppressed communities. Von Rad has pointed the way in some respects. In his Old Testament Theology he has shown that theological knowledge in the Old Testament is not rational, based on concepts (1962: 116). In short it is not *episteme* but *daʿat*. Theology in the Old Testament is not an abstract body of knowledge which one can learn by heart and pass on, but a process in which one has to be involved, a way in which ever new decisions have to be taken, a response to the concrete challenges of history which cannot be divorced and abstracted from them.

How do we arrive at such a new approach? In developing a new approach to Old Testament theology we need to draw on the basic characteristics of *daʿat* which we have outlined above.

The Contextual Nature of Old Testament Theology

Whereas Gabler emphasized religious ideas to the detriment of history, a new approach towards Old Testament theology shaped by the poor and marginalized as dialogue partners needs to understand it within the context of the social, economic, and political history of Israel. Following Geertz, we need "thick description" (1973: 6–7) in which the study of inscription is no longer "severed from the study of inscribing, the study of fixed meaning" no longer severed "from the study of social processes that fix it" (1983: 32). Thereby the social sciences become important not only for History of Israel and History of Israelite Religion but also for Old Testament Theology. The watertight compartments which developed between the disciplines after the First World War, especially through the influence of Dialectical Theology (cf. esp. Eissfeldt), need to be broken up. Theology, too, not only Israelite Religion, needs to be seen as embedded in the socio-economic and cultural history of the people of Israel. This refiguration would certainly represent a "sea change" (Geertz 1983: 34) in [[234]] our notion of what Old Testament theology means and of what we need to know in order to be relevant for our own context.

The Conflictual Nature of Old Testament Theology

Walter Brueggemann (1983) is possibly the first to have introduced sociological categories into the discipline of Old Testament Theology. Brueggemann draws on an insight by Claus Westermann (pp. 9–34) that the Old Testament does not speak about God uniformly, but in at least two different ways, namely the saving God in the context of history and the blessing God in the context of creation. He links these two different modes of speaking of God to two different trajectories, the one derived from Moses, the other from the Davidic monarchy. The theology in the royal trajectory supports the monarchy and the privileged upper class, while in the Mosaic trajectory, which Brueggemann also calls the "liberation trajectory," the focus is on God's justice and the concern for the poor.

By linking different modes of theologizing in the Old Testament to different social groups, Brueggemann has contributed significantly to the Old Testament theology debate, but his own proposal is not satisfactory. By using the term trajectory he remains within the paradigm initiated by Gabler. One gets the impression that the two trajectories run alongside each other without interaction. The concept trajectory does not yet take us into the actual struggles and conflicts out of which ideas and traditions ultimately derive. We have to go a step further and ask how theologies interact, how they function in the communicative process of ancient Israelite society.

The Role of Theology in the Communicative Process

What is being communicated by the theology which has found expression in the Old Testament? One answer is: power. Robert B. Coote and Mary P. Coote try to demonstrate that the Bible is the product of ruling classes. They argue that there is an inextricable link between the biblical text and political power. "The history of scripture is a history of power, and of powerful organizations" (p. 3). Ruling elites have always used religion to support and legitimate their own interests. It was no different in Israel. Those who wrote did so to satisfy the needs for legitimation of Judahite kings and the ruling class.

There are, of course, many Old Testament texts which seem to support Cootes and Cootes' view. Old Testament scholarship has done particularly fruitful research into the Jerusalem cult traditions and the role of Israelite royal ideology. Drawing on Durkheim's theory of ritual, Lukes [[235]] has suggested that many rituals can be seen as modes of exercising, or seeking to exercise, power along the cognitive dimension as crucial elements in the "mobilization of bias" (pp. 289, 301). This could be seen as an apt description of the ritual of the temple of Jerusalem considering the theology of the royal psalms and the role of the king in the state cult (cf. von Rad 1966).

Nevertheless, Cootes and Cootes' view is highly one-sided and simplistic. Without going into details I want to highlight three areas in which serious questions have to be raised about this whole conception. There is first of all the negative evaluation of the Israelite monarchy in many of the Old Testament sources, especially the Deuteronomistic History. To explain this with reference to the frequent change in dynasties and the antagonisms between those in power begs more questions than it answers.

Secondly, Cootes and Cootes always refer to the Old Testament laws as royal laws, David's laws (p. 28), Hezekiah's laws (p. 55), Josiah's laws (p. 61), written down in the royal scriptorium at the king's command. But they do not answer the question, why it is that the monarchy plays no role in the Old Testament law codes apart from Deut 17:14–17, which severely restricts the king's power. Why is it that, unlike all other ancient Near Eastern law codes which were promulgated by kings, the Old Testament resolutely affirms that Moses alone is the lawgiver of all the law codes? All law ultimately derives from the revelation of the Law on Mount Sinai. The information that Moses' name is given to the author of David's law in order to give absolute authority to David's rule; that David is identified with Moses (p. 30) is speculation not borne out by an exegesis of the texts.

The third area where serious questions need to be asked is Cootes and Cootes' view of prophecy. In order to give plausibility to their thesis that all of the Old Testament literary works have been written by scribes reflecting the views of the ruling class, they have to downplay the role of the prophets. It is important to note their use of terminology. They consistently refrain from using the accepted term "prophet" and, instead, use the term "saint" possibly accompanied by an epithet, e.g., "eccentric" of Elijah (p. 44), to emphasize their marginal role. This is to ignore the textual evidence in favour of an unnuanced schema of a hegemonic Bible.

The three contentious areas, the role of the monarchy, the significance of Law, and the importance of prophecy, seem rather to point in a different direction than Cootes and Cootes want us to take. They are indications that we do not have in the Old Testament a uniform theology supporting state power, but rather, as Brueggemann has affirmed, a complex picture of contending theologies, including a theology that challenges and resists state power, a resistance theology.

The Role of the Theologians

[[236]] In order to understand the dynamics of this resistance theology in the social conflicts of ancient Israel, we have to consider the social groups which have been the bearers of resistance theology. In this context Max Weber's theory of rationalisation can provide a useful model.

Weber investigated the role of ethics and rationalization as the basis of social action. According to Weber, rational reflection, and this means in our context theological reflection, can involve on the one hand "the intellectual elaboration and deliberate sublimation of cultured man's 'inner compulsion' not only to understand the world as a 'meaningful cosmos' but also to take a consistent and unified stance toward it." According to Roth and Schluchter (p. 15), "this type of rationalism may be called *metaphysical-ethical rationalism*."

It can also refer "to the achievement of a methodical way of life. Here rationalism is the consequence of the institutionalization of configurations of meaning and interest." Roth and Schluchter call this rationalism a *practical rationalism*. Weber was especially interested in the way both interact to lead to social action.

In his *Ancient Judaism* (pp. 169–74; 205–18; 223–25; 235) Weber advanced the thesis that Israelite intellectuals were responsible for developing an alternative form of theology which could oppose and challenge the dominant theology communicated by state ritual. Although the term "intellectual" is really a modern concept (cf. Kippenberg: 70), Weber uses it to characterize a certain group in ancient Israel which were educated enough to be considered part of the ruling class, but who specifically took up the cause of the uneducated, the poor and the oppressed. They became the educators of the lower classes and gave expression to an ideology which served their basic interests. In this connection Weber mentions three groups which provided an alternative theology: Levites, prophets, and lay intellectuals. An Old Testament Theology will not only have to consider the content of their theology, but also the conflicts and problems to which their theology responded.

Old Testament Theology as Story Telling

The Old Testament tells a story. Von Rad was right when he emphasized this point over against those who felt that the task of Old Testament theology was the systematic presentation of Israel's religious ideas. It seems to me that we need to tell the story of how Israel obtained its deepest theological insights, how its theology was formed in the context of conflict and opposition. I do not believe that we should only tell the story which Israel itself told, as von Rad suggested, because that story is but the end product of a much more dramatic story (including contending stories). [[237]] The confessional formulae which von Rad believed to have stood at the beginning of Israel's tradition history are the culmination of [[a]] long process of struggle, conflict, and theological reflection. We need to look at the historical context, at the groups involved in the process, and to employ the tools supplied by the social sciences to understand that process. And we need ourselves to be involved, seeking to understand God's will and purpose for us in our own context if we wish to gain daʿat, a knowledge of God, based on the biblical witness, which is helpful and dynamic for the manifold challenges in our time.

The task of writing a theology of the Old Testament, then, cannot simply consist in gathering the religious ideas of the Old Testament and bringing them into a systematic order, but in treating the theology of the Old Testament we have to take cognizance of the context in which these insights were formulated. To attempt such a task for the whole of the Old Testament would be a massive undertaking. The objective should therefore be much more modest. We should concentrate on one central issue which proved of decisive significance for the development of Israel's theology, even if we have to recognize that not everything in the Old Testament will be covered. That issue, in my opinion, is the establishment of a hegemonic theology, on the one hand, which is challenged by a new type of theology, on the other.

This theology is not ready at hand, but is only formulated and developed in the process of resistance and opposition. In order to make that theology relevant for our own situation, we would have to retell the story of this theology, concentrating not only on theological ideas or theological traditions, but taking into consideration the historical context and the various social groups and their struggles which gave rise to those traditions. Such a theology could serve as a model for struggles of resistance and theological reflection arising out of struggles in our own South African context.

Works Consulted

Brueggemann, Walter
  1983 "Trajectories in Old Testament Literature and the Sociology of Ancient Israel." Pp. 306–33 in *The Bible and Liberation: Biblical and Social Hermeneutics*. Ed. Norman K. Gottwald. Maryknoll: Orbis.
  1984 "Futures in Old Testament Theology." *Horizons in Biblical Theology* 6: 1–11.
Cochrane, James R.
  1993 "Foreword." Pp. 7–10 in *Jesus Is Tricky and God Is Undemocratic: The Kindom of God in Amawoti* by Graham Philpott. Pietermaritzburg: Cluster.
Coote, Robert B., and Mary P. Coote
  1990 *Power, Politics and the Making of the Bible: An Introduction*. Minneapolis: Fortress.
Eissfeldt, Otto
  1926 "Israelitisch-jüdische Religionsgeschichte und alttestamentliche Theologie." *Zeitschrift für die alttestamentliche Wissenschaft* 44: 1–12.
Frostin, Per
  1988 *Liberation Theology in Tanzania and South Africa. A First World Interpretation*. Studia Theologica Lundensis 42. Lund: Lund University Press.
Geertz, Clifford
  1973 *The Interpretation of Cultures: Selected Essays*. New York: Basic.
  1983 *Local Knowledge: Further Essays in Interpretive Anthropology*. New York: Basic.
Gibellini, Rosino
  1987 *The Liberation Theology Debate*. Trans. John Bowden. London: SCM.
Gutiérrez, Gustavo
  1983 *The Power of the Poor in History*. London: SCM.
Hasel, Gerhard F.
  1974 "The Problem of the Center in the Old Testament Theology Debate." Zeitschrift für die alttestamentliche Wissenschaft 86: 65–82.
  1985 "Major Recent Issues in Old Testament Theology." *JSOT* 31: 31–53.
  1991 *Old Testament Theology: Basic Issues in the Current Debate*. Revised and expanded fourth edition. Grand Rapids: William B. Eerdmans.
Kippenberg, Hans G.
  1991 *Die vorderasiatischen Erlösungsreligionen in ihrem Zusammenhang mit der antiken Stadtherrschaft: Max-Weber-Vorlesungen 1988*. Suhrkamp Taschenbuch Wissenschaft 917. Frankfurt: Suhrkamp.

Lukes, Steven
  1975   "Political Ritual and Social Integration." *Sociology* 9: 289–308.
Marglin, Stephen
  1990   "Losing Touch: The Cultural Conditions of Worker Accommodation and Resistance." Pp. 217–82 in *Dominating Knowledge: Development, Culture, and Resistance.* Ed. Frédérique Apffel Marglin and Stephen A. Marglin. WIDER Studies in Development Economics. Oxford: Clarendon.
Philpott, Graham
  1993   *Jesus Is Tricky and God Is Undemocratic: The Kin-dom of God in Amawoti.* Pietermaritzburg: Cluster.
Roth, Guenther, and Wolfgang Schluchter
  1979   *Max Weber's Vision of History: Ethics and Methods.* Berkeley: University of California Press.
Segundo, J. L.
  1985   "The Shift within Latin American Theology." *Journal of Theology for Southern Africa* 52:17–29.
von Rad, Gerhard
  1962   *Old Testament Theology. Vol. I: The Theology of Israel's Historical Traditions.* New York: Harper & Row.
  1966   "The Royal Ritual in Judah." Pp. 222–31 in *The Problem of the Hexateuch and Other Essays.* Edinburgh: Oliver & Boyd.
Weber, Max
  1952   *Ancient Judaism.* Trans. H. H. Gerth and D. Martindale. London: George Allen & Unwin.
Westermann, Claus
  1982   *Elements of Old Testament Theology.* Atlanta: John Knox.
Wolff, Hans Walter
  1964   "'Wissen um Gott' bei Hosea als Urform der Theologie." Pp. 182–205 in *Gesammelte Studien zum Alten Testament.* Theologische Bücherei 22. München: Chr. Kaiser.
Zimmerli, Walther
  1969   "Erkenntnis Gottes nach dem Buche Ezekiel." Pp. 41–119 in *Gottes Offenbarung, Gesammelte Aufsätze zum Alten Testament.* Theologische Bücherei 19. 2d ed. München: Chr. Kaiser.
  1978   *Old Testament Theology in Outline.* Edinburgh: T. & T. Clark.

A native of Glasgow, Scotland, James Barr has been professor of Old Testament at the universities of Edinburgh and Manchester, Princeton Theological Seminary, Oxford, and Vanderbilt University. He is currently Distinguished Professor of Hebrew Bible Emeritus at Vanderbilt. In 1991, he delivered the Gifford Lectures, in Edinburgh. Barr's work has ranged widely and his critical eye on biblical scholarship, including Old Testament theology, has proved very keen. He has inveighed particularly against Childs and Brueggemann, among those included in this volume.

Selected Writings by Barr

1966   *Old and New in Interpretation*. London: SCM / New York: Harper & Row.
1973   *The Bible in the Modern World*. London: SCM / New York: Harper & Row.
1977   *Fundamentalism*. Philadelphia: Westminster.
1980   *The Scope and Authority of the Bible*. London: SCM / Philadelphia: Westminster.
1983   *Holy Scripture: Canon, Authority, Criticism*. Philadelphia: Westminster.
1988   The Theological Case against Biblical Theology. Pp. 3–19 in *Canon, Theology, and Old Testament Interpretation: Essays in Honor of Brevard S. Childs*. Edited by Gene M. Tucker, David L. Petersen, and Robert R. Wilson. Philadelphia: Fortress.
1993a   *The Garden of Eden and the Hope for Immortality*. Minneapolis: Fortress.
1993b   *Biblical Faith and Natural Theology: The Gifford Lectures, Edinburgh 1991*. Oxford: Oxford University Press.
1999   *The Concept of Biblical Theology: An Old Testament Perspective*. Minneapolis: Fortress.
2000   *History and Ideology in the Old Testament: Biblical Studies at the End of a Millennium*. London: Oxford University Press.

Writings about Barr

Balentine, Samuel E., and John Barton (editors)
1994   *Language, Theology and the Bible: Essays in Honour of James Barr*. Oxford: Clarendon.

James Barr
"Real" Theology and Biblical Theology

Excerpted with permission from James Barr, *The Concept of Biblical Theology: An Old Testament Perspective* (Minneapolis: Fortress, 1999), pp. 58–62, 74–76, 240–43, 246–49, 251–52. Some footnotes have been omitted.

A Wider Spectrum

[[58]] To sum up, then: it is mistaken to suppose that the field of Old Testament theology is identical with the enterprise of writing (or reading) largish volumes with the title of *Theology of the Old Testament* (or a similar title). It is by no means certain that the production of such volumes is essential to the discipline. Old Testament theology might be sustained and carried forward on the basis of essays on particular aspects, studies of terms and concepts, and also of major studies which have an overlap with Old Testament theology but are not concentrated upon it. Indeed, there are some reasons for thinking that the discipline would go forward better if it [[were]] seen in this way. It is likely that Old Testament [[59]] theology, far from being definitively located in the production of large volumes dedicated purely to this theme, is rather an aspect which is likely to be present, in varying proportions, in almost all activity of study of the Bible and comment upon it.

The matter is of central importance. Biblical theology or Old Testament theology is in essence not a book but a *level* of scholarship. Whether it is possible to represent this entire level in one book, i.e., whether one can encapsulate in a single definitive statement this variety of subjects and approaches, is an interesting practical question, but not one that affects the total status of biblical theology as an undertaking.

It may thus have been a misfortune for the subject that Eichrodt, and many others after him, in setting before us the ideal of a *synthetic* or *comprehensive* study as opposed to an analytic one, which in itself might be quite a justifiable principle, allowed it (perhaps inadvertently) to seem that the production of a single-book statement was the real task and goal of the subject. On the contrary, such books may have the character more of *suggestions, hypotheses, possible alignments of evidence*, and in this sense be actually *subsidiary* to the main course of thought in biblical theology, of which main course these books are only one manifestation among others.

For this there is an important theoretical reason: in order to be comprehensive, a book must also be, paradoxically, *selective*. On such a subject, any single book that aspires to be comprehensive must also by the same token be *selective*. No book, however long, can contain all the material or even give references to all of it. Equally, there are many different ways in which the materials may be *grouped, ordered and classified*, and many differing degrees in which each element can be either emphasized or treated as marginal. The books that appear, therefore, even accepting their high quality and even

449

leaving aside the various criticisms which may be directed against each, are statements of individual approaches and hypotheses rather than definitive expressions of what biblical theology is. It is not necessarily a fault, but part of the nature of the undertaking, that the unsympathetic reader will be able to perceive gaps in the evidence cited: naturally, the writer will have to *know* all the evidence, in so far as that is humanly possible, but to *present* it all is more than can be demanded.

The question, often posed, of "methodology" in writing a work on biblical theology is thus a relatively unimportant one. There is no such thing as a "right" methodology for carrying out such a task.[1] The differences of ordering and approach in the various works surveyed in the last chapter are not a matter of fault or defect; rather, they are what is to be expected. Certainly there are questions of principle, of "methodology" if one wants to call it so, in such matters as perceiving the theology implied by a text, or relating it to the theology of some other text: these are of real importance, and the question [[60]] of ordering and organizing the individual book about it is of much lesser importance.

A realization of this might do much to obviate some of the criticism and opposition with which biblical theology has sometimes had to contend. The idea of someone writing a book which aspires to be "the" theology of the Old Testament has something grandiose about it which tends to invite mockery. Can anyone really put together the essentials, perhaps even the totality, of such a theology within a few hundred pages? Does not the very title suggest a claim to definitiveness, to ultimate authority? Does it not suggest that the author, however he or she may differentiate their work from that of doctrinal theology, is implying a claim to ultimate authority similar to that which (some) doctrinal theology claims? Studies of a particular theme, or aspect, or text, may be able to avoid that sort of criticism. Thus, for instance, many Christian theologies of the Old Testament have aspired to establish some sort of connection with the New. This fact, however understandable, has in turn provoked some scepticism toward such theologies, for by their own comprehensive nature and design they have given the impression of stating "the" one true relation between the Testaments. A study of some particular theme, on the other hand, can pass more easily from the Hebrew Bible into the post-biblical era and thence into the New Testament, without suggesting that the relations thus traced constitute "the" essential connection between Old and New. No one doubts that *some* themes or aspects are enunciated in the Old and reactualized or recontextualized in the New. Such a limited and partial study can therefore—at least in principle—successfully perform a function which, when attempted by the full-scale one- or two-volume Theology of the Old Testament, is likely to meet with questioning or opposition. Moreover, as

---

1. This has some degree of agreement with the position of Childs in *Old Testament Theology in a Canonical Context* [[London: SCM, 1985]] 15, but differs in that the logic of his work seems to me to require the opposite, i.e., that the canon *would* provide the one right methodology. [[. . .]]

has been said above, the comprehensiveness of the full Theologies also implies a selectivity within the material, and this possible weakness can at least in part be overcome by a more partial and limited study, which can seek to handle *all* the material relevant to that particular theme and consider it in a variety of aspects—say, textual, historical, sociological and so on—for which the comprehensive Theology does not have space.

This has great importance, for it shows that the detailed work of biblical theology is closer to the normal activity of exegesis than is commonly realized: it is, I suggest, a "level" within the latter rather than a special and separate activity. There is nothing wrong with the special activity of writing a book called "a Theology" of the Old Testament or the New, but it is not the paradigm for the activity of biblical theology in essence; rather it is a special case, which in fact is dependent on a large number of limited and particular studies that may not be mentioned but are presupposed.

If I am right, it means that Old Testament (or biblical) theology is not a matter of the production of large and comprehensive volumes. Nor is it an [[61]] activity sharply separated from other kinds of study that concern the Bible. It does not have strict rules to demarcate it from other kinds and levels of biblical study. On the contrary, biblical (or Old or New Testament) theology is a level of study that is present in varying degree in all sorts of teaching, courses, texts, dictionaries, encyclopedias, articles and books. Information and scholarship of any kind—historical, linguistic, textual, cultural, comparative—can at any point move into the position of significance for biblical theology. Anyone who wishes can, of course, refrain from making that transition, and can decide simply to keep out of the area of biblical theology. Many scholars do this. There is no harm in it: they simply refrain from entering into certain questions, as they are entitled to do. But their work remains as work that may potentially be significant in the field of biblical theology.

The variety of forms that the total enterprise of biblical theology can take has a further important consequence. It means that there can be no such thing as the one appropriate method for biblical theology. Even if a regulative method could be worked out for writing a complete "Old Testament Theology," that method would not be regulative for other formats. For instance, a complete Theology, seeking to cover the entire Old Testament, would be forced to use an approach both synthetic and selective, there being no other way to cover the ground required. On the other hand someone writing a monograph on some particular theological aspect, let us say the theology of war and peace or the theology of the restoration period with Haggai and Zechariah, would almost necessarily have to provide completeness of coverage along with historical location of the materials to be used. For some sorts of enquiry, such as the Hebrew idea of humanity or of body and soul, the question of historical difference might prove to be unimportant (at least until the Hellenistic period), while for others, such as the idea of monotheism, a historical framework with dating of different sources would very likely prove necessary. In general, one cannot predict what sort of method will be needed until the outlines of the particular question have been examined for each case.

. . . .

Difference from Doctrinal Theology

[[62]] Central to all discussion of Old Testament theology (or of New Testament theology, or of biblical theology) is the question: how does it differ from doctrinal (dogmatic, systematic) theology?

It is customary to begin with the distinction as defined by Gabler in the late eighteenth century. Doctrinal (in his words dogmatic) theology was didactic and philosophical: it taught what was to be believed. While doctrinal theology used the Bible and depended on it, it had to be influenced also by other factors, such as philosophy and church tradition. Biblical theology was historical; it concerned what the biblical authors in their own time had believed.

This might seem clear enough, but further distinctions made the difference more obscure. "True" biblical theology was "thus conceived as a purely descriptive task: a true and accurate description of the religion (religious ideas) of the Bible in its various periods and contexts and in a systematic and historical presentation."[2] There was also a "pure" biblical theology, "a systematic presentation of God's eternal truths or the unchanging ideas found in the Bible which were valid for all times."[3] Here "the descriptive task moves to the level of the normative task." Within biblical theology there was something that appeared to attain to supreme and authoritative status.

Here then, in this early attempt to define biblical theology, we find present one of the antinomies which has continued to bedevil the subject down to the present day—not least, as we shall see, because the problem has not been properly faced by biblical theologians themselves. On the one hand it is recognized that normative status and prescriptive function belong to doctrinal theology, while the scope of biblical theology lies within the historical thinking of the biblical writers in their own time; on the other hand there is an expectation that the work of biblical theology will somehow produce insights of maximal theological status and authority.

. . . .

Conclusion [[74]]

1. Biblical theology has the Bible as its horizon: its source material is the biblical text, its subject is the theology which lies behind or is implied by the Bible, and its scope is determined by the meanings as known and implied within the time and culture of the Bible. In this sense Gabler was right in saying that biblical theology was historical in character. This does not mean, however, that it consists of nothing more than historical research.

2. [[John H. Hayes and F. Prussner *Old Testament Theology: Its History and Development* (London: SCM / Atlanta: John Knox, 1985) 63.]]

3. [[Ibid.]] On this, see D. Ritschl, " 'Wahre,' 'reine' oder 'neue' Biblische Theologie? [[Einige Anfragen zur neueren Diskussion um 'Biblische Theologie,' " *JBTh* 1, (1986) 135–50]].

2. Doctrinal theology, however much it works with the Bible and acknowledges the Bible as authoritative, is not primarily *about* the Bible: it is primarily about God and its horizon is God. Its task is to elucidate, explain, and make intelligible and consistent the regulative principles which influence or control the action and the speech of the religious community. Even given the maximum authority of the Bible, the Bible is not the sole or even the sole controlling factor in its work. Its work is related to later traditions, to philosophy (as Gabler said) and to natural theology (as Jacob said), and to the modern situation. The ultimate reason for this is that the source of doctrinal theology is not the Bible. It would be more correct to say that the source of doctrinal theology is the tradition of regulative decisions which had a part in the formation of the biblical texts. Or, in other words, the prime and ancient paradigm for doctrinal theology is not the Bible but the Creed. The extant creeds are, of course, historically later than the completion of the Bible; logically, however, they have precedence, because they represent something that, in earlier forms, antedated the Bible.

[[75]] I am here disagreeing, therefore, with Emil Brunner when he began the second chapter of his *The Divine-Human Encounter* with the sentence "The source and norm of all Christian theology is the Bible." This, he goes on, "is the presupposition . . . for my attempt to work out the opposition between the biblical understanding of truth and the general, rational understanding of truth as determined by the Object-Subject antithesis."[4] The Bible may in a certain sense be the norm, or rather one of the norms; but it cannot, strictly speaking, be the source. The source is a theological tradition which *preceded* the Bible and accompanied it, guiding and influencing its utterances, as well as following it. Precisely its ability to identify and describe this tradition, or at least its aspiration to do so, is the justification and meaning of biblical theology.

Robert Morgan is thus right in writing:

> The dependence of both the Bible and theology upon a prior revelation of God, and the denial that theology consists simply in deductions from the Bible, can be confirmed by recalling that Christian theology antedated the Christian Bible. The beginnings of Christian theology can be traced within the New Testament to a period before it was described as either "Christian" or "theology."[5]

The same thing, we must add, would be true, *mutatis mutandis*, for the Hebrew Bible. This insight is of vital importance for the conception of biblical theology.

Doctrinal theology does indeed have a scriptural test which affects its status. But the test is not whether a doctrinal theology is full of biblical exegesis

4. E. Brunner, *The Divine-Human Encounter* [[London: SCM, 1944]] 30 [[. . .]].

5. R. Morgan, "The Bible and Christian Theology," in J. Barton (ed.), *The Cambridge Companion to Biblical Interpretation* [[Cambridge: Cambridge University Press, 1998]] 117.

or not, or whether it is derived from the Bible or can be proved by the Bible—on the contrary, many of the great doctrines could never be "proved" from the Bible. The test is rather whether the theology can provide matrices suitable for the interpretation of the Bible. The suitability of these matrices is not any better proved by massive exegesis of the Bible than by the explication of other modes in which the Bible may be integrated into theology.

3. The effect of dialectical theology in some of its forms was to diminish the distance between biblical and doctrinal theology; this coincided with a biblicistic view of theology on the part of many biblical scholars. It was, however, a misunderstanding of dialectical theology: in many respects the major dialectical theologians took the opposite view.

4. Precisely because biblical theologians have not seriously faced the fact of a doctrinal theology that is quite different in type and operational mode from their own work, they have given little thought to the nature of doctrinal theology and have not tried to converse meaningfully with it. The tendency to think that it would be good to merge biblical and doctrinal theology as far as possible is a symptom and a result of this failure.

5. I mention here another aspect which will be discussed later, but must be [[76]] mentioned here because it concerns the relation between doctrinal and biblical theology: it remains a serious question how far any sort of "biblical theology" is really and authentically *theology*. Biblical theologians cannot rightly justify this title by simply *asserting* that their work is, as they see it, "theological." For the question how far it is really theology depends not on their assertions but on the judgment of the doctrinal theologians, whose province "theology" in the proper sense of the word it is. We will return to this below, Chapter 15 [[excerpted below—ed.]]

The distinction between doctrinal theology and biblical theology is therefore very important. That is not to say that the two may not be mixed up. They may very well be mixed up, in the sense that considerations on both levels may occur together. But even if thus mixed up, they have to be clearly distinguished. Ideas that may be creative in biblical theology may often come out of the older theological tradition, which is primarily doctrinal. Ideas formed within biblical theology may require to be considered in doctrinal theology. Biblical theologians may well wish to point out ways in which doctrinal theology could better orientate itself in relation to the Bible. Doctrinal theologians may wish to point out to biblical theologians consequences in their concepts—say of "history," or of "tradition," or of "parable"—which have not been taken into account. All this is the more the case because "biblical theologians" and "doctrinal theologians" are not, in essence, two different sets of people: rather the terms signify, not always but at least sometimes, two different sets of operations, which may go on in the same mind. But the maintenance of the distinction remains very important.

Some such position as this, I submit, will provide adequate differentiation between biblical theology and doctrinal theology. Further justification and elaboration of it will be added in later chapters.

. . . .

"There Is No 'Theology of the Old Testament'"

[[240]] The person from whom I quote these words was not a rabid zealot for historical criticism, but the influential dogmatic theologian Emil Brunner; they were published in German in 1941, in English in 1946.[6]

That so strong a statement to this effect came from *Brunner*—surely then still the best-known and most accepted voice of dialectical theology in the English-speaking world—is surprising.[7] Did anyone pay attention to it? Most biblical theologians, I imagine, remained quite unaware of it until much later, or are still unaware of it. The phrase and its impact had widely escaped notice, at least until scholars were reminded of it by Smend's article of 1982. Nor do I remember it being quoted or discussed in all the many discussions of biblical theology in which I took part in the intervening years. Such a remark falls like a shower of icy water upon the head of those enthusiastic for biblical theology. For surely, in pressing for the development of their rapidly growing discipline, they were confident that Brunner and his theological emphasis supported them. In this, it seems, they were wrong. And if they were wrong about Brunner, then very likely this implied Barth also: for, though these two disagreed in many things, it is quite likely that in this particular point Brunner was expressing common ground, as will be shown shortly.

Although the great theologians of dialectical theology, Brunner and Barth, did very much to inspire the rise of modern biblical theology, they themselves were distinctly cool towards any idea of such a discipline. Their thinking did not depend on it and they did not build it into the structure of their thinking.

A lack of enthusiasm for biblical theology on the part of doctrinal theologians has been noticed before. Thus Childs in his *Biblical Theology in Crisis* properly notes (64–65) the critical article of Langdon Gilkey, "Cosmology, Ontology, and the Travail of Biblical Language."[8] And, more generally, Childs correctly writes that with the dissolution of "the amorphous category of 'neo-orthodoxy,'"

---

6. E. Brunner, *Revelation and Reason* (Philadelphia: Westminster, 1946) 290. See especially R. Smend, "Theologie im Alten Testament" [[in *Verificationen: Ebeling FS* (Mohr, 1982) = *Die Mitte des Alten Testaments*, 104–17]]. Interestingly, R. Rendtorff has recently, in *JBTh* 10 (1995) 37 [["Die Hermeneutik einer kanonischen Theologie des Alten Testaments: Prolegomena," 35–44]] said precisely the opposite: "A sentence like 'the Old Testament has no theology' is in my eyes simply nonsense," but without reference to Brunner or anyone else who has uttered the remark.

7. On the central position of Brunner in the beginnings of the Biblical Theology Movement, cf. Childs, *Biblical Theology in Crisis* [[Philadelphia: Westminster, 1970]] 17, who mentions this same book as one of his two most influential.

8. [[Langdon Gilkey, "Cosmology, Ontology, and the Travail of Biblical Language," *JR* 41 (1961) 194ff.]]

The effect of the breakdown of one dominant theological position was increasingly to isolate the biblical theologians from the active support of the systematic theologians. (p. 78)[9]

[[241]] But Childs' presentation does not make clear that this was no new development: something like this had been the feeling of most doctrinal theologians over a long time, and still is today. Gilkey's sharply-focussed article was specially relevant because it addressed a particular weakness specific to biblical theology. But it, and Childs' presentation of it, did not make clear that this was only one aspect of a more general scepticism on the part of doctrinal theologians, which had prevailed throughout the rise and apogee of modern biblical theology. Only a small minority of them were enthusiastic for biblical theology or had confidence in its products. Taking together all currents of Christian doctrinal theology, neo-orthodoxy was never so very dominant, and for many the dependence of biblical theology upon it was a good reason for scepticism towards the latter. As I will show, even within neo-orthodoxy, scepticism towards biblical theology goes back to the foundational thinkers like Barth and Brunner themselves. Certainly, my own contacts and conversations with doctrinal theologians were an important source of confidence in the criticisms of biblical theology that I advanced.

Theologians proper, doctrinal or dogmatic theologians, never really gave full support to what biblical theologians have been trying to do. They did not much want what Old Testament and New Testament theologians were seeking to provide, and when they saw what had been provided they did not much like it. To quote from an earlier article of my own:

> The fall from grace of biblical theology was welcomed with warm acclamation by a very large number of leading theologians; its demise, if it was a demise, was greeted with cordial accents of joy.[10]

At the very least it can be stated: biblical theology, whether of the Old or New Testament or of both, can no longer be assured of the acceptance and support of doctrinal (dogmatic, systematic) theology. Indeed, as a matter of fact, it never had such support. If it is to succeed, it has to show why it should gain that support.

I must say that I have had difficulty in convincing people of this. None of my writings relevant to biblical theology has been more misunderstood than the article which I have just quoted.[11] Let me put it again in simple words. In

---

9. Childs adds that as a result "Biblical theologians were forced to do their own theology."

10. J. Barr, "The Theological Case against Biblical Theology" [[in G. M. Tucker, D. L. Petersen, and Wilson (eds.), *Canon, Theology and Old Testament Interpretation: Childs FS* (Philadelphia: Fortress, 1988) 3–19]]: 5.

11. Cf. among others Reventlow in *ThR* 61 (1996) 123 [[H. Graf Reventlow, "Der Konflikt Zwischen Exegese und Dogmatik: Wilhelm Vischers Ringen um den 'Christus im AT,'" in *Textgemäss: Würthwein FS* (Göttingen: Vandenhoeck & Ruprecht, 1979) 110–22]]; Reumann, *Promise and Practice*, 9 [[John Reumann (ed.), *The Promise and Practice of Biblical Theology*

that article I am not saying that *I* have theological arguments against biblical theology. I am reporting the fact that *doctrinal theologians* have arguments against it. I knew, after all, though I refrained from saying so, that I had Barth and Brunner on my side. It was from them, after all, that I got the freedom to be critical of biblical theology without thinking that I was thereby ruining the biblical basis of faith. We biblical scholars are often urged to work with doctrinal theologians and I think I have done so more than most people. When I have done so, this is what I have found. With few exceptions, they are [[242]] sceptical of the idea of biblical theology. They do not think that they stand in need of any such thing and they do not think highly of what has been produced by it thus far.[12] They do not believe that biblical theology has a secure standing *as a form of theology*, or as an ancillary support necessary for theology. In this I am not expressing my own opinion: I am stating what I have heard from doctrinal theologians. If this is not the case, and if doctrinal theologians are longing for biblical theology to proceed and to assist them in their endeavours, I shall be delighted to retract what I have said. All I can say is that my own experience has been otherwise. Thus Hans Frei, much quoted in recent biblical theology as a source of inspiration, himself personally told me how pleased he was by the "destruction of biblical theology" (or similar terms) in the 1960s. The whole point of this, therefore, is not an "attack" on biblical theology by me but an indication to biblical theologians that their arguments for their discipline have to be directed towards meeting the distrust and scepticism of many doctrinal theologians. Far from agreeing with these sceptical positions, I have planned the arguments of this book precisely with the hope and intention of going some small distance towards meeting them. My own opinion is that the scepticism of doctrinal theologians towards biblical theology is short-sighted, and that biblical theology will have to be recognized in the long run as an important and indeed an essential component in the total structure of theology.

I should also point out that the question at issue is not whether doctrinal theologians can or should interpret the Bible or not. In my opinion they both

---

(Minneapolis: Fortress, (1991)]]; Childs, *Biblical Theology*, 370, who appears to say that the article "denigrates the value of biblical theology as lacking the integrity of a true discipline." There is nothing in the article to this effect. So also Hasel in Ollenburger et al., *Flowering*, 374 [[B. Ollenburger, E. A. Martens, and G. F. Hasel, *The Flowering of Old Testament Theology* (Winona Lake, Ind.: Eisenbrauns, 1992)]], who quotes this article as evidence for the statement that: "For Barr, biblical theology [and Old Testament theology] is descriptive, and clearly not normative or prescriptive." But in the passage referred to I say *"let us suppose"* that this is so. I put this forward as one of "two main extreme possibilities." On the next page I say that this understanding is "unrealistic." These things are *suppositions* for discussion, not statements of my own opinion.

12. In this sense I think a theology that is more abstracted from biblical detail, like Tillich's (or indeed like some of the later writings of T. F. Torrance, on which cf. Childs, *Biblical Theology*, 406, is *formally speaking* just as appropriate as a matrix for biblical interpretation as a theology full of pieces of exegesis, such as Barth's. This is relevant to the argument of F. Watson, *Text and Truth*, 4. [[(Francis Watson, *Text and Truth: Redefining Biblical Theology* [Edinburgh: T. & T. Clark / Grand Rapids: Eerdmans, 1997]).]]

can and should and normally do, though a theology that is more abstracted from biblical detail is also perfectly possible. But *of course* theologians may and should interpret the Bible. That is not the question. The question is whether there is, or should be, a "biblical theology" which seeks to bring together the entire biblical witness, or large portions of it, as a sort of intermediate activity between normal exegesis of individual texts and the regulative decision-making of doctrinal theology. That is a quite different question.

Why then does an uncertainty of this kind exist? We return to Brunner's emphatic statement: "There is no 'theology of the Old Testament.'"

What was Brunner's argument? He had been arguing for several pages that one must recognize the *differences* of doctrine (*Lehre*) in the various parts of the Bible. The most important of these is the difference between the teaching of Jesus and that of the apostles. Similarly, it is impossible to reconcile the teachings of Paul and James, of John's Gospel and the Johannine Apocalypse, if one takes them just as teachings or doctrines. They complement each other, but they do so just because they disagree, not because they say the same thing. Faith benefits from them all because faith is not directed to a uniform doctrine or teaching but to a *person*.

Similarly, Brunner goes on, there is no "theology of the Old Testament." It is [[243]] often difficult to know what the doctrinal content of Old Testament passages is at all. Even if one does know, there is such a difference of levels and ideas that one would be much embarrassed if one tried to reach a unitary picture. The most primitive lies alongside the most sublime; there are irreconcilable differences between rival tendencies; there is material that is more or less ossified (*erstarrtes*) and material that is living. Who can bring the priestly and the prophetic, the archaic and the post-exilic, under one title? Thus "the contrasts seem to mock at every view of a unity" [[Brunner, *Revelation and Reason*, 319]] and so "anyone who attempts a scientific unitary view of this differentiated and contradictory material will have to suffer shipwreck."

. . . .

Does the Bible Contain Theology?

[[246]] Another way of putting the question is to ask whether the Bible in fact *contains* "theology." Non-theological opponents of Old Testament theology had long made this argument: the material of the Old Testament is not "theology." "Theology" is foreign to it. Jewish opinion, as we shall see, is often the same. Some schools of opinion in the history of religion have also been reluctant to admit the existence of theology in the Hebrew Bible. And even those committed to Old Testament theology often found it necessary to add the qualification that, of course, the Old Testament (and the New) is not "a theological textbook." Brunner's strongly-expressed arguments seem likewise to imply that little, if anything, of the Old Testament material should count as "theology." To this formulation of the question we now turn.

One who has been cautious about saying that anything in the Bible is actually "theology" is Gerhard Ebeling in his famous and basic article on the idea of biblical theology:[13]

> A further thing that has become problematical is the application of the concept "theology" to the actual content of the Bible. . . . [From a certain angle] there would be real sense in speaking of theology even in the New Testament, above all in Paul and the author of the Fourth Gospel. On the other hand it would be questionable to describe, say, the preaching of the individual Old Testament prophets as theology. But it is certainly capable of theological explication. From this the conclusion follows that although the Bible for the most part does not contain theology in the strict sense, yet it does press for theological explication.[14]

In more recent times Dietrich Ritschl, under the chapter title "The Fiction of a Biblical Theology," wrote:

> The question is whether the Bible contains theology in the sense that contemporary theology could get its content directly from it or find a model for [[247]] its work in the way in which the Bible presents things. Certainly parts of the biblical writings were "theology" in a particular way for the believers of their time. But that does not mean that the theological content could be transferred directly to later times or situations. Strictly speaking, most parts of the Bible cannot be transferred. The wisdom literature in the Old Testament and in the New may be an important exception.

> Only approximations to theology in the sense of theorizing with a view to regulative statements are present in the biblical writings. Only with qualifications and under certain conditions can we talk of "the theology of Deutero-Isaiah," of Lucan or Johannine "theology"; it is easier to speak of Pauline theology because in Paul there are detailed declarations, arguments and definitions that we can follow. And yet even in comparison with the christologies, doctrines of the Trinity, doctrines of the church, of grace, of man and so on, the letters of Paul are theology only in the inauthentic sense of the word.[15]

Still less can we seek an overall biblical theology. . . .

13. Gerhard Ebeling, "The Meaning of 'Biblical Theology,'" [[*JTS* 6 (1955) 210–24 = *Word and Faith* (London: SCM / Philadelphia: Fortress, 1963) 79–97]].

14. The question raised here by Ebeling seems not to be discussed in Berkhof's *Christian Faith* [[Hendrikus Berkhof, *Christian Faith* (Grand Rapids: Eerdmans, 1979)]].

15. D. Ritschl, *The Logic of Theology*, 68; wording of the English slightly altered by me. Ritschl may well have altered his view of these matters more recently—see his article in *JBTh* 1 (1986) 135–50—but the view as stated by him in his *The Logic of Theology* remains suitable as a starting point for discussion. [[D. Ritschl, *The Logic of Theology* (London: SCM, 1986), ET of *Zur Logik der Theologie* (Munich: Chr. Kaiser 1984).]]

Not only, then, is much of the Bible not theology: even more, attempts at "an overall biblical theology" are *particularly* to be discouraged. These remarks indicate serious difficulties for biblical theologians. They have mostly come to believe, and believe passionately, that much of the content of the Bible constitutes theology or can be read as theology—not, perhaps, historical remarks taken in themselves, like the years of the reign of this king or that, but certainly the narratives of patriarchs, the accounts of battles, the religious exhortations, the prophetic speeches of warning; and even more certainly the stories in the Gospels, the teaching of the Pauline letters. Even more, they have mostly thought that by presenting an "overall picture" of the Bible as a whole they would be expressing the essentials of its theology. Now theologians tell us that little or none of this material is theology and that individual approximations are better than an overall picture, which should not be sought after. Biblical theologians have often scouted such objections, for they thought that they must come either from historical-critical scholars, a familiar source of error, or from theologians of "liberal" tradition, who could be trusted to misrepresent the Bible. But here they find that these objections come from theologians of high centrality and of deep concern for the traditional theology of the church. Thus, far from it being the case that biblical scholars, by becoming biblical theologians, are coming closer to the great theological work of the church; they may actually be contradicting its most respected leadership.

There are indeed objections which have to be considered. Hans Hübner in his stimulating *Biblische Theologie des Neuen Testaments*[16] has taken up and discussed the points made by Ebeling (see Vol. 1, 24ff.). Can one not perceive, he asks, a [[248]] *theological* conception underlying the narrative representations of the Gospels (p. 26)? These conceptions show clearly theologically reflective and argumentative features, and to such a degree that one can speak of the respective theologies of the individual Synoptic evangelists. "Naturally the theology of the New Testament authors is not academic theology in the modern sense, but the spiritual achievement of these men is theologically reflective argumentation" (p. 26). He concludes: "The New Testament is thus a highly theological book" (p. 28).

It seems to me, however, that Hübner is wrong in this and that Ebeling was right. *Of course* the Synoptic Gospels are "theological": that is not to be doubted. So is the New Testament as a whole. They imply theology and, as Ebeling and Brunner before him said, they invite theological explication. But that a text is theological is not the same as saying that it is *theology*. The content of most parts of the Synoptic Gospels is not theology. Theology may well be implicit in them, but a text is theology only when theology is made explicit in it. One way of expressing the task of biblical theology, or of theological exegesis, is to say that it seeks to make explicit the implicit theology of the

---

16. [[H. Hübner, *Biblische Theologie des Neuen Testaments* (3 Vols.; Göttingen: Vandenhoeck & Ruprecht, 1990–95.)]]

texts. But this is needed precisely because the texts themselves for the most part are not theology. If they were theology, in the proper sense, there would be no need for a discipline such as biblical theology.

The distinction between implicit and explicit, as made above, seems to me to be important. If we think of a text as *being* theology, we mean that its theology is explicit. When the theology is implicit, it means that the theology is not *stated* by the text. The theology is in someone's mind, but even there is, perhaps, not explicit. The text may, however, be adequate evidence of the implicit theology.

Where Then Can All This Lead?

The first direction in which it must lead is towards a rethinking by biblical theologians of what they mean when they talk of "theology" in the Bible. If the biblical material is not (for the most part) "theology," then what is it? And, what is it that biblical theologians are looking for, or constructing, if it is not "theology," at least "in the authentic sense"?

This is not easy to answer. Let me make an attempt. The biblical theologian seeks to study the intellectual and cultural world-image that lies behind the individual texts and their individual meanings. He or she considers the presuppositions from which the writers (and later readers) may have started, the connections with other concepts which have been used elsewhere, or with concepts that might have been used but are avoided, the general world-picture that may have been assumed, the network of connections and indications that may have been involved.

Biblical theology partakes, therefore, of the nature of exegesis rather than that of theology in the proper sense. Exegesis is not, and cannot ever be, a discipline [[249]] that is purely and only theology: where people seek to make it so, it is likely to be bad exegesis. It is a discipline in which factors of language, of literary form, of history, of environing culture, or knowledge of geography and other *realia*, intertwine and from which theological conclusions may be drawn. Biblical theology belongs to the same category but with two differences: its aim is usually not the sequential following out of the individual text, e.g., Genesis or Luke, but quest for common factors shared—and usually only partly shared—by a number of texts: and because of this common scope it may come rather closer to the appearance of theology than to the appearance of normal sequential exegesis. The common factors involved, say, in the very various utterances of the Hebrew Bible about "creation" look a little as if they were a "theology of creation." The procedure does not require the assumption that the texts themselves "are theology" or that all, or even the main part, of the content of the Bible "is theology."

Indeed we have to accept the verdict of doctrinal theologians that only very little of the Bible, whether in Old Testament or New, "is theology." Religious opinions, expressions and aspirations, however strongly expressed, are not thereby theology. Theology is a reflective activity in which the content of

religious expressions is to some extent abstracted, contemplated, subjected
to reflection and discussion, and deliberately reformulated. Much of the
Bible does not have this character.

. . . .

Conclusions [[251]]

1. It must be accepted that most of the material of the Bible is not "theology" in any direct or authentic sense; biblical theology therefore cannot be
validated simply by arguing that the Bible itself is, or contains, theology.

2. "Biblical theology" is an aspect of exegesis, directed towards individual
texts, parts of texts and interrelations between texts, with reference to theological relations and references that they imply and/or express and with
openness to questions of truth-values as represented within the Bible, within
the environing world cultures, and within the religious/theological traditions
that existed before it and were developed afterwards, within Judaism, Christianity and other relevant systems. It should therefore be aware of, and welcome, its difference from what is really theology.

3. It is likely that a certain progression towards "theology" can be seen
within the Bible; a particularly important stage in this movement is marked
by contact with Greek language and thought, and is evidenced especially in
some "apocryphal" books like Wisdom, and in Paul and John. But it is likely
that in ancient times in Israel, as marked in early texts and as lying even far-
ther in the past antecedent to the texts, decisions were made that also had
the character of "theology." Both this fact, and the fact that many biblical elements were a sort [[252]] of "theology" for their own time, support the understanding that an historical perspective is necessary for any biblical theology.

4. It should be clearly admitted by those working in biblical theology that
the case in favour of their discipline, however it is defined, has not been satisfactorily established and remains precarious, and this from the most central
theological point of view. Most important are the arguments of doctrinal theologians, who see the enterprise as an amateurish attempt of pious biblical
scholars to do the work of theology on the basis of their own biblical exper-
tise alone,[17] and thus as a fundamentally biblicistic illusion. From this point
of view it can be argued that biblical scholars would contribute more to theology if they pursued the aspects of biblical study for which they themselves
are uniquely equipped and gave less attention and effort to work in the realm
that must belong to theology proper. It may well be that these arguments can
be overcome, but one should not expect that they will be easily overcome.

17. I repeat from above, Childs' remark that "Biblical theologians were forced to do
their own theology."

R. W. L. MOBERLY

b. 1952

The Bible, Theology, and Faith

R. W. L. Moberly is Lecturer in Theology at the University of Durham. G. I. Davies supervised his dissertation at Cambridge, where Moberly completed his doctoral work in 1981. His work, which ranges across both Testaments into theology, has brought together critical exegesis and religious convictions.

Selected Writings by Moberly

1983   *At the Mountain of God: Story and Theology in Exodus 32–34.* Journal for the Study of the Old Testament Supplements 22. Sheffield: JSOT Press.

1992a   *The Old Testament of the Old Testament: Patriarchal Narratives and Mosaic Yahwism.* Overtures to Biblical Theology. Minneapolis: Fortress.

1992b   *From Eden to Golgotha: Essays in Biblical Theology.* South Florida Studies in the History of Judaism 52. Atlanta: Scholars Press.

1999   Theology of the Old Testament. Pp. 452–78 in *The Face of Old Testament Studies: A Survey of Contemporary Perspectives.* Edited by David W. Baker and Bill T. Arnold. Grand Rapids: Zondervan.

2000   *The Bible, Theology, and Faith: A Study of Abraham and Jesus.* Cambridge Studies in Christian Doctrine. Cambridge: Cambridge University Press.

2001   The Christ of the Old and New Testaments. Pp. 184–99 in *The Cambridge Companion to Jesus.* Edited by Markus Bockmuehl. Cambridge Companions to Religion. Cambridge: Cambridge University Press.

R. W. L. Moberly
Suspicion and the Rule of Faith

Excerpted with permission from R. W. L. Moberly, *The Bible, Theology, and Faith: A Study of Abraham and Jesus* (Cambridge: Cambridge University Press, 2000), pp. 38–44, 177–83, 232–38.

The Bible and the Question of God

[[38]] Our argument is that the question of what may count as truth in relation to God requires a searching rethinking of the nature of biblical and theological study. This is not to argue that only theologians or believers may properly study the Bible. Nor is it to deny that there are many questions other than the question of God which may fruitfully be studied within the Bible. Nor is it to suppose that the question of God could be studied without indispensable reference to much of the not-very-overtly theological content within the Bible (this rootedness of the reality of God within the realities of human life being one of the significant points at issue in the much used and abused assertion that Christianity is inescapably an historical religion). The point is rather that if the question of religious truth is seen to be foundational to the study of the Bible as Bible (however much other questions may also properly be addressed), then criteria for articulating, clarifying, disputing, and appropriating such truth are not matters for optional afterthought but should be integral to scholarly engagement.

How then might we proceed? In broadest terms I wish to advocate the kind of strategy which was famously expressed in the twentieth century by Karl Barth (1960) when he appealed to Anselm as a model of theological method; that is, to reach behind Enlightenment conceptions of truth and method (while still learning from them) to classic (not just Reformation) Christian conceptions of biblical and theological study with corresponding protocols for speech about God; to recognize that the last two centuries have been times not only of gain but also of loss, and to try to recover some of that loss without forfeiting the important gains. I conclude, therefore, with an outline of some basic elements of historic Christian hermeneutics, all of which I have sought (with what degree of success the reader must judge) to exemplify in the textually based discussions in the rest of this book.

The basic premise is that the question of God, around which the content of the Bible, and of Jewish and Christian faiths, revolves, is always [[39]] simultaneously a question about humanity.[1] This is not to concede to the suspicion that talk about God is, at heart, only a coded projection of talk about humanity. It is rather to affirm that an understanding of God, as the Bible depicts God, and a self-understanding of humanity, with corresponding implications

---

1. This biblical and patristic understanding was, not surprisingly, foundational also for Bultmann, who recast it in an existentialist way (1969).

for how people live, are necessarily interrelated dimensions of a complex reality. From this much follows.

Interpreting the Bible in Relation to the Question of God: Some Hermeneutical Presuppositions

First, biblical interpretation becomes inseparable from the question of how people live. That is, no matter how elaborate and sophisticated the technical skills which are brought to the task, and no matter how rigorous the use of these skills must be, the interpretation of the Bible is not detached from basic human questions of allegiance and priorities, of spirituality and ethics—"How should we, how should I, live? What should we, what should I, live for?" Such questions are not only about individuals and their possible choices, but raise also corporate and structural concerns to do with the configurations of life which shape people and provide the working assumptions, constraints, and possibilities which people consciously and unconsciously absorb.

In classic theological parlance, such an understanding of biblical interpretation is "faith seeking understanding." One characteristic way in which this was expressed by the Fathers is found in the dictum of Evagnus, "If you are a theologian, you will pray truly, and if you pray truly, you are a theologian."[2] This concisely articulates the understanding that theology requires personal engagement with that reality of which one speaks. This is itself rooted in the Bible's own presentation of the matter. The classic Old Testament formulation is "The fear of YHWH is (the beginning of) wisdom"[3] on which von Rad (1972: 67) succinctly comments:

> There is no knowledge which does not, before long, throw the one who seeks the knowledge back upon the question of his self-knowledge and his self-understanding. . . . The thesis that all human knowledge comes back to the question about commitment to God is a statement of [[40]] penetrating perspicacity. It has, of course, been so worn by centuries of Christian teaching that it has to be seen anew in all its provocative pungency. . . . It contains in a nutshell the whole Israelite theory of knowledge.

Within the New Testament the classic formulation is the words of Jesus in John 7:16–17: "My teaching is not my own but his who sent me. If anyone is willing to do his will, then he will know about the teaching—whether it is from God or whether I am speaking solely from myself" (my translation). Down the ages this text has been basic to an understanding of Christian theology as "faith seeking understanding."[4] It is not necessary to engage with the many

2. *On Prayer: 153 Texts*, §61.
3. Prov 1:7; 9:10; 15:33; Ps 111:10; Job 28:28.
4. So, for example, Augustine comments: "Understanding is the reward of faith. Therefore do not seek to understand in order to believe, but believe that you may understand. . . . What is 'If any man be willing to do his will?' It is the same thing as to believe" (*Homilies on Gospel of John* 29:6).

uses to which the text has been put in order to observe that it directly addresses the key question of the relationship between historical, descriptive religious statements (Jesus, according to the evangelist, says such and such) and
theology as "dogmatic," as confessing affirmation (what Jesus says truly reveals
God). Jesus' words enunciate what may reasonably be seen as a general principle, that a certain kind of knowledge (whether particular human words truly
derive from, and refer to, God) is not attainable apart from an engagement of
the person which is more than just an intellectual or rational exercise. What
this might mean, especially when "faith" is not construed in an unduly narrowed sense, is one of the prime concerns of the present discussion.[5] It is not
surprising, however, that a significant discussion of biblical hermeneutics
should stress that "there is . . . a sense in which the articulation of what the
text might 'mean' today, is a necessary condition of hearing what the text
'originally meant' (Lash 1986: 81); or that some recent work on the nature of
theology reintegrates theology with spirituality (McIntosh 1998); or that some
attempts to reformulate the task of biblical interpretation should direct attention to the character of the interpreter and the question of how one develops
wisdom (which puts in a moral and theological form some of the valid insights
of reader-response theory) (Fowl and Jones 1991; Fowl 1998).

Secondly, there is the issue, already mentioned, of the sheer difficulty of
speaking of God, since God is not a "person" or "object" accessible to scientific [[41]] examination. The Bible, to be sure, regularly depicts God with a
host of analogies drawn from known life. Yet at the same time it sees the mis-
direction of human responses to God, supremely in the form of idolatries of
one kind or other, as a fundamental and recurrent problem. The extensive
analogies for God do not, therefore, make genuine encounter with God in
any way easy or straightforward. A sense of the problematic nature of religious language as such is not often made explicit within the Bible.[6] In this
the Bible differs from much subsequent theology, which regularly emphasizes
the inadequacy of human understanding with regard to God and stresses the
need for apophatic denial to complement the affirmative use of analogy.[7] But
this should not lead one to overlook that this issue is constantly implicit

---

5. This issue has also, of course, been in one way or another a foundational concern of
liberation theology with its special attention to the social and political dimensions of faith.

6. For a study of a possible exception, see Moberly 1998. Other relevant biblical passages would range from the sweeping poetic vision of the incomparability of God in Isa
40:12–31 to Jesus' blunt response to James and John that, in asking for seats of honour beside Jesus in his kingdom/glory, "You do not know what you are asking" (Matt 20:22//Mark
10:38).

7. Donald MacKinnon (1987: 12) observes, "In . . . the schools, it became a commonplace that in speech about God, we continually swing between an anthropomorphism that
ultimately reduces the divine to the status of a magnified human worldly reality, and an agnosticism which continually insists that where God is concerned, we may only confidently
affirm that we do not know what we mean when we speak of him; nor indeed do we know
how the concepts we apply to him latch onto his being, borrowed or developed as they are
from the familiar world of our experience. Always agnosticism was judged less perilous than
anthropomorphism."

within the Bible. Recent renewed appreciation of the role of metaphor and symbolism within religious language has made significant contributions to biblical study, not least in the work of Paul Ricoeur (see, for example, Ricoeur 1978). Much of the burgeoning narrative theology in biblical study is, in essence, a rediscovery of something about religious language and discourse which was almost wholly obscured when it was too readily assumed that certain kinds of critical historiography provided the norms for understanding and assessing the biblical writers' depiction of their history. In a complementary way, the Bible regularly assumes the problematic nature of the actual use of language about God. On the one hand, people who speak for God may fail to do so truly (the so-called problem of false prophecy), while on the other hand those who hear words which do truly speak of God may fail to understand that this is the case, or to respond appropriately (the problem, in biblical idiom, of a hardened heart and/or a stiffened neck, of eyes that see without seeing and ears that hear without hearing). We shall see, in the next chapter, that a form of this problem is basic to a *locus classicus* for biblical interpretation, that is the story of the road to Emmaus.

[[42]] A third presupposition, which follows from that just mentioned, is that of "mystery."[8] Here the sense of mystery is not that of a puzzle which ceases to be a puzzle as soon as enough information becomes available (which is the nature of many philological and historical problems), but rather that of something whose intrinsic depth cannot be exhausted—simply expressed, the more you know, the more you know you do not know. Many famous and central biblical passages have regularly been understood to come in this category—such as "I AM WHO I AM," "YHWH is one," "the word became flesh," "God is love," and the double commandment to love God with heart, soul, mind, and strength and one's neighbour as oneself; and much more besides could also be considered in this light. The use of "mystery" in this context should not function prematurely to pre-empt or close down discussion ("that is a mystery—we must not question it too closely").[9] Rather it should open up interpretation that moves beyond the possible position and meaning of such texts within a history of religious thought (which is often the primary concern of biblical commentators) to an engagement with the meaning and truth of the content which may draw on many disciplines and may be explored

---

8. See, e.g., Louth 1983: 66–71,144–47; Kasper 1989: 19–31.

9. It must however be recognized that this is a not uncommon perception of how it does function. See, for example, Oden 1987. Oden comments upon appeal to "the mysterious" that "within the theological tradition—at least as this bears upon and shapes biblical study—explanation by reference to the inexplicable is hardly unusual. Outside this tradition, that which is apparently inexplicable is rather that which cries out for explanation" (p. viii); and "the apparently inexplicable presents a challenge and not a solution" (p. 160). He offers a discussion of the Jacob narrative as a case in point, where premature appeal by theologians to the mystery of divine election has mystified aspects of the story which can be explained by social anthropology. One may readily concede that theologians sometimes appeal to mystery when the real issue is either laziness or incomprehension. But, as ever, abuse does not remove right use.

through a wide range of media (poetry, picture, music, imaginative story, drama), and not least in prayer and the living of life (for it is the faithful lover who best understands the meaning of love).

Finally (though my sequence is not in order of priority), there is the "rule of faith." It was very early recognized that study and scrutiny of the biblical texts need not lead to God, or might lead to a defective understanding of God. The rule of faith was formulated in the early Church concurrently with the process of canonical recognition and compilation. The purpose of the rule of faith, which was in due course summarized in the creeds, is to guide readers so that they may discern that truth of God in Christ to which the Church, through its scripture, bears witness.[10] In an historic Christian understanding, formation of canon, rule of faith, and [[43]] creeds are mutually related and integral to the quest of recognizing truth about God. In general terms, guidelines such as a rule of faith embodies are obviously integral to the health of the never-ending dialectic between an authoritative text and a community which seeks to conduct itself in the light of that text.

The notion of a rule of faith, of course, regularly excites suspicion and hostility among professional biblical scholars, as being a tool for prejudgment, manipulation or coercion, and just plain bad scholarship—to say what texts "must" mean on the grounds of post-biblical dogmas, and to attempt to marginalize or silence those who have the courage to show that biblical texts do not necessarily mean what later tradition has thought them to mean. There are, sadly, so many examples of a rule of faith being used thus that an attempt to gain a fresh hearing for it is not an easy task.[11]

How then might a rule of faith be understood? It sets the biblical text within the context of the continuing life of the Christian Church where the one God and humanity are definitively understood in relation to Jesus Christ. In this context there is a constant interplay between the biblical text and those doctrinal, ethical, and spiritual formulations which seek to spell out its implications. The concerns in this are at least twofold. On the one hand, the initial concern is not so much to explain the Bible at all (in senses familiar to philologist or historian) as to preserve its reality as authoritative and canonical for subsequent generations, so that engagement with the God of whom it speaks, and the transformations of human life which it envisages, remain enduring possibilities; that is, to say "God is here." On the other hand, the interest is not so much the history of ideas and religious practices (though this remains an important critical control) as the necessities of hermeneutics and theology proper, that is, the question of what is necessary to enable succeeding generations of faithful, or would-be faithful, readers to penetrate and grasp the meaning and significance of the biblical text; that is, to say "God is here" in such a way that the words can be rightly understood without lapse into idolatry, literalism, bad history, manipulation, or the numerous other

10. A valuable recent account is Blowers 1997.

11. For some of the issues concerning a trinitarian rule of faith see Heron 1991; Webster 1998; and the collection of essays in Miller 1997.

pitfalls into which faith may stumble. It is when the Christian community fails sufficiently to grasp the implications of its own foundational text that a rule of faith changes role from guide to inquisitor.

[[44]] In sum, the presuppositions just mentioned set a context for the exercise of the appropriate technical skills (linguistic, historical) and the engagement with substantive existential issues (ideological, moral, theological) which directs them to a particular goal—using the biblical text to engage with the question of God, with a view to the transformation of human life through engagement with God in Christ, understood not as some kind of optional or sectarian religious exercise, but as engagement with the deepest accessible truth about human existence.

. . . .

Genesis 22 as Manipulative Religious Propaganda?

[[177]] If the initial point about the potential significance of hermeneutics of suspicion is to be taken seriously, it does not suffice to show, on primarily exegetical grounds, the inadequacies of the accounts above. Rather, I need to attempt my own suspicious reading of Genesis 22, one which builds on the exegetical foundations laid, and so is not open to rebuttal on the simple ground of exegetical inadequacy. Only then can the issues which suspicion raises be appropriately engaged with. What follows is a preliminary attempt to do this with one kind of suspicion.

The interpretation in chapter 3 did not just try to elucidate the meaning of Genesis 22 as a paradigmatic narrative portrayal within the Old Testament of the primary Hebrew category for appropriate human response to God, the "fear of God," in relation to the important concepts of divine testing, seeing/providing, and blessing. It also sought to point out the wider resonances and associations that have become associated with that portrayal: on the one hand, "Sinai," that is God's gift of *torah* to Israel, representing definitive insight into the nature of God and his will for Israel; on the other hand, "Zion," the place chosen by God to be the focus of God's presence on earth within the temple built by Solomon, the place where God's people are to gather in worship.

This synthesis of "Sinai" and "Zion" is not peculiar to Genesis 22 but in fact represents the canonical shape of the Old Testament more generally. For the book of Deuteronomy gives definitive expression to the exclusive nature of the relationship between God and Israel which is given content by *torah*, and requires that the relationship be given symbolic enactment in a place prescribed by God—a place which could at an early stage be Shechem but which definitively becomes Jerusalem in the book of Kings. Thus, among other things, Genesis 22 presents *in nuce* what Deuteronomy and the deuteronomistic history—not to mention the Chronicler's history, many of the prophets, and many of the psalmists—present *in extenso*: Israel's fulfilment of *torah* through obedient sacrificial worship in the Jerusalem temple. Genesis 22 is thus a hermeneutical key to the Hebrew scripture.

What is one to make of this? One move is to point out that such a harmonious consensus does not fully represent the realities of Israel's history where the nature of *torah* and the significance of Jerusalem were contested. To be sure, the Old Testament itself explicitly recognizes that the role of Jerusalem was contested. But it presents it in such a way that in the mind of the reader there should be no real contest, because Jeroboam's [[178]] establishment of Bethel and Dan were idolatrous acts of apostasy akin to Israel's paradigmatic apostasy with the golden calf at Sinai, while God's choice of Jerusalem is rooted in the faithful response to God of Israel's ancestor Abraham.[12] The Old Testament presents a one-sided, and at times anachronistic, account of disputes over Jerusalem. It has thus been one of the strengths of modern reconstructions of the history of Israel and its religion to show that history as characterized by a far greater complexity than the present shape of the Old Testament would suggest.

This, among other things, raises the question of the status of the present shape of Old Testament history. Apart from its use as a source to reconstruct a history different from itself, what is it in itself? Is it (to put it crudely) other than religious propaganda on behalf of the Jerusalem establishment, related to particular moments in Israel's history, perhaps the reform of Josiah and/or the struggle to reestablish Jerusalem after the exile? And even as the expression of a Jerusalemite perspective, is it other than the work of a small, nonrepresentative, scribal elite, whose claims to privilege have been foisted on others even within their own constituency?

Specifically, is Genesis 22 an example of the Jerusalem establishment validating itself through the appropriation of the prestigious figure of Abraham (and thereby invalidating any rival sanctuary)? Is it not implying that valid, God-ordained sacrificial worship as specified in *torah* takes place in Jerusalem (and not elsewhere)? Does it not convey the message that appropriate human response to God, the "fear of God," can best be shown by those who follow the example of Abraham in coming to Jerusalem (and thereby bringing money and resources to the Jerusalem establishment)? Does not Abraham's unquestioning obedience to God imply that true worshippers should be similarly unquestioning (and thereby should not challenge the privileged Jerusalem establishment)? Does not the focus on Abraham and the absence of Sarah imply a religious system where all significant action is a male preserve (leaving women invisible and powerless)? Is not therefore Genesis 22 a fine example of religious propaganda and ideology, which is interesting as a document of ancient religious history but cannot, and should not, have any further significance for a person in the modern world?

It will be obvious to the reader of this book that the final conclusion is not one which I hold, and so I will outline one possible response. But a [[179]] suspicious reading must be taken seriously, lest it be supposed that a Christian appropriation of Israel's literature as Old Testament scripture is undertaken in ignorance of the kinds of consideration that are often urged

---

12. David also is a foundational figure in 2 Samuel 24.

against it. Moreover, since a responsible historical awareness must allow that the answers to the above questions may be in some sense affirmative—they are all possible, and not necessarily invalid, implications of the text—such questions can help a Christian use of scripture be aware of some of its own possible implications.

Limitations of Suspicious Interpretation of Genesis 22

With regard to a narrative such as Genesis 22, there are three particular limitations to thoroughgoing suspicion.[13] One is a reluctance to enter into the narrative world in its own right and to take the irreducibility of the narrative with full seriousness. The irreducibility of the narrative is not just a point about literary genre, true of any narrative—that it cannot be transposed into another idiom or genre without loss. It is also a point about narrative as the vehicle of moral and theological discourse, in which certain moral and theological concerns are explored and conveyed precisely through their embodiment in narrative. Because a suspicious reading tends to see the narrative as a disguise for something else, it can be difficult to take seriously the issues of the narrative as genuine issues in their own right.

In the story of Genesis 22 the crucial thing is the relationship of a human being with God in an extreme situation of human relinquishment and divine provision, where the language and imagery readily become a metaphor for a multiplicity of situations, the more so when the story resonates with its wider canonical context (as the history of interpretation indicates). If the story is *really* about unquestioning obedience to a self-serving Jerusalemite male religious hierarchy, then this simply undercuts the imaginative world of the narrative, except in so far as one can think of ingenious ways in which it could be put to self-serving uses by the hierarchy. But this is a reductive approach to the text, in which one is unlikely to take seriously the question whether the fear of God, as displayed by Abraham, is indeed an appropriate human response to God, which may be promoted in paradoxical ways by God himself. If one knows in advance of each rereading what the text really means, it will [[180]] only ever convey what is already known; the ability of the text to surprise, disturb, or challenge is safely neutralized (as also, of course, in many reading strategies other than the suspicious). The suspicion can become a mirror image of the very complacency it set out to challenge.

A second consequence, which follows from the first, is that thoroughgoing suspicion lacks adequate criteria for assessing in what way the content of the story might, in some important sense, be true. Or rather, there is a tendency to judge it primarily by two criteria: the "historical" ("It never really happened like that anyway"), and the "socio-political" ("What happens in the story makes no difference to what really matters"). The first wholly excludes moral and theological, not to mention imaginative, criteria; and easily adopts an oversimple understanding of the complex relationships between text and

---

13. Of course, a more qualified suspicion requires greater nuance in evaluation.

the living of the "fear of God" in ancient Israel/Judah which has given rise to the text. The second tends to restrict significant criteria to those which in one way or another relate to often hidden structures of power and money and gender, which preserve themselves and manipulate others the more successfully the more they are hidden. Thus to focus on Abraham's act of obedience and God's blessing at a place given the pious-sounding name "YHWH sees," diverts attention from struggles over money and power within the Jerusalem priesthood and the use of a story about Abraham's piety to validate Jerusalem against its rivals.

The difficulty here is not just that such struggles are inevitably to some extent the product of the modern interpreter's imagination, compensating for exiguous hard evidence with generous extrapolations from the interpreter's own understanding of ecclesiastical politics to show what "must have been" the case (the perennial problem of interpreters discovering their own face at the bottom of the well). Even more important is a prejudgement of precisely the crucial issue of "what really matters." It is one thing to criticize those who stress a narrowly defined personal piety at the expense of any critical understanding of, or engagement with, the social, economic, and political dimensions of institutional, not least religious, life. It is another thing to undervalue the realities of personal encounter with the living God or to dismiss its foundational nature for human existence. Because by its nature much suspicion is concerned with "structural" questions about language and social role,[14] it may be insensitive to those dimensions of human life such as loyalty or trust which are [[181]] either "on the surface" or, in so far as they touch the depths of human persons, may remain largely oblique to the discourses of social power.

A third limitation is that a suspicious reading of the text tends to have difficulty with doing justice to the processes of recontextualization, and in particular with the metaphorical reconstrual of religious language, which are present within the canonical text. The further the content of the text moves from its original setting, the less plausible at least some suspicions become. We have already noted this phenomenon with reference to the construal of child sacrifice as a metaphor. Further, one might reflect upon the logic of the various ways in which Genesis 22 characteristically functions in Jewish and Christian contexts *post* 70 A.D. and the destruction of the temple in Jerusalem. Most obviously, for Christians (and differently within rabbinic Judaism) worship in the Jerusalem temple ceases to be significant in the same ways as once it was. This is not just for the historical reason of the destruction of the temple. More decisive for a Christian view is the understanding, encapsulated (as we will see) within the narrative of Matthew's Gospel, that Jesus replaces the temple as the unique and privileged place of encounter between God and humanity. This means, among other things, that Jerusalem goes the way of child sacrifice and retains its significance primarily as a symbol. It is symbolic

---

14. Suspicions about self-deception in relation to God on a personal level tend to operate on a more psychological basis, which requires separate discussion.

of many things, but in Christian thought it especially symbolizes the Church, to which the Old Testament language of God's election and judgment is often transferred. The geographical location of the place God chooses for acceptable worship, where "God sees/provides," is no longer capable of any straightforward definition—in terms of the biblical text, the symbolic language of Moriah and "YHWH sees" is more or less detached from its particular realization within Jerusalem and seen as open to realization within any number of other contexts where God is truly worshipped. It is not that geographical locations no longer have any significance—for the histories of Rome, Constantinople, Canterbury, Geneva, and the many places of Christian pilgrimage (including Jerusalem!) would tell against any such simplification—but that any one place does not, and cannot, have the kind of significance that Jerusalem has within the Old Testament. To be sure, the Church is in no way immune to, but rather requires, suspicious critique (and, as already noted, much of the suspicious critique formulated as historical hypothesis is a projection of contemporary suspicions). The point is that when Christians appropriate the Old Testament in the light of Christ an understanding of the biblical text may be transformed in subtle and far-reaching ways. What to the unsympathetic may [[182]] appear an ever-shifting evasiveness (and can at times be such) may be a searching attempt to penetrate the significance of symbols in such a way as to enable continuity in the midst of change. In any case, the evaluation of such processes cannot meaningfully be carried out in isolation from consideration of the actual ways of living which they promote.

In short, the question of "God," and what it means to speak responsibly of God in relation to the interpretation of the Bible, is too difficult and demanding an issue to be easily resolved by transposition into the categories of ideological suspicion (however salutary these may be against idolatrous and self-deceiving tendencies). The moral passion of the suspicious critique can become as one-sided and inadequate to human life as the position it is meant to challenge. Yet one responsibility of the biblical interpreter is at least to imagine in a disciplined way, and convey to others, what it might mean for the fear of God to have the kind of importance that Hebrew scripture attributes to it; and for the Christian theologian there are further questions as to the appropriation of such an imagining within the realities of contemporary life.

Conclusion

From the perspective of interpreting Genesis 22 as scripture, one primary critical norm in assessing the story is that which it itself offers, that is the fear of God, as explained and displayed within the text. To the charge that religious people act self-seekingly, as the satan said of Job, and as Abraham himself apparently displays on occasion, the answer is that *this* is what true religion entails: a trusting obedience of God which means relinquishing to God that which is most precious (sacrifice Isaac, the beloved son); a self-dispossession of that on which one's identity and hopes are most deeply based (sacrifice Isaac, the long-awaited bearer of God's promise and Abraham's hopes for the future); a recognition that response to God may be as costly, or even more costly, at the end of one's life as it was earlier on (Abraham must relinquish his future as once he relinquished his past); a recognition that the outcome of obedience is unknown and cannot be predicted in advance (a test is not "only" a test, but is a real test); and a recognition that the religious community to which one belongs and which tells this as one of its foundation stories can only become complacent at the expense of the essence of its identity.

To say all this is not to deny the institutional realities of the Jerusalem temple as underlying the present form of Genesis 22. It is rather to say [[183]] that, to the extent that the institutional forms of a religious community, whose purpose is to enable and preserve openness and responsiveness to God ("fear of God"), become devoted to maintaining their own existence at the expense of the very qualities they exist to foster, they deserve no less than the full critical impact of their own identifying charter.

. . . .

Biblical Interpretation within the Context of a Trinitarian Rule of Faith

[[232]] We argued at the outset for the importance of contextualizing biblical interpretation within a rule of faith if the question of God is to be able to be approached in any way adequately. We may now reflect a little more fully upon what is, and is not, entailed by such a context, in development of the preceding remarks about "letter" and "spirit."

When Matthew's portrayal of Jesus is set within the context of a trinitarian rule of faith, this is not (or should not be) remote speculation about metaphysics, or alien imposition upon the first-century Jewish humanity of Jesus (an imposition from which biblical scholars need regularly to liberate Jesus). Rather, what is at stake is an account of the nature of God that is inseparable from the particularity and specificity of Israel's account of human nature in relation to God. As already emphasized, the interrelatedness of accounts of God with accounts of humanity is fundamental to the biblical witness of both Old and New Testaments: what we believe about God is inseparable from what we believe about ourselves (and vice versa). Where Christians part company from Jews is in the affirmation that these beliefs find their truest form in the Jesus to whom the New Testament bears witness. The human transformation, which Jews and Christians agree that confession of the one God entails, is for Christian faith supremely given content and shape by Jesus more than by *torah* (although much of *torah* remains foundational). And an understanding of God is reformulated so as to incorporate Jesus and the Holy Spirit, so that it becomes (in one way or another) trinitarian.

In general terms, the doctrines of Trinity and Incarnation are an attempt to formulate a kind of context of understanding of the Bible as a whole, where the scriptures of Israel lead on to the apostolic witness to [[233]] the person of Jesus Christ, who is taken to represent the decisive self-revelation and action of Israel's God. The doctrine of the Trinity is rooted in a primary, and uncontroversial, dimension of Israel's scriptures, that the God of Israel is best understood in relational terms. Within the Old Testament, these relational terms are always in the context of God's dealings with his creation, primarily human beings (and the absence of classic mythology—stories about the divine realm in its own right—is a striking corollary of the Old Testament's austere refusal to speak of God other than in engagement with the created order). Within the New Testament, relationships between God and people are mediated by, and focussed in, the person of Jesus in a way that is without precedent within Israel's scriptures, despite significant analogies in prophetic texts. What the doctrines of Trinity and Incarnation do is to extend a relational account of God to God's very identity, in terms of the relationship between Father and Son and Holy Spirit.

The ramifications of historic and renewed contemporary debate about understanding the Trinity obviously lie beyond our present scope. However, the kind of approach I am trying to articulate needs at this stage only a short restatement of a classic trinitarian understanding. To state a complex matter briefly: over time, two specific terms became central to patristic theology and spirituality in regard to the Trinity: first, *kenosis*, and secondly, *perichoresis*. *Kenosis*, "self-emptying," rooted in the terminology of Phil 2:7, attempts to express what it means for Jesus as Son of God to be a human being in a life culminating in crucifixion. *Perichoresis*, "interpenetration," attempts to express the relationship between Father, Son, and Spirit, and to say what must be the case if the relationship between Father and Son, as exemplified within the gospels, is an enduring reality in the being of God. Both terms were developed in attempts to spell out the implications of the New Testament. And both terms were seen (with qualifications) as applicable as well to humanity as to God—for in Jesus, in significant respects, what is true of God is true of humanity, and what is true of humanity is also true of God. One can thus re-express *kenosis* and *perichoresis* by saying that they are accounts of the nature of God which are also, in effect, accounts of what it means for humanity to become truly itself, for such becoming is realized through transformation by the Spirit into the likeness of God. "Self-emptying," the process of learning to live by trust in the Father, is an essential corollary to "interpenetration," the process of having one's being defined [[234]] through relationship to God and to others, such that relationship in love becomes the essence of one's being.[15]

How does this relate to the specifics of biblical interpretation? First, in general terms, to read the Bible in the light of a trinitarian rule of faith—or, alternatively expressed, in the light of Christ, for it is in Christ that the trinitarian understanding of God and humanity is displayed and focussed—is not

15. This discussion has tended to emphasize the potential continuity between Abraham and Jesus and the life of faith today, and has not as such focussed on those senses in which Christians understand Jesus as having been and done that which no one else can be or do, that is, the nature and meaning of incarnation and atonement. But the purpose of the discussion is not to deny such uniqueness, but rather to reestablish a context within which such uniqueness might be an important issue with which to engage.

a matter of imposing anachronisms on the biblical text. It is not an exercise in scouring the Old Testament for covert or oblique references to Jesus or the Trinity (making much, for example, of divine self-reference with a plural form in Gen 1:26; Isa 6:8), or of making the writers of the New Testament hold a christology which approximates ever more closely to Nicene or Chalcedonian definitions. Rather, it is to contextualize the Bible within a continuing attempt to realize that of which it speaks and so to bring a certain kind of concern to bear on the reading of the text. This concern is focussed in a particular understanding of God and humanity, which is used heuristically in reciprocal interchange between text and reader.

More specifically, the linkage between the *kenosis* of Philippians 2 and the *kenosis* of an orthodox Christian understanding of God is not dependent on the supposition that Philippians 2 depicts the incarnation of the pre-existent Christ (which it may, or may not, do). The incarnation affirms that what characterizes Jesus in his life, death, and resurrection characterizes God, indeed that it is definitive of God's very being. The trinitarian corollary of this is that Jesus' relationship to God as Son to Father is an enduring reality within God, to which the Spirit gives access. My thesis is that the biblical passages studied express an understanding of God and humanity in which identity, integrity, and growth in relationship revolve around the paradoxes of a certain kind of self-giving (*kenosis*) to enable life in profound interrelationship (*perichoresis*). On the one hand, the biblical text gives content to human life in relation to God, while on the other hand a contemporary attempt to live faithfully likewise gives content, and the interplay between the two enables genuine human growth and transformation.

We have seen how in Genesis 22 the dynamics of Abraham's relationship [[235]] with God are given content by the particular terms "fear of God," "test," "see/provide," and "bless" in relation to the offering of Isaac, and these terms and concepts were set as fully as possible within their Old Testament context of meaning. Likewise the portrayal of Jesus in Matthew's Gospel was explicated by working with the narrative context and development of the gospel, in terms of what the text as a first-century text means. The dialectical relationship between exegesis of these texts and an understanding of God and humanity in terms of *kenosis* and *perichoresis* works in various ways. It was my own intellectual and experiential grasp (such as it is) of this Christian understanding which enabled my discussion of the biblical text to engage in some way with those realities of which the text speaks, for it is a presupposition which suggests a particular kind of questioning of the text and is open to a particular kind of pattern of things—though this pre-understanding itself arises out of prolonged engagement with the biblical text, and the learning of the appropriate intellectual and moral disciplines of interpretation. On the assumption that the trinitarian account of God and humanity represents an ultimate truth, I have sought to articulate how the biblical writers themselves understood and expressed the dynamics of relationship with God; not (I hope) prematurely conforming the text to some procrustean pattern, but rather respecting the particularities of the Genesis and Matthean texts while being enabled to see something of the profundity of the ways in which they articulate paradigms of human life in relationship with God.

If the context of a rule of faith thus enables better penetration into the content of the biblical text, the biblical text should also challenge the adequacy of the various ways in which that rule of faith is articulated and practised (which brings us back in a different way to the legitimate concerns of suspicious readings of the text). In general terms, Abraham's self-dispossession in obedience to God and Jesus' refusal to use God's power to his own advantage both should disqualify any use of the rule of faith (in power seeking or manipulative or coercive ways) which undercuts that which the rule of faith represents in the first place; the Church cannot be permitted to try to sustain itself by those very means which Jesus renounced and upon whose renunciation the value of the Church's life is predicated. This, to be sure, will rarely be straightforward, both because of the inherent complexities of life and human nature, and because the Christian faith does require a certain kind of insistence that certain things (including a particular and public configuration of texts and life and thought) be maintained for potentially true speech about God and [[236]] humanity to be possible. Such an insistence can easily be heard to be (and can easily become) a denial of the integrity and value of other contexts and perspectives, rather than the maintaining of a wider and deeper reality through participation in which other contexts can maintain their particularity and integrity and yet be transformatively enriched.

In terms of possible implications of the biblical text for an understanding of God, a trinitarian theology must remember always to keep the Old Testament and gospel narratives in the foreground. Trinitarian theology always tends to locate in eternity that which was achieved in time. The appearance of Jesus on earth in his life, death, and resurrection is a new thing within history (however much the way is prepared within Israel), yet because that which Jesus is and does accomplishes and realizes a supreme truth about human life and God, and that supreme truth is understood to be definitive of God, then what God is in Jesus is reasoned to characterize God as he has been and as he will be. This process is already visible within John's Gospel, where the events of the passion come to characterize the ministry of Jesus as a whole, and where the Logos who becomes flesh in Jesus is present with God "in the beginning." Yet the Synoptic Gospels resolutely focus on the achievement in time. At a climactic moment in Luke's Gospel, where Jesus, returned from the realm of the dead, could make definitive pronouncement about the nature of God and a world beyond this one, the focus is wholly and solely upon that which Israel already has in its scripture in relation to the known person of Jesus as suffering messiah. Within Matthew's Gospel, Jesus must appropriate ever more deeply the givenness of his sonship through faithfulness when tested, and the cost of not using God's power for himself grows greater until it culminates in dereliction while being put to death. Both the Lukan and the Matthean accounts presuppose and intensify a pattern of true relationship found already in Abraham and in the Old Testament more generally. The tensions between time and eternity within trinitarian understanding are part of the mystery of God, where the theologian's task is not to dissolve the tensions but to depict them faithfully. The contribution of this study is to redescribe some of the dimensions of the definitive achievement in time as the primary articulation and realization of that which one believes to be true in eternity.

Secondly, a trinitarian theology which keeps the Old Testament and gospel narratives in the foreground will not articulate an account of God which disengages God from demanding and paradoxical relationality. Accounts of God as "suffering" have been widely articulated in recent [[237]] years, as a way of trying to speak about God that does not detach God from the realities and extremities of life, yet it is a form of speaking about God that the Bible itself does not adopt (except perhaps incidentally). That is not necessarily a fault, for "suffering" may in certain ways capture something integral to the biblical picture. Nonetheless, the Bible's own preferred term for speaking of the engaged God is "love" (*ḥesed*, *agape*) and related terms (grace, faithfulness, etc.), and one of the continuing theological tasks is to clarify the meaning of these terms and to remove misunderstandings, not least through taking seriously the narrative form in which the moral and theological content is regularly depicted. Attention to the narrative portrayal of the nature and development of the "love" between God and Abraham in Genesis 22, and between Father and Son within Matthew's Gospel, is therefore an element in the continuing task of articulating a trinitarian understanding of God and humanity (for although Genesis 22 does not use *ḥesed* to characterize God, nor does Matthew characterize God with *agape*, the question is whether the gracious and demanding portrayals of God in these contexts respectively may not appropriately be depicted by these summative concepts).

The Question of God in Relation to the Human

One of the basic issues at the outset of our discussion was the question of God, where we noted both the importance of the issue and the way in which it is regularly marginalized or elided in biblical study because of a fundamental intellectual and cultural shift which has characterized the growth of modernity. Although it is not possible here in any way to trace or analyse the nature of the shift, I hope one general observation may be permitted. This concerns the change in content attributed to "God," which may perhaps be summed up in Pope's famous lines: "Know then thyself, presume not God to scan; the proper study of mankind is Man." This assumes a concept of God which would have been baffling to most biblical writers (possibly excepting Qoheleth) and to most theologians from the second to the sixteenth centuries. For them, knowing oneself and knowing God would not have been alternatives (the former implicitly attainable, the latter speculative and inconclusive), but rather interrelated facets of the one task of growing into human maturity in which God is the foundation for true human potential. Once God is understood as a speculative (and, in other contexts, heteronomously threatening) accessory to autonomous human life, it is hardly surprising if the question of God recedes from the public agenda.

[[238]] The bafflement which Pope's lines would have generated can be well illustrated from our exegesis in chapters 2, 3, and 6. In these various texts a recurrent issue is the way in which the biblical writers juxtapose and interrelate divine action and human action. In the Emmaus story, the divine action of withholding and giving sight is not conceived arbitrarily but in relation to human engagement with the meaning of scripture and the sharing of a meal. Perception of the risen Jesus is an action of God correlated with particular kinds of human actions (classically understood as means of grace). In Genesis 22 God's testing enables Abraham to become that which the Old Testament holds out as the moral and spiritual goal for humanity in general and Israel in particular. The affirmation about divine action, that God sees/provides, only becomes definitive when Abraham embodies appropriate human response to God, and likewise the divine action of blessing is renewed and integrated with Abraham's obedience on this basis. In Matthew's Gospel it is the divine initiative which calls Jesus Son which constitutes the context for the continuing appropriation by Jesus of the true meaning of his sonship in response to continued testing. It is the unreserved responsiveness of Jesus to his Father which enables Jesus to receive the gifts of God, supremely the unlimited divine power which can only be received by the one who has learned to embody its true meaning. Within this overall portrayal, there is the recurrent sense that what God the Father and Jesus the Son give to others is both a matter of their initiative and a matter of appropriate human attitude and action—the simple receive what is withheld from the wise, so that what is withheld from an abusive high priest is given (in differing ways) to Peter and the centurion.

What is striking in all this is both the profound reciprocity of divine and human action, and the way in which divine action enables human life to grow to its fullest potential. In other words, these biblical texts all consistently illustrate the general axiom about the interrelatedness of meaningful speech about God with protocols of human responsiveness, in which God is neither heteronomous threat to human integrity nor arbitrary speculation but rather that summoning and challenging presence and power who is foundational to true humanity.

References

Barth, Karl 1960, *Anselm: Fides Quaerens Intellectum*, London, SCM Press (ET from German of 1930, 1958).

Blowers, Paul 1997, "The *Regula Fidei* and the Narrative Character of Early Christian Faith," *Pro Ecclesia* 6/2: 199–228.

Bultmann, R. 1969, "What Does It Mean to Speak of God?" in Bultmann, R., *Faith and Understanding*, London, SCM Press, pp. 53–65 (ET from German of 1925).

Fowl, Stephen 1998, *Engaging Scripture*, Oxford, Blackwell.

Fowl, Stephen, and Jones, L. Gregory 1991, *Reading in Communion: Scripture and Ethics in Christian Life*, London, SPCK.

Heron, A. 1991, "The Biblical Basis for the Doctrine of the Trinity" in Heron, A. (ed.), *The Forgotten Trinity*, Inter-Church House, London SE17RL, BCC/CCBI.

Kasper, Walter 1989, "Revelation and Mystery: The Christian Understanding of God" in Kasper, Walter, *Theology & Church*, London, SCM Press, pp.19–31 (ET from German of 1987).

Lash, Nicholas 1986, "What Might Martyrdom Mean?" in Lash, Nicholas, *Theology on the Way to Emmaus*, London, SCM Press, pp.75–92.

Louth, Andrew 1983, *Discerning the Mystery: An Essay on the Nature of Theology*, Oxford, Clarendon Press.

McIntosh, Mark 1998, *Mystical Theology*, Oxford, Blackwell.

MacKinnon, Donald 1987, "The Inexpressibility of God" in MacKinnon, Donald, *Themes in Theology: The Three-Fold Cord*, Edinburgh, T. & T. Clark, pp.11–19.

Miller, P. 1997, *Theology Today* 54/3.

Moberly, R. W. L. 1998, " 'God Is Not a Human That He Should Repent' (Numbers 23:19 and 1 Samuel 15:29)" in Beal, Timothy, and Linafelt, Tod (eds.), *God in the Fray: A Tribute to Walter Brueggemann*, Minneapolis, Fortress Press, pp. 112–23.

Oden Jr, Robert 1987, *The Bible without Theology: The Theological Tradition and Alternatives to It*, San Francisco, Harper & Row.

Rad, Gerhard von 1972, *Wisdom in Israel*, London, SCM Press (ET from German of 1970).

Ricoeur, Paul 1978, *The Rule of Metaphor: Multi-disciplinary Studies of the Creation of Meaning in Language*, London, Routledge (ET from French of 1975).

Sandys-Wunsch, J., and Eldredge, L. 1980, "J. P. Gabler and the Distinction between Biblical and Dogmatic Theology: Translation, Commentary, and Discussion of His Originality," *Scottish Journal of Theology* 33: 133–58.

Webster, John 1998, "Hermeneutics in Modern Theology: Some Doctrinal Reflections," *Scottish Journal of Theology* 51/3: 307–41.

MARK G. BRETT

b. 1958

The Future of Old Testament Theology

Mark G. Brett graduated from the University of Queensland, Princeton Theological Seminary, and Sheffield University, where he earned his Ph.D. He is currently Professor of Hebrew Bible at Whitley College, University of Melbourne. Brett's research has conversed with contemporary work in philosophy, theology, and the social sciences. His consideration of Old Testament theology and its future also draws attention to contextual, social, and moral issues (thus theological ones) particular to Australia and instructive beyond it.

Selected Writings by Brett

1991 *Biblical Criticism in Crisis? The Impact of the Canonical Approach on Old Testament Studies.* Cambridge: Cambridge University Press.

1996 (editor) *Ethnicity and the Bible.* Leiden: Brill.

1998 Biblical Studies and Theology: Negotiating the Intersections. *Biblical Interpretation* 6: 131–41 (and guest editor of the issue).

2000a *Genesis: Procreation and the Politics of Identity.* London: Routledge.

2000b Canonical Criticism and Old Testament Theology. Pp. 63–85 in *Text in Context: Essays by Members of the Society for Old Testament Study.* Oxford: Oxford University Press.

2000c The Future of Old Testament Theology. Pp. 465–88 in *Congress Volume: Oslo 1998.* Edited by André Lemaire and Magne Sæbø. Vetus Testamentum Supplements 80. Leiden: Brill.

Mark G. Brett
The Future of Old Testament Theology

Excerpted by permission from "The Future of Old Testament
Theology," *Congress Volume: Oslo 1998* (edited by André Lemaire
and Magne Sæbø; VTSup 80; Leiden: Brill), 469–88. Some footnotes have been omitted.

[[469]] To summarize my argument so far, I have been suggesting that the discipline of Old Testament theology is quite capable of dealing with contradictions in scripture, as long as it does not succumb to modernist abstractions,
and as long as it places theological contradictions within the context of wider
discussions concerning the complexities of literary form and competing testimony. But to say that divine reality cannot be domesticated by conceptual
abstraction and determinate testimony is actually to say nothing new. Post-
structuralist theology, in both its Christian and Jewish forms, is simply the
most recent expression of this very old theme. It seems to me that the [[470]]
substantive issue facing us today is not how to protect ourselves from the abstractions of dogmatics, but rather, how we are to *evaluate* both the undeniable diversity of the biblical canon and its multifarious influences throughout
history. And this is a task we share with systematic theologians, or at least
with those theologians who are not bound by pre-fabricated dogmatic systems. The focus should not simply be on the contradictions in scripture but
also on the contradictions of its *Wirkungsgeschichte* [['history of effects']]. I
would argue that we need a value-oriented style of research which deals with
both ends of the hermeneutical problematic, both the diversity of the canon
and the diversity of interpretative communities.

There are many possible ways of approaching these hermeneutical complexities, but it is interesting to note the clearly contrary solutions proposed
by two American biblical critics, J. J. Collins and Jon Levenson. To paint the
contrast with broad brush strokes, I would say that Collins has proposed a revision of the Enlightenment approach, while Levenson can be taken to represent a "postmodern" position, for want of a better term.[1]

While this is not the place to tell the complex story of the Enlightenment, it may be worthwhile to pause for a moment and draw an analogy between our current situation and that of the seventeenth century. Spinoza's
Tractatus theologico-politicus contains a modern biblical theology conceived in
a climate of ecclesial fragmentation and violence. There were good political
reasons for the Enlighteners' philosophical flight from religious authority,
and Spinoza rigorously applied the new rationalism to the study of the Bible,

---

1. The sense in which I use this problematic category will be clarified below. At this
point, however, it needs to be said that not all versions of postmodernism are simply relativ-
ist (see, e.g., Allen 1989; Ward 1997b). Certainly, I do not mean to attribute relativism to Levenson's position.

in part because he was concerned to address the political disorder of the day (Stout 1981). An Enlightenment thinker like Spinoza was well aware of religious diversity; that was precisely what his *Tractatus* was designed to overcome by means of its quest for a universal sub-stratum of reason; the denial of a reader's particularity was at least in part a political strategy carefully crafted in response to the violent expression of religious differences in the seventeenth century. Historical criticism, as Spinoza practised it, attempted to create a neutral space between different religious traditions.

[[471]] In J. J. Collins's essay "Is a Critical Biblical Theology Possible?" (1990), he continues to see this quest for neutrality as a virtue, although he recognizes that historical criticism does not possess the kind of objectivity that has often been associated with it. It is distinguished, however, by a tradition of self-criticism and by stringent attempts to be impartial. Collins argues that historical criticism is also the indispensable framework for biblical theology: it provides the broadest basis for discussing "the meaning and function of God-language," and it is the most widely accepted medium of exchange between scholars of different religious traditions (1990: 14–15).

In his important article "Why Jews Are Not Interested in Biblical Theology," Jon Levenson (1993a) has argued, to the contrary, that insofar as Jewish and Christian biblical scholars bracket their religious commitments in the cause of neutrality, the dialogue between them does not count as Jewish-Christian dialogue. There are two inter-related facets of his argument. First, in attempting to privatize religious commitments, we discover that hidden assumptions have been smuggled in under the cover of objectivity. Walther Eichrodt, in his *Theology of the Old Testament*, for example, adopted the formulaic intention to "avoid all schemes which derive from Christian dogmatics" but, in the very same chapter, was able to speak of the "torso-like appearance of Judaism in separation from Christianity" (Eichrodt 1961: 26, 33). Explicit rejection of Christian dogmatics does not, in itself, signal the absence of Christian prejudices. Or to put the point another way, *claims* on objectivity are not themselves evidence of objectivity.

This kind of example does not, however, directly contradict Collins's argument; it simply demonstrates that the rhetoric of objectivity has been frequently misused, not that the ideal of objectivity is inherently flawed. But the second facet of Levenson's argument is more telling: scholarship focussed exclusively on ancient Israel has little significance for a dialogue between Christians and Jews whose identities are formed by a great number of *post*-biblical traditions. We need a rigorous scrutiny of the history of biblical interpretation in both Christian and Jewish tradition (cf. Sawyer 1996; Sæbø 1996), since this history has also influenced the construction of religious identities, and only a wooden version of Protestantism would assume that the biblical literature should always over-ride other forms of religious tradition.

I would want to add one other supporting observation to Levenson's argument. It is not just that Eichrodt's attempt to avoid Christian [[472]] features of his readerly identity was unsuccessful; he also seems paradoxically to have over-estimated the effects of a theological framework on studies of the

Hebrew Bible. One would just need to consider the radically different effects of kerygmatic theology on Brevard Childs and Walther Zimmerli (Childs 1969; Motte 1995) to realize that a single theological framework can produce highly diverse effects on biblical theology. To take another example, process theology has been an influence on both Terence Fretheim's study of divine suffering (1984) and on Robert Gnuse's recent book on polytheism and monotheism in Israel (1997). Yet Fretheim's work is essentially literary while Gnuse's is based primarily on archaeology. Process theology has determined neither the method nor the results. And thus we would need to confess that theological reflection need not be the straitjacket it might have been in the past.

What, then, are the alternatives to Collins's modernist proposal to obscure the particularities of scholarly identity and theological orientation? Levenson has made a good case for making theological commitments clear in advance, thus inviting the reader to evaluate the relationship between an argument and the bias that may lie behind it. He is not averse to historical research; the critique is only directed against a purely descriptive objectivism which has been characteristic of historical criticism. His own contribution to Jewish-Christian dialogue in *The Death and Resurrection of the Beloved Son* is a fine example of how questions about the relationship between the Testaments can shape historical study, and the historical work has, in turn, provoked genuinely ecumenical theological reflection.[2]

There are, however, many different ways in which readerly identities and commitments might be expressed in scholarly research. For example, some methodological studies in the social sciences have argued that cross-cultural understanding necessarily entails, at decisive points, comparisons and contrasts with the interpreter's own culture. Perspicuous comparisons and contrasts need not become ethnocentric *imposition*, distorting the process of understanding. On the contrary, disciplined cultural contrasts may be necessary, lest unexamined assumptions be unconsciously imported into the interpretative task. This view has been argued perhaps most rigorously by Charles Taylor (Taylor 1985; cf. Craffert 1996).

[[473]] Also in line with Levenson's stance, the so-called "new historicist" movement in literary criticism suggests (in contrast to the objectivism of the older historicism) that a critic's representation of the past will frequently entail a normative dimension. In particular, new historicists often provide an implicit, or explicit, critique of dominant cultures in critical attempts to recover voices rendered marginal by cultural elites (Greenblatt and Gunn 1992).[3] Furthermore, the older historicist idea that "all cultures are equally

2. For further discussion of Jewish contributions to theology of the Hebrew Bible, see Rendtorff (1993: 31–45), Kalimi (1996) and Sweeney (1998).

3. Rainer Albertz's two volume history of Israelite religion has affinities with the new historicist quest to illuminate the marginal voices displaced by the dominant culture, especially insofar as he differentiates between popular piety and official religion. Albertz has ignited a fresh round of debates on the normative value of Israelite religion by arguing that it is "more theological" than Old Testament theologies (1995: 23). See the discussion in the *Jahrbuch für Biblische Theologie* 10 (1995).

valuable" can be seen as implicitly ethnocentric insofar as, in advance of any actual dialogue, it presumes that one already has the values to make such a judgment (Taylor 1992). In short, some normative judgments are quite appropriate in scholarship, and a purely neutral stance may be dubious on ethical grounds, especially in cases like Eichrodt's *Old Testament Theology* where normative interests have been masked.

This kind of point has also been made, in a different way, in feminist scholarship. While their interpretative methods and results are diverse, feminist critics are united in a normative attitude which has been neatly summarized by Phyllis Trible: feminism "opposes the paradigm of domination and subordination in all forms, most particularly male over female" (1989: 28).[4] Marie-Theres Wacker (1995:140) similarly speaks of gender equality as the "fundamental conviction" of feminist research—whether the research is historical or literary—and she defends the scholarly validity of a consciously biased decision to focus on women's experience. Such a "confessional" stance in no way invalidates feminist contributions within the university as a whole, nor within biblical scholarship in particular. In principle at least, there is nothing inherently wrong with evaluative perspectives within biblical studies, whether these are ethical or theological. The substantive question is whether a normative stance has been well argued or not. Clearly, the interpretative practices of feminism are major contributors in contemporary arts and human sciences, and they inevitably entail normative judgments.[5] To prohibit normative [[474]] judgments just because the literature at issue was the Bible, would be puzzling in the extreme.

. . . .

[[477]] And this brings us to some fundamental questions for the future of Old Testament theology, which should precede any questions of method: What *purposes* does it serve? For *whom* is such theology written? In my view, there is no general answer to these questions, but the lack of a universalizable answer certainly does not imply that the questions are irrelevant. Already in his *Religionsgeschichte Israels*, Rainer Albertz commented that an important place could come to be occupied by a theological approach which started from the burning problems of the present, but he noted that this is not the customary way biblical theology has been conceived thus far (1994: 17).

There are actually several studies which have been conceived in this way, and speaking from my own context in Australia, Habel's book is among the most significant. We are currently enmeshed in some of the most important political struggles in our history about the nature of national identity, and it is of crucial importance to note that Habel's book *The Land is Mine* is dedicated to Eddie Mabo and the Aboriginal people of Australia. In June 1992, the Australian High Court ruled that Mabo's native title claim on his ancestral land in

---

4. Ollenburger (1995: 99) calls this a confessional stance, and the language is not simply metaphorical. Trible (1981: 281) says that "Theologically, the rule of male over female constitutes sin."

5. The same point could be made, *mutatis mutandis*, for postcolonialism.

the Murray Islands was valid, over-turning the colonialist doctrine of *terra nullius* which envisaged the entire continent in the eighteenth century as effectively empty. This ruling opened the way for all crown land in Australia to be subject to native title claims. Habel's book is designed as an overture to theological reflection on land rights and reconciliation with the indigenous people. His method is primarily descriptive in that he seeks to analyse the contours of six different biblical ideologies, looking at whose interests are being served by the images of land and God, without committing himself to any view of contemporary applicability. He does, however, briefly mention that some have drawn hermeneutical analogies between, for example, the theology of the jubilee and the Australian Aboriginal claims on their ancestral heritage. Elsewhere he has claimed that the Abraham narratives embody the most appropriate theology for immigrants (Habel 1992).

My own research on nationalism and ethnicity has, similarly, been [[478]] exploring the relationship between dominant cultures, ethnic minorities and indigeneity. But unlike Habel or Watson, it seems to me theologically unnecessary to maintain a methodologically purist focus on the canonical form of biblical texts. For example, if one were to compare Habel's work on Leviticus 25–27 with a recent historical study on the Holiness Code, provided by Jan Joosten, one finds considerable agreement between the two. Joosten's work supports an interpretation of the Holiness Code as essentially an agrarian ideology, and his more detailed observations could hardly be declared irrelevant to theological concern simply because Joosten's monograph is conceived within an historical-critical paradigm.

One could wonder, perhaps, whether there was anything theologically interesting about the fact that Joosten dates the Holiness Code in the period of the monarchy, while Habel's method prevents him from being firm on any date at all. The difference seems to be a modest one, but there are some ideological questions arising. Jeffrey Fager, for example, has argued that "the inclusion of the jubilee in the Priestly Code may be seen an attempt to aid the returning exiles in regaining the land they were forced to abandon" (1993: 111). This would locate the text within the social interests of the returnees from Babylon. Joosten's date, on the other hand, would seem to promote the interests of peasant farmers during the monarchy.

But, of course, the two approaches are not mutually exclusive: a text which initially served the interests of peasant farmers could have been reshaped to serve the interests of the exiles. That is to say, a single text can be put to various ideological purposes, and a text passed down by tradition may be far removed from the ideological matrix of its production. This phenomenon of textual "distanciation" has been developed in the hermeneutical literature by both Hans-Georg Gadamer and Paul Ricoeur, and I have argued elsewhere (1991: 123–48) that it lies behind the logic of the canonical approach as developed by Brevard Childs. Similarly, Sandra Schneiders (1989) has argued that because the biblical text has a surplus of meaning which makes it susceptible to multiple interpretations beyond those imagined by its authors, it is able to elude the grasp of the social prejudices which produced it.

Even Phyllis Bird's work on Genesis 1 (1981), which interprets the text primarily within the framework of the Priestly tradition, suggests that the gender-inclusive language of the divine image has implications not foreseen by P.

[[479]] This kind of observation should be taken further, I would suggest, because it is surely of theological relevance to know precisely what implications were in fact drawn out in the history of interpretation. As is well known, the *Wirkungsgeschichte* [['history of effects']] is contradictory: many examples demonstrate a tradition oppressive to women, yet the *imago dei* [['image of God']] has sometimes been put to liberating uses. With regard to creation theology generally, Walter Brueggemann has often argued that creation theology in ancient Israel characteristically suited the interests of the powerful. Yet the situation is clearly different today: ecological theology is inimical to the interests of trans-national capital, and in his recent Old Testament theology Brueggemann has conceded biblical creation theology may well have a fresh contribution to make in our present context (1997: 163).[6] It is clear, then, that theological reflection upon scripture will need to deal with the influence of the Bible down through history, and there are even good reasons for thinking that this influence is at least as significant as the ideological contestations behind the canonical texts.

But against Childs, Watson, and perhaps even Habel, I do not see that a theologian committed to the burning questions of the day should adopt a methodological purism which relinquishes any interest in historical criticism. Moreover, if biblical scholars have been labouring under the assumption that *systematic* theologians will only be interested in theology in the narrow sense (explicit biblical discourse about God), it is time to put this assumption to rest. Schubert Ogden, for instance, begins his recent discussion of theology and biblical interpretation by noting that many scholars would distinguish between *religion* as a first-order activity of referring to God (in the Psalms, for example) and *theology* as critical reflection on a particular religion. Thus, "Old Testament theology" might be conceived as critical reflection on the history of Israelite religion. Yet Ogden wants to be more inclusive than this: he wants to say that theology is not simply critical reflection on a "religion," it also engages with other so-called secular forms of praxis and culture. Thus, Christian theology reflects upon the explicit expressions of biblical faith, but it may also include critical reflection on the social and cultural frameworks within which that faith is expressed (1996: 175).

[[480]] On his view, ideological criticism becomes part of theology itself, not a deeper and wider context for a narrowly conceived, and canonically regulated, *depositum fidei* [['deposit of faith']]. Many systematic theologians are therefore interested in ideology (note, however, the differences between Milbank 1990 and Chapman 1995), not simply in theology in the narrow sense. While affirming the relative integrity of both biblical studies and systematics, Werner Jeanrond (1996), for example, calls for a mutually-critical dialogue

6. This kind of argument has been advanced by, among others, Anderson (1994: 11–31), Lohfink (1994:1–17), and Hiebert (1996).

between the disciplines, explicitly welcoming *Ideologiekritik* [['critique of ideology']] as an interpretative practice indispensable to systematic theology. The theological enterprise is not threatened by the question of ideology, partly because biblical scholars are no longer expected to provide the foundations of systematics.[7] Although some biblical scholars, including Habel, tend to construe Old Testament theology as primarily concerned with explicit biblical discourse about God, systematic theologians are not necessarily so restricted in their focus. "Theological reflection" encompasses much more than "theology" in Habel's narrow sense.

Even in contemporary *hermeneutical* theology, the Bible is hardly given an unquestioned foundational role. For example, David Tracy represents the schools of "mediating" or "correlational" theology in which there is a mutually-critical dialogue between classic texts and contemporary experience. Lindbeck's "intratextual" theology, on the other hand, has often been understood as less dialogical: he construes doctrine as a kind of grammar of scripture and suggests that scripture should "absorb the world," rather than the other way around. This gives a clear priority to biblical frameworks, as was the case with the old Biblical Theology Movement, but Lindbeck insists that these may be supplanted or displaced "for the sake of greater faithfulness, intelligibility or efficaciousness" (1989: 182). The biblical tolerance of slavery is a paradigm case where critique is necessary, he suggests. Even where Lindbeck advocates the logical priority of the biblical narrative, as in his argument for ecclesiology as "Israelology" (1989), he does not assume that the Bible is straight-forwardly relevant today. He finds it necessary to argue carefully for the applicability of this biblical model, comparing and contrasting it with traditional Christian ecclesiologies, and identifying the features of our contemporary context that make it newly appropriate. In particular, in arguing that [[481]] Christians see themselves as part of Israel's story, he is careful to avoid any implications of supercessionism.

While some would see an affinity between "intratextual" theology and the canonical approach (Brett 1991: 156–64), it is important to see this affinity in a wider context: there is as much diversity amongst systematic theologians as there is amongst biblical scholars, and different styles of biblical criticism will be suited to different theological projects (see Kelsey 1975; Ollenburger 1995). Some of the recent historical works on Israelite religion may be as valuable for systematic theology as works which carry in their title "Old Testament theology" or "biblical theology." If Old Testament theology incorporates the study of ideology, then the case for blending theological reflection with the history of religion is greatly strengthened, as is the case for the disciplined use of the social sciences (cf. Mayes 1989; Milbank 1990; Chapman 1995). If, on the other hand, a theologian regards the biblical *narratives* as constitutive of contemporary religious identity, then narrative criticism may be more informative (Frei 1974; Perdue 1994: 23 1–62). In this

---

7. Cf. Ritschl (1986) who criticizes Claus Westermann for still assuming, as Gabler did, that biblical studies can provide such foundations.

respect, the dispute in biblical studies over the significance of "history" has its parallel also in systematic theology.

In a word, Old Testament theology is likely to be as pluralistic as any of its disciplinary neighbours, whether literary theory, systematic theology, or the social sciences. As we become more influenced by the tones of postmodernism, we will no doubt become less interested in grand comprehensive visions which suit no particular context, and more used to working with modest goals, particular perspectives, and concrete ethical and political issues. And as the example of land theology in Australia makes clear, a contextually-shaped set of interpretative interests should promote both a study of the diversity of biblical theologies, and the diversity of their reception. Thus, a postcolonial ideology critic is likely to renounce the Deuteronomic conceptions of war against the prior inhabitants of Canaan,[8] especially given their disastrous *Wirkungsgeschichte*, and endorse [[482]] an analogy between a jubilee theology and the return of indigenous people to their ancestral homelands. Such a vision of redemption is highly local, and it does not apply directly to urban Australians, nor even to many urban Aboriginals.[9] But the jubilee theology is itself caught up in a complex history of ideology, and it

8. In examining the command in Deuteronomy 7 to exterminate the indigenous peoples, Dennis Olson's canonical reading of the wider context in chaps. 7–9 is immensely illuminating. The burden of these chapters, according to Olson, is not just foreign divinities but the "gods" of militarism (chap. 7), economic power (chap. 8), and self-righteous moralism (9:1–10:22). Specifically in relation to chap. 7, many translations have obscured the connections in the Hebrew between 7:7 (Yʜᴡʜ's affection not being the result of the Israelites being numerous) and 7:17 (Israel's fear of the nations who are more numerous). What unifies the chapter is the demythologizing of numerical strength, the ancient foundation of military pride. But however illuminating such a theological exegesis may be, it does not address the postcolonialist's ethical concern for indigenous peoples. Another mode of explanation, advanced in particular by Norbert Lohfink (1982: 17–37) and Georg Braulik (1992: 147–51), would locate Deuteronomic theology specifically within a seventh century ideology of *ressentiment*—a complex mixture of envy and critique which apparently allowed the Deuteronomic theologians to borrow the suzerainty treaty genre, as well as the discourse of violence, from the Assyrian empire and bend them to serve nationalist Israelite purposes (cf. Brett 1995). Yet even this complex reconstruction, which fits neatly within the interests of postcolonial theories of ideology, in no way lessens the actual history of the impact of these texts on indigenous peoples in many contexts of colonization (see further Donaldson 1996).

9. This endorsement of a local vision of redemption suggests that the land-based focus of much Old Testament thinking need not be superseded by Christianity, as suggested by A. H. J. Gunneweg, e.g., when he comments on the uses of Gen 15:6 in Romans 4 and Galatians 3: "So werden die Überlieferungen entschränkt bis hin zur universalen paulinischen Theologie, welche auch das Konkretum von Land und Nachkommenschaft hinter sich lässt" [['Thus will the traditions be unfolded into the universal Pauline theology, which also leaves behind the concrete matters of land and descendants']] (1993: 51–52). This not only begs the questions articulated by political and ecological theology, it also recycles an uncritical view of the meaning of universalism (see Levenson 1996). An Aboriginal Christian would resonate with Gunneweg's description of Patriarchal religion wherein the promise of land, taken wholly in its concrete sense is, at the same time, a cipher for "Leben, Heil, Lebenserfüllung, Identitätsfindung, Menschwerdung des Menschen" [['life, wholeness, fulfillment, discovery of identity, people becoming fully human']] (1993: 50).

retains, for example, a negative attitude towards foreign slaves (Lev 25:44–46). Thus, both Deuteronomy and Leviticus should be deconstructed, as Julia Kristeva suggests, by other biblical norms that mark the Israelites with a "primal inscription of foreignness" (Exod 23:9 and the related texts; see Kristeva 1993: 23; Brett 1995: 157–63).

Precisely this example from Kristeva illustrates that even if we give up the modernist desire for completeness and "totality," we can still ask how the various parts of the canon, or aspects of Israelite tradition, relate to each other and to the religious traditions which preserve them. When, for example, Brueggemann describes human obedience as a proper response to YHWH'S sovereignty, glory and self-regard, he gives an accurate description of one aspect of biblical tradition. But such a description would be one-sided. When he says that God enters into a pathos-filled relationship with Israel, risking solidarity in a way "which seems regularly to qualify, if not subvert, [[483]] Yahweh's sovereignty and self-regard," Brueggemann has captured another part of biblical tradition (1997: 296). But when he goes on to say that a mature humanity also needs the courage of self-regard and self-assertion,[10] as well as the confidence to yield to the divine partner, this fresh idiom provides a valuable re-framing of the other perspectives. A knowledge of both Christian and Jewish tradition then becomes essential to his theological evaluation of this set of issues: as a result of the tradition's failure to grasp the pathos and vulnerability of YHWH's fidelity,

> the dominant Christian tradition has not fully appreciated the way in which the dialectic of assertion and abandonment in the human person is a counterpart to the unsettled interiority of Yahweh's sovereignty and fidelity. It seems to me that the classical Christian tradition must relearn this aspect of the interaction of God and human persons from its Jewish counterpart. (1997: 459)

Here the Hebrew Bible scholar steps out of the safety of descriptive discourse and invites the widest range of ecumenical critique.

Once one begins to encompass the wider canvas of biblical texts and post-biblical traditions, all the questions of contemporary hermeneutics return. If Old Testament theology is to include critical reflection on Israelite and Christian religion in all its diversity, then the scope of the task is inherently inter-disciplinary and dialogical. It is too large a task for scholars who work individualistically. Even Brueggemann has narrowed his task somewhat—in implicit agreement with Childs—insofar as he regards the history of Israelite religion as largely irrelevant to his theological task; the diversity of the *biblical* testimonies is Brueggemann's over-riding concern (1997: 123, 264). Scholars such as Albertz and Gnuse would not agree with this canonical

---

10. Brueggemann's phrase the "courage to assert" echoes Robert Davidson's title *The Courage to Doubt* (1983). Of relevance here are the traditions such as Job's complaints, the Psalms of lament, and Jeremiah's confessions, within which we find vigorous arguments with God.

framing of the task, and they would have Schubert Ogden's view of theological reflection to support them. However, I have argued that insofar as we
have a discipline called Old Testament Theology (or "Theology of the Hebrew Bible"), it should include an awareness of ideology and encompass both
the biblical texts and their *Wirkungsgeschichte*, without privileging any particular method of interpretation. Whether this is a theologically valuable enterprise is [[484]] a question practitioners in the field will need to debate not
only with Christian theologians, but also with Jewish scholars and philosophers who have now joined the conversation.

Bibliography

Albertz, R.
  1994 *A History of Israelite Religion in the Old Testament Period Vol. 1.* London:
        SCM. Trans. of *Religionsgeschichte in alttestamentlicher Zeit.* Göttingen: Van-
        denhoeck & Ruprecht, 1992.
  1995 "Religionsgeschichte Israels statt Theologie des Alten Testaments" *JBTh*
        10, pp. 3–24.
Allen, D.
  1989 *Christian Belief in a Postmodern World.* Louisville: Westminster / John
        Knox.
Anderson, B. W.
  1994 *From Creation to New Creation: Old Testament Perspectives.* Minneapolis: For-
        tress.
Bird, P. A.
  1981 "'Male and Female He Created Them': Gen. 1:27b in the Context of the
        Priestly Account of Creation" *HTR* 74: 129–59. Reprinted in *Missing Per-
        sons and Mistaken Identities: Women and Gender in Ancient Israel.* Minneapo-
        lis: Fortress, 1997, pp. 123–54.
Braulik, G.
  1992 *Deuteronomium II 16,8–34,12.* Würzberg: Echter Verlag.
Brett, M. G.
  1991 *Biblical Criticism in Crisis?* Cambridge: Cambridge University Press.
  1995 "Nationalism and the Hebrew Bible" in J. W. Rogerson *et al.* (eds.), *The
        Bible in Ethics.* Sheffield: JSOT Press, pp. 136–63.
Brueggemann, W.
  1997 *Old Testament Theology: Testimony, Dispute, Advocacy.* Minneapolis: Fortress.
Chapman, M.
  1995 "Ideology, Theology and Sociology: From Kautsky to Meeks" in J. W. Rog-
        erson *et al.* (eds.), *The Bible in Ethics.* Sheffield: JSOT Press, pp. 41–65.
Childs, B. S.
  1969 "Karl Barth as Interpreter of Scripture" in D. L. Dickerman (ed.), *Karl
        Barth and the Future of Theology.* New Haven: Yale Divinity School Assoc.,
        pp. 30–39.
Collins, J. J.
  1990 "Is a Critical Biblical Theology Possible?" in W. Propp *et al.* (eds.), *The He-
        brew Bible and Its Interpreters.* Winona Lake: Eisenbrauns, pp. 1–17.

Craffert, P.
1996 "On New Testament Interpretation and Ethnocentrism" in M. G. Brett (ed.), *Ethnicity and the Bible*. Leiden: Brill, pp. 449–68.
Donaldson, L. (ed.)
1996 *Postcolonialism and Scriptural Interpretation: Semeia 75.*
Eichrodt, W.
1961 *Theology of the Old Testament Vol. 1*. London: SCM. Trans. of *Theologie des Alten Testaments, Teil I*. Stuttgart: Klotz, ⁶1959.
Fager, J.
1993 *Land Tenure and the Biblical Jubilee: Uncovering Hebrew Ethics through the Sociology of Knowledge*. JSOTS 155; Sheffield: JSOT Press.
Frei, H.
1974 *The Eclipse of Biblical Narrative*. New Haven: Yale.
Fretheim, T.
1984 *The Suffering of God: An Old Testament Perspective*. Philadelphia: Fortress.
Gnuse, R.
1997 *No Other Gods: Emergent Monotheism in Israel*. JSOTS 241; Sheffield: JSOT Press.
Greenblatt, S., and Gunn, G. (eds.)
1992 *Redrawing the Boundaries: The Transformation of English and American Literary Studies*. New York: Modern Language Association.
Gunneweg, A. H. J.
1993 *Biblische Theologie des Alten Testaments*. Stuttgart: Kohlhammer.
Habel, N.
1992 "Peoples at Peace: The Land Ideology of the Abraham Narrative" in N. Habel (ed.), *Religion and Multiculturalism in Australia*, Adelaide: Australian Association for the Study of Religion, pp. 336–49.
1995 *The Land Is Mine: Six Biblical Land Ideologies*. Minneapolis: Augsburg.
Handelman, S.
1991 *Fragments of Redemption: Jewish Thought and Literary Theory in Benjamin, Scholem and Levinas*. Bloomington: Indiana University Press.
Hart, K.
1989 *The Trespass of the Sign: Deconstruction, Theology and Philosophy*. Cambridge: Cambridge University Press.
Hiebert, T.
1996 *The Yahwist's Landscape: Nature and Religion in Early Israel*. Oxford: Oxford University Press.
Jeanrond, W.
1996 "Criteria for New Biblical Theologies" *Journal of Religion* 76: 233–49.
Joosten, J.
1996 *People and Land in the Holiness Code: An Exegetical Study of the Ideational Framework of the Law in Lev. 17–26*. VTS 17; Leiden: Brill.
Kalimi, I.
1998 "History of Israelite Religion or Old Testament Theology? Jewish Interest in Biblical Theology" *SJOT* 11: 100–123.
Kelsey, D.
1975 *The Uses of Scripture in Recent Theology*. London: SCM.

Kristeva, J.
1993   *Nations without Nationalism.* New York: Columbia University Press.
Levenson, J.
1993a *The Hebrew Bible, the Old Testament and Historical Criticism.* Louisville: Westminster / John Knox.
1993b *The Death and Resurrection of the Beloved Son: The Transformation of Child Sacrifice in Judaism and Christianity.* New Haven: Yale.
1996   "The Universal Horizon of Biblical Particularism," in M. G. Brett (ed.), *Ethnicity and the Bible.* Leiden: Brill, pp. 143–69.
Lindbeck, G.
1989   "The Church" in G. Wainright (ed.), *Keeping the Faith.* London: SPCK, pp. 179–201.
Lohfink, N.
1982   *Great Themes from the Old Testament.* Edinburgh: T&T Clark. Trans. of *Unsere Grossen Wörter: Das Alte Testament zu Themen dieser Jahre.* Freiburg: Herder, 1977.
1994   *Theology of the Pentateuch.* Edinburgh: T&T Clark. Trans. from *Studien zum Pentateuch* and from *Studien zum Deuteronomium und zur deuteronomistischen Literatur.* Stuttgart: Katholisches Bibelwerk, 1988 and 1990.
Mayes, A.
1989   *The Old Testament in Sociological Perspective.* London: Marshall Pickering.
Milbank, J.
1990   *Theology and Social Theology.* Oxford: Blackwell.
Motte, J.
1995   *Biblische Theologie nach Walther Zimmerli.* Frankfurt: Peter Lang.
Ogden, S.
1996   "Theology and Biblical Interpretation" *Journal of Religion* 76: 172–88.
Ollenburger, B. C.
1995   "Old Testament Theology: A Discourse on Method" in S. J. Kraftchick *et al.* (eds.), *Biblical Theology: Problems and Perspectives.* Nashville: Abingdon, pp. 81–103.
Olson, D.
1994   *Deuteronomy and the Death of Moses.* Minneapolis: Fortress.
Perdue, L.
1994   *The Collapse of History: Reconstructing Old Testament Theology.* Minneapolis: Fortress.
Rendtorff, R.
1993   *Canon and Theology: Overtures to an Old Testament Theology.* Minneapolis: Fortress. Trans. of *Kanon und Theologie: Vorarbeiten zu einer Theologie des Alten Testaments.* Neukirchen-Vluyn: Neukirchener Verlag, 1991.
Ricoeur, P.
1976   *Interpretation Theory: Discourse and the Surplus of Meaning.* Fort Worth: Texas Christian University.
1980   "Toward a Hermeneutic of the Idea of Revelation" in Ricoeur *Essays on Biblical Interpretation,* ed. Lewis S. Mudge. Philadelphia: Fortress, pp. 73–118.
Ritschl, D.
1986   " 'Wahre', 'reine' oder 'neue' Biblische Theologie?" *JBTh* 1: 135–50.

Sæbø, M. (ed.)
1996 *Hebrew Bible/Old Testament: The History of Its Interpretation Vol. 1.* Göttingen: Vandenhoeck & Ruprecht.

Sawyer, J.
1996 *The Fifth Gospel: Isaiah in the History of Christianity.* Cambridge: Cambridge University Press.

Schneiders, S.
1989 "Feminist Ideology Criticism and Biblical Hermeneutics" *BTB* 19: 3–10.

Stout, J.
1981 *The Flight from Authority: Religion, Morality and the Quest for Autonomy.* Notre Dame: University of Notre Dame Press.

Sweeney, M. A.
1998 "Reconceiving the Paradigms of Old Testament Theology in the Post-Shoah Period" *Bib.Int.* 6: 142–61.

Taylor, C.
1985 "Understanding and Ethnocentrism" in Taylor, *Philosophy and the Human Sciences.* Cambridge: Cambridge University Press, pp. 116–33.
1992 "The Politics of Recognition" in A. Gutman (ed.), *Multiculturalism and the Politics of Recognition.* Princeton: Princeton University Press, pp. 25–73.

Trible, P.
1978 *God and the Rhetoric of Sexuality.* Philadelphia: Fortress.
1989 "Five Loaves and Two Fishes: Feminist Hermeneutics and Biblical Theology" *Theological Studies* 50: 279–95.

Wacker, M.-T.
1995 "'Religionsgeschichte Israels' oder 'Theologie des Alten Testaments'—(k)eine Alternative?" *JBTh* 10: 129–55.

Ward, G. (ed.)
1997 *The Postmodern God.* Oxford: Blackwell.

Appendix

JOHANN P. GABLER

b. 1753   d. 1826

An Oration on the Proper Distinction between Biblical and Dogmatic Theology and the Specific Objectives of Each

Johann P. Gabler studied theology at the universities of Jena and Göttingen. In 1785 he became professor of theology at the University of Altdorf. His inaugural lecture there, in 1787, came to be seen as biblical theology's founding document, especially since it argued for a "proper distinction" between biblical and dogmatic theology. Gabler intended the distinction to serve dogmatic theology and, thereby, the church and its ministers.

Writings about Gabler

Knierim, Rolf
  1995   On Gabler. Pp. 495–556 in *The Task of Old Testament Theology: Substance, Method, and Cases*. Grand Rapids: Eerdmans.
Merk, Otto
  1972   *Biblische Theologie des Neuen Testaments in ihrer Anfangszeit*. Marburg: Elwert.
Morgan, Robert
  1987   Gabler's Bicentenary. *Expository Times* 98: 164–68.
Sæbø, Magne
  1987   Johann Philipp Gablers Bedeutung für die biblische Theologie. *Zeitschrift für die Alttestamentliche Wissenschaft* 99: 1–16.
Sandys-Wunsch, John, and Laurence Eldredge
  1980   J. P. Gabler and the Distinction between Biblical and Dogmatic Theology: Translation, Commentary, and Discussion of His Originality. *Scottish Journal of Theology* 33: 133–58.

Johann P. Gabler
on Biblical Theology

Excerpted with permission from John Sandys-Wunsch and Laurence Eldredge, "J. P. Gabler and the Distinction between Biblical
and Dogmatic Theology: Translation, Commentary, and Discussion of His Originality," *Scottish Journal of Theology* 33 (1980) 133–
44. Translated by John Sandys-Wunsch and Laurence Eldredge.
The translators provide helpful commentary (pp. 148–58), which
is not reprinted here.

Translators' Introduction

[[133]] Gabler's inaugural address *De justo discrimine theologiae biblicae et dogmaticae regundisque recte utriusque finibus* was written in a very complex, classically-
based Latin, but the ideas he expressed were those of eighteenth-century Enlightenment theology. The responsibility for this translation was shared in that
Dr Eldredge dealt with the philological and idiomatic sense of the Latin, and
Dr Sandys-Wunsch filled in the theological background to Gabler's thought.
Dr Sandys-Wunsch alone is responsible for the commentary and discussion.

There is evidence that the address was published in 1787, but this edition
may no longer be extant. The text used in this translation is that given in the
second volume of Gabler's *Kleinere Theologische Schriften* (Ulm: 1831), pp. 179–
98, edited by his sons after his death. For convenience of reference we have
indicated approximately the pagination from this volume in the body of our
translation [[marked with a double slash followed by the page number; as
throughout this book, page numbers of the reprint source are in double
brackets]].

An excellent translation into German is found in Otto Merk, *Biblische Theologie des neuen Testaments in ihrer Anfangszeit* (Marburg: Elwert, 1972), pp. 273–
84. We have, however, on occasion differed from him in matters falling into
that grey area that lies between etymology and interpretation. There is also a
partial translation into English in W. G. Kümmel, *The New Testament: The History of the Investigation of Its Problems* (London: S.C.M., 1973), pp. 98–100.

Footnotes with Latin numerals are Gabler's; those with Arabic numerals
are ours. Gabler's footnotes have been altered in two respects; they have
been numbered consecutively [[134]] and the bibliographical details they contain have been enriched where possible.

Conventions referring to deceased scholars in the eighteenth century do
not translate well into English. Faced with the choice between incongruity
and anachronism we have opted for the latter; for example, 'the late Professor Zachariae' instead of 'the blessed Zachariae'.

An Oration

ON THE PROPER DISTINCTION BETWEEN BIBLICAL
AND DOGMATIC THEOLOGY AND THE SPECIFIC
OBJECTIVES OF EACH

which was given on March 30, 1787, by Magister Johann
Philipp Gabler as part of the inaugural duty of the Professor
Ordinarius of Theology in Alma Altorfina

Magnificent Lord, Rector of the Academy;
Most Generous Lord, prefect of this town and surrounding area;
Most revered, learned, experienced and esteemed men;
Most excellent and most celebrated professors of all faculties;
Patrons of the college, united in your support;
and you, students, a select group with respect to your nobility
    of both virtue and family;
Most splendid and worthy audience of all faculties:

All who are devoted to the sacred faith of Christianity, most worthy listeners, profess with one united voice that the sacred books, especially of the New Testament, are the one clear source from which / /180 all true knowledge of the Christian religion is drawn. And they profess too that these books are the only secure sanctuary to which we can flee in the face of the ambiguity and vicissitude of human knowledge, if we aspire to a solid understanding of divine matters and if we wish to obtain a firm and certain hope of salvation. Given this agreement of all these religious opinions, why then do these points of contention arise? Why these fatal discords of the various sects? Doubtless this dissension originates in part from the occasional [[135]] obscurity of the sacred Scriptures themselves; in part from that depraved custom of reading one's own opinions and judgments into the Bible, or from a servile manner of interpreting it. Doubtless the dissension also arises from the neglected distinction between religion and theology; and finally it arises from an inappropriate combination of the simplicity and ease of biblical theology with the subtlety and difficulty of dogmatic theology.

Surely it is the case that the sacred books, whether we look at the words alone or at the concepts they convey, are frequently and in many places veiled by a deep obscurity—and this is easily demonstrated; for one thing it is self-evident and for another a host of useless exegetical works proclaims it. The causes of this state of affairs are many: first the very nature and quality of the matters transmitted in these books; second, the unusualness of the individual words and of the mode of expression as a whole; third, the way of thinking behind times and customs very different from our own; fourth and finally, the ignorance of many people of the proper way of interpreting these books, whether it is due to the ancient characteristics of the text as a whole or to the language peculiar to each scriptural writer. / /181 But before this audience it is of little importance to describe each and every one of these causes, since it is self-evident that the obscurity of the Holy Scriptures, whatever its source, must give rise to a great variety of opinion. Also one need not discuss at length that unfortunate fellow who heedlessly dared to attribute some of his own most insubstantial opinions to the sacred writers themselves—how he increased the unhappy fate of our religion! There may even be some like him who would like to solidify the frothiness of such opinions about the sacred authors; for it is certainly something to give a divine appearance to their human ideas. Those completely unable to interpret correctly must inevitably inflict violence upon the sacred books; truly we even notice that often the wisest and most skilled of interpreters goes astray, so much so that, disregarding the laws of correct interpretation, they indulge their own ingenuity for its own sake. And let us not think then that it is suitable and legitimate for those who use the sacred words to tear what pleases them from its context in the sacred Scriptures; for it happens again and again that, when they cling to the words and do not pay attention to the mode [[136]] of expression peculiar to the sacred writers, they express something other than the true sense of these authors. And if they continue to use metaphors when the context demands universal notions, then they may persuade themselves to say that some meaning which they brought to the sacred texts in the first place, actually comes from the sacred texts.[i]

/ /182 Another cause of discord, a most serious one, is the neglected distinction between religion and theology; for if some people apply to religion what is proper to theology, it is easy to understand that there would be enormous room for the sharpest differences of opinion, and these differences will be even more destructive because each party to the quarrel will only with great reluctance surrender what he considers to pertain to religion. However, after the work of Ernesti, Semler, Spalding, Toellner, and others, most recently the venerable Tittmann[ii] has shown us brilliantly that there is considerable difference between religion and theology. For, if I may quote this excellent scholar, religion is passed on by the doctrine in the Scriptures, teaching what each Christian ought to know and believe and do in order to secure happiness in this life and in the life to come. Religion then, is everyday, transparently clear knowledge; but theology is subtle, learned knowledge, surrounded by a retinue of many disciplines, and by the same token derived not only from the sacred Scripture but also from elsewhere, especially from the domain of philosophy and history. It is therefore a field elaborated by human discipline and ingenuity. It is also a field that is advanced by careful and discriminating observation / /183 that experiences various changes along with other fields. Not only does theology deal with things proper to the

---

i. The best things to read in this connexion are the observations truly and learnedly made by the late immortal J. A. Ernesti in his learned work *Pro grammatica interpretatione librorum sacrorum* and *De vanitate philosophantium in interpretatione librorum sacrorum*, in *Opuscula Philologica* (2nd ed.; Leiden, Luchtman, 1764) 219–32 and 233–51; and the very distinguished Morus in *Prolus. de discrimine sensus et significationis in interpretando* (Leipzig, 1777).

ii. C.C. Tittmann, *Progr(amm) de discrimine theologiae et religionis* (Wittemberg, 1782).

Christian religion, but it also explains carefully and fully all connected matters; and finally it makes a place for them with the subtlety and rigor of logic. But religion for the common man has nothing to do with this abundance of literature and history.

[[137]] But this sad and unfortunate difference of opinion has always been and, alas, always will be associated with that readiness to mix completely diverse things, for instance the simplicity of what they call biblical theology with the subtlety of dogmatic theology; although it certainly seems to me that the one thing must be more sharply distinguished from the other than has been common practice up to now. And what I should like to establish here is the necessity of making this distinction and the method to be followed. This is what I have decided to expound in this brief speech of mine in so far as the weakness of my powers allows and in so far as it can be done. Therefore, most honored listeners of all faculties.[1] I strongly beg your indulgence. Would you grant me open ears and minds and be so kind as to follow me as I venture to consider these increasingly important matters. I pray and ask each and every one of you for your attention as far as is necessary so that I may speak my mind as clearly as possible.

There is truly a biblical theology, of historical origin, conveying what the holy writers felt about divine matters; on the other hand there is a dogmatic theology / /184 of didactic origin, teaching what each theologian philosophises rationally about divine things, according to the measure of his ability or of the times, age, place, sect, school, and other similar factors. Biblical theology, as is proper to historical argument, is always in accord with itself when considered by itself—although even biblical theology when elaborated by one of the disciplines may be fashioned in one way by some and in another way by others. But dogmatic theology is subject to a multiplicity of change along with the rest of the humane disciplines; constant and perpetual observation over many centuries shows this enough and to spare. How greatly the churches of the learned differ from the first beginnings of the Christian religion; how many systems the fathers attributed to each variety of era and setting![2] For history teaches that there is a chronology and a geography to theology itself. How much the scholastic theology of the Middle Ages, covered with the thick gloom of barbarity, differs from the discipline of the fathers! Even after the light [[138]] of the doctrine of salvation had emerged from these shadows, every point of difference in theology was endured even in the purified church, if I may refer to Socinian and Arminian factions. Or if I may refer to the Lutheran church alone, the teaching of Chemnitz and Gerhard is one thing, that of Calov another, that of Museus and Baier another, that of Budde another, that of Pfaff and Mosheim another, that of Baumgarten another, that of Carpov another, that of Michaelis and Heilmann another, that of Ernesti and Zachariae another, that of Teller another, that of

---

1. A.O.O.H. Presumably an abbreviation for *Auditores omnium ordinum honorabiles*.

2. The translation here represents a conjectural emendation of the untranslatable Latin text. *Quanta* has been added before *Patres*.

Walch and Carpzov another, that of Semler another, and that of Doederlein finally another. But the sacred writers are surely not so changeable that they should in this fashion be able to assume these different types and forms of theological doctrine. What I do not wish to be said, however, / /185 is that all things in theology should be considered uncertain or doubtful or that all things should be allowed according to human will alone. But let those things that have been said up to now be worth this much: that we distinguish carefully the divine from the human, that we establish some distinction between biblical and dogmatic theology, and after we have separated those things which in the sacred books refer most immediately to their own times and to the men of those times from those pure notions which divine providence wished to be characteristic of all times and places, let us then construct the foundation of our philosophy upon religion and let us designate with some care the objectives of divine and human wisdom. Exactly thus will our theology be made more certain and more firm, and there will be nothing further to be feared for it from the most savage attack from its enemies. The late Professor Zachariae did this very capably,[iii] but I hardly need to remind you of the fact that he left some things for others to emend, define more correctly, and amplify. However, everything comes to this, that on the one hand we hold firmly to a just method for cautiously giving shape to our interpretations of the sacred authors; and on the other that we rightly establish the use in dogmatics of these interpretations and dogmatics' own objectives.

The first task then in this most serious matter is to gather [[139]] carefully the sacred ideas and, if they are not expressed in the sacred Scriptures, let us fashion them ourselves from passages that we compare with each other. In order that the task proceed productively and that nothing is done fearfully or with partiality, / /186 it is necessary to use complete caution and circumspection in all respects. Before all else, the following will have to be taken into account: in the sacred books are contained the opinions not of a single man nor of one and the same era or religion. Yet all the sacred writers are holy men and are armed with divine authority; but not all attest to the same form of religion; some are doctors of the Old Testament of the same elements that Paul himself designated with the name 'basic elements';[3] others are of the newer and better Christian Testament. And so the sacred authors, however much we must cherish them with equal reverence because of the divine authority that has been imprinted on their writings, cannot all be considered in the same category if we are referring to their use in dogmatics. I would certainly not suggest that a holy man's own native intelligence and his natural way of knowing things are destroyed altogether by inspiration. Finally since especially in this context it is next asked what each of these men felt about divine things (this can be understood not from any traditional appeal to divine

iii. G. T. Zachariae in his noted work *Biblische Theologie* (5 vols.; Göttingen and Kiel, 1771, 1772, 1774, 1775, 1786).

3. The expression from Gal 4:9 is cited in Greek in Gabler's text. It is translated here as Gabler understood it but many modern commentators would interpret it otherwise.

authority but from their books) I should judge it sufficient in any event that we do not appear to concede anything which lacks some proof. I should also judge that when it is a case of the use in dogmatics of biblical ideas, then it is of no consequence under what authority these men wrote, but what they perceived this occasion of divine inspiration clearly transmitted and what they perceived it finally meant. That being the case it is necessary, unless we want to labour uselessly, to distinguish among each of the periods in the Old and New Testaments, each of the authors, and each of the manners of speaking / /187 which each used as a reflection of time and place, whether these manners are historical or didactic or poetic. If we abandon this straight road, even though it is troublesome and of little delight, it can only result in our wandering into some deviation or uncertainty. Therefore we [[140]] must carefully collect and classify each of the ideas of each patriarch—Moses, David, and Solomon, and of each prophet with special attention to Isaiah, Jeremiah, Ezekiel, Daniel, Hosea, Zachariah, Haggai, Malachi, and the rest; and for many reasons we ought to include the apocryphal books for this same purpose; also we should include the ideas from the epoch of the New Testament, those of Jesus, Paul, Peter, John, and James. Above all, this process is completed in two ways: the one is in the legitimate interpretation of passages pertinent to this procedure; the other is in the careful comparison of the ideas of all the sacred authors among themselves.

The first of these two involves many difficulties.[iv] For not only must we consider here the linguistic problem of the language then in use, which in the New Testament is both graeco-Hebrew and the vulgar Greek of the time; we must also consider that which is peculiar to each writer; that is, the uses of the meaning that a particular word may have in one certain place whether / /188 that meaning be broader or narrower. Also we should add the reason for the divergence of these uses and explain, if possible, the common meaning in which several instances of the same word fall together.[v] But we must also investigate the power and reason of the meaning itself; what is the primary idea of the word, and what merely added to it. For the interpreter who is on his guard must not stop short at the primary idea in the word, but he must also press on to the secondary idea which has been added to it either through long use or through ingenuity or through scholarly use of the word, and in so doing one may certainly make the most egregious of blunders. Let us not by applying tropes[4] forge new dogmas about which the authors themselves never thought. Not only in prophetic or poetic books but also in the writings of the Apostles there are often improper uses of words which should

iv. The late Professor Ernesti warned us of this problem in his distinguished fashion in his two works *De difficultatibus N.T. recte interpretandi* and *De difficultate interpretationis grammatica N.T.*, in *Opuscula Philologica*, 198–218 and 252–87.

v. That excellent man S. F. N. Morus in his *Prolus. de nexu significationum eiusdem verbi* (Leipzig, 1776) has taught us what caution must be observed in interpreting the relationship amongst meanings of the same word.

4. This is a technical term referring to allegorical or similar methods of extracting a 'spiritual' meaning from a text.

be traced either to an abundance of genius or to the traditional usage of opponents, or to the use of words familiar to the first [[141]] readers.[vi] Up to now this is mostly done when we are comparing carefully many opinions of the same author, such as Paul; in comparing many things and words, //189 we reduce to one idea and thing the many passages which, although variously expressed, show the same meaning. Morus [vii] recently showed and illustrated all this in a distinguished fashion—a very great man whose reputation is his monument. Finally one must properly distinguish whether the Apostle is speaking his own words or those of others; whether he is moved only to describe some opinion or truly to prove it; and if he wants to do the latter, does he repeat the argument from the basic nature of the doctrine of salvation, or from the sayings of the books of the Old Testament, and even accommodating them to the sense of the first readers? For although the opinions of the Apostles deserve our trust, so that we may easily get along without some part of their argument, the first readers nonetheless wanted the proofs that were appropriate to their own sense and judgment. Therefore, it is of great interest whether the Apostle proposes some opinion as a part of Christian doctrine or some opinion that is shaped to the needs of the time, which must be considered merely premises, as the logicians call them. If we rightly hold on to all these things, then indeed we shall draw out the true sacred ideas typical of each author; certainly not all the ideas, for there is no place for everything in the books that have come down to us, but at least those ideas which the opportunity or the necessity for writing had shaped in their souls. Nonetheless, there is a sufficient number of ideas, and //190 usually of such a kind that those that have been omitted can then be inferred without difficulty, if they constitute a single principle of opinion expressly declared, or if they are connected to the ideas that are stated in some necessary fashion. This process, however, requires considerable caution.

At this point we must pass on to the other part of the task, namely to a careful and sober comparison of the various parts attributed to each testament. Then, with Morus, the best of men, as our guide, each single opinion must be examined for its [[142]] universal ideas, especially for those which are expressly read in this or that place in the Holy Scriptures, but according to this rule: that each of the ideas is consistent with is own era, is own testament, is own place of origin, and is own genius. Each one of these categories which is distinct in cause from the others should be kept separate. And if this cautionary note is disregarded, it may happen that the benefit from the universal ideas will give way to the worst sort of damage to the truth, and it will render useless and will destroy all the work which had been brought together in diligently isolating the opinions of each author. If, however, this comparison with the help of the universal notions is established in such a way that for each author his own work remains unimpaired, and it is clearly revealed

---

vi. The distinguished J. A. Noesselt did this in his *Disp. de discernenda propria et tropica dictione* (Halle, 1762).

vii. That great man dealt with this first in his *Disp. de notionibus universis in Theologia* and then in his *Prog. de utilitate notionum universarum in Theologia* (Leipzig, 1782).

wherein the separate authors agree in a friendly fashion, or differ among themselves; then finally there will be the happy appearance of biblical theology, pure and unmixed with foreign things, and we shall at last have the sort of system for biblical theology that Tiedemann elaborated with such distinction for Stoic philosophy.

When these opinions of the holy men / /191 have been carefully collected from Holy Scripture and suitably digested, carefully referred to the universal notions, and cautiously compared among themselves, the question of their dogmatic use may then profitably be established, and the goals of both biblical and dogmatic theology correctly assigned. Under this heading one should investigate with great diligence which opinions have to do with the unchanging testament of Christian doctrine, and therefore pertain directly to us; and which are said only to men of some particular era or testament. For among other things it is evident that the universal argument within the holy books is not designed for men of every sort; but the great part of these books is rather restricted by God's own intention to a particular time, place, and sort of man. Who, I ask, would apply to our times the Mosaic rites which have been invalidated by Christ, or Paul's advice about women veiling themselves in church? Therefore the ideas of the Mosaic law have not been designated for any dogmatic use, neither by Jesus and his Apostles nor by reason iself. By the same token we must diligently investigate what in the books of the New Testament was said as an accommodation to the ideas or the [[143]] needs of the first Christians and what was said in reference to the unchanging idea of the doctrine of salvation; we must investigate what in the sayings of the Apostles is truly divine, and what perchance merely human. And at this point finally the question comes up most opportunely of the whys and wherefores of theopneustia.[5] This matter, to be sure very difficult, is, in my opinion at least, rather incorrectly inferred from the sayings of the Apostles, in which they make mention of a certain divine inspiration, since these individual passages are very obscure and ambiguous. / /192 However, we must beware, if we wish to deal with these things with reason and not with fear or bias, not to press those meanings of the Apostles beyond their just limits, especially since only the effects of the inspirations and not their causes, are perceived by the senses. But if I am judge of anything, everything must be accomplished by exegetical observation only, and that with constant care, and compared with the things spoken of and promised by our Saviour in this matter. In this way it may finally be established whether all the opinions of the Apostles, of every type and sort altogether, are truly divine, or rather whether some of them, which have no bearing on salvation, were left to their own ingenuity.

Thus, as soon as all these things have been properly observed and carefully arranged, at last a clear sacred Scripture will be selected with scarcely any doubtful readings, made up of passages which are appropriate to the

---

5. This is a transcription of the term Gabler uses in Greek script. 'Theopneustia' was often used for 'inspiration' in the eighteenth-century debates on the subject.

Christian religion of all times. These passages will show with unambiguous words the form of faith that is truly divine; the *dicta classica*[6] properly so called, which can then be laid out as the fundamental basis for a more subtle dogmatic scrutiny. For only from these methods can those certain and un-doubted universal ideas be singled out, those ideas which alone are useful in dogmatic theology. And if these universal notions are derived by a just inter-pretation from those *dicta classica*, and those notions that are derived are carefully compared, and those notions that are compared are [[144]] suitably arranged, each in its own place, so that the proper connexion and provable order of doctrines that are truly divine may stand revealed; truly when the re-sult is biblical theology in the stricter sense of the word / /193 which we know the late Zachariae to have pursued in the preparation of his well-known work.[7] And finally, unless we want to follow uncertain arguments, we must so build only upon these firmly established foundations of biblical theology, again taken in the stricter sense as above, a dogmatic theology adapted to our own times. However, the nature of our age urgently demands that we then teach accurately the harmony of divine dogmatics and the principles of human reason; then, by means of art and ingenuity by which this can happen, let us so elaborate each and every chapter of doctrine that no abundance is lacking in any part—neither subtlety, whether in proper arrangement of pas-sages or the correct handling of arguments, nor elegance in all is glory, nor human wisdom, primarily philosophy and history. Thus the manner and form of dogmatic theology should be varied, as Christian philosophy especially is,[viii] according to the varity both of philosophy and of every human point of view of that which is subtle, learned, suitable and appropriate, elegant and graceful; biblical theology iself remains the same, namely in that it deals only with those things which holy men perceived about matters pertinent to reli-gion, and is not made to accommodate our point of view.[8]

viii. J. G. Toellner, *Theologische Untersuchungen* (Riga, 1772) 1.264ff.

6. This is a technical expression that refers to the standard collection of proof texts in the orthodox theology of the eighteenth century. G. T. Zachariae had been the first to chal-lenge the usefulness of these lists of texts isolated from their context.

7. Here our translation differs from Merk's 'biblical theology in a stricter sense than Zachariae followed'. The Latin is ambiguous at this point, but in the next sentence the ex-pression 'stricter sense' is used without any direct comparison. Furthermore, Gabler is very dependent on Zachariae here in his reference to the *dicta classica* and therefore he seems to be making this remark in connexion with rather than as a contrast to Zachariae's position. At all events there is no real difference between Gabler's and Zachariae's approach to biblical theology on this point.

8. The remainder of Gabler's address is not concerned with biblical theology but with the polite formalities of the occasion. Merk translates this section in his work.

SOURCES

The following books and articles are cited in the editor's essays and notes.

Adam, A. K. M.
  1995   *What Is Postmodern Biblical Criticism?* Minneapolis: Fortress.
  2001   *Postmodern Interpretations of the Bible: A Reader.* St. Louis: Chalice.

Albertz, Rainer
  1994   *A History of Israelite Religion in the Old Testament Period.* 2 volumes. Translated by John Bowden. Minneapolis: Fortress.
  1995a   Religionsgeschichte Israels statt Theologie des Alten Testaments! Plädoyer für eine forschungsgeschichtliche Umorientierung. *Jahrbuch für biblische Theologie* 10: 3–24.
  1995b   Hat die Theologie des Alten Testaments doch noch eine Chance? *Jahrbuch für biblische Theologie* 10: 177–88.

Albertz, Rainer, Hans-Peter Muller, Hans W. Wolff, and Walther Zimmerli (editors)
  1980   *Werden und Wirken des Alten Testaments: Festschrift für Claus Westermann zum 70. Geburtstag.* Göttingen: Vandenhoeck & Ruprecht / Neukirchen-Vluyn: Neukirchener Verlag.

Albertz, Rainer, Friedemann W. Golka, Jürgen Kegler (editors)
  1989   *Schöpfung und Befreiung: Für Claus Westermann zum 80. Geburtstag.* Stuttgart: Calwer.

Ammon, Christoph F. von
  1801-2 *Biblische Theologie.* 3 volumes. 2d edition. Erlangen: Palm.

Anderson, Bernhard W.
  1971   The Crisis in Biblical Theology. *Theology Today* 28: 321–27.
  1976   Introduction. Pp. 9–28 in Will Herberg, *Faith Enacted as History: Essays in Biblical Theology.* Edited by Bernhard W. Anderson. Philadelphia: Westminster.
  1986   *Understanding the Old Testament.* 4th edition. Englewood Cliffs, New Jersey: Prentice-Hall.
  1987   *Creation versus Chaos: The Reinterpretation of Mythical Symbolism in the Bible.* 2d edition. Philadelphia: Fortress.
  1994   *From Creation to New Creation: Old Testament Perspectives.* Overtures to Biblical Theology. Minneapolis: Fortress
  1999   *Contours of Old Testament Theology.* Minneapolis: Fortress.

Anderson, Bernhard W. (editor)
  1984   *Creation in the Old Testament.* Issues in Religion and Theology 6. Philadelphia: Fortress.

Baab, Otto J.
1949   *The Theology of the Old Testament*. New York: Abingdon-Cokesbury.

Balentine, Samuel E., and John Barton (editors)
1994   *Language, Theology and the Bible: Essays in Honour of James Barr*. Oxford: Clarendon.

Barr, James
1961   *Semantics of Biblical Language*. London: Oxford University Press.
1961–62 Recent Biblical Theologies, VI: G. von Rad's *Theologie des Alten Testaments*. *Expository Times* 73: 142–46.
1966   *Old and New in Interpretation*. London: SCM / New York: Harper & Row.
1973   *The Bible in the Modern World*. London: SCM / New York: Harper & Row.
1977   *Fundamentalism*. Philadelphia: Westminster.
1980   *The Scope and Authority of the Bible*. London: SCM / Philadelphia: Westminster.
1983   *Holy Scripture: Canon, Authority, Criticism*. Philadelphia: Westminster.
1993a   *The Garden of Eden and the Hope for Immortality*. Minneapolis: Fortress.
1993b   *Biblical Faith and Natural Theology: The Gifford Lectures, Edinburgh 1991*. Oxford: Oxford University Press.
1999   *The Concept of Biblical Theology: An Old Testament Perspective*. Minneapolis: Fortress.
2000   *History and Ideology in the Old Testament: Biblical Studies at the End of a Millennium*. London: Oxford University Press.

Bauer, Bruno
1838–39 *Kritik der Geschichte der Offenbarung: Die Religion des Alten Testaments in der geschichtlichen Entwicklung ihrer Principien*. 2 volumes. Berlin: Dummler.

Bauer, Gerhard Lorenz
1796   *Theologie des alten Testaments oder Abriss der religiösen Begriffe der alten Hebräer von den altesten Zeiten bis auf den Anfang der christlichen Epoche: Zum Gebrauch akademischer Vorlesungen*. Leipzig: Weygand.
1799   *Entwurf einer Hermeneutik des Alten und Neuen Testaments*. Leipzig: Weygand.
1801   *Beylagen zur Theologie des alten Testaments, enthaltend die Begriffe von Gott und Vorsehung nach den verschiedenen Büchern und Zeitperioden entwickelt: Kann als ein zweyter Theil der Theologie des alten Tetaments angesehen werden*. Leipzig: Weygand.
1838   *The Theology of the Old Testament; or, A Biblical Sketch of the Religious Opinions of the Ancient Hebrews: From the Earliest Times to the Commencement of the Christian Era. Extracted and Translated from the Theologie des alten Testaments of Georg Lorenz Bauer* (London: Charles Fox, 1838). [Note: this translation is of Bauer's 1801 *Beylagen*, not of his 1796 *Theologie*]

Baumgarten-Crusius, Ludwig F. O.
1828   *Grundzüge der biblischen Theologie*. Jena: Frommann.

Benecke, Heinrich
1883   *Wilhelm Vatke in seinem Leben und seinen Schriften*. Bonn: Emil Strauss.

Benz, Ernst
1983   *The Mystical Sources of German Romantic Philosophy*. Translated by Blair R. Reynolds and Eunice M. Paul. Pittsburgh Theological Monographs n.s. 6. Allison Park, Pennsylvania: Pickwick.

Boadt, Lawrence
    2001   Review of *Teologia dell'Antico Testamento,* by Marco Nobile. *Catholic Biblical Quarterly* 63: 124–25.

Brett, Mark G.
    1991   *Biblical Criticism in Crisis? The Impact of the Canonical Approach on Old Testament Studies.* Cambridge: Cambridge University Press.
    2000a   *Genesis: Procreation and the Politics of Identity.* London: Routledge.
    2000b   Canonical Criticism and Old Testament Theology. Pp. 63–85 in *Text in Context: Essays by Members of the Society for Old Testament Study.* Oxford: Oxford University Press.
    2000c   The Future of Old Testament Theology. Pp. 465–88 in *Congress Volume: Oslo 1998.* Edited by Andre Lemaire and Magne Sæbø. Vetus Testamentum Supplements 80. Leiden: Brill.

Brett, Mark G. (editor)
    1996   *Ethnicity and the Bible.* Leiden: Brill.

Breukelman, Frans H.
    1980   *Bijbelse theologie I/1: Schriftlezing.* 3d edition. Kampen: Kok.

Brömse, Michael
    1984   W. Vatkes philosophische Theologie im Streit der Polemik und Apologie. Pp. 129–45 in *Vergessene Theologen des 19. und frühen 20. Jahrhunderts: Studien zur Theologiegeschichte.* Edited by Eilert Herms and Joachim Ringleben. Göttinger theologische Arbeiten 32. Göttingen: Vandenhoeck & Ruprecht.

Brueggemann, Walter
    1991   *Interpretation and Obedience: From Faithful Reading to Faithful Living.* Minneapolis: Fortress.
    1992   *Old Testament Theology: Essays on Structure, Theme, and Text.* Edited by Patrick D. Miller. Minneapolis: Fortress.
    1993   *Texts under Negotiation: The Bible and Postmodern Imagination.* Minneapolis: Fortress.
    1997   *Theology of the Old Testament: Testimony, Dispute, Advocacy.* Philadelphia: Fortress.
    1998   Theology of the Old Testament: A Prompt Retrospect. Pp. 307–20 in *God in the Fray: A Tribute to Walter Brueggemann.* Edited by Tod Linafelt and Timothy K. Beal. Minneapolis: Fortress.
    1999   The Role of Old Testament Theology in Old Testament Interpretation. Pp. 70–88 in *In Search of True Wisdom: Essays in Old Testament Interpretation in Honour of Ronald E. Clements.* Edited by Edward Ball. Journal for the Study of the Old Testament Supplements 300. Sheffield: Sheffield Academic Press.
    2002   *The Land: Place as Gift, Promise, and Challenge in Biblical Faith.* Overtures to Biblical Theology. 2d edition. Minneapolis: Fortress.
    2003   *Awed to Heaven, Rooted in Earth: Prayers of Walter Brueggemann.* Edited by Edwin Searcy. Minneapolis: Fortress.

Buber, Martin
    1950   *Two Types of Faith.* Translated by Norman P. Goldhawk. London: Routledge & Paul.
    1967   *The Kingship of God.* Translated by Richard Schiemann. London: Allen and Unwin.

Bultmann, Rudolf
1955   *Theology of the New Testament.* 2 volumes. Translated by Kendrick Grobel. New York: Scribner.

Burrows, Millar
1946   *An Outline of Biblical Theology.* Philadelphia: Westminster.

Butler, James T., Edgar W. Conrad, and Ben C. Ollenburger (editors)
1985   *Understanding the Word: Essays in Honor of Bernhard W. Anderson.* Journal for the Study of the Old Testament Supplements 37; Sheffield: JSOT Press.

Chapman, Stephen B.
2000   *The Law and the Prophets: A Study in Old Testament Canon Formation.* Forschungen zum Alten Testament 27. Tübingen: Mohr Siebeck.

Childs, Brevard S.
1970   *Biblical Theology in Crisis.* Philadelphia: Westminster.
1974   *The Book of Exodus: A Critical, Theological Commentary.* Old Testament Library. Philadelphia: Westminster / London: SCM.
1979   *Introduction to the Old Testament as Scripture.* Philadelphia: Fortress.
1984   *The New Testament as Canon: An Introduction.* Philadelphia: Fortress.
1986   *Old Testament Theology in a Canonical Context.* Philadelphia: Fortress.
1992   *Biblical Theology of the Old and New Testaments.* Minneapolis: Fortress.

Clements, Ronald E.
1969   *God's Chosen People: A Theological Interpretation of the Book of Deuteronomy.* Valley Forge, Pennsylvania: Judson / London: SCM.
1970   Theodorus C. Vriezen: An Outline of Old Testament Theology. Pp. 121–40 in *Contemporary Old Testament Theologians.* Edited by Robert B. Laurin. Valley Forge, Pennsylvania: Judson.
1976   *One Hundred Years of Old Testament Interpretation.* Philadelphia: Westminster. [British edition: *A Century of Old Testament Study* (Guildford: Lutterworth)]
1978   *Old Testament Theology: A Fresh Approach.* New Foundations Theological Library. Atlanta: John Knox / London: Marshall, Morgan & Scott.
1990   *Wisdom for a Changing World: Wisdom in Old Testament Theology.* Berkeley, California: BIBAL.
1992   *Wisdom in Theology.* Grand Rapids: Eerdmans.
1996   *Old Testament Prophecy: From Oracles to Canon.* Westminster John Knox.

Cölln, Daniel G. C. von
1836   *Die biblische Theologie des Alten Testaments.* Volume 1 of *Biblische Theologie.* Leipzig: Barth.

Collins, John J.
1990   Is a Critical Biblical Theology Possible? Pp. 1–17 in *The Hebrew Bible and Its Interpreters.* Edited by William H. Propp, Baruch Halpern, and David N. Freedman. Winona Lake, Indiana: Eisenbrauns.

Crenshaw, James L.
1978   *Gerhard von Rad.* Makers of the Modern Theological Mind. Waco, Texas: Word.

Cross, Frank M., Werner E. Lemke, and Patrick D. Miller Jr. (editors)
1976   *Magnalia Dei, The Mighty Acts of God: Essays on the Bible and Archaeology in Memory of G. Ernest Wright.* Garden City, New York: Doubleday.

Davidson, Andrew B.
1904   *The Theology of the Old Testament*. Edited by S. D. F. Salmond. International Theological Library. Edinburgh: T. & T. Clark / New York: Scribner.

Davies, G. Henton
1970   Gerhard von Rad: Old Testament Theology. Pp. 63–89 in *Contemporary Old Testament Theologians*. Edited by Robert B. Laurin. Valley Forge, Pennsylvania: Judson.

Dentan, Robert C.
1950   *Preface to Old Testament Theology*. Yale Studies in Religion 14. New Haven: Yale University Press.
1963   *Preface to Old Testament Theology*. Revised edition. New York: Seabury.

Deurloo, Karel
2000   Biblische Theologie in Grundworten. *Zeitschrift für dialektische Theologie* 16: 89–92.

Diestel, Ludwig
1869   *Geschichte des Alten Testamentes in der christlichen Kirche*. Jena: Mauke.

Donner, Herbert, Robert Hanhart, and Rudolf Smend (editors)
1977   *Beiträge zur Alttestamentlichen Theologie: Festschrift für Walther Zimmerli zum 70. Geburtstag*. Göttingen: Vandenhoeck & Ruprecht.

Eichrodt, Walther
1929   Hat die Alttestamentliche Theologie noch selbständige Bedeutung innerhalb der Alttestamentlichen Wissenschaft? *Zeitschrift für die Alttestamentliche Wissenschaft* 47:83–91. [English translation on pp. 21–29 above]
1933   *Gott und Volk*. Volume 1 of *Theologie des Alten Testaments*. Leipzig: Hinrichs.
1935   *Gott und Welt*. Volume 2 of *Theologie des Alten Testaments*. Leipzig: Hinrichs.
1939   *Gott und Mensch*. Volume 3 of *Theologie des Alten Testaments*. Leipzig: Hinrichs.
1961   *Theology of the Old Testament*. Volume 1. Translated by John A. Baker. Philadelphia: Westminster / London: SCM.
1962   *Gott und Volk*. 7th edition. Volume 1 of *Theologie des Alten Testaments*. Stuttgart: Klotz / Göttingen: Vandenhoeck & Ruprecht.
1964   *Theologie des Alten Testaments*. Volumes 2 and 3. 5th edition. Stuttgart: Klotz / Göttingen: Vandenhoeck & Ruprecht.
1967   *Theology of the Old Testament*. Volume 2. Translated by John A. Baker. Philadelphia: Westminster / London: SCM.
1969   *Religionsgeschichte Israels*. Bern: Francke.

Eissfeldt, Otto
1926   Israelitisch-jüdische Religionsgeschichte und Alttestamentliche Theologie. *Zeitschrift für die Alttestamentliche Wissenschaft* 44: 1–12. [English translation on pp. 12–20 above]

Fishbane, Michael
1989   *The Garments of Torah: Essays in Biblical Hermeneutics*. Bloomington: Indiana University Press.
1998   *The Exegetical Imagination: On Jewish Thought and Theology*. Cambridge: Harvard University Press.

Flanagan, James W., and Anita W. Robinson (editors)
1975　　　*No Famine in the Land: Studies in Honor of John L. McKenzie.* Missoula, Montana: Scholars Press / Claremont: Institute for Antiquity and Christianity.

Fohrer, Georg
1972　　　*Theologische Grundstrukturen des Alten Testaments.* Theologische Bibliothek Töpelmann 24. Berlin: de Gruyter.

Frymer-Kensky, Tikva
2000　　　The Emergence of Jewish Biblical Theologies. Pp. 109–22 in *Jews, Christians, the Theology of the Hebrew Scriptures.* Edited by Alice Ogden Bellis and Joel S. Kaminsky. Atlanta: Society of Biblical Literature.

Gabler, Johann P.
1980　　　An Oration on the Proper Distinction between Biblical and Dogmatic Theology and the Specific Objectives of Each. Translated by John Sandys-Wunsch and Laurence Eldredge. *Scottish Journal of Theology* 33: 134–44. [reprinted on pp. 497–506 above]

Gammie, John G., Walter A. Brueggemann, W. Lee Humphreys, and James M. Ward (editors)
1978　　　*Israelite Wisdom: Theological and Literary Essays in Honor of Samuel Terrien.* New York: Scholars Press for Union Theological Seminary.

Garcia Cordero, Maximiliano
1970　　　*Teología de la Biblia.* Volume 1: Antiguo Testamento. Madrid: Católica.

Gelin, Albert
1948　　　*Les Idées maîtresses de l'Ancien Testament.* Lectio Divina 2. Paris: Cerf.
1955　　　*The Key Concepts of the Old Testament.* Translated by George Lamb. New York: Sheed & Ward.

Gerstenberger, Erhard S.
1988　　　*Psalms Part 1, with an Introduction to Cultic Poetry.* Forms of the Old Testament Literature. Grand Rapids: Eerdmans.
1996　　　*Yahweh the Patriarch: Ancient Images of God and Feminist Theology.* Translated by Frederick J. Gaiser. Minneapolis: Fortress.
2000　　　Conflicting Theologies in the Old Testament. *Horizons in Biblical Theology* 22: 120–34.
2001　　　*Psalms, Part 2, and Lamentations.* Forms of the Old Testament Literature. Grand Rapids: Eerdmans.
2002　　　*Theologies in the Old Testament.* Translated by John Bowden. Minneapolis: Fortress.

Gerstenberger, Erhard S., and Wolfgang Schrage
1981　　　*Woman and Man.* Translated by Douglas W. Stott. Nashville: Abingdon.

Gese, Hartmut
1974　　　*Vom Sinai zum Zion: Alttestamentliche Beiträge zur biblischen Theologie.* Munich: Kaiser.
1977　　　Tradition and Biblical Theology. Pp. 301–26 in *Tradition and Theology in the Old Testament.* Edited by Douglas A. Knight. Philadelphia: Fortress.
1981a　　*Essays on Biblical Theology.* Translated by Keith Crim. Minneapolis: Augsburg.
1981b　　Wisdom, Son of Man, and the Origins of Christology: The Consistent Development of Biblical Theology. *Horizons in Biblical Theology* 3: 23–57.
1983　　　*Zur biblischen Theologie: Alttestamentliche Vorträge.* 2d edition. Munich: Kaiser.

1987   Die dreifaltige Gestaltwerdung des Alten Testaments. Pp. 299–328 in *Mitte der Schrift? Ein jüdisch-christliches Gespräch.* Edited by Martin Klopfenstein, Ulrich Luz, Shemaryahu Talmon, and Emanuel Tov. Bern: Peter Lang.

Gnuse, Robert K.
2001   *The Old Testament and Process Theology.* St. Louis: Chalice.

Goldingay, John
1987   *Theological Diversity and the Authority of the Old Testament.* Grand Rapids: Eerdmans.
2003   *Old Testament Theology, Volume One: Israel's Gospel.* Downers Grove, Ill.: InterVarsity.

Goshen-Gottstein, Moshe H.
1987   Tanakh Theology: The Religion of the Old Testament and the Place of Jewish Biblical Theology. Pp. 617–44 in *Ancient Israelite Religion: Essays in Honor of Frank Moore Cross.* Edited by Patrick D. Miller Jr., Paul D. Hanson, and S. Dean McBride. Philadelphia: Fortress.

Gottwald, Norman K
1970   W. Eichrodt: Theology of the Old Testament. Pp. 23–62 in *Contemporary Old Testament Theologians.* Edited by Robert B. Laurin. Valley Forge, Pennsylvania: Judson.

Gramberg, Carl P. W.
1829–30 *Kritische Geschichte der Religionsideen des Alten Testaments.* 2 volumes. Berlin: Duncker & Humblot.

Gunkel, Hermann
1913   *Reden und Aufsätze.* Göttingen: Vandenhoeck & Ruprecht.
1926–27 The "Historical Movement" in the Study of Religion. *Expository Times* 38: 532–36.

Gunneweg, Antonius H. J.
1993   *Biblische Theologie des Alten Testaments: Eine Religionsgeschichte Israels in biblisch-theologischer Sicht.* Stuttgart: Kohlhammer.

Hävernick, Heinrich A. C.
1848   *Vorlesungen über die Theologie des Alten Testaments.* Edited by Heinrich A. Hahn. Erlangen: Heyder.
1863   *Vorlesungen über die Theologie des Alten Testaments.* 2d edition. Edited by Hermann Schultz. Frankfurt: Heyder & Zimmer.

Hanson, Paul D.
1986   *The People Called: The Growth of Community in the Bible.* San Francisco: Harper & Row.

Hausmann, J., and H.-J. Zobel (editors)
1992   *Alttestamentlicher Glaube und biblische Theologie: Festschrift für Horst Dietrich Preuss.* Stuttgart: Kohlhammer.

Hartlich, Christian, and Walter Sachs
1952   *Der Ursprung des Mythosbegriffes in der modernen Bibelwissenschaft.* Tübingen: Mohr.

Hasel, Gerhard F.
1991   *Old Testament Theology: Basic Issues in the Current Debate.* 4th edition. Grand Rapids: Eerdmans.
1992   The Future of Old Testament Theology: Prospects and Trends. Pp. 373–83 in *The Flowering of Old Testament Theology: A Reader in Twentieth-Century Old Testament Theology, 1930–1990.* 1st edition. Edited by Ben C. Ollen-

burger, Elmer A. Martens, and Gerhard F. Hasel. Sources for Biblical and Theological Study 1. Winona Lake, Indiana: Eisenbrauns.

Hayes, John H., and Frederick C. Prussner

1985   *Old Testament Theology: Its History and Development.* Atlanta: John Knox / London: SCM.

Heinisch, Paul

1940   *Theologie des Alten Testaments.* Bonn: Peter Hanstein.

1950   *Theology of the Old Testament.* Translated by William G. Heidt. Collegeville, Minnesota: Liturgical Press.

Hermisson, Hans-Jürgen

2000   *Alttestamentliche Theologie und Religionsgeschichte Israels.* Leipzig: Evangelischer Verlag.

Heschel, Abraham Joshua

1955   *God in Search of Man: A Philosophy of Judaism.* Cleveland: World / Philadelphia: Jewish Publication Society.

1962–65 *Theology of Ancient Judaism.* London: Soncino. [Hebrew]

Hinson, David F.

1976   *The Theology of the Old Testament.* Theological Education Fund Study Guides 15. London: SPCK.

Hofmann, Johann C. K. von

1841–44 *Weissagung und Erfüllung im Alten und im Neuen Testamente: Ein theologischer Versuch.* 2 volumes. Nördlingen: Beck.

1852–56 *Der Schriftbeweis: Ein theologischer Versuch.* 2 volumes. Nördlingen: Beck.

1880   *Biblische Hermeneutik.* Edited by W. Volk. Nördlingen: Beck.

1959   *Interpreting the Bible.* Translated by Christian Preus. Minneapolis: Augsburg.

House, Paul R.

1988   *Zephaniah: A Prophetic Drama.* Journal for the Study of the Old Testament Supplements 69. Sheffield: Almond.

1990   *The Unity of the Twelve.* Journal for the Study of the Old Testament Supplements 97. Sheffield: Almond.

1998   *Old Testament Theology.* Downers Grove, Illinois: InterVarsity.

House, Paul R. (editor)

1992   *Beyond Form Criticism: Essays in Old Testament Literary Criticism.* Sources for Biblical and Theological Study 2. Winona Lake, Indiana: Eisenbrauns.

Imschoot, Paul van

1954–56 *Théologie de l'Ancien Testament.* 2 volumes. Tournai: Desclée & Cie.

1965   *God.* Volume 1 of *Theology of the Old Testament.* Translated by Kathryn Sullivan and Fidelis Buck. New York: Desclée.

Ingraffia, Brian D.

1995   *Postmodern Theory and Biblical Theology: Vanquishing God's Shadow.* New York: Cambridge University Press.

Irwin, William A.

1945   The Reviving Theology of the Old Testament. *Journal of Religion* 25: 235–46.

Jacob, Edmond

1955   *Théologie de l'Ancien Testament: Revue et augmentée.* Paris: Delachaux & Niestlé.

1958   *Theology of the Old Testament.* Translated by Arthur W. Heathcote and Philip J. Allcock. New York: Harper / London: Hodder & Stoughton.

1968 *Théologie de l'Ancien Testament: Revue et augmentée.* 2d edition. Paris: Delachaux & Niestlé.

1970 *Grundfragen alttestamentlicher Theologie.* Franz Delitzsch-Vorlesungen 1965. Stuttgart: Kohlhammer.

Janowski, Bernd

2002 Theologie des Alten Testaments: Plädoyer für eine Integrative Perspektive. Pp. 241–76 in *Congress Volume: Basel, 2001.* Edited by André Lemaire. Vetus Testamentum Supplements 92. Leiden: Brill.

Kaiser, Gottlieb P. C.

1813–21 *Die biblische Theologie.* 3 volumes. Erlangen: Palm.

Kaiser, Otto

1993 *Der Gott des Alten Testaments. Theologie des Alten Testaments 1: Grundlegung.* Göttingen: Vandenhoeck & Ruprecht.

1998 *Der Gott des Alten Testaments: Wesen und Wirken. Theologie des Alten Testaments 2.* Göttingen: Vandenhoeck & Ruprecht.

2003 *Der Gott des Alten Testaments: Wesen und Wirken. Theologie des Alten Testaments 3: Jahwes Gerechtigkeit.* Göttingen: Vandenhoeck & Ruprecht.

Kaiser, Walter C., Jr.

1978 *Toward an Old Testament Theology.* Grand Rapids: Zondervan.

1981 *Toward an Exegetical Theology: Biblical Exegesis for Preaching and Teaching.* Grand Rapids: Baker.

1983 *Toward Old Testament Ethics.* Grand Rapids: Zondervan.

1995 *The Messiah in the Old Testament.* Grand Rapids: Zondervan.

Kaiser, Walter (with Moisés Silva)

1994 *An Introduction to Biblical Hermeneutics: The Search for Meaning.* Grand Rapids: Zondervan.

Kalimi, Isaac

2002 *Early Jewish Exegesis and Theological Controversy: Studies in the Shadow of Internal and External Controversies.* Assen: Van Gorcum.

Kayser, August

1886 *Die Theologie des Alten Testaments in ihrer geschichtlichen Entwicklung dargestellt.* Edited by E. Reuss. Strassburg: Schmidt & Bull.

Keel, Othmar

2001 Religionsgeschichte Israels oder Theologie des Alten Testaments? Pp. 88–109 in *Wieviel Systematik erlaubt die Schrift? Auf der Suche nach einer gesamtbiblischen Theologie.* Edited by Frank-Lothar Hossfeld. Freiburg: Herder.

Kelsey, David H.

1975 *The Uses of Scripture in Recent Theology.* Philadelphia: Fortress / London: SCM.

Kessler, Rainer, Kerstin Ulrich, Milton Schwantes, and Gary Stansell (editors)

1997 *"Ihr Völker alle, klatscht in die Hände!": Festschrift für Erhard S. Gerstenberger zum 65. Geburtstag.* Exegese in unserer Zeit 3. Münster: LIT-Verlag.

Kim, Wonil, Michael Floyd, and Marvin A. Sweeney (editors)

2000 *Reading the Hebrew Bible for a New Millenium: Form, Concept and Theological Perspective.* Volume 1. Philadelphia: Trinity.

Kittel, Gisela

1989 *Der Name über alle Namen 1: Biblische Theologie / AT.* Göttingen: Vandenhoeck & Ruprecht.

Kittel, Rudolf
1921   Die Zukunft der Alttestamentlichen Theologie. *Zeitschrift für die Alttestamentliche Wissenschaft* 39: 84–99.
Knierim, Rolf
1992   *Text and Concept in Leviticus 1:1–9: A Case in Exegetical Method.* Forschungen zum Alten Testament 2. Tübingen: Mohr.
1995   *The Task of Old Testament Theology: Substance, Methods and Cases.* Grand Rapids: Eerdmans.
2000   On the Task of Old Testament Theology. Pp. 21–31 in *Reading the Hebrew Bible for a New Millenium: Form, Concept and Theological Perspective.* Volume 1. Edited by Wonil Kim, Michael Floyd, and Marvin A. Sweeney. Philadelphia: Trinity. [On Biblical Theology, pp. 11–20; Comments on the Task of Old Testament Theology, pp. 33–41]
Köberle, Justus
1906   Heilsgeschichtliche und religionsgeschichtliche Betrachtungsweise des Alten Testaments. *Neue kirchliche Zeitschrift* 17: 200–222.
Köhler, Ludwig
1935   *Theologie des Alten Testaments.* Tübingen: Mohr.
1953   *Theologie des Alten Testaments.* 3d edition. Tübingen: Mohr.
1957   *Old Testament Theology.* Translated by A. S. Todd. Philadelphia: Westminster / London: Lutterworth.
König, Eduard
1992   *Theologie des Alten Testaments kritisch und vergleichend dargestellt.* Stuttgart: Belser.
Kraeling, Emil G.
1955   *The Old Testament since the Reformation.* London: Lutterworth.
Kraftchick, Steven J.
1995   Facing Janus: Reviewing the Biblical Theology Movement. Pp. 54–77 in *Biblical Theology Problems and Perspectives: In Honor of J. Christiaan Beker.* Edited by Steven J. Krafthick, Charles D. Myers Jr., and Ben C. Ollenburger. Nashville: Abingdon.
Laurin, Robert B. (editor)
1970   *Contemporary Old Testament Theologians.* Valley Forge, Pennsylvania: Judson.
Lehman, Chester K.
1971   *Old Testament.* Volume 1 of *Biblical Theology.* Scottdale, Pennsylvania: Herald.
Levenson, Jon D.
1985   *Sinai and Zion: An Entry into the Jewish Bible.* San Francisco: Harper & Row.
1988   *Creation and the Persistence of Evil.* San Francisco: Harper & Row.
1993a   *The Hebrew Bible, the Old Testament, and Historical Criticism.* Louisville: Westminster / John Knox.
1993b   *The Death and Resurrection of the Beloved Son: The Transformation of Child Sacrifice in Judaism and Christianity.* New Haven: Yale University Press.
1997   *Esther: A Commentary.* The Old Testament Library. Louisville: Westminster John Knox.
Linafelt, Tod, and Timothy K. Beal (editors)
1998   *God in the Fray: A Tribute to Walter Brueggemann.* Minneapolis: Fortress.

Lohfink, Norbert
2001   Alttestamentliche Wissenschaft als Theologie? 44 Thesen. Pp. 13–47 in
         *Wieviel Systematik erlaubt die Schrift? Auf der Suche nach einer gesamtbibli-
         schen Theologie.* Edited by Frank-Lothar Hossfeld. Freiburg: Herder.
Long, Burke O.
1997   *Planting and Reaping Albright: Politics, Ideology, and Interpreting the Bible.*
         University Park: Pennsylvania State University Press.
McKenzie, John L.
1956   *The Two-Edged Sword: An Interpretation of the Old Testament.* Milwaukee:
         Bruce.
1965   *Dictionary of the Bible.* New York: Bruce / London: Collier-Macmillan.
1974   *Theology of the Old Testament.* Garden City, New York: Doubleday.
Martens, Elmer A.
1981   *God's Design: A Focus on Old Testament Theology.* Grand Rapids: Baker.
         [British edition: *Plot and Purpose in the Old Testament* (Leicester: Inter-
         Varsity)]
1986   *Jeremiah.* Believers Church Bible Commentary. Scottdale, Pennsylvania:
         Herald.
1992   The Multicolored Landscape of Old Testament Theology. *The Flowering of
         Old Testament Theology: A Reader in Twentieth-Century Old Testament Theol-
         ogy, 1930–1990.* 1st edition. Edited by Ben C. Ollenburger, Elmer A. Mar-
         tens, and Gerhard F. Hasel. Sources for Biblical and Theological Study 1.
         Winona Lake, Indiana: Eisenbrauns.
1994   The Oscillating Fortunes of "History" within Old Testament Theology.
         Pp. 313–40 in *Faith, Tradition, and History: Old Testament Historiography in
         Its Near Eastern Context.* Edited by A. R. Millard, J. K. Hoffmeier, and Da-
         vid W. Baker. Winona Lake, Indiana: Eisenbrauns.
1997a   The Flowering and Floundering of Old Testament Theology. Pp. 169–81
         in *A Guide to Old Testament Theology and Exegesis.* Edited by Willem A.
         VanGemeren. Grand Rapids: Zondervan.
1997b   *Old Testament Theology.* Bibliographies 13. Grand Rapids: Baker.
1998   *God's Design: A Focus on Old Testament Theology.* 3d edition. North Rich-
         land Hills, Texas: D. & F. Scott.
1997c   Yahweh's Compassion and Ecotheology. Pp. 234–48 in *Problems in Bibli-
         cal Theology: Essays in Honor of Rolf Knierim.* Edited by H. T. C. Sun, K. L.
         Eades, James M. Robinson, and Garth I. Moller. Grand Rapids: Eerd-
         mans.
2001   Reaching for a Biblical Theology of the Whole Bible. Pp. 83–101 in *Re-
         claiming the Old Testament: Essays in Honour of Waldemar Janzen.* Edited by
         Gordon Zerbe. Winnipeg: CMBC.
Marti, Karl
1897   *Geschichte der israelitischen Religion.* 3d edition. Strassburg: Schmidt &
         Bull.
Merk, Otto
1972   *Biblische Theologie des Neuen Testaments in ihrer Anfangszeit.* Marburg:
         Elwert.
Minear, Paul
1944   Wanted: A Biblical Theology. *Theology Today* 1: 47–58.

Moberly, R. W. L.
1983 At the Mountain of God: Story and Theology in Exodus 32–34. Journal for the Study of the Old Testament Supplements 22. Sheffield: JSOT Press.
1992a *The Old Testament of the Old Testament: Patriarchal Narratives and Mosaic Yahwism.* Overtures to Biblical Theology. Minneapolis: Fortress.
1992b *From Eden to Golgotha: Essays in Biblical Theology.* South Florida Studies in the History of Judaism 52. Atlanta: Scholars Press.
1999 Theology of the Old Testament. Pp. 452–78 in *The Face of Old Testament Studies: A Survey of Contemporary Perspectives.* Edited by David W. Baker and Bill T. Arnold. Grand Rapids: Zondervan.
2000 *The Bible, Theology, and Faith: A Study of Abraham and Jesus.* Cambridge Studies in Christian Doctrine. Cambridge: Cambridge University Press.
2001 The Christ of the Old and New Testaments. Pp. 184–99 in *The Cambridge Companion to Jesus.* Edited by Markus Bockmuehl. Cambridge Companions to Religion. Cambridge: Cambridge University Press.

Möller, Wilhelm, and Hans Möller
1938 *Biblische Theologie des Alten Testaments in heilsgeschichtlicher Entwiklung.* Zwickau: Johannes Herrmann.

Morgan, Robert
1987 Gabler's Bicentenary. *Expository Times* 98: 164–68.

Müller, Hans-Peter
1992 Bedarf die alttestamentliche Theologie einer philosophischen Grundlegung? Pp. 342–51 in *Alttestamentlicher Glaube und biblische Theologie: Festschrift für Horst Dietrich Preuss.* Edited by J. Hausmann and H.-J. Zobel. Stuttgart: Kohlhammer.

Munson, Thomas N.
1975 Biographical Sketch of John L. McKenzie. Pp. 1–13 in *No Famine in the Land: Studies in Honor of John L. McKenzie.* Edited by James W. Flanagan and Anita W. Robinson. Missoula, Montana: Scholars Press / Claremont: Institute for Antiquity and Christianity.

Murphy, Roland E.
1997 Reflections on a Critical Biblical Theology. Pp. 265–74 in *Problems in Biblical Theology: Essays in Honor of Rolf Knierim.* Edited by Henry T. C. Sun and Keith L. Eades. Grand Rapids: Eerdmans.

Noack, Ludwig
1853 *Die biblische Theologie.* Halle: Pfeffer.

Nobile, Marco
1998 *Teologia dell'Antico Testamento.* Logos, Corso di Studi Biblici 8/1. Leumann (Turin): Elle di Ci.

Noble, Paul R.
1995 *The Canonical Approach: A Critical Reconstruction of the Hermeneutics of Brevard S. Childs.* Leiden: Brill.

Ochs, Peter (editor)
1993 *The Return to Scripture in Judaism and Christianity: Essays in Postcritical Interpretation of Scripture.* New York: Paulist Press.

Ochs, Peter, and Nancy Levene (editors)
2002 *Textual Reasonings: Jewish Philosophy and Text Study at the End of the Twentieth Century.* Grand Rapids: Eerdmans.

Oehler, Gustaf F.
  1845   *Prolegomena zur Theologie des Alten Testaments*. Stuttgart: Leisching.
  1873–74 *Die Theologie des Alten Testaments*. 2 volumes. Edited by Hermann Oehler. Tübingen: Heckenhauer.
  1874–75 *Theology of the Old Testament*. 2 volumes. Translated by Ellen D. Smith and Sophia Taylor. Edinburgh: T. & T. Clark.
  1883   *Theology of the Old Testament*. 2 volumes. 2d edition. Translated by Ellen D. Smith and Sophia Taylor. Edinburgh: T. & T. Clark / New York: Funk & Wagnalls.

Oeming, Manfred
  1987   *Gesamtbiblische Theologien der Gegenwart*. 2d edition. Stuttgart: Kohlhammer.

Ollenburger, Ben C.
  1985   Biblical Theology: Situating the Discipline. Pp. 37–62 in *Understanding the Word: Essays in Honor of Bernard W. Anderson*. Edited by James T. Butler, Edgar W. Conrad, and Ben C. Ollenburger. Journal for the Study of the Old Testament Supplements 37. Sheffield: JSOT Press.
  1992   From Timeless Ideas to the Essence of Religion. Pp. 3–19 in *The Flowering of Old Testament Theology: A Reader in Twentieth-Century Old Testament Theology, 1930–1990*. 1st edition. Edited by Ben C. Ollenburger, Elmer A. Martens, and Gerhard F. Hasel. Sources for Biblical and Theological Study 1. Winona Lake, Indiana: Eisenbrauns.
  1995   Old Testament Theology: A Discourse on Method. Pp. 81–103 in *Biblical Theology Problems and Prospects: In Honor of J. Christiaan Beker*. Edited by Steven J. Kraftchick, Charles D. Myers, and Ben C. Ollenburger. Nashville: Abingdon.
  1999   Theology, Old Testament. Pp. 562–68 in *Dictionary of Biblical Interpretation*. Edited by John H. Hayes. Nashville: Abingdon.
  2000   Review Essay: The History of Israel Contested and Revised. *Modern Theology* 16: 529–40.
  2003   Discoursing Old Testament Theology. *Biblical Interpretation* 11: 612–28.

Ollenburger, Ben C. (editor)
  1991   *So Wide a Sea: Essays on Biblical and Systematic Theology*. Elkhart, Indiana: Institute of Mennonite Studies.

Olson, Dennis T.
  1998   Biblical Theology as Provisional Monologization: A Dialogue with Childs, Brueggemann, and Bakhtin. *Biblical Interpretation* 6: 162–80.

Pannenberg, Wolfhart (editor)
  1968   *Revelation as History*. Translated by David Granskou. New York: Macmillan.

Patrick, Dale
  1999   *The Rhetoric of Revelation in the Hebrew Bible*. Overtures to Biblical Theology. Minneapolis: Fortress.

Payne, John Barton
  1962   *The Theology of the Older Testament*. Grand Rapids: Zondervan.

Penchansky, David
  1995   *The Politics of Biblical Theology: A Postmodern Reading*. Macon, Georgia: Mercer University Press.

Perdue, Leo G.

1994   *The Collapse of History: Reconstructing Old Testament Theology*. Overtures to Biblical Theology. Minneapolis: Augsburg Fortress.

Porteous, Norman

1951   Old Testament Theology. Pp. 311–45 in *The Old Testament and Modern Study*. Edited by H. H. Rowley. London: Oxford University Press.

Preuss, Horst Dietrich

1968   *Jahweglaube und Zukunfsterwartung*. Stuttgart: Kohlhammer.

1984   *Das Alte Testament in christlicher Predigt*. Stuttgart: Kohlhammer.

1991   *JHWH's Erwählendes und verpflictendes Handeln*. Volume 1 of *Theologie des Alten Testaments*. Stuttgart: Kohlhammer.

1992   *Israels Weg mit JHWH*. Volume 2 of *Theologie des Alten Testaments*. Stuttgart: Kohlhammer.

1995–96   *Theology of the Old Testament*. 2 volumes. Translated by Leo G. Perdue. Old Testament Library. Louisville: Westminster John Knox.

Procksch, Otto

1950   *Theologie des Alten Testaments*. Gütersloh: Bertelsmann.

Rad, Gerhard von

1957   *Die Theologie der geschichtlichen Überlieferungen Israels*. Volume 1 of *Theologie des Alten Testaments*. Munich: Chr. Kaiser.

1960   *Die Theologie der prophetischen Überlieferungen Israels*. Volume 2 of *Theologie des Alten Testaments*. Munich: Chr. Kaiser.

1962a   *The Theology of Israel's Historical Traditions*. Translated by David M. G. Stalker. Volume 1 of *Old Testament Theology*. New York: Harper & Row / Edinburgh: Oliver & Boyd. [Reprinted in 2001 with an introduction by Walter Brueggemann]

1962b   *Die Theologie der geschichtlichen Überlieferungen Israels*. Volume 1 of *Theologie des Alten Testaments*. 4th edition. Munich: Chr. Kaiser.

1965a   *The Theology of Israel's Prophetic Traditions*. Translated by David M. G. Stalker. Volume 2 of *Old Testament Theology*. New York: Harper & Row / Edinburgh: Oliver & Boyd.

1965b   *Die Theologie der prophetischen Überlieferungen Israels*. Volume 2 of *Theologie des Alten Testaments*. 4th edition. Munich: Chr. Kaiser.

1966   *The Problem of the Hexateuch and Other Essays*. Translated by E. W. T. Dickens. Edinburgh: Oliver & Boyd.

1972   *Wisdom in Israel*. London: SCM / Nashville: Abingdon.

Rendtorff, Rolf

1993   *Canon and Theology: Overtures to an Old Testament Theology*. Overtures to Biblical Theology. Minneapolis: Fortress.

1996   Recent German Old Testament Theologies. *Journal of Religion* 76: 328–37.

1999   *Kanonische Grundlegung*. Volume 1 of *Theologie des Alten Testaments: Ein kanonischer Entwurf*. Neukirchen-Vluyn: Neukirchener Verlag.

2001   *Thematische Entfaltung*. Volume 2 of *Theologie des Alten Testaments: Ein kanonischer Entwurf*. Neukirchen-Vluyn: Neukirchener Verlag.

Rendtorff, Rolf, and Klaus Koch (editors)

1961   *Studien zur Theologie der Alttestamentlichen Überlieferungen*. Neukirchen-Vluyn: Neukirchener Verlag.

Reventlow, Henning Graf

1985   *Problems of Old Testament Theology in the Twentieth Century*. Translated by John Bowden. Philadelpia: Fortress / London: SCM.

1986   *Problems of Biblical Theology in the Twentieth Century.* Translated by John
        Bowden. Philadelphia: Fortress / London: SCM.
Riehm, Eduard K. A.
1889   *Alttestamentliche Theologie.* Edited by Karl Pahncke. Halle: Strien.
Robinson, H. Wheeler
1946   *Inspiration and Revelation in the Old Testament.* Oxford: Clarendon.
Rogerson, John W.
1991   *W. M. L. de Wette, Founder of Modern Biblical Criticism: An Intellectual Biography.* Sheffield: JSOT Press.
Rosenzweig, Franz
1970 [1921]   *The Star of Redemption.* Translated by William W. Hallo. Notre Dame:
        University of Notre Dame.
Rowley, Harold H.
1956   *The Faith of Israel: Aspects of Old Testament Thought.* Philadelphia: Westminster / London: SCM.
Sæbø, Magne
1982   Eichrodt, Walther. Pp. 371–73 in volume 9 of *Theologische Realenzyklopädie.* Berlin: de Gruyter.
1987   Johann Philipp Gablers Bedeutung für die biblische Theologie. *Zeitschrift
        für die Alttestamentliche Wissenschaft* 99: 1–16.
Sailhamer, John H.
1992   *The Pentateuch as Narrative: A Biblical-Theological Commentary.* Grand Rapids: Zondervan.
1995   *An Introduction to Old Testament Theology: A Canonical Approach.* Grand
        Rapids: Zondervan.
1996   *Genesis Unbound: A Provocative New Look at the Creation Account.* Sisters,
        Oregon: Multnomah.
2002   Biblical Theology and the Composition of the Hebrew Bible. Pp. 25–37
        in *Biblical Theology: Retrospect and Prospect.* Edited by Scott J. Hafemann.
        Downers Grove, Illinois: InterVarsity.
Sanders, James A.
1978   Comparative Wisdom: L'Oeuvre Terrien. Pp. 3–14 in *Israelite Wisdom:
        Theological and Literary Essays in Honor of Samuel Terrien.* Edited by John
        G. Gammie, Walter A. Brueggemann, W. Lee Humphreys, and James M.
        Ward. New York: Scholars Press for Union Theological Seminary.
Sandys-Wunsch, John, and Laurence Eldredge
1980   J. P. Gabler and the Distinction between Biblical and Dogmatic Theology:
        Translation, Commentary, and Discussion of His Originality. *Scottish Journal of Theology* 33: 133–58.
Schertz, Mary H.
1991   Biblical Theology and Feminist Interpretation: A Dinosaur at the Freedom March? Pp. 65–78 in *So Wide a Sea: Essays on Biblical and Systematic
        Theology.* Edited by Ben C. Ollenburger. Elkhart, Indiana: Institute of
        Mennonite Studies.
Schmid, Hans Heinrich
1977   Unterwegs zu einer neuen biblischen Theologie? Anfragen an die von
        H. Gese und P. Stuhlmacher vorgetragenen Entwürfe biblischer Theologie. Pp. 75–95 in *Biblische Theologie heute: Einführung, Beispiele, Kontroversen.*
        By Klaus Haacker et al. Biblisch-theologische Studien n.s. 1. Neukirchen-Vluyn: Neukirchener Verlag.

Schmid, Johannes H.
1988   *Biblische Theologie in der Sicht heutiger Alttestamentler: Hartmut Gese, Claus Westermann, Walther Zimmerli, Antonius Gunneweg.* 2d edition. Giessen: Brunnen.
Schmidt, Werner H.
1982   *Alttestamentlicher Glaube in seiner Geschichte.* 4th edition. Neukirchener Studienbücher 6. Neukirchen-Vluyn: Neukirchener Verlag.
1983   *The Faith of the Old Testament: A History.* Translated by John Sturdy. Philadelphia: Westminster.
Schmitt, Hans-Christoph
2001   *Theologie in Prophetie und Pentateuch.* Beiheft zur Zeitschrift für die Alttestamentliche Wissenschaft 310. Berlin: de Gruyter.
Schreiner, Josef.
1995   *Theologie des Alten Testaments.* Die neue Echter Bibel: Ergänzungsband 1 zum Alten Testament. Würzburg: Echter.
Schultz, Hermann
1869   *Alttestamenthche Theologie: Die Offenbarungsreligion auf ihrer vorchristlichen Entwicklungstufe.* 2 volumes. Frankfurt am Main: Heyder & Zimmer.
1878   *Alttestamentliche Theologie: Die Offenbarungsreligion auf ihrer vorchristlicher Entwicklungstufe.* 2d edition. Frankfurt: Heyder & Zimmer.
1892   *Old Testament Theology: The Religion of Revelation in Its Pre-Christian Stage of Development.* 2 volumes. Translated by John A. Paterson. Edinburgh: T. & T. Clark.
1895   *Old Testament Theology: The Religion of Revelation in Its Pre-Christian Stage of Development.* 2d edition. 2 volumes. Translated by John A. Paterson. Edinburgh: T. & T. Clark.
1896   *Alttestamentliche Theologie: Die Offenbarungsreligion auf ihrer vorchristlicher Entwicklungstufe.* 5th edition. Frankfurt: Heyder & Zimmer.
Seitz, Christopher, and Kahtryn Greene-McCreight (editors)
1999   *Theological Exegesis: Essays in Honor of Brevard S. Childs.* Grand Rapids: Eerdmans.
Sellin, Ernst
1933   *Alttestamentliche Theologie auf religionsgeschichtlicher Grundlage.* 2 volumes. Leipzig: Quelle & Meyer.
Shaffer, Elinor S.
1975   *"Kubla Khan" and the Fall of Jerusalem: The Mythological School in Biblical Criticism and Secular Literature, 1770–1880.* Cambridge: Cambridge University Press.
Smart, James D.
1943   The Death and Rebirth of Old Testament Theology. *Journal of Religion* 23: 1–11, 125–36.
Smend, Rudolf
1958   *Wilhelm Martin Leberecht de Wettes Arbeit am Alten und am Neuen Testament.* Basel: Helbing & Lichtenhahn.
1962   Universalismus und Particularismus in der Alttestamentlichen Theologie des 19. Jahrhunderts. *Evangelische Theologie* 22: 169–79.
1970   Die Mitte des Alten Testaments. *Theologische Studiën* 101. Zurich: Evangelischer Verlag. [Reprinted, pp. 40–84 in *Gesammelte Studien.* Beiträge zur Evangelischen Theologie 99. Munich: Chr. Kaiser]

1989   *Deutsche Alttestamentler in Drei Jahrhunderten.* Göttingen: Vandenhoeck & Ruprecht.

Smith, Ralph L.
1993   *Old Testament Theology: Its History, Method, and Message.* Nashville: Broadman & Holman.

Spieckermann, Hermann
2000   God's Steadfast Love: Towards a New Conception of Old Testament Theology. *Biblica* 81: 305–27.
2001   *Gottes Liebe zu Israel: Studien zur Theologie des Alten Testaments.* Forschungen zum Alten Testaments 33. Tübingen: Mohr Siebeck.

Spriggs, David G.
1974   *Two Old Testament Theologies: A Comparative Evaluation of the Contributions of Eichrodt and von Rad to Our Understanding of the Nature of Old Testament Theology.* Studies in Biblical Theology 2/30. London: SCM / Naperville, Illinois: Allenson.

Stade, Bernhard
1899   Über die Aufgabe der biblischen Theologie des Alten Testaments. Pp. 77–96 in *Ausgewählte akademische Reden und Abhandlungen.* Giessen: Ricker. [Reprinted from *Zeitschrift für Theologie und Kirche* 3 (1893) 31–51]
1905   *Die Religion Israels und die Entstehung des Judentums.* Volume 1 of *Biblische Theologie des Alten Testaments.* Tübingen: Mohr (Siebeck).

Staerk, Willy
1923   Religionsgeschichte und Religionsphilosophie in ihrer Bedeutung für die biblische Theologie des Alten Testaments. *Zeitschrift für Theologie und Kirche* 31: 289–300.

Steudel, Johann C. F.
1840   *Vorlesungen über die Theologie des Alten Testaments.* Edited by Gustaf F. Oehler. Berlin: Reimer.

Steuernagel, Carl
1925   Alttestamentliche Theologie und Alttestamentliche Religionsgeschichte. Pp. 266–73 in *Vom Alten Testament: Karl Marti zum siebzigsten Geburtstage.* Edited by Karl Budde. Beiheft zur Zeitschrift für die Alttestamentliche Wissenschaft 41. Giessen: Alfred Töpelmann.

Stoebe, Hans J., Johann J. Stamm, and Ernst Jenni (editors)
1970   *Wort-Gebot-Glaube: Beiträge zur Theologie des Alten Testaments—Walther Eichrodt zum 80. Geburtstag.* Abhandlungen zur Theologie des Alten und Neuen Testaments 59. Zurich: Zwingli.

Sun, Henry T. C., and Keith L. Eades (editors)
1997   *Problems in Biblical Theology: Essays in Honor of Rolf Knierim.* Grand Rapids: Eerdmans.

Sweeney, Marvin A.
2000   Reconceiving the Paradigms of Old Testament Theology in the Post-Shoah Period. Pp. 155–72 in *Jews, Christians, the Theology of the Hebrew Scriptures.* Edited by Alice Ogden Bellis and Joel S. Kaminsky. Atlanta: Society of Biblical Literature.

Terrien, Samuel L.
1978   *The Elusive Presence: Toward a New Biblical Theology.* Religious Perspectives 26. San Francisco: Harper & Row.
1981   The Play of Wisdom: Turning Point in Biblical Theology. *Horizons in Biblical Theology* 3: 125–53.

1996   *The Iconography of Job through the Centuries: Artists as Biblical Interpreters.* University Park: Pennsylvania State University Press.

2003   *The Psalms: Strophic Structure and Theological Commentary.* Grand Rapids: Eerdmans.

Toews, John E.

1980   *Hegelianism: The Path toward Dialectical Humanism, 1805–1841.* Cambridge: Cambridge University Press.

Trible, Phyllis

1978   *God and the Rhetoric of Sexuality.* Overtures to Biblical Theology 2. Philadelphia: Fortress.

1984   *Texts of Terror: Literary-Feminist Readings of Biblical Narratives.* Overtures to Biblical Theology. Philadelphia: Fortress.

1989   Five Loaves and Two Fishes: Feminist Hermeneutics and Biblical Theology. *Theological Studies* 50: 279–95.

1993   Treasures Old and New: Biblical Theology and the Challenge of Feminism. Pp. 32–56 in *The Open Text: New Directions for Biblical Study.* Edited by Francis Watson. London: SCM.

1994   *Rhetorical Criticism: Context, Method, and the Book of Jonah.* Guides to Biblical Scholarship. Minneapolis: Fortress.

1995   *Feminist Approaches to the Bible.* Symposium at the Smithsonian Institution. Washington, D.C.: Biblical Archaeology Society.

Troeltsch, Ernst

1913   The Dogmatics of the "Religionsgeschichtliche Schule." *American Journal of Theology* 17: 1–21.

Tsevat, Matitiahu

1986   Theology of the Old Testament: A Jewish View. *Horizons in Biblical Theology* 8/2: 33–50.

1987   Theologie des Alten Testaments: Eine jüdische Sicht. Pp. 329–41 in *Mitte der Schrift? Ein jüdisch-christliches Gespräch.* Edited by Martin Klopfenstein, Ulrich Luz, Shemaryahu Talmon, and Emanuel Tov. Bern: Peter Lang.

Tucker, Gene M., David L. Petersen, and Robert R. Wilson (editors)

1988   *Canon, Theology, and Old Testament Interpretation: Essays in Honor of Brevard S. Childs.* Philadelphia: Fortress.

Unnik, W. C. van, and A. S. van der Woude (editors)

1966   *Studia Biblica et Semitica: Theodoro Christiano Vriezen . . . Dedicata.* Wageningen: Veenman & Zonen.

Vatke, Johann K. W.

1835   *Die Religion des Alten Testaments nach dem kanonischen Büchern entwickelt.* Volume 1 of *Die biblische Theologie wissenschaftlich dargestellt.* Berlin: Bethge.

Vaux, Roland de

1972   Is It Possible to Write a "Theology of the Old Testament"? Pp. 49–62 in *The Bible and the Ancient Near East.* London: Darton, Longman & Todd.

Vos, Geerhardus

1948   *Biblical Theology: Old and New Testaments.* Grand Rapids: Eerdmans.

Vriezen, Theodorus C.

1949   *Hoofdlijnen der Theologie van het Oude Testament.* Wageningen: Veenman & Zonen.

1958   *An Outline of Old Testament Theology.* Translated by S. Neuijen. Boston: Branford / Oxford: Blackwell.

| 1966 | *Hoofdlijnen der Theologie van het Oude Testament.* 3d edition. Wageningen: Veenman & Zonen. |

1966   *Hoofdlijnen der Theologie van het Oude Testament.* 3d edition. Wageningen: Veenman & Zonen.

1970   *An Outline of Old Testament Theology.* 2d edition. Translated by S. Neuijen. Newton, Massachusetts: Branford / Oxford: Blackwell.

Westermann, Claus

1967   *Basic Forms of Prophetic Speech.* Translated by Hugh C. White. Philadelphia: Westminster.

1978a   *Blessing: In the Bible and in the Life of the Church.* Translated by Keith Crim. Overtures to Biblical Theology. Philadelphia: Fortress.

1978b   *Theologie des Alten Testaments in Grundzügen.* Göttingen: Vandenhoeck & Ruprecht.

1979   *What Does the Old Testament Say about God?* Edited by Friedemann W. Golka. Atlanta: John Knox / London: SCM.

1980a   *Promises to the Fathers: Studies on the Patriarchal Narratives.* Translated by David E. Green. Philadelphia: Fortress.

1980b   *The Psalms: Structure, Content, and Message.* Translated by Ralph D. Gehrke. Minneapolis: Augsburg.

1982   *Elements of Old Testament Theology.* Translated by Douglas W. Stott. Atlanta: John Knox.

1984–86   *Genesis: A Commentary.* 3 volumes. Translated by John J. Scullion. Minneapolis: Augsburg / London: SPCK.

Wette, Wilhelm M. L. de

1813   *Biblische Dogmatik Alten und Neuen Testaments.* Volume 1 of *Lehrbuch der christlichen Dogmatik.* Berlin: Realschulbuchhandlung.

1831   *Biblische Dogmatik Alten und Neuen Testaments.* 3d edition. Volume 1 of *Lehrbuch der christlichen Dogmatik.* Berlin: Reimer.

1846   *Die biblische Geschichte als Geschichte der Offenbarungen Gottes.* Berlin: Reimer.

Whybray, R. N.

1987   Old Testament Theology: A Non-existent Beast? Pp. 168–80 in *Scripture: Meaning and Method—Essays Presented to Anthony T. Hanson for His Seventieth Birthday.* Edited by Barry P. Thompson. Hull: Hull University.

Wittenberg, Gunther H.

1988   *King Solomon and the Theologians.* Pietermaritzburg: University of Natal Press.

1991   *I Have Heard the Cry of My People: A Study Guide to Exodus 1–15.* Bible in Context 1. Pietermaritzburg: Institute for the Study of the Bible with Cluster Publications.

1993   *Prophecy and Protest: A Contextual Introduction to Israelite Prophecy.* Bible in Context 2. Pietermaritzburg: Institute for the Study of the Bible with Cluster Publications.

1996   Old Testament Theology: For Whom? *Semeia* 73: 221–40.

2000   Alienation and "Emancipation" from the Earth: The Earth Story in Genesis 4. *The Earth Story in Genesis.* The Earth Bible. Edited by Norman C. Habel and Shirley Wurst. Sheffield: Sheffield Academic Press / Cleveland, Ohio: Pilgrim.

Wolff, Hans W. (editor)

1971   *Probleme biblischer Theologie: Gerhard von Rad zum 70. Geburtstag.* Munich: Chr. Kaiser.

Wright, G. Ernest
  1952   *God Who Acts: Biblical Theology as Recital.* Studies in Biblical Theology 8.
            London: SCM / Chicago: Regnery.
  1969a   *The Old Testament and Theology.* New York: Harper & Row.
  1969b   History and Reality: The Importance of Israel's "Historic Symbols" for
            the Christian Faith. Pp. 176–99 in *The Old Testament and Christian Faith.*
            Edited by Bernhard W. Anderson. New York: Herder and Herder.
  1970   Historical Knowledge and Revelation. Pp. 279–303 in *Translating and Un-
            derstanding the Old Testament.* Edited by H. T. Frank and W. L. Reed. Nash-
            ville: Abingdon.
Wright, G. Ernest, and Reginald H. Fuller
  1957   *The Book of the Acts of God: Contemporary Scholarship Interprets the Bible.*
            Garden City, New York: Doubleday.
Zimmerli, Walter
  1971   *Man and His Hope in the Old Testament.* Translated by G. W. Bowden. Stud-
            ies in Biblical Theology 2/20. London: SCM / Naperville, Illinois: Allen-
            son.
  1972   *Grundriss der Alttestamentlichen Theologie.* Theologische Wissenschaft 3.
            Stuggart: Kohlhammer.
  1976   *The Old Testament and the World.* Translated by John J. Scullion. Atlanta:
            John Knox.
  1978   *Old Testament Theology in Outline.* Translated by David E. Green. Atlanta:
            John Knox / Edinburgh: T. & T. Clark.
  1979–83   *Ezekiel: A Commentary on the Book of the Prophet Ezekiel.* 2 volumes. Trans-
            lated by Ronald E. Clements and James D. Martin. Edited by Frank M.
            Cross, Klaus Baltzer, Leonard J. Greenspoon, and Paul D. Hanson.
            Hermeneia. Philadelphia: Fortress.
  1982   *I Am Yahweh.* Translated by Douglas W. Stott. Edited by Walter Bruegge-
            mann. Atlanta: John Knox.
  1985   *Grundriss der Alttestamentlichen Theologie.* 5th edition. Theologische Wis-
            senschaft 3. Stuggart: Kohlhammer.
Zimmerli, Walter (editor)
  1932   *Psychopannychia, von Joh. Calvin.* Leipzig: Scholl.

INDEX OF AUTHORS

INDEX OF SCRIPTURE

New Testament